The Vanishing Present

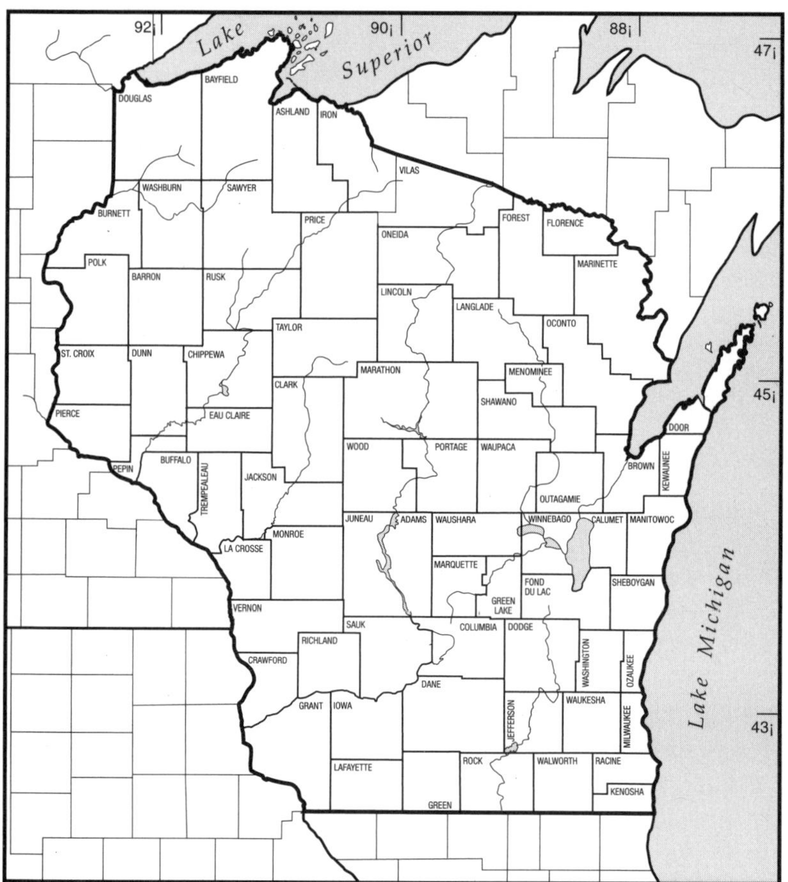

Counties of Wisconsin

The Vanishing Present: Wisconsin's Changing Lands, Waters, and Wildlife

Edited by Donald M. Waller and Thomas P. Rooney

The University of Chicago Press :: Chicago and London

The University of Chicago Press, Chicago 60637
The University of Chicago Press, Ltd., London

Paperback edition 2010
Printed in the United States of America

19 18 17 16 15 14 13 12 11 10   2 3 4 5 6

ISBN-13: 978-0-226-87173-8 (paper)
ISBN-10: 0-226-87173-8 (paper)

Library of Congress Cataloging-in-Publication Data

The vanishing present: Wisconsin's changing lands, waters, and wildlife /
edited by Donald M. Waller and Thomas P. Rooney.
p. cm.
Includes bibliographic references and index.
ISBN-13: 978-0-226-87171-4 (cloth: alk. paper)
ISBN-10: 0-226-87171-1 (cloth: alk. paper)
1. Ecological succession—Wisconsin. 2. Biological diversity—Wisconsin.
I. Waller, Donald M. II. Rooney, Thomas P.
QH105.W6V36 2008
577'.1809775—dc22

2007045306

∞ The paper used in this publication meets the minimum requirements
of the American National Standard for Information Sciences—Permanence
of Paper for Printed Library Materials, ANSI Z39.48-1992.

Contents

Part Four: Changing Animal Communities

Part Five: Nature Meets Us: The Social and Political Context

Part Six: Trajectories

Conclusion

Contributors

Unless otherwise noted, the city, state, and zip code for all University of Wisconsin–Madison addresses are Madison, WI 53706.

James P. Bennett, Institute for Environmental Studies, University of Wisconsin–Madison

Janine Bolliger, Division of Landscape Dynamics and Management, Swiss Federal Institute of Forest, Snow and Landscape Research, CH-8903 Birmensdorf, Switzerland

Stephen M. Born, Department of Urban and Regional Planning, University of Wisconsin–Madison

Matthias Bürgi, Swiss Federal Institute of Forest, Snow and Landscape Research, CH-8903 Birmensdorf, Switzerland

Stephen R. Carpenter, Center for Limnology, University of Wisconsin–Madison

John R. Cary, Department of Wildlife Ecology, University of Wisconsin–Madison

Gary S. Casper, Casper Consulting, 4677 State Rd. 144, Slinger, WI 53086

Dave Cieslewicz, 210 Martin Luther King, Jr. Blvd., Rm. 403, Madison, WI 53703

Scott Craven, Department of Wildlife Ecology, University of Wisconsin–Madison

Mike Dombeck, College of Natural Resources, University of Wisconsin–Stevens Point, Stevens Point, WI 54481

Les Ferge, 7119 Hubbard Ave., Middleton, WI 53562-3231

Gary Fewless, Department of Natural and Applied Sciences, University of Wisconsin–Green Bay, Green Bay, WI 54311

Rich Henderson, Wisconsin Department of Natural Resources, 3911 Fish Hatchery Rd., Madison, WI 53711

John H. Idzikowski, University of Wisconsin–Milwaukee, PO Box 413, Milwaukee, WI 53201

Emmet J. Judziewicz, Department of Biology, University of Wisconsin–Stevens Point, Stevens Point, WI 54481

S. Kelly Kearns, Bureau of Endangered Resources, Wisconsin Department of Natural Resources, PO Box 7921, Madison, WI 53707

James F. Kitchell, Center for Limnology, University of Wisconsin–Madison

Christopher J. Kucharik, Center for Sustainability and the Global Environment, Nelson Institute for Environmental Studies, University of Wisconsin–Madison

Mark K. Leach, Sigurd Olson Environmental Institute, Northland College, 1411 Ellis Ave., Ashland, WI 54806

Lawrence A. Leitner, Southeastern Wisconsin Regional Planning Commission, PO Box 1607, Waukesha, WI 53187-1607

Nina Leopold Bradley, Aldo Leopold Foundation, E12919 Levee Rd., Baraboo, WI 53919

Daniel L. Lindner, U.S. Department of Agriculture Forest Products Laboratory, 507 Highland Ave., Madison, WI 53705

John Lyons, Wisconsin Department of Natural Resources, 1350 Femrite Dr., Monona, WI 53716

John J. Magnuson, Center for Limnology, University of Wisconsin–Madison

David W. Marshall, Wisconsin Department of Natural Resources, 3911 Fish Hatchery Rd., Madison, WI 53711

Jeff T. Maxted, Center for Limnology, University of Wisconsin–Madison

Jim Meeker, Department of Biology, Northland College, 1411 Ellis Ave., Ashland, WI 54806

Curt Meine, International Crane Foundation, E-11376 Shady Lane Rd., PO Box 447, Baraboo, WI 53913

David J. Mladenoff, Department of Forest Ecology and Management, University of Wisconsin–Madison

Michael J. Mossman, Wisconsin Department of Natural Resources, 1350 Femrite Dr., Monona, WI 53716
Matthew P. Nelsen, Department of Botany, University of Wisconsin–Madison
Stanley A. Nichols, Department of Environmental Sciences, University of Wisconsin–Extension, and Wisconsin Geological and Natural History Survey, 3817 Mineral Point Rd., Madison, WI 53705
Charles M. Pils, Wisconsin Department of Natural Resources (retired)
Kenneth W. Potter, Department of Civil and Environmental Engineering, University of Wisconsin–Madison
David Rogers, Department of Botany, University of Wisconsin–Madison
Thomas P. Rooney, Department of Biological Sciences, 3640 Colonel Glenn Hwy., Wright State University, Dayton, OH 45435
David W. Sample, Wisconsin Department of Natural Resources, 1350 Femrite Dr., Monona, WI 53716
Greg G. Sass, Center for Limnology, University of Wisconsin–Madison
Robert M. Scheller, Conservation Biology Institute, 136 SW Washington, Corvallis, OR 97333
Lisa A. Schulte, Department of Natural Resource Ecology and Management, Iowa State University, Ames, Iowa 50011-3221
Emily H. Stanley, Center for Limnology, University of Wisconsin–Madison
Stanley A. Temple, Department of Wildlife Ecology, University of Wisconsin–Madison
Monica G. Turner, Department of Zoology, University of Wisconsin–Madison
Timothy Van Deelen, Department of Wildlife Ecology, University of Wisconsin–Madison
M. Jake Vander Zanden, Center for Limnology, University of Wisconsin–Madison
Donald M. Waller, Department of Botany, University of Wisconsin–Madison
Susan Will-Wolf, Department of Botany, University of Wisconsin–Madison
Sarah D. Wright, Department of Botany, University of Wisconsin–Madison
Adrian P. Wydeven, Wisconsin Department of Natural Resources, 875 S. 4th Ave., Park Falls, WI 54552
Joy B. Zedler, Department of Botany, University of Wisconsin–Madison

Illustrations

Plates

Following page 210

1 Assembling the Puzzle

Donald M. Waller and Thomas P. Rooney

Touchstones

We who admire nature often have a favorite place we return to—a walk or run along a lake or marsh, a favorite fishing hole or tree stand, or perhaps a view or wooded path. Our reasons for choosing these and the spots themselves vary greatly, reflecting our own diversity and our various reasons for getting outside. If we visit these spots at different times of year or in different weather, we appreciate the changes that grace any spot in a temperate climate like ours. Our familiarity with one place heightens our ability to perceive the changes that occur there. Although we may have practical reasons to return to our favorite place, it often has a value for us that transcends its immediate utility. This significance tends to grow over time as we become more familiar with it. Aldo Leopold's shack along the Wisconsin River became far more than a weekend retreat for his family or a location to hunt. Particular places provide a touchstone for us that resonate, enriching our lives in a way that "real estate" or summed geographical statistics do not.

Those who return to particular places time and again often are the first to notice changes. A storm topples a line of trees, favoring the seedlings below. A stream seems to be filling in with silt. Deer or grouse appear more, or less, abundant than in previous years. Migrant birds may appear to return earlier than before. Are these changes real, reflecting broad trends across the land, or are they only brief and inconsistent deviations, part of the normal range of variation? Such questions occur to any observant person. They also occur with increasing frequency to scientists concerned with the cumulative impacts of changes in land use, invading species, and accelerating shifts in regional and global climates. In a few short years, questions about change that might have once been regarded as entertaining chat have emerged as some of the most compelling questions being asked in science.

As Leopold himself made clear, those who study natural systems professionally are hardly immune to a love of favorite places. However, we also have practical reasons to value particular places. Like hunters or fishermen, we often gain decided advantages by returning to the same spot. We notice more subtle or cryptic forms of life, for example. We can more easily track the things that change and those that remain the same. Field biologists often talk of reference sites or lakes. We value the power of permanent quadrats and survey transects for detecting changes in the populations and communities we study (Billick and Price, forthcoming). These are our touchstones, with the "home court advantage" applying at least as much in field biology as it does in sports.

In this book, we explore questions about the kinds, nature, and extent of the changes going on in the landscapes around us. Is climate change affecting when flowers bloom? Are our lakes and streams getting cleaner? Are invading species threatening native species? Which species benefit and which decline as habitat patches grow smaller and roads and suburbs push outward? Many seek answers to these questions from the vantage point of their particular experience and perhaps their favorite place. Such observations and opinions provide valuable perspective (as well as rich sources for discussion). Scientists, however, are trained not to rely too much on any single observation or source of information. Instead, we prefer replicated observations, controlled comparisons, long time series, and large sample sizes. Unfortunately, these are rarely available. Many of the changes that surround us are difficult to perceive because they are subtle or occur gradually. In addition, we usually lack adequate baselines. This elevates the value of those baselines we do have, the touchstone places we are intimately familiar with, and the particular individuals whose extensive field experience gives us the perspective that most of us lack.

History as Context

Wisconsin is changing. The past is gone, except as captured in our memories, records, and artifacts. The present is measurable, but rapidly fading into the past. To understand the present, in ecology as in other endeavors, we need history. Here, we provide background and historical context for understanding the ecological changes that surround us. This is not simple, as the present and recent past are often cloaked by the absence of reliable details. Documenting change hinges on how well we can unveil the invisible present (see chapter 3).

Two things are noteworthy about ecological systems—diversity and change. Biologists delight in the diversity of ecosystems and their favorite taxonomic groups of species. Here, you will find a sampling of that diversity and a taste of that delight. This book emphasizes the diversity of habitats and species in Wisconsin, sharing the enthusiasm of its biologist authors. Our main point, however, is to use this knowledge of our state's natural history to evaluate the changes these habitats and species are undergoing. This is a harder task, as we don't perceive change except with reference to some preexisting state. We can only detect and discuss change when we have a reference system or baseline to compare with current conditions. Not until Aldo Leopold traveled to the Sierra Madre in Mexico did he understand how pervasively grazing had degraded rangelands of the American Southwest. Unfortunately, such reference systems are growing ever scarcer. These are so scarce, in fact, that ecologists commonly refer to the "missing baseline problem."

Biotic diversity can itself be cleaved along two planes. The first reflects the wide range of habitats we find in our state—forests, streams, prairies, lakes, savannas, dunes, bogs, bluffs, and so on. These include the special places that you may know well and that draw so many to our state each year. The second plane reveals the broad variation we see among living groups. When visiting any given habitat, one naturalist will tune her ear for birds or frogs, another will scan the ground for footprints or burrows, and still others will study any available flower, leaf, or bark surface. Anyone can distinguish a mouse from a frog and a moss from a flowering plant, but knowing just which mouse, frog, moss, or flower one sees soon becomes an absorbing (and, for some, a lifelong) challenge. We have striven to present both these planes of diversity in this book. You will find chapters on your favorite habitats as well as (we hope) your favorite groups of plants or animals. We also include chapters on how these pieces of diversity fit together and interface with human systems.

We recognize and accept change in our own lives and in our communities and institutions. We also accept change in the natural areas around us. Change is natural to all ecosystems. Rivers meander and flood, ponds fill in, prairies burn, woods mature or are flattened in a storm, and dunes migrate. Plants and animals are generally adapted to these natural changes and are often remarkably resilient to them. In contrast, many of these same species are peculiarly susceptible to various forms of human disturbance. Artificial impoundments doom wild rice beds, a clear-cut exposes and kills a patch of Braun's holly fern, and vehicles flatten thousands of animals on our highways each year. Shifts in the type, frequency, scale, and intensity of disturbance are changing most of the natural communities around us. Thus, we face another task—namely, to evaluate how Wisconsin's waters, lands, and wildlife are responding to a rising tide of human impacts. As you glimpse this bigger picture of ecological change, we hope you take time to ponder what these changes portend for our state's and our children's future.

The Puzzles of History and Ecology

To solve a jigsaw puzzle, we fit many pieces together into a coherent whole. We often refer to the picture on the box and begin by assembling the edges into a frame as the picture and frame give us contexts to see how the pieces fit. Jigsaw puzzles lacking pieces or a reference picture present a frustrating challenge.

Ecologists and historians also work on puzzles. They work diligently to assemble jumbles of seemingly disconnected facts into bigger and more coherent pictures of a complex system. Furthermore, these pictures keep shifting. Lacking a reference picture and some of the pieces leaves much room for differences in arrangement, emphasis, and interpretation. Fitting even a few pieces together can present a challenge. Perhaps this accounts for why ecology and history both emphasize context and value theory—these provide frames and set boundaries.

One reason ecologists study history is to understand and interpret the present. History is often highly relevant for understanding what species occur where, making biogeography an explicitly historical field (Cox and Moore 1993; Brown and Lomolino 1998). Paleoecologists emphasize how plant species swept to and fro across our postglacial landscapes, reforming communities in new combinations as migrations interacted with shifts in climate (e.g., Davis 1969). "Neo"-ecologists also find value in history, reconstructing the dynamics of particular sites and regions (e.g., Henry and Swan 1974; Kline and Cottam 1979). Despite these obvious roles of history in ecology, the science was long dominated by equilibrium theories that taught a generation of ecologists to ignore history whenever they could. As the pendulum swung back to reemphasize the value of historical analysis, we have seen a renaissance of historical studies (Gates et al.

1983; Loucks 1983; Whitney 1987, 1990; Tallis 1991; Foster et al. 1992; Matlack 1994; Orwig and Abrams 1994; Dey 2002; Flinn and Marks 2004). Symmetrically, environmental history has emerged in recent decades to emphasize the power of ecology to inform our understanding of historical change (Pyne 1982; Cronon 1983, 1991; Flader 1983; Worster 1993; Diamond 1997, 2005).

Assembling the Pieces

In this book, we strove to assemble enough pieces to build a reasonably complete picture of ecological change in the Midwest in the early 21st century. Finding the right pieces and assembling them have proved challenging. We began without a box or a cover picture, and we were missing many of the pieces. Realizing that this was too daunting a task to tackle by ourselves, we sought out colleagues with a remarkable range of expertise. Some brought pieces about birds, others about lakes, and others about lichens. Within these covers, you will find the thoughts of noted ecologists, ornithologists, herpetologists, limnologists, ichthyologists, botanists, and entomologists. Our authors, in turn, gathered yet more pieces, searching through the academic literature, filing cabinets, museum collections, agency reports, and historical documents. Each has assembled their part of the puzzle as best they could. To avoid leaving you with only isolated pieces, we also asked our authors to step back from their immediate results to ponder how their results fit with other patterns and connect to the broader picture of ecological change.

Although our first concern is with biotic change, we also sought ideas about how lands, water, and wildlife are managed. Professional land stewards and wildlife managers are particularly well placed to provide these pieces. As land-use policies clearly affect patterns of land use and their impacts, we also solicited essays from two policy leaders unusually well informed on environmental issues: an environmental planner and the mayor of Madison. Finally, to provide explicit perspectives on how history and ecology interact, we summarize "The Big Picture" in our final chapter. While the puzzle doubtless remains incomplete, we hope you find enough pieces here to enlarge your understanding of ecological change in this region.

The Nature of Ecological Change

What do we mean by ecological change? Many today are rightfully concerned about the serious environmental changes that surround us in-

Components of Overall Environmental Change, as Enumerated by Vitousek (1992)

This book focuses mainly on the three highlighted components.

- Change in composition of the atmosphere
- Climate change
- Decreased stratospheric ozone and increased UV
- *Ecological change*
  - > *Cumulative land use change*
  - > *Decreased biodiversity*
  - > *Biological invasions*
- Regional shifts in atmospheric chemistry

cluding global climate change in its various forms, the ozone hole, and regionally significant issues like acid rain. We explore climate change in one chapter describing changes in phenology at Leopold's shack property and in another that explores the consequences of warming for Wisconsin's forests. However, we mainly focus on three other types of ecological change: cumulative changes in land use, declines in biological diversity, and biotic invasions. These represent what we label ecological change, a subset of a broader class of human-accelerated, global, environmental changes (see sidebar).

Why focus on human-driven ecological changes? We know from the Millennium Ecosystem Assessment (www.maweb.org) that ecosystems have changed more rapidly and extensively in the past 50 years than in any comparable period in human history. These changes continue to accelerate. Growing demands for food, fresh water, timber, fiber, and fuel are driving a huge and largely irreversible loss in the diversity of life on Earth. The persistence and evolution of most large mammals is in doubt globally. So far, most people feel that these changes have generally improved the quality of life for humanity. These gains, however, have come at a steep price and cannot continue indefinitely. As we learn more each year about the global and regional consequences of the habitat changes humans have wrought, we face new and increasingly complex problems that increasingly threaten the quality of life for future generations. Ecological change will increasingly affect the price and availability of essentials like food, energy, minerals, water, and timber. Ecological degradation, particularly in fragile environments, has clearly contributed to the collapse of nation-states (Diamond 2005). Today, habitat losses and degradation threaten most natural communities. Remaining patches are becoming ever more isolated and fragile. Climate changes are poised to dramatically affect biological diversity (Thomas et al. 2004). Shifts in climates, storms, and runoff patterns combine with fluctuating microbe, parasite, and animal populations to increasingly threaten human health. These are not hypothetical or distant threats. High rainfall washed parasites from large animal feedlots into the water supply of Milwaukee in 1991 driving a deadly outbreak of *Cryptosporidium* that killed over 100 people (Mac Kenzie et al. 1994). We see parallel increases in the threats posed by Lyme disease, West Nile virus, hantavirus, and so on, increasingly exacerbated by climate and land-use change (Patz et al. 2005). Changes in habitat quality, connectivity, and weather are also interacting to increase the frequency and severity of wildfires and floods. Ecological change has never been more important or more relevant.

Ecological changes occur at variable rates across various spatial and temporal scales. This heterogeneity delights and vexes ecologists. Ecologists have been reasonably successful in understanding the population dynamics of particular species of interest and interactions among a few species over short periods of time. Likewise, paleoecologists often piece together long-term shifts in geographical ranges and community composition. We have had far less success in tracing ecological shifts over the medium term of decades to a century or two. This is the interval that John Magnuson (1990) refers to as the "invisible present," inspiring our title. He explores these ideas further in chapter 3.

Why Focus on Wisconsin?

Rather than attempt to describe the global ecological changes under way, we confine our attention here to the particular north temperate lands and waters known as Wisconsin. Straddling temperate forest and grassland biomes, our state contains prairie, oak savanna, and forest in the south, forests and many lakes in the north, and abundant wetlands and rivers throughout. Wisconsin is our touchstone. During the last 200 years of explosive human population growth, our ancestors exploited the abundant natural resources they found, modified and often obliterated habitats, and introduced many new species, deliberately and inadvertently. The changes under way here are significant precisely because they are ordinary. While specific changes differ from place to place in when and how fast they occur, overall patterns of change are distressingly similar. What is happening in our typical midwestern state is happening everywhere. We focus on the changes going on here in Wisconsin because they present a synecdoche for changes under way across North America and around the world. Human activities and population growth are driving massive shifts in land cover and use, urbanization and sprawl, and declines in wild habitats and species. Such pervasive processes deserve scrutiny wherever they occur and increase the generality and relevance of our conclusions.

We have a second reason to focus on Wisconsin. We are fortunate here to inherit remarkable compendiums of high-quality historical data. The historical reports, archives, museum collections, monitoring reports, wildlife harvest records, and other data we have inherited from earlier researchers combine to provide a fuller picture of earlier conditions than can be reconstructed in most other places. These baselines exist because of commerce and science. Our fullest picture of pre-European settlement vegetation comes from the General Land Office Survey in the early to mid-19th century that noted the vegetation while subdividing the land into the grid of townships, ranges, and sections that now define our land (see chapter 2). In the early to mid-20th century, individual scientists and teams worked hard to collect and assemble data in their quest to understand natural systems. Edward A. Birge and Chancey Juday were intent to learn all that they could about temperate lakes from their reference lakes in southern and northern Wisconsin, founding North American limnology along the way. John T. Curtis and his students and colleagues roamed the state widely, collecting remarkably detailed data from over 1,000 sites to understand how plant species sort themselves out into the forests, prairies, savannas, and wetlands that once covered our state. Aldo Leopold recorded details about just when plants bloomed and animals came or went at his shack beginning in the 1930s. We now use these and other records to assess land use and climate change, animal and plant invasions, shifts in the distribution and abundance of species and habitats, and the suitability of sites for ecological restoration.

Traditionally, most of our research efforts have been isolated, leading to fragmented pictures of change. Bird researchers might be aware of shifts in vegetation structure, but not of changes in plant species composition. Botanists, in turn, would rarely know what shifts were occurring in butterfly and moth populations. This is not for a lack of interest. Rather, specialists are always busy. Recently, however, ecologists have sought to link their results more effectively together to provide fuller pictures of ecological change. We have new tools to sharpen our picture including landscape ecology, geospatial analysis, shared databases, and meta-analyses of results from multiple studies. Linked studies and comprehensive reviews of existing data are allowing us to evaluate the significance of ecological changes across broader geographical scales (e.g., the Millennium Assessment; Noss et al. 1995; Noss and Peters

1995). Scientific meetings are now devoted to understanding ecological change. This book results from one such meeting. With support from the National Science Foundation, we met in Madison in the fall of 2004 to hear each others' stories and tell our own. Our goal was not only to put the pieces you see in this book together but also to broaden our collective view of ecological change. We found that perspectives from geography and history enrich and complement our view of ecology.

Is Our Vision Dimming?

The picture we assemble here is, of course, fading. Books take time to write, yet ecosystems continue to change, often in unpredictable ways. The picture you find here is provisional and impermanent. We considered it important nevertheless to take stock of what we know now and to assemble as full a picture as we could. Opportunities to assemble and interpret data fade as those who collected it age. Baselines and records disappear. Opportunities to observe, record, and experiment may also decline. If we are to make sense of the changes ahead, we need to assess where we have been and where we are now. With the records in this book, we hope to provide a foundation for periodically updating our understanding of change and what to expect in the future. Neglecting these tasks only clouds the picture, causing us to lose sight of the lessons it might teach.

Our Readers

We hope this book is accessible to all those who share our interests in how landscapes, waters, and wildlife populations have changed and continue to change in response to shifts in climate, interactions among species, and growing pressures from human population growth and land use. To that end, we explain terms and ideas and avoid jargon whenever possible. We also often omit qualifying terms like "may" and "might" common in the scientific literature. Although scientists recognize these terms to mean that inferences and interpretations are likely, others often take such terms to imply that we are merely guessing. We sought to avoid such potential misunderstandings and accept responsibility for sometimes blurring the important distinction scientists make between certain and probable outcomes.

As humans continue to modify, convert, destroy, and fragment the habitats that surround us, we confront a key question—namely, how and when will humans devise truly sustainable cultures? Despite being preeminent "ecosystem engineers," we have yet to fully perceive the scale of the changes we are causing or comprehend how they will ultimately affect other species and ourselves. We face unprecedented challenges not only in comprehending these changes but also in modifying human activities to ameliorate their impacts. We trust that those reading this book share our concern for sustaining the beauty and grace of Wisconsin's lands, waters, and wildlife. To achieve that will not be easy. As a small step in that direction, we dedicate this book to the field biologists and conservation professionals who work to monitor, understand, and protect Wisconsin's natural areas. Their expertise is hard-won, and their dedication and efforts are never fully compensated. To express our dedication in concrete terms, we and the University of Chicago Press are allocating many of the royalties earned by this book to the Endangered Resources Fund of the Wisconsin Department of Natural Resources. While other worthy causes exist, this organization plays several key roles, overseeing our State Natural Areas program (one of the oldest in the country) and efforts to conserve the habitats and conditions essential to the survival of our native plants and animals. Sadly, fulfilling these roles now largely depends on annual public charity via an income tax check-off and license plate revenues. The professionals that staff this state bureau and the state's lands, waters, and wildlife deserve more stable and sustained support for their crucial efforts.

References

Billick, I., and M. V. Price, eds. Forthcoming. The ecology of place: Contributions of place-based research to ecological and evolutionary understanding. Chicago: University of Chicago Press.

Brown, J. H., and M. V. Lomolino. 1998. Biogeography. 2nd ed. Sunderland, MA: Sinauer Assoc.

Cox, C. B., and P. D. Moore. 1993. Biogeography: An ecological and evolutionary approach. 5th ed. Boston: Blackwell Scientific.

Cronon, W. 1983. Changes in the land: Indians, colonists, and the ecology of New England. New York: Hill and Wang.

———. 1991. Nature's metropolis: Chicago and the Great West. New York: W. W. Norton.

Davis, M. 1969. Palynology and environmental history during the Quaternary Period. American Scientist 57:317–332.

Dey, D. 2002. Fire history and postsettlement disturbance. Pp. 46–59 in W. J. McShea and W. M. Healy, eds. Oak forest ecosystems: Ecology and management for wildlife. Baltimore: Johns Hopkins University Press.

Diamond, J. 1997. Guns, germs, and steel: The fates of human societies. New York: W. W. Norton.

———. 2005. Collapse: How societies choose to fail or succeed. New York: Viking.

Flader, S. L., ed. 1983. The Great Lakes forest: An environmental and social history. Minneapolis: University of Minnesota Press.

Flinn, K. M., and P. L. Marks. 2004. Land-use history and forest herb diversity in Tompkins County, New York, USA. Pp. 81–96 in O. Honnay, K. Verheyen, B. Bossuyt, and M. Hermy, eds. Forest biodiversity: lessons from history for conservation. Wallingford, UK: CABI.

Foster, D. R., T. Zebryk, P. Schoonmaker, and A. Lezberg. 1992. Post-settlement history of human land-use and vegetation dynamics of a *Tsuga canadensis* (hemlock) woodlot in central New England. Journal of Ecology 80:773–786.

Gates, D. M., C. H. D. Clarke, and J. T. Harris. 1983. Wildlife in a changing environment. Pp. 52–80 in S. L. Flader, ed. The Great Lakes forest: An environmental and social history. Minneapolis: University of Minnesota Press.

Henry, J. D., and J. M. A. Swan. 1974. Reconstructing forest history from live and dead plant material—an approach to the study of forest succession in southwest New Hampshire. Ecology 55:772–783.

Kline, V. M., and G. Cottam. 1979. Vegetation response to climate and fire in the driftless area of Wisconsin. Ecology 60:861–868.

Loucks, O. L. 1983. New light on the changing forest. Pp. 17–32 in S. L. Flader, ed. The Great Lakes forest: An environmental and social history. Minneapolis: University of Minnesota Press.

Mac Kenzie, W. R., N. J. Hoxie, M. E. Proctor, M. S. Gradus, K. A. Blair, D. E. Peterson, J. J. Kazmierczak, D. G. Addiss, K. R. Fox, J. B. Rose, and J. P. Davis. 1994. A massive outbreak in Milwaukee of Cryptosporidium infection transmitted through the public water supply. New England Journal of Medicine 331:161–167.

Magnuson, J. 1990. Long term research and the invisible present. BioScience 40:495–501.

Matlack, G. R. 1994. Plant species migration in a mixed-history forest landscape in eastern North America. Ecology 75:1491–1502.

Noss, R. F., E. T. LaRoe III, and J. M. Scott. 1995. Endangered ecosystems of the United States: A preliminary assessment of loss and degradation. Biological Report No. 28, National Biological Service, U.S. Department of the Interior, Washington, DC.

Noss, R. F., and R. L. Peters. 1995. Endangered ecosystems: A status report on America's vanishing habitat and wildlife. Washington, DC: Defenders of Wildlife.

Orwig, D. A., and M. D. Abrams. 1994. Land-use history (1720–1992), composition, and dynamics of oak-pine forests within the Piedmont and Coastal Plain of northern Virginia. Canadian Journal of Forest Research 24:1216–1225.

Patz, J., D. Campbell-Lendrum, T. Holloway, and J. A. Foley. 2005. Impact of regional climate change on human health. Nature 438:310–317.

Pyne, S. J. 1982. Fire in America: A cultural history of wild land and rural fire. Princeton, NJ: Princeton University Press.

Tallis, J. H. 1991. Plant community history. London: Chapman and Hall.

Thomas, C. D., A. Cameron, R. E. Green, M. Bakkenes, L. J. Beaumont, Y. C. Collingham, B. F. Erasmus, M. Ferreira de Siqueira, A. Grainger, L. Hannah, L. Hughes, B. Huntley, A. S. v. Jaarsveld, G. F. Midgley, L. Miles, M. A. Ortega-Huerta, A. T. Peterson, O. L. Phillips, and S. E. Williams. 2004. Extinction risk from climate change. Nature 427: 145–148.

Vitousek, P. M. 1992. Global environmental change: An introduction. Annual Review of Ecology and Systematics 23:1–14.

Whitney, G. G. 1987. An ecological history of the Great Lakes forest of Michigan. Journal of Ecology 75:667–684.

———. 1990. The history and status of the hemlock-hardwood forests of the Allegheny plateau. Journal of Ecology 78:443–458.

Worster, D. 1993. The wealth of nature: environmental history and the ecological imagination. New York: Oxford University Press.

Part One: Perspectives

In recent years, we see growing recognition among ecologists that human activity has played an important role in shaping the natural world and continues to do so. With this in mind, we begin our book at Man Mound. Curt Meine reminds us that European explorers were not the first people to set foot in Wisconsin, only the most recent. They were preceded by the Mississippian culture, who in turn were preceded by the Woodland societies, the Archaic cultures, and before that, Paleo-Indians. Man Mound was just one of thousands of earthworks left by the Woodland Indians. Meine further reminds us that the current inhabitants are not the only ones that have profoundly shaped the natural world. Paleo-Indians contributed to the extinction of many large mammals several thousand years ago, greatly diminishing a fauna that resembled the current species found in the African Serengeti.

Today, humans often accomplish in decades what typically takes natural processes thousands of years (Russell 1997). Meine argues that many of the changes we have seen in Wisconsin can be traced to a single historical event: the Land Survey. The division of the land into townships, ranges, and sections in the 19th century completely reordered the land and our view of it. The boundary lines followed no natural or man-made features. Although wounded by the Land Survey, Man Mound was later protected by the efforts of ordinary, dedicated citizens living on this reordered land. We inherit a land divided by the Land Survey; how we proceed from here is up to us.

The eminent ecologist (and University of Wisconsin limnology alum) Gene Likens noted that careful, reliable, long-term observations will contribute significantly to ecology in coming decades (Likens 1989). Chapters 3 and 4 illustrate how careful observations in Wisconsin are advancing our understanding of the consequences of global warming. John Magnuson examines the duration of ice cover on Madison's Lake Mendota each winter and how this period has grown shorter, particularly in recent decades. In one recent winter, ice lasted only 95 days. Alone, this fact seems trivial. It becomes interesting, however, when viewed through the lens of history. Nina Leopold Bradley and Sarah Wright pick up where Aldo Leopold left off, examining a long time series of careful observations on when natural events occur each year. By comparing Aldo's records of when the first robin arrived each spring, and so on, with the timing of those events today, they document a radical shift in climate. Neither the first person to record Lake Mendota's ice duration nor Aldo Leopold anticipated how their records could be used to document the effects of global warming. Yet without their careful record keeping, we would be oblivious to these changes, trapped in John Magnuson's "invisible present." Fortunately, we see that efforts to collect systematic data continue to expand, including more citizen science efforts like the Audubon Society's annual Christmas Bird Count and Operation Ruby Throat (organized by the Hilton Pond Center for Piedmont Natural History). Given all the kinds of change that appear to be occurring, the data collected via these efforts seems destined to become useful in ways that we can barely imagine today.

References

Likens, G. E. 1989. Long-term studies in ecology: approaches and alternatives. New York: Springer-Verlag.

Russell, E. W. B. 1997. People and the land through time: linking ecology and history. New Haven, CT: Yale University Press.

2

The View from Man Mound

Curt Meine

Take Wisconsin Highway 33 to Baraboo. On the east edge of town, turn north on County Road T, and go up the hill. (The hill is the north gunnel of the canoe-shaped Baraboo Hills). One mile up you will come to a crossroad. To the west, it is called City View Road. To the east, it is Man Mound Road. Turn right. The road is straight; it follows the half-section line. Go past the farm fields, woodlots, and houses for a little more than two miles. You'll see a sign on the right for Man Mound Park.

This small roadside park protects something unique: a human-shaped effigy mound. At the time of Native/European contact in what is now Wisconsin, the landscape contained an estimated 15,000–20,000 Indian mounds. A succession of native societies had constructed the mounds over a 2,000-year period, from about 800 BC to 1200 AD (Birmingham and Eisenberg 2000). They were as distinguishing an attribute of the Wisconsin landscape as its glacial features. No other part of North America had so rich a concentration of these ancient earthworks.

Over the last century and a half, agriculture and development have obliterated at least three-fourths of Wisconsin's Indian mounds. Of just nine known mounds built in the shape of a human or humanlike figure, Man Mound is the only one that survives in a relatively intact state. A local land surveyor, William Canfield, first described it in

1859. The "man" of Man Mound measured out at 218 feet from head to foot (the head being extended by two projections variously described as antlers, horns, a headdress, or elongated ears). Increase Lapham, reporting Canfield's find that same year, deemed it "the most strange and extraordinary [artificial earthwork] yet brought to light." To Lapham's eyes, the mound captured the figure "in the act of walking, and with an expression of boldness and decision which cannot be mistaken" (Lapham 1859, 365).

Man Mound has not survived whole. The public land survey marked out these six square miles of Wisconsin—Township 12 North, Range 7 East—in September 1845. The half-section boundary line that Man Mound Road now follows intersected the mound at its "legs." As that boundary line became (presumably) a field border or perhaps a wagon trail, then a dirt road, and then a paved road, the mound's lower legs were destroyed. Around the turn of the twentieth century the threat of the plow reached Man Mound. Local citizens and state organizations launched a campaign that led, in 1908, to creation of the park to safeguard the remainder of the mound.

The Man Mound itself is only about three-feet high. Respect demands that one not stand atop it. But the view it affords has nothing to do with its height and everything to do with its historic and symbolic significance. This figure has been surveying its landscape for perhaps 1,000 years, walking the shifting border between prairie and forest. Over its flanks plant and animal populations have ebbed and swelled. It has seen long-tenured species disappear and newcomers arrive. It has persisted through the evolving lifeways of varied human communities and cultures. It witnessed the comings and goings of its Woodland Indian builders and later bands of modern Native Americans. It watched as trappers and traders—including one Jean Baribault—worked their way up the Baraboo River. Its amputation marked the arrival of European settlers, the imposition of the land survey's abstract order upon the land, and the rank commodification of nature. And just when further change in the form of the plow was about to vanquish the mound, an ethic of caring took hold, allowing the Man to continue along "in the act of walking."

From Man Mound, we can look out and see that the history of Wisconsin's natural and human communities is woven together on Wisconsin's landscape. From here we can try to discern patterns in that relationship. We can appreciate that change is constant, but neither uniform nor random, varying by type, cause, rate, duration, scale, and impact. We can recognize the reality of ecological change over 12,000 years of human inhabitation. We can appreciate the magnitude of the change that came with the redefinition of land over the last century and a half, and especially with the land survey's initial reduction of the land to our possession.

Beyond History's Horizon

In *The Contested Plains,* his study of the transformations that the clash of Native and Euro-American cultures brought to the central Great Plains, historian Elliott West writes (1998, 33): "The changes brought by Europeans were so great that they usually are called the start of history itself, the breaking of a slumbering spell. They were not that, but the consequences of that first contact came so fast and ran so deep that they made for a material and imaginative revolution." What West describes with regard to the mixed-grass prairies of the mid-continent holds for the prairie-savanna-forest borderland of Wisconsin as well. The history of environmental change in Wisconsin did not begin when Wisconsin's original inhabitants encountered European explorers, trappers, and missionaries. However, that moment of cultural contact remains a profound demarcation line. Man Mound, frozen in time, disfigured, yet still in motion, is an apt point from which to consider the consequences of first contact and the "material and imaginative revolution" that ensued.

Such matters are of more than passing interest. Over the last 20 years the words *nature* and *wilderness* have been corralled within quotation marks. Those quotation marks mean to say: "Your assumptions about what *nature* is, and your mythologies concerning *wilderness,* need to be revisited." The critique reflects varied insights, claims, and contentions, offered from multiple perspectives: from environmental historians dissatisfied with environmentalism's seeming attachment to romantic notions of a static, pristine, unpeopled, and ahistoric landscape; from ecologists and other natural scientists who have come to place greater emphasis on the dynamism of ecosystems; from environmental ethicists concerned with the causes and consequences of the strict polarization of people and nature; from Native Americans, geographers, and anthropologists frustrated that the historical role of native peoples has too often been ignored, disregarded, or misunderstood; from resource managers with a pragmatic need to rethink the context of land management decisions; and from opportunists in the culture wars who saw here a chance to drive in ideological wedges and skewer political foes. We are talking, then, about something deeper than definitions. We are dealing with fundamentals: our view of the world, our place within it, and what we ought to do about it.

The reinterpretation of the human-nature relationship and its trajectory through time has generated extensive debate (e.g., Cronon 1995; Soulé and Lease 1995; Callicott and Nelson 1998; Vale 2002). That debate revolves around our comprehension of *change* itself and our recognition of the relative importance of humans as agents of change. In the New World, these matters require critical understanding of Native American demographics, dispersal, movement and settlement patterns, resource use and management practices (especially hunting, agriculture, and the use of fire), cultural innovations, and belief systems. It inevitably entails ambiguity, since detailed knowledge of these factors often lies, and will forever remain, beyond history's horizon.

Within that circle of ambiguity, the pendulum of opinion has swung. The "myth of the pristine landscape" has been debunked and discredited (Denevan 1992). In its place, a radically different account arose, one that sees in the pre-Columbian New World, not *wilderness,* not in fact a *New* World at all, but an "omnipresent humanized landscape" (Vale 1999, 2002, 2). Thus, for example, journalist Charles Mann (2002, 41, 50)—in an article tellingly entitled "1491"—writes that "in 1492 Columbus set foot in a hemisphere thoroughly dominated by humankind." Indian-set fires "shaped" the short-grass plains over millennia into "vast buffalo farms." By implication, any notion of restoring "pre-settlement" landscapes must entail "creat[ing] the world's largest garden." In the absence of the pristine, the human rules.

Tom Vale (2002, xiii, 2) suggests that the pendulum has in fact swung too far, that we are now in fact in the thrall of a new "myth of the humanized landscape" that also fails to describe with sufficient accuracy the character of pre-Columbian America. "The debate," Vale writes, "typically focuses on the polar assertions that the continent was either a 'natural landscape' or a 'human-modified landscape.'" In contrast, Vale stresses "the logic of an intermediate position—some areas were humanized, some were not." Recognizing that human alterations of nature vary in intensity, over scales of time and space, by ecosystem type and by region, Vale has made the case for a more nuanced appreciation of "humanized effects in a mosaic over the [pre-Columbian] landscape."

That mosaic would not have been fixed. Its patches would have shifted in time and in space, and would have done so constantly, starting with the moment human beings first crossed into the hemisphere. Indeed, the arrival of people in the Americas was but a late stage in the diaspora of the genus *Homo* out of Africa. By the time *Homo sapiens* ventured across Beringia, the species had left behind it a long trail of ecosystem impacts (Tudge 1996; Diamond 1997; MacPhee 1999). Over more than a dozen post-Beringia and pre-Columbian millennia, America's native populations waxed and waned, warred and allied, jostled for territory, expanded and contracted ranges, evolved changing technologies, adapted to new places, and adopted new lifeways. Native empires arose and receded. Across those millennia, the impact of such cultural flux on the biota and on ecological processes likewise varied by time and place (Martin and Szuter 1999; Flannery 2001). Their impacts intensified and faded. In short, "1491" is an artificial fixed end point, just as "1492" is an artificial fixed beginning point.

As we try to assess and calibrate ecological change in Wisconsin, what does our gaze beyond history's horizon suggest?

Pre-Nicolet Wisconsin

We can begin by reviewing the broad narrative of Wisconsin's past.

Here, 1634—the year that the Ho-Chunk received Jean Nicolet on the shores of Green Bay—is the operative analog for 1492. That first confirmed contact was heavy with portents for the Ho-Chunk; for the nearby Menominee, and Potawatomi; for the Ojibwe, Ottawa, Sauk, Mesquakie, Mascouten, Miami, and Kickapoo who, uprooted as conflict engulfed the East, came west to Wisconsin; and for the lands and waters, plants and animals that shared the Wisconsin landscape. But pre-Nicolet Wisconsin was hardly isolated or immune to change. As Patty Loew notes (2001, 12), "Even before their actual arrival in the western Great Lakes region, Europeans had already touched the lives of the Native people"—through the effects of the eastern conflicts, intertribal trade, intracontinental migrations, and disease outbreaks.

Wisconsin has always been a landscape in motion, though the relative pace and motive forces have varied. Ecological change had been a constant and continuing fact since humans first arrived in the landscape now known as Wisconsin. We may in fact look back even beyond the human horizon. The recurrent glacial advances of the Pleistocene of course refashioned our topography and altered our biota in lasting ways. But we were also home to the refugium landscape of the unglaciated Driftless Area. Its special history would have lasting consequences. Which is to say, its unusual immunity to recent geological change (in the form of glaciers) in fact made it a vital factor in subsequent ecological change.

Norman Fassett and John Curtis were fascinated by the biogeographical legacy of the Driftless Area—its rare plant communities, relict species, and special habitats. Curtis (1959, 14) identified 34 "plants endemic in the Driftless Area or whose range in Wisconsin is restricted to that region." Evidence suggested that the Driftless Area "was at least partially covered with vegetation at all times and that it formed the source for the bulk of the plant cover which later spread out over the remaining parts of the state as these were deglaciated." We continue to learn about various biotic legacies of the Driftless Area. Kevin Rowe and others, for example, have recently determined that most of the eastern chipmunks in Illinois and Wisconsin are descendents of a population that endured the Wisconsinan glacial phase in the Driftless Area and then expanded its range as the ice sheets receded.

The end of the Pleistocene brought sweeping changes to the continent. In Wisconsin, as plants and chipmunks were moving outward from the Driftless Area, people were moving in. Their arrival coincided with a changing climate and the famous disappearance of so many members of the North American Pleistocene megafauna—powerful predators like the dire wolf, giant short-faced bear, and saber-toothed cat; massive herbivores like the mastodon, woolly mammoth, and giant beaver; ground sloths, glyptodons, cheetahs, and camels, and horses. At least 35 large mammal species went extinct in North America between 12,000 and 9,000 years ago. "This wave of extinctions," E. C. Pielou (1991, 251) writes, "is one of the most noteworthy, and most puzzling, events in ecological history."

Scientists have vigorously debated the causes of these extinctions for decades (Martin and Klein 1984; MacPhee 1999; Grayson and Meltzer 2002). In particular, their arguments have revolved around human predation as a—some say, *the*—leading factor behind the demise of the megafauna (climate and environmental change and commensal-carried diseases being the other prime suspects). Tim Flannery (2001, 205), a strong believer that these species disappeared largely at the end of the elegant Clovis spear points, notes that "regardless of whether human hunters or climate change caused the extinctions, the event is without parallel in North American prehistory." And the consequences, too, would be profound: cascading effects involving the surviving fauna; responses in ecosystem structure, function, and composition; and a changed habitat (and resource base) for the newly arrived people.

By 10,000 years before present, the ice sheets had melted back from Wisconsin, and the modern flora began to constitute itself on the opened land. Subsequent changes in climate would have a large and continuing impact on the extent of grassland and forest, and the location of the savanna between them, across the region (Davis 1977). About 8,500 years ago a warming and drying phase, the Hypsithermal, had begun. Grasslands expanded and forests contracted northeastward. Over the millennia, the shifting prairie-forest ecotone would reflect the dynamic interplay of changing temperatures, precipitation and humidity levels, vegetation types, fuel production, and fire frequency and severity (Baker et al. 1992; Camill et al. 2003, Williams et al. 2004). Some of those fires were set by people. When, where, how often, and with what effects have also long been matters of vigorous research and unresolved debate.

As Wisconsin's biomes responded to its fluctuating climate, pre-Nicolet cultures also changed constantly and continually. Wisconsin is home to the oldest known site of butchered mammoths in North America, in Kenosha County (Overstreet and Kolb 2003). The remains have been dated to between 12,500 and 13,500 years ago. The butchers at this important site were pre-Clovis Paleo-Indians. For the next 5,000 years, Paleo-Indian peoples moved about the landscape in small family groups; hunted animals and gathered plants; crafted stone spear points and knives; built temporary shelters and exchanged goods; and cremated and buried their dead. Their tenure overlapped that of the people of the Archaic culture (8000–100 BC), who hunted the abundant post-Pleistocene game populations; experimented with rudimentary agriculture; traded in Lake Superior copper, Atlantic seaboard seashells, and Yellowstone obsidian; developed rituals and cemeteries; and initiated the tradition of mound building.

The Archaic cultures in turn overlapped with the early Woodland societies. The Woodland Indians inhabited Wisconsin from 500 BC into the second millennium AD. These were the mound builders, occupying more clearly defined territories, establishing Wisconsin's first villages, trading extensively, growing garden crops, cultivating corn, shaping pottery, and symbolizing their inner lives in their ceramics and mounds. Then came the Mississipian people who built the largest Native American settlement in North America, the great city at Cahokia, in what is now Illinois, and whose hinterland extended upriver into Wisconsin. The Missisippian culture in Wisconsin is best known for the large platform mounds at its outpost site at Aztalan, where activity peaked around 1150 AD. Cahokia and Aztalan would fade within a century, but the Upper Mississipian people would remain in the landscape. They are thought to be ancestors to the modern Ho-Chunk, and perhaps the Menominee and other Native American tribes (Birmingham and Eisenberg 2000).

Through 14 pre-Nicolet millennia, then, native people hunted, gathered, trapped, fished, mined, settled, farmed, and burned lands throughout Wisconsin. These activities have altered the land in ways known, unknown, and suspected, and no doubt in ways yet to be understood. But change is not uniform in time or space. We can denote key periods of intense change. We can identify other periods of relative stability.

Even if our view beyond the horizon is hazy, we can still perceive prehistoric natural phenomena and human activities that produced resonant ecological echoes. From Man Mound we can see ecological change over not just one but multiple temporal thresholds.

Bounding the Land

And yet—not all thresholds are equal. Other chapters in this book focus on the impact of the subsequent four centuries of Euro-American influence on Wisconsin's life-forms and landscapes. Change in this period has come in rapid waves, from many directions, with complex crosscurrents. But of all the events of this period, none has reordered the land and its life on such a scale, with such lasting and monumental consequences, as the one so poignantly apparent at Man Mound: the advent of the public land survey (Johnson 1976; Linklater 2002; Meine 2004).

In *Nature's Metropolis* (1991, 102) William Cronon succinctly summarized the purpose of the land survey: it aimed "to turn land into real estate by the most economically expedient method. By imposing the same abstract and homogeneous grid pattern on all land, no matter how ecologically diverse, government surveyors made it marketable." The land survey in Wisconsin was carried out between 1833 and 1866. The actual act of surveying the grid lines had little immediate physical effect. But in subdividing and bounding the land—legally, politically, economically, and imaginatively—it would reshape the biological diversity, ecosystems, and human communities of Wisconsin in profound ways.

Because we are so accustomed to seeing the land through the survey's gridded lens, its legacies are easily overlooked. They are paradoxically both subtle and obvious, minute and extensive. They are written in the manifold stories of Wisconsin places. A few examples:

- Gaze down from the air above the Menominee Forest border and note the sharp division between tribal and nontribal lands. The survey line is an obvious ecological boundary, but it is an economic and cultural boundary as well.
- Look at early maps of the southwestern Wisconsin mining district or the French lots along the Fox and Mississippi rivers: the lands outlined in the presurvey maps and described in Indian treaties obviously had no uniform square grid lines. Lakes, streams, and wetlands were the most important features of the early maps. The geography of the Indian mounds reflects this. Almost all were located in gathering places near water.

- Wisconsin agriculture was built between the lines of subdivided property. Agricultural conversion and intensification happened rapidly in southern and eastern Wisconsin—the first portions of the state to be surveyed—as the prairies, savannas, and wetlands were turned to wheat farming, then to dairying. The fresh survey lines plainly did not cause the conversion, but it made the process far more rapid, efficient, and complete than it might otherwise have been. Even the main ditch through Horicon Marsh follows a north-south section line, an emblem of the changes that have affected wetland communities across Wisconsin.
- Neither did the new survey lines cause the post–Civil War decimation of the northern pineries, but there too they speeded the process. The direct impacts of the white pine logging boom are the stuff of conservation legend, but the indirect environmental impacts deserve accounting as well. They would include the era's epic fires, modification of forest soil flora and fauna, extensive soil erosion and stream sedimentation, changes in the fish and stream invertebrate fauna, and widespread construction of water control structures across the northern half of Wisconsin.
- The grid would invite its own response in the form of innovative conservation practices on the farm. The pioneering watershed rehabilitation project that began at Coon Valley in 1933 would, in effect, defy the grid. The innovations developed there—the adoption of a whole-watershed approach, working of the land along contours, the protecting and restoring waterways, the integration of farm management plans—helped to open a new phase in the conservation movement (Leopold 1935). The whole effort might be seen as an exercise in refitting rectangular land parcels into watershed-shaped realities.
- We can read the grid in other stories out of Wisconsin's conservation tradition. Aldo Leopold's wildlife management ideas were very much a response to the fragmentation, simplification, and intensified management of midwestern farms. His appreciation of edge effects in *Game Management* (1933) derived not from any desire to *fragment* intact ecological communities but to *restore* some semblance of biological diversity along field borders and fencelines within a thoroughly converted agricultural landscape. Later, John Curtis (1956) would use the ecological history of Cadiz Township in Green County as, quite literally, the textbook example of landscape fragmentation.

We could, of course, multiply these examples by as many lines and land parcels as the survey etched into the surface of Wisconsin. These few serve to make a simple point: the land survey has facilitated immense changes in human activity in a relatively short period of time. Those activities over the last century and a half have affected biological diversity, ecological processes, and environmental features to varying degrees, at varied temporal and spatial scales, and the effects will forever be with us.

How might we think more critically about the role of the land survey in shaping Wisconsin's landscapes and biodiversity? We can identify an array of possible approaches:

- A *community approach* would emphasize the survey's direct and indirect effects on Wisconsin's various ecological communities, for example, the southern deciduous forests, sedge meadows, or oligotrophic lakes (following Hoffman 2002).
- A *landscape/scalar approach* would emphasize the survey's effects over a range of embedded spatial scales, for example, along a fencerow; on the farm property that contains it; along the stretch of the Wisconsin River containing many such farms; or within the Central Sands region containing many such landscape features.
- A *hierarchic approach* would emphasize the survey's effects at the different levels of biological organization, from the genetic structure to the population level, to the community and ecosystem level, and finally up to the level of landscapes and biomes.
- A *functional approach* would emphasize the survey's effects on ultimate and proximate causes and processes of environmental change (see the sidebar).

Over the last two decades, conservation biologists have used these same approaches to comprehend the challenges of conserving and restoring biological diversity in flexible and creative ways. They may also serve as diagnostic tools for understanding historic (and prehistoric) ecological change.

Gaining Perspective

We live with, and *within,* the survey's legacy. So all-encompassing are the ways in which it reordered Wisconsin, it is challenge enough just to gain perspective on it. From Man Mound, we might gain that perspective.

The task of land surveying was relatively straightforward and uncomplicated; the task of understanding its lasting impact on our land,

The Functional Analytic Approach

"First-order" effects:

- Human population growth, settlement, distribution, and movement
- Change in land tenure and jurisdiction; privatization and commodification of land
- Establishment of property lines and boundaries
- Change in land uses

"Second-order" effects:

- Parceling and fragmentation of land
  - > Changes in disturbance regimes: fire, flooding, and so on
  - > Changes in flora and fauna: for example, genetics; distribution; reproduction; behavior; dispersal, migration, and movement; species richness; extirpations and extinctions; and invasive species
  - > Changes in ecological processes: for example, pollination, grazing, and predation
  - > Establishment of borders and edges
- Human resource use
  - > Facilitation of resource overexploitation: forests, fish, game species, and so on
  - > Land use: agriculture, forestry, fishing, transportation (roads), and urbanization and subdivision
  - > Land management: exploitation, conversion, protection, restoration, and planning

"Third-order" effects:

Soil erosion and sedimentation

- Air, water, and soil pollution
- Water: alterations (ditching, draining, and damming)
- Altered lake shoreline vegetation

our lives, and our future is not. The survey was, in its original conception, an audacious act of the Enlightenment imagination. It requires a different type of imagination, one that aspires to something beyond expedience and abstraction, to see beyond the grid. It requires appreciation of the cultural harvest (to borrow Leopold's phrase) that land, in all its diverse expressions, yields.

Here, too, the story of Man Mound offers hope. Increase Lapham, in his 1859 report, cautioned that "it would be idle to attempt to speculate upon the object and the meaning of the strange mound here represented. The reader may indulge his own imagination on that subject, and he will perhaps arrive at as near the truth as could the most profound antiquary" (368). The meaning that Man Mound's builders invested in it is one of those mysteries that must remain beyond history's horizon. For Lapham, it suggested motion, boldness, and decisiveness. It may yet open our imaginations, and offer new meanings.

Modern students have noted that Man Mound is distinguished by more than its unique shape. As noted above, almost all other effigy mounds occur near water. Man Mound by contrast walks through uplands some distance from any permanent water. This has prompted speculation that the mound might have served some exceptional ceremonial function for its Woodland Indian engineers. Evidently they sought, and found, a cultural harvest in this special place. And in 1908, a peak year in the nascent conservation movement, a later, very different society found extraordinary cultural value in the same place.

At Man Mound, the geographies of the ancient Native Americans and recently arrived Euro-Americans intersected. At their point of intersection, damage was done. At that same point of intersection, a healing was also begun.

References

Baker, R. G., L. J. Maher, C. A. Chumbley, and K. L. Van Zant. 1992. Patterns of Holocene environmental changes in the midwestern United States. Quaternary Research 37:379–389.

Birmingham, R. A., and L. E. Eisenberg. 2000. Indian Mounds of Wisconsin. Madison: University of Wisconsin Press.

Callicott, J. B., and M. P. Nelson, eds. 1998. The Great New Wilderness Debate. Athens: University of Georgia Press.

Camill, P., C. E. Umbanhowar, Jr., R. Teed, C. E. Geiss, J. Aldinger, L. Dvorak, J. Kenning, J. Limmer, and K. Walkup. 2003. Late-glacial and Holocene climatic effects on fire and vegetation dynamics at the prairie-forest ecotone in south-central Minnesota. Journal of Ecology 91(5):822–836.

Cronon, W. 1991. Nature's Metropolis: Chicago and the Great West. New York: W. W. Norton.

———, ed. 1995. Uncommon Ground: Toward Reinventing Nature. New York: W. W. Norton.

Curtis, J. T. 1956. The modification of mid-latitude grasslands and forests by man. Pp. 721–736 in W. L. Thomas, ed. Man's Role in Changing the Face of the Earth. Chicago: University of Chicago Press.

———. 1959. The Vegetation of Wisconsin: An Ordination of Plant Communities. Madison: University of Wisconsin Press.

Davis, A. M. 1977. The prairie-deciduous forest ecotone in the Upper Middle West. Annals of the Association of American Geographers 67:204–213.

Denevan, W. 1992. The pristine myth: The landscape of the Americas in 1492. Annals of the Association. of American Geographers 82:369–385.

Diamond, J. 1997. Guns, Germs and Steel: The Fates of Human Societies. New York: W. W. Norton.

Flannery, T. 2001. The Eternal Frontier: An Ecological History of North America and Its Peoples. New York: Grove Press.

Grayson, D. K., and D. J. Meltzer. 2002. Clovis hunting and large mammal extinction: a critical review of the evidence. Journal of World Prehistory 16:313–359.

Hoffman, R. 2002. Wisconsin's Natural Communities: How to Recognize Them, Where to Find Them. Madison: University of Wisconsin Press.

Johnson, H. B. 1976. Order upon the Land: The U.S. Rectangular Land Survey and the Upper Mississippi Country. New York: Oxford University Press.

Lapham, I. 1859. Man-shaped mounds of Wisconsin. Pp. 365–368 in Report and Collections of the State Historical Society of Wisconsin for the Years 1857 and 1858, Fourth Annual Report. Madison, WI.

Leopold, A. 1933. Game Management. New York: Scribner's Sons.

———. Coon Valley: An adventure in cooperative conservation. *American Forests* 41(5):205–208.

Leow, P. 2001. Indian Nations of Wisconsin: Histories of Endurance and Renewal. Madison: Wisconsin Historical Society Press.

Linklater, A. 2002. Measuring America: How an Untamed Wilderness Shaped the United States and Fulfilled the Promise of Democracy. New York: Walker.

MacPhee, R. D. E., ed. 1999. Extinctions in Near Time: Contexts, Causes, and Consequences. New York: Plenum Press.

Mann, C. 2002. 1491. Atlantic Monthly 289(3):41–53.

Martin, P. S., and R. G. Klein, eds. 1984. Quaternary Extinctions: A Prehistoric Revolution. Tucson: University of Arizona Press.

Martin, P. S., and C. R. Szuter. 1999. War zones and game sinks in Lewis and Clark's West. Conservation Biology 13:36–45.

Meine, C. 2004. Inherit the grid. Pp. 187–209 in Correction Lines: Essays on Land, Leopold, and Conservation. Washington, DC: Island Press.

Overstreet, D. F., and M. F. Kolb. 2003. Geoarchaeological contexts for Late Pleistocene archaeological sites with human-modified woolly mammoth remains in southeastern Wisconsin, U.S.A. Geoarchaeology 18(1):91–114.

Pielou, E. C. 1991. After the Ice Age: The Return of Life to Glaciated North America. Chicago: University of Chicago Press.

Rowe, K. C., E. J. Heske, P. W. Brown, and K. N. Paige. 2004. Surviving the ice: northern refugia and postglacial colonization. Proceedings of the National Academy of Sciences 101(28):10355–10359.

Soulé, M. E., and G. Lease, eds. 1995. Reinventing Nature? Response to Postmodern Deconstructionism. Washington, DC: Island Press.

Tudge, C. 1996. The Time before History: 5 Million Years of Human Impact. New York: Simon and Schuster.

Vale, T. 1999. The myth of the humanized landscape: An example from Yellowstone National Park. Wild Earth 9(3):34–40.

———. 2002. Fire, Native Peoples, and the Natural Landscape. Washington, DC: Island Press.

West, E. 1998. The Contested Plains: Indians, Goldseekers, and the Rush to Colorado. Lawrence: University Press of Kansas.

Williams, J. W., B. N. Shuman, T. Webb III, P. J. Bartlein, and P. L. Leduc. 2004. Late-Quaternary vegetation dynamics in North America: Scaling from taxa to biomes. Ecological Monographs 74(2):309–334.

3 The Challenge of Unveiling the Invisible Present

John J. Magnuson

Change is all around us; the challenge is to see it or perhaps to remember it. Often we seem locked in an invisible present (Magnuson 1990) and an invisible place (Swanson and Sparks 1990), oblivious to long-term changes occurring across the landscape. Even qualitatively our memories are fallible. Were hickory nuts less abundant this year than last? How abundant were they a decade ago, or when we were children? Quantitatively our sense of change is usually just plain wrong. Consider the statement: "In winter 1999–2000 Lake Monona in the Madison area did not freeze over." Is that correct? Actually the shortest recorded ice duration to date on Lake Monona was 47 days, and it occurred in the winter of 1997–98. It was actually Lake Mendota (figure 3.1) that some allege did not freeze over. In fact, it was ice covered for only 21 days in the winter of 2001–2.

Lake Mendota Ice Example

We can recall the past and sense change only when we keep records. Lake Mendota's ice cover provides a good example (Robertson 1989; Magnuson 1990; Magnuson et al. 2003, 2006b). Recently, in the winter of 2005–6, ice cover persisted for 95 days (figure 3.2, top). By itself,

FIGURE 3.1 A view of Madison and the Wisconsin state capital from Governors Island across the ice forming on Lake Mendota in winter, December 20, 2003. (Photo by author.)

this is a rather uninteresting fact that provides no sense of change—the invisible present.

When we view 10 years of records, we see that the 2005–6 winter was longer than average. Ice cover ranged from 21 to 119 days, and the apparent decline in ice cover at 3.7 days per decade is uncertain.

Across 50 years, we see that ice cover in 2005–6 was about average for those years and that ice cover declined rapidly at 6.4 days per decade. The trend is apparent even given the high interyear variability in weather.

With the full length of observation from 1855–56 to 2005–6, we see that even though ice cover in 2005–6 was about average for the most recent 10 years, it was shorter than each of the first 20 years of record. We also see that ice cover shortened by 1.9 days per decade over the 150 years or more slowly than over the last 50 years. Over the 150 years, ice covered Lake Mendota for as long as 161 days in 1881. The four longest ice cover years were before 1900, and the three shortest occurred in the last 10 years. The trend again is apparent even given the high interyear variability in weather.

By itself, even this long record from Lake Mendota tells us nothing about how pervasive this trend is. Any single site risks leaving us in an "invisible place" (Swanson and Sparks 1990). Madison is unique in many ways; perhaps our loss of lake ice is simply another idiosyncrasy. This, however, proves not to be the case. We have long ice records for other lakes in Wisconsin (Magnuson et al. 2003) and across the Great Lakes region (Kling et al. 2003). We also have records for lakes and streams throughout the Northern Hemisphere (Magnuson et al. 2000). Ice durations are decreasing around the globe; this conclusion is possible only when we are not constrained by information from a single location and thus lost in the invisible place (figure 3.3).

Collectively, simple observations of ice cover over the last 150 years from around the Northern Hemisphere reveal a systematic pattern that leads us to conclude that warming is under way. We are losing winters as we knew them. Ice cover turns out to be as sensitive an indicator of warming as the miner's canary was for poor air. The ice records allow another conclusion: lake and stream ecosystems already are being altered physically by climate warming in immediate, observable ways.

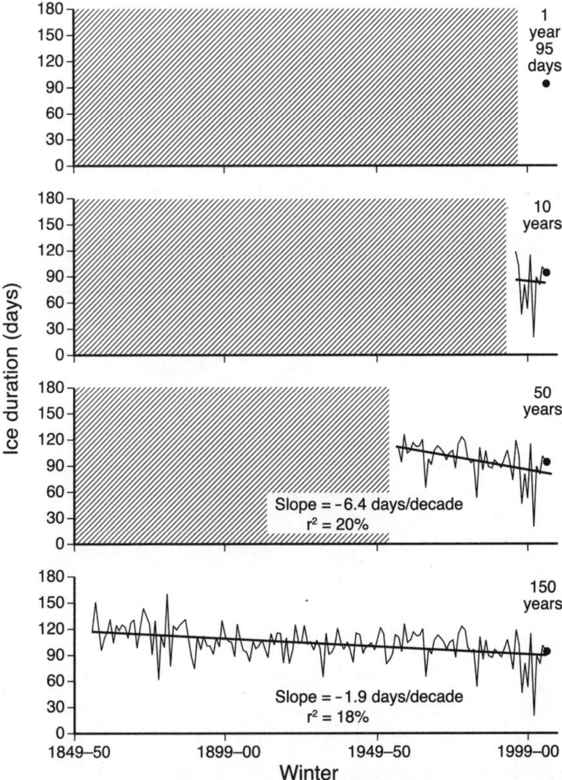

FIGURE 3.2 The invisible present exemplified by opening up a long-term record of ice duration on Lake Mendota at Madison, Wisconsin, from the winter of 2005–6 to the winter of 1855–56 (data available at http://lterquery.limnology.wisc.edu/index.jsp?project_id=LTER1).

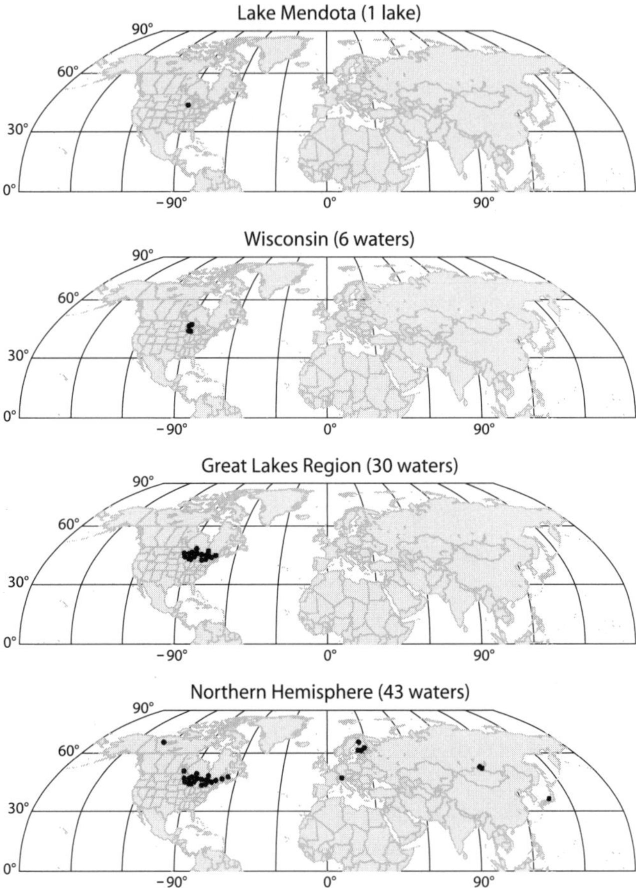

FIGURE 3.3 The invisible place exemplified by the increasing spatial array of waters on which we have published long-term data. Data range from one specific lake to 43 waters throughout the Northern Hemisphere (Magnuson et al. 2000; Kling et al. 2003; Magnuson et al. 2003). Forty of the 43 sites have long-term linear trends toward warming.

Being an Elder at a Young Age

As we expand our view to include longer periods and broader areas, we lift the veil from the invisible present and invisible place. We gain a vantage point for glimpsing the changes going on around us. With this comes insights that we usually associate with age and wisdom. Cultures have always depended on sages and elders whose wide experience gave them deep understanding and perspective. With this capacity, we might hope that our own culture will gain perspective on patterns of global change as well and be able to make informed policy decisions. The idea that knowledge and wisdom come from a longer temporal and broader spatial view of the world is not new as we see in some of my favorite quotations (see sidebar).

REGARDING TIME

Time is sort of a river of passing events, and strong is its current; no sooner is a thing brought to sight than it is swept by and another takes its place, and this too will be swept away.

Marcus Aurelius, Emperor of Rome, 121–80 [1673, chap. 4, 43]

Time is but the stream I go a-fishing in.

Henry David Thoreau [1854, 155]

Thinking Like a Mountain . . . Only the mountain has lived long enough to listen objectively to the howl of a wolf.

Aldo Leopold [1949, 129]

We are always acting on what has just finished happening. It happened at least 1/30th of a second ago. We think we are in the present, but we aren't. The present we know is only a movie of the past.

Tom Wolfe [1968, 145]

It takes a leap of the imagination to . . . accelerate . . . a process of change in the environment enough to see it in a more familiar frame and thus discern its meaning. **Al Gore [1992, 42]**

REGARDING SPACE

The field cannot be well seen from within the field

Ralph Waldo Emerson [1909, 161]

It is helpful to stand at some distance from any large pattern we are trying to comprehend. **Al Gore [1992, 43]**

REGARDING TIME AND SPACE TOGETHER

Any great work of art . . . revives and readapts time and space, and the measure of its success is the extent to which it makes you an inhabitant of that world—the extent to which it invites you in and lets you breathe its strange, special air. **Leonard Bernstein [1958, 159]**

A fundamental characteristic of complex human systems [is that] "cause" and "effect" are not close in time and space [yet] most of us assume, most of the time, that cause and effect are close in time and space. **Peter M. Senge [1990, 63]**

Although the ice-cover data point to global changes, many of the changes occurring in lakes are more local or temporary. For invasions of exotic species into lakes, the appropriate scale might be the regional drainage network. For excess nutrient inputs, it might be the lake's watershed. Knowing the spatial imprint of a driver of change is important and helps ascribe the cause as well as the appropriate human response to change.

The Challenge

Long-term observations and measurements come from people making individual efforts or working as part of some larger volunteer or professional group. These efforts are often organized as a result of scientific interest, management concerns, or legal obligations to monitor environmental impacts. Much of this activity is focused at field stations, in established research and educational programs, or in government and nongovernment organizations. Records range from yesterday's gage height in a stream to analyses of thousands of years of charcoal or pollen records in lake sediment. Each such activity faces challenges in generating, sustaining, and analyzing useful long-term records. What should be measured? Where? How should measurements be documented? What should be done to make the data secure and available? How can measurements and their documentation survive between generations of observers, scientists, budget cycles, and administrations?

One complex challenge is to coordinate our information over time and across landscapes. How can we coordinate and plan our records to create a meaningful and interpretable whole? *Waters of Wisconsin* (WASAL 2003) lists and identifies 66 data sets from "Aerial Photography" (State Cartographers Office) to "Lakes, North Temperate Lakes Long-Term Ecological Research" (Center for Limnology, University of Wisconsin–Madison) to "Wetland Losses—Permitted" (Wisconsin Department of Natural Resources). WASAL also lists and identifies 38 separate volunteer monitoring programs for amphibians, birds, butterflies, exotics, fish, Best Management Practices in forestry, groundwater, health and water, lakes, rivers, watersheds, and wetlands. Who combines these data to ponder them collectively?

Often we fail to face these challenges explicitly leaving a collage of segmented local observations. *Waters of Wisconsin* (WASAL 2003) discussed these challenges and made four relevant recommendations to improve our abilities to monitor and manage aquatic ecosystems and resources. Consider replacing "water" with "ecological system" in these quoted passages to cover the scope of "Vanishing Wisconsin":

- "The state of Wisconsin—working in partnership with federal, tribal, and local governments; the private sector; nonprofit organizations—should maintain the state's long-term commitment to and capacity for effective water monitoring. The goal of the state of Wisconsin should be *to develop and maintain the most cost-effective, efficient, well organized, and responsive water monitoring, data collection, and information management system possible.*"
- "The state of Wisconsin, in partnership with relevant state, tribal, federal, and private entities, should explore options for improving coordination of water information within the state and identifying key research and monitoring needs."
- "To help make information on Wisconsin's waters more available and useful to educators, state legislators, local officials, and other decision makers, the state of Wisconsin should coordinate and prepare a regular 'State of Wisconsin's Waters.' "
- "To make information on Wisconsin's waters more accessible to the public, institutions engaged in gathering and analyzing such information should collaborate in developing a web-based, interactive repository of documented water status and trend data."

Sustaining a long-term series of measurements is always a challenge. Yet some individuals, groups, and programs are remarkably successful. The following examples range from volunteer self-initiated records to institutionalized formal programs.

Since 1958, my friend Tug Juday had been collecting ecological data on the northern Wisconsin lake where he now lives. His daughter Patricia stepped in to help in recent years. They have shared these data with the University of Wisconsin's Center for Limnology.

Each year, huge numbers of volunteer birders participate in local Christmas Bird Counts (http://www.audubon.org/bird/cbc/) organized by the National Audubon Society. Frank Chapman began these counts on Christmas Day in 1900 with 27 enthusiastic birders. Today, there are 50,000 participants, and the data can be queried on a Web interface. These data have proven to be useful in many unanticipated ways.

Noe Woods at the western entrance to the University of Wisconsin Arboretum was mapped in 1948, providing a known baseline for comparing sampling methods (Cottam and Curtis 1949, 1956; Curtis 1959). Since then, Noe Woods has been resurveyed and remapped many times in the training of new generations of ecologists through field exercises. The goal of Grant Cottam's early "Oak Integration Study" (Loucks and Curtis 1993) was to understand succession in southern Wisconsin oak forests. This work contributed to the careers of many eminent ecologists, including O. Loucks, G. Goff, and B. McCune (McCune and Cottam 1985; Loucks and Curtis 1993). The tradition continues with T. Givnish who continues to have classes remap Noe Woods every five years. These data are available by request from the University of Wisconsin Arboretum. The long-term data from Noe Woods reflect the spirit of most working ecologists driven by a desire for knowledge. They also reflect the hard work, foresight, and dedication required to establish and maintain data sets beyond normal funding and personal time frames. These data continue to increase in value as they contribute to our understanding of ecological change.

Since 1981, the Center for Limnology has intensively studied a suite of lakes near the University of Wisconsin's Trout Lake Station in Vilas County, Wisconsin as part of the Long-Term Ecological Research (LTER) program funded by the National Science Foundation (http://lternet.edu/). The site focuses on studies of north temperate lakes (http://www.limnology.wisc.edu/) and is one of 26 terrestrial and aquatic sites being studied intensively in the United States, Antarctica, Puerto Rico, and even in French Polynesia. To address the challenges of long-term research, we document sample sites, place measurement protocols on the Web, back up the data securely, and make it freely available on the Web (Magnuson et al. 2006a). We also work to coordinate and interpret data across the entire LTER network. Our Wisconsin research program has persisted for 26 years, surviving six bouts of peer review, shifts in research focus, use of new technologies, and new students and lead investigators. To retain vitality and persist within the NSF-LTER system, we have had to maintain the old while embracing the new, retain continuity and reliability of the long-term research, balance program growth with manageability, and continually synthesize while making site- and system-specific advances (Magnuson et al. 2006b).

Each of the above examples portrays success in helping unveil the invisible present and place. Each reflects individual effort, willingness to collaborate with others, and sharing that is driven by common goals. All make their data freely available. Some recognize that monitoring, per se, is not the purpose. The use of the records for decision making, scientific information, education, or even personal enjoyment is the fundamental purpose.

Ecological changes will continue to occur across the landscape. Our challenge is to unveil the "invisible present and place" through long-term measurement and monitoring so that we can understand and learn from the past, better imagine the future, and shape a future of choice.

References

Bernstein, L. 1958. What makes opera great. Vogue, December.

Cottam, G., and J. T. Curtis. 1949. A method for making rapid surveys of woodlands by means of randomly selected trees. Ecology 30:101–104.

———. 1956. The use of distance measures in phytosociological sampling. Ecology 37:451–460.

Curtis, J. T. 1959. The Vegetation of Wisconsin. Madison: University of Wisconsin Press.

Emerson, R. W. 1909. Essay X—Circles. Vol. 5. In C. W. Eliot, ed. The Harvard Classics: Essays and English Traits. New York: P. F. Collier & Son.

Gore, A. 1992. Earth in the Balance, Ecology and the Human Spirit. Boston: Houghton Mifflin.

Kling, G. K., K. Hayhoe, L. B. Johnson, J. J. Magnuson, S. Polasky, S. K. Robinson, B. J. Shuter, M. M. Wander, D. J. Wuebbles, D. R. Zak, S. C. Lindroth, S. C. Moser, and M. L. Wilson. 2003. Confronting Climate Change in the Great Lakes Region: Impacts on Our Communities and Ecosystems. Cambridge, MA: Union of Concerned Scientists; Washington DC: Ecological Society of America.

Leopold, A. 1949. Thinking like a mountain. Pp. 129–133 in A Sand County Almanac and Sketches Here and There. New York: Oxford University Press.

Loucks, O. L., and J. T. Curtis. 1993. Integration studies of the dry-mesic quercus community in Southern Wisconsin. In J. S. Fralish, R. P. McIntosh, and O. L. Loucks, eds. John T. Curtis: Fifty Years of Wisconsin Plant Ecology. Madison: Wisconsin Academy of Sciences, Arts and Letters.

Magnuson, J. J. 1990. Long-term ecological research and the invisible present. BioScience 40:495–501.

Magnuson, J. J., B. J. Benson, T. K. Kratz, D. E. Armstrong, C. J. Bowser, A. C. C. Colby, T. W. Meinke, P. K. Montz, and K. E. Webster. 2006a. Origin, operation, evolution, and challenges. Pp. 280–320 in J. J. Magnuson, T. K. Kratz, and B. J. Benson, eds. Long-Term Dynamics of Lakes in the Landscape. New York: Oxford University Press.

Magnuson, J. J., T. K. Kratz, and B. J. Benson. 2006b. Long-Term Dynamics of Lakes in the Landscape. New York: Oxford University Press.

Magnuson, J. J., J. T. Krohelski, K. E. Kunkel, and D. M. Robertson. 2003. Wisconsin's waters and climate: Historical changes and possible futures. Transactions of the Wisconsin Academy of Sciences, Arts and Letters 90:23–36.

Magnuson, J. J., D. M. Robertson, B. J. Benson, R. H. Wynne, D. M. Livingstone, T. Arai, R. A. Assel, R. G. Barry, V. Card, E. Kuusisto, N. G. Granin, T. D. Prowse, K. M. Stewart, and V. S. Vuglinski. 2000. Historical trends in lake and river ice cover in the Northern Hemisphere. Science 289(5485):1743–1746; errata, 2001, Science 291(5502):1254.

Marcus Aurelius [Emperor of Rome, 121–80]. 1673. Meditations, translated out of the original Greek, with notes by Meric Casaubon. 4th ed. London: Charles Harper.

McCune, B., and G. Cottam. 1985. The successional status of a southern Wisconsin oak woods. Ecology: 66:1270–1278.

Robertson, D. M. 1989. The use of lake water temperature and ice cover as climatic indicators. Ph.D. thesis, University of Wisconsin–Madison.

Senge, P. M. 1990. The Fifth Discipline, the Art & Practice of the Learning Organization. New York: Doubleday/Currency.

Swanson, F. J., and R. E. Sparks. 1990. Long-term ecological research and the invisible place. BioScience 40:502–508.

Thoreau, H. D. 1854. Walden, or, Life in the Woods. Boston: Ticknor and Fields.

Wisconsin Academy of Sciences, Arts and Letters (WASAL). 2003. Waters of Wisconsin: The Future of Our Aquatic Ecosystems and Resources. Madison: WASAL.

Wolfe, T. 1968. The Electric Kool-Aid Acid Test. New York: Farrar, Straus and Giroux.

4

Thinking Like a Flower: Phenology and Climate Change at the Leopold Shack

Sarah D. Wright and Nina Leopold Bradley

No single person embodies the legacy of conservation in Wisconsin better than Aldo Leopold. His beloved classic *A Sand County Almanac* is treasured as much for its landmark ethical ideas and literary merit as for the ecological principles it pioneered. Millions of readers have doted on the Central Sands of Wisconsin where the Leopold family built their now-famous "shack," welcomed the return of cranes, and stooped to the ground to inspect the tiny *Draba* flower. "He who hopes for spring with upturned eye never sees so small a thing as Draba," reads a line from the "April" chapter of *A Sand County Almanac* (1949, 29).

A Sand County Almanac is not just an elegant narrative of the backyard soap operas played out by woodcocks or a series of elegies to the native flora. It has endeared those of us who cannot "live without wild things" because it challenges us to *see* in ways that deepen our connection to the landscapes we inhabit. By paying attention to the comings and goings of geese and keeping track of what's in flower, we come closer to realizing Aldo Leopold's vision of a Land Ethic, and our role in the "biotic community." As he puts it, "We can be ethical only in relation to something we can see, feel, understand, love, or otherwise have faith in" (1949, 251). Even tiny flower buds serve to demonstrate how environmental problems are global in scope, connecting climate warming to the plants and animals where we live.

The Phenological Legacy of the Leopolds

Leopold often encouraged his students to keep a phenological journal to gain a clearer understanding of the biotic community. Phenology, or the study of biological cycles, explores the seasonal rhythms of events—such as flowering, fruiting, bird migration, and animal reproduction—in order to discern potential relationships between these events and abiotic cues such as climate or the amount of daylight at a given time of the year. In short, phenologists attempt to uncover the "clock" that makes ecosystems tick. This interdisciplinary science transcends the "invisible present" by being both rooted in the present and interpreting events in the context of the past. Leopold's gift for "thinking like a mountain," contemplating the present from the vantage of history, suited him well to the study of phenology.

The Leopolds made phenology a family affair, resulting in extensive records on phenological events at the "shack" (now the Leopold Memorial Reserve in Fairfield Township, Sauk County, Wisconsin). Aldo Leopold recorded phenological events from 1935 to 1945, summarized in an article in *Ecological Monographs* (Leopold and Jones 1947). Beginning in 1976, his daughter, Nina Leopold Bradley, and her husband Charlie, resumed marking the dates of blooms and birdsongs at the Reserve. These two sets of data, collected in the same location over the span of nearly 70 years, offer a unique opportunity to assess the effects of climate warming on phenophases, or life cycles, of plants and animals in Wisconsin. Results from 1976 to 1998 were previously published (Bradley et al. 1999). Here, we present only the data collected from 1994 to 2004, to incorporate the most recent data and to compare data from equal windows of time.

Phenology: The "Horizontal Science"

"Phenologists are a heterogeneous lot, and have found shelter under diverse intellectual roof-trees," Leopold noted (Leopold and Jones 1947, 83). He described phenology as a "horizontal science" that incorporates information from many disciplines within the biological and agricultural sciences: "Whoever sees the land as a whole is likely to have an interest in it" (Leopold and Jones 1947, 83). President Thomas Jefferson is a notable phenologically minded figure: in his instructions to Meriwether

Lewis prior to the famed Lewis and Clark expedition, Jefferson includes "the dates at which particular plants put forth or lose their flower, or leaf, times of appearance of particular birds, reptiles, or insects" as "objects worthy of notice" along the channel of the Missouri River (http://wiki.monticello.org/mediawiki/index.php/Preparations_for_the_Lewis_and_Clark_Expedition). Henry David Thoreau is also known to have kept detailed phenological records in his journals. Phenological observations have been used for centuries to maximize crop production, prepare for seasonal allergies, and anticipate optimal bird-watching conditions. Today, this ancient science is used to track the effects of climate warming on organisms and to make predictions about the future health of ecosystems.

Long-term records on climate, such as those that document temperature and precipitation, are common; however, similar records on phenological cycles of organisms are rare. A few well-known sets of data have been studied to correlate weather with the life cycles of plants and animals. For example, two English scientists have examined data on "indications of spring" spanning over 200 years collected by the Marsham family (Sparks and Carey 1995). Several generations of the Smiley family kept records of first blooms and arrivals of birds at their upstate New York inn (Oglesby and Smith 1995). More recently, observers at the Rocky Mountain Biological Laboratory in western Colorado have tracked local climate conditions such as snowfall as well as phenological cycles of birds, mammals, and wildflowers at this high-altitude field station since the 1970s (Inouye et al. 2000). The study described in this chapter is similar to these studies, in that it uses data recorded over many decades to discern changes in the average dates of first blooms and arrivals of birds over time.

Even though long-term phenological records are uncommon, some scientists have devised innovative ways to study the effects of climate warming on organisms. A clever study conducted in Boston used dated herbarium specimens to track advances in flowering dates over time (Primack et al. 2004). Meta-analysis, or synthesis of a large number of scientific studies, can be a powerful tool to combine large volumes of information and construct a "big picture" of how organisms are responding to climate warming (Root et al. 2003). Other studies simulate the warming events of the recent past by conducting experiments to mimic the increases in ambient temperature that organisms are likely to face within the next several decades, in order to predict how they might respond to continued warming. For example, Price and Waser (1998) found that subalpine plants grown with electric heaters that simulated climate warming bloomed earlier than plants grown without artificial heat, probably due to earlier timing of snowmelt.

Many studies confirm a warming trend over the last several decades. According to the Intergovernmental Panel on Climate Change (IPCC), which compiles studies on climate change from a variety of scientific disciplines, the 1990s were "very likely" the warmest decade and 1998 was the warmest year since 1861 (IPCC 2001). The report notes that global average temperatures have increased by 0.6°C over the course of the 20th century and are predicted to increase by 1.4°C to 5.8°C for the period 1990–2100. While the IPCC finds that climate warming is already occurring on a global scale, the panel predicts that warming will elicit the most pronounced effects on biological cycles at higher elevations and latitudes (2001). Locally, Wisconsinites have noticed that our lakes freeze later and thaw earlier than in the past (Magnuson et al. 2000; also see chapter 3). Bradley et al. (1999) use the average date of ice melt in Madison's Lake Mendota as a reliable baseline to indicate advances in the arrival of spring.

With warmer temperatures and earlier springs, we expect some organisms to respond by advancing their life cycles. Organisms whose rhythms are closely connected with temperature—for example, whose reproductive cycles are set to a seasonal "clock" or whose food sources vary in abundance with temperature—tend to respond to warmer average temperatures by starting their life functions earlier in the spring or remaining active longer into the fall. Some organisms, though, may not be as sensitive to or may be less able to respond to changing temperatures, sticking to the same "routine" regardless of when warm spring days arrive or the chillier days of fall begin. The phenological data collected by the Leopolds offers us an opportunity to evaluate which organisms fall into each category.

The Data: Birds and Blooms at the Leopold Memorial Reserve

The Leopold records of phenological events at the shack represent a "natural" warming experiment that measures changes in life cycles in response to higher temperatures. We compared events for which there were at least 3 observations from 1935–45 and 3 from 1994–2004. This yielded a total of 108 events; of those, 75 were dates of first bloom, 27 were first or last sightings of birds, and 6 were climate events such as last frost and thawing of lakes. For each event, an average Julian date was calculated for 1935–45 and for 1994–2004. The average date of each event in the 1930s and 1940s was then subtracted from its average date over the past

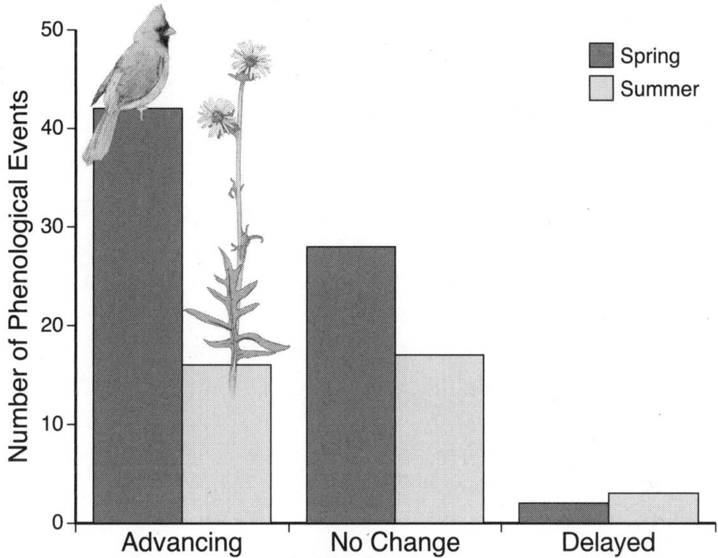

FIGURE 4.1 Shift in spring and summer phenological events between 1935–45 and 1994–2004. Significantly more organisms respond to climate warming than would be expected due to random chance ($t = 7.76$, $p < 0.0001$). In addition, advanced events are more likely to occur in the spring ($G = 65.65$, $p < 0.001$). The trend toward earlier life cycles is significant in the summer ($G = 12.64$, $p < 0.01$), but far less striking than the spring shift.

10 years. We report this difference in terms of weeks in order to convey the importance of these changes in terms that are meaningful relative to our human "clock."

We defined an organism as "advancing" its life cycle if the difference between its average Julian date in 1935–45 and in 1994–2004 was one week or more—that is, if a bird arrived or a plant bloomed at least one week earlier in 1994–2004 than it did in 1935–45. An event was defined as showing no change if it was neither one week earlier nor one week later in 1994–2004 than in 1935–45 and "delayed" if it occurred at least one week later in 1994–2004 than it did in 1935–45. We also grouped data into "spring" and "summer" categories, based on whether the event's overall average date of occurrence fell before or after the summer solstice, June 21. Five events that occurred in the autumn were included in the summer category.

Many phenological events occur at least a week earlier today than they did 70–80 years ago (figure 4.1), with the average life cycles advancing 7.64 days. Shifts are more pronounced in the spring than the summer, consistent with climatic measurements that show that the spring months are heating up to a greater extent than the summer months.

Plants on the "Move"

What biological mechanisms might explain these shifts? We expect plants with C3 photosynthetic pathways (typical for most temperate-zone plants) to respond to warming temperatures by advancing their life cycles. This is because net photosynthesis peaks at moderate temperatures. At low temperature, enzyme activity (and hence the rate of photosynthesis) is sluggish. Net photosynthesis then increases at moderate temperatures but plateaus, or even decreases, under hot conditions. This occurs because the machinery of photosynthesis saturates at high temperatures and light levels while respiration (the use of sugars and starches to provide energy) continues to increase. High temperatures also bring more water loss as leaves open their stomata for evaporative cooling. Furthermore, some plants are sensitive to exposure to too much light or too little water, stresses more likely to occur in the summer months. Because plants cannot move in space, they "move" in time, to take advantage of the climate conditions most conducive to a successful life cycle.

One noteworthy plant whose date of first bloom has advanced by nearly three weeks between 1935–45 and 1994–2004 is the compass plant. This species once grew among the prairie plants in the graveyard visited by Aldo Leopold in the "July" chapter of *A Sand County Almanac.* "Heretofore unreachable by scythe or mower, this yard-square relic of original Wisconsin gives birth, each July, to a man-high stalk of compass plant," Leopold wrote. During the 1930s and 1940s, compass plant began to bloom, on average, on July 15; today, it would no longer find its place within the "July" chapter, as its average date of first bloom over the last 10 years is June 26.

Some of the earliest bloomers—the showy flowers that make up Wisconsin's spring flora—seem to debut in concert with the last frost of the season. The average marsh marigold first flowers just one day later than the average date of the last frost. Both events have advanced by 1.5 weeks between 1935–45 and 1994–2004. Other early emerging plants include Dutchman's breeches and large-flowered trillium, both of which now bloom 2 weeks earlier (in 1994–2004) than in 1935–45. Most spring-blooming woodland wildflowers must take advantage of the abundant light that passes through leafless treetops in April and May and complete most of their growth and flowering before the canopy fills in and shades the forest floor. Such plants may have evolved to follow temperature cues to guide their early emergence. In general, plants that are nonwoody, early bloomers show a more pronounced response to climate warming than late-blooming or woody plants (Walther et al. 2002).

Because each species has evolved to thrive within a specific range of temperatures, climate warming may differentially affect species with varying thresholds of heat tolerance, ultimately causing shifts in plants' geographic ranges and in composition of plant communities. For example, Harte and Shaw (1995) demonstrated that heat-tolerant sagebrush dominated sections of an alpine meadow where the soil was warmed with a heater, while wildflowers fared badly. As temperatures continue to climb, it is possible that plants for which Wisconsin is the southern edge of their range may go locally extinct if they do not advance their life cycle to avoid heat stress.

Climate Change on the Wing

Previous studies suggest that temperature may affect the timing of migration (Temple and Cary 1987) and egg laying in birds and may potentially shift ranges of distribution for some species (for a review, see Crick 2004). We expect short-distance migrants or year-round residents to have life cycles cued by temperature and therefore respond quickly to warmer temperatures. Long-distance migrants, in contrast, typically rely on photoperiod as they cannot sense climate conditions in Wisconsin. A previous study by Temple and Cary demonstrated that while long-distance migrants' flight schedules were not correlated with temperature over a period of five years, short distance migrants passed through southern Wisconsin significantly earlier in warmer years. The present study found similar trends: although a handful of short-distance migrants such as the brown-headed cowbird and fox sparrow showed no change in arrival date between 1935–45 and 1994–2004, short-distance migrants were overwhelmingly the most notable "advancers." For example, the Canada goose arrived five weeks earlier, on average, in 1994–2004 than in 1935–45, the northern cardinal sang its first song four weeks earlier, and the American robin arrived three weeks earlier. Of the 18 short-distance migrants and residents whose phenology was recorded, 11 advanced their life cycle by at least one week, 5 showed no change, and 1 autumn migrant, the white-throated sparrow, delayed its arrival from the north by one week.

In contrast, only one neotropical migrant, the indigo bunting, has advanced its life cycle by arriving at least one week earlier in recent years compared with the 1930s and 1940s (the great blue heron, whose long-distance migration flight path does not quite reach the neotropics, also advanced its arrival by more than one week). The rose-breasted grosbeak and Baltimore oriole nearly made our "phenological cutoff" by arriving six days earlier. The great crested flycatcher and wood thrush, however, maintain about the same spring schedule between the two data sets. These birds may be cued by signals such as photoperiod, rather than temperature, or may experience too little warming in their wintering grounds to trigger early migration.

Implications of Climate Change for Relationships among Species

What happens if interacting species respond differently to climate warming? What will be the implications for relationships between organisms that have been fine-tuned over the course of evolutionary time? These questions have yet to be fully explored, but it is clear that the answers will vary widely among species. One interaction that appears to have remained intact occurs between the eastern phoebe and the skunk cabbage. These species have responded in concert to warmer spring temperatures. In the 1930s and 1940s, the average date of first bloom for the skunk cabbage was April 1, with eastern phoebes arriving, on average, six days later. In the period 1994–2004, the skunk cabbage bloomed exactly two weeks earlier, on March 18. The eastern phoebe matched this advancement precisely, arriving at the Leopold Memorial Reserve, on average, on March 24.

This striking synchrony in phenology between the phoebe and the skunk cabbage corresponds well with observations recounted by a young Aldo Leopold in a letter to his mother from boarding school. Describing a bird-watching venture with his new binoculars in what he calls the Far Woods, he writes, "The above mentioned tract contains a great deal of Skunk Cabbage, now in full blossom and buzzing with carrion flies and other insects. Accordingly, the Phoebes were there in force, and I actually detected one sitting on a flower and contentedly snapping up all visitors in the way of insects" (Leopold Archives, Leopold Memorial Reserve). Indeed, the skunk cabbage radiates both heat and stink from its flowers, luring insect pollinators to linger inside. Both the skunk cabbage and the phoebe seem to have adapted to warmer temperatures by altering their life cycles in tandem to maximize resource capture.

Mismatches also occur between organisms' phenophases and the resources they need to survive. In Europe, great tits feed their young caterpillars hatched in rotting wood. The caterpillars have hatched earlier in recent years, reflecting increased spring temperatures. However, great tits have not responded to warmer temperatures, laying their eggs and rearing their young on the same average dates as in the past. The result is that young today are born after the peak of caterpillar hatching, leaving baby great tits hungry (Visser et al. 1998).

Though we did not measure insect phenophases in our study, insects are expected to respond readily to climate change, as many of the trees they feed on produce leaves earlier with warmer springs. Birds that feed primarily on insects but do not respond to climate warming may suffer. Neotropical migrant birds in particular appear less able to respond to warmer temperatures, as their migration is usually based on stable cues such as day length. The disjunction between the rates of change in these birds' wintering and breeding grounds, coupled with their reliance on internal cues to trigger migration, hamper their ability to adjust to changing climatic conditions that could impair breeding success and thus the ultimate survival of some species (Both and Visser 2001). Inouye and colleagues (2000) report that while the growing seasons are lengthening at lower altitudes, they have not changed significantly at high altitudes. As a result, the American robin is arriving earlier at high altitudes, as much as 65 days before the snow melts to uncover sources of food.

Such asynchronies may lead to selection to change phenological characteristics. For example, the mismatch between the reproductive cycles of birds and their insect prey may act to favor birds that lay and incubate their eggs earlier or produce one brood in a season instead of two in order to ensure that there is sufficient food for each chick (Crick 2004). However, selective pressure can only result in rapid adaptation when there is sufficient genetic variation in a population and when such genetic traits are not too tightly coupled to other traits subject to other kinds of selection. In other words, adaptation requires the existence of at least a few "weirdo" individuals that happen to exhibit the trait that is desirable under new environmental conditions—in this case, great tits that happen to lay their eggs earlier.

We have yet to discover whether there is enough genetic diversity within populations of great tits to facilitate adaptation to the constraints posed by climate warming or to discern in general which characters define the "winning" and "losing" organisms in ecosystems undergoing climate change. Generalists, or "weedy" species, that thrive over a wide range of environmental conditions may have a competitive edge over more specialized species in the face of environmental change. As the case of the great tits and caterpillars demonstrates, a change in the life cycle of one organism may have consequences for a series of food chain interactions. "This interdependence between the complex structure of the land and its smooth functioning as an energy unit is one of its basic attributes," wrote Leopold in "The Land Ethic," his landmark essay at the end of *A Sand County Almanac.* "When a change occurs in one part of the circuit, many other parts must adjust themselves to it" (1949, 254). We have much to learn about which parts of the circuits will be able to adjust and which will not and how ecosystems as a whole might change as a result.

Rebirth of Phenology: Opportunities for Education and Collaboration

Certainly, there are far too many questions about the impact of climate warming on life cycles and far too many species to measure for scientists alone to characterize these ecological changes. Phenology is a promising field not only because it provides some of the most striking, easy-to-see indicators of the effects of climate change on biota but also because it offers a unique opportunity for cooperation between "citizen scientists," students, and the scientific community. As University of Wisconsin–Milwaukee geography professor Mark Schwartz notes, the field of phenology is experiencing a rebirth, as the problem of climate change has renewed interest in this interdisciplinary, on-the-ground science. He highlights the potential for phenological studies to provide critical information about the responses of individual species to climate change at a local level that can be used in conjunction with information from satellite images to construct models of regional climate change (Schwartz 1999).

Schwartz is president of the Wisconsin Phenological Society. He advocates integrating phenological research with education. Events such as first blooms and first arrivals can be easily measured and serve to heighten students' and volunteers' awareness of environmental dynamics. They can also be incorporated into scientific studies. Another long-running program that has successfully connected volunteer monitors with scientists is the Wisconsin Checklist Project, which compiled weekly bird observations from throughout the state to produce *Wisconsin Birds: A Seasonal and Geographical Guide* (Temple, Cary, and Rolley 1997). This book is an indispensable guide for birders, showing the probability of finding each species according to the time of year and location.

Other programs across North America offer opportunities for people interested in phenology to get involved in monitoring their favorite species. For example, the PlantWatch program, based at the University of Alberta, collects data on spring flowering times from volunteers and students on 14 key indicator species of plants (see Beaubien 1996). Some groups, such as Operation Ruby Throat, focus on tracking a single species that draws a significant following—in this case, the ruby-throated hummingbird—while others, like the Vermont Climate Change project, focus on a handful of conspicuous local events, such as the turning of fall foliage and the blooming of lilacs, as well as the occurrence of Lyme disease as a proxy indicator of deer tick abundance. The idea is to identify repeatable, distinctive, significant local events that are easy to consistently measure from one observer to another and from year to year. Leopold knew that "there is value in any experience that reminds us of our dependency on the soil-plant-animal-man food chain, and of the fundamental organization of the biota" (1949, 212). Engaging in phenological studies is definitely a valuable way of both learning about the impacts of climate warming on the organisms with which we share our food chain and cultivating an ethical relationship with them.

A Gentler Kind of Change

Aldo Leopold described ecosystems as "circuits" of energy, complex networks of life whose sustenance depends on the continued flow of resources among diverse components. He saw that "evolution is a long series of self-induced changes, the net result of which has been to elaborate the flow mechanism and to lengthen the circuit." Additions and subtractions have certainly always been part of the interaction among organisms, as some adapt and persist and others die out. "Evolutionary changes, however, are usually slow and local," he warned. "Man's invention of tools has enabled him to make changes of unprecedented violence, rapidity, and scope" (1949, 254). Indeed, climate warming is acting as a selective agent of unprecedented scale. This chapter has recounted some of the ongoing tales of adaptation and disruption that continue to play out.

While Leopold fingers human "tools" as inflicting rapid, violent change, he also recognizes how tools allow us to look back on history and see our place within it. The tools themselves are neither inherently destructive nor constructive: the nature of their impact depends on how they are used. We would do well to heed the advice of Wisconsin's most prominent conservationist, to develop a land ethic that permits us to understand our past, perceive our vanishing present, and change our attitudes and actions in a way that preserves the future. Leopold ends *A Sand County Almanac* with these words: "We shall hardly relinquish the shovel, which after all has many good points, but we are in need of gentler and more objective criteria for its successful use" (1949, 263–64). The study of phenology exposes the unfolding saga of environmental change that we have unwittingly staged. Such discoveries suggest that we should employ our shovels carefully to get to the root of our ecological history and lay the foundation for more sustainable, mindful communities. The *Draba* and the geese demand no less of us.

References

Beaubien, E. 1996. PlantWatch, a model to stimulate phenology in school classes. Phenology and Seasonality 1:33–35.

Both, C., and M. E. Visser. 2001. Adjustment to climate change is constrained by arrival date in a long-distance migrant bird. Nature 411:296–298.

Bradley, N. L., C. A. Leopold, J. Ross, and W. Huffaker. 1999. Phenological changes reflect climate change in Wisconsin. Proceedings of the National Academy of Sciences 96:9701–9704.

Crick, H. Q. P. 2004. The impact of climate change on birds. Ibis 146: 48–56.

Harte, J., and R. Shaw. 1995. Shifting dominance within a montane vegetation community: Results of a climate warming experiment. Science 267:876–880.

Inouye, D. W., B. Barr, K. B. Armitage, and B. D. Inouye. 2000. Climate change is affecting altitudinal migrants and hibernating species. Proceedings of the National Academy of Sciences 97:1630–1633.

Intergovernmental Panel on Climate Change (IPCC). 2001. IPCC Third Assessment Report. Climate Change 2001: Synthesis Report, Summary for Policymakers. Available at http://www.grida.no/climate/ipcc%5Ftar/vol4/english/pdf/spm.pdf.

Leopold, A. 1949. A Sand County Almanac, with Essays on Conservation from Round River. New York: Oxford University Press; Ballantine Books, 1966. Citations are to the Ballantine edition.

Leopold, A., and S. E. Jones. 1947. A phenological record for Sauk and Dane Counties, Wisconsin, 1935–1945. Ecological Monographs 17(1):83–123.

Magnuson, J. J., D. M. Robertson, B. J. Benson, R. H. Wynne, D. M. Livingstone, T. Arai, R. A. Assel, R. G. Barry, V. Card, E. Kuusisto, N. G. Granin, T. D. Prowse, K. M. Stewart, and V. S. Vuglinski. 2000. Historical trends in lake and river ice cover in the Northern Hemisphere. Science 289(5845):1743–1746.

Oglesby, R.T., and C. R. Smith. 1995. Climate change in the Northeast. Pp. 390–391 in T. LaRue, G. S. Farris, E. E. Puckett, P. D. Doran, and M. J. Mae, eds. Our Living Resources. Washington, DC: U.S. Department of the Interior National Biological Service.

Price, M. V., and N. M. Waser. 1998. Effects of experimental warming on plant reproductive phenology in a subalpine meadow. Ecology 79(4):1261–1271.

Primack, D., C. Imbres, R. B. Primack, A. J. Miller-Rushing, and P. Del Tredici. 2004. Herbarium specimens demonstrate earlier flowering times in response to warming in Boston. American Journal of Botany 91(8):1260–1264.

Root, T. L., J. T. Price, K. R. Hall, S. H. Schneider, C. Rosenzweig, and J. A. Pounds. 2003. Fingerprints of global warming on wild animals and plants. Nature 421:57–60.

Schwartz, M. D. 1999. Advancing to full bloom: planning phenological research for the 21st century. International Journal of Biometeorology 42:113–118.

Sparks, T. H., and P. D. Carey. 1995. The responses of species to climate over two centuries: An analysis of the Marsham phenological record, 1736–1947. Journal of Ecology 83:321–329.

Temple, S. A., and J. R. Cary. 1987. Climatic effects on year-to-year variations in migration phenology: A WSO project. Passenger Pigeon 49:70–75.

Temple, S. A., J. R. Cary, and R. Rolley. 1997. *Wisconsin Birds: A Seasonal and Geographical Guide.* 2nd ed. Madison: University of Wisconsin Press.

Visser, M. E., A. J. van Noordwijk, J. M. Tinbergen, and C. M. Lessells. 1998. Warmer springs lead to mistimed reproduction in great tits (*Parus major*). Proceedings of the Royal Society of London 265:1867–1870.

Walther, G. R., E. Post, P. Convey, A. Menzel, C. Parmesan, T. J. C. Beebee, J. M. Fromentin, O. Hoegh-Guldberg, and F. Bairlein. 2002. Ecological responses to recent climate change. Nature 416:389–395.

Part Two: Changing Plant Communities

To understand changes in Wisconsin's lands and wildlife, we begin by examining the changes that have occurred in our plant communities. All species show an affinity for particular sites or habitats. Ask a good bird-watcher where to go to observe Blackburnian warblers, and she is likely to direct you to an extensive tract of old coniferous forest. Ask a land manager how to double the number of sharp-tailed grouse, and he will probably recommend doubling the amount of habitat for the species. Because the distribution and abundance of animals ultimately depends on the amount and configuration of suitable habitat available, changes in plant communities have far-reaching effects. But plant communities provide far more than habitat for animals; plants interact with each other, the animals, fungi, protists, and bacteria, above- and belowground, as well as with soils, water, and the atmosphere. In this part we examine shifts in both habitats and plant species composition within those habitats in an effort to understand shifts in the terrestrial ecosystems that surround us.

In the next chapter, forest ecologists David Mladenoff, Lisa Schulte, and Janine Bolliger explore why the types of forests we see vary from place to place and over time. They rely on two types of historic records: the layers of sediment from lake bottoms that contain a 10,000-year accumulation of pollen grains and the written records from the individuals that conducted Wisconsin's public land survey in the mid-1800s. We see that forests change constantly, through time and across space. The interplay of climate, the physical environment, natural events, and human history has shaped, and continue to shape, the forests that we see today.

Chapters 6–8 make extensive use of a remarkable set of baseline data collected by John Curtis and his students. Professor Curtis was a botanist initially interested in orchids and physiology who transformed himself into one of the best-known plant ecologists of his day (Fralish, McIntosh, and Loucks 1993). He sought to test how plant communities were structured and how they responded to gradients in physical conditions by carefully documenting community composition and species abundances at hundreds of sites dispersed throughout the state. His landmark book *The Vegetation of Wisconsin* (Curtis 1959) stands as a monument to their efforts and remains in print and in use as a textbook today. Although it was not their intent, the data they collected in the 1940s and 1950s created unique opportunities in Wisconsin to evaluate long-term (50-year) changes in our prairies, savannas, forests, and other communities.

We revisted the same sites these early researchers surveyed to uncover exactly the slow and sometimes subtle shifts in ecological conditions that are the focus of this book. In our contribution (chapter 6) to Part two, we report, for example, that most forests in northern Wisconsin have lost native plant species; that weedy, nonnative plants have begun to invade; and that these processes contribute to a pattern of "biotic homogenization" wherein sites are coming to resemble each other in composition. While several factors doubtless affect these trends, the loss of mature forest habitats combined with overabundant deer clearly contribute.

Dave Rogers, Tom Rooney, and Rich Henderson then examine corresponding changes in southern Wisconsin forests. They report even greater declines in native plant diversity since the Curtis surveys, greater invasions of exotics, and more homogenization. Forest fragmentation and deer clearly play roles here, but so do the changes set in motion 150 years ago when fire suppression allowed oak woodlands to replace oak savannas. As tree canopies close with succession, these oak woodlands are further displaced by maples and other, more shade-tolerant trees. Shadier understories that rarely burn exclude, in turn, the oak seedlings that could regenerate oak woodlands along with the sun-loving forest herbs that once thrived there.

Northland College ecologist Mark Leach next examines what is left of our prairies. Like savannas, the tall-grass prairies that once dominated the landscapes of southern Wisconsin have become one of the most threatened ecosystems in the country with less than 0.1% remaining (Noss et al. 1995). Many are aware of the remarkable efforts being invested in restoring prairie and savanna habitats (Stevens 1995). Fewer are aware of the fact that our precious few small remnant patches of prairie have lost many of their native species since the 1950s. Despite the depressing numbers, Leach hopes that the patterns these losses reveal will help us learn how to better manage both the old and new prairies now under our care. Interest in science-based prairie restoration is growing, translating into some on-the-ground success stories.

University of Wisconsin–Stevens Point botanist Emmet Judziewicz then, in chapter 9, explores how the isolated plant communities of two archipelagos in the Great Lakes are changing. Both the Apostle Islands in Lake Superior and the Grand Traverse Islands in Lake Michigan have undergone great changes over the past 150 years, and both face similar threats (primarily from deer and invasive plants) today. The differences are also informative, leading Judziewicz to note that the changes on the unprotected Grand Traverse Islands are more pronounced and have left the archipelago more biotically impoverished. While these islands may seem remote from most of us, they also stand as a synecdoche for the isolated patches of habitat that increasingly surround us.

Our final two chapters in this part examine changes in a group of small plants that rarely draw our attention—lichens. In fact, although botanists traditionally study lichens, they are not really plants but rather a symbiosis between a fungus and a photosynthetic partner (algae and/or cyanobacteria). Lichens come in several beautiful forms, as these chapters and plates 12 and 13 illustrate, but most are not conspicuous enough to grab public attention. This is a pity, as they have much to teach us. Because lichens seldom receive much attention, even from most botanists, we have limited data to work with. U.S. Geological Survey botanist Jim Bennett explores the "missing data" problem in detail, highlighting how little we actually know about the state's lichen flora. In fact, he estimates that scientists still have only identified 85% of the species that occur in the state. In undercollected areas of the state, we may never know what once existed. Our ignorance also creates an ironic paradox: our lichen flora may continue to lose species even as our knowledge of the lichen flora and species lists grow. Lichenologists Suzy Will-Wolf and Matt Nelsen then review some of what we know about lichens and their sensitivity to substrates and environmental conditions. They draw on both direct and indirect lines of evidence to infer that our lichen flora has declined considerably in quantity and quality. The resurvey findings they report reveal conspicuous declines, including the disappearance of half the lichen species that once occurred in Madison over the past century. They also note the conspicuous losses and biotic homogenization of bark lichens near a coal-fired power plant in central Wisconsin. Where lichen data are unavailable, they use changes in habitat to infer how the abundances of slow-growing species must have declined with the loss of mature trees and old growth forests.

Thus, we see that Wisconsin's plant communities and habitats have undergone cataclysmic changes in response to shifts in climate, the physical environment, natural events, and human history. What is changing is the relative impact of these factors and the rates of biological change. Human activities on the land increasingly drive ecological change, directly and often indirectly. We hope these glimpses behind the curtain of the invisible present will help us to understand the nature and extent of the changes we exert on plant communities and inform our efforts to protect and restore our remaining natural habitats.

References

Curtis, J. T. 1959. The vegetation of Wisconsin. Madison: University of Wisconsin Press.

Fralish, J. S., R. P. McIntosh, and O. L. Loucks, eds. 1993. John T. Curtis: Fifty years of Wisconsin plant ecology. Madison: Wisconsin Academy of Sciences, Arts and Letters.

Noss, R. F., E. T. LaRoe III, and J. M. Scott. 1995. Endangered ecosystems of the United States: A preliminary assessment of loss and degradation. Biological Report No. 28. Washington, DC: U.S. Department of the Interior, National Biological Service.

Stevens, W. K. 1995. Miracle under the oaks: The revival of nature in America. New York: Pocket Books.

5

Broad-Scale Change in the Northern Forests: From Past to Present

David J. Mladenoff, Lisa A. Schulte, and Janine Bolliger

Some years ago, after giving a talk to citizens in northwest Wisconsin on forest change, I (Mladenoff) was pointedly questioned by an attendee. She was upset by the premise that the northern Great Lakes states' forests are changing, and always have been. She related how her family had owned rural forest land with a cabin on a lake since she was young and that the forest had been beautiful white birch trees "forever." She was upset that the birch forest was now dying and seemed to see me, and my message, as likely causes of this. She wanted to know why the forest was now changing and what would replace the forest if it was "dying."

This conversation was eye-opening and revealed several important things to me. One was that I had failed to communicate several key intended messages, at least to some. In particular, I had failed to explain that the white birch forest had not been there forever but was mostly about 70 years old. The trees originated when birch seeds had the opportunity to germinate and grow in the full sunlight they require, following logging of the original pine forest and subsequent slash fires. The trees were now getting old, nearing the end of their lives, and had recently been hard-hit by disease and drought. To this landowner in her mid-50s, however, the birches *had* been there forever based on her own experience.

Further, I had clearly not communicated a larger issue—that not only do forests change constantly, but that what occurs varies from place to place. The fact that the neighbor's land across the small lake did not have a dying birch forest could reflect several possible causes. The land may not have burned at the same time, the site may have had different soils, or it may not have had significant, original commercial forest to log. The different exposures of the neighbor's land (north vs. her south) meant that hers was drier and more suitable to the dry-adapted oaks rather than birch, a species that requires constant soil moisture to grow well. Also, I had not conveyed that the Great Lakes states' forest was heterogeneous—forests in northern Wisconsin were not all old-growth pine either.

This experience emphasized how important it is to clarify the ways in which our perspective in terms of time and space influence what we study and how we identify which factors shape our subjects. We should strive to articulate this not only in our scientific articles but also in our public talks.

Changes in a landscape (including this particular birch forest) usually involve many intertwined factors. These factors include species-specific properties (like the life span of birches), the environment (e.g., drought or soil type), natural disturbances like fire and wind, and human influences like logging. All these factors act at various scales across the landscape and through time. Changes occur over months, years, decades, centuries, and thousands of years. Drought during a summer month, for example, may act as a short-term trigger for changes in the birch forest, whereas soils and slopes generally remain the same for millennia. Environments also vary across space, reflecting local site factors and differences in history. These differences may be sharp and local, as when they reflect different glacial formations or soils, or more gradually distributed through our region, as with differences in climate.

We will first provide a framework for recent change and the factors that shape Wisconsin's landscape. In a later chapter, we assess potential future changes in our northern forests.

Environmental Factors That Shape Landscapes

The vegetation of a region or landscape reflects several factors. Climate, geology, and the overall physical environment vary over broad scales and long periods of time. These set broad limits for the plants and animals that inhabit our forests. Within this context, disturbances like wind, floods, and fires act more locally and temporarily to reset the successional clock and favor species adapted to more open conditions.

Climate. On a global scale, climate (primarily seasonal patterns of temperature and precipitation) tends to determine dominant patterns of vegetation (e.g., tundra, rain forest, and desert). The forest cover of the northern Great Lakes states reflect a seasonal climate and moderate precipitation. Northern Minnesota is colder than northern Wisconsin, favoring more boreal (evergreen) forests. To the west and south, drier conditions tend to favor grassland plains and prairies, particularly where fires are allowed to burn.

Climate also varies over time. Within our region, climate has varied dramatically and at several scales. Several times over the past 1 million years, glaciers covered most of our state. The most recent episode ended just over 10,000 years ago. Since then, we have had warmer and cooler periods, as well as droughts and wet periods. Within these, we also find particular years that may be hot, cold, wet, or dry. Such climatic episodes can greatly affect vegetation, as when dry spells increase the frequency or intensity of fires. Despite this variation, our climate has generally favored forests in northern Wisconsin. Precipitation and temperature continue to vary as they have for thousands of years (though recent trends clearly indicate warmer conditions; see chapter 4).

How does climate affect vegetation? "Evapotranspiration" includes the direct evaporation of water from soils and the water that is taken up by plants and transpired through their leaves. Higher temperatures increase evapotranspiration, favoring plants adapted to drier conditions. Sandy soils that allow most water to infiltrate away before plants can use it also favor drought-adapted plants.

Physical Environment. Glaciers sculpted our region. Most of Wisconsin was glaciated from about 25,000 to 10,000 years ago (plate 1) meaning we have a young landscape, geologically speaking. Without mountains, glaciers were free to flatten, scar, and mold the physical landscapes in all but the southwestern region of Wisconsin. Our rolling topography, eskers, drumlins, kettle-holes, patches of sand, and wet clay soils all reflect the action of glaciers and their deposits. These patterns of topography and soil created a template for plants to colonize and for soil to develop. The template is much older in southwestern Wisconsin, where glaciers have not occurred for more than a million years. We call this the "Driftless Area" because it lacks glacial deposits (Dott and Attig 2004).

Where the glaciers advanced and retreated, soils are recent. Cool temperatures in our northern forest region slowed soil development. Across the Great Lakes states, variation in surficial geology and soils due to glaciation interacts with climate resulting in varying conditions for plants. While all plants need water and nutrients, some plants are more tolerant of drought or nutrient-poor conditions than others. Clay and silty soils hold far more water than sandy soils. Sandy loam soils of intermediate texture often favor the broadest number of plant species, being neither too dry nor too wet. Over time, soil variability interacts with variability in climate to create a heterogeneous landscape with variable conditions for plants, as with the dry to moist gradients shown in plate 2.

Disturbance. The climate and physical environment provide the template for the vegetation, forming limits to what *can* grow. However, disturbances like fire, windthrow, insects, disease, and flooding also affect natural systems. In our region, disturbances often determine which plants actually grow at a site. Disturbances vary in intensity and frequency, with slight disturbances only altering plant growth and competition in minor or temporary ways. More severe disturbances can obliterate all plant life at a site. For example, a light ground fire in a forest may kill only small seedlings on the forest floor whereas a crown fire can kill all trees. Wind storms also vary in their impacts, sometimes only breaking branches or toppling a few trees. Other times, they flatten extensive areas of forest. Certain tree caterpillar outbreaks can defoliate broad-leaved deciduous trees, but the trees soon reflush new leaves, causing little mortality. Defoliators of needle-leaved evergreens, however, can cause considerable mortality. Older trees are generally more susceptible to wind, insects, and disease often creating dead and downed wood that can make older forests vulnerable to fires. Weather also clearly affects the likelihood of various disturbances. Because disturbances interact in complex ways, climate change will surely shift disturbance regimes. For example, windthrow and mortality from insects and disease all kill trees, increasing the risk of fire. Let us also stress that these dynamics do not "kill" forests but rather represent part of a natural cycle. As trees die, they create favorable conditions for new trees.

Vegetation Responses: Colonization, Succession, and Change. Physical environments also affect patterns of species abundance. Jack pine grows well on droughty, infertile sandy soils. Hemlock and sugar maple prefer moist, loamy soils. White pine is intermediate, growing across a range of soils but does best on somewhat sandy soils of moderate fertility. Over thousands of years, plant death and decomposition add organic matter to the soil, improving its ability to retain moisture and nutrients.

This process gradually allows more species to occur at a site. Tree species differ particularly in how they respond to light. Aspen, paper birch, jack pine, and bur oak all require open, high light conditions. Hemlock, sugar maple, and beech, in contrast, persist and grow well (if slowly) beneath the canopy of other trees. Other species including many pines and oaks thrive under medium light.

Trees also differ in how much water and nutrients they require, how they disperse their seeds, how well they resprout after damage, and how long they live. For example, aspen's very small, wind-blown seeds travel for miles but require open sites without taller competitors if they are to germinate and establish. They grow quickly, particularly where fires have cleared away the competition, but will not thrive under the shade of other species. Under full light, they form dense patches of stems.

Thus we see that the traits trees have interact with various kinds of disturbances and more gradual changes over space and time in their environment to create the complex quilt of forests that we find in Wisconsin.

Changes since the Last Ice Age

How have we learned about Wisconsin's early forests? Paleoecologists strive to understand how our vegetation has changed in the northern Great Lakes states. They generally rely on analyses of pollen and charcoal taken from sediment cores drilled into the bottoms of deep lakes. Under the right conditions, these sediments slowly accumulate silt that includes enough wind-blown pollen to give us a good idea of what trees covered the nearby landscape at various times in the past. By dating these sediment layers, they can track shifts in the abundance of pollen of the dominant plant species. Our large number of lakes favors this kind of research, providing a fairly detailed picture of how vegetation has changed over the last 10,000 years.

The forests we see and know now did not recolonize en masse. Some tree species invaded quickly, whereas others moved more slowly. As the glaciers receded, cold conditions and poor soils lacking organic matter favored those plants best able to disperse long distances and colonize these open sites. Species with wind-dispersed seeds including grasses and trees like aspen and willow dominate the record from this time. Slowly maturing plants with larger, heavier seeds invaded later, as did those that depend on better soils and warmer, longer growing seasons. Thus, white pine, oak, and maple did not appear for several thousand years. Eastern hemlock arrived last, reaching its current range limit in northwestern Wisconsin about 3,000 years ago.

Climates and vegetation in our region also underwent several successive periods of change since the end of the Wisconsin glaciation (Webb et al. 1983). South of the retreating ice lay a climate similar to northern boreal regions today with permafrost, poor drainage, and frequent wet soil conditions. Open, tundra-like conditions alternated with open forests of spruce, fir, jack pine, and some hardwoods such as elm and willow. Large continental areas of tundra like those that exist today did not exist. This mix of vegetation lasted until about 8,000 years ago.

The warmest and driest period since the glacier occurred during the "Hypsithermal," about 7,000 to 4,000 years ago. During this period, prairies stretched much further east than they do now. Shorter cooler and warmer periods followed. During cool periods, boreal species such as spruce became more abundant. The recent period from about 1,100 to 700 years ago was relatively warm, followed by a cool period spanning 600 years. In the last century, temperatures again began to warm, with dramatically higher temperatures over the last 30 years. Average temperatures are now only about 1°C cooler than they were during the Hypsithermal. Our weather continues to vary daily, monthly, and from year to year. Nevertheless, the dramatic increases in temperatures around the world in recent decades strongly imply that future forests in Wisconsin will differ greatly from those of today. These changes in climate have important implications for our biota (see chapters 3, 4, and 31).

Human Impact as a Factor in Shaping Landscapes

Early Human Influence. People occupied Wisconsin soon after the ice retreated (Stoltman and Baerreis 1983; Cleland 1992). These Paleo-Indians preceded and differed from more recent Native American peoples (Cleland 1992). They hunted grazing animals such as caribou as well as the initially quite diverse but now extinct megafauna (like the mastodon, mammoth, and giant beaver).

While these early peoples may not have had dramatic direct impacts on the vegetation, they indirectly altered plant cover by hunting the large grazing animals. Vegetation was also responding to the warming climate. Paradoxically, seasonal extremes became more pronounced, with summers becoming hotter and winters colder. Scientists disagree on the relative importance of hunting and climate change in contributing to the extinction of many large mammals, although many believe both contributed to this dramatic extinction event (see chapter 2).

The warming climate (peaking 7,000 to 4,000 years ago) also favored growth in the human population. Seasonal droughts increased the likelihood of wildfires developing wherever lightning or people ignited vegetation. In the north, fire favored pines and oaks on the sandier soils. These species demand less water and fewer nutrients and respond favorably to fire. In the south and southwest of the state, more moderate climates favored higher human populations. Warmer summers with more drought there favored fires. Fire-dependent prairie, open oak savanna, and oak woodland came to dominate the south.

Wisconsin's indigenous inhabitants used fire to signal neighboring tribes, drive game animals, create habitat, and promote the growth of useful plants (Stoltman and Baerreis 1983). Fishing became important along the Great Lakes and at some inland locations (Cleland 1992). Seasonal concentrations of people probably resulted in large, localized clearings. Still later, people planted crops, creating more clearings. In southern Wisconsin, the longer growing season enabled people to grow corn, boosting population levels, enabling larger settlements, and creating larger impacts. Seasonal movement and hunting and gathering still occurred with bison, elk, and deer serving as common staples.

Pre-European Vegetation. Over the past 3,000 years, the climate, vegetation, and forests have been fairly stable. Growing Native American populations greatly influenced vegetation up until the period of contact with Europeans, who brought devastating diseases and displaced most Indians over the last 200 years (Cleland 1992).

The best picture we have of the region's vegetation is based on information collected by the U.S. General Land Office surveyors doing the original land survey in the mid-1800s. This survey delineated the township and section lines that define most land ownership boundaries today (chapter 2). Surveyors used trees to mark boundaries every half mile (804 m), noting the species (by common names), size (diameter estimate), and distance and bearing (direction) from the corner. A picture of the pre-European landscape emerges when these trees are mapped (Schulte and Mladenoff 2001).

A general classification of pre-European vegetation for the Great Lakes states reflects the integration of regional climate, physical environment, and disturbance (plate 3). Note the northwest to southeast pattern. Climate (temperature and moisture) does not vary along a strictly north-south gradient, so prairie is more abundant to the west and south, and forest to the north. The forests furthest north in the region, in northeastern Minnesota, contain more pine, aspen-birch, and spruce-fir, reflecting the combined effects of lower temperatures and drier conditions. In this regional context, Wisconsin's vegetation is intermediate between those of Minnesota and Michigan with more prairie and savanna than Michigan and more northern hardwoods than Minnesota. These forests had similar levels of windthrow disturbance, but northern Minnesota had more regular fires that Wisconsin and Michigan and correspondingly more pine and aspen-birch forest (Frelich 2002). Insect disturbances were also more common in Minnesota as the common spruce-fir forests are highly susceptible to defoliating insects.

Maps of Wisconsin's pre-European vegetation (plates 4 and 5) reflect variation in the state's environmental conditions and patterns of disturbance (Schulte et al. 2002; Bolliger and Mladenoff 2005). Comparing the habitat type map (plate 2) with the vegetation shows that the south was dominated by open oak savannas and oak woodlands with scattered prairies. The north and areas inland from the Lake Michigan shoreline were more densely forested. Tree species present in the north and east suggest less frequent fire, though this varied across the region. The broad, green area across the north (mesic to wet-mesic in plate 2) contained hemlock, sugar maple, and yellow birch. Beech was common but is now confined to areas along Lake Michigan where fire was rare. Aspen was scattered patchily across the north at this time as its populations tracked intermittent disturbances. It was more common in regions dominated by fires and pines, but nowhere was it as abundant as it is today. Abundant patches of wetland or lowland (swamp) forest of tamarack, cedar, spruce, and fir were common especially in the north, reflecting our legacy of a glaciated landscape.

Pines (jack, red, and white) dominated the dry, sandy outwash plain soils of northwestern, north central, and northeastern Wisconsin as well as the center of the state once covered by glacial Lake Wisconsin (plates 2 and 5). Generally, jack pines occupied the poorest, drought-prone soils in the northwest and central sand plains where fires typically occurred every 50–100 years. Red pines occupied areas where severe fires were a bit less frequent (perhaps every 100–200 years) but where light ground fires may have occurred every decade or so. Red pines occurred commonly with jack and white pines. White pine was the most abundant pine, occurring where ground fires were less frequent. It reached its greatest abundance on more fertile soils than the other pines, intermediate between the other pines and the hemlock-hardwoods. Windthrow was more important in the white pine and hemlock-hardwood regions where fire was less frequent. Older and larger trees are more susceptible to wind. The hemlock-hardwood region was strongly controlled by wind with older trees beginning to blow down after 100–300 years. More catastrophic blowdowns, where all canopy trees were toppled, were less frequent but were important (Frelich and Lorimer 1991; Schulte and Mladenoff 2005). In general, 60%–70% of the northern forests were mature and old growth, with larger, older trees than present in recent times (Frelich and Lorimer 1991). Local variation existed within these general patterns with trees occurring in mixtures across the landscape (Curtis 1959).

Landscape Changes following Euro-American Settlement. Euro-American settlement that really began in the 1830s in southern Wisconsin soon spread north and west. Agriculture and pastures quickly replaced the prairies and oak savanna of the south (chapter 8). Logging in northern Wisconsin began in the mid-1800s, soon radically transforming those landscapes to a region that became known as the "cutover" (chapters 6 and 24). While old-growth pine forests are usually associated with these Northwoods, hemlock, yellow birch, and sugar maple were in fact far more dominant (plates 5 and 6). While these mature, tall, conifers and hardwoods dominated northern forests, other conifers also occurred frequently, including white cedar, balsam fir, and white and black spruce. Tamarack, the only conifer that drops its leaves in our area, was the fourth most abundant tree species recorded in the land survey, which seems remarkable given its scattered distribution today. Conifers differ from broad-leaved deciduous species in having resinous needles and branches. These slow rates of nutrient cycling in the soil, allowing flammable litter to accumulate and profoundly altering habitat conditions for other plants and animals.

Fires, farming, and timber harvest enabled broad-leaved deciduous species to replace conifers as the dominant group of species. The intense slash fires that followed the devastating original logging were more extensive and severe than previous fires in the region (chapter 24). These intense fires killed many tree seedlings and saplings and sometimes burned up crucial soil organic matter as well. The bare mineral soil that remained favored species with small, wind-dispersed seeds such as aspen and paper birch. Misguided attempts to farm this cutover land in some parts of the north mostly failed due to the short growing season, poor soils, and other factors. By the 1930s, many farms were abandoned, and effective fire suppression allowed more aspen and other early successional tree species to become established. In some regions, however, farming persists and is successful (plate 4).

Aspen became valuable for paper pulp and continues to comprise a large component of today's forests (plate 7). The abundance of aspen forests peaked in the 1950s and has been declining since, though recent inventories show this trend leveling off. On the moist, mesic soils we now find only scattered small remnants of the former hemlock-hardwood forest, the once dominant forest type. Hemlock has declined so much as to be ecologically absent from most sites, existing only at 0.5% of its former abundance (Eckstein 1980). After logging, hemlock lost seed sources, suffered from fires, and lost seedlings to deer browsing. On drier sites, pine is replacing aspen. On mesic soils, sugar maple has come to dominate. Yellow birch, once codominant with hemlock and sugar maple, has declined nearly as much as hemlock. Thus, we see a general pattern of replacement with mature conifer forests dominated by large trees replaced first by widespread, young aspen forest, and now, increasingly, sugar maple. While this has favored species like deer, these dramatic habitat losses and changes have decimated many other species.

The extent to which our forests have changed over the past 150 years surprises many people. It is often assumed that the north regained its original forests, escaping the agriculture that has so transformed the rest of our region. However, agriculture (largely dairy farming) has replaced forests along much of the southern band of the former forest (plates 4 and 5). Similarly, agriculture and urbanization have eliminated most of the eastern forests along Lake Michigan from Door Peninsula south to Illinois. Only in the unglaciated topography of the southwest have forests remained scattered, and even increased, among sinuous patches of farmland and pasture. Here, the original prairies and oak savannas have gone in two directions, being replaced by either farms or dense forest with declines in fire frequency following settlement (chapters 7 and 8). Prairies and savannas do not persist here without fire. Population growth and continuing changes in land use over the past 50 years are creating a second wave of change (plate 8) that we are only beginning to understand.

In addition to these dramatic losses of original forest cover, our forests have also experienced radical changes in disturbance. Trees that once had a chance to grow to majestic proportions are now commonly felled after 40–100 years for use as wood and fiber by humans. Commercial logging for species like aspen and red pine usually involves clear-cutting, which removes all the trees present at a site. Mixed hardwoods are more usually harvested via "selection cutting," which removes some subset of the trees present. Except in the case of whole-tree harvesting (for biomass energy production), logging "tops" and debris are left behind, providing nutrients and structure that can help seedlings to establish. As trees die and leaves accumulate, microbes and soil organisms decompose the organic matter to create soil, enabling future plant growth. Soil reflects a cycling of organic matter—there is no "waste" in natural ecosystems. Accumulations of forest biomass also represent stockpiles of carbon. Plants take up carbon dioxide (CO_2), fixing the carbon in the form of new tissues and releasing oxygen. When they decompose or burn, CO_2 is released. Before complex carbohydrates are broken down, substantial amounts of carbon can accumulate in trunks, coarse woody debris, roots, and forest soils. Because CO_2 is a major greenhouse gas, there is considerable interest in the fate of forest carbon. The more carbon remains as plant tissue, not decomposing or burning, the more carbon is sequestered and the less CO_2 is released to the atmosphere to contribute to global warming. Conserving forests with high productivity and large pools of live and dead biomass represents a key approach for slowing global warming.

Loss of forest cover also affects key aspects of habitat structure affecting many smaller plants and the animals that occur in our forests. Terrestrial, wetland, and aquatic systems are all affected when forests are dominated by younger and smaller trees with few dead snags or fallen logs. Upland forests and those along rivers contribute nutrients and plant litter to aquatic systems sustaining invertebrates, fish, and the birds and mammals that depend on these. These forests also buffer lakes and streams from human disturbances while adding structure in the form of logs and branches that improve habitat for many fish.

Sustainable Forest Management

Changes across Wisconsin's landscapes have radically altered our original vegetation. Some forests have partly recovered but remain quite different than they were. This has significant consequences. Most forests in the state are now managed. Even forest stands protected as parks or reserves are not free of human impacts. Increasingly, we recognize that active management may be needed to restore some of these forests. Yet it is often unclear how much restoration is possible, given how altered our systems have been for over 100 years, changes in natural processes, species loss, and a changing climate (chapter 31).

Management is gradually becoming more ecological with a broad search for more sustainable forms of forestry (Franklin 1993; Andersson et al. 2000). We see increasing emphasis on managing forests using ecosystem management, a framework to conserve, protect, or restore entire ecological systems, including their structure and function. These approaches strive to unite concerns for ecology with social and economic objectives. This intersection of applied science and land management requires scientists and managers to confront a broad suite of issues from maintaining biodiversity to sustaining economies by providing services and products for public needs. Ideally, ecosystem management will sustain both natural diversity and the resources we depend on. Such efforts must be tailored to specific landscapes and forest types, emphasizing our need for more information on ecosystem structure and function.

References

Andersson, F. O., K.-H. Feger, R. F. Hüttl, N. Kräuchi, L. Mattsson, O. Sallnäs, and K. Sjöberg. 2000. Forest ecosystem research—priorities for Europe. Forest Ecology and Management 132:111–119.

Bolliger, J., and D. J. Mladenoff. 2005. Quantifying spatial classification uncertainties of the historical Wisconsin landscape (USA). Ecography 28:141–153.

Cleland, C. E. 1992. Rites of conquest: The history and culture of Michigan's Native Americans. Ann Arbor: University of Michigan Press.

Curtis, J. T. 1959. The vegetation of Wisconsin: An ordination of plant communities. Madison: University of Wisconsin Press.

Dott, R. H., Jr., and J. W. Attig. 2004. Roadside geology of Wisconsin. Missoula, MT: Mountain Press.

Eckstein, R. G. 1980. Eastern hemlock (*Tsuga canadensis*) in north central Wisconsin. Research Report 104. Wisconsin Department of Natural Resources, Madison.

Franklin, J. F. 1993. Preserving biodiverstiy: Species, ecosystems, or landscapes? Ecological Applications 3:202–295.

Frelich, L. E. 2002. Forest dynamics and disturbance regimes. Studies from temperate evergreen-deciduous forests. Cambridge: Cambridge University Press.

Frelich, L. E., and Lorimer C. G. 1991. A simulation of landscape-level stand dynamics in the northern hardwood region. J. Ecol. 79: 223–233.

Schulte, L. A., and D. J. Mladenoff. 2001. The original U.S. Public Land Survey records: Their use and limitations in reconstruction pre-European settlement vegetation. Journal of Forestry 99:5–10.

———. 2005. Severe wind and fire regimes in northern forests: Historical variability at the regional scale. Ecology 86:431–445.

Schulte, L. A., D. J. Mladenoff, and E. V. Nordheim. 2002. Quantitative classifications of a historic northern Wisconsin (USA) landscape: Mapping forests at regional scales. Canadian Journal of Forest Research 32:1616–1638.

Stoltman, J. B., and D. A. Baerreis. 1983. The evolution of human ecosystems in the eastern United States. Pp. 252–298 in H. E. Wright, Jr., ed. The Holocene. Vol. 2. Minneapolis: University of Minnesota Press.

Webb, T. III, E. J. Cushing, H. E. Wright, Jr. 1983. Holocene changes in the vegetation of the Midwest. Pp. 142–165 in H. E. Wright, Jr., ed. The Holocene. Vol. 2. Minneapolis: University of Minnesota Press.

6

Plant Species Diversity in the Once and Future Northwoods

Thomas P. Rooney and Donald M. Waller

For many, Wisconsin conjures up images of the great Northwoods—a patchwork quilt of woods, lakes, wetlands, and bogs (plates 4 and 5). Here were the tall pines that attracted loggers during the Paul Bunyan era. The logs from these trees were piled into giant stacks each winter to be released in spring into the region's rivers, swollen by snowmelt, for a quick trip down to the booming sawmills. Here, they became lumber for the farms, towns, and cities of the Midwest (Cronon 1991). Today, an extensive forest once again covers much of the northern third (over 64,000 km^2, or 24,700 sq miles) of the state. The timber industry is still here as well, though it focuses far more on pulp and engineered wood products like oriented strand board. Increasing throngs of vacationers and second-home owners now see the region's forests and lakes as their playground. Year-round tourism and recreation are now poised to eclipse timber as the primary economic engine of the north. Ironically, all these tourists create ever-more developed environments complete with roads, shopping centers, and indoor water parks that threaten to isolate them from, and degrade, the very nature that attracted them in the first place.

How is today's northern forest different from what greeted the voyageurs? How is it changing in response to these continuing and new uses? Change has always been part of this landscape, as we learned in the last chapter, but changes over the past 150 years appear greater than in any other 150-year period since the glaciers retreated (Whitney 1994). In addition, the rates and types of changes occurring now appear unusual. Despite its current expanse and seeming good health, the Northwoods is losing species and remains a shadow of its former self. Because we lack data from the primeval forests and the great cutover period in the late 19th century, we instead focus on changes over the late 20th century and what these portend for the future. We are fortunate here in having the exceptional baseline data collected by John Curtis and his students in the 1950s. These data allow us to perceive gradual shifts in Wisconsin's forests with more precision than is possible almost anywhere else.

Ice Age to Cutover to Conservation

As the glaciers receded, our region was dominated at first by a permafrost-free tundra shrubland (Pielou 1991). At that time, North America was home to more species of large mammal than any continent in the world. This quickly changed once humans crossed the Bering land bridge into North America about 14,000 years ago. So many large species of mammals went extinct (see chapter 2) that we now have fewer large mammals than any other continent. Most scientists agree that hunting by Paleo-Indians contributed to the extinction of mammoths, camels, giant ground sloths, mastodons, and other large animals (Martin 1973; Foreman 2004). Had these megagrazers and seed dispersers survived to modern times, we might well find a different forest from that which we see today (Flannery 2001).

Over the next several thousand years, glaciers retreated further as the climate warmed. Plants responded to this warming trend by migrating (chapter 5). Plant species associated with tundra moved north and disappeared from the state, replaced by the invading boreal forest plants. Temperate species now associated with the northern hardwoods forest then colonized from the south and east. Today, boreal species are only found in the coldest parts of the state. With additional climate change, they may well disappear altogether.

Euro-American settlement accelerated changes in the Northwoods. As noted above, early loggers felled extensive stands of red and white pine to feed the many sawmills and growing demand. Soon, railroads crisscrossed the landscape, connecting markets for the heavier hardwoods to their source. This ensured that remaining forests would be clear-cut in what became known at the great cutover. Within a few decades, millions of acres of old-growth forest were felled (Griffith 1906;

Whitney 1994). The cutover also spawned intense slash fires through the 1890s to the 1930s. These were often intense enough to consume all the organic matter in the topsoil (Solberg 1961), sterilizing soils and suppressing the regrowth of seedlings and saplings (Griffith 1906; Whitney 1994). Proposals to reforest these cutover lands sparked controversy at the time. Many considered such efforts to be idealistic and unprofitable given the then still plentiful forests to the north and west. Others argued that the plow would follow the axe, as it had in southern Wisconsin. Initially, the University of Wisconsin and state legislature encouraged agriculture in the region (Solberg 1961). Many hoped that a foundation of agriculture would attract immigrants with settlers building roads and schools that would then attract industry and laborers (Turner 1920). However, the short growing seasons and infertile soils of the Northwoods proved ill suited for agriculture. Hopes for an agricultural empire in northern Wisconsin collapsed before half of the land was tilled or pastured (Barry et al. 2001). This is fortunate, as tilled and pastured lands support far lower plant diversity than forested sites that were never cleared (Bellemare et al. 2002). Such effects of agriculture persist for centuries (Dupouey et al. 2002).

In the wake of the "cut and run" era came new concern for acquiring and protecting public forest land. Citizens that witnessed the great cutover demanded reforms that eventually led to the federal Forest Preserves (later the National Forests) and game protection laws like the Lacey and Migratory Bird Treaty acts. The new discipline of forestry recognized forests as a renewable resource important for protecting watersheds and wildlife rather than simply capital to be liquidated. Wisconsin began a system of state forest reserves despite the fact that some viewed this as a waste of tax dollars.

As farming collapsed, young forests sprung up on their own. Pioneer species, including aspen, paper birch, and red oak, reclaimed cutover lands and abandoned croplands and pastures. Many of these recovering forests lacked the standing snag trees and large rotting logs that typify the forests that regenerate after natural disturbances such as forest fires or windstorms. Such biological legacies provide structure and substrate that provide vital habitats for both plants and animals. Seedlings of many trees, including hemlock, yellow birch, and northern white cedar are found most commonly growing on rotting logs and other coarse woody debris. Owls, bats, and woodpeckers nest in standing snags, and mammals like the pine marten make their dens in or beneath hollow trees or logs.

Wildlife also underwent dramatic changes in the late 19th and early 20th century (see chapter 18). Elk and moose were extirpated, and top carnivores including cougar, wolf, and wolverine disappeared with bounty hunting. White-tailed deer were hunted to extinction throughout most of southern Wisconsin and became rare in the north. Deer populations reached a low in the state around 1915 when only 5,000 animals were harvested (Bersing 1956). As concerns for conservation grew, the state developed restrictive game laws based on strict seasons and enforced bag limits. Deer seasons were cancelled every other year between 1925 and 1935. These devices (together with favorable habitat conditions and scarce predators) led to rapid population growth. By the 1930s, deer were so abundant in some places that they eliminated their best sources of food. By 1942, deer population peaked in the Northwoods, and thousands of animals starved (Leopold et al. 1947). Record numbers of deer (over 100,000) were harvested in 1943, 1949, 1950, and 1951 (Bersing 1956). Ironically, such harvests seem small by today's standard as deer populations have rebounded all over the state. Hunters now often harvest over 500,000 deer per year (over 600,000 in 2000).

Where Is Forest Diversity?

Wisconsin has only a few dozen species of native trees with fewer than 15 typically found within a hectare (2.5 acres) of land. In contrast, there are hundreds of herbaceous species in the Northwoods, including showy lilies and orchids, delicate ferns, and grasslike sedges. Thus, to find most of the plant diversity in our forests, cast your gaze to the forest floor.

Tree species tend to grow at sites with particular conditions. Each of these canopy types, in turn, tends to have a distinctive set of understory plant species. Trees often reflect a site's topography and soil fertility. Lowland trees, for example, thrive in waterlogged soils. Black spruce and tamarack commonly occur around bogs and on other nutrient-poor sites. Northern white cedar and black ash populate swamps on richer sites. Each type of lowland forest has an understory that includes some distinctive species. In upland forests, jack, red, and white pines dominate dry, infertile sites, while eastern hemlock and "northern hardwoods" like sugar maple, basswood, yellow birch, and white ash grow on fertile sites. Again, these forests differ in far more than just the trees. Some trees (like trembling aspen, red maple, and red oak) and herbs (like wild lily of the valley) are found in many sites that span a range of nutrient conditions. Although such generalists are common, they represent the minority of species. Many more species are sparse to rare, occurring only in particular habitats. This basic fact has profound implications that we explore below.

Baselines

What baselines exist for tracking ecological change? Ecologists have generally been creative in exploiting various kinds of data as baselines, including floristic surveys, herbarium specimens, land survey records, and old-growth forests. Floristic surveys compile a full list of all the plants that occur in a specific location such as a park, natural area, county, or state. A few floristic surveys extend beyond a list to include information on whether a species is common, uncommon, or rare. Because species colonize and disappear from sites, floristic surveys change over time, allowing ecologists to infer "turnover." Herbarium specimens provide solid evidence on which species occurred where, creating a baseline similar to floristic surveys. Botanists collect herbarium specimens in order to document which species are present in various locations and to study patterns of geographic and taxonomic variation. Ecologists use herbarium specimens to track the spread of invasive species, relocate populations of interest, map the distribution of species, and compile lists of all the plants present in a particular area. Land survey records provide a different kind of baseline for tracking ecological change. When the General Land Office surveyed the state's lands, surveyors noted the general vegetation and tree species closest to every section and half-section line. This has allowed ecologists to reconstruct the distribution of forest and plant communities just at the time Wisconsin was being settled (plate 5). Other ecologists use the few remaining old-growth forests to obtain yet another kind of baseline. Instead of relying on historical data, ecologists can sample these relicts from the past and directly compare them with the younger, second growth forests that dominate our landscapes today (Scheller and Mladenoff 2002). Aldo Leopold (1966) stressed this scientific value of wilderness as a "baseline of normality."

Early botanical work in the Northwoods focused on identifying which species were present and collecting herbarium specimens paying little attention to the abundance of species except for trees. Staring in the 1940s, however, ecologists began to collect data on plant abundances more systematically, creating a reliable baseline for tracking change. Ecological surveys differ from floristic surveys in that they provide quantitative data not only on where species occur but also on their abundance at these sites. Botanist John Curtis of the University of Wisconsin was one of the first and most industrious of the mid-20th-century ecologists seeking to describe plant community composition and structure along environmental gradients. He and his students fanned out across the state in the 1940s and 1950s, surveying over 1,000 sites across all the major community types in Wisconsin. Curtis (1959) summarized this remarkable work in his landmark book, *The Vegetation of Wisconsin*. Their work in the Northwoods sampled forests that had managed to escape the axe, plow, and grazing, although most were selectively logged. Although these stands hardly represent the original forest, they provided the closest approximation possible.

Plant Community Dynamics

Our research group has resurveyed forests in northern Wisconsin in recent years to gain a clearer picture of just how Northwoods plant communities have changed over the past 50 years. We use the Curtis era data as a baseline to track changes not only in which species are there but also in their abundance and in overall community composition. This work is providing valuable insights into the nature and extent of long-term ecological change.

We face a paradox in the Northwoods: herbarium records reveal that the total number of plant species in the region has increased over the past 150 years, yet the number of species present at any given site has usually declined. The increase in overall species diversity reflects the colonization of hundreds of nonnative (exotic) plant species combined with an absence of native species extinction. Colonization can occur quickly. If a few seeds of the highly invasive Japanese stilt grass (currently not found in the Northwoods) stick to a hiker's shoe in Illinois, fall off in the Northwoods, and plants become established, colonization has occurred. Total species diversity in the Northwoods increases by one, even if the species is only found at one site. By contrast, extinction is usually a slow process (though still rapid relative to historic extinctions). The Indian cucumber root may once have been present at thousands of sites throughout the Northwoods but is now found at only few dozen sites. Despite these many local losses, the species is not (yet) extinct in Wisconsin. It will remain a part of the Northwoods flora until the last individual from the last population disappears. Because colonization is fast and extinction is slow, plant species diversity is increasing at large spatial scales throughout the United States and elsewhere even at it declines locally (McKinney 2002).

At the same time, particular species are disappearing from particular places while a small number of generalist species replace those lost. The extirpation of species in the Northwoods was noted as early as the 1880s, when botanists were unable to relocate species where they were known to occur previously (Swezey 1883). Species were sometimes lost due to habitat destruction. Other times they disappeared for unknown reasons. Species continued to disappear through the 20th century. We found that an average of one native species disappeared from any particular upland mesic forest stand every 12 years between 1950 and 2000 (Rooney et al. 2004). Over the same period, common plant species increased in abundance, while many rare species disappeared and a handful of nonnative species invaded. In other words, the conservation value, or quality, of species present at sites declined. Although these declines are conspicuous in the data, they occurred gradually and are too subtle for most to have noticed them.

We can use these data to estimate how quickly biotic impoverishment is occurring in the Northwoods. Of the 67 sites surveyed by Curtis in 1950, 62 (92%) persisted to 2000. Similarly, an average of 85% native species persisted at each of these surviving sites (Rooney et al. 2004), and sites retained 93% of their original floristic quality. Including all these effects, we estimate that Northwoods plant communities retain only about 73% of the biological value (cover, diversity, and quality) they had 50 years ago.

What Drives Biotic Impoverishment?

By tracking a number of local communities we gain a sensitive indicator of regional biotic quality (and impoverishment). Examining several places simultaneously allows us to identify recurring patterns and separate the idiosyncratic changes operating at one or a few sites from the general patterns operating across sites. Examining changes in the abundance of many species over these many sites also gives us clues as to the mechanisms driving these changes. Consistent declines in fire-dependent species, for example, suggest that the loss of fires may be threatening the persistence of many species.

Figure 6.1 summarizes our thinking about how various factors interact to cause declines in habitat quantity and quality and native plant species diversity in the Northwoods. Many of these factors have causes of their own. We know that deer influence plant communities (plate 10). Hemlock and northern white cedar seedlings face extremely high mortality in areas with higher deer densities (Rooney et al. 2000, 2002). Areas without deer hunting (including some parks) experience plant species losses four times greater than elsewhere (Rooney et al. 2004). We also see that the particular plant species that have declined the most (nutritious lilies, orchids, and most forbs) and increased the most (grasses, sedges that tolerate herbivory, and some fibrous protected ferns) reflect the impacts of hungry deer (Wiegmann and Waller 2006). Collectively,

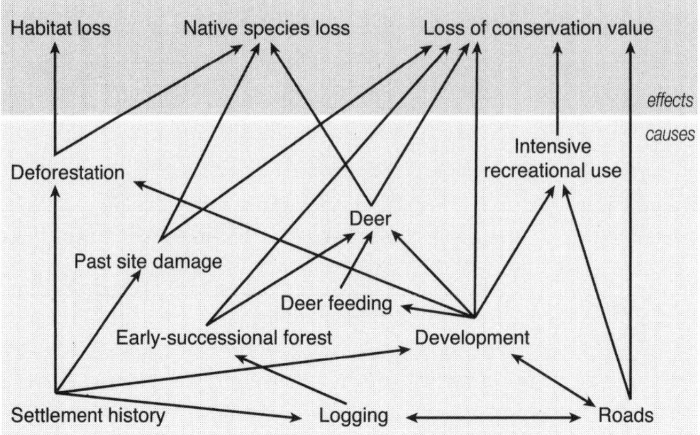

FIGURE 6.1 The loss of conservation value in the Northwoods, occurring through many indirect and unintentional pathways.

deer appear to be the primary driver of the major shifts we have documented in Northwoods plant communities.

Deer populations have grown across the region in response to abundant clearings and early successional forest. Both hunters and nonhunters also love to feed deer in Wisconsin, boosting overwinter survival in recent years (as have warming temperatures). Increases in the number of vacation homes are also reducing deer-hunting opportunities in many areas as private owners post their land. Some hunters may be less willing to drive and walk long distances into remote areas to hunt. Although the Department of Natural Resources is now struggling to increase hunter effort and effectiveness (e.g., by issuing additional doe permits), their success so far has been limited. Collectively, all these trends boost local deer populations at the expense of native species diversity. As the public learns more about these results and the important ecological role that hunters play, we hope to see less winter feeding and more support for the hunting of does and yearlings.

Logging remains the dominant land use in the Northwoods and will continue to play an important role in the future. When the presettlement forest was liquidated a century ago, both old-growth forests and old-growth legacies (like large-diameter dead wood) were eliminated. Current forestry practices throughout most of the state are designed to provide a mix of forest products, so trees seldom reach ages found in old-growth forests. Unlike lichens (chapter 11) and fungi (see sidebar), we have no evidence to suggest that there are any Wisconsin plants that depend exclusively on old growth (Scheller and Mladenoff 2002), though many occur at higher abundances in such habitats.

Inferring Change in Wisconsin's Fungal Populations

Daniel L. Lindner

Baseline population data do not exist for most species of fungi in Wisconsin, making it difficult to determine whether populations have changed over time. This situation is common for many other "obscure" species groups, including bacteria, spiders, and mollusks. Although it is tempting to discount such creatures due to their small size and cryptic nature, these species often play critical roles in basic ecosystem processes. This is because small creatures dominate terrestrial ecosystems in terms of both the number of different species present and overall biomass. Although individually small, these species have large effects on ecosystems.

Two approaches can be taken to infer changes in fungal populations following European settlement. The first examines current stands of unmanaged, old-growth forest to determine which species live there and to compare these populations with those found in managed or more heavily disturbed forests. Instead of tracking a group of sites over time, this technique examines a group of differently managed sites on the landscape at one time. Although this is one of the best tools available, remaining old-growth forests do not fully represent the unmanaged, unfragmented landscape that existed in presettlement times. Nonetheless, this technique gives one of the best windows into the past, showing what fungal populations may have been like before the forests of northern Wisconsin were clear-cut in the late 19th and early 20th centuries.

This approach revealed two species of wood-inhabiting fungi that are consistently associated with old-growth, northern hardwood forests: the black and white crust fungus, which causes a canker rot on yellow birch, and the saffron-colored polypore, which decays large-diameter sugar maple logs. The mossy maple polypore, an important forest pathogen, was more abundant in managed stands, particularly stands that had been clear-cut at some time (Czederpiltz 2001). These wood-decay fungi produce cavity trees used by many mammal and bird species during foraging and breeding (Samuelsson et al. 1994). Specialized animals, especially some beetles and flies, also rely on these fungal reproductive structures as places to feed and reproduce. Although wood decay fungi are rarely considered in conservation or management plans, these species were previously an integral part of old-growth forest systems, contributing to the production and decay of the large amounts of dead wood in old-growth stands.

The second approach for inferring change comes from our understanding of fungal life cycles. Many fungi depend on specific plant host species for growth and reproduction and cannot survive without their specific host plant. If these host plants decline or disappear from certain areas, the fungi associated with these plants also disappear. This might have happened to the Huron sulphur shelf, a bright orange, edible shelf-fungus that grows on large-diameter hemlock trees. This species was named after the Huron Mountains of Michigan, where it was only recently discovered (Burdsall and Banik 2001). To date, the Huron sulphur shelf has only been found in old-growth forests in the Upper Peninsula of Michigan, although specimens have been collected very close to the Wisconsin border in the Sylvania Wilderness Area (Czederpiltz 2001). This species was probably common in northern Wisconsin's hemlock-dominated presettlement forests (plate 6). Its dependence on large-diameter hemlock trees, however, appears to have made it a very rare species today.

The Huron sulphur shelf may be just one of many fungi that have become rare or extinct in Wisconsin due to a loss of large-diameter conifer species. In one of the first surveys of Wisconsin's fungi, Neuman (1914, 85) reported that the quinine fungus "has been reported by various collectors as found on larch in the northern part of the state" and noted a perennial fruiting body in the University of Wisconsin herbarium measuring 65 cm (2.1 ft) in height with at least 70 annual growth rings! Fruiting bodies of this size require very large, old trees. This species is now thought to be extirpated in the Midwest. The last known collection made in this region occurred in 1974, from a large-diameter hemlock in the Huron Mountains.

The quinine fungus has several uses. It was important to the Tlingit, Haida, and Tsimshian peoples of the Northwest Coast, who used it for medicinal and ritual purposes (Blanchette et al. 1992). Shamans considered this woody fungus to have strong supernatural powers and carved spirit figures from it to use in various rituals. Such figures were placed as guardians on gravesites. Early herbalists also used this fungus as a cure-all. Its use continued into the twentieth century, with pharmaceutical companies employing it as an antiperspirant to relieve the night sweats associated with tuberculosis. Because this fungus frequently grows in the upper reaches of tall trees, quinine collectors sometimes dislodged large fruiting bodies using rifles (Arora 1986). Although it has no antimalarial properties, the fungus was used as a quinine substitute due to its bitter taste. It does contain agaric acid and agaricin, has styptic (antibleeding) and purgative properties, and remains a potential source of novel chemical compounds (Blanchette et al. 1992).

The Huron sulphur shelf and quinine fungus were probably common in northern Wisconsin when large-diameter conifers still dominated much of the landscape. Knowledge of the habitat requirements for these large, obvious fungi suggests that there may also be many smaller, less obvious species that rely on large-diameter trees. These fungi may also have suffered undocumented declines. More fungal surveys of Wisconsin's remaining old growth are needed to determine which species are still present and whether population sizes are large enough to support these interesting, if often unnoticed, forest dwellers.

REFERENCES

Arora, D. 1986. Mushrooms demystified: A comprehensive guide to the fleshy fungi. 2nd ed. Berkeley, CA: Ten Speed Press.

Blanchette, R. A., B. D. Compton, N. J. Turner, and R. L. Gilbertson. 1992. Nineteenth century shaman grave guardians are carved *Fomitopsis officinalis* sporophores. Mycologia 84:119–124.

Burdsall, H. H., Jr., and M. Banik. 2001. The genus *Laetiporus* in North America. Harvard Papers in Botany 6:43–55.

Czederpiltz, D. L. L. 2001. Forest management and the diversity of wood-inhabiting polyporoid and corticioid fungi. Doctoral diss., University of Wisconsin–Madison.

Neuman, J. J. 1914. The Polyporaceae of Wisconsin. Wisconsin Geological and Natural History Survey, Bulletin No. XXXIII, Scientific Series No. 10. Madison, Wisconsin.

Samuelsson, J., L. Gustafsson, and T. Ingelög. 1994. Dying and dead trees: A review of their importance for biodiversity. Uppsala, Sweden: Swedish Threatened Species Unit.

When logging operations follow best management practices, direct impacts to rare, logging-sensitive plant species (like the goblin fern) can be minimized. However, logging also contributes to biotic impoverishment in indirect ways. We already noted that an abundance of early successional forest boosts deer populations to the detriment of many plant species. Logging operations also depend on an extensive road network, providing habitat and invasion routes for invasive species. Spotted knapweed and orange hawkweed are now seen frequently along logging roads with hawkweed beginning to invade forest interior habitat. Logging roads also provide access for cars, hikers, bird-watchers, hunters, and all-terrain-vehicle riders. Invasive plant seeds then hitchhike along via tires, trailers, undercarriages, boots, and clothing. As invasive plants outcompete and displace native plant species, conservation value declines. Areas with recreational access experience more soil compaction, vegetation damage, and invasive species than less used areas. Garlic mustard is highly invasive and has already taken over many woods in southern Wisconsin. Although it remains uncommon in the Northwoods, we have begun to see it along dirt roads, at trail heads, and in unsurfaced parking lots and campgrounds.

Although complex, figure 6.1 tells an incomplete story. At broad scales, global climate change has begun to affect the Northwoods. Warm winters favor overwinter deer survival much as winter feeding does, amplifying deer impacts. Habitat fragmentation probably threatens many species, slowing recolonization and recovery from disturbances that might otherwise not pose much of a threat. Novel pests and pathogens also continue to appear (see chapter 30). White-pine blister rust has decimated white pine populations for more than a century, slowing their recovery. Climatic warming and the hemlock wooly adelgid could doom eastern hemlock from its remaining strongholds in the north (plate 6). Acid rain or terrestrial eutrophication (nitrogen inputs) could also be stressing Northwoods trees. A diagram like figure 6.1 presents a rather static view of biotic impoverishment given that many causes exist and that these can interact in complex ways (and at various scales). The Northwoods is dynamic, with complicated feedback between causes and effects, novel interactions, delayed responses, and unpredictable behavior. Still, the figure captures several key interactions driving ecological change in the Northwoods and plainly shows how human activities are linked to biotic impoverishment.

Trajectories

> In the final stages the communities completely dominated by man are composed of a small number of extremely vigorous, highly specialized weeds of cosmopolitan distribution, whose origin and distribution are in themselves a man-induced phenomena. The subfinal stages are a mixture of these weeds and the most aggressive elements of the native flora. **Curtis 1956**

Fifty years ago, John Curtis foresaw how native plant communities respond to human population and economic growth. In a sense, the history of the Northwoods flora resembles the history of western Europe's flora, with increases in weedy species and declines in high conservation value species over time. The changes that took place in Europe thousands of years ago, however, are occurring far more rapidly now in the Northwoods. Because the future is difficult to predict (chapter 28), we must consider the current trajectory of impoverishment as a baseline for the future rather than a concrete prediction of what will occur. Trends could well accelerate, decelerate, or shift direction.

The changes we are documenting in northern forests reflect in part what has happened here in the past (Carpenter 2002). Reinvasions of forest plants after the glacier retreated provided the species pool. The great cutover a century ago and exploding white-tailed deer populations continue to shape the composition of today's flora. They will continue to do so for the next several decades, even if deer populations are brought under control. Decisions made today likewise will shape the future flora. This year's residential and commercial development, road construction, and pulpwood operations will create ecological legacies likely to persist long into the future. Novel changes just staring to take place like global warming, altered snow and rain patterns, and the appearance of new pathogens, herbivores, and invasive species will further affect future forest communities (Foster and Aber 2004). How much additional development will occur in the Northwoods? What new conservation and restoration strategies will be deployed, and when? The high degree of uncertainty we face here suggests that we be cautious and conservative in managing our forests. We also benefit from using our imagination in scenarios as a tool to understand the drivers and consequences of possible future changes to the Northwoods flora (chapter 28).

What We Know

Existing conservation measures are failing to protect the flora. State parks that restrict hunting lost more native plant species over the last 50 years (more than 50%) than any other land use we examined. National forest lands, with their multiple-use, sustained-yield mandate, also exhibit slightly above average rates of species loss. Few places we studied showed both increases in native species richness and improved floristic quality through time. Interestingly, these occurred disproportionately on the Lac du Flambeau, Ojibwa, and Menominee tribal lands. This suggests that we should study and learn from their land and wildlife management practices.

Given the limited successes and outright failures of many existing conservation strategies, some conservation biologists are beginning to think about strategies applied at the continental scale. The "rewilding" approach emphasizes the importance of protecting large wild areas, maintaining functional habitat corridors, and maintaining or restoring ecologically effective densities of large carnivores (Soulé and Terborgh 1999; Foreman 2004). Rewilding is an ambitious and demanding conservation strategy. It will require that all parties—individual property owners, tribal governments, land conservancies, lake associations, zoning boards, natural areas and natural resources managers, regional planning commissions, and conservation groups—look beyond the boundaries that most interest them to embrace a larger, regional conservation strategy. Similar shifts in perspective have begun in Florida, the Rockies, and the Southwest. Success, however, will require commitment, cooperation, and coordination.

Rewilding is happening both on its own and with some help from conservationists. Wolves have successfully recolonized the Northwoods on their own (chapter 18), and cougars may follow. In cedar swamps within wolf pack territories, deer are wary and/or less abundant, allowing plant growth to recover. Ecologists with the U.S. Forest Service are working to identify, protect, and connect high quality natural communities on the Chequamegon and Nicolet National Forests. Barry and others (2001) examined the current state of "wildness" in the Northwoods, identifying candidate areas to restore connectivity (plate 11). Many steps still remain. The Northwoods still needs ecologically effective large blocks of habitat to support wide-ranging species and landscape-scale processes. Conservation biology is often viewed as idealistic (as forestry was a century ago), impractical, and unprofitable. We disagree. Forests are both a renewable resource and a complex ecosystem to be managed conservatively.

Humans have acted as agents of change in the Northwoods since the glaciers receded. While human caused changes in this region are not new, the rates of change are. Some of this change is encouraging. Careful management on tribal lands, for example, has retained forest structure and sustained floristic quality. The question remains, however: Will the rest of the Northwoods continue to become more crowded, commercial, and intensively managed, ensuring further biotic losses, or can we sustain its beauty, diversity, and natural value? If we succeed in taming the Northwoods, we will have failed.

References

Barry, G. R., T. P. Rooney, S. J. Ventura, and D. M. Waller. 2001. Evaluation of biodiversity value based on wildness: A study of the western Northwoods, Upper Great Lakes, USA. Natural Areas Journal 21:229–242.

Bellemare J., G. Motzkin, and D. R. Foster. 2002. Legacies of the agricultural past in the forested present: An assessment of historical land-use effects on rich mesic forests. Journal of Biogeography 29:1401–1420.

Bersing, O. S. 1956. A century of Wisconsin deer. Madison: Wisconsin Conservation Department.

Carpenter, S. R. 2002. Ecological futures: Building an ecology of the long now. Ecology 83:2069–2083.

Cronon, W. 1991. Nature's metropolis: Chicago and the Great West. New York: W. W. Norton.

Curtis, J. T. 1956. The modification of mid-latitude grasslands and forests by man. Pages 721–736 in W. L. Thomas, ed. Man's role in changing the face of the Earth. Chicago: University of Chicago Press.

———. 1959. The vegetation of Wisconsin. Madison: University of Wisconsin Press.

Dupouey J. L., E. Dambrine, J. D. Laffite, and C. Moares. 2002. Irreversible impact of past land use on forest soils and biodiversity. Ecology 83:2978–2984.

Flannery, T. 2001. The eternal frontier: An ecological history of North America and its peoples. New York: Atlantic Monthly Press.

Foreman, D. 2004. Rewilding North America: A vision for conservation in the 21st century. Washington DC: Island Press.

Foster, D. R., and J. D. Aber. 2004. Forests in time. New Haven, CT, and London: Yale University Press.

Griffith, E. M. 1906. First annual report of the state forester of Wisconsin. Madison, WI: Democrat Printing Co.

Leopold, A. 1966. A Sand County Almanac with essays on conservation from Round River. New York: Ballantine Books.

Leopold, A., L. K. Sowls, and D. L. Spencer. 1947. A survey of overpopulated deer ranges in the United States. Journal of Wildlife Management 11:162–177.

Martin, P. S. 1973. The discovery of America. Science 179:969–974.

McKinney, M. L. 2002. Do human activities raise species richness? Contrasting patterns in United States plants and fishes. Global Ecology and Biogeography 11:343–348.

Pielou, E. C. 1991. After the ice age: The return of life to glaciated North America. Chicago: University of Chicago Press.

Rooney, T. P., R. J. McCormick, S. L. Solheim, and D. M. Waller. 2000. Regional variation in recruitment of eastern hemlock seedlings and saplings in the Upper Great Lakes, USA Ecological Applications 10:1119–1132.

Rooney, T. P., S. L. Solheim, and D. M. Waller. 2002. Factors influencing the regeneration of northern white cedar in lowland forests of the Upper Great Lakes region, USA. Forest Ecology and Management 163:119–130.

Rooney, T. P., S. M. Wiegmann, D. A. Rogers, and D. M. Waller. 2004. Biotic impoverishment and homogenization in unfragmented forest understory communities. Conservation Biology 18:787–798.

Scheller, R. M., and D. J. Mladenoff. 2002. Understory species patterns and diversity in old-growth and managed northern hardwood forests. Ecological Applications 12:1329–1343.

Solberg, E. D. 1961. New laws for new forests. Madison: University of Wisconsin Press.

Soulé, M. E., and J. Terborgh, eds. 1999. Continental conservation. Washington DC: Island Press.

Swezey, G. D. 1883. Catalogue of the phaenogamous and vascular cryptogamous plants of Wisconsin. Geology of Wisconsin 1:376–395.

Turner, F. J. 1920. The significance of the frontier in American history. Ithaca, NY: Cornell University Press.

Whitney, G. G. 1994. From coastal wilderness to fruited plain: A history of environmental change in temperate North America from 1500 to the present. New York: Cambridge University Press.

Wiegmann, S. M., and D. M. Waller. 2006. Biotic homogenization in forest understories: Identity and traits of historical "winners" and "losers." Biological Conservation 129:109–123.

7

From the Prairie-Forest Mosaic to the Forest: Dynamics of Southern Wisconsin Woodlands

David Rogers, Thomas P. Rooney, and Rich Henderson

When Chief Blackhawk looked over the land in the early 19th century, he gazed upon complex mosaic of prairie, savanna, and forest (plates 5 and 9), a landscape shaped by fire. In places where fires were frequent and intense enough, open prairie persisted. Other areas with less frequent or intense fires were occupied by oak savanna. Where fires were frequent but of low intensity, oak woodland developed—patches of oak-hickory forest with white oak saplings in an otherwise open understory. Oak savanna and woodland graded into each other with no clear line of demarcation. Together, prairie, oak savanna, and oak woodland occupied 75% of the landscape.

Mature forests also developed and persisted but only where fires were rare. Because fires generally moved with prevailing winds from west to east, lakes and topographic features often served as natural firebreaks allowing forests along eastern lake shorelines. Moist forest also established in ravines throughout the Baraboo Hills and portions of the Driftless Area, reflecting the rugged topography and favorable microclimate (Kline and Cottam 1979). The forests that were the most protected from fire supported southern mixed hardwood trees, including maple, basswood, beech, elm, white ash, and other fire-intolerant species. Collectively, southern mixed hardwoods covered about a quarter of this landscape with major concentrations along the

Lake Michigan shoreline and at the confluence of the Mississippi and St. Croix rivers (Curtis 1959; Anderson et al. 1996). These species were thus ready to colonize any oak woodland that went unburned for long, initiating a transition toward more southern mixed hardwood forest across the region following European settlement.

To understand the other southern forests one must understand the overriding importance of fire. Unlike many eastern U.S. forests, forests here seldom represented an end state of succession. Instead, fires recurred in regular cycles that would reset the successional clock. Fires occurred commonly in southern Wisconsin where a slightly warmer and drier climate (plate 2) tipped the balance to favor fires more than in the north. Indigenous Indians reinforced, modulated, and amplified these patterns. Indians used fire extensively to signal neighboring tribes, clear land, and increase the quantity and quality of economically important plants, from berries to basket-making materials. Fire improved the quality of forage for ungulates like deer and elk. Ground fires also sustained an impressive diversity of plants within these forests. By reducing densities of shrubs and other clonal species, subcanopy trees, and the trees that cast denser shade like maple, fires favored a rich array of herbaceous species (Leach and Givnish 1996). Fires also removed oak leaf litter, which can hinder the growth and reproduction of many ground layer plant species. The quilt of interspersed prairies and forests created a broad range of environmental conditions. This particularly reflected variation in the amount of sunlight reaching herbaceous plants from shady forest understories to exposed open prairies. This, in turn, often favored more adaptations to drought in prairie plants. Even small areas often supported mixtures of forest and prairie plants. Some of this diversity represented vestiges from previous vegetation, while other species were new arrivals. Disturbance and environmental variation combined to create one of the most diverse plant communities in the region (Weiher and Howe 2003).

A Century of Change: 1850–1950

When Euro-Americans colonized southern Wisconsin, they drastically altered the mosaic. While the destruction of the prairie by the plow is an obvious legacy (chapter 8), the suppression of fires by settlers had similarly drastic and lasting consequences (Curtis 1956). Without fire, the savannas and woodland began a slow transition to southern mixed hardwood forest. Shade-tolerant, fire-sensitive trees were no longer kept at bay and out of the oak forests and savannas. The fire-driven, dynamic vegetation mosaic ceased to exist. A landscape where forests and woodlands had graded into savannas and prairies morphed into a landscape where pockets of closed forest occurred scattered among open agricultural fields and towns. Farmers often valued these patches of closed forest as they provided a continuous supply of timber, fuel wood, nuts, fruits, and wild game. The decline of "sun-loving" savanna and open woodland plants was scarcely noticed.

In addition to their origin, two other factors greatly influence the structure and composition of present day forests in southern Wisconsin. The first is forest fragmentation. Where there was once a continuous habitat mosaic covering the region, the creation of cropland, pasture, towns, and urban areas isolated the southern forests from one another, greatly reducing the free movement of plants and animals among stands. Previously, disturbance or some other factor would regularly eliminate a species from a stand but individuals could easily migrate from nearby unaffected areas to reestablish a population. Ecologists call this the "rescue effect." Smaller, isolated stands, however, lack unaffected areas from which migrants can come. Instead, common and persistent species still present in the stand would tend to replace those species that were eliminated, diminishing species diversity (Curtis 1956). A second important factor also stems from the growing isolation of these stands. Plants adapted to woodland in the vegetation mosaic persisted because they were adapted to disperse well following fires. These conditions favored short generation times, fire tolerance, and the ability to disperse long distances (Curtis 1956). In the absence of fire, individuals persist at the same place for much longer periods of time, favoring traits that allow plants to compete in shady environments rather than tolerate fire or disperse long distances. This ecological "regime shift" favored a different set of adaptive traits.

Fifty Years of Change: 1950–2000

Under the leadership of John Curtis, the Plant Ecology Laboratory (PEL) group intensively surveyed forests throughout southern Wisconsin in the 1940s. They encountered a broad range of forest types, with oaks particularly abundant (Curtis and McIntosh 1951). Many of the oak forests had origins in savanna, as attested by the abundance of open-grown oaks within them (Curtis 1959). Oak seeds were abundant, and the scarcity of deer through the early 20th century favored oak seedling survival. During this time, seeds from other tree species were sparse. Box elder and green ash were still largely confined to lowland and floodplain forests, while hackberry, maples, ash, and other fire-intolerant species only colonized slowly from the few mixed hardwood forests present in the landscape. "Sun loving" shrubs were abundant in southern forests, especially gray dogwood and American hazelnut. The ground layer contained abundant honewort, sweet cicely, black snakeroot, and bedstraws.

In the early 2000s, we revisited 132 PEL southern forest sites. We expected some loss of sites, particularly where we found new residential developments with names like "Oak Acres" sprouting in place of the forests they supplanted. In all, 88% of the forests Curtis and colleagues sampled persisted. The remaining 12% became cropland, pasture, or, more usually, a residential or commercial development. The forests that did persist changed a lot. Oaks are still present at most sites but are not as common as they once were. Nearly all the oaks we encountered were large canopy trees with seedlings and saplings conspicuously absent. On the rare occasions we encountered oak saplings, they invariably grew on coarse soils, under pine plantations, and sometimes on steep slopes. Canopy oaks now vie for position with competing maples, elms, black cherry, bitternut hickory, and other fire-intolerant species (figure 7.1). Researchers are not surprised by this shift from oaks to fire-intolerant species. Curtis and McIntosh (1951) predicted it, and studies from other locations support this prediction (Larsen 1953; Lorimer 1984; McCune and Cottam 1985). Red maple and black cherry have become far more common now.

In addition to these changes in the canopy, southern Wisconsin forests are losing discouraging amounts of vascular plant diversity in their shrub and ground layers. Our preliminary analyses reveal that of the 288 plant taxa encountered in 1950, 96 taxa (33%) were not present in 2003. We encountered 52 new plant taxa in 2003, 30 native taxa and 22 nonnative taxa. This represents a 15% decline in the regional species pool. Four out of every five sites lost species through time, with the average site losing 26% of its native plant taxa richness. Even if nonnative new species are added, the average site still lost 22% of its plant diversity over the last 50 years. Even our smallest sampling unit, the one-square-meter quadrat, now contains, on average, 28% fewer plant taxa. In contrast, exotic plants are steadily invading southern Wisconsin forests. In 1950, only 29 stands (26%) had at least one exotic species but by 2003, 93 sites (82%) did. On average, the relative abundance of exotic species has tripled (from 2% to 6%), and sites support seven times as many exotic species relative to all taxa present.

Aside from these declines in native species and increases in exotics, we also see that forest understory communities in southern Wisconsin are converging in species composition. The extent of this "biotic homogenization" is evident from the fact that the average species similar-

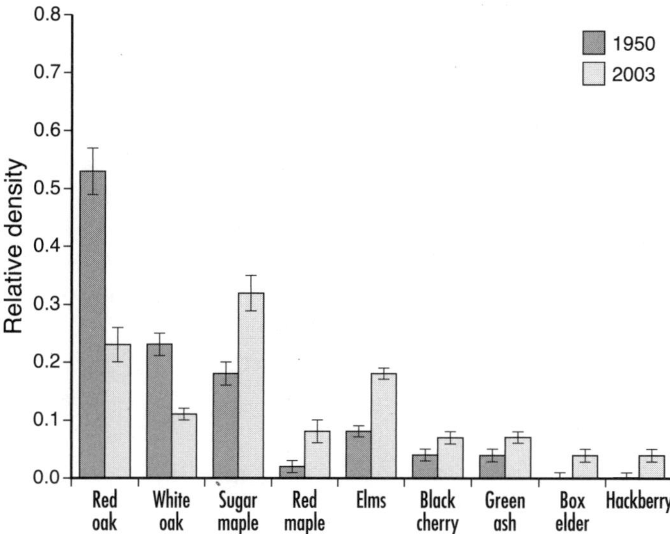

FIGURE 7.1 Changes in the density and importance value of common tree taxa in southern Wisconsin upland forests. Red oak includes black oak, white oak includes bur oak, and elms includes American and slippery elms.

ity among sites has increased from 31% in 1950 to 36% in 2003. While we initially expected this convergence to reflect the invasion of exotic species, it actually reflects increases in a few common native plants at least as much (when we look at native taxa only, average among site similarity increased from 31% to 37%). Furthermore, we were surprised to learn that rates of species loss and biotic homogenization over sites only weakly reflect the presence and abundance of exotic species. In fact, sites that were most heavily invaded by exotics actually had, on average, lower rates of native species loss than uninvaded sites. This unexpected finding may reflect the fact that exotic species are still invading these sites and may not yet be abundant enough to greatly affect local native species. This finding also illustrates how important it is to have data from many sites. With data from only a single invaded site, we might erroneously attribute a decline in species diversity to the invasion of exotic species. While invasive exotic species can and do drive native species losses elsewhere (and may yet do so in these forests), we do not yet have evidence of such impacts in these upland forests.

If exotic invasion is not driving native species loss, what is? Changes in the shrub layer provide a clue. The relative abundance of shrubs has increased 21% since 1950, and we see the greatest losses in species just where these increases in shrubs and other understory woody plants is greatest. Craig Lorimer and colleagues (1994) found a similar relationship. The survival and growth rates of oak seedlings decline greatly wherever there is a dense shrub layer. Some shrubs, like the hazelnuts and gray dogwood, occupy frequently burned sites. While fire kills the aboveground parts, they resprout from their roots. In the absence of fire, these pioneer shrubs are eventually outcompeted by chokecherry and other fire-intolerant shrubs. As shrubs proliferate, they cast additional shade, reducing the number of individuals and their growth rates in the ground layer. Shrubs also cause soils to retain more moisture. Both the shade and this additional soil moisture reduce the likelihood of fire, further favoring late-successional tree seedlings over oaks and other early successional species. This successional process is therefore self-reinforcing.

Fire Suppression and Succession: A Driving Force

We see that the suppression of fires in southern Wisconsin forests has driven forest succession in a direction that has contributed to both species declines and biotic homogenization. We used techniques developed by Wisconsin ecologists (Curtis and McIntosh 1951; Curtis 1959; Peet and Loucks 1977) to characterize the successional state of each stand in both 1950 and 2003. Without fires or other disturbance, succession gradually transforms an oak savanna into an oak woodland, which then succeeds to a multilayered oak forest and finally a maple forest. These changes can be captured via a numeric "continuum index" that places early successional oak savannas at one end (1) and late successional sugar maple forests at the other (10). We assign values to each stand, based on which tree species are present, their relative abundances, and how shade tolerant they are. Using this approach, we find the successional state of the average stand has indeed shifted greatly (from 5.1 to 6.4) between 1950 and 2003. These changes are also reflected in standing wood. Increases in both average density and basal area boosted wood volume almost 30% (to an average of 34.2 cubic meters per hectare).

These shifts in succession are related to species losses. Late successional forests in 1950 lost more plant species than early successional forests. Losses are also greater in forests that have changed the most due to succession. Shifts in the identity of species through time provide additional evidence that species losses are being driven by succession. As expected, sun-adapted species characteristic of the oak mosaic, including the narrow, thick-leaved sedges, grasses, and bedstraws show marked declines in both the number of sites they occupied and their abundance. In contrast, shade-tolerant and fire-intolerant species with thin, broad leaves persist and have gained in abundance.

Land Use

As Aldo Leopold noted, we write our intentions onto the landscape with the axe and the plow. Not all the southern forests are used or managed in the same way. Perhaps the most important factor influencing the fate of southern forests are the decisions that individual landowners or land managers make in managing their land. Some exploit forest stands for their value as timber to maximize short-term economic gain. Many private tracts and most state parks are set aside for their own sake and for future generations. Many of the state natural areas and Nature Conservancy holdings are actively managed to maintain their outstanding ecological properties or unique species. Many property owners practice and take pride in good stewardship, promoting timber extraction within the broader context of maintaining the character of the property and the sustainability of the resource.

Our research sheds some light on the effects of logging on southern forests. We were able to divide our sites into 71 stands that had a history of logging in recent decades and 43 that did not. Interestingly, the stands that had been logged had more species at both the site and quadrat levels (19% and 26%, respectively). Thus, logged stands appear to be losing species at only two-thirds the rate of unlogged stands. While some might interpret this as evidence that logging boosts forest understory diversity, long-term effects are less certain. We also compared rates of species loss and biotic homogenization between 30 stands that were logged prior to the 1950s (Rogers 1959) and 84 stands that showed no sign of logging at that time. Over the last 50 years, stands that had been logged before the 1950s showed almost twice the rate of species loss that unlogged stands did. Thus, logging may increase understory diversity in the short term but then increase longer-term declines in diversity as stands mature. Of course, not all logging is equal. The timing of timber cuts, how many and which trees are removed, and the equipment used and associated disturbances all influence just how a site will be affected. Sites subject to rapid and extensive cutting to maximize short-term gain often suffer high rates of exotic invasion and conspicuous declines in floristic quality. However, careful removals of single trees or small groups of trees (selection harvest) or partial overstory removals ("shelterwood" cuts) can recreate habitat conditions similar to those found in the original oak mosaic. We therefore predict that such harvesting methods (particularly if combined with understory fires) could reduce rates of species loss and maintain higher floristic quality while improving prospects for oak regeneration.

What is happening in the state parks? Overall, we found that lands formally "protected" tended to experience greater rates of invasion by exotics, native species losses, and reductions in floristic quality. We found the same surprising, sad, and ironic finding in northern forests (chapter 6). If these areas are protected from logging and development, why are they not retaining diversity? We suspect that roads, parking lots, campgrounds, and heavy human visitation and use combined with a lack of fire and canopy disturbance reduce the conservation value of these lands. Many parks also historically banned hunting, contributing to locally high deer populations and associated impacts (chapter 19). We conclude that many parks need careful management and restrictions on human access and use if they are to avoid further biotic impoverishment.

Landscape Effects

So far, we have evaluated changes within forest stands as though only local conditions (like soils, succession, light, and deer) matter. In reality (as is so often true in ecology), context also matters. In particular, analyses of landscape conditions show that surrounding land use and land cover strongly affect local forest dynamics. Most notably, stands with more forest cover within 5 km lost species more slowly (and suffered less biotic homogenization) than similar stands isolated within agricultural or suburban landscapes. Likewise, stands with higher densities of roads and houses lost native species faster (and floristic quality declined more) than forests surrounded by fewer houses and roads. Regional trends mirror these local patterns. Stands in the sparsely populated Driftless Area lost fewer native species, gained exotics, and underwent biotic homogenization more slowly than stands in the southeast. This does not strictly reflect glacial history. Even within the glaciated southeast, smaller patches of forest lost species faster than large patches and those with higher road and housing densities gained more exotics. Thus, we all, via our collective land use decisions, affect the biotic composition of the natural communities around us even if we never give it any thought.

The Future

Unless we greatly reduce our collective human footprint on the land, the southern forests appear destined to continue losing uncommon native species until they contain only species that thrive in human-disturbed habitats. To avoid this scenario, we need to craft a regional strategy to restore and maintain remnant oak woodlands and savannas in a mosaic that could effectively conserve viable populations of the species that once lived here. It is, of course, neither desirable nor practical to restore conditions to just what Curtis and colleagues saw and recorded in the 1950s. Those data represent but one snapshot at a time when succession was already eliminating species characteristic of the mosaic (Curtis 1956).

Because most forests in southern Wisconsin are privately owned, any viable conservation plan for southern Wisconsin forests will need to include incentives for these owners. Private owners also operate with fewer constraints than public land managers, allowing those interested to move beyond benign neglect by managing their land using more active and ecologically enlightened approaches. Groups like the Blue Mounds Area Project are providing expertise and encouraging landowners to move in this direction. We also advocate providing additional incentives for landowners, such as a federal or state program to reduce woodland exotics, restore oak woodland remnants, and protect viable populations of declining species. Landowners pursuing such management should receive favorable breaks on property taxes (see chapter 27).

Promoting oak regeneration will also require us to reduce deer densities at least locally and create high-light understory environments to favor oak saplings and associated ground layer plants. Owners with woodlots that contain large canopy oaks and no oak regeneration should consider logging out nearly every hackberry, ash, box elder, and maple from the stand, along with most native and every exotic shrub. They might also experiment with fire, plant oak saplings, and work with reputable foresters to restore oak. We also recommend that the state natural areas program discourage, or at least limit, visitation to many of the state natural areas. People unintentionally bring exotic species seeds to these areas on their cars, shoes, and clothing. Many state natural areas would benefit by reducing the number of hiking trails and parking spaces. This, however, presents us with a dilemma. Public visits help build political support for the funds needed to administer and manage our natural areas program. Visits also serve an educational role—visitors learn how important it is to restore and manage oak ecosystems. For the moment, it is not too late to recover many limited populations of the woodland and savanna species that thrive under open conditions. Time, however, is of the essence. The longer we wait, the more populations are lost and the more labor intensive and expensive restoration becomes.

If we ultimately fail to conserve and restore the southern oak mosaic, what will be lost? We will still have forestland capable of producing timber. This forest will continue to function, capturing solar energy, absorbing carbon dioxide, cycling nutrients, and pumping water. But this forest will be an impoverished place, harboring exotic plants and persistent and aggressive native species. Reflecting on the future of southern forests, John Curtis (1956, 734) wrote, "A premium is placed on those species that can resist the particular pressure [of people] and still maintain their populations. All others tend to decline or disappear." While he was writing about plants, the same holds true for all species. With the loss of oak trees, many oak-specific bark-dwelling lichens will disappear (chapter 11). Red-headed woodpeckers, flickers, and a whole suite of open oak woodland birds will become less abundant. Likewise, the loss of a diverse understory flora will go on to reduce the diversity of insect pollinators and herbivores, including butterflies and moths (chapter 23). Acorns are a key resource that feed many mammals, birds, and insects. As Leopold noted, while these are things many people assume they can live without, others of us know we cannot.

References

Andersen, O., T. R. Crow, S. M. Lietz, and F. Stearns. 1996. Transformation of a landscape in the upper mid-west, USA: The history of the lower St. Croix River valley, 1830 to present. *Landscape and Urban Planning* 35:247–267.

Curtis, J. T. 1956. The modification of mid-latitude grasslands and forests by man. Pages 721–736 in C. O. Sauer, M. Bates, and L. Mumford, eds. Man's role in changing the face of the earth. Chicago: University of Chicago Press.

———. 1959. The vegetation of Wisconsin: An ordination of plant communities. Madison: University of Wisconsin Press.

Curtis, J. T., and R. P. McIntosh. 1951. An upland forest continuum in the prairie-forest border region of Wisconsin. *Ecology* 32:476–496.

Kline, V. M., and G. Cottam 1979. Vegetation response to climate and fire in the driftless area of Wisconsin. *Ecology* 60:861–868.

Larsen, J. A. 1953. A study of invasion by red maple of an oak woods in southern Wisconsin. *American Midland Naturalist* 49:908–914

Leach, M. K., and T. J. Givnish. 1996. Ecological determinants of species loss in remnant prairies. *Science* 273:1555–1558.

Lorimer, C. G. 1984. Development of the red maple understory in northeastern oak forests. *Forest Science* 30:3–22.

Lorimer, C. G., J. W. Chapman, and W. D. Lambert. 1994. Tall understorey vegetation as a factor in the poor development of oak seedlings beneath mature stands. *Journal of Ecology* 82:227–237.

McCune, B., and G. Cottam. 1985. The successional status of a southern Wisconsin oak woods. *Ecology* 66:1270–1278.

Peet, R. K., and O. L. Loucks. 1977. A gradient analysis of southern Wisconsin forests. *Ecology* 58:485–499.

Rogers, D. J. 1959. Ecological effects of cutting southern Wisconsin woodlots. Ph.D. diss., University of Wisconsin–Madison.

Weiher, E., and A. Howe. 2003. Scale-dependence of environmental effects on species richness in oak savannas. *Journal of Vegetation Science* 14:917–920.

8

Savanna and Prairie: Requiem for the Past, Hope for the Future

Mark K. Leach

Have you ever reflected on times when your skepticism melted, giving way to glowing admiration? In 1988 the manager of a planned recreation trail hired me to document rare plants and native vegetation along a recently abandoned railroad right-of-way. This big, blond, local fellow, Steve Hubner, despite some virulent opposition, had preserved the 76 km (47 mi) corridor between Monroe and Mineral Point. He couldn't tell a lousewort from a fleabane, but he knew a lot of other things, such as the fact that old railroad rights-of-way sometimes harbor rare prairie and savanna plants. The Gratiot to Mineral Point section was built in 1856 and 1857, and the Monroe to Gratiot section was built in 1880 and 1881. The 30.5 m (100 ft) right-of-way between the two fencerows probably protected some places from the plow and the cow. Steam locomotives caused fires, and before the railroad, the First Peoples burned the area. The original land survey records showed that much of southern Wisconsin had been sparsely wooded by oaks (plate 9), while many other places had no trees at all (plates 3 and 4). Steve knew all this, but his knowledge and enthusiasm seemed directed toward hound dogs, trapping, skinning, hunting, chasing coyotes, and raising blond kids. I doubted that he had any personal interest in sissy things like flowers.

During several late afternoons Steve found me while I searched for plants. He would hand me a cold can of beer and start asking, "Which plants are interesting here? What's the name of this one? I've always wondered what it is. Nobody around here knows this stuff." I thought, maybe he really is interested. I began showing him how to identify plants that indicate original savannas, prairies, and wetlands. Showing him how the large leaves lined up north-south, I told Steve, "This one is compass plant. This is a sign that we can find many other prairie plants nearby. Look. Here's vernal sweet grass. I don't find that often. The First Peoples make braids of this to burn like incense. For this site I have an old list of plants found here by Henry Greene, the renowned prairie expert, in 1948." We found most of the species on Henry's list. Some we didn't find—like the prairie parsley (listed as a threatened species in the state; Hubner and Leach 1995).

On a different afternoon, Steve pulls up in his pickup truck and asks, "What the hell are these weirdo plants?" I replied, "They are rattlesnake master. Thousands of years ago people used them to make rope sandals. I'm glad to see some here. They and some of these other plants indicate this is a patch of unplowed, rich-soil prairie: the kind that has all but vanished from Wisconsin." Steve examined the plants silently, then looked far across the rolling pastures and cornfields before saying, "Hell, Mark—I know where that gull-darn rattlesnake crappin' master grows up the yin-yang!"

Some days later, Steve's pickup truck bounced down a rutted lane between fields of ripening corn. Leaving the truck, Steve and I squeezed through two barbed-wire fences and crossed a dry washout. We stopped among the Holsteins, busy grazing the vegetation to a centimeter of the ground. This was it? The place with all the rattlesnake master? I was skeptical. Steve said that this pasture was far from the barn and, therefore, infrequently grazed. There wasn't enough of any plant remaining for me to identify. I guessed that this pasture probably had a few prairie plants but was unlikely to be remarkable.

Out of his own pocket, Steve leased and fenced about 8 hectares (20 acres). He took me back the following summer. "Steve, this is the real thing. Incredible. A real mesic prairie!" With every few steps I saw more plants that you rarely find outside of a fragment of original prairie, including rare species I had never seen before.

Steve caught the prairie bug. Since the 1980s, he has been active in the Prairie Enthusiasts, one of several grassroots organizations protecting and restoring savanna and prairie. Hundreds of people have also caught that bug, resulting in a remarkable upsurge in the conservation of native landscapes. Nonetheless, I remain skeptical that what remains of original Wisconsin can maintain its species composition and ecosystem functions for even the next 25 years. My skepticism stems from two big problems. Steve Hubner puts it this way, "First big problem is people. In 2004 I tried to get the caretakers of two prairie cemeteries excited about the rarity of what they have. So what did they do? They herbicided everything, including the state-threatened wild quinine. Know what they said? 'We don't want no rare plants so the DNR [Department of Natural Resources] can tell us what to do.'" Sadly, no federal or state agency has or has ever had the authority to protect plants on private land in the United States. Steve went on to cite another problem: "You'd think nature would work with us—we save places, cut brush, pull weeds, burn—but she keeps throwing us problems." Steve rather quickly discovered lessons that many conservationists take years to learn, if they learn them at all.

Ecology of Wisconsin's Oak Savanna and Prairie

Wisconsin's savannas and prairies grew where the climate could support forests, but frequent fire kept them open. On a continental scale, midwestern oak savanna occurred in a band stretching from western Minnesota to Illinois and Missouri to central Texas. This band, sometimes called the Prairie-Forest Border, lies between the prairies of the arid Great Plains and the forests of the humid East. In Wisconsin, the band lies southwest of the Tension Zone. Within the band was once a complex mosaic of vegetation types (see plate 3). In places sheltered from fire, such as northeast edges of lakes, grew lush forests of fire-intolerant sugar maple, American elm, and basswood. The aptly named village of Maple Bluff lies on the northeast shore of Lake Mendota. Typically on flat land and on southwest-facing slopes, fires consumed all woody plants, creating the essentially treeless areas we call prairie. However, fire-tolerant oaks populated most of the region (see sidebar on p. 106 and figure 8.1).

There are no clear lines separating prairie, savanna, and woodland (or forest). I loosely define prairie as grassy vegetation with no or very few large trees. In Wisconsin, I think of prairies as places in the savanna where the trees are far apart. In woodlands and forests the trees are tight together so their crowns form a continuous canopy, allowing little light to reach the smaller plants below. The oak savanna trees are more widely spaced and have low horizontal branches that receive light from the side. This spacing results in a complex shifting mosaic of

Soil Response to Reestablishment of Prairie Communities in Southern Wisconsin

Christopher J. Kucharik

The loss of prairie and oak savanna had impacts beyond individual species. The transformation eventually led to a 40%–60% loss of soil organic matter (Kucharik et al. 2001; figure 8.1). Even after 150 years; the average observed soil carbon content (25 cm depth) of nine prairie remnants in Dane County was three times higher than that of soils under traditional row crop systems. The constant aeration of soils through tillage practices, combined with the loss of the extensive root production systems associated with prairies, contributed to a net release of carbon dioxide from these soils to the atmosphere and increased topsoil loss through erosion. Soil organic matter, which is largely composed of carbon, is essential to maintaining soil structure, water-holding capacity, nutrient retention, and buffering against degrading management practices.

To help combat the deterioration of soil and water resources due to widespread agricultural land use, over 250,000 hectares of land in Wisconsin have been enrolled in the Conservation Reserve Program (CRP) since 1986, with 80% of this area planted in prairie vegetation. Researchers are now interested in how to deliberately return large quantities of carbon into degraded soils, because it helps rejuvenate fertility and potentially mitigates an enhanced greenhouse effect. Thus, the obvious question arises: How successful have prairie restoration efforts in Wisconsin been at replenishing key soil resources? Unfortunately, some planted prairies, even after 20 years, are not returning significant quantities of carbon back into soils (Brye, Gower, et al. 2002; Brye and Kucharik, 2003). Moreover, soils uptake carbon slowly. In CRP-planted prairies, most of the carbon uptake was confined to the top 5 cm of soil (Kucharik et al. 2003). These findings imply that functional restoration is not the same as prairie plant restoration; reestablishing native vegetation does not assure reestablishment of important ecosystem processes. To achieve more complete restorations, we will need to focus on belowground processes just as much—and maybe more—than the aboveground community structure (Brye, Norman, and Gower et al. 2002).

REFERENCES

Brye, K. R., S. T. Gower, J. M. Norman, and L. G. Bundy. 2002. Carbon budgets for a prairie and agroecosystems: Effects of land use and inter-annual variability. Ecological Applications 12:962–979.

Brye, K. R., and C. J. Kucharik. 2003. Carbon sequestration in two prairie topochronosequences on contrasting soils in southern Wisconsin. American Midland Naturalist 149:90–103.

Brye, K. R., J. M. Norman, and S. T. Gower. 2002. Assessing the progress of a tallgrass prairie restoration in southern Wisconsin. American Midland Naturalist 148:218–235.

Kucharik, C. J., K. R. Brye, J. M. Norman, J. A. Foley, S. T. Gower, and L. G. Bundy. 2001. Measurements and modeling of carbon and nitrogen cycling in agroecosystems of southern Wisconsin: Potential for SOC sequestration during the next 50 years. Ecosystems 4:237–258.

Kucharik, C. J., J. A. Roth, and R. T. Nabielski. 2003. Statistical assessment of a paired-site approach for verification of C and N sequestration on Wisconsin Conservation Reserve Program (CRP) land. Journal of Soil and Water Conservation 58:58–67.

---

sun and shade for the shorter plants. Most of Wisconsin's oak woodlands sprang up when fires stopped and, today, are actually overgrown former savannas or prairies (see chapter 7). According to John Curtis (1959), at the time of settlement, oak savannas covered far more area than prairie (2.2 million vs. 850,000 hectares).

Many of the same plants grow in both oak savannas and prairie, but a given area of savanna often has more species than the same area of prairie (Leach and Givnish 1999). Prairie vegetation is typically dominated by a few species of warm-season grasses, such as big bluestem

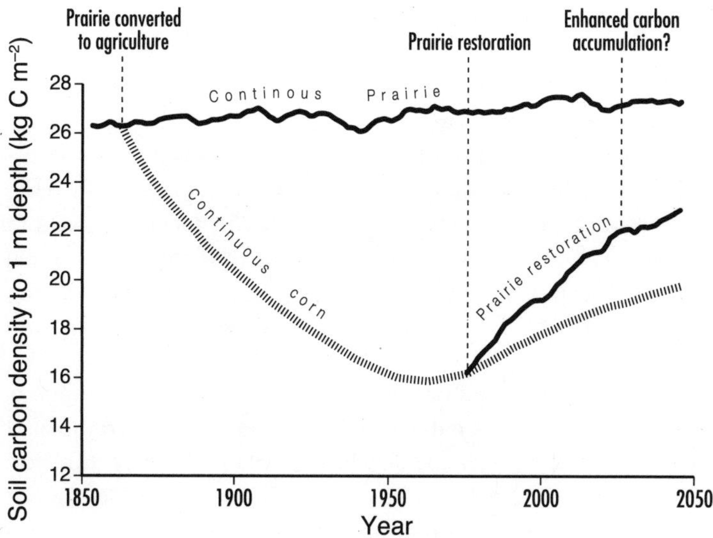

FIGURE 8.1 Soil carbon density.

and Indian grass. These warm-season grasses are well suited for hot, bright, drought-prone, frequently burned places. They typically do not grow as well in the shade of the savanna oaks. The bulk of plant diversity in both savanna and prairie is composed of hundreds of species of herbaceous plants collectively called forbs. Compared to grasses, forbs have broader leaves and showier flowers. In open prairie, warm season grasses coexist with many species of forbs. In the savanna shade, the warm season grasses occupy less space, leaving more room for forbs. Since there are many species of forbs, more room means more species per area.

Without regular fires, trees and shrubs quickly invade prairies and oak savannas. Soon, insufficient light reaches the herb layer, and the number of native plant species decreases sharply. Often, a few native species persist: wild geranium, jack-in-the-pulpit, Virginia creeper, and white avens. These are joined by some of the weedier members of our woodland flora, such as the native white snakeroot and the European weed garlic mustard. Most such places lack nearby seed sources for true forest species, depleting their conservation value (see chapter 7) .

Direct and Indirect Drivers of Change

It didn't take long for domestic grazing animals and the steel plow—both introduced during the 19th century—to destroy over 99.9% of Wisconsin's original prairie vegetation (Curtis 1959). Today, nearly all of Wisconsin's prairie exists as small remnants of a few hectares or less. It's not clear how much of the savanna was lost. Many savannas on steep and rocky places survived direct destruction, only to become overgrown woodlots and forests (chapter 7).

Human arrogance and ignorance still drive savanna and prairie losses. There is no social norm calling for their protection. Prairie cemeteries in Lafayette County are poisoned with herbicide. A farmer plows a remnant prairie in Waukesha County to spite the DNR officials offering to buy and protect it. Homes are built in highly restorable savannas and on prairie remnants. Gardeners dig up wild plants. And so goes the prairie and savanna.

An optimist might point out that by the end of the 20th century, only one plant species, Mead's milkweed, has been extirpated from Wisconsin's savannas and prairies and note the efforts under way to restore it in the wild. However, as Hugh Iltis, one of Wisconsin's elder statesmen of conservation, says, "An optimist is someone who has not yet heard the bad news." The 21st century could witness considerable loss of plant species, as has already occurred in Milwaukee County (chapter 25). Biologists, including myself, are concerned that a quarter or more of the savanna-prairie flora is declining and may soon vanish (Henderson and Sample 1995; Milbauer and Leach 2007). Indirect and underrecognized processes contribute to this ongoing loss of plant diversity. As Steve Hubner pointed out, nature follows her own rule and does not always cooperate with conservation efforts.

Hidden Losses over Time

Ecologists use a variety of approaches to document long-term change. In Wisconsin, we have a special opportunity to track changes in prairie vegetation by using the baseline data collected 50 years ago for over 200 prairie sites by John Curtis (1959) and his colleagues. Revisiting these sites allows us to document how plant species have come, gone, increased, and decreased in recent decades. Tom Givnish, Michelle Milbauer, and I relocated 74 of these sites that were still intact enough to sample. We recorded all the species present while also noting habitat size and fire history (see Leach and Givnish 1996). We then compared patterns in these shifts in abundance with plant traits and site conditions to cast light on what is driving the changes we observe in these remnant prairies.

The first thing we noticed was a dramatic loss of plant populations (all the individuals of a species present at a site represent one population). While Curtis and others found 4,377 populations over these 74 sites in the 1950s, we could not relocate 1,662 (38%) of these. This represents an average loss of 22.5 species per site. About two-thirds of the losses appear related to the size of the remnant prairie, its original species richness, and the time interval between sampling. Smaller vegetation remnants (and those that originally contained more species, not surprisingly) have lost the most species. Furthermore, these species losses have grown over time. Some of the "losers," or species experiencing population losses, include purple prairie clover and pussy-toes (69% lost); prairie cinquefoil, prairie panic grass, and sky-blue aster (63% lost); and shooting star, prairie sunflower, and prairie thistle (over 50% lost).

These losses provide a prime example of a lag between the cause of change and when we observe that change. Altering the landscape from extensive savanna-prairie to one with only scattered fragments of savanna-prairie happened over a hundred years ago. However, the "extinction debt" implicit in this loss and fragmentation of habitats is still being paid. Following habitat fragmentation, species losses can occur slowly over decades. Without nearby populations to recolonize the site, populations can die out for good. Also, the loss of prairie plant populations can be accelerated by new, weedier species arriving by immigration, reducing space and resources for species originally present (Milbauer and Leach 2007). Examples of species gaining in abundance include native species like river grape, Canada goldenrod, gray dogwood, evening primrose, Virginia creeper, and box elder, and introduced species including Kentucky bluegrass, Queen Anne's lace, smooth brome grass, and quackgrass.

Population Size

Small populations of plants suffer declines from various factors including chance events, the inability to attract pollinators, and crosses between related individuals (inbreeding). Sparse populations with only a few individuals are particularly at risk. Michelle Milbauer and I didn't know how many individuals were in plant populations a half-century ago in the 21 sites we studied. However, John Curtis's data sometimes provided a convenient substitute—namely, the frequency at which they encountered each species across multiple sampling plots. For example, when John Curtis and Henry Greene visited prairie number 9 in 1947, they recorded the names of all the plants rooted within 20 of these one-square-meter plots (termed quadrats). They found side-oats grama grass in all 20 quadrats, for a frequency of 100%. Most species are scarcer, and Curtis and Greene recorded 11 species only found in a single quadrat. Knowing that they might overlook other sparsely scattered species, Curtis and Greene also surveyed outside the quadrats where they recorded another 21 species. These small populations clearly had a frequency of less than 5%. From these data, we discovered that smaller populations are far less able to persist. Of the populations that occurred in two or more quadrats, 31% disappeared, but an even larger and more disturbing fraction (64%) of the smaller populations were lost. Curiously, the pattern was the same in both fire-managed and unburned prairies. Thus, most populations appear to be at risk even in the seemingly intact remnants of Wisconsin's natural savannas and prairies.

Species with Problems and Problem Species

The characteristics of species affect their fate. In our study of 55 prairie remnants, Tom Givnish and I discovered particularly high losses in those species that fix nitrogen, are short in stature, or produce small seeds (Leach and Givnish 1996). Why did this occur? It may reflect fire suppression. Nitrogen tends to be scarce after fires (when it is volatilized from plant material). Fire also stimulates the growth of warm-season grasses that extract nitrogen from the soil. In contrast, a lack of fires causes dead plant material to accumulate in a thick mulch layer, retaining nitrogen and choking out short plants and small seedlings. These dynamics tend to favor species that can fix nitrogen after fires.

Michelle Milbauer and I also explored how species' fidelity to intact versus human-impacted habitats affected how well prairie plants persisted. Botanists in the Midwest have ranked Wisconsin's native plants into 11 classes based on how limited they are to rare and undisturbed habitats. Species like compass plant and rattlesnake master gain a high "coefficient of conservatism" (8–10) reflecting the fact that they are restricted to high quality fragments of original vegetation. In contrast, weedy plants like giant ragweed that are widespread even in degraded habitats get low scores (0–3). We found that, if fires did not recur at least once every five years, remnant specialized species declined and were replaced by habitat generalists. In fact, habitat generalist species have increased at every spatial scale (i.e., one square meter, 20 square meters, the whole site, and all 21 sites combined). The net effect has been an overall average increase in the number of native species that tend to occur at a site. Lost populations of "conservative" prairie plants are being replaced by these weedy native plants. After half a century, prairie remnants remain full of plants, yet many of the species we are most concerned with conserving have been replaced by the same plants we encounter along roadsides, in pastures, and in degraded habitats.

Why are generalists replacing specialists? Our few remaining savanna and prairie fragments are small and correspondingly only able to sustain small populations of habitat specialists. These small, isolated populations are vulnerable to the vagaries of local disturbance and changing weather and water conditions. Remnant savannas and prairies now also lack the fires and herds of elk that may have once checked populations of their competitors or opened up favorable sites for seed germination and seedling growth. Instead, these "islands" of habitat are surrounded by a hostile "sea" of farms, roads, and sprawling suburbs. Most of the seeds these prairie and savanna plants produce are doomed by landing on fields, roadsides, or other unsuitable patches. At the same time, their populations fail to recruit seedlings from afar as conditions are less suitable and most nearby potential source populations have died out. Thus, smaller and increasingly isolated populations tend to sink lower until they wink out, one by one. In contrast, weedy and widespread habitat generalist species (including many exotic invaders) thrive in our disturbed landscapes. As their populations soar, their seeds rain down upon our remnant prairies and savannas, exploiting tiny open patches. While fires every few years help to maintain habitat specialists, they do little to slow this steady immigration of habitat generalists.

From Skepticism to Hope

Neither human nor nature's behaviors will be easy to steer in a more ecologically sustainable direction. In the short run, expect populations losses to accerlate, more remnant communities to be destroyed, and, future human generations to experience less of nature's beauty. However, many smart, energetic, creative people are dedicated to turning things around. They spend their weekends and holidays protecting and restoring the best of wild Wisconsin. They raise money to buy the places they love. They form grassroots efforts with names like the Prairie Enthusiasts (http://www.theprairieenthusiasts.org) and the Blue Mounds Area Project (http://www.bluemounds.org). While well-intentioned people can make things worse by enthusiastically doing the wrong thing, these organizations show significant foresight in incorporating research and education into their restoration practice. Each year more people learn that they can foster environmentally sustainable behaviors in ways that are fun and that help build the kind of society most of us want. I admire all this energy pouring into saving and restoring our remnant savanna and prairie ecosystems. I see prairie restorations under way along highways and bike trails, on church properties, in school yards, adjacent to retention ponds, and on private lands. Steve Hubner told me the other day, "My kids are taking me out to cut brush on the prairie. We want the place to look nice, so their kids—if they have any—have something to appreciate."

We may doubt whether we can ever regain the beauty savannas and prairies once gave our landscapes (see sidebar on p. 113). We certainly face dire social and ecological challenges. Yet support for savanna and prairie conservation and restoration is growing, even with few federal or state incentives. Imagine what could be accomplished if there were sufficient prairie conservation and restoration incentives. Grassland birds might stage an impressive recovery (see chapter 21). Semiwild elk might punctuate the landscape. Large areas of recovering savanna and prairie might help reduce dangerously high levels of atmospheric carbon dioxide (see sidebar on p. 106). Rather than vanish into a forgotten past, the recovery of prairies and savannas could provide us with a great conservation success story.

The view from this mound, as well as from the flat near the summit of the eastern mound, surpasses description! An ocean of prairie surrounds the gazer, whose vision is not limited to less than thirty or forty miles; this great sea of verdure is interspersed with delightfully varying undulations like the vast waves of the ocean and every here and there sinking in the hollows, or cresting the swells, appear spots of wood, large groves, extensive ranges of timber, small groups of trees, as if planted by the hand of art, for ornamenting this naturally splendid scene! Over this extended view in all directions are scattered the incipient farms of the settlers, with their luxuriant crops of wheat and oats, whose yellow sheaves, already cut, form a beautiful contrast with the waving green of the Indian corn, and the smooth dark lines of the potato crop. Throughout the prairie the most gorgeous variety of flowers are seen rising above the thickly set grass, which in large and small patches has here and there been mowed for hay, all presenting a curious chequered appearance of the table beneath us. The mineral flower, the tall bright purple, and red feather, the sunflower, the yellow broom, the golden rod, the several small and beautiful flowers interspersed with the grass, rendered the scene indescribably beautiful. . . . This picture is not exaggerated; it fails of the original beauty, in the attempt to describe that scene which is worth a journey of a thousand miles to contemplate in the calm sunset of a summer day, as I have viewed it from the top of the Platte mounds.

William Rudolph Smith. 1838. Pp. 92–94 in Observations of the Wisconsin Territory. Philadelphia: E. L. Carey & A. Hart. Reprinted in 1975 (New York: Arno Press).

References

Curtis, J. T. 1959. The Vegetation of Wisconsin: An Ordination of Plant Communities. Madison: University of Wisconsin Press.

Henderson, R., and D. Sample. 1995. Grassland communities. pp. 116–129 in J. Gomoll, S. Holtz, R. Isenring, M. Jesko, L. Komai, B. Les, and W. McCown, eds. Wisconsin's Biodiversity as a Management Issue. Madison: Wisconsin Department of Natural Resources.

Hubner, S., and M. Leach. 1995. Prairie parsley reappears following brush cutting and burning (Wisconsin). Restoration and Management Notes 13(2):209–210.

Leach, M. K., and Givnish, T. J. 1996. Ecological determinants of species loss in remnant prairies. Science 273:1555–1558.

———. 1999. Gradients in the composition, structure, and diversity of remnant oak savannas in southern Wisconsin. Ecological Monographs 69:353–374.

Milbauer, M. L., and M. K. Leach. 2007. Influence of species pool, fire history, and woody canopy on plant species density and composition in tallgrass prairie. Journal of the Torrey Botanical Society 134(1):53–63.

9 Plant Communities of Great Lakes Islands

Emmet J. Judziewicz

What can islands tell us about the rate and extent of ecological change in isolated plant communities? In Wisconsin, we are fortunate to have two archipelagoes with different ecological histories and trajectories to study and compare: the Apostle Islands (hereafter AI) located in Lake Superior and the Grand Traverse Islands (hereafter GTI) in Lake Michigan. I have done extensive fieldwork in both island groups since 1990. Much of what I summarize here draws from two technical papers (for AI, Judziewicz and Koch 1993; for GTI, Judziewicz 2002).

The islands range in size from a few tenths of a hectare to almost 6,000 ha. The AI, located off the northern tip of Wisconsin's Bayfield Peninsula, are unusual in their regular spacing and relatively similar size and topography. The GTI vary more but are derived from similar dolomitic limestone and are spread in a line between Michigan's Garden Peninsula and Wisconsin's Door Peninsula. In both archipelagoes, microclimates play prominent roles, especially in the spring. Midday temperatures in the interior of the larger, relatively high islands may be 10°C higher inland than at lake level.

Apostle Islands

History. People have lived on the AI for many centuries. Native Americans settled Madeline Island long before the

French explorers and traders began visiting the islands in the early 17th century. Lighthouses were built on five islands in the late 1800s. Nearby "reservations" of uncut forest survived on Devils, Outer, and Raspberry islands, and these give us an idea of what the original (presettlement) vegetation was like in this archipelago. Logging began in the mid-19th century and continued for a century until this National Lakeshore was designated in 1970. Today the AI is largely covered with luxuriant second-growth forest, except for parts of Madeline Island where old agricultural fields are gradually reverting to forest.

Ecological and Floristic Studies. Systematic ecological studies of AI forests began with the University of Wisconsin Plant Ecology Laboratory project led by John T. Curtis. He and his students, including Edward Beals, were able to visit 18 islands and measure vegetation parameters in 76 sample plots during the years 1955–58 (Beals et al. 1960; Beals and Cottam 1960). From 1990 to 1992, I surveyed the vegetation of 1,424 upland forest plots (circular with an area of 0.01 ha) regularly spaced throughout the archipelago (Judziewicz and Koch 1993). I also collected approximately 4,000 plant specimens. Thus, the flora of the chain (809 vascular plant species) is well documented.

Forest Communities. Before European settlement, about 90% of the AI were covered by an upland mixed coniferous/hardwood forest dominated by hemlock, white pine, sugar maple, yellow birch, and white birch (Brander 1978). On poorly drained sites or places exposed to the prevailing winds where windthrow is a major factor, balsam fir and white cedar were important trees. Quaking aspen and white spruce were minor components of these upland forests. After logging, the forest composition changed. The large white pines were removed during the 1880s to the early 1900s, followed by the large hemlocks, yellow birch, and sugar maples. Nearly all old-growth stands were gone by 1950. Severe slash fires often followed logging, burning large sections of some islands (Beals and Cottam 1960). This favored short-term increases in species like quaking aspen, white birch, and red maple.

Hemlock occurs at its northwestern range limit in these islands and is not a dominant tree except in a few small, relict stands. Regeneration is rare. White pines are limited to maturing second-growth stands on sandscapes and scattered supercanopy individuals on all islands. Sugar maple, a species that thrives on well-drained upland soils on many islands, appears to have benefited from the decline of other species and is the only forest tree exhibiting good seedling and sapling recruitment. The abundance of early successional trees like aspen and white birch increased dramatically in the decades after logging, but most of these stands are now mature or in decline. White birch, sugar and red maples, balsam fir, and white cedar are presently the most important tree species.

Outer Island is both large (3,232 ha) and the most remote AI. Importantly, it has never had deer. The presettlement forest was dominated by large hemlock, white pine, and yellow birch. White cedar and sugar maple were also important. Logging started in the late 19th century with pine cutting, but the most intensive episodes occurred in the 1920s in the southern half of the island (with devastating fires following the slash) and in the late 1940s and early 1950s in the northern half (a selective cut with no fires afterward). This difference in disturbance history between the northern and southern halves of Outer Island is reflected in the differential abundance of many common species. Yellow birch, sugar maple, and especially hemlock are more common in the north, while white birch, quaking aspen, balsam fir, red oak, and red maple are more common in the south. Canada yew is common and locally dominant in the north but scarcer in the south. A 75 ha stand of hemlock/hardwoods located in the northwestern corner of the island was never logged because it was part of the lighthouse reservation. This stand is a benchmark tract of old growth in the archipelago and, indeed, in the Great Lakes region. Individual hemlock, yellow birch, and sugar maple trees approach 1 m in diameter, and there are scattered supercanopy white pines. Yew and mountain maple form a dense understory with an abundance of coarse woody debris. Palatable lilies, like white mandarin, are frequent on deer-free islands such as Outer but rare on the mainland. We see no evidence of any beaver activity in a 1939 air photo of Outer Island. However, by the 1950s, beaver were common all over the island. With the maturation and depletion of aspen, declines in beaver numbers became evident by the 1970s. Currently, there are few active lodges.

In the understory of the presettlement forest, Canada yew was the dominant shrub (figure 9.1) on many, if not all, the AI. After World War II, a severe irruption of white-tailed deer (perhaps intentionally introduced by hunters), which prefer yew to nearly any other food (Curtis 1961; Allison 1990), led to the near extirpation of yew from many AI. As deer became common in the late 1940s and peaked in the mid-1950s (chapter 19), yew suffered accordingly. Deer populations were subsequently curtailed by liberal hunting seasons as well as a series of severe winters in the late 1960s (Brander and Bailey 1983). Today yew is still dominant only on those islands without a history of deer irruptions.

FIGURE 9.1 Dense Canada yew understory on North Twin Island, Apostle Islands National Lakeshore, Wisconsin, July 1, 1990. This island was never logged and never supported a deer population. (Photo by author.)

These deer-free islands include Outer, North Twin, Raspberry, York, Eagle, and Devils. On islands with very low current yew cover, irruption-era deer harvest densities ranged from 0.4 to 2.8 per sq km. Fires also contributed to the loss of yew as on the southern half of Outer Island where fires following logging. Foster (1993) noted a similar absence of yew in the area severely burned by the Peshtigo Fire of 1871.

Sandscapes. The sandscapes of the AI are some of the most extensive and diverse on Lake Superior. Sandscapes originated in different ways and include true sand spits, or strips of beach that extend into deeper water (Cat and Outer islands); cuspate forelands, or triangular points or capes made from sediment deposits (as on Raspberry and South Twin islands); barrier beaches (Big Bay and Amnicon Bay on Madeline Island); tombolos, or spits or bars connecting an island to a mainland (York Island); a double tombolo (Presque Isle Point on Stockton Island); beaches (Justice Bay on Sand Island); and the barrier spit on Long Island that forms, disappears, and reforms every few decades (Nuhfer and Dalles 1987). A typical sandscape has a series of zones: a beach devoid of vegetation, active dunes, interdunal hollows (sometimes with ephemeral pools or ponds), stabilized dunes or beach ridges (sometimes covered with pine savannas or forests), and, often, a filled-in lake basin covered with bog or alder thicket vegetation.

Presque Isle Point is one of the few examples of a double tombolo on the Great Lakes. The Julian Bay beach lake dunes are dominated by beach grass and have all the other common associates of dune communities. This large sandscape is remarkable in the Great Lakes region in its complete absence of exotic plants. At the southern end there is a red pine savanna with a lichen heath understory (figure 9.2), which is the best remaining example of this community type in Wisconsin. Fires regularly burned in the closed beach ridge pine forests all along Presque Isle Bay, initiated by both lightning and burning by Native Americans to increase blueberry crops. Swain and Winkler (1983) found evidence for nine separate fires during the past two centuries, most recently in 1860, 1880, 1895, and 1925. Fires have been suppressed since about 1940.

Boreal Habitats. About a third of the AI's coast consists of Precambrian sandstone ledges and bluffs. Several rare boreal or subarctic plants occur here, mostly on north-facing cliffs moistened by seepage as on Devils, Otter, and Outer islands, but also on mossy boulders moistened by wave splash as on Ironwood Island. The Devils Island population of butterwort relies on a constant supply of moisture from seepage joints and appears to have remained stable during surveys made in 1980, 1991, 1996, and 2001. In contrast, butterwort populations on Iron-

FIGURE 9.2 Great Lakes barrens on Presque Isle Point, Stockton Island, Apostle Islands National Lakeshore, Wisconsin, July 1, 1990. Red pine is the dominant. This community has been maintained by lightning-caused and anthropogenic fires. (Photo by author.)

wood Island depend on wave splash and appear to be more affected by hot summers and water-level fluctuations (Judziewicz 1997). The rayless ragwort population on North Twin Island also depends on wave splash for its moisture. This population suffered a steep decline from 1991 to 1996 and had yet to recover as of 2002.

Exotic (Nonnative) Plants. An estimated 173 exotic vascular plant species exist in the AI (Judziewicz and Koch 1993). However, few of these species appear to pose serious problems for native communities. Probably the biggest threat is the population of purple loosestrife that appeared on the Long Island sand cut in the 1980s. The National Park Service (NPS) has conducted a decade-long eradication campaign that has, at least, prevented the spread of this population. A more menacing recent invader is spotted knapweed. So far, the dunes of the AI have escaped infestation by this species. However, it did appear for the first time in 1999 in sand near a dock on Stockton Island. Spotted knapweed may have been inadvertently introduced there by NPS personnel due to an infestation at the NPS equipment yard in Little Sand Bay on the Wisconsin mainland.

Grand Traverse Islands

History. Stretching from Wisconsin's Door Peninsula to Michigan's Garden Peninsula, these Lake Michigan and Green Bay islands are largely underlain by Silurian dolostone that outcrops along shorelines as high, white cedar–dominated cliffs (on west coasts), low wave-washed shelves (east coasts), and occasional interior escarpments. Most islands experienced intensive human use in the 19th century in the form of fishing, logging, and farming, but have now recovered to second- or third-growth forests of beech and sugar maple. An exception is Washington Island, the largest in the archipelago, which has a permanent population and extensive current and former farm land.

Ecological and Floristic Studies. Although there have been no systematic inventories of the plant communities of the GTI, there have been many forays to the archipelago to collect plants including intensive field work between 1997 and 1999 (Judziewicz 2002). The flora of these islands consists of 797 plant species.

Forest Communities. These islands were originally dominated by beech, sugar maple, quaking aspen, birches, hemlock, and basswood (in or-

FIGURE 9.3 Cobble glade community of deer-browsed white cedar on Little Summer Island, Grand Traverse Islands, Michigan, May 29, 1998. A similar community occurs along the north coast of Washington Island. (Photo by author.)

der of their abundance in the General Land Office survey notes of the 1830s and 1840s). Presumably, there were also large individual white pines. Butternut was an important forest tree at least through the 1920s on Washington Island (Fuller 1927) but then declined due to logging and disease. Today mesic forests are found in the interiors of the eight islands greater than 100 ha in size. Deer herbivory restricts the regeneration of most tree species except beech, which is unpalatable to deer. Deer also reduce the abundance and survival of many understory herbs (e.g., lilies and orchids) on large islands. Fuller (1929) once described the calypso orchid as "locally abundant" and noted that they were used to decorate gravestones on Memorial Day. This species has not been relocated on the island for over 50 years in spite of intensive searches. Another dramatic example of deer impacts is the obvious browse line visible in the dolostone-cobble white cedar communities found along the coasts of Washington and Little Summer islands (figure 9.3).

Deer have been repeatedly introduced to tiny Plum (108 ha) and Poverty (78 ha) islands. These publicly owned lands are regarded by some residents as "deer farms" for their private hunting privileges. In 1999, feral hogs were introduced to Plum Island in anticipation of an autumn "pig shoot." These introductions have seriously damaged plant communities on these islands.

Sandscapes. Sandscapes on the GTI are not as well developed as on the AI. Small dune complexes may have regional endemic plants such as dune thistle and Lake Huron tansy, but these are declining, probably due to intensive human use of Great Lakes beaches. For example, a small dune system on Rock Island is presently dominated by beach grass, mixed with rare species such as dune goldenrod and seaside spurge. Photographs from the 1930s show intact dunes with white cedar seedlings and juniper heaths that do not exist today. The last known location in Wisconsin for Lake Huron tansy occurred on this very beach but was trampled by beachgoers. It has not been seen there since 1972.

Bird Islands. Several small (less than 10 ha) islands in Green Bay and Lake Michigan have been colonized by nesting colonies of water birds (principally herring gulls and double-crested cormorants) starting in the 1970s. Urea deposits from these colonies have destroyed most of the white cedar, white birch, and balsam fir trees that originally occurred here (Hogg and Morton 1983). Since the tree kill, shrubs with bird-dispersed berries like red-berried elder, red raspberry, and red-osier dogwood have become dominant. The understory consists of rank native and exotic herbs such as catnip, motherwort, and nettles (figure 9.4). An example of a "bird island" is Pilot Island, a one-hectare tract with a lighthouse, built in 1851,

FIGURE 9.4 Pilot Island, Grand Traverse Islands, Wisconsin, July 22, 1999. The island was invaded by colonial water birds in the 1970s and 1990s; a dead white cedar forest overtops a dense shrub layer of dogwood, elder, and raspberry. (Photo by author.)

that is now abandoned to the birds and elements. Photographs show the station and the surrounding white cedar and white birch forest to be in good condition during the 1970s. By 1999, the forest was skeletal. The island is now dominated by weedy shrubs and herbs.

Exotic Plant Species. At least 161 exotic plant species are present on the GTI (Judziewicz 2002). These island forests face serious threats from exotic plant species. Garlic mustard has been marching north for years, and now dominates woods near campgrounds on the Door Peninsula. It is spread by vehicle traffic (including logging equipment) and hikers and campers who inadvertently introduce the seeds on boots and tents from farther south. For many campers on a Door County outing, the next stop after Peninsula State Park is often Rock Island State Park. Garlic mustard was first detected there on a tent pad in 1997, as well as on Washington Island.

On sandscapes, spotted knapweed has become a common and unmanageable threat, as, for example, on the barrens near the airstrip on Chambers Island (where it was absent in 1961). Dolostone cliff plant communities are threatened by the proliferation of common hound's-tongue, a coarse herb with burlike fruits that are abundantly dispersed on clothing or on the fur of deer. The herb is locally common on many dolostone cliffs, as well as in mesic woods that have been disturbed by heavy cutting or high deer populations.

The Future of the Archipelagos

Both the Apostle and Grand Traverse islands have experienced major changes over the past century and a half, including a dramatic shift in forest composition. As these forests recovered from their initial deforestation, hardwoods have usually won out over conifers. White pine and especially hemlock have yet to recover to presettlement levels and may not. The lack of hemlock regeneration in island forests is a mystery and occurs even on islands that have never had deer or have had their deer populations extirpated. Sugar maple is now substantially more important in the second-growth forests of the AI than in presettlement times. In the GTI, where deer browse is greater, beech has increased even more than maple.

After 1945, deer irrupted on all of the GTI larger than about 10 ha (25 acres) and on about half of the AI. On several islands, deer were subsequently extirpated either intentionally (via hunting, as on several of the AI and Chambers Island), natural processes (range degradation combined with severe winters), or both. Deer browsing has nearly eliminated Canada yew from the forest understory on all the GTI and about half of the AI. Canada yew appears to recover slowly from such browsing. On Rocky Island (AI), deer were gone by 1960, but yew has yet to recover. Herbaceous plants have also been decimated by abundant deer, particularly orchids and lilies in the GTI. On the smallest islands (less than 5–10 ha) in both archipelagoes, plant communities have shifted and simplified drastically since about 1975 in response to enormous increases in colonial water birds like herring gulls and double-crested cormorants.

Invasive exotic plant species have become a major threat to the integrity of plant communities on many of the GTIs. The main culprits are garlic mustard, spotted knapweed, and common hound's-tongue. In the AI, invasives are not yet problematic, although purple loosestrife is an issue on Long Island, and spotted knapweed has now established on Stockton Island. Finally, there is evidence that disjunct northern (boreal or arctic-alpine) species such as rayless ragwort may be declining in the AI.

Direct human impacts are also evident in these island systems. Fire suppression since about 1925 in the AI and on Chambers Island (GTI) has adversely affected fire-adapted pine barrens and savanna communities. For example, the original pine barrens along the western side of Presque Isle Point on Stockton Island (AI) is now a dense, even-aged red pine stand sheltering a popular campground. Great Lakes dune communities have been similarly devastated by human foot and vehicular traffic on the GTI.

Changes can occur quickly on islands. Conifers, particularly hemlock and Canada yew, appear likely to remain at low levels in the AI and the GTI for at least the next century. Further human development on Chambers, Washington, and Detroit islands (GTI) is likely to bring more vacation homes, more trails, more deer, more exotics, and further degradation of these plant communities unless measures are taken to protect them. Such measures are evident in the Apostle Islands National Lakeshore where recent legislation (2004) extended wilderness area protection to many of these islands.

References

Allison, T. D. 1990. Pollen production and plant density affect pollination and seed production in *Taxus canadensis*. *Ecology* 71: 516–522.

Beals, E. W., and G. Cottam. 1960. The forest vegetation of the Apostle Islands, Wisconsin. *Ecology* 41:743–751.

Beals, E. W., G. Cottam, and R. J. Vogl. 1960. Influence of deer on vegetation of the Apostle Islands, Wisconsin. *Journal of Wildlife Management* 24:68–80.

Brander, R. B. 1978. Apostle Islands tree diameters listed in the General Land Office Survey, 1852–1857. Report prepared for the National Park Service, Bayfield, WI.

Brander, R. B., and M. M. Bailey. 1983. Environmental assessment: Natural resources inventory and management, Apostle Islands National Lakeshore, Wisconsin. Report prepared for the National Park Service, Bayfield, WI.

Curtis, J. T. 1961. *The Vegetation of Wisconsin.* Madison: University of Wisconsin Press.

Foster, D. K. 1993. *Taxus canadensis* Marsh: Its range, ecology, and prospects in the state of Wisconsin. MS thesis, Department of Botany, University of Wisconsin–Madison.

Fuller, A. M. 1927. A botanist afield on Washington Island. *Milwaukee Public Museum Yearbook* 6:66–78.

Hogg, E. H., and J. K. Morton. 1983. The effects of nesting gulls on the vegetation and soil of islands in the Great Lakes. *Canadian Journal of Botany* 61:3240–3254.

Judziewicz, E. J. 1997. Final report on inventory and monitoring of rare vascular plants at Apostle Islands National Lakeshore. University of Wisconsin–Madison report to National Park Service, Bayfield, WI.

———. 2002 [as 2001]. Flora and vegetation of the Grand Traverse Islands (Lake Michigan), Wisconsin and Michigan. *Michigan Botanist* 40: 81–208.

Judziewicz, E. J., and R. G. Koch. 1993. Flora and vegetation of the Apostle Islands National Lakeshore and Madeline Island, Ashland and Bayfield Counties, Wisconsin. *Michigan Botanist* 32:43–189.

Nuhfer, E. B., and M. P. Dalles. 1987. A guidebook to the geology of Lake Superior's Apostle Islands National Lakeshore (and nearby areas of the Bayfield Peninsula of Wisconsin). Published by the authors, Platteville, WI.

Swain, A. M., and M. Winkler. 1983. Forest and disturbance history at Apostle Islands National Lakeshore. *Park Science* 3:3–5.

10 Patterns in Wisconsin Lichen Diversity

James P. Bennett

One hundred and fifty years ago, anyone traveling cross-country in Wisconsin found lichens growing in abundance. Beard lichens hung from the trees, orange bush lichens (plate 13) adorned shrubs and small trees in the southern counties, and lung lichens draped the giant tree trunks of the Northwoods (plate 12). Today, our only abundant lichens are weedy species on the trunks and branches of hardwoods and some rocks. Only a few northern bogs and mature maple and coniferous forests support a diverse and abundant lichen flora. Six species that we know used to occur in Wisconsin have disappeared. One species was last collected in 1884, while others were collected until recently. Methuselah's and the bushy beard lichens that once adorned the trunks of mature trees throughout the state have not been seen in decades. Our ancestors enjoyed a world full of thrilling plant diversity, but our world is becoming biologically simpler and monotonous.

A common theme in this book is the "missing baseline" problem—that without data on how abundant species were in the past and how they were distributed we cannot infer changes in their distribution and abundance. We particularly face this problem with lesser-known and undersurveyed groups like lichens. We face an even deeper level of uncertainty with lichens—namely, which species are here? Compilations of Wisconsin lichens list 726 species in 180 genera (Thomson 2003; Bennett and Wetmore 2004; Bennett 2006). This is about 70 species fewer than reported from Minnesota and Michigan (Bennett and Wetmore 2004). Does Wisconsin really have fewer lichen species than neighboring states of similar size and ecological conditions? And why, if we know lichens have gone extinct in Wisconsin, do we continue to discover new species? What ecological changes can we infer in this inconspicuous but ecologically important group?

What Are Lichens, and Why Are They Important?

Lichens are small, nonvascular plantlike organisms composed of a fungus and an alga growing symbiotically. They occur on the surfaces of vascular plants, rocks, soil, and many man-made structures. They are ubiquitous but often overlooked because they are inconspicuous. Most lichens grow quite slowly compared with higher plants but can be very long lived. Some form crustlike coatings on surfaces (crustose types); others have leafy lobes (foliose) or form complex shrubby or filamentous structures (fruticose). Lichens reproduce by producing fungal spores from various shaped, fruiting bodies or by small powdery or granular particles containing both the fungal and algal components. Because they grow slowly, most lichens species require stable substrates and lots of time to become established. Cutting mature forests can therefore contribute to the decline of several species (chapter 11).

Although lichens do not provide humans with food, shelter, or clothing, they do provide important ecosystem services. Many break down rocks into soil. Others fix nitrogen, increasing nutrient capture. Lichens also provide food for many animals and nesting material for certain birds. Some insects camouflage themselves as lichens to escape predation. Although often overlooked, lichens are an integral and beautiful part of our natural world (plate 12).

Because lichens are physiologically active most of the year and lack means to exclude pollutants, lichens are quite sensitive to air pollution, making them sensitive indicators of air quality. Fruticose and foliose species are exposed to the atmosphere, making them more sensitive than crustose types. Lichens on trees are similarly more vulnerable than those on soil and rocks. Sulfur dioxide, nitrogen oxides, and heavy metals kill sensitive lichens at low concentrations. The symbiotic algae are especially sensitive. When they die, the lichen partnership breaks down. Air pollution in southern Wisconsin was severe from 1900 until about 1990, eliminating many species. Since then, air pollution controls have reduced sulfur dioxides and other emissions considerably allowing some sensitive lichens to return. Encouragingly, an orange bush lichen was found in 1999 in Dane County.

Lichens and Lichenology

Although lichenology has a distinguished history in Wisconsin (Thomson 2003), we lack adequate collections from many areas. In general, the northern lichen flora is better known than the flora in southern Wisconsin. For example, over 80% of the species rated as imperiled or rare come from the northern part of the state. Of the 41 species of macrolichens (foliose and fruticose life forms) being considered for protection as rare and endangered species, almost 60% occur in the northern part of the state (Bennett and Wetmore 2004). These represent 7% of the lichen flora of the state. Some 38 of these 41 species are rare only in Wisconsin, not our neighboring states of Michigan and Minnesota.

We might conclude that northern lichens are more threatened than those in the south. However, this pattern could also simply reflect the fact that we know northern lichens better. This explanation is supported by several observations. First, the six lichen species now extinct in the state are not from the north (Bennett and Wetmore 2004) and appear to have disappeared from Wisconsin due to habitat destruction and air pollution. These stresses are more severe in the south as expected, given that human impacts scale with population density.

Human impacts thus lead us to expect that lichen diversity will decline in the more populous counties of southeastern Wisconsin. Indeed, Ashland County in northwestern Wisconsin has the highest number of recorded species (291), while Milwaukee and the other populous counties of southeastern Wisconsin have few (figure 10.1). However, this pattern confounds differences in human impacts with differences in sampling effort. Our most complete lichen surveys come from the Apostle Islands National Lakeshore (Wetmore 1990) and St. Croix National Scenic Riverway (Wetmore and Bennett 2004) in northwestern Wisconsin. Only one species has been recorded in Kenosha County, while an unusually high number of lichen species has been recorded for populous Dane County (where several lichenologists reside). This leads to a startling conclusion—namely, that the number of species noted in various parts of Wisconsin reflects the intensity of collecting rather than the actual number of lichen species present in that region (figure 10.2).

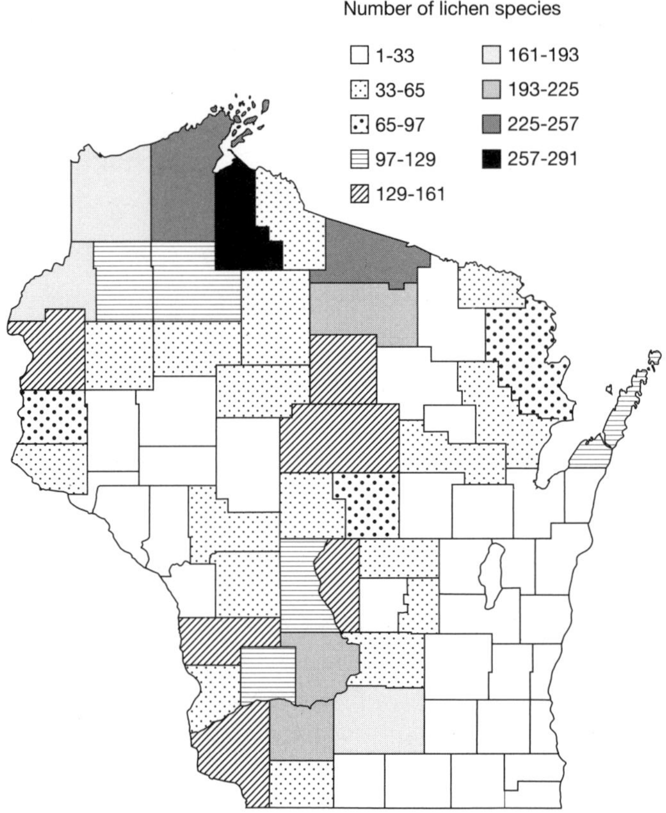

FIGURE 10.1 Number of lichen species identified, by county.

In general, we expect the number of species found in any sample to scale with the number of specimens collected (Gotelli and Colwell 2001). Only a large sampling effort can overcome this effect to provide an accurate picture of lichen diversity. A total of 7,320 lichens were collected in Wisconsin before 2003 (Thomson 2003). This sounds like a lot but is only one-fifth the number of lichens collected in Minnesota (C. Wetmore, personal communication with author) and about half those collected in Michigan (A. Fryday, personal communication with author). Thus, we expect fewer species to have been recorded. In addition, collecting has been uneven, being focused in the northern counties, along the Wisconsin River, and in several southwestern counties (figure 10.2). Crustose life forms also appear to be undercollected as only 32% of lichens reported from Wisconsin are crustose, while 52% of lichen genera across North America are.

Can we disentangle the effects of human impacts, area, and collecting effort on lichen species diversity? Using a statistical approach (multiple regression), I find that the number of lichen species reported for a county increases in direct proportion with the number of lichens collected there (as expected). In contrast, total area, human population density, forested acreage, farm acreage, road mileage, temperature, and precipitation do not appear to influence lichen diversity at the county level (once collecting is accounted for). We clearly have yet to fully characterize lichen species diversity in Wisconsin.

If lichens remain undercollected, we should expect to find new species with additional effort. This is indeed the case. Lichenologists working in northern counties recently uncovered 47 species new for Wisconsin. My collections on limestone bluffs along the Mississippi River also uncovered species new to the state. I have uncovered species new to their county and even the state almost every time I collect in State Natural Areas in the southwestern part of the state. We can conclude that much

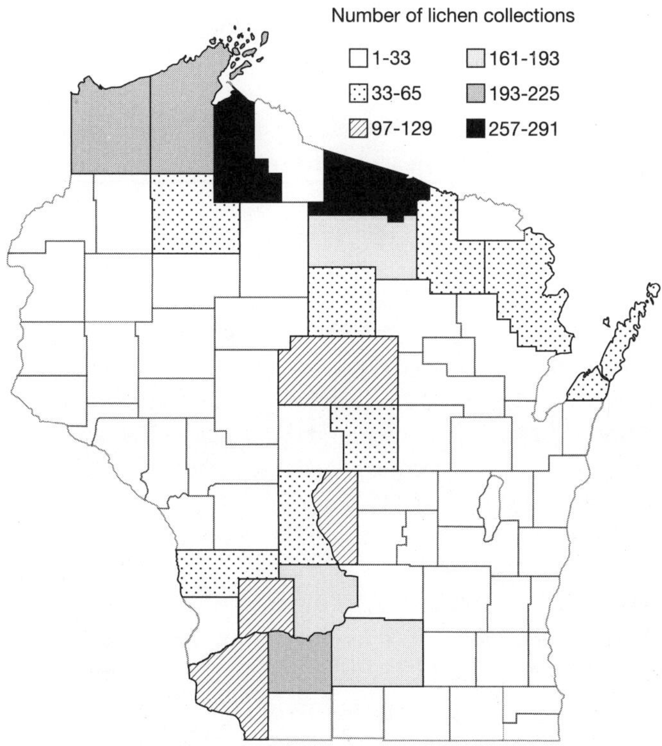

FIGURE 10.2 Number of lichen collections, by county.

of Wisconsin has yet to be sampled adequately enough to characterize background levels of species diversity. Without this baseline, we are clearly handicapped in our ability to infer change in these communities. In the next chapter, Will-Wolf and Nelsen explore how some particular lichen communities have changed. Although rare species are overlooked when they occur outside these plots, such resurveys give us an important glimpse into how these communities are changing.

Our Uncertain Future

Despite living in an age of information, we remain surprisingly ignorant both of Wisconsin's original lichen flora and just how it has changed. A inventory of the entire state would provide an invaluable baseline for future comparisons. With so few lichenologists and so many unexplored areas, we have yet to discover many rare species. Rare lichens can only be found by diligently searching special habitats. Additional surveys and collecting are particularly needed from the southeastern and west-central portions of Wisconsin (e.g., Marathon County). Such surveys provide an important complement and context for resurveying relatively common species in permanent plots like the studies described in the following chapter.

The future of lichenology in Wisconsin depends on building from our currently limited knowledge. If the state were comprehensively surveyed, I would expect the number of lichen species known from Wisconsin to increase from 726 species to 750–800 species, more similar to Minnesota and Michigan. Such gains, however, would clearly reflect improvements in our knowledge, not actual increases in the number of species present. Without full surveys, we may lose species before we discover them. While these species may occur in neighboring states, their rarity in Wisconsin makes them vulnerable. Biologists refer to such losses as "Centinelan" extinctions after a ridge in Ecuador that was logged just after botanists collected specimens that revealed many unique and previously unknown local species (Wilson 1992).

The future of lichens in Wisconsin is precarious. Historical records and our knowledge of how lichens respond to air pollution and dense human settlement clearly indicate that many lichens are declining statewide. In the south, few species sensitive to human disturbance remain. In the north, rare species can still be found, but lumbering and recreational development pose immediate threats. To retain our natural legacy of lichens, we need both better surveys in lesser-known areas and better conservation of the species we already know are threatened.

References

Bennett, J. P. 2006. New or overlooked Wisconsin lichen records. Evansia 23(2):28–33.

Bennett, J. P., and C. M. Wetmore. 2004. Proposed list of extinct, rare and/or endangered macrolichens in Wisconsin. *Mycotaxon* 89:169–180.

Gotelli, N. J., and R. K. Colwell. 2001. Quantifying biodiversity: Procedures and pitfalls in the measurement and comparison of species richness. *Ecology Letters* 4:379–391.

Thomson, J. W. 2003. *Lichens of Wisconsin.* Madison: Wisconsin State Herbarium, Department of Botany, University of Wisconsin.

Wetmore, C. M. 1990. Lichens of Apostle Islands National Lakeshore. *Michigan Botany* 29: 65–73.

Wetmore, C. M., and Bennett, J. P. 2004. *2003 Lichen Studies in St. Croix National Scenic Riverway.* Final Report. St. Croix National Scenic Riverway, St. Croix Falls, Wisconsin.

Wilson, E. O. 1992. *The Diversity of Life.* New York: W. W. Norton.

11 How Have Wisconsin's Lichen Communities Changed?

Susan Will-Wolf and Matthew P. Nelsen

How have Wisconsin's lichen communities changed in recent decades? Surprisingly few people could give us a reasonable answer. In addition, species records and data are scant. Nevertheless, the inferences we can draw are shocking. Consider the lung lichen (figure 11.1B), an indicator of clean air and old-growth forest found in southern Wisconsin as recently as 1940. Although still present in the north, it has vanished from the south. Its range contraction raises questions: Have other lichens suffered similar fates? What has been lost, and why? To answer these questions we rely on both direct and indirect lines of evidence. Many lichen communities have suffered major losses in cover and diversity over the past 50 to 150 years. Nevertheless, remnants and other lichen communities remain intact, providing an opportunity for us to conserve and restore lichen communities via thoughtful management.

Lichen Biology and Ecology

Lichens can form colorful patches on rocks and tree trunks but are often overlooked. As noted in the preceding chapter, lichens represent symbioses between a fungus and an alga or cyanobacterium. The photosynthetic partner provides the fungus with carbohydrates, while the fungus absorbs water and protects the algae from harmful radiation and

FIGURE 11.1 *A,* Tightly attached, crustose growth form: a rim-lichen (trees). (Photos by C. Lipke and K. Elliot.) *B,* Flat, leaflike foliose growth form: lung lichen (trees). (Photo by M. Trest.) *C,* Tufted/hanging fruticose growth form: 1892 Wisconsin State Herbarium specimen of an orange bush lichen (trees). (Photo by C. Lipke and K. Elliot.) Foliose and fruticose lichens are considered macrolichens.

herbivores. We also learned that lichens are generally grouped by appearance into three general forms: crustose—tightly attached or embedded in substrate and appearing "painted on"; foliose—flattened, leaflike, and loosely attached to their substrate; and fruticose—three-dimensional tufted, stalked, or hanging forms springing from their substrate (figure 11.1).

Most lichens grow slowly, and some can live hundreds of years. They compete poorly with plants other than mosses, growing mostly where plants cannot. Lichens obtain most of their nutrients from the air. Because they are long lived and absorb airborne compounds, lichens are often used to monitor air quality.

Wisconsin's lichens occur on three main substrates: rocks, soil, and woody plants. Woody substrates host the most lichen species, followed by rocks, with fewer found on soil. Most lichens on woody substrates are found in forests and woodlands, though they can also occur on isolated woody plants or even bare wood, buildings, and fence posts. Ground lichens are found mostly on dry, nutrient-poor soils where plants are sparse. On richer, moister soils, ground lichens are found along with mosses on decomposing wood. Rock lichens occupy a range of rock types where they sometimes also co-occur with mosses or liverworts.

Assessing Change in Lichen Communities

The lichen communities of Wisconsin are better characterized than those of some states, with organized collections beginning in the 1850s (Thomson 2003). As noted in the preceding chapter, nearly 700 species have been found in the state so far (Wisconsin State Herbarium 2007), yet Wisconsin lacks records for more than 100 species found in Minnesota and Michigan and new state and county records continue to appear (Lay 2004; Nelsen 2005; Bennett 2006).

We can estimate changes in lichen communities by tracking changes in their available substrates (like plant communities), studying relationships between lichen communities and habitat conditions (moisture, forest age, air quality, etc.), or by directly measuring change at specific locations over time. We can also seek to link the changes we observe in lichen communities to changes we see in habitat and environmental conditions (Will-Wolf et al. 2004).

Direct estimates of change in Wisconsin remain sparse, but the gradual accumulation of excellent baseline data gives us more opportunities to conduct resurveys. Studies like those mentioned above that started in the 1950s give us quantitative data on distribution and abundance of lichens from many habitats and localities (table 11.1; figure 11.2). By resurveying these sites, we can quantify changes through time.

Culberson (1955a) documented bark-dwelling lichen communities at many sites in northern Wisconsin as an extension of John Curtis's (1959) extensive ecological surveys. In similar fashion, Beals (1965) and Hale (1955) surveyed lichens on trees in south-central and southern Wisconsin. The explicit links between Hale's (1955) and Culberson's (1955a) surveys and Curtis's (1959) data on vascular plant communities make these data and sites particularly valuable. Foote (1966) studied

Table 11.1 Studies that support quantitative description (at least frequency across sites) of lichen community composition, organized by Bailey's ecoregion sections

Bailey's ecoregion section	Tree lichens	Rock lichens	Ground lichens
Southern Superior Uplands	Culberson (1955a) [1]; Newberry (1974) [3]; Newberry (1976) [4]; Makholm (1994) [5]; Jesberger (1973) [7]; Will-Wolf, Westad, and Czlapinski (2002) [10]; Wetmore (1990) [11]; Wetmore (1993) [12]	Makholm (1994) [5]; Wetmore (1990) [11]; Wetmore (1993) [12]	Makholm (1994) [5]; Wetmore (1990) [11]; Wetmore (1993) [12]
Northern Great Lakes	Culberson (1955a) [1]		
Southern Great Lakes Morainal	Culberson (1955a) [1]; Hale (1955) [2]; Makholm (2003) [6]; Will-Wolf (1980) [8]; Will-Wolf et al. (2005) [8]; Nelsen et al. (2007) [17]; Beals (1965) [18]		Looman (1964) [14]
Central Loess Plains	Hale (1955) [2]		
North Central U.S. Driftless and Escarpment	Culberson (1955a) [1]; Hale (1955) [2]; Makholm (2003) [6]; Will-Wolf (1980) [8]; Will-Wolf et al. (2005) [8]; Will-Wolf (1988) [9]; Cole (1977) [13]	Foote (1963) [15]; Foote (1966) [16]; Armstrong (1968) [19]	Looman (1964) [14]; Lechowicz and Adams (1974) [20]

Note: Study numbers shown in square brackets are keyed to figure 11.2, which shows specific regional locations of studies.

lichens on southern Wisconsin sandstone and limestone rock outcrops, focusing on how lichens respond to substrates and each other.

Why Are Lichen Communities Changing?

Changes in lichen communities are ultimately linked to the effects of environmental pollution and habitat destruction, fragmentation and alteration. When habitats disappear or are fragmented, lichen communities lose the substrates and associated microhabitats they depend on. Habitat losses started in the mid-1800s in Wisconsin and were well advanced by 1950, particularly in southern Wisconsin (Curtis 1959). This makes it hard to infer early impacts on lichen communities. For instance, nearly half of the bark macrolichens Cheney collected in the Madison area before 1900 (Thomson 1998) were missing by 2000 (Nelsen et al. 2007). Lichen surveys since 1950 are thus examining a diminished lichen flora, making it likely that some species were lost before being documented.

Habitat losses and alteration continue. Most lichen communities today occur in forests and woodlands where conditions are linked to land use and management. Continued urbanization destroys and fragments

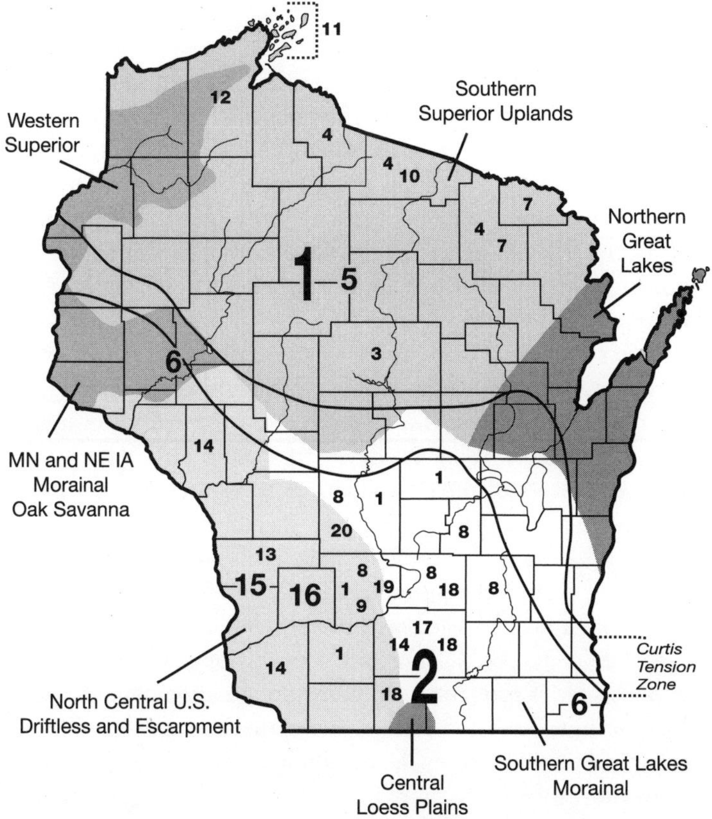

FIGURE 11.2 Locations of Wisconsin lichen studies since 1950 that support quantitative description of lichen community composition by habitat. See table 11.1 for authors of studies, by number code. Studies 1 and 2 (indicated with numerals in large-sized font) included many sites broadly spread across either northern or southern Wisconsin. Medium-sized numerals mark studies that included sites scattered across several counties in a region, while small-sized numerals indicate study plots within a county. Shaded areas are Bailey's Ecoregion Sections (Bailey et al. 1994; USDA Forest Service 2007). The long diagonal zone is John Curtis's (1959) "tension zone" dividing the state into more northern or more southern plant communities and species. This division is also relevant for lichen species and communities (Culberson 1955b; Thomson 2003).

woodland habitats as well as boosting levels of air pollution. Only the most tolerant lichen species are found in large urban areas. The continued conversion of dry savanna and prairie to more closed-canopy woodland via fire suppression threatens sun-loving prairie and savanna lichen communities as well. Although we have not documented the effects of white-tailed deer browsing on lichens, Wisconsin's mounting deer herd has dramatically affected our plant communities (Waller and Alverson 1997; chapter 19; plate 10). Effects of deer on lichens should be studied particularly in northern Wisconsin wooded bogs and cedar swamps where abundant lichens might provide food for hungry deer in winter.

Losses in Savanna and Prairie. Savanna-dependent lichen communities have declined with the loss of over 98% of the midwestern savanna. Sadly, we have found no early lists of savanna lichens in Wisconsin. Modern data on upper-midwestern savanna lichen communities (Wetmore 1981, 1983 [for Minnesota]; Makholm 2003) suggest this community supported 20–40 relatively common and widespread bark species with little hint of savanna specialists. However, tufted orange bush lichen (figure 11.1C; plate 13) has a distribution that matches former savanna and is now declining throughout its range (Brodo et al. 2001; Nelsen 2005).

Losses of remnant dry savannas, prairies, and barrens in southern and southwestern Wisconsin and failures to consistently manage these communities with fire have eliminated habitat for many sun-loving lichens of soil and rocks. While we have little quantitative data regarding ground lichen species of these habitats, several—such as the earthscale lichen (Looman 1964; Rosentreter and Belnap 2001)—are now rare (Thomson and Will-Wolf 2000; Bennett and Wetmore 2004). Some ground lichens, such as the tufted *Cladonias,* are fire sensitive (Schulten 1985; Wetmore 1981) yet need the open patches of bare ground created by fires (Neher et al. 2003). Thus, fire suppression may affect *Cladonia* habitat. Such species probably exhibit metapopulation dynamics similar to the Karner blue butterfly. These species are sensitive to local habitat loss and fragmentation as they depend on interspersed patches of different ages to allow them to colonize burned patches and mature before the next fire (Will-Wolf and Stearns 2000). Extending and actively managing our remaining savannas and dry prairies should benefit these lichens. Prescribed burn plans should also consider that ground lichens require fire refuges to serve as sources for recolonization after fires. Losses of oak and pine savanna in northern Wisconsin have been less extensive (chapter 5). Nevertheless, fire suppression also allows these sites to become shadier, reducing habitat for sun-loving lichens.

An interesting countertrend to the loss of former savanna habitat is the appearance of new "savanna-like" habitat in cities and suburbs. The lichens found on urban and suburban trees and wood (unpainted fence posts and buildings) are widespread and can also be found in many other open habitats and forest edges, as well as in some midwestern savanna remnants (Wetmore 1981, 1983; Makholm 2003). These lichens probably represent the most common, widely dispersed, and pollution tolerant of savanna bark lichens.

Losses in Forest and Wooded Wetlands. The extensive permanent reduction of southern Wisconsin forests and the temporary reduction of northern Wisconsin forests between the 1850s and approximately 1930 likely caused some lichen species to disappear from these communities. Older trees and forests have distinct and often more diverse lichen communities. For lichens restricted to older forests, the conversion of the old-growth northern Wisconsin landscape to one dominated by younger forests constitutes habitat loss (Will-Wolf, Esseen, and Neitlich 2002). Lung lichen (figure 11.1B) is a world-wide "flagship" species and indicator for old-growth forests free of air pollution. Studies have shown that it has limited ability to disperse to new habitats, making it sensitive to habitat fragmentation (Thomson 1990; Sillett et al. 2000; Brodo et al. 2001; Walser 2004). Although it disappeared from southern Wisconsin by 1940 (Will-Wolf 1988), lung lichen is still widespread in the north. However, populations are smaller in young managed stands than in old-growth stands (Will-Wolf, Westad, and Czlapinski 2002). Lung lichen is currently on several conservation watch lists and the subject of global conservation efforts.

Several rare and endangered lichens in Wisconsin are found primarily in old growth forests (Thomson and Will-Wolf 2000; Cameron 2002; Will-Wolf, Westad, and Czlapinski 2002; Bennett and Wetmore 2004). Methuselah's beard lichen (plate 12) has almost disappeared from Wisconsin (Thomson 2003; Bennett and Wetmore 2004) perhaps because its interior mature forest habitats are now rare. Will-Wolf, Westad, and Czlapinski (2002) found that 10% of lichens observed in northern Wisconsin are restricted to older forests and several other groups (small, shade-loving, tufted, and nitrogen-fixing lichens including lung lichens) are more diverse in older forests (figure 11.3*A*). One quarter of the species found are most abundant in older forests, though lichen groups differ in how they respond to forest age (figure 11.3*B*).

Many lichen species restricted to old-growth forests may have restricted dispersal ability, so only nearby younger trees are colonized. Others, such as the pin lichens that are common on snags, old bark, and

Northern WI macrolichen groups

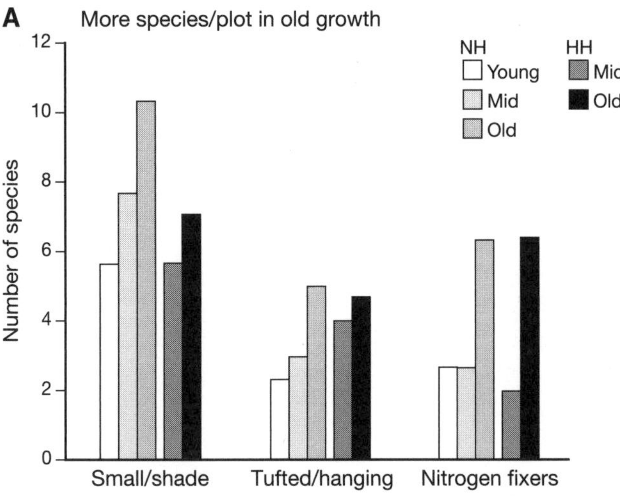

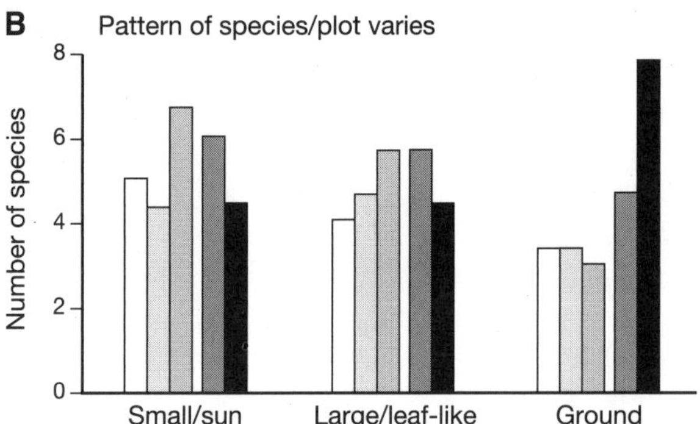

FIGURE 11.3 Northern Wisconsin old growth study: results from nine northern hardwoods (NH) forests dominated by sugar maple and six hemlock-hardwood (HH) forests on moist upland sites in northeastern Wisconsin and the Upper Peninsula of Michigan (Will-Wolf, Westad, and Czlapinski 2002). Old-growth forests stands (Old) are more than 250 years old; medium aged stands (Mid) are about 80 years old and uneven-aged; young stands (Young) are 40–50 years old and even-aged. *A,* Macrolichen groups with more species in old-growth stands. Tufted/hanging and nitrogen-fixing lichens are also much more abundant in old-growth stands. *B,* Macrolichen groups whose pattern of response to stand age differs between NH and HH stands.

old wood (Selva 1994), may be limited to microhabitats found mainly in old forests. These latter species might eventually increase their range and abundance if forests are managed to maintain old-forest characteristics. Will-Wolf, Westad, and Czlapinski (2002) identified several structural characteristics that could benefit lichens in managed forests. These include maintaining islands of large old trees, creating medium-sized gaps, retaining large downed wood in several decay stages, and maintaining diverse tree species.

Shifts in tree communities may also be affecting bark lichen communities. The forest lichen studies listed in table 11.1 demonstrate that lichen communities differ substantially among oaks, conifers, aspen, maples, and other tree species. Conifers, in particular, harbor a lichen flora distinct from deciduous trees (Culberson 1955a). The barks of conifers, oaks, and other species differ significantly in acidity, water-holding capacity, and other factors important for lichens. Declines in the abundance of oaks in southern Wisconsin and conifers in the north along with increases in maples throughout the state are all causing shifts in the relative abundance of lichen communities.

One study directly measuring changes in lichen communities through time reveals large changes. In 2003, Will-Wolf and others (2005) resampled 24 sites from a 1974–78 study of bark lichen communities on red, black, or Hill's oak near a coal-fired power plant in south-central Wisconsin (Will-Wolf 1980). Differences in lichen species composition among sites have declined over this period. Sites in 2003 are, on average, 12% more similar to each other than they were in 1974. This finding resembles the "biotic homogenization" we see in our forest communities (Rooney et al. 2004). Large leaflike lichens have decreased, small leaflike lichens have increased. Crust lichens in general have increased, though several fertile crust rim-lichens have decreased (figure 11.4*A*). These changes appear less related to the power plant than to increases in shade from black cherry, red maple, and other non-oak trees (figure 11.4*B*). Such dramatic changes suggest that we should resurvey the Hale (1955) and Culberson (1955a) sites where paired Curtis plots would allow us to evaluate whether changes in lichen communities are coupled to wider changes in trees or communities.

Pollution and Physical Impacts on Lichens

Air pollution directly affects lichen communities. In large urban areas, lichen communities are dominated by pollution-tolerant species. Two types of air pollution affect lichens in Wisconsin: acidic compounds produced in urban and industrial areas and nonacidic compounds from agricultural areas. Urban and industrial areas with elevated levels of sulfur dioxide, nitrogen oxides, particulates, and/or heavy metals typically show reduced lichen diversity and shifts in lichen composition due to acidification (Nimis et al. 2002). Major single-point sources that produce

Alliant-Columbia Power Plant Resurvey

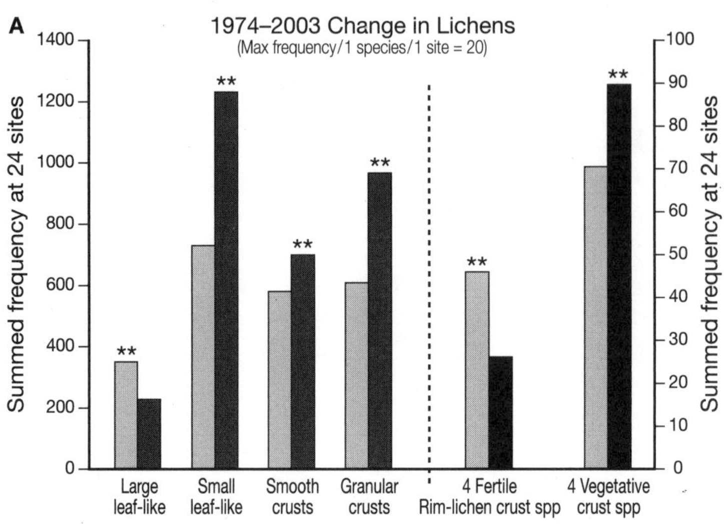

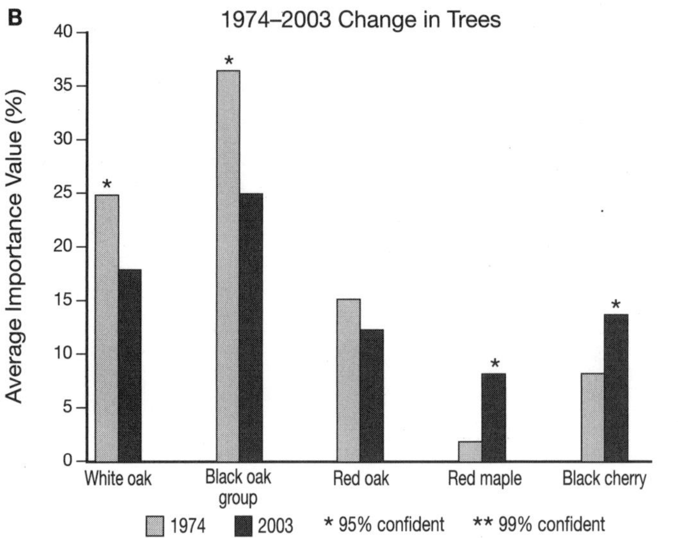

FIGURE 11.4 Changes from 1974 to 2003 in frequency of lichens (*A*) and percentage importance of trees (*B*) from resurvey of 24 oak woods sites near the Alliant-Columbia Power Plant, south-central Wisconsin (Will-Wolf et al. 2005). *A,* Each lichen group includes four or more species. *B,* Red oak is the most common of the black oak group tree species; this group was sampled for lichens. Red maple is the most common of the late successional trees that increased over time. Black cherry is the most common of the disturbance tolerant tree species that increased over time.

these pollutants include coal-fired power plants, pulp paper mills, and other factories (Wisconsin studies: Newberry 1974; Will-Wolf 1980). Common nonpoint sources include automobiles and home heating. Many industrial point sources in Wisconsin reduced their emissions by the mid-1990s (EPA 2007; Wisconsin DNR 2007). Will-Wolf and others (2005) found that emissions from a south-central Wisconsin power plant had fewer effects on lichens than did changing forest composition and structure. Diffuse regional air pollutants from urban areas and neighboring states, have also declined since the 1980s but remain high in southeastern Wisconsin (Makholm and Mladenoff 2005; NADP 2007).

Agricultural pollutants such as ammonia (from fertilizers and livestock) and dust create nutrient-rich, high-pH conditions that favor nutrient-tolerant lichen species and eliminate sensitive lichens. Many lichen communities in southern Wisconsin have been subjected to both agricultural and urban/industrial pollution, further impoverishing lichen communities. Lichen communities in southeastern Wisconsin are less diverse and lack many sensitive species found elsewhere in the state (Makholm 2003). Although not yet quantified, these lichen communities have also presumably been homogenized as less tolerant species characteristic of particular habitats were eliminated.

Recreational rock climbing can also physically damage lichen communities, removing larger lichen species and changing composition (Nuzzo 1996; Farris 1998; McMillan and Larson 2002). Although we still lack studies here, we expect heavily used areas, like Devil's Lake State Park, to show locally large impacts. Water quality problems, such as siltation, pollution, and eutrophication, could also affect shoreline rock lichen communities. This, too, needs further study.

Summary and Conclusions

To sum up, direct evidence shows that in south-central Wisconsin oak forests large leaflike lichens and sun-loving crust lichens are decreasing while shade-tolerant small leaflike lichens and most crusts on oak trunks in south-central oak forests are increasing, resulting in homogenization of lichen communities. Indirect evidence suggests declines across the state in nitrogen-fixing lichens, lichen communities of conifer and oak trees, and forest lichens like the lung lichen that depend on old-growth conditions. Lichen diversity near agricultural pollution or major sources of urban and industrial pollution is conspicuously lower than near unaffected areas. Lichen communities of rock outcrops have probably also been affected in some places by increased shading, rock climbing, and water and air pollution over the last 50 years. Some lichen species were probably lost from our northern forests as a result of widespread logging and burning between the 1860s and 1920s while others were lost from southern Wisconsin savannas and dry prairies as those habitats were decimated between 1850 and 1950.

Based on these lines of evidence, we foresee continued declines for the already restricted old-growth forest lichens unless old forests are conserved and younger forests are managed to enhance old-forest structural features. Lichen communities in southeastern Wisconsin will decline further and become more homogenous if habitat fragmentation and urban, industrial, and agricultural pollution are not ameliorated. We also predict continued losses of oak- and conifer-associated lichens state-wide with associated biotic homogenization.

How can we better conserve lichen communities in Wisconsin? There is much we do not know. Nevertheless, one obvious step would be to conserve all remaining old-growth forest stands. It would also be very informative to resurvey the Hale and Culberson sites, which could generate direct evidence of how forest lichen communities are changing across the state. Such resurveys would help us to identify which habitat or management features are associated with sustaining lichen diversity. We also need follow-up studies to test how maintaining old-growth characteristics in managed forests acts to maintain lichens. For other lichen communities, we know too little to suggest how to specifically manage for lichens. Nevertheless, it seems likely that managing these ecosystems for diversity generally (or for certain "umbrella" species) could act to sustain lichen diversity. We particularly recommend studies in savanna remnants and restorations to investigate how soil lichens interact with plant community structure, composition, and fire management.

References

Armstrong, P. K. 1968. Cryptogam communities on quartzite of Devil's Lake, WI. M.S. thesis, University of Chicago.

Bailey, R. G., P. E. Avers, T. King, W. H. McNab, eds. 1994. Ecoregions and subregions of the United States (map; 1:7,500,000). Washington, DC: U.S. Department of Agriculture Forest Service. With supplementary table of map unit descriptions, compiled and edited by W. H. McNab and R. G. Bailey.

Beals, E. W. 1965. Ordination of some corticolous cryptogamic communities in south-central Wisconsin. Oikos 16:1–8.

Bennett, J. P. 2006. New or overlooked Wisconsin lichen records. Evansia 23:28–33.

Bennett, J. P., and C. M. Wetmore. 2004. Proposed list of extinct, rare and/or endangered macrolichens in Wisconsin. Mycotaxon 89:169–180.

Brodo, I. M., S. D. Sharnoff, and S. Sharnoff. 2001. Lichens of North America. New Haven and London: Yale University Press.

Cameron, R. P. 2002. Habitat associations of epiphytic lichens in managed and unmanaged forest stands in Nova Scotia. Northeastern Naturalist 9:27–46.

Cole, M. S. 1977. The ecology of lichens and bryophytes in the Kickapoo River Valley, southwestern Wisconsin. Ph.D. thesis, University of Wisconsin–Madison.

Culberson, W. L. 1955a. The corticolous communities of lichens and bryophytes in the upland forests of northern Wisconsin. Ecological Monographs 25:215–231.

———. 1955b. Qualitative and quantitative studies on the distribution of corticolous lichens and bryophytes in Wisconsin. Lloydia 18:25–36.

Curtis, J. T. 1959. The Vegetation of Wisconsin. Madison: University of Wisconsin Press.

Environmental Protection Agency (EPA). 2007. EPA AirData: Access to air pollution data. Available at http://www.epa.gov/air/data/index.html. Accessed October 2007.

Farris, M. A. 1998. The effects of rock climbing on the vegetation of three Minnesota cliff systems. Canadian Journal of Botany 76:1981–1990.

Foote, K. G. 1963. Bryophyte and lichen vegetation of rock outcrops in the driftless area of Wisconsin. Ph.D. thesis, University of Wisconsin–Madison.

———. 1966. The vegetation of lichens and bryophytes on limestone outcrops in the driftless area of Wisconsin. Bryologist 69:265–292.

Hale, M. E. 1955. Phytosociology of corticolous cryptogams in the upland forests of southern Wisconsin. Ecology 36:45–63.

Jesberger, J. A. 1973. An ordination of corticolous lichen communities in the Popple River Basin of northern Wisconsin. Wisconsin Academy of Sciences, Arts and Letters 61:267–284.

Lay, E. 2004. Wisconsin lichens and lichenicolous fungi collected during the 2002 Tuckerman Lichen Workshop. Evansia 21:17–35.

Lechowicz, M. J., and M. S. Adams. 1974. Ecology of *Cladonia* lichens. I. Preliminary assessment of the ecology of terricolous lichen-moss communities in Ontario and Wisconsin. Canadian Journal of Botany 52:55–64.

Looman, J. 1964. The distribution of some lichen communities in the prairie provinces and adjacent parts of the Great Plains. Bryologist 67:209–224.

Makholm, M. M. 1994. The Forest Monitoring Network: Maple stand lichen survey. Madison: Wisconsin Department of Natural Resources, Bureau of Air Management Report. PUBL-AM-126–93.

———. 2003. Assessing air pollution impacts: Biomonitoring with lichens and mosses. Ph.D. thesis, University of Wisconsin–Madison.

Makholm, M. M., and D. J. Mladenoff. 2005. Efficacy of a biomonitoring (moss bag) technique for determining element deposition trends on a mid-range (375 km) scale. Environmental Monitoring and Assessment 104:1–18.

McMillan, M., and D. W. Larson. 2002. Effects of rock climbing on the vegetation of the Niagara Escarpment in southern Ontario, Canada. Conservation Biology 16:389–398.

National Atmospheric Deposition Program (NADP). 2007. Isopleth Maps [data for 1986–2005]. Available at http://nadp.sws.uiuc.edu/isopleths. Accessed October 2007.

Neher, D. A., T. Walters, E. Tramer, T. R. Weicht, R. M. Veluci, K. Saiya-Cork, S. Will-Wolf, J. Toppin, J. Traub, and J. R. Johansen. 2003. Biological soil crust and vascular plant communities in a sand savanna of Northwestern Ohio. Journal of the Torrey Botanical Society 130:244–252.

Nelsen, M. P. 2005. Additions to the lichen flora of Wisconsin with new records of rare species. Michigan Botanist 44:188–191.

Nelson, M. P., S. Will-Wolf, and A. Gargas. 2007. One hundred years of change in corticolous lichens of Madison, Wisconsin. Evansia 24 108–112.

Newberry, G. 1974. The influence of a sulfate-process paper mill on corticolous lichens. Bryologist 77:561–576.

———. 1976. Corticolous epiphytes in north central Wisconsin bogs. Ph.D. thesis, University of Wisconsin–Madison.

Nimis, P. L., C. Scheidegger, and P. A. Wolseley, eds. 2002. Monitoring with Lichens—Monitoring Lichens. Dordrecht: Kluwer Academic Publishers.

Nuzzo, V. A. 1996. Structure of cliff vegetation on exposed cliffs and the effect of rock climbing. Canadian Journal of Botany 74:607–617.

Rooney, T. P., S. M. Wiegmann, D. A. Rogers, and D. M. Waller. 2004. Biotic impoverishment and homogenization in unfragmented forest understory communities. Conservation Biology 18: 787–798.

Rosentreter, R., and J. Belnap. 2001. Biological soil crusts of North America. Pages 31–50 in J. Belnap and O. L. Lange, eds. Biological Soil Crusts: Structure, Function, and Management. Berlin: Springer-Verlag.

Schulten, J. A. 1985. The effects of burning on the soil lichen community of a sand prairie. Bryologist 88:110–114.

Selva, S. B. 1994. Lichen diversity and stand continuity in the northern hardwoods and spruce-fir forests of northern New England and western New Brunswick. Bryologist 97:424–429.

Sillett, S. C., B. McCune, J. E. Peck, T. R. Rambo, and A. Ruchty. 2000. Dispersal limitations of epiphytic lichens result in species dependent on old-growth forests. Ecological Applications 10:789–799.

Thomson, J. W. 1990. Lichens in old-growth woods in Wisconsin. Bulletin of the Botanical Club of Wisconsin 22:7–10.

———. 1998. Two Wisconsin lichen collections over 100 years old. Evansia 15:84–90.

———. 2003. Lichens of Wisconsin. Madison: Wisconsin State Herbarium, Department of Botany, University of Wisconsin–Madison.

Thomson, J. W., and S. Will-Wolf. 2000. Lichenized fungi which may warrant listing for protection. Wisconsin State Herbarium. Available at http://www.botany.wisc.edu/wislichens/lichenTAB-A.htm. Accessed October 2007.

U.S. Department of Agriculture (USDA) Forest Service. 2007. Ecoregions Information. Vector digital data from U.S. Geological Survey, Reston, VA. Available at http://www.fs.fed.us/rm/analytics/publications/ecoregions-information.html. Accessed October 2007.

Waller, D. M., and W. S. Alverson. 1997. The white-tailed deer: A keystone herbivore. Wildlife Society Bulletin 25:217–226.

Walser, J.-C. 2004. Molecular evidence for limited dispersal of vegetative propagules in the epiphytic lichen *Lobaria pulmonaria*. American Journal of Botany 91:1273–1276.

Wetmore, C. M. 1981. Lichen studies on Allison Savanna. Journal of the Minnesota Academy of Science 47:2–3.

———. 1983. Lichen survival in a burned oak savanna. Michigan Botanist 22:47–52.

———. 1990. Lichens of Apostle Islands National Lakeshore, Wisconsin. Michigan Botanist 29:65–73.

———. 1993. Lichens and air quality in Chequamegon National Forest Rainbow Lake Wilderness Area. Final Report to U.S. Department of Agriculture Forest Service and Northeastern Area State and Private

Forestry, Forest Health Protection. Contract 42–649. St. Paul, MN.

Will-Wolf, S. 1980. Structure of corticolous lichen communities before and after exposure to emissions from a "clean" coal-fired generating station. Bryologist 83:281–295.

———. 1988. Bark cryptogam communities of Baxter's Hollow and Pine Glen Sauk County, Wisconsin. Report to the Nature Conservancy, Wisconsin Academy of Science, Arts and Letters, and Wisconsin Department of Natural Resources, Madison.

Will-Wolf, S., P.-A. Esseen, and P. Neitlich. 2002. Monitoring biodiversity and ecosystem function: Forests. Pp. 203–222 in P. L. Nimis, C. Scheidegger, and P. A. Wolseley, eds. Monitoring with Lichens—Monitoring Lichens. Dordrecht: Kluwer Academic Publishers.

Will-Wolf, S., D. L. Hawksworth, B. McCune, H. J. M. Sipman, and R. Rosentreter. 2004. Assessing the biodiversity of lichenized fungi. Pp. 173–195 in G. M. Mueller, G. F. Bills, and M. S. Foster, eds. Biodiversity of Fungi: Inventory and Monitoring Methods. San Diego: Elsevier Academic Press.

Will-Wolf, S., M. M. Makholm, J. Roth, M. P. Nelsen, A. H. Reis, and M. T. Trest. 2005. Lichen bioaccumulation and bioindicator study near Alliant-Columbia generating facility. Final Project Report to Focus on Energy Environmental Research Program and Wisconsin Department of Natural Resources, Madison, WI. Available at http://www.focusonenergy.com/page.jsp?pageId=1680⒫. Accessed October 2007.

Will-Wolf, S., and F. Stearns. 2000. Dry soil oak savanna in the Great Lakes region. Pp. 135–154 in R. C. Anderson, J. S. Fralish, and J. Baskin, eds. The Savanna, Barrens, and Rock Outcrop Communities of North America. New York: Cambridge University Press.

Will-Wolf, S., K. Westad, and A. Czlapinski. 2002. Lichen communities of managed and old growth forests in the Great Lakes States. Report to the Section of Wildlife and Forestry Research of the Wisconsin Department of Natural Resources, Madison.

Wisconsin Department of Natural Resources (DNR). 2007. Historical air emissions information for years 1985–2005. Available at http://www.dnr.state.wi.us/org/aw/air/emission/historical_emissions/index.htm. Accessed October 2007.

Wisconsin State Herbarium. 2007. Wisconsin Lichens. Available at http://www.botany.wisc.edu/wislichens/. Accessed October 2007.

Part Three: Changing Waters and the Land-Water Interface

Some speed across it on a boat, some glide across it in a canoe. Some sit silently next to it in a duck blind. Many explore the life beneath its surface with only a line and hook. Others prefer to watch the life on its surface and shoreline through binoculars. Many find their strongest connection to nature here. People pay a premium to buy property or rent a cottage next to it. Wisconsin's waters retain their magical pull for us as they have for centuries.

No one disputes that Wisconsin's waters are extraordinary in their number, abundance, and importance to the state, its wildlife, and its people (WASAL 2003). Lakes, rivers, and wetlands connect the clouds and atmospheric water to groundwater and, ultimately, to the oceans. They also connect to each other and to the land, translating land use patterns into water quality issues. Like the lands that surround them, Wisconsin's waters reflect many broad-scale ecological changes over the past two centuries. In this part, we explore several dimensions of these changes.

Limnologists Jim Kitchell and Greg Sass begin this part by recounting the tumultuous changes experienced by aquatic food webs in Lakes Superior and Michigan. Once abundant fisheries in both lakes have crashed due to overexploitation and successive invasions of nonnative species. New prized fisheries involving imported salmon have sprung up to replace those that depended on native species like the lake trout. Fish populations in each Great Lake have responded to these ecological changes in both similar and different ways, suggesting lessons on how we might manage these ecosystems.

For most, the mention of fish in Wisconsin's waters brings to mind images of sport fish like bass, walleye, muskellunge, and northern pike. Ichthyologists Dave Marshall and John Lyons remind us, however, that most of our 147 native species of fish are not game species. Neither the public nor fisheries managers know much about the biology of these minnows, suckers, darters, and mooneyes. However, these nongame fish often indicate the health of streams and lakes. Sadly, many species show sharp declines since the 1970s. Urbanization, lakeshore development, and agricultural runoff appear to be the main culprits. Marshall and Lyons recommend a "safe haven" strategy to protect the best fish communities that remain and urge us to incorporate the needs of fish into broader restoration programs.

Some of the state's most majestic wetlands occur along the shores of Lakes Michigan and Superior. Ecologists Jim Meeker and Gary Fewless describe these systems, noting that their diversity often hinges on regular disturbance events including shifts in water depth. They also note how hard it is to separate changes in these wetlands that represent these natural cycles and "pulse stability" from those due to long-term directional changes. Habitat destruction has already eliminated half the wetlands in Wisconsin, and alterations in land use and hydrology continue to degrade many of those that persist. Our wetlands are also experiencing unprecedented waves of invasion from exotic plant species like reed canary grass and purple loosestrife threatening native wetland species and wetlands along both lakeshores.

Wetland ecologist Joy Zedler and hydrologist Ken Potter next examine changes in inland wetlands beginning with their glacial origins, extending through the past century of draining, filling, and dredging and ending with current efforts to protect wetlands. They find it remarkably difficult to estimate just how wetland acreage and quality have changed over the past 50 years given the scarcity of reliable baseline data. Like coastal wetlands, herbaceous wetlands face an onslaught of invasive species like reed canary grass whose impacts are often amplified by shifts in surface and groundwater flow, sedimentation, and livestock grazing. Although these threats are partially countered by federal and state policies to protect wetlands, we need further research if we are to succeed in the challenging task of restoring more wetlands.

Aquatic plants occur commonly in nearly all of Wisconsin's 14,000 lakes. Aquatic botanist Stan Nichols informs us that these communities are changing, too. The "missing baseline" problem prevents us from seeing more than a few decades into the past, but we can learn a lot by looking at historic accounts, recent changes, and detailed case studies. Key threats to lake plant communities include shoreline development, heavy boat traffic, nutrient runoff, and consequent lake eutrophication and turbidity. Many invasive species capitalize on these conditions, forcing more elaborate efforts to control the excessive growth of invasive lake plants and algae. Lake plant communities also sometimes surprise scientists as when a previously degraded community recovers beyond what we might expect. After this chapter was written, a study on carp exclusion in Lake Wingra resulted in improvements in water clarity that greatly exceeded the most optimistic predictions. Such surprises give us hope and insights into how we might manipulate lake ecosystems to improve conditions.

The Wisconsin River strongly shaped the state's history. Shortly after the fur trade began, towns appeared along the river's shores. Before the railroads and interstates, it was a major commercial route. Today it generates electricity, powers the paper industry, and provides many opportunities for recreation. Ecologists Monica Turner, Emily Stanley, Matthias Bürgi, and David Mladenoff trace the ecological history of this mighty river, providing a new twist on Heraclitus's famous quote about never being able to step into the same river twice. Land uses along this river's long watershed have changed dramatically over the past 200 years. This "hardest working river in America" has also experienced radical changes in response to all the dams and levees that have been constructed in and along it to control water flows and limit flooding. Together, these changes have altered sediment flows, nutrient loads, and water quality with effects extending all the way to the Gulf of Mexico. Changes in flooding and nutrients have also greatly altered floodplain vegetation with reciprocal effects on water quality.

Collectively, these stories reinforce the view that Wisconsin's waters have undergone massive changes parallel to those seen in the great cutover of our northern forests a century ago. However, although the great cutover left us with graphic images of change, the similar scale and impact of changes in aquatic ecosystems have generally been less graphic. The reader who views our waters and the land-water interface through this lens of history will soon see the need for more effective conservation and restoration strategies for these precious habitats.

Reference

Wisconsin Academy of Sciences, Arts and Letters (WASAL). 2003. Waters of Wisconsin: The future of our aquatic ecosystems and resources. Madison: WASAL. Available at http://www.wisconsinacademy.org/wow/.

12

Great Lakes Ecosystems: Invasions, Food Web Dynamics, and the Challenge of Ecological Restoration

James F. Kitchell and Greg G. Sass

The waters of Lake Superior and Lake Michigan have experienced many of the same historical events, but these events changed the lake ecosystems in profoundly different ways. Restoration of native fish communities in Lake Superior is deemed one of the major successes of resource management. Management of the Lake Michigan ecosystem brought a substantial but different kind of success, and future management will likely sustain certain exotic species, effectively keeping it in a very different state. This chapter reviews the key events of their common past and offers a view of their divergent future.

The rapid influx of European immigrants brought major ecological changes to the Laurentian Great Lakes. The implements of change included the axe, the plow, the hook, and the net. After the region's forests were harvested to grow midwestern cities, the plow was put to native soils. The resulting erosion loads increased to levels that changed the rivers, streams, and nearshore habitats into inhospitable places. This, in turn, provoked institutional responses aimed at preventing and reversing cultural eutrophication.

The hook and the net also played important roles. Although Indians fished these waters for millennia (Bogue 2000), engine-powered boats, metal hooks, and nets made of synthetic fiber spread across the region during the early 20th century, providing much more efficient ways to fish. Native fish populations soon felt the effects of growing commercial fisheries that fueled the local economies for hundreds of coastal towns.

A growing parade of invasive species also followed the technology that enhanced commerce. During the 19th century, completion of the Erie and Welland canals bypassed Niagra Falls, a natural barrier that separated the Great Lakes from the Atlantic Ocean. As shipping developed through a series of lock and dam systems, both the path and the vectors (ballast water) brought a continuing series of new exotics. The Great Lakes have already been successfully invaded by 172 exotics (Ricciardi 2001), including species at every trophic level. Some of those have been particularly important agents of ecological change. Many native species responded to their effects, as has recently been documented (Madenjian et al. 2002; Bronte et al. 2003; Harvey et al. 2005; Johnson 2005).

As the Great Lakes ecosystems changed, two important agencies led efforts to restore ecological conditions. The International Joint Commission (http://www.ijc.org/en/home/main_accueil.htm) is primarily focused on water quality issues, while the Great Lakes Fishery Commission (GLFC; http://www.glfc.org/) focuses on fishery resources and their ecological basis. The history, goals, and progress of these agencies can be accessed from their Web sites. Both were formed by international agreements, and both share continuing interests in the issues surrounding exotic species.

In this chapter, we focus on major changes in the food web dynamics of Lakes Superior and Michigan that arose due to fisheries management programs and nonnative species invasions. We emphasize both native and nonnative species representing three trophic levels:

1. Top predators in the food web (sea lamprey, stocked Pacific salmon, the native lake trout, and their prey)
2. Expansion of invading zooplankton-feeding fishes (alewife and rainbow smelt) at the middle of the food web
3. Declines in primary productivity following the invasion by zebra mussels

We caution readers about such a general, short summary. A sentence or two herein can represent decades of hard-won data, complex trophic interactions in diverse biological communities, and unresolved controversies. This chapter reflects our perspective.

The Sea Lamprey

The sea lamprey is a parasitic fish that feeds on the blood of other fish. It was the first major invader of the Great Lakes, entering Lake Erie from the Hudson River as the Erie Canal was completed. The Welland Canal provided a second point of access through the direct connection it established between Lake Ontario and Lake Erie. Sea lamprey first appeared in the early 19th century and, over the course of about a century, became fully established in all of the Great Lakes. Although there were native lamprey species in the Great Lakes, they matured at small sizes following a period of feeding on host fishes. Unlike native lampreys, the sea lamprey grows to much larger sizes. Native fish species had no history of coexistence with such a large parasite. Because of its size and feeding rate, it effectively acts as a predator to kill most host fishes of weight less than 3 kg.

Like commercial fisheries and recreational anglers, the sea lamprey seeks out the largest fish. This invader presented a new mortality agent for local fish stocks already diminished in number and average size due to the growing commercial fisheries. Lake trout, the apex predator in all pre-invasion food webs, declined and was successively extirpated from Lakes Ontario, Erie, Huron, and Michigan. In a sequence of similar causes and the consequent declining body sizes, many other native fishes (including burbot, lake whitefish, ciscoes, and lake herring) declined or disappeared owing to the combined effects of fishing and sea lamprey parasitism.

To respond to this growing problem, a binational treaty between the United States and Canada formed the GLFC in 1955 and charged it with two goals: (1) restore the native fish community and (2) find a solution to the sea lamprey crisis. By 1958 an effective lampricide was developed and first applied to the streams of western Lake Superior that served as nursery habitat for larval sea lamprey. Lampricide use gradually spread to the east until the Lake Ontario streams were regularly treated by the 1970s. Suppression of the sea lamprey and restoration of native fish communities became the common goal of regional fishery management agencies whose activities were coordinated through the GLFC. While fishery restrictions and sea lamprey control reduced the levels of mortality to many fishes, they were not 100% effective. Sea lampreys still persist, but only at 5%–10% of their former abundance.

Lake Trout

Before sea lamprey could be effectively controlled, the lake trout disappeared from Lake Michigan. The loss of this apex predator triggered a number of changes in the food web. Prior to extirpation, individuals from some lake trout stocks were preserved in hatcheries (Page et al. 2004). Starting in the 1960s, these hatchery fish provided the source for stocking programs intended to restore natural populations. In Lake Michigan, little natural reproduction of lake trout occurs today. Fisheries scientists disagree on what causes are responsible for the lack of success in this restoration effort (Madenjian et al. 2002).

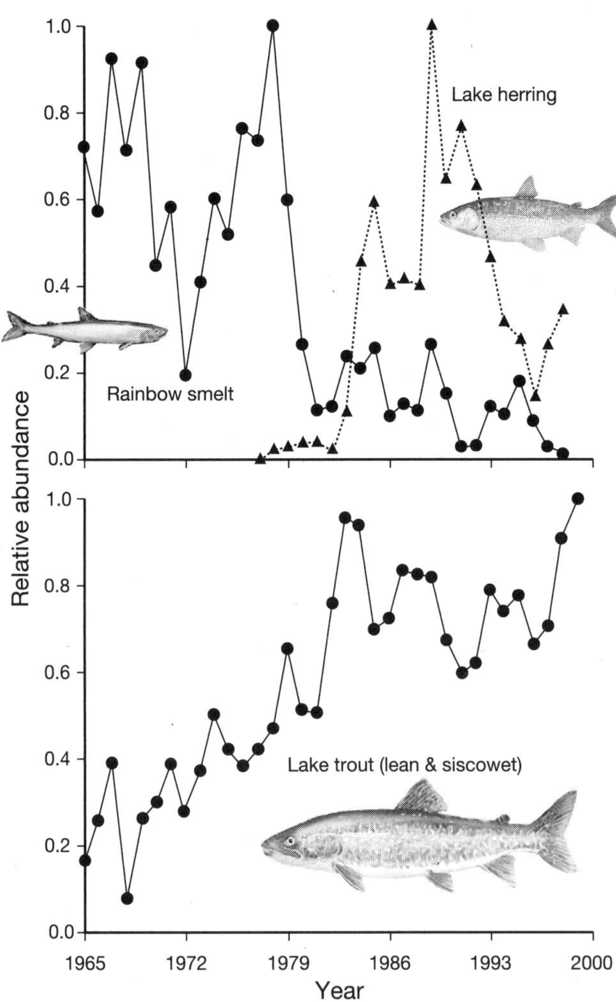

FIGURE 12.1 Relative abundance of rainbow smelt, lake herring, and lake trout (lean and siscowet) in Lake Superior during 1965–99. Data are based on and redrawn from Bronte et al. (2003).

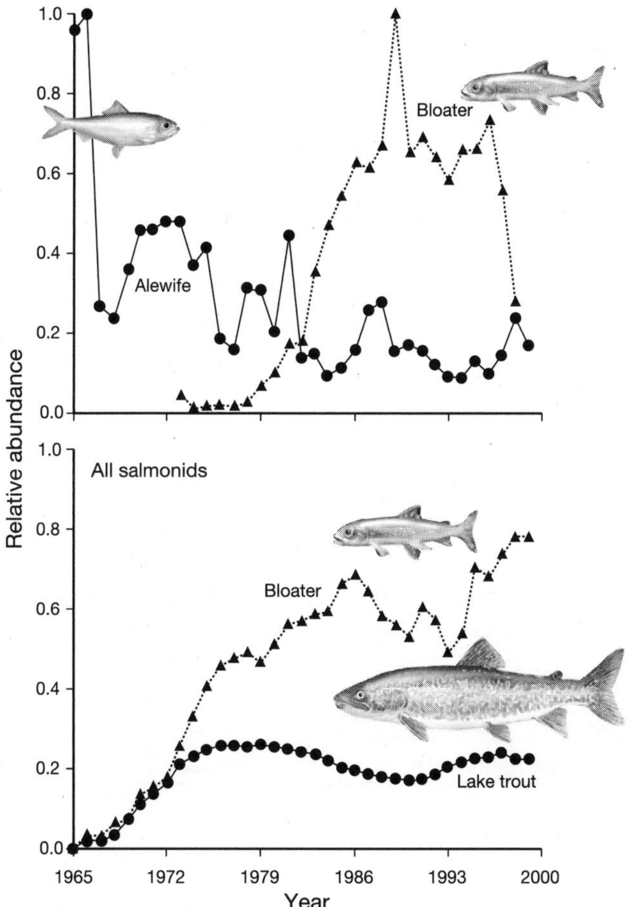

FIGURE 12.2 Relative abundance of alewife, bloater (deepwater cisco), and stocked salmonids including lake trout in Lake Michigan during 1965–2000. Data are based on and redrawn from Kitchell (1991) and Madenjian et al. (2002).

Lake Superior lake trout populations were severely reduced but did not disappear. Lake trout were stocked in Superior to accelerate restoration. With high natural reproduction rates, the native stocks gradually recovered. Stocking programs ceased in areas where native stocks were deemed fully recovered (Bronte et al. 2003).

Recovery of native lake trout in Lake Superior is a remarkable success (figure 12.1). Lake trout abundance now approximates that of the virgin stock; it might even be in excess of carrying capacity for this ecosystem (Ebener 2005; Harvey et al. 2005) as evidenced by declining growth rates of individual fish. However, there is irony and contradiction in this success story. Most of the lake trout biomass can be found in the "siscowet" type that occupy deep, cold-water habitats. These trout were only modestly affected by the sea lamprey and fishing pressure, both of which are more prevalent in shallow water habitats. Siscowet is a name of Ojibwa origin and translates as "cooks itself." This fish can be 30%–70% fat by weight and will catch fire when placed close to a flame. This species has little commercial value and is held in low regard by recreational anglers. Siscowet make up 80%–90% of the native lake trout biomass in today's Lake Superior and exceed the combined biomass of all other salmonids in the lake (Bronte et al. 2003). Similarly, the population of another native deepwater piscivore, the burbot, has increased in tandem with lake trout. Siscowet lake trout and burbot populations are at or above those estimated before commercial fishery development and sea lamprey invasion, reflecting a restoration success. However, their demand for prey resources is large, while their benefit to current fisheries is small (Harvey and Kitchell 2000; Harvey et al. 2003).

Lake trout in Lake Michigan differ from those in Lake Superior in two important ways: they have not reestablished self-sustaining populations and are largely maintained through continued stocking efforts (figure 12.2), and they exist in a food web now dominated by exotics. The alewife is now a dominant prey species, and introduced Pacific salmon now compete with lake trout for prey.

Alewife and Rainbow Smelt

Like the sea lamprey, alewife and rainbow smelt are native to the Atlantic Ocean. The alewife is also thought to have invaded through direct access provided by the Erie Canal. Alewife successfully colonized each of the four lower lakes, but never became established in the cold, ultraoligotrophic Lake Superior. In contrast, rainbow smelt were purposely introduced into Crystal Lake in Michigan's lower peninsula in the 1900s, then spread downstream into Lake Michigan and into the other Great Lakes. Alewife and rainbow smelt entered ecosystems where predators like the lake trout were severely depleted by sea lamprey and fishery effects. Both exotic fishes flourished and became very abundant. Both had strongly negative ecological effects as they compete with native forage fishes and prey on their larval stages (Kitchell and Crowder 1986; Hansson et al. 1997).

Alewife abundance in Lake Michigan reached exceptional levels. At its peak in the 1960s, predation by alewife depleted the zooplankton community (figure 12.2). Alewife populations soon crashed, with extensive die-offs clogging power plant and municipal water intakes. Beaches were littered with dead adults, and the odor of decomposing fish wafted miles inland. These conditions are estimated to have cost millions of dollars in tourist revenues and required expensive engineering additions designed to protect water intake structures.

In Lake Superior, rainbow smelt replaced the native cisco species as the dominant predator of zooplankton. Ciscoes had been greatly reduced by fishery exploitation, and lake trout populations were low. The recovery of the native lake trout stocks increased predation pressure on smelt. The current abundance of smelt is 10%–20% of that at the maximum (figure 12.1), enabling many native fishes to recover in response (Harvey et al. 2005).

A recreational fishery for rainbow smelt flourished for a time in both Lake Michigan and Lake Superior, but the burgeoning success of alewife soon diminished rainbow smelt populations in Lake Michigan. Fishery managers then faced a weighty problem: the loss of lake trout and other native fish enabled exotics to become abundant, creating profound ecological consequences. To control these nuisance species, they looked to Pacific salmon.

Pacific Salmon: The Solution

Several attempts to stock Pacific salmon species in the Great Lakes during the early part of the 20th century failed. In the early 1960s, fishery scientists intensified salmon stocking in Lake Michigan. They hoped to use salmon as a biological control agent for the alewife problem while establishing a recreational fishery to replace the extirpated lake trout. Coho and Chinook salmon were specifically selected because their distribution and behavior offered the greatest potential for predatory impact on alewife. By the late 1980s, stocking rates approached 15 million juvenile salmon and trout per year with lake trout accounting for about 25% of the total (figure 12.2). The results were remarkable. Alewife populations declined to half or less of their former abundance, abating the massive die-offs. In response, native species including the bloater or deepwater cisco (figure 12.2) and some sculpin species recovered. Zooplankton community structure returned to dominance by large *Daphnia* and, during the middle 1980s, developed to levels where grazing pressure by zooplankton promoted a twofold increase in summer water clarity relative to times when alewife were most abundant (Kitchell and Carpenter 1987; Madenjian et al. 2002).

For two decades following the mid-1960s, salmon stocking increased in response to public demand and the demonstrated success in Lake Michigan. Coastal towns experienced an economic boom based on an angling industry estimated at $3–$4 billion in annual revenues for the Great Lakes. Waterfront hotels, restaurants, boutiques, and marina development prospered as anglers traveled from distant states such as Oregon, Washington, and Iowa. Although resource economists argue about the dimension and sources of this economic development, nearly all agree that the reversal of a devastated fishery to one with an elevated to substantial public value is a miracle of fishery management.

Much the same salmon-stocking policy and its consequent economic benefits occurred in Lake Superior communities, although stocking rates were much lower, up to 4 million per year and, of that, 50% were lake trout. Instead of alewife, the forage base was the rainbow smelt. As salmon and lake trout increased, smelt declined, allowing recovery of many native species, especially the lake herring (figure 12.1) (Bronte et al. 2003; Cox and Kitchell 2004). As with Lake Michigan, public enthusiasm for salmon stocking grew, but these efforts eventually came into conflict with a larger set of constraints.

Pacific Salmon: The Problem

Salmon-stocking practices presented two ecological challenges. First, because of strong public encouragement, salmon abundance was not largely determined by the prey base but by the rate at which legislatures and fishery management agencies could allocate funds for hatchery development. This system is uncoupled from natural predator-prey abundance cycles, effectively making prey highly vulnerable to overexploitation because of artificially high predator abundances. Early cautions about the consequence of overstocking the system (Stewart et al. 1981) were generally met with bemused disregard by fishery managers riding on a rising wave of public support—a rare experience for most resource managers!

Salmon stocking succeeded in controlling alewife in Lake Michigan, reducing densities to 10%–20% of peak abundance (figure 12.2). Based on a mixture of advice and evidence, managers constrained and reduced stocking rates to levels that continue to both support recreational fisheries and reduce the adverse ecological effects of alewife. Along the way, a profound event confirmed this wisdom. In the 1980s, large numbers of dead or dying adult salmon appeared on local beaches shortly after the highest stocking rates on record. The two interactive components were deduced as cause and effect. Intensive salmon culture practices promoted the development and spread of bacterial kidney disease. This disease killed many fish already stressed by an insufficient supply of alewife prey. At about this time, researchers documented a substantial recruitment from streams and rivers where salmon had naturalized and developed self-sustaining reproduction.

In the public mind, dead alewives were replaced by dead salmon—not a desirable outcome. Managers recognized the consequences of density-dependent constraints, the disease outbreak that followed, and reduced stocking levels accordingly. According to Bill Horns of the Wisconsin Department of Natural Resources (personal communication with authors), current densities of alewife and salmon-stocking practices have equilibrated in ways that sustain the highest salmon catch rates on record. Reduced salmon stocking produced better fishing.

The second challenge revolved around the conflict created by the general goal of restoring native fish communities. Like any ecosystem, the ecological productivity of these lakes is limited. Eventually, heavier stocking of hatchery-reared fish can exceed the ability of existing food webs to support these top predators. Although additional salmon initially filled an ecological vacuum, they soon began to encounter ecological constraints. Too many salmon and trout can yield too few alewife, creating intensified competition among the stocked predators.

Lake trout stocking continues in Lake Michigan where fisheries biologists hope to restore a naturally reproducing population. However, public enthusiasm for the salmon fishery constrains this restoration effort, reflecting the finite productivity of the food web and trade-offs among management efforts. The same dilemma persists in Lakes Huron, Erie, and Ontario. Unlike Lake Michigan, the residual populations of lake trout in Lake Superior established and sustain a full recovery of native stocks. Like Lake Michigan, salmon stocking created an expectant public whose angling preferences continue to favor salmon.

Ironically, Lake Superior fishery managers face a different dilemma—a plague of riches. The recovery of siscowet and burbot, a victory for restoration efforts, created tremendous feeding pressure on smaller fish while offering little benefit to fisheries. Salmon also developed naturalized populations in Lake Superior streams and rivers. Competition with salmon for limited prey, exacerbated by declines in rainbow smelt and consequent increases in lake herring, are slowing the recovery of near-shore "lean" lake trout (Kitchell et al. 2000). Although increasing the stock of lake herring is consistent with restoring traditional fisheries, adult herring grow to be larger than adult smelt allowing them to avoid predation by salmon and lake trout (Mason et al. 1998; Bronte et al. 2003; Ebener 2005). Managers continue this long-term experiment as they seek to titrate salmon stocking against the inherent constraints of the fishery and their desire to continue restoring native fish.

Zebra and Quagga Mussels

The changes discussed so far reflect "top-down" ecological effects—how apex predators influence other species as their effects cascade down through food webs. At the same time, however, other invasions are shifting trophic interactions from below. Zebra and quagga mussels, in particular, are shifting food webs from the "bottom-up," creating changes in Great Lakes ecosystems that are as profound as introduced fish.

Zebra mussels were first discovered in Lake St. Clair during 1988 but spread quickly to shallow, warm, and productive habitats near shorelines throughout the Great Lakes (Mills et al. 1993; see also Great Lakes Net Web site, available at http://www.great-lakes.net/envt/flora-fauna/invasive/zebra.html). Soon thereafter, the quagga mussel invaded deeper, colder offshore waters. Both of these mussel species hitchhiked here in ship ballast water from their native homes in eastern Europe. Both have a life cycle that differs from that of our native mussels in that they have an immature pelagic (veliger) stage that enables them to disperse rapidly. Both soon attach to solid substrates and consume large amounts of phytoplankton and small zooplankton by efficiently filtering the water. The extent of their colonization is limited by a combination of factors including habitat productivity, temperature, and the presence of enough dissolved calcium to build their shells (chapter 29). The lack of calcium limits their extent in Lake Superior, although they occupy a few shallow, productive bays like Duluth harbor and Thunder Bay.

In the lower Great Lakes, zebra mussel numbers can exceed thousands per square meter. They are extremely dense in productive, warm areas such as western Lake Erie, Lake Huron's Saginaw Bay, Lake Michigan's Green Bay, and most nearshore areas. They encrust any solid substrate. Barnacles and their equivalents create a similar fouling problem in marine environments, but this has been a wholly new problem in the Great Lakes. Zebra mussels fouling municipal water intakes, docks, piers, buoys, and the bottoms of boats has inflated annual removal and maintenance costs to millions of dollars. Windrows of dead and broken mussel shells on once beautiful, inviting beaches now cut bare feet and cause a negative public response similar to the alewife die-offs. However, unlike alewife, we do not appear to have any means to control these species.

Zebra mussels are having immense ecological impacts. They encrust and smother native mussel species. Their filtering activity removes phytoplankton and deposits both feces and pseudofeces (undigested organic matter) on the substrate, creating an enriched benthic boundary layer and a water column depleted of algae. Understanding their bottom-up impacts on food webs continues to be a major research challenge (Strayer et al. 2004). By consuming large quantities of phytoplankton, zebra mussels often improve water clarity. In western Lake Erie, the water has become twice as clear, surpassing the gains wrought by the Clean Water Act! Because this increased clarity favors the growth of submerged plants (macrophytes; chapter 16), zebra mussels have greatly altered the shallow-water habitat structure in places like Green Bay.

In deeper water habitats where quagga mussels have become abundant, we see large declines in a benthic amphipod, *Diporeia hoyi,* that fed on lake bottom sediments. This shrimplike crustacean once densely covered lake bottoms at densities of thousands per square meter providing an important food source for many fishes. In some areas of Lake Michigan, *Diporei* has now virtually disappeared (Madenjian et al. 2002) with similar declines in all the other Great Lakes except Superior. Because the quagga mussel is a recent invader, we do not yet know what their long-term ecological impacts will be.

Zebra mussels create a new type of benthic habitat type that actually facilitates the success of other invaders from eastern Europe. The round goby invaded shortly after zebra mussels, aggressively occupying zebra mussel beds and displacing native benthic fishes. According to Tim Johnson of the Ontario Ministry of Natural Resources (personal communication with authors), round goby is now the most abundant forage fish in Lake Erie. This ability of one invader (the zebra mussel) to create favorable ecological conditions for additional invaders like the round goby is sometimes referred to as an "invasional melt-down" (Ricciardi 2001). As with alewife and rainbow smelt, gobies are becoming important components of local food webs.

The Future

A 2005 symposium on food web interactions in the lake and other recent reports offer warnings about the future of Lake Michigan. Stocked salmon have naturalized and now reproduce in local streams. This has boosted the recruitment of new piscivores, especially Chinook salmon, even though salmon-stocking rates remain steady. This unexpected and ill-documented increase in salmon abundance is leading to a collapse of the alewife population in Lake Huron. At the same time, high populations of zebra and quagga mussels are radically changing benthic environments and eliminating important food sources (*Diporeia)* for some native fish. However, native yellow perch, walleye, and lake trout populations are having remarkable recent recruitment success reflecting, we assume, reduced interactions with alewife (Hansson et al. 1997).

Other efforts at restoration may further confound our ability to manage Great Lakes food webs. Dam removals on tributary streams are increasing rapidly (Stanley et al. 2002), allowing sea lamprey and spawning salmon to colonize new river habitats. These also remove barriers to the dispersal of other exotics (chapter 29). With history as a teacher and the Great Lakes as a lesson, we should expect more surprises as new invaders appear and succeed.

Summary

The Great Lakes have followed somewhat different time lines but often parallel trajectories of profound ecological change wrought by two powerful causes—exploitation by commercial fisheries and invasion by exotic species. The Lake Michigan fishery is now a salmon-dominated system, marked by some success in restoring native species and changes brought by the continuing parade of new exotics. Similar events unfolded in Lakes Huron, eastern Lake Erie, and Lake Ontario. Lake Superior reflects a great success in restoring native stocks. In terms of public utility, Lake Michigan and Lake Superior are now in remarkably better ecological condition than in their recent past.

In our view, the futures of Lakes Michigan and Superior will continue to diverge. Lake Michigan supports an important recreational fishery for stocked salmon with alewife as the primary prey resource. This will likely continue but, as in Lake Huron, we may see increased naturalization of Chinook salmon as they adapt to recruit from local streams and rivers with consequent impacts. As predation levels increase, managers will face challenges in how to set stocking rates as they seek to titrate predator-prey interactions. Native fishes appear likely to continue recovering in Lake Superior. Lake herring populations are likely to become the primary forage species as predation increases, providing a base to support native fishes like lake trout as rainbow smelt decline. Management there needs to balance the developing commercial fisheries with tribal fishery rights and the interests of recreational anglers.

Both researchers and managers face challenging trade-offs as they seek to understand and manage the dynamic food webs of the Great Lakes. Their efforts will continue to be constrained by the basic productivity of these lakes and the surprises sprung by new exotic species. Success in adaptively managing these systems will need to include vigilant sea lamprey control, greater understanding of the effects wrought by recent invaders, and improved efforts and methods to employ fishery management as a tool to regulate food web interactions.

References

Bogue, M. B. 2000. Fishing the Great Lakes: An Environmental History, 1783–1933. Madison: University of Wisconsin Press.

Bronte, C. R., M. P. Ebener, D. R. Schreiner, D. S. DeVault, M. M. Petzold, D. A. Jensen, C. Richards, and S. J. Lozano. 2003. Fish community change in Lake Superior, 1970–2000. Can. J. Fish. Aquat. Sci. 60:1552–1574.

Cox, S. P., and J. F. Kitchell. 2004. Lake Superior ecosystem, 1929–1998: Simulating alternative hypotheses for recruitment failure of lake herring (*Coregonus artedi*). Bull. Mar. Sci 74:671–684.

Ebner, M. P., ed. 2005. The State of Laker Superior in 2000. Ann Arbor, MI: Great Lakes Fishery Commission.

Hansson, S., D. M. Post, J. F. Kitchell, and T. S. McComish. 1997. Predation by yellow perch (*Perca flavescens*) in southern Lake Michigan—A model analysis. Proceedings of the International Symposium on the Role of Forage Fishes in Marine Ecosystems, University of Alaska Sea Grant, Anchorage.

Harvey, C. J., S. P. Cox, and J. F. Kitchell. 2005. Food webs. Pp. 113–117 in M. P. Ebener, ed. The State of Lake Superior in 2000. Ann Arbor, MI: Great Lakes Fishery Commission.

Harvey, C. J., and J. F. Kitchell. 2000. A stable isotope evaluation of the structure and spatial heterogeneity of a Lake Superior food web. Can. J. Fish. Aquat. Sci. 57:1395–1403.

Harvey, C. J., S. T. Schram, and J. F. Kitchell. 2003. Trophic relationships among lean and siscowet lake trout in Lake Superior. Trans. Am. Fish. Soc. 132:219–228.

Johnson, T. B. 2006. Trophic linkages in the Lake Superior food web: A synthesis of empirical and modeling studies, 1970–2003. In M. Munawar and J. H. Leach, eds. The State of Lake Superior. Ecovision World Monograph Series. Backhuys, the Netherlands.

Kitchell, J. F. l991. Salmonid carrying capacity: Estimates and experiences in the Great Lakes of North America. Pp. 59–66 in R. J. Svrjcek, eds. Marine Ranching: Proceedings of the Seventeenth U.S.-Japan Meeting on Aquaculture, Ise, Japan, 1988. National Oceanic and Atmospheric Administration Technical Report NMFS 102. Washington, DC: National Marine Fisheries Service.

Kitchell, J. F., and S. R. Carpenter. 1987. Piscivores, planktivores, fossils and phorbins. Pp. 132–146 in W. C. Kerfoot and A. Sih, eds. Predation: Direct and Indirect Impacts on Aquatic Communities. Hanover, NH: University Press of New England.

Kitchell, J. F., S. P. Cox, C. J. Harvey, T. B. Johnson, D. M. Mason, K. K. Schoen, K. Aydin, C. Bronte, M. Ebener, M. Hansen, M. Hoff, S. Schram, D. Schreiner, and C. J. Walters. 2000. Sustainability of the Lake Superior fish community: Interactions in a food web context. Ecosystems 3:545–560.

Kitchell, J. F., and L. B. Crowder. 1986. Predator-prey interactions in Lake Michigan: Model predictions and recent dynamics. Env. Biol. Fish. 16:205–211.

Madenjian, C. P., G. L. Fanhnenstiel, T. H. Johengen, T. H. Nalepa, H. A. Vanderploeg, G. W. Fleischer, P. J. Schneeberger, D. M. Benjamin, E. B. Smith, J. R. Bence, E. S. Rutherford, D. S. Lavis, D. M. Robertson, D. J. Jude, and M. P. Ebener. 2002. Dynamics of the Lake Michigan food web, 1970–2000. Can. J. Fish. Aquat. Sci. 59:736–753.

Mason, D. M., T. B. Johnson, and J. F. Kitchell. 1998. Consequences of prey fish community dynamics on lake trout (*Salvelinus namaycush*) foraging efficiency in Lake Superior. Can. J. Fish. Aquat. Sci. 55: 1273–1284.

Mills, E. L., J. H. Leach, J. T. Carlton, and C. L. Secor. 1993. Exotic species in the Great Lakes: A history of biotic crises and anthropogenic introductions. J. Great Lakes Res. 19:1–54.

Page, K. S., K. T. Scribner, and M. Burnham-Curtis. 2004. Genetic diversity of wild and hatchery lake trout populations: Relevance for management and restoration in the Great Lakes. Trans. Am. Fish. Soc. 133:674–691.

Ricciardi, A. 2001. Facilitative interactions among the aquatic invaders: Is an "invasional meltdown" occurring in the Great Lakes? Can. J. Fish. Aquat. Sci. 58:2513–2525.

Stanley, E.H., M. A. Luebke, M. W. Doyle, and D. W. Marshall. 2002. Short-term changes in channel form and macroinvertebrate communities following low-head dam removal. J. North Am. Benthol. Soc.: 21:172–187.

Stewart, D. J., J. F. Kitchell, and L. B. Crowder. 1981. Forage fishes and their salmonid predators in Lake Michigan. Trans. Am. Fish. Soc. 110:751–763.

Strayer, D. L., K. A. Hattala, and A. W. Kanhle. 2004. Effects of an invasive bivalve (*Dreissena polymorpha*) on fish in the Hudson River estuary. Can. J. Fish. Aquat. Sci. 61:924–941.

13 Documenting and Halting Declines of Nongame Fishes in Southern Wisconsin

David W. Marshall and John Lyons

Wisconsin has a rich native fish fauna of 147 species, but most of these are little-known "nongame" species. Although sport fish and other fish of direct economic impact have been thoroughly studied in Wisconsin, most nongame fishes receive little attention from resource managers and the general public. The occurrence and abundance of many of these sensitive species declined following European settlement, illustrating a major deterioration of aquatic ecosystems (Becker 1983). More recent and ongoing declines in these species indicate that environmental conditions continue to worsen (Lyons 1989, 1996; Lyons et al. 2000). We now use the diversity and distribution of nongame fish sensitive to environmental degradation (table 13.1) as indicators for the health of streams and lakes.

Our knowledge of the distribution of most Wisconsin nongame fishes is limited because they have not been frequently surveyed. Between 1974 and 1980, the Wisconsin Department of Natural Resources (WDNR) conducted the Fish Distribution Study (Fago 1992). Although this was comprehensive by most standards, only half of the state's watersheds were surveyed before funding cuts terminated the study. More recently, the WDNR began a new statewide fish survey (overseen by Lyons) in part to allow a rewrite of the landmark *Fishes of Wisconsin* book (Becker 1983). We are using results from this Fishes of Wisconsin

Table 13.1 Sensitive species found in study streams or lakes during the Fish Distribution Study or the Fishes of Wisconsin Survey

Common name	Scientific name	NHI status	Lake shore species
American brook lamprey	*Lampetra appendix*		
Brook trout	*Salvelinus fontinalis*		
Redside dace	*Clinostomus elongatus*	Special concern	
Redfin shiner	*Lythrurus umbratilis*	Special concern	
Pugnose shiner	*Notropis anogenus*	Threatened	X
Blackchin shiner	*Notropis heterodon*		X
Blacknose shiner	*Notropis heterolepis*		X
Ozark minnow	*Notropis nubilus*	Threatened	
Carmine shiner	*Notropis percobromus*		
Pugnose minnow	*Opsopeodus emiliae*	Special concern	X
Lake chubsucker	*Erimyzon sucetta*	Special concern	X
Northern hog sucker	*Hypentilium nigricans*		
Banded killifish	*Fundulus diaphanus*	Special concern	X
Starhead topminnow	*Fundulus dispar*	Endangered	X
Rock bass	*Ambloplites rupestris*		X
Smallmouth bass	*Micropterus dolomieu*		X
Rainbow darter	*Etheostoma caeruleum*		
Iowa darter	*Etheostoma exile*		X
Least darter	*Etheostoma microperca*	Special concern	X
Banded darter	*Etheostoma zonale*		
Mottled sculpin	*Cottus bairdii*		X

Source: Modified from Lyons 1992.
Note: Species considered rare by the Wisconsin Natural Heritage Inventory (NHI) are indicated by NHI status. An "X" indicates species that often occur in the nearshore area of southern Wisconsin lakes.

Survey to document how Wisconsin's aquatic ecosystems have changed over the last 30 years.

Here, we compare results of these two surveys to examine how nongame fishes have declined in selected small streams and lakes in the southernmost quarter of Wisconsin. This region is generally the most densely populated with a landscape dominated by intensive agriculture and urbanization (plates 4 and 8). Although some high-quality aquatic ecosystems remain, our findings suggest that, if current trends continue, the future of these ecosystems is precarious. We therefore propose a conservation strategy to help protect these ecosystems and their fish faunas.

Declines in Nongame Fishes in Streams since the 1970s

Small streams, with their limited volumes of water, are especially vulnerable to pollution and other forms of environmental degradation. This makes the nongame fishes that inhabit these streams reliable indicators of environmental health (Lyons 1992; Lyons et al. 1996). Except for trout streams, most small streams lack sport fish populations. Consequently, most are ignored with respect to water quality monitoring, biological assessment, and environmental protection. We use nongame fish data

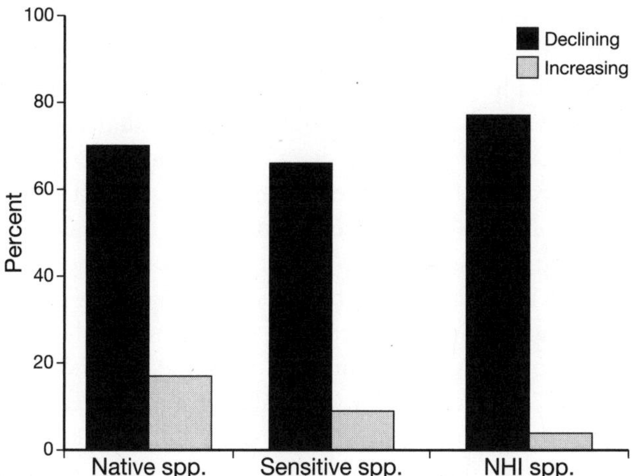

FIGURE 13.1 Changes in small stream occurrences of native, sensitive, and Wisconsin Natural Heritage Inventory rare fishes since the 1970s.

to estimate changes in environmental health in these southern Wisconsin streams. As part of the Fishes of Wisconsin Survey, we sampled 46 streams in 1998 and 2000 that were originally sampled during the Fish Distribution Study in 1974–80. We attempted to duplicate the Fish Distribution Survey methods, visiting the same locations during the same seasons and using the same gear and effort. We focused on changes that had occurred in native species richness and the distribution of rare species (table 13.1) as defined by Wisconsin's Natural Heritage Inventory.

We found substantial drops in both native species diversity and the abundance of rarer species over the 25 years between the two samplings (figure 13.1). Species richness declined in 70% of the 46 streams surveyed. The Fish Distribution Study encountered rare species in 54% of the streams, but we found them in only 13%. Five species recorded during the Fish Distribution Study were not found in the Fishes of Wisconsin Survey. Declines were most pronounced for environmentally sensitive species such as the redside dace and redfin shiner.

We believe that shifts in land use, especially increased urbanization and agricultural intensification, were the main causes of these declines. Urban and suburban areas have expanded faster than population growth in many of the study watersheds. Even relatively small increases in urban land use, particularly impervious surfaces like roofs, roads, and parking lots, are associated with sharp declines in many sensitive fish species (Wang et al. 2000, 2003).

Agriculture was the dominant land use in most of the watersheds, and intensive agriculture is negatively correlated with the diversity of sensitive fish (Wang et al. 1997). Fish communities are particularly affected by nutrient loading, sedimentation, and habitat destruction. Of particular concern are livestock manure spills and runoff, which are believed to be responsible for declines in many fish species in southern Wisconsin (Lyons 1996). Sensitive fish species are commonly extirpated within local watersheds subject to persistent manure management problems. Although these data are often anecdotal, we believe that excessive manure runoff or spills have affected several of our study watersheds.

The losses of fish species that we documented in small headwater streams indicate a worsening of the health of these systems. These declines in the health of small tributary streams attract little publicity but ultimately determine the character and quality of larger navigable waters with more obvious and direct social and economic value (Meyers et al. 2003).

Declines in Nongame Fishes in Lakes since the 1970s

After observing major declines in fish diversity in small streams, we looked for changes in fishes in lakes. Previous studies of the Madison lakes, especially Lake Mendota, had shown major losses of small littoral-zone fishes (Lyons 1989; Magnuson and Lathrop 1992; Magnuson et al. 1994). In 2004, as part of the Fishes of Wisconsin Survey, we seined nearshore areas of 13 lakes in southeastern Wisconsin to capture small-bodied fishes, replicating Fish Distribution Study samples from 1974–80. Water quality was good in 12 of the 13 lakes with conditions ranging from mesotrophic to slightly eutrophic. The other lake was highly eutrophic. Most of the lakes were calcareous, and water quality had not changed substantially for decades.

The 2004 study revealed dramatic declines in native species richness and in sensitive species (figure 13.2), including certain darters, minnows, and topminnows associated with lake nearshore areas (table 13.1). Native species richness dropped in 11 of the 13 lakes (85%), and sensitive and rare species in 9 (69%). Many of the sensitive species that disappeared, such as pugnose shiner (threatened), blackchin shiner, blacknose shiner, banded killifish (special concern), Iowa darter, and least darter (special concern), share a strong affinity for aquatic vegetation (Becker 1983; Lyons 1989; see also plate 15). Their demise may thus reflect losses and changes in nearshore vegetated habitats.

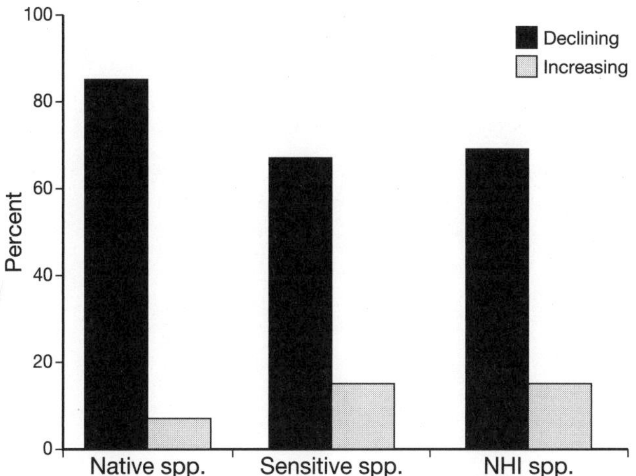

FIGURE 13.2 Changes in lake shoreline occurrences of native, sensitive, and Wisconsin Natural Heritage Inventory rare fishes since the 1970s.

Similar declines in nearshore lake fishes, including these six vegetation-associated species, have been documented elsewhere in Wisconsin and the Midwest and have been attributed to deteriorating habitat quality, particularly vegetated habitat, caused by shoreline development (Bryan and Scarnecchia 1992; Jennings et al. 1999, 2003; Schindler et al. 2000). Shoreline development occurs when terrestrial vegetation and nearshore aquatic vegetation are removed or highly modified. It is associated with house construction, beach development, and the installation of docks and piers. Interestingly, we found the highest number of native and sensitive species in the most eutrophic lake—the lake with the worst water quality. However, this lake had the least developed shoreline and lowest pier density.

We believe that pier distribution and density may be a useful and easily quantified index of the extent and degree of human impacts on lake shorelines. Piers directly shade aquatic plant habitat reducing growth rates (Loflin 1995; Engel and Pederson 1998; Burdick and Short 1999; Shafer 1999). In 2004, the WDNR studied pier shading in two of the 13 study lakes (Garrison et al. 2005). Light intensity averaged 4% of surface levels under piers, compared with about 40% at uncovered sites, enough to support abundant aquatic vegetation. Low light under piers either completely eliminated aquatic plants or favored sparse densities of shade-tolerant wild celery. Aquatic invertebrates were correspondingly less abundant under piers. Juvenile sunfishes and other small fishes

FIGURE 13.3 Habitat preference for juvenile sunfishes and nongame species based on minnow-trap catch rates.

were nearly four times more abundant among unshaded aquatic vegetation than under piers (figure 13.3).

Piers also act as focal points for human access and use of lakes, leading to additional changes in nearshore habitats. More and bigger piers are associated with increased motorboat use, the reinforcement or armoring of shorelines, mechanical and chemical removal of macrophytes, and exotic species invasions, all of which damage nearshore habitats (Engel 1985; Engel and Pederson 1998; Asplund and Cook 1997; Jennings et al. 1999, 2003; chapter 16). Piers modify lake shorelines and littoral zones in both direct and indirect ways that ultimately expose nongame fishes to unusually high rates of predation. We are now examining changes in pier densities between 2004 and the 1970s, based on aerial photos. Preliminary analyses indicate that pier numbers have increased in every lake.

The demise of small-bodied nongame fishes from the shorelines of southern Wisconsin lakes speaks volumes about the seemingly schizophrenic approach to lake management adopted by society and the tug-of-war between private property interests and the Wisconsin Public Trust Doctrine. This doctrine holds that state waters are owned in common by all the citizens of the state and are held in trust by the WDNR. On the one hand, as the holder of the trust, the WDNR is mandated to protect the natural lake environment and promote its sustainable use for aesthetics, fisheries, recreation, and biodiversity conservation, now and in the future. On the other hand, many property owners have a "suburbanized" view of nature and expect (and work toward) open, "weed-free" water and manicured shorelines, often conflicting directly with the WDNR's aesthetic, fishery, and biodiversity goals and actions. Our results suggest that if the "suburbanization" of southern Wisconsin lakeshores continues, many of the natural values of our lakes will decline.

"Safe Havens" to Protect Fish Diversity

As human land use intensifies and unspoiled aquatic habitat shrinks in southern Wisconsin, the future of many sensitive fish species is in doubt. To protect and sustain these species, we recommend that the state establish a network of relatively undeveloped and undegraded "safe havens" to provide habitat for these fishes. They represent an irreplaceable part of Wisconsin's natural heritage and should not be lost from the region. Several existing safe havens serve as models for such a network. In Walworth and Waukesha counties in southeastern Wisconsin, the 672 ha Lulu Lake Natural Area encompasses 38 ha Lulu Lake and a portion of the Mukwonago River. These waters are buffered with extensive wetlands, and the Mukwonago River system supports a variety of rare and sensitive native fishes including the starhead topminnow (endangered), pugnose shiner, longear sunfish (threatened), lake chubsucker (special concern), banded killifish, and least darter.

The Lower Wisconsin State Riverway in southwestern Wisconsin is another example of a safe haven. Some of the most interesting and unusual fish species in the upper Midwest dwell within this river system, which stretches 148 km from the Prairie du Sac Dam to the Mississippi River. Of Wisconsin's 147 native species, 98 are found within the Riverway, which retains a largely natural character and in some ways resembles the place that Native Americans and early French explorers canoed centuries ago (Lyons 2005; chapter 17). The Riverway contains a diversity of habitats including a channel braided by islands and sandbars and numerous off-channel floodplain lakes. The main channel holds ancient species such as the silver lamprey, paddlefish (threatened), lake sturgeon (special concern), and shovelnose sturgeon and healthy populations of sensitive rare species such as the blue sucker (threatened) and western sand darter (special concern).

The floodplain lakes along the river support both riverine and lake fishes. Although these lakes are geologically distinct from the southeastern glacial lakes we sampled in 2004, shoreline habitat issues are the same. The floodplain lakes are mostly undeveloped. Aquatic plants are abundant, and the heavily wooded shores provide habitat for birds, reptiles, and fish. The floodplain lakes support numerous sensitive fish including starhead topminnow, pirate perch (special concern), mud darter (special concern), and least darter. In contrast to the southeastern glacial lakes, nearly every seine haul in these floodplain lakes yields one or more rare or sensitive species from the blankets of aquatic plants or woody snags.

Many of our fish species would become more secure if additional refuges similar to Lulu Lake and the Lower Wisconsin Riverway could be established to protect and restore similar high-quality habitats elsewhere. One landscape scale restoration currently under way in southwestern Wisconsin that aims to create new safe havens is the Military Ridge Prairie Heritage Area. Although the primary goals of this restoration are to protect remnant prairies and migratory grassland bird habitat, grasslands management has also benefited local trout streams. Watershed nutrient models predict that there has been an 84% phosphorus reduction and a 38% reduction in surface runoff as croplands have been converted to grasslands. Still, some nitrate problems persist (chapter 17). Water quality has improved, as warm and "dirty" surface runoff has been replaced with cold "clean" groundwater flow. Trout and other sensitive cold-water indicators such as mottled sculpin and American brook lamprey have increased as warm water and environmentally tolerant species have declined (Marshall et al., in press). Coldwater Index of Biotic Integrity (Lyons et al. 1996) scores have improved, increasing from 10–20 (poor) in 1974–75 to 60–70 (good) by 2001–3.

The safe haven strategy should be applied to those remaining small watersheds and lakeshores in southern Wisconsin that still have relatively intact habitat and fish populations. Key terrestrial riparian and upland habitats must be protected from certain types of agricultural and urban land uses. Habitats can be protected either through public acquisition and management of land or development of long-term preservation plans on private lands. Whether a public-acquisition or private-preservation approach is taken, safe havens must be established quickly in southern Wisconsin, as current trends suggest that within less than a generation there may be no sensitive nongame fishes left to protect.

Conclusions

We briefly described two examples, one for streams and the other for lakes, of how fish biodiversity continues to decline in southern Wisconsin as natural habitats are modified or destroyed. The fishes most clearly affected are small and inconspicuous and have no apparent utility to most people, so their passing has thus far been little noticed or mourned. But the disappearance of nongame species is an early warning sign that Wisconsin's aquatic ecosystems are in trouble. Establishing safe havens of relatively intact natural habitat is perhaps the only way that remnant populations of nongame fishes can be preserved. But are we as a society willing to save southern Wisconsin's nongame fish fauna? The outcome of the conflict between two diametrically opposed worldviews may well answer this question. One worldview is that nongame species offer no direct economic benefit and that the costs to protect or restore their habitats are not warranted. The other worldview is that human life is enriched by the biodiversity of fish (and other organisms) and that we all profit from the functioning ecosystems that these species require. We hope that more people will adopt this second view. Ultimately, our shared existence with nongame fishes may benefit human society in ways we cannot yet fully understand.

References

Asplund, T. R., and C. M. Cook. 1997. Effects of motor boats on submerged aquatic macrophytes. Journal of Lake and Reservoir Management 13:1–12.

Becker, G. C. 1983. Fishes of Wisconsin. Madison: University of Wisconsin Press.

Bryan, M. D., and D. L. Scarnecchia. 1992. Species richness, composition, and abundance of fish larvae and juveniles inhabiting natural and developed shorelines of a glacial Iowa lake. Environmental Biology of Fishes 35:329–341.

Burdick, D. M., and F. T. Short. 1999. The effects of boat docks on eelgrass beds in coastal waters of Massachusetts. Environmental Management 23:231–240.

Engel, S. 1985. Aquatic community interactions of submerged macrophytes. Wisconsin Department of Natural Resources, Technical Bulletin No. 156, Madison.

Engel, S., and J. L. Pederson. 1998. The construction, aesthetics, and effects of lakeshore development: A literature review. Wisconsin Department of Natural Resources, Research Report No. 177, Madison.

Fago, D. 1992. Distribution and relative abundance of fishes in Wisconsin. VIII. Summary report. Wisconsin Department of Natural Resources, Technical Bulletin No. 175, Madison.

Garrison, P. J., D. W. Marshall, L. Stremick-Thompson, P. L. Cicero, and P. D. Dearlove. 2005. Effects of pier shading on littoral zone habitat and communities in Lakes Ripley and Rock, Jefferson County. Wisconsin Department of Natural Resources Research Report No. ISS PUB-SS-1006 2005, Madison.

Jennings, M. J., M. A. Bozek, G. R. Hatzenbeler, E. E. Emmons, and M. D. Staggs. 1999. Cumulative effects of incremental shoreline habitat modifications on fish assemblages in north temperate lakes. North American Journal of Fisheries Management 19:18–27.

Jennings, M. J., E. E. Emmons, G. R. Hatzenbeler, C. Edwards, and M. A. Bozek. 2003. Is littoral habitat affected by residential development and land use in watersheds of Wisconsin lakes? Lake and Reservoir Management 19:272–279.

Loflin, R. K. 1995. The effects of docks on seagrass beds in the Charlotte Harbor Estuary. Florida Scientist 58:198–205.

Lyons, J. 1989. Changes in the abundance of small littoral-zone fishes in Lake Mendota, Wisconsin. Canadian Journal of Zoology 67:2910–2916.

———. 1992. Using the index of biotic integrity (IBI) to measure environmental quality in warmwater streams of Wisconsin. U.S. Forest Service, North Central Forest Experiment Station, General Technical Report 149, St. Paul, MN.

———. 1996. Recent decline in the distribution and abundance of slender madtom (*Noturus exilis*) in Wisconsin. Journal of Freshwater Ecology 11:415–419.

———. 2005. Fish assemblage structure, composition, and biotic integrity of the Wisconsin River. American Fisheries Society Symposium 45:345–363.

Lyons, J., P. A. Cochran, and D. Fago. 2000. Wisconsin fishes 2000. Status and distribution. Madison: University of Wisconsin Sea Grant Institute.

Lyons, J., L. Wang, and T. D. Simonson. 1996. Development and validation of an index of biotic integrity for coldwater streams in Wisconsin. North American Journal of Fisheries Management 16: 241–256.

Magnuson, J. J., B. J. Benson, and A. S. McLain. 1994. Insights on species richness and turnover from long-term ecological research: Fishes in north temperate lakes. American Zoologist 34:437–451.

Magnuson, J. J., and R. C. Lathrop. 1992. Historical changes in the fish community. Pp. 193–227 in J. F. Kitchell, ed. Food web management: A case study of Lake Mendota. New York: Springer-Verlag.

Marshall, D. W., A. H. Fayram, J. C. Panuska, J. Baumann, and J. Hennessy. In press. Positive effects of agricultural land use changes on cold water fish communities in southwest Wisconsin. North American Journal of Fisheries Management.

Meyer, J. L., L. A. Kaplan, D. Newbold, et al. 2003. Where rivers are born: The scientific imperative for defending small streams and wetlands. Washington, DC: American Rivers and Sierra Club.

Schindler, D. E., S. I. Geib, and M. R. Williams. 2000. Patterns of fish growth along a residential development gradient in north temperate lakes. Ecosystems. 3:229–237.

Shafer, D. J. 1999. The effects of dock shading on the seagrass *Halodule wrightii* in Perdido Bay, Alabama. Estuaries 22(4):936–943.

Wang, L., J. Lyons, and P. Kanehl. 2003. Impacts of urban land cover on trout streams in Wisconsin and Minnesota. Transactions of the American Fisheries Society 132:825–839.

Wang, L., J. Lyons, P. Kanehl, R. Bannerman, and E. Emmons. 2000. Watershed urbanization and changes in fish communities in southeastern Wisconsin streams. Journal of the American Water Resources Association 36:1173–1189.

Wang, L., J. Lyons, P. Kanehl, and R. Gatti. 1997. Influences of watershed land use on habitat quality and biotic integrity in Wisconsin streams. Fisheries 22(6):6–12.

14 Change in Wisconsin's Coastal Wetlands

Jim Meeker and Gary Fewless

We come to a bay 25 miles around (Chequamegon Bay). In it there is a channel where we take a great store of fish: sturgeons of vast bigness and pike seven feet long.

Pierre Esprit Radisson 1658

We soon reached the (southern) extremity of the Baye des Puants (Green Bay) . . . to enter a river (Fox River). This river is beautiful at its mouth—full of geese, ducks, teal and other birds attracted there by the wild rice.

Father Jacques Marquette 1673

: : :

Native Americans favored the coastal wetlands of Wisconsin. Not only did the habitats associated with these wetlands teem with fish and game, the wetlands themselves also served as interchanges for river highways to the interior used for trading. Later, European explorers used these routes to ply the fur trade. It is hard to spend time in these wetlands today without wondering how they looked to visitors prior to the French encounter. Consider this the next time you cross the Bong Bridge connecting Superior to Duluth or the Tower Drive Bridge over the Fox River in Green Bay.

Here, we describe the ecology of these key areas and how they have changed in parallel with other aspects of Wisconsin's natural heritage. A few early inventories of coastal wetlands give us a glimpse into the past. These include the exhaustive Herdendorf, Hartley, and Barnes (1981) study of coastal wetlands across the Great Lakes. These wetlands connect hydrologically to the adjacent lakes by embayments and rivers. When water levels on the big lakes change, denizens of these wetlands are affected as their water levels are tied to these lake levels. Other wetlands are connected to the lakes through groundwater exchange. Although these ground-fed wetlands do not respond as fast to shifts in lake water levels, shifting water tables still cause substantial changes over time.

Wetland Types

Coastal wetlands of Wisconsin vary considerably from the southwestern shore of Lake Michigan up to the south shore of Lake Superior. Along the western shores of Lake Michigan and Green Bay, the most conspicuous wetlands are large marshes at river mouths (plate 14), but along the Lake Superior shoreline, peatlands are common with only occasional marshes. Where rivers empty into the Great Lakes, they carry silt and sand, forming barrier beaches, sand spits, and deltas. All these deposits act to protect developing vegetation from the energy of the lakes. Some "drowned wetlands" are completely submerged when lake levels rise. These are most common at the western end of Lake Superior and southern Lake Michigan.

While a few huge original wetlands complexes accounted for over half the original wetland acreage in Wisconsin, most coastal wetlands are small, often covering less than 100 ha (Herdendorf et al. 1981). The larger complexes included the marshes at the lower end of Green Bay, and, on Lake Superior, the wetlands at the mouth of the St. Louis River (near the present day cities of Duluth and Superior) and within Chequamegon Bay. Unfortunately, most of these major wetland complexes near cities have since been drained or filled (plate 14).

Pulse Stability in Coastal Wetlands

Coastal wetlands are unique and ecologically different from interior marshes and bogs in part because they experience periodic fluctuations in water level. Daily shifts due to wind (seiches) as well as seasonal and multiyear fluctuations occur, creating what biologists term "pulse stability"—a system completely dependent on regular disturbance events (Odum 1969). Such flooding and dewatering maintains the health and viability of these coastal wetlands by flushing them of accumulated detritus, exposing and oxidizing sediments from time to time, and preventing dominance by any one species. The year-to-year changes provide the most important pulses for driving shifts in vegetation. Over longer time scales, however, all the species that occupy these marshes are sustained.

Water levels also fluctuate over longer time periods with periodic highs every 30 years or so in Lake Superior and every 20 years in Lake Michigan. These fluctuations average about 0.5 m on Lake Superior and 1.0 m on Lake Michigan. These fluctuations present a special challenge for those monitoring long-term changes in vegetation in coastal wetlands, as it becomes important to separate these natural cycles and the ensuing vegetation responses from more systematic shifts like those resulting from human disturbance or climate change. We recognized this when monitoring wetlands on the Apostle Islands during the high water year of 1996 and the low water year of 2002. Controlling for the effects of water levels at the time of sampling is difficult. In the Apostle Islands, wide-leaf cattail declined from the high to the low water year, while shrub species increased over the same drawdown. Upland shrubs and grasses usually increase during low water times but are replaced by emergent vegetation better adapted to flooding when waters become high again. Our challenge, then, is to disentangle patterns generated by pulse stability from those generated by directional, long-term change. Lake Superior dropped to an historic low point in September 2007, perhaps reflecting increased evaporation and reduced precipitation due to climate change.

Human-Induced Changes to the Wetland Ecosystems

In addition to the natural, usually cyclical, change in Great Lakes coastal wetlands, there has been considerable change in response to human activities since European settlement. Some coastal wetlands were completely lost to actions like filling or dredging for shoreline and marina development. Other wetlands have been lost indirectly and unintentionally through activities, like road construction. Remaining wetlands often contain a severely degraded flora and fauna. Few wetlands appear to be similar to their presettlement condition. Here, we describe the natural and human-induced changes in three Wisconsin coastal wetlands: Lake Superior, Green Bay, and Lake Michigan exclusive of Green Bay.

Lake Superior Coastal Wetlands

The uplands along the Lake Superior coastline have changed dramatically since settlement. Gone are most of the large white pine, white spruce, and white cedars that fringed the lake. Some of the original wetlands experienced the same fate. This is particularly true at the very head of the lake. Here, the Nemagi, Pokegama, and St. Louis rivers and numerous smaller streams empty into embayments protected from the lake by long sand spits (Wisconsin Point and Minnesota Point). Dredging and filling eliminated much of what was probably the largest wetland complex on Lake Superior. It is difficult to estimate the proportion of wetlands destroyed, but acres of peatland have vanished. Many functional wetland marshes along the St. Louis River and in Allouez Bay have developed where peat lands once occurred, but these do not replace what has been lost. In addition, most remaining coastal wetlands are seriously altered.

Transitions from Peatlands to Marshlands. How have the remaining coastal wetlands along the Great Lakes changed since European settlement? One remnant peatland, at the eastern end of Allouez Bay near the town of Superior, gives us clues to this process of change. Whereas small thin-leaved, "wiregrass" sedges (predominantly the woolly fruit sedge) still dominate the less disturbed peatlands of the Bayfield peninsula and Apostle Islands, they barely persist at Allouez Bay. Instead, a rogues' gallery of tall, aggressive exotic plants have invaded, including narrow-leaved cattail, common reed grass, purple loosestrife, and, at higher elevations, reed canary grass. The smaller sedges will eventually be lost from this site. This "peatland-to-marsh" transition, already complete in many Lake Ontario wetlands, is still progressing in several Lake Superior coastal wetlands. The process is advanced at Allouez Bay and Fish Creek (near Ashland). At Fish Creek, as much as a meter of eroded sediment has been transported from the upper watershed and deposited near the mouth since the cutover at the beginning of the last century (Fitzpatrick and Knox 2000). The nutrient enrichment associated with these sediments spurs the growth of invading plants, displacing native species and contributing to the loss of these peatlands (chapter 15).

You can still see the initial stages of peatland-to-marsh transition along the Sioux River as it enters Lake Superior north of Washburn. Sediment cores from the developing marshes on the west side of Highway 13 tell a revealing story. Here, sediment-laden annual floodwaters are temporarily impounded, spilling over the remnant wiregrass sedge peatlands. The cores contain much more sand, silt, and clay than the peat cores collected across the highway. Road construction contributed to these changes. Trapped behind the impervious road, the Sioux River floodwaters spread out and deposit sediment on the west side of the highway, while the peatlands on the east side escape these sediments. On the west side, marsh species like bur-reed and cattail are now quite abundant with only a few relict wiregrass sedge stems. In contrast, wiregrass sedges still dominate the nonimpacted peatland.

In addition to the changes in peatland vegetation, submerged and floating aquatic communities in deep marshes of St. Louis/Allouez and Chequamegon Bay were greatly modified due to shading and physical disturbance by rafts of logs and other logging debris discarded from the myriad sawmills that once dotted the shorelines. Today, there are only sparse aquatic plant beds in Chequamegon Bay. At one time, this area probably supported both wild celery in the deeper water and bulrushes and spikerushes in the shallows, much like the present day vegetation in the nearby Kakagon Sloughs and Bad River wetland complex.

Newcomers—Changes in Floristics due to Invasive Species. Not all peatlands have become marshes. In some seemingly intact peatlands, the arrival of aggressive exotic species is driving floristic changes. At Bark Bay on the Bayfield peninsula, for example, common reed grass is invading (Lynch and Saltonstall 2002). Wisconsin Department of Natural Resources stewards of this natural area have initiated a "cut and dab" herbicide treatment to reduce its abundance. These treatments appear effective but will probably have to be continued for the foreseeable future. A similar situation is unfolding in the Kakagon/Bad River wetland complex as both common reed and narrow-leaved cattail invade. This complex lies wholly within the Bad River Reservation and represents the best remaining large wetland mosaic on the Great Lakes. Nevertheless, it, too, is changing. In the mid-1980s, purple loosestrife was first observed in the Kakagon complex. Although herbicide treatments have reduced its numbers, narrow-leaved cattail appears to be replacing it. While neither of these species may threaten the Bad River tribe's wild rice resource, it is distressing to witness such invasions even in this impressive wetlands complex.

Lake Michigan Shoreline Exclusive of Green Bay

Much of the Lake Michigan shoreline from the Illinois border to the tip of Door County is steep and exposed to strong wave action, precluding the development of wetlands. Before European settlement, most wetlands occurred at the mouths of larger rivers and in sheltered bays along

Door County. While most of these marshes have been lost, a few remain, most notably at the mouth of the Kewaunee and Ahnapee rivers.

The largest coastal wetlands once occurred in Door County from Clay Banks north to Whitefish Bay and again from Baileys Harbor north to Newport State Park. Now, the only significant large, nonforested wetlands along this shoreline can be found in the sheltered bays (e.g., Moonlight, North, and Rowleys bays). Here, the vegetation forms distinct zones like the sparse, deepwater emergent marsh that occurs in standing water up to a meter in depth. This zone is dominated by hardstem bulrush, although submergent and floating leaved species also occur in scattered patches. Moving landward, a shallow marsh and/or a sedge meadow zone is often followed by alder or wet shrubs and finally the conifer swamps.

Door County's Rich Botanical Heritage—the Ridges Sanctuary, Toft Point, and Mud Lake. The Ridges Sanctuary together with the adjacent Toft Point Natural Area and Mud Lake Wildlife area protect a large and diverse wetlands complex. These well-known wetlands occur in concentric swales between ridges laid down historically when lake levels were advancing and retreating over the last 1,000 years. The swales encompass a range of conditions, from standing water to moist soil, and from open sun to complete shade. This variety of environmental conditions spread across sites of different ages creates a diversity of habitats that support an impressive array of plant species that are rare throughout most of Wisconsin. Winds off the cool waters of Lake Michigan provide a cool, moist climate that supports plants more commonly found further north. Conifer swamps occur together with calcareous sedge-dominated wetlands, resembling rich boreal fens.

Except for some upland forests at Toft Point, most of this area was logged. Some areas subsequently burned, but the forests have never been converted to other land uses. Thus, the hydrology remains largely intact, and the land has been managed as a natural area since the 1930s. Although this wetlands complex has been altered by human activities, it still supports considerable biodiversity and is of great conservation importance. A similar but smaller set of ridges and swales are preserved within Point Beach State Park in Manitowoc County and at Jackson Harbor Ridges on Washington Island in the Grand Traverse chain (chapter 9). Another similarly valuable wetland complex occurs within the low ridge and swale topography adjacent to Lake Michigan at Chiwaukee Prairie in Kenosha County.

Green Bay

A large proportion of the wetlands on Lake Michigan occur along the west shore of Green Bay where the nearly level contour is well suited to form wetlands. Early French settlers described vast marshes of wild rice here, along with extensive swamps of conifers, black ash, and speckled alder. Some reports described "rushes," "reeds," or "grasses" for the wetlands, but these labels are used loosely even today. The deepwater marshes were probably similar to those that remain in the Kakagon Sloughs of Lake Superior where wild rice and pickerelweed are abundant. Surveyors' notes from 1832–66 describe extensive swamps of tamarack, white cedar, black ash, and speckled alder. Large areas of marsh, wet prairie, and probably sedge meadow occurred as well. These wetlands likely included the widespread native wetland species still found there today like tussock, lake, and water sedges; blue-joint grass; Joe-pye weed; and swamp milkweed.

Green Bay wetland vegetation surveys from the early 1940s noted large populations of wild rice, wild celery, hard-stem bulrush, soft-stem bulrush, three-square bulrush, bur-reed, and common arrowhead. These species probably occurred here before European settlement. At that time, beavers must have played a major role in the rivers and streams along Lake Michigan by retaining water in ponds, trapping suspended sediments, and slowing water flows to Green Bay. Since then, the removal of beaver via trapping may have dramatically affected stream flows and thus coastal wetlands, but we have no way of knowing just what these changes are.

Widespread logging proceeded quickly in the region over the last half of the 19th century into the early 20th century. With logging came widespread change. Forest cover was lost and dams were constructed to float logs to downstream mills and ports. These sawmills deposited huge volumes of bark, sawdust, and other wood wastes directly into nearby streams and lakes. Logging also brought giant slash fires in the Lake Michigan watershed, including the famous Peshtigo Fire of 1871. Reports describe how the peat burned for weeks where the swamps once stood, killing seed-producing trees and destroying many of the soils that might have otherwise allowed the swamps to recover (Wells 1983).

During the early settlement period, water-based transportation provided the most cost-effective way to export resources, especially timber. After the logging boom, settlers established farms and homes through the watershed. As the population grew, so did the road network. Seasonal flooding of roads was reduced by constructing roadside ditches designed to accelerate the flow of water away from the land and into nearby lakes and rivers. These ditches also drained the coastal wetlands and continue to do so. Together, this lumbering, the fires, and these shifts in hydrology exacted a heavy toll on the vegetation, converting extensive swamps of white cedar, tamarack, black spruce, and black ash into disturbed forests dominated by cottonwood, green ash, American elm, and crack willow.

The open wetlands of Green Bay also underwent substantial changes since European settlement. The Bosley (1978) report on the Green Bay wetlands estimated that 60% of the coastal marshes were lost following settlement along with an even larger percentage of the coastal swamps. Sadly, the extensive wild rice populations that once stretched many kilometers along the shore are now gone from Green Bay. We are not sure why, but declines in water quality and the introduction of carp are prime suspects (chapter 16).

Newcomers—Invasive Species. A dramatic new element has appeared in Lake Michigan's coastal wetlands—invasive plants. These species are displacing native plants, causing catastrophic change in coastal wetlands including protected areas and high-quality remnants. In recent decades, extensive marshy areas have been overrun by nearly pure stands of reed canary grass (as has happened elsewhere; see chapter 15). Common reed grass invaded even more strikingly during a recent episode of low water in Lake Michigan. Since the late 1990s, hundreds of acres of exposed lakebed and adjacent marsh and wet meadow have become dominated by common reed, excluding almost all other species in these shallow marsh and sedge meadow communities. Judging from areas that have been invaded for several years, many native species may disappear from this region. Purple loosestrife is also invading shallow marsh and wet meadow areas near Green Bay. While it is a not as pervasive as reed canary grass and common reed grass, it too will probably displace native species, including cattails and most other plants of the shallow marsh and sedge meadow communities. Flowering rush, a more recent invasive, is not yet a serious problem in coastal wetlands but has become strongly invasive elsewhere. Because it tolerates deeper water than these other invasive species, it may threaten other marsh zones previously free of invasive plants.

Large areas previously in sedge meadow, shrub carr, alder thicket, and wet forest have now been infested by thick stands of glossy buckthorn. In many places, wet forest canopies are still dominated by native species, but the understory is dominated by glossy buckthorn. The future of these wetlands is in jeopardy and many wetland plants will be severely reduced or lost entirely in these systems if current trends continue. These invasive plants are collectively reducing wetland habitats for native species, dramatically reducing biodiversity. Unfortunately, many still do not fully appreciate the serious threat to natural ecosystems posed by continuing expansions in populations of invasive species.

Can We Restore Wisconsin's Coastal Marshes?

Much of the degradation we see in Wisconsin's coastal marshes reflects shifts in the hydrology of streams, lakes, and the Great Lakes themselves. It will be difficult or impossible to restore our coastal wetlands if we do not first restore this function. Although dams are accepted features along many of our state's riverways, dams and levees are also now being removed in an effort to restore normal flows and normal fluctuations in flow (chapters 12 and 17). Once we restore hydrologic processes, it should be possible to restore coastal wetlands. However, opinions as how to preserve and restore coastal wetlands differ widely among interested parties, reflecting the tension that surrounds many conservation efforts.

Which coastal wetlands should we strive to restore first? Northern coastal marshes are fairly intact and have fewer problems related to invasive species and degraded water quality. This suggests that northern coastal wetlands might represent a wise investment of conservation dollars. Their size, high quality, and promise make them cheaper to protect and restore than more degraded wetlands. In addition, human population pressures are less pronounced, and it is certainly easier to prevent invasions of exotic species than to eradicate them once they arrive (chapter 30). However, the Lake Michigan wetlands are more in need of immediate protection. The large human population in the watershed could support a large citizen-based monitoring program, extensive invasive species control efforts, and opportunities for environmental education. Thus, there are good arguments for restoring wetlands along the shores of both Great Lakes, assuming that funding agencies, resource managers, and conservation organizations also recognize these needs and are willing to provide the support so desperately needed.

References

Bosley, T. R. 1978. Loss of wetlands on the west shore of Green Bay. Transactions of the Wisconsin Academy of Sciences, Arts, and Letters 66:235–245.

Fitzpatrick, F. A., and J. C. Knox. 2000. Spatial and temporal sensitivity of hydrogeomorphic response and recovery to deforestation, agriculture, and floods. Physical Geography 21:89–108.

Herdendorf, C. E., S. M. Hartley, and M. D. Barnes, eds. 1981. Fish and wildlife resources of the Great Lakes coastal wetlands within the United States. U.S. Fish and Wildlife Service Report No. FWS/OBS-81/02-v1–6, Fort Snelling, MN.

Lynch, E. A., and K. Saltonstall. 2002. Paleoecological and genetic analyses provide evidence for recent expansion of native *Phragmites australis* populations in a Lake Superior wetland. Wetlands 22:637–646.

Odum, E. P. 1969. The strategy of ecoystem development. Science 164: 262–270.

Wells, R. 1983. Fire at Peshtigo. Madison, WI: Northword.

15 Southern Wisconsin's Herbaceous Wetlands: Their Recent History and Precarious Future

Joy B. Zedler and Kenneth W. Potter

A Wetland by Any Name Is Just as Sweet

Readers of this book, you are probably acutely aware that wetlands are of critical importance. But few know that the term "wetland" is quite new (Zedler et al. 1998). In his classic analysis of Wisconsin's vegetation, John Curtis (1959) referred to wet plant communities by a variety of names, but wetlands was not one of them. He treated those with woody vegetation (shrub carrs and alder thickets) in a section with savannas, and herbaceous wetlands in a section entitled "lesser communities." These latter are our focus, and unlike Curtis we consider them to be "greater communities" in terms of the ecosystem services they provide, such as wildlife habitat, water filtering, and flood abatement.

Curtis (1959) recognized five types of herbaceous wetlands. Fens are open areas with wet, peaty soils that are usually alkaline due to the seepage of calcareous groundwater. Grasses and forbs dominate fens. Bogs are similarly wet and open but their water and peat is acidic (usually due to *Sphagnum* moss), and they are dominated by herbs and low shrubs. Sedge meadows occur on wet organic soils and are dominated by sedges. Wet prairies are dominated by grasses and water-tolerant prairie plants. Marshes have standing water and are usually dominated by emergent cattails and/or reeds. At the same time Curtis was working,

Wisconsin's Game Management Division (GMD) was busily mapping wetlands in 14 southeastern counties, identifying seven types of wetland: fresh meadow, shallow marsh, deep marsh, pothole, bog, shrub swamp, and timber swamp (GMD 1960–63). Since then, Amon and others (2002) recognize five herbaceous wetland types largely consistent with Curtis (bogs, fens, meadow, wet prairie, and marsh) based on differences in water flow, saturation, inundation, fluctuation in water levels, conductivity, and organic to mineral content of soil.

In this chapter, we describe the origin of Wisconsin's wetlands and characterize changes in herbaceous wetlands, mostly since the 1950s. This is a challenge, as historical documentation is slim. Curtis (1959) characterized southern sedge meadows using only 44 sites, and his description of fens relies on just six. Regrettably, the only data available are species lists by site, and his book devotes fewer than 20 pages to the herbaceous wetlands of southern Wisconsin. Fortunately, scattered descriptions of the state's fens, meadows, bogs, and marshes have appeared since 1959. In 1974, Jim Zimmerman joined Barbara Bedford and Elizabeth Zimmerman in compiling descriptions of Dane County wetlands. In the 1980s, Carol Johnston (1982, 1984) conducted the state's second major wetland inventory, although it lacks details of species composition. Various other scientists contributed accounts of wetlands, for example, Carpenter's (1995) and Reed's (2002) treatises on fens, Middleton's (2002a, 2002b) work on sedge meadows, and work on Great Lakes coastal wetlands by Meeker and Fewless (chapter 14) and Frieswyk and Zedler (2007). Extensive mapping and assessment of wetlands in southeastern Wisconsin (SEWRPC 1997) provide more recent data. Accounts of wetland plants appear in standard floras (Fassett 1957, updated by Crow and Hellquist 2000; Eggers and Reed 1997). More information about wetland animals can be found in several sources (Hobbs and Jass 1988; Hilsenhoff 1995; Christoffel et al. 2001; Legler et al. 2003; see also the bibliography in Thompson and Luthin 2004).

Despite a history of loss, numerous Wisconsin wetlands remain. While many high quality sites persist, evidence points to degradation over the past 50 years. In this chapter, we describe the region's vanishing wetland heritage, evaluate current conditions, and identify strategies for effective wetland conservation and restoration.

Hydrogeomorphology of Southern Wisconsin Wetlands

During the Pleistocene, glacial ice eroded hilltops and deposited the sediment in low areas, effectively blocking many streams and rivers. After the ice melted, large glacial lakes formed. The force exerted by these massive lakes eventually cut through the sediments deposited by the glaciers, partially or fully draining glacial lakes (Martin 1965; Bedford et al. 1974; Clayton and Attig 1989). Groundwater gradually rose to barely cover the flat basins left by the glaciers and glacial lakes. Where water was sufficiently shallow, vegetation moved into these wet areas, creating wetlands. Glaciers deposited different kinds of soils in different areas influencing the kinds of vegetation that colonized. The abundance and diversity of wetlands throughout much of Wisconsin today reflects the actions of glaciers over the past million years.

Groundwater flows provide the major source of water for Wisconsin wetlands. During wet periods, however, these wetlands also receive surface water from precipitation and from the overflow of adjacent streams and lakes. A small number of wetlands formed in depressions that were never subsequently drained by streams. These unique, isolated wetlands receive water primarily from precipitation and surface runoff instead of groundwater.

In the unglaciated portion of southwestern Wisconsin, wetlands are much less abundant. Here, wetlands formed in stream valleys and in river floodplains (Novitzki 1982). The rugged topography of the Driftless Area generally favored the formation of natural springs. Today, springs serve as a primary source of groundwater to the large number of small wetlands in this region.

A recent study of wetland surface features (or geomorphology) by McDermott et al. (2007) shows how important the underlying geology, water flow, and soils are in shaping the wetland biota. Three wetland types are found in Cherokee Marsh. The difference in elevation among these types is minor, but groundwater supply rates and soils are very different. For example, a fen overlies fine sand at 5 feet below the surface with a continuous discharge of low-nutrient groundwater. In contrast, marsh overlies silt loam where surface soils become stagnant and nutrients accumulate. The sedge meadow occurs between the two, with 3.5 feet of peat overlying silty sand and medium sand layers. Groundwater influence is intermediate, with a late-season drawdown. The historical patterns of water flow and sediment deposition have lasting effects on wetland vegetation.

Wetland Losses

Wetlands are destroyed when they are drained, filled, or dredged. According to Dahl (1990), Wisconsin lost 46% of its total wetland area between the 1780s and 1980s, declining from 9.8 to 5.3 million acres. The exact timing of these losses is difficult to determine. Many wetlands were drained and filled following the passage of the federal Swamp Lands Act of 1850, but the program was notoriously corrupt. States routinely overstated the amount of land reclaimed under the Act as a way to increase budget revenues (Vileisis 1997). Changes in some wetlands have been documented. In 1852, a noteworthy tamarack swamp and wet meadow known as Buena Vista Marsh covered over 51,000 acres. A century later, only a quarter of the marsh supported wetland vegetation (figure 15.1; Zedler 1966). In 14 southeastern counties, about 33% of the wetland area was lost between the 1930s and the 1950s (table 15.1). SEWRPC (1997) reports a 40% loss for seven southeastern counties between 1836 and 1990, ranging from a 70% in Milwaukee County to 0.2% in Ozaukee County.

Detailed maps of 14 southeastern Wisconsin counties derived from 1950s era aerial photographs identify over 25,000 wetlands, covering almost 570,000 acres (GMD 1960–63). The largest area (55%) was occupied by fresh meadow, with timber swamp, shallow marsh, and shrub swamp each contributing 13%, deep marsh about 6%, and potholes and bogs under 1% (table 15.2). Comparing this with a less detailed inventory in 1934–39 indicates that counties lost varying amounts ranging from 12% for Jefferson County to 55% for Green County and 62% for Kenosha County during the preceding two decades. Size distributions (table 15.3) show that 29% of wetlands were less than 2 acres in size, while 13% of the region's wetlands exceeded 40 acres. About 40% of the wetlands had some history of livestock grazing.

We wondered if the state's most recent wetland inventory (based mostly on 1978 aerial photos; Johnston 1982, 1984; Johnston and Meysembourg 2002) would reveal further losses in wetland area, so we asked Jennifer Koehler to calculate wetland areas for the counties inventoried by GMD (1960–63). Answering this question became more difficult than we expected. Because wetlands were classified differently in the 1980s, we could not directly compare acreages of wetland types between the two time periods. Still, we were surprised to see total wetland area increase by 26% over the 24-year period (table 15.3). In discussions with Carol Johnston and others, we learned that the later surveys were more inclusive of wetlands, in part because mappers are now better able to identify wetlands from air photos. As a result, we cannot distinguish the increase due to different mapping criteria from real, on-the-ground increases in wetlands.

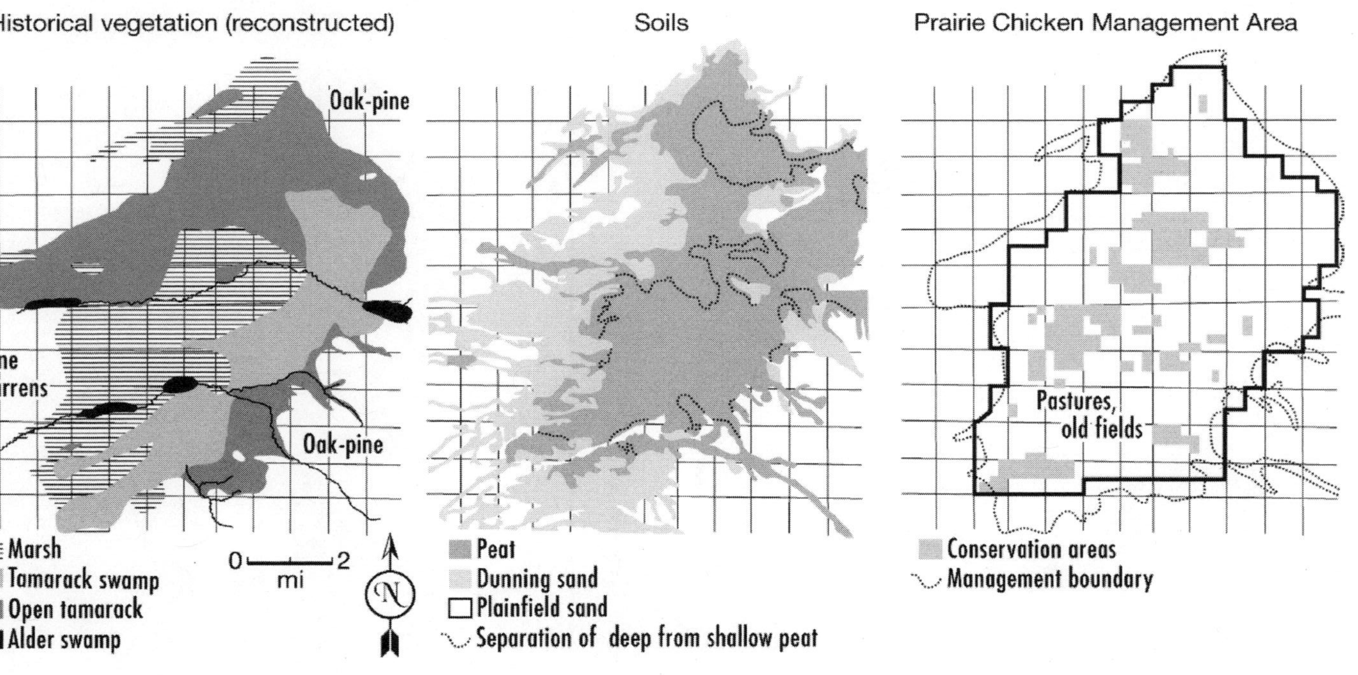

FIGURE 15.1 Changes at Buena Vista Marsh. Buena Vista Marsh covered about 51,546 acres of south-central Wisconsin in 1852; a century later, only 26% of the site was wet enough to support wetland vegetation, due to drainage for crops and pastures, subsequent peat fires, and agricultural activities (Zedler 1966).

Table 15.1 Summary of data from the Wisconsin Wetland Inventory: Area and sites

County	1934–39 (acres)	1954–59 (acres)	Area difference (%)	1954–59	
				No. of sites	No. grazed
Columbia	63,763	55,181	−13.4	2,445	941
Dane	67,277	44,599	−33.7	1,988	1,023
Dodge	127,279	89,378	−29.8	2,382	1,156
Fond du Lac	63,393	52,770	−16.8	1,855	899
Green	15,777	7,135	−54.8	562	362
Green Lake	59,312	44,435	−25.1	1,152	756
Jefferson	76,963	67,920	−11.7	2,747	366
Kenosha	20,615	10,159	−62.5	1,896	459
Marquette	84,614	69,418	−18.1	1,681	396
Racine	14,932	10,159	−31.9	1,317	250
Rock	33,775	20,311	−39.9	1,330	391
Walworth	36,115	27,254	−24.5	1,443	830
Waukesha	55,481	40,891	−26.3	1,852	730
Winnebago	47,368	32,550	−31.3	877	577
Total	746,049	562,001	−24.67	21,631	8,677

Source: Game Management Division (1960–63), based on air photos taken in 1934–39 and in 1954–59 (plus on-the-ground visits).

Table 15.2 Summary of data from the Wisconsin Wetland Inventory: Types of wetlands

Value	Fresh meadow	Shallow marsh	Deep marsh	Pothole	Shrub swamp	Timber swamp	Bog
Area							
Total (acres)	307,005	76,477	33,537	3,749	70,809	74,685	904
% of total	54.6	13.6	6.0	0.7	12.6	13.3	0.2
Count							
Total no.	10,492	7,274	601	1,429	2,963	2,178	118
% of total	52.0	36.0	3.0	7.0	15.0	11.0	1.0

Source: Game Management Division (1960–63), based on air photos taken in 1934–39 and in 1954–59 (plus on-the-ground visits).
Note: Fresh meadow = smartweeds, grasses, sedges, forbs, and sometimes burreed; shallow marsh = cattails, river rush, bulrushes, and spikerushes; deep marsh = similar to shallow marsh but water from 0.5 to 3 feet deep during growing season; shrub swamp = alder, willow, dogwoods, etc.; timber swamp = tamarack, black spruce, black ash, balsam, etc.; pothole = pond or stock watering area with grass and/or weeds; bog = leatherleaf, cranberries, and Labrador tea.

In addition to being about 30 years old, the 1978 inventory reveals little about wetland quality. We do not know if some wetland types are being lost more rapidly than others, or the extent to which their condition has degraded. The 1978 inventory reveals that emergent/wet meadow remained the most extensive wetland type (49%), followed by forested

Table 15.3 Wetland size distributions in 1950–59 and 1978–86 for 14 southeastern Wisconsin counties

	Size (acres)						
Period	0–2	3–5	6–10	11–20	21–40	41–80	>80
1950–59							
Total no.	6,282	3,922	3,684	3,452	2,655	1,535	1,201
% of total	29.0	18.1	17.0	16.0	12.3	7.1	6.0
1978–86							
Total no.	11,966	7,947	7,753	6,782	4,440	2,078	1,214
% of total	34.4	22.8	22.3	19.5	12.8	6.0	3.5

Sources: The earlier data are from Game Management Division (1960–63); the later data were calculated by J. Koehler at our request.

Note: Data for 1978–86 were reported for polygons in all counties; additional point data for wetlands greater than 2 acres were available for only five of the 14 counties. Hence the proportion of small wetlands is underestimated.

(18%) and scrub/shrub (18%) types. Size data reveal that many small wetlands may be replacing fewer large ones (table 15.3).

The limitations of existing data sources point to the need for standardized inventory and monitoring if we are to effectively track changes in wetland type, area, and quality. For a subset of counties, SEWRPC (1997) inventories wetlands every five years. An expanded inventory and monitoring system that sampled within watersheds and among ecoregions could provide many insights into how wetlands are changing. Standard audits at 10-year intervals would greatly augment the occasional documentation of change over time (e.g., Zedler 1966; Vogl 1969). Such regular surveys would also allow us to confidently evaluate the cumulative effects of policy, management, climate change, and inadvertent impacts to wetlands at a broad scale.

Wetland Degradation I: Environmental Disturbances

Many remaining wetlands exhibit varying degrees of degradation. Some wetland impacts are due to direct manipulation of wetland systems. Other impacts are indirect, reflecting the pressures of population growth and the intensification of land use.

Wetlands can be altered directly in several ways including mowing and livestock grazing, creating cranberry farms, discharging heated effluent into wetlands, manipulating water levels, channelizing creeks, and building roads. In the late 1950s, livestock grazing occurred commonly in wetlands (table 15.1). Middleton (2002a) documented the detrimental effects of cattle on sedge meadows on her family farm near Lodi by comparing four sites. One site served as an ungrazed reference site, one was heavily grazed since about 1900, another was lightly grazed, and one was heavily grazed until 1977, when it was fenced and allowed to recover. She found that the reference site remained shrubless, while shrubs invaded grazed areas as sedges were eaten and the tussocks were shortened by hoof damage. Hence, "Cattle grazing promoted the invasion of woody species such as gray dogwood and ultimately set the stage for the development of a shrub carr in the recovery sedge meadow" (Middleton 2002a, 97). Besides grazing wet meadows, farmers often mowed them for hay, especially during dry growing seasons. As these farmers shifted to alfalfa cultivation, shrubs invaded abandoned hay meadows (White 1965).

In western Wisconsin, wetlands were flooded and planted to create cranberry farms. Simultaneously, nearby wetlands were affected by water-level manipulations and materials discharged from cranberry farms (Jorgensen and Nauman 1994). Near Portage, the discharge of heated water from a power plant completely eliminated a large area of marsh vegetation (Ellison and Bedford 1995). In Madison, drainage, channelization of creeks, and road construction in the Monona Wetlands Conservancy altered hydrologic conditions, shifting vegetation toward invasive species (Owen 1999).

Wetlands are further altered by the combination of fire suppression and surface water management. In large areas around Lake Winnebago, water-level management has altered extensive areas of native cattail marshes (Bodensteiner and Gabriel 2003; Hu et al. 2003). Although common reed has replaced cattails in some areas, the reed marshes are now declining. Plant rhizomes are damaged by ice in winter when lake levels are lowered and by heat and anoxia in summer when water levels are raised. Where dams stabilize the water levels, nearby wetland vegetation is degraded. Vogl (1969) concluded that alternating flooding during wet years and fire during drought years kept the state's marshes, sedge meadows, and wet prairies from being invaded by woody vegetation. If he was correct, modern efforts to reduce flooding and eliminate fire are further diminishing herbaceous wetlands. Smaller, lower quality wetlands filter and store less floodwater, recharge less groundwater, provide less and poorer habitat for wildlife, and support fewer native species (SEWRPC 1997).

Agricultural development in the Driftless Area led to extensive soil erosion (Knox 2002). More than half of this eroded soil never left the watershed as most was deposited on stream and river floodplains (Beach 1994). Today, several meters of eroded soil covers the original floodplain (Knox 2002). This undoubtedly degraded the floodplain's wetlands but these impacts are undocumented. In the rest of the state, soil erosion due to agricultural development has been less severe but is still a cause of significant wetland degradation.

Upstream, off-site disturbances such as agriculture and urbanization runoff increase the nutrient, sediment, and toxic contaminant loads to wetlands (Owen 1999; Werner and Zedler 2002; Zedler 2003). Owen (1995, 1999) noted that surface water flows in the Nine Springs watershed increased 20-fold between 1850 and 1990, while groundwater sources likely decreased. The combined effect of excess water, nutrients, and sediments created ideal habitat for invasive plant species (Maurer and Zedler 2002; Kercher and Zedler 2004). By the time that invasive plants are dominant, most of the native species have been extirpated (Kercher et al. 2007; Frieswyk et al. 2008).

Wetland Degradation II: Invasive Species

Invasive species are a major threat facing Wisconsin's ecosystems, including wetlands (see chapter 30). Invasive graminoids, such as hybrid cattail, reed canary grass, and common reed, tend to form single-species stands, excluding native species (Owen 1999; Kercher and Zedler 2004). Nutrient enrichment, often in the form of fertilizers transported in surface water, reduces overall plant species diversity. In the Arboretum's Gardner Marsh, Isa Woo found that lawn fertilizer additions enabled the hybrid cattail to expand its distribution and double its biomass (Woo and Zedler 2002). Historically, this diverse meadow was dominated by bluejoint grass and sedges, with cattails limited to small areas (Irwin 1973). Today, invasive cattails form single-species stands across much of the marsh and the sedge meadows are limited to small areas (Woo and Zedler 2002). With cattails "on the march," it is only a matter of time before the remaining sedge meadow and its diversity of native plants will be lost. Frieswyk et al. (2008) expect many of Wisconsin's coastal wetlands to follow a similar path as invasive cattails thrive across a broader range of hydrological conditions than do native sedge meadow species. The increasing dominance by invasive cattails in Peter's Marsh, Green Bay, demonstrates that coastal wetlands are quite vulnerable and might degrade rapidly in the near future (chapter 14).

The invasive reed canary grass appears to be responsible for the greatest loss in quality of southern Wisconsin wetlands. This highly invasive strain was likely introduced from Europe. It has become so abundant and widespread that Wisconsin Department of Natural Resources (WDNR) can map it from space (Bernthal and Willis 2004). Of the

737,000 acres of wetlands evaluated, 11% were in a heavily degraded condition, with over 80% cover of reed canary grass. The 2004 WDNR inventory covers wetlands across the southern half of the state, excluding only the Lake Michigan coastal counties and five counties on the western border. Compared with reed canary grass, purple loosestrife is a distant second-place invader of wetlands, dominating less than 5% of Wisconsin's wetlands. In a separate WDNR study, reed canary grass was found in 57 of the 74 small (less than 4 acres) depressional wetlands sampled in 2000 and classified as abundant to dominant in over half of the sites where it occurred (Lillie et al. 2002).

Reed canary grass benefits from nutrients (Maurer and Zedler 2002), sedimentation (Werner and Zedler 2002) and hydrological disturbance (Maurer et al. 2002; Miller and Zedler 2003; Kercher et al. 2007). It is prone to form single species stands where sediments accumulate and transform tussock meadows into more uniform floodplains. Experiments back up this assertion. Kercher et al. (2007) found that continuous flooding, high nutrient inputs, and the addition of nutrient-rich sediment interact to accelerate reed canary grass invasion. The invasion process involved two steps. Flooding killed many of the native wet prairie species, opening the canopy and making more light available for reed canary grass growth (Lindig-Cisneros and Zedler 2002).

Bernthal and Willis (2004) found a correlation between the fraction of wetlands dominated by reed canary grass and the fraction of agricultural land use in the watershed. They assert that reed canary grass is the state's "single most dominant plant in emergent, open canopy wetlands, and should be considered of great concern for wetland managers" (Bernthal and Willis 2004, 39). Many of the wetlands with heavy dominance by reed canary grass are in Dodge, Dane, Green, Green Lake, and Jefferson counties—five counties that GMD realized had wetlands at risk of losing wildlife habitat in 1960, although there is no indication that GMD recognized the impending threat of invasive plants. Elsewhere, Barnes (1999) documented rapid expansion of reed canary grass within the lower Chippewa River. Nearly all of the lowest elevations of a small island became dominated by reed canary grass between 1981 and 1996, while native plant species declined.

Where reed canary grass and cattails dominate, fewer species occur and the species that do persist are of low floristic quality. In field sites where hydrological disturbance has occurred (via culverts and drainage ditches) and in plots where reed canary grass is present, floristic quality is lower than in reference sites lacking the invader (Kercher et al. 2007). The same is true for native species coexisting with native species versus invasive cattails (Frieswyk et al. 2008). In contrast to the invasive species, our native tussock sedge actually facilitates the co-occurrence of other species, including species of high floristic quality. It does this by building tussocks that support the growth of other species. A larger surface area of tussocks supports more species (Werner and Zedler 2002; Peach and Zedler 2006). When sediments bury tussocks, invasive species can colonize. We expect the trend toward invasive species dominance to continue. Southern Wisconsin's herbaceous wetlands are at great risk of losing all but the most aggressive native plants. Bluejoint grass, marsh milkweed, swamp aster, Joe-pye-weed, sneezeweed, and a few sedges and rushes might be the only plants that persist in the wake of current invaders.

Can Restoration Reverse Degradation?

The United States has pledged to increase both the quantity and quality of wetlands (National Wetlands Policy Forum 1988). With drainage for agriculture a major cause of wetland loss and increased nutrient-enriched runoff a major cause of degradation among remaining wetlands, this will be challenging. Although Wisconsin takes full advantage of federal funds earmarked for restoring wetlands (e.g., Wetland Reserve Programs), few of the state's restored wetlands have been evaluated scientifically. Restoring water to sites is relatively easy; restoring the full complement of native species and ecosystem services is more difficult. Although many landowners show more interest in open water than vegetated wetlands (Kitchen 2002), there is demand for information on how to restore wetlands ecologically. The Wisconsin *Wetland Restoration Handbook* was first published in 2000 and is already in its second edition (Thompson and Luthin 2004).

Few studies have characterized how restored wetlands differ from natural ones (Hunt et al. 1996, 1997, 1999). Owen and others (1989) and Ashworth (1997) reported on wetlands restored by the Wisconsin Department of Transportation following the construction of a causeway for Madison's beltline highway. The mitigation project involved replacing fill with salvaged sedge meadow soil (and its seed bank). The restoration sites were initially diverse, although cattail was a major component (Owen et al. 1989). Five years after construction, both restoration sites had more species than the reference site (Ashworth 1997). Wetlands biologist Quinten Carpenter (personal communication) noted that following a series of flood years, the restored area became dominated by invasive cattails. Similarly, cattail cover in 11 constructed wetlands in southeastern Wisconsin increased from 15% to 55% in three years, leading Reinartz and Warne (1993) to predict the sites would become single-species cattail marshes. Weedy plant species are likewise abundant in hundreds of shallow isolated wetlands in Ozaukee County.

While creating and restoring former wetlands represents a major challenge, wetlands that are less disturbed show more promise for regaining biodiversity. Middleton (2002b) employed burning to reduce shrub cover in formerly grazed sedge meadows near Lodi. While fire had little effect on woody plants, herbaceous species richness was enhanced, including the appearance of some species not seen in decades. Kost and De Steven (2000) also used fire to sustain forb diversity in sedge meadows. Fire shows promise for maintaining plant diversity, but burning is a two-edged sword. Many invasive plants exploit the gaps created by fire. High light conditions facilitate germination of reed canary grass seeds (Lindig-Cisneros and Zedler 2002) and establishment of vegetative propagules that float into such openings (Maurer and Zedler 2002).

The Future

Remaining wetlands face multiple threats. Many have hydrologic regimes that are either disrupted or face disruption. Channel dredging and straightening have lowered water tables, altering the frequency and duration of overbank flooding. Upstream development has introduced summer runoff to systems that historically experienced summer drawdown. Agricultural development has led to high sediment and nutrient loads, facilitating the growth of aggressive invasive plants. Increasingly, urbanization and groundwater pumping near cities is lowering groundwater levels, reducing groundwater discharge to wetlands. Few of these impacts can be easily abated. Summer runoff, for example, will be hard to limit, although restoring wetland vegetation along stream channels will often improve the functioning of wetlands.

Because most of the state is not public land, the future of wetland functioning lies in the hands of rural and urban private landowners. We hope that the current trend for Wisconsin landowners to enroll increasing areas of their property in wetland protection programs will continue. Still, setting aside wetlands is only the first step. In most cases, we need to restore and manage both individual wetlands and networks of wetlands throughout entire landscapes.

Invasive plants are a serious, widespread threat to the integrity of remaining wetlands. Without substantial progress in controlling the most aggressive species (reed canary grass, invasive cattails, purple loosestrife, and common reed), diverse wetlands will continue to shift toward impoverished, single-species stands. A key strategy for slowing degradation of wetlands is to restore wetlands in strategic locations within watersheds (Knutson et al. 1999; Richardson and Gatti 1999; Zedler 2003). A recent group of University of Wisconsin Water Resources Management students recommends evaluating wetland resources at the approximate 100 square-mile watershed scale. They suggest identifying significant remnant wetlands, then seeking upstream sites to restore where wetlands could reduce nutrient and sediment exports. Two watersheds within the Upper Rock River Basin offer models for strategic wetland restoration.

We have few data on wetland biodiversity or how it has changed through time. Because the state's wetland heritage is poorly quantified, we recommend mapping and tracking the quantity and quality of remaining wetlands, by type, within watersheds. A subset of each should then be intensively tracked for plant and animal diversity, soils, and water quality and hydrology.

We support efforts by the state to retain viable populations of all extant native species. Where remnant wetlands are too small to sustain populations, we suggest using novel approaches to manage populations. For example, we could introduce and grow native species in wet depressions along freeway rights-of-way, storm water basins, golf courses, and city parks (Bonilla-Warford and Zedler 2002). To prevent invasive species from displacing the planted natives, we should better publicize the benefits of our rich wetland biodiversity heritage, encourage gardening of public wetland areas, and adopt better pest control measures as they become available.

Wisconsinites should be proud of their wetland heritage as well as their recent history of wetland protection. Wisconsin has retained more of its original wetlands than many other states. Extensive wetlands here still sustain plant and wildlife diversity. Wisconsin was also the first state to protect isolated wetlands after the Supreme Court's recent ruling that such wetlands were not regulated by the Clean Water Act. The WDNR's Natural Areas include many wetlands of several types throughout the state (WDNR 2003). The Nature Conservancy also protects other wetlands, particularly in the Mukwonago River watershed and at Quincy Bluff. Other nongovernmental organizations are also conserving wetlands. The pride we take in these conservation efforts should not make us complacent, however. To maintain the diversity and function of wetlands, we need continual reconnaissance, vigilance, and stewardship.

References

Amon, J. P., C. A. Thompson, Q. J. Carpenter, and J. Miner. 2002. Temperate zone fens of the glaciated Midwestern USA. Wetlands 22: 301–317.

Ashworth, S. M. 1997. Comparison between restored and reference sedge meadow wetlands in south-central Wisconsin. Wetlands 17: 518–527.

Barnes, W. J. 1999. The rapid growth of a population of reed canarygrass (*Phalaris arundinacea* L.) and its impact on some riverbottom herbs. Journal of the Torrey Botanical Society 126:133–138.

Beach, T. 1994. The fate of eroded soil: Sediment sinks and sediment budgets of agrarian landscapes in southeastern Minnesota, 1851–1988. Annals of the Association of American Geographers 84:5–28.

Bedford, B. L., E. Zimmerman, and J. Zimmerman. 1974. *The Wetlands of Dane County, Wisconsin.* Madison: Dane County Regional Planning Commission and Wisconsin Department of Natural Resources.

Bernthal, T. W, and K. G. Willis. 2004. Using Landsat 7 imagery to map invasive reed canary grass (*Phalaris arundinacea*): A landscape level wetland monitoring methodology. U.S. Environmental Protection Agency Region V, Wisconsin Department of Natural Resources Publication No. SS-992-2004, Madison.

Bodensteiner, L. R., and A. O. Gabriel. 2003. Response of mid-water common reed stands to water level variations and winter conditions in Lake Poygan, Wisconsin, USA. Aquatic Botany 76:49–64.

Bonilla-Warford, C. M., and J. B. Zedler. 2002. Potential for using native plant species in stormwater wetlands. Environmental Management 29:385–394.

Carpenter, Q. 1995. Toward a new definition of calcareous fen for Wisconsin (USA). Ph.D. diss., University of Wisconsin–Madison.

Christoffel, R., R. Hay, and M. Wolfgram. 2001. *Amphibians of Wisconsin.* Madison: Wisconsin Department of Natural Resources Bureau of Endangered Resources.

Clayton, L., and J. W. Attig. 1989. Glacial Lake Wisconsin. Boulder, CO: Geological Society of America.

Crow, G. E., and C. B. Hellquist. 2000. Aquatic and Wetland Plants of Northeastern North America: A Revised and Enlarged Edition of Norman C. Faett's "A Manual of Aquatic Plants." Vols. 1 and 2. Madison: University of Wisconsin Press.

Curtis, J. T. 1959. The Vegetation of Wisconsin. Madison: University of Wisconsin Press.

Dahl, T. 1990. Wetlands: Losses in the United States 1780's to 1980's. Washington, DC: U.S. Department of the Interior, Fish and Wildlife Service.

Eggers, S. D., and D. M. Reed. 1997. Wetland Plants and Plant Communities of Minnesota and Wisconsin. 2nd ed. St. Paul, MN: U.S. Army Corps of Engineers.

Ellison, A. M., and B. L. Bedford. 1995. Response of a wetland vascular plant community to disturbance—A simulation study. Ecological Applications 5:109–123.

Fassett, N. C. 1957. *A* Manual of Aquatic Plants. 2nd ed. Madison: University of Wisconsin Press.

Frieswyk, C. B., C. Johnston, and J. B. Zedler. 2008. Quantifying and qualifying dominance in vegetation. Journal of Great Lakes Research 33:125–135.

Frieswyk, C. B., and J. B. Zedler 2007. Vegetation change in Great Lakes coastal wetlands: Deviation from the historical cycle. Journal of Great Lakes Research 33(2):360–380.

Game Management Division (GMD). 1960–63. Wisconsin Wetland Inventory. Madison: Game Management Division, Wisconsin Conservation Department. (Thirteen separate reports covering 14 counties.)

Hilsenhoff, W. I. 1995. Aquatic Insects of Wisconsin: Keys to Wisconsin Genera and Notes on Biology, Habitat, Distribution and Species. Madison: Natural History Museums Council, University of Wisconsin.

Hobbs, H. H., III, and J. P. Jass. 1988. The Crayfishes and Shrimp of Wisconsin. Milwaukee: Milwaukee Public Museum.

Hu, S. F., A. O. Gabriel, and L. R. Bodensteiner. 2003. Inventory and characterization of wetland habitat on the Winnebago Upper Pool Lakes, Wisconsin, USA: An integrated multimedia-GIS approach. *Wetlands* 23:82–94.

Hunt, R. J., D. P. Krabbenhoft, and M. P. Anderson. 1996. Groundwater inflow measurements in wetland systems. Water Resources Research 32:495–507.

———. 1997. Assessing hydrogeochemical heterogeneity in natural and constructed wetlands. Biogeochemistry 39:271–293.

Hunt, J. J., J. F. Walker, and D. P. Krabbenhoft. 1999. Characterizing hydrology and the importance of ground-water discharge in natural and constructed wetlands. Wetlands 19:458–472.

Irwin, H. A. 1973. A natural history study of East Marsh of the University of Wisconsin Arboretum. M.S. thesis, University of Wisconsin–Madison.

Johnston, C. A. 1982. Wetlands in the Wisconsin landscape. Wisconsin Academy Review 29:8–11.

———. 1984. Mapping Wisconsin's wetlands. Wisconsin Natural Resources 8:4–6.

Johnston, C. A., and P. Meysembourg. 2002. Comparison of the Wisconsin and National Wetlands Inventories. Wetlands 22:386–405.

Jorgensen, E. E., and L. E. Nauman. 1994. Disturbance in wetlands associated with commercial cranberry (*Vaccinium macrocarpon*) production. American Midland Naturalist 132:152–158.

Kercher, S. M., C. B. Frieswyk, and J. B. Zedler. 2003. Effects of sampling teams and estimation methods on the assessment of plant cover. Journal of Vegetation Science 14:899–906.

Kercher, S. M., A. Herr-Turoff, and J. B. Zedler. 2007. Understanding invasion as a process: The case of *Phalaris arundinacea* in wet prairies. Biological Invasions 9:657–665.

Kercher, S. M., and J. B. Zedler. 2004. Multiple disturbances accelerate invasion of reed canary grass (*Phalaris arundinacea* L.) in a mesocosm study. Oecologia 138:455–464.

Kitchen, A. 2002. An assessment of landowner participation and habitat accomplishments. Partners for Fish and Wildlife Program Monitoring Report for Wisconsin, U.S. Fish and Wildlife Service, Wisconsin Private Lands Office, Madison.

Knutson, M. G., J. R. Sauer, D.A. Olsen, M. J. Mossman, L. M. Hemesath, and M. J. Lannoo. 1999. Effects of landscape composition and wetland fragmentation on frog and toad abundance and species richness in Iowa and Wisconsin, USA. Conservation Biology 13: 1437–1446.

Knox, J. C. 2002. Agriculture, erosion, and sediment yields. Pp. 482–500 in A. R. Orme, ed. The Physical Geography of North America. Oxford: Oxford University Press.

Kost, M. A., and D. De Steven. 2000. Plant community responses to prescribed burning in Wisconsin sedge meadows. Natural Areas Journal 20:36–45.

Legler, K., and D. Legler, with D. Westover. 2003. Color Guide to Dragonflies of Wisconsin. Sauk City, WI: Karl Legler.

Lillie, R. A., P. Garrison, S. I. Dodson, R. A. Bautz, and G. LaLiberte. 2002. Refine and expansion of wetland biological indices for Wisconsin. Wisconsin Department of Natural Resources, Madison.

Lindig-Cisneros, R. A., and J. B. Zedler. 2002. Relationships between canopy complexity and germination microsites for *Phalaris arundinacea L.* Oecologia 133:159–167.

Martin, L. 1965. The Physical Geography of Wisconsin. Madison: University of Wisconsin Press.

Maurer, D. A., and J. B. Zedler. 2002. Differential invasion of a wetland grass explained by tests of nutrients and light availability on establishment and vegetative growth. Oecologia 131:279–288.

McDermott, A., J. M. Bahr, Q. J. Carpenter, and R. H. Hunt. 2007. The importance of subsurface geology for water source and vegetation communities in Cherokee Marsh, Wisconsin. Wetlands 27:189–202.

Middleton, B. 2002a. Nonequilibrium dynamics of sedge meadows grazed by cattle in southern Wisconsin. Plant Ecology 161:89–110.

———. 2002b. Winter burning and the reduction of *Cornus sericea* in sedge meadows in southern Wisconsin. Restoration Ecology 10:723–730.

Miller, R. C., and J. B. Zedler. 2003. Responses of native and invasive plants to hydroperiod and water depth. Plant Ecology 167:57–69.

National Wetlands Policy Forum. 1988. Protecting America's Wetlands: An Action Agenda. Washington, DC: The Conservation Foundation.

Novitzki, R. P. 1982. Hydrology of Wisconsin Wetlands. USGS Information Circular No. 40. Madison: U.S. Geological Survey.

Owen, C. R. 1995. Water-budget and flow patterns in an urban wetland. Journal of Hydrology 169(1–4):171–187.

———. 1999. Hydrology and history: Land use changes and ecological responses in an urban wetland. Wetlands Ecology and Management 6:209–219.

Owen, C. R., Q. J. Carpenter, and C. B. DeWitt. 1989. Evaluation of Three Wetland Restorations Associated with Highway Projects. Madison: Wisconsin Department of Transportation.

Peach, M. A., J. B. Zedler. 2006. How tussocks structure sedge meadow vegetation. *Wetlands* 26:322–335.

Reed, D. M. 2002. Environmental correlates of vegetation types in southeastern Wisconsin fens. Ph.D. diss., University of Wisconsin–Milwaukee.

Reinartz, J. A., and E. L. Warne. 1993. Development of vegetation in small created wetlands in southeastern Wisconsin. Wetlands 13:153–164.

Richardson, M. S., and R. C. Gatti. 1999. Prioritizing wetland restoration activity within a Wisconsin watershed using GIS modeling. Journal of Soil and Water Conservation. 54:537–542.

Southeastern Wisconsin Regional Planning Commission (SEWRPC). 1997. A regional natural areas and critical species habitat protection and management plan for southeastern Wisconsin. SEWRPC, Waukesha, WI.

Thompson, A., and C. Luthin. 2004. Wetland Restoration Handbook for Wisconsin Landowners. Madison: Bureau of Integrated Science Services, Wisconsin Department of Natural Resources.

Vileisis, A. 1997. Discovering the Unknown Landscape: A History of America's Wetlands. Washington, DC: Island Press.

Vogl, R. J. 1969. One hundred and thirty years of plant succession in a southeastern Wisconsin lowland. Ecology 50:248–255.

Werner, K. J., and J. B. Zedler. 2002. How sedge meadow soils, microtopography, and vegetation respond to sedimentation. Wetlands 22: 451–466.

White, K. L. 1965. Shrub carrs of southeastern Wisconsin. Ecology 46: 286–303.

Wisconsin Department of Natural Resources (WDNR). 2003. Wisconsin, naturally: A guide to 150 great State Natural Areas. WDNR, Publication No. PUB-ER-115 2003, Madison.

Woo, I., and J. B. Zedler. 2002. Can nutrients alone shift a sedge meadow towards dominance by the invasive *Typha x glauca*? Wetlands 22: 509–521.

Zedler, J. B. 1966. Buena Vista Marsh in historical perspective. M.S. thesis, University of Wisconsin–Madison.

———. 2003. Wetlands at your service: Reducing impacts of agriculture at the watershed scale. Frontiers in Ecology and Environment 1:65–72.

Zedler, J. B., M. Fellows, and S. Trnka. 1998. Wastelands to wetlands: Links between habitat protection and ecosystem science. Pp. 69–112 in P. Groffman and M. Pace, eds. Successes, Limitations and Frontiers in Ecosystem Science. New York: Springer-Verlag.

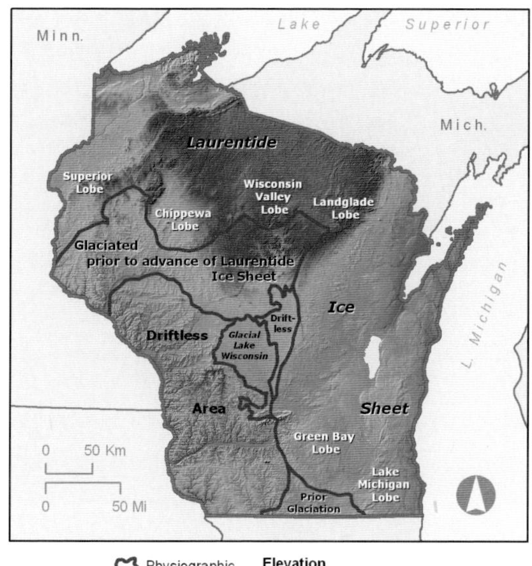

PLATE 1 The physiographic regions and glacial landscape of Wisconsin. (© D. Mladenoff. Maps in plates 1–8 by T. Sickley, Forest Landscape Ecology Lab, University of Wisconsin–Madison.)

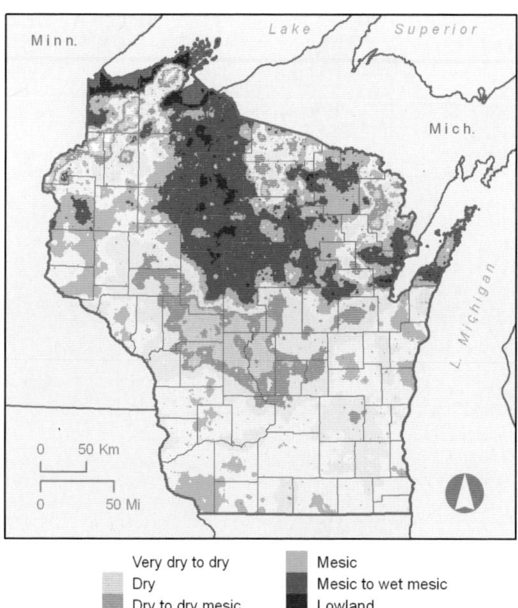

PLATE 2 A generalized classification of Wisconsin, by soils, temperature, and precipitation. Classification is based on the combined influence of soils, temperature, and precipitation on susceptibility of habitats to fire and drought, as interpreted through the presence of forest understory plant species. (© D. Mladenoff, modified from S. Dahir, Wisconsin Department of Natural Resources.)

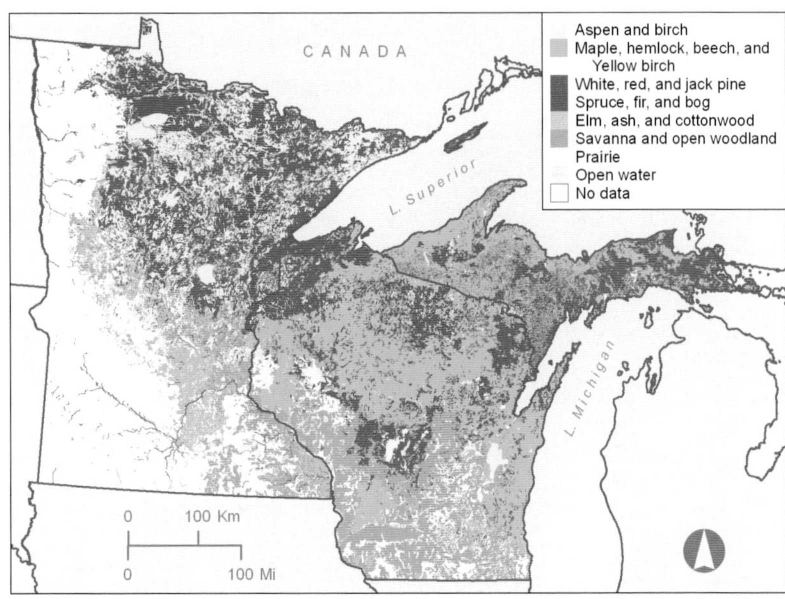

PLATE 3 Pre-European settlement vegetation of the northern Great Lakes States. (Courtesy of U.S. Forest Service Great Lakes Assessment.)

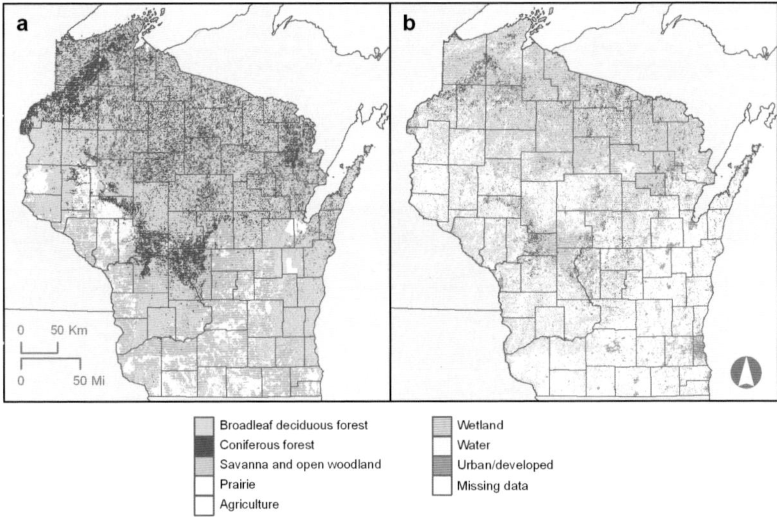

PLATE 4 Vegetation and land cover change in Wisconsin, from the mid-1800s to the 1990s. *a,* Generalized pre-European vegetation classes derived from U.S. Government Land Office Survey data (1832–65). (© D. Mladenoff.) *b,* Current generalized vegetation and land cover classes derived from Landsat satellite data (Data from Wisconsin Department of Natural Resources, Wisconsin Initiative for Statewide Cooperation on Landscape Analysis and Data, 1996.)

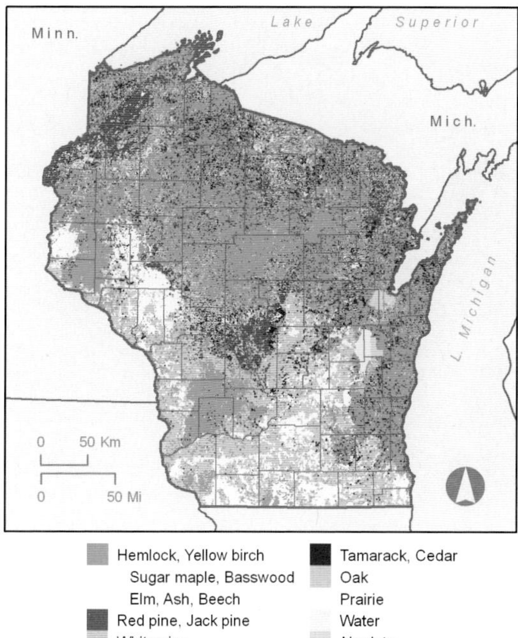

PLATE 5 Forest type classes, from U.S. Government Land Office Survey data (1832–65). (© D. Mladenoff.)

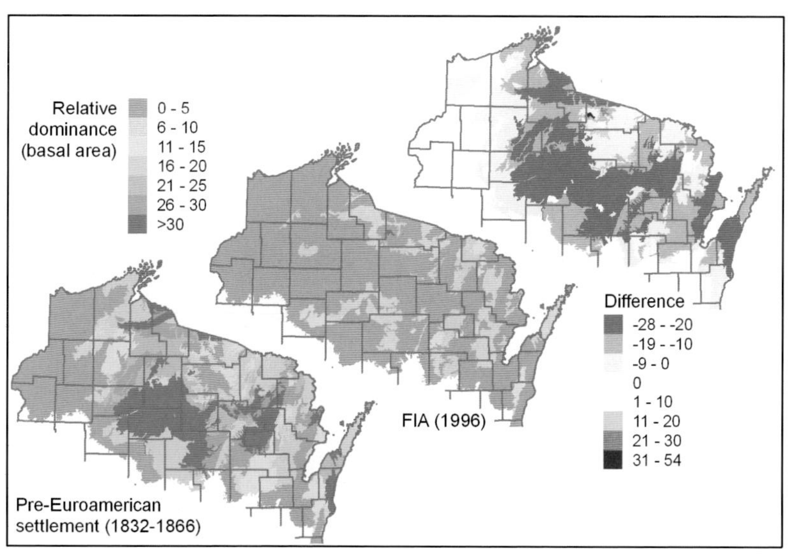

PLATE 6 Changes in the distribution and abundance of eastern hemlock, from the mid-1800s to the 1990s. (© D. Mladenoff.)

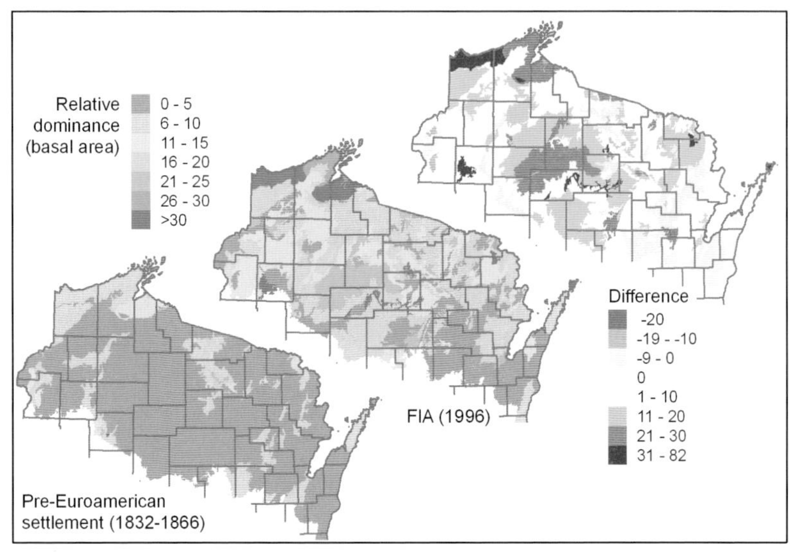

PLATE 7 Changes in the distribution and abundance of aspen, from the mid-1800s to the 1990s (© D. Mladenoff.)

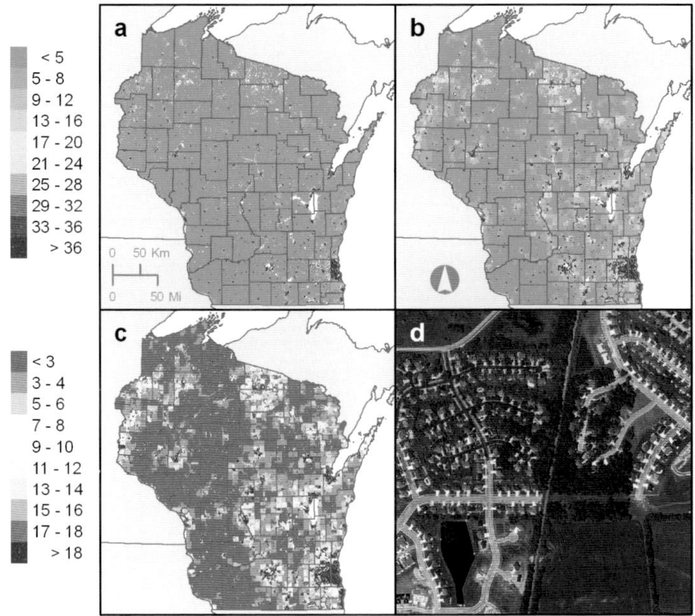

PLATE 8 Number of houses per square mile, in 1940 (*a*) and 2000 (*b*). *c,* Percent housing density change, 1940–2000. (Data from V. Radeloff and R. Hammer, University of Wisconsin–Madison). *d,* Aerial photo showing sprawl on the land. (Photo by T. Rooney.)

PLATE 9 A section of an oak savanna. Oak savanna once covered millions of acres in southern Wisconsin. Less than 0.01% of Wisconsin's original oak savannas remain, making it one of the most endangered ecosystems in the United States. (Photo by T. Rooney.)

PLATE 10 A deer exclosure. At high densities, large grazers like white-tailed deer have the potential to completely alter native plant communities. The fenced area, or deer exclosure, reveals how vegetation developed when protected from deer for 14 years. (Photo by T. Rooney.)

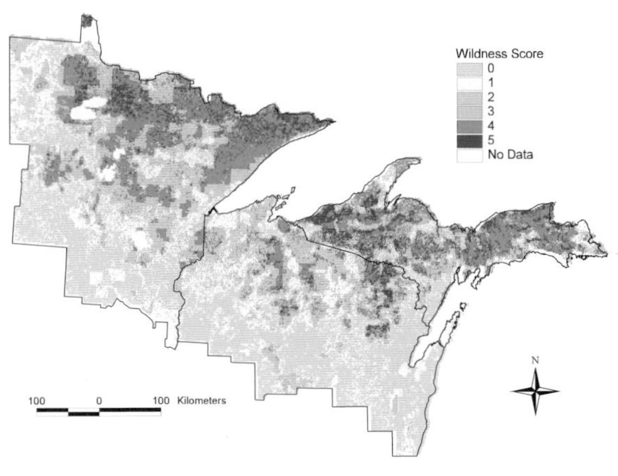

PLATE 11 A human disturbance gradient throughout the Northwoods region. (Reprinted by permission from *Natural Areas Journal* 21[2001]:229–242.)

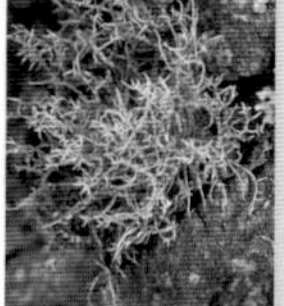

Usnea rubicunda

Cladonia acuminata

Parmotrema perforatum

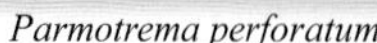

Extinct & Endangered Lichens of Wisconsin

Hypogymnia tubulosa

Ephebe lanata

Peltigera venosa

Usnea longissima

Menegazzia terebrata

PLATE 12 Endangered and extinct lichens of Wisconsin. (Composite image courtesy of J. Bennett.)

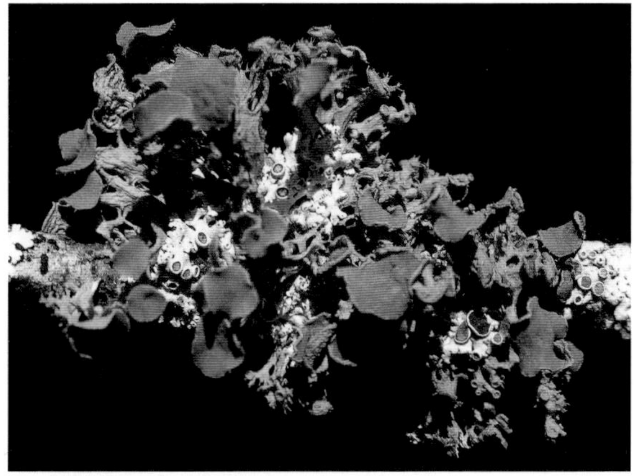

PLATE 13 The tufted orange bush lichen. This lichen occurs in oak savanna. Like its habitat, it is now very rare throughout the state. (Photo by T. Esslinger.)

PLATE 14 Peshtigo Harbor (*a*) and Atkinson's Marsh (*b*). Peshtigo Harbor is a relatively intact coastal wetland complex along Lake Michigan. Atkinson's Marsh is an example of a degraded coastal wetland complex along Lake Michigan at the mouth of the Fox River. (Photos by G. Fewless.)

PLATE 15 An undeveloped lake shoreline in northern Wisconsin. Deadfalls, emergent and floating-leaved plants, and undeveloped shoreline provide critical habitat for many species of wildlife, including amphibians and nongame fish. (Photo by T. Rooney.)

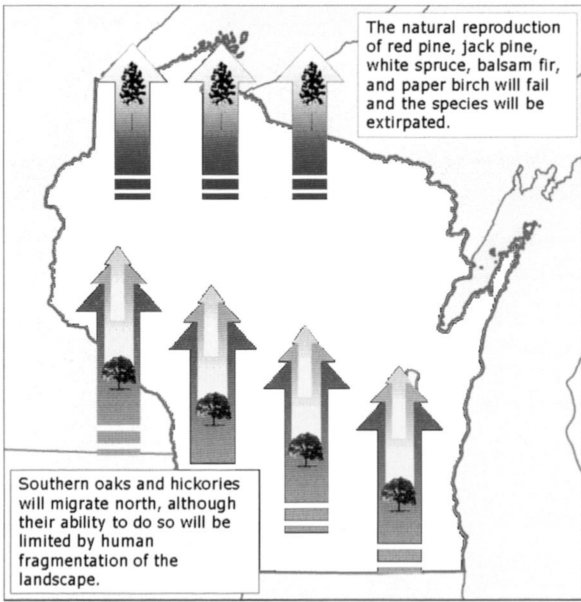

PLATE 16 Projected impacts of climate change on Wisconsin forests. (Courtesy of R. Scheller.)

16

Shifting Plants in Wisconsin Lakes

Stanley A. Nichols

Describing a Madison canoe trip from Lake Monona down the Yahara River, R. G. Thwaites (1902) said that "a long hard pull through close-grown patches of reeds and lily pads" and "dense tangles of wild rice, reeds, and rushes; water-lilies abound everywhere; the crystal clear water is thickly studded with great rosettes . . . bearing arrow-shaped leaves." Dead Lake (as Madison's Lake Wingra was known in the 1870s) was marshy on all sides with wild rice and wild celery. Rowley (in Sachse 1965) said that "the shores of the lake were shallow and one had to push a boat through a hundred yards of weeds and cattails before reaching open water." These statements paint a vivid picture of some southern Wisconsin lakes and lake plants in the late 1800s and early 1900s.

What Is a Lake Plant?

Macroscopic aquatic plants are collectively known as macrophytes, in contrast to microscopic plants like phytoplankton (plate 15). They form four ecological groups based on life form: (1) submergent, (2) free-floating, (3) floating-leaved, and (4) emergent. These differ in habitat, structure, morphology, and how they acquire resources. Plants within a group often share a similar set of adaptations to their environment. Submergent species include quillworts, mosses, wild celery, and water-milfoils. They face special problems obtaining light for photosynthesis and must obtain carbon dioxide from the water where it is much less available than it is in air. Free-floating macrophytes float on or just under the water surface. Free-floating species in Wisconsin include the small duckweeds and a liverwort. Subject to the whims of wind, waves, and currents, they are usually found in quiet embayments. Floating-leaved macrophytes, such as water lilies, root in the lake bottom but have leaves that float on the water surface. As these plants can be ravaged by wind and waves, they are usually found in protected areas. Emergent macrophytes such as reeds and cattails root in the lake bottom and are submersed in water through their basal portion but extend upper leaves into the air. They are usually found in shallower water as along lake margins.

Lake plant surveys and herbarium data show that we have about 150 species of lake plants in Wisconsin (Nichols and Martin 1990; Nichols 1999a). About 20% of these are emergent, 13% are floating-leaved, 60% are submergent, and 7% are free-floating (though some species fit in more than one category). Our most common macrophytes include coontail, stonewort, waterweed, white water lily, large-leaf pondweed, floating-leaf pondweed, sago pondweed, flat-stem pondweed, slender naiad, spatterdock, common arrowhead, and wild celery (Nichols and Martin 1990). Most other species are uncommon. At least 11 taxa are classified as endangered, threatened, or species of special concern (Wetter et al. 2001). Our lake flora also includes nonnative species like curly-leaf pondweed and Eurasian water milfoil.

Lakescapes—Islands of Water in a Sea of Land

Lakes resemble islands in that they are isolated. Wisconsin has about 14,500 islands of water spread over a sea of land. Our lakes vary widely in size, shape, chemistry, and origin (Lillie and Mason 1983). Lakes largely reflect processes operating in the surrounding landscape, providing insights into which macrophytes occur in a given lake and why. Land surely acts as a barrier among these water islands, limiting the dispersal of aquatic plants. We know little about how most aquatic plants disperse except for the species we often transport.

Lakes differ in size, shape, depth, stratification, water sources, drainage type, water quality, and watershed characteristics (Lillie and Mason 1983). These tend to vary regionally across the state, though individual lakes may not reflect regional conditions. Omernick and Gallant (1988)

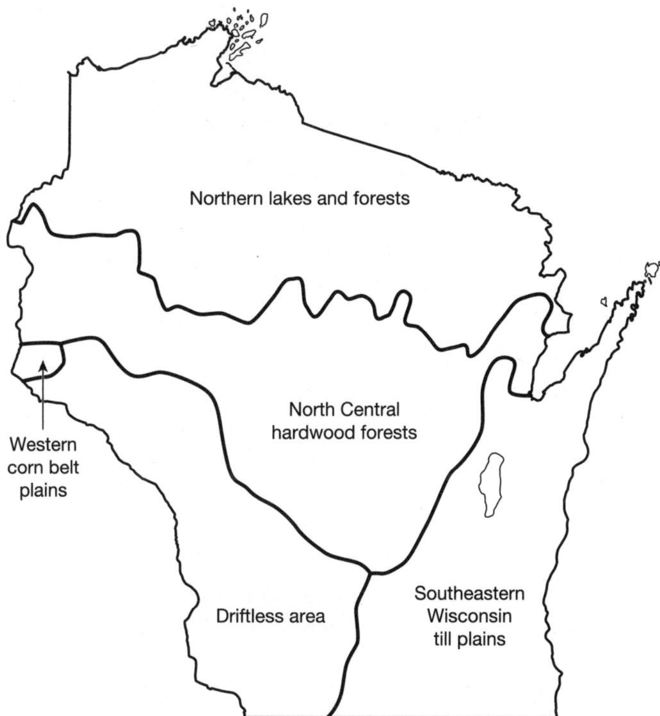

FIGURE 16.1 Ecoregions of Wisconsin, adapted from Omernick and Gallant (1988).

divided the state into five "ecoregions" on the basis of land-use factors, landforms, potential natural vegetation, and soils: the Northern Lakes and Forests, the North Central Hardwood Forests, the Southeastern Wisconsin Till Plains, the Driftless Area, and a pocket of the Western Corn Belt (figure 16.1; see also plate 1).

The Northern Lakes and Forests region has the most lakes, particularly those larger than 10 ha and more than 2 m deep. These lakes are often clear, being low in nutrients and productivity, though some are stained brown by humic acids. In the North Central Hardwood Forest region, lakes also tend to be unproductive with few nutrients. However, the lakes here are generally smaller (few exceed 40 ha) and more alkaline (like lakes in the southern region; water quality remains very good in this region). In the Southeastern Wisconsin Till Plains, lakes tend to be alkaline (due to carbonate bedrock), higher in nutrients, and correspondingly cloudy and more productive. With higher human densities, we also see more human impacts. Water quality varies and is often below statewide averages. The Driftless Area contains only a few lakes, consisting of shallow impoundments or oxbow lakes occurring along rivers. Water quality tends to be poor. Lillie and Mason (1983) provide further descriptions of our lakes and their chemistry.

Baselines—Past Lake Plant Surveys

We know little about lake vegetation before European settlement. Surveys of Wisconsin's lake plants began in the late 1800s. An 1893 survey recorded plants from the Dane County lakes (Cheney and True 1893), but its utility is limited as plants were not always matched to the lake they came from and we don't know how complete these surveys were. Quantitative studies of lake plant distributions began with a survey of Madison's Lake Mendota in the summer of 1912 (Denniston 1921), followed soon by additional surveys of Lake Mendota and Big Green Lake (Rickett 1921, 1924). Additional surveys in the 1930s and early 1940s described plant communities, distribution, productivity, and succession for several lakes in northern Wisconsin. Some lakes were surveyed as part of county economic inventories. Nichols and Martin (1990) identified 448 lakes in 50 Wisconsin counties with pre-1980 lake plant surveys.

Ecological analyses of lake plant communities began in the summers of 1952 and 1953 when Swindale and Curtis (1957) related species groupings of large, submerged lake plants to environmental gradients within and among lakes. Macrophyte data continue to accumulate for lakes included in the Long-Term Ecosystem Research program, the Wisconsin Department of Natural Resources (WDNR) Ambient Lake Monitoring program, the U.S. Geological Survey (USGS) long-term monitoring of Mississippi River pools, and studies by individuals. Electronic databases of lake and river plant information are available from the University of Wisconsin Center for Limnology (http://limnology.wisc.edu/) and the USGS Upper Midwest Environmental Sciences Center (http://www.umesc.usgs.gov/). Such studies serve several uses including regulation, lake management, planning, and science studies of ecological change.

Assessing Change

How are macrophyte communities changing? Are these communities deteriorating? The floristic quality index, or FQI (Nichols 1999b), and the aquatic macrophyte community index, or AMCI (Nichols et al. 2000) both measure the quality of lake plant communities but are based on different criteria. The FQI provides a standardized metric for comparing

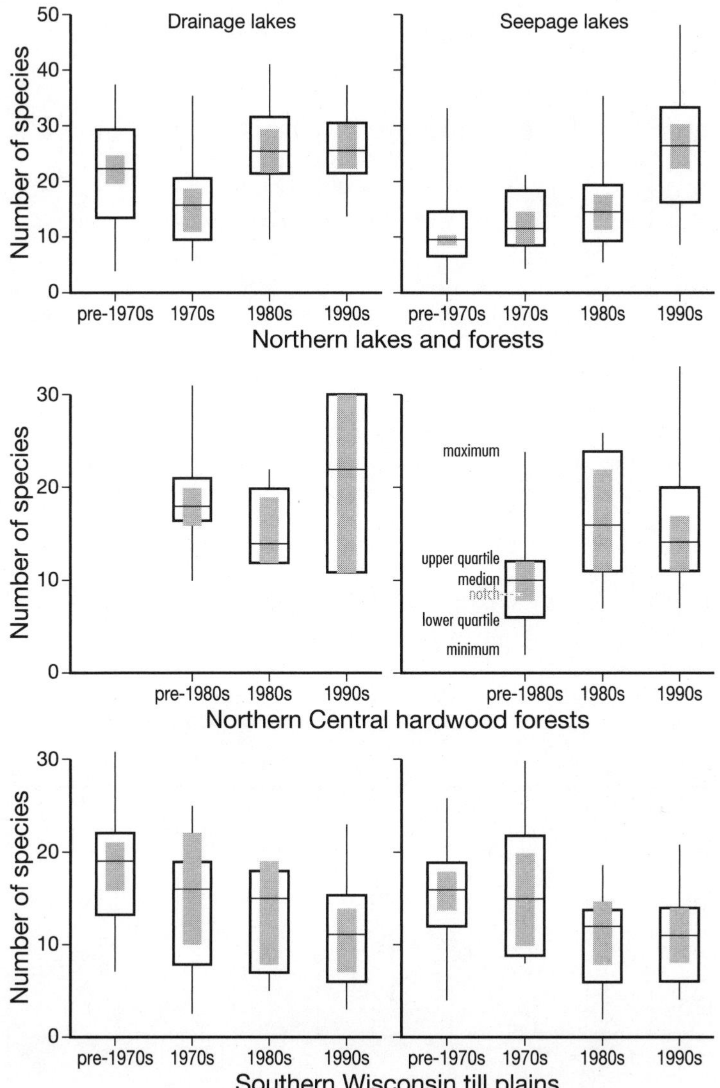

FIGURE 16.2 Number of species by ecoregion, water source, and time period for Wisconsin lake plant communities.

quality based on the identity of each species at a lake. The AMCI is a composite index that weights species diversity, the fraction of the littoral zone vegetated, the maximum depth of plant growth, and the relative frequencies of submerged, sensitive, and exotic species. For both the FQI and AMCI, higher values indicate higher-quality communities.

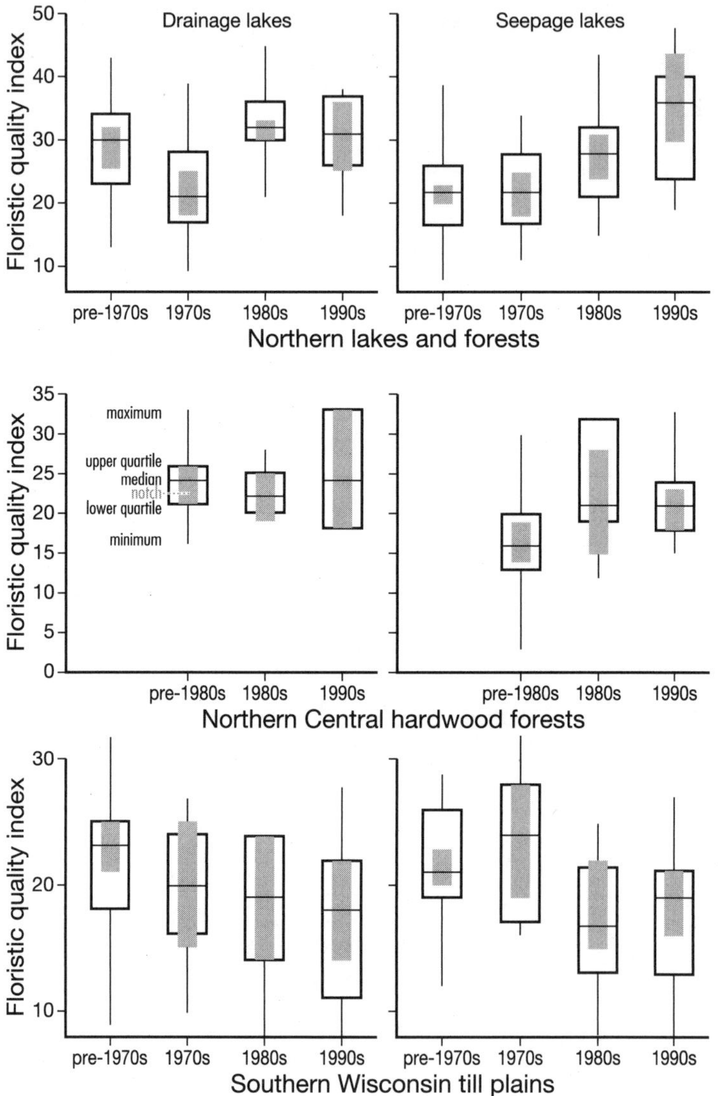

FIGURE 16.3 Floristic quality index by ecoregion, water source, and time period for Wisconsin lake plant communities.

I have studied changes in lake macrophyte communities since the 1960s (Nichols 2001). Both FQI and species richness have varied since then, reflecting differences among ecoregions and whether they were drainage or seepage lakes (figures 16.2 and 16.3).

The AMCI tell a slightly different story. AMCI values have increased steadily in the Northern Lakes and Forests seepage lakes, with the largest increase occurring between the 1980s and the 1990s. In contrast, sensitive species have declined 28% in the North Central Hardwood seepage lakes with similar declines in Southeastern Wisconsin Till Plains drainage lakes. Community quality in the Northern Lakes and Forests and the North Central Hardwoods Forests ecoregions show few strong trends. If anything, quality may be increasing in the Northern Lakes and Forests and in seepage lakes in the North Central region. However, increases in macrophyte community quality might not signal increased water quality. Increased sediment and nutrient inputs and increased boat access to isolated oligotrophic (nutrient poor) lakes may have temporarily enhanced the macrophyte community, although this might be an early stage of long-term degradation. Most changes in the Southeastern Wisconsin Till Plains lakes would have occurred prior to the baseline data collected in the late 1960s. The little data we do have suggests large changes; Nichols and Lathrop (1994) found that 19 of 59 taxa or roughly one-third of species that occurred in the Madison area lakes were not found after 1960. The macrophyte communities in the Till Plains are probably the most disturbance tolerant in the state.

Although changes in some individual lakes have been dramatic, regional changes may be too slow to determine without a longer period of analysis. With floristic turnover rates of 2.6%–3.5% per year, it would take around 10 years to disentangle seasonal and sampling variability from directional change (Nichols 1997).

Impacts and Threats

Macrophyte communities have also changed in ways not captured by the FQI or AMCI. Dams and dredging have changed water levels. Excess nutrients from human activities (e.g., runoff from farm fields) continue to pollute many surface waters. Users often struggle to control the ensuing nuisance growths of aquatic plants. Fishermen, boaters, and other users augment recreational pressure on lakes. The traffic among lakes have opened many lakes to invasions by introduced plant and animal species (see chapter 29).

Water Level Alterations, Wind, and Waves. European settlers dammed streams to make impoundments and lake outlets to raise water levels to generate hydropower or transport logs. Small impoundments, or mill ponds, often acquired recreational value after they outlived their commercial utility. Over time, they filled with sediment, became weed choked, and lost their recreational value. Larger river systems were also dammed, forming some of the state's larger lakes, like the Chippewa and Petenwell flowages. Some of these flowages developed extensive beds of aquatic vegetation, especially in the newly flooded shallows. Water-level fluctuations, wind and wave action, and ice scouring often worked in concert to destroy aquatic vegetation. The demise of lake vegetation in the Upper Winnebago Pool lakes provides a classic case study (Kahl 1993). Water drawdowns, especially during winter, favor the development of a drawdown-tolerant vegetation (Beard 1973; Nichols 1975a, 1975b).

Dredging began soon after European settlement. Dredging influences lake plant communities by making the habitat too deep for plant growth and turning shallows into dry land. Chancey Juday (1914) described the first dredging of Monona Bay in Madison: "until recently the shallows were filled with a large amount of vegetation and the swamp along the shore was slowly advancing into the bay. But a few years ago the shallow portions were deepened by dredging and the shores were much improved by filling the swamps, thus counteracting the natural processes." By 1920, 1536 ha of marsh and 90 ha of lakebed were filled in the Madison area (Mollenhoff 1982).

Exotic Species. Common carp were intentionally introduced into state waters in the 1880s. Lathrop et al. (1992) report carp were introduced into the Madison area lakes between 1887 and 1893. By 1913, Cahn (1915) observed carp to "abound" in Lake Wingra. A record carp harvest of 803 kg/ha was removed from Lake Waubesa in 1938 (Lathrop et al. 1992). These numbers equal or far exceed the density of 72 kg/ha known to destroy aquatic vegetation (Robel 1961; King and Hunt 1967). Vander Zanden and Maxted (chapter 29) discuss additional impacts of carp.

Curly-leaf pondweed appeared in the state in 1905 (Ross and Calhoun 1951). It prefers soft substrates, shallow water, and is often associated with degraded water quality. It is a serious nuisance species in some lakes, and the annual July dieback leads to secondary problems like increased algae blooms.

Eurasian water-milfoil (EWM) was probably introduced into the state in the early 1960s. Early detection of the species was difficult because it resembles the native spiked water-milfoil. It is most often found in the southern half of the state. The likelihood or severity of a milfoil invasion in a lake appears related to amount of dissolved carbon (Buchan and Padilla 2000), total phosphorus (Madsen 1998), and distance from a lake with a known infestation (Johnstone et al. 1985; Nichols and Buchan 1997). This species often becomes abundant after invading, and in some lakes it accounts for over 90% of the vegetation present. However, dominance in many lakes declines after 10–15 years, as in Lake Wingra in Madison (Carpenter 1980). The cause of these declines is not certain, but the milfoil weevil may play a role (Lillie and Helsel 1997). Declines occur independent of aquatic plant management techniques (Helsel et al. 1999).

Spiny naiad is a plant found in the high pH lakes in southeastern Wisconsin. In Nagawicka Lake, Waukesha County, spiny naiad had a frequency of occurrence of 50% in 1987. Presently, it doesn't appear to be migrating to other ecoregions. The Nagawicka Lake population declined 80% by 1993 for reasons unknown.

Purple loosestrife, reed canary grass, narrow-leaved cattail, flowering rush, and other emergent plants often form large monotypic colonies in lake shallows. Because they are depth limited they usually pose the greatest threat to adjacent or isolated wetlands. Flowering rush has only a limited distribution in the state and doesn't appear to spread as rapidly as in some adjacent states. Loosestrife beetles are being used to reduce purple loosestrife infestations around lakeshores.

Zebra mussels surround the waters of the state and are starting to be found in inland lakes. An important impact at high mussel population is a noticeable improvement in water clarity, allow aquatic plants to grow at greater depths.

Invasive species exploit several modes of human transport. Plant fragments adhere to boats, boat trailers, floatplanes, and fishing gear. Aquarium discards, fish stocking, and nursery stock provide other pathways of invasion. Sometimes the spread is intentional, as occurs with water gardening, scientific transplant experiments, and agriculture (Johnstone et al. 1985). Les and Mehrhoff (1999) noted that of the 17 species of nonindigenous aquatic plants found in southern New England, 13 escaped from cultivation. New invasive plants continue to appear in the state. Recently, Frank Koshere of the WDNR reported water hyacinth from a wastewater treatment pond and **water-lettuce** in a stream in northern Wisconsin during the summer of 2002. Human transport is probably responsible for both introductions.

Aquatic Plant Management—Harvesting and Herbicides. Both mechanical harvesting and herbicides are used to manage exotic species and treat excessive vegetation growth in direct or high-use areas. The long-term community changes are not known. The resulting community can be

(1) dominated by species not present immediately prior to management, (2) dominated by species that were dominant immediately prior to management, or (3) dominated by species that were present but not common before management (Wade 1990). Nicholson (1981) found that slow-growing, sexually reproducing plants that regenerate poorly from fragments are most impacted by harvesting. Our native pondweeds fall into this group. Conversely, species that grow rapidly after cutting and regenerate from fragments are likely to become more dominant after harvesting. The invasive EWM benefits from frequent harvesting. Herbicides change lake plant community structure depending on herbicide dose, formulation, timing of application, mode of attack (systemic vs. contact), and susceptibility of the treated species.

Shoreline Development and Boat Traffic. The impacts of home developments on shorelines are complex. Some are obvious; all aquatic vegetation is often removed to improve shoreline access, develop swimming beaches, and construct seawalls. Nevertheless, macrophyte abundance has increased in most northern Wisconsin lakes since European settlement because lakefront development increases nutrient and sediment inputs (Garrison and Wakeman 2000). In Little Bearskin Lake, Oneida County, Garrison and Winkelman (1996) concluded that the area of macrophyte coverage had not changed since settlement times, but the density of macrophyte growth had increased.

Motorboats also influence lake plant communities. Asplund and Cook (1997) examined the impact of motor boating by constructing boat exclosures in Lake Ripley. After a single growing season, species composition was similar between the experimental and control plots, with stonewort and spiny naiad being the predominant species. However, protected areas had much greater plant cover and biomass than unprotected areas. They determined that motorboats reduced plant biomass by sediment scouring and direct cutting of the plants. Slow no-wake restrictions on the eastern shore of Long Lake, Fond du Lac County, resulted in the recovery of stonewort (Asplund and Cook 1999). However, motorboat restrictions are not a cure-all; restrictions on Big Green Lake in Green Lake County failed protect a bulrush bed (Asplund and Cook 1999).

Eutrophication and Turbidity—Poor Water Clarity. Eutrophication-triggered algal blooms reduce water clarity, reducing habitat quality for many lake plants (Phillips et al. 1978). Species differ in their susceptibility to turbidity, with sago pondweed being among the most tolerant (Engel and Nichols 1994). Even minor changes in nutrient conditions can cause shallow lakes to abruptly switch from being macrophyte dominated to algae dominated (the alternate stable state hypothesis; Scheffer et al. 1993; chapter 28). Most of Rice Lake in Polk County is less than 1.5 m deep. Historically it had clear water, abundant wild rice and submerged species, and many fish. By 1988 it became highly eutrophic as a result of the cumulative impacts of increased water levels caused by beaver damming the outlet stream, wind, erosion, ice heaving, runoff from adjacent farms, and nutrient inputs from the Milltown wastewater treatment plant. Wild rice disappeared and the submerged plant community became dominated by sago and floating-leaf pondweeds. Initial efforts to restore vegetation to Rice Lake failed, but water quality improved after 1996. A steady increase in submergent macrophyte coverage and density was observed each year from 1996 to 1999. An 1999 survey found submergent macrophytes present in 100% of the sampling sites, compared with 31% in 1987 and 51% in 1989 (Engel and Nichols 1994; Roesler 2000). Diversity recovered by 2002.

Why did this lake recover? An upgrade of Milltown wastewater treatment from primary treatment to secondary treatment occurred in 1978. If this played a role, it illustrates the long time lags between improving the quality of water discharge and in-lake changes. Changes in agricultural practices in the watershed also probably contributed to water quality improvements. Since the late 1980s, the number of cattle in the watershed declined by 75%. At the same time, areas of erosion-prone cropland were enrolled in the Conservation Reserve Program, and conventional tillage was largely replaced by conservation tillage (Roesler 2000). A recently constructed tertiary wastewater treatment plant in Milltown will probably contribute to the future long-term health of Rice Lake.

Hope for the Future

Aquatic Plant Community Restoration. Because of the vital role plants play in the aquatic ecosystem there is a growing interest in restoring aquatic plant communities. Aquatic plant restoration may (1) improve fish and wildlife habitat (chapter 13), (2) reduce shoreline erosion and bottom turbulence, (3) buffer nutrient fluxes, (4) shade shorelines, (5) reduce nuisance macrophyte and algae growth, (6) treat storm water and wastewater effluent, (7) replace exotic invaders with native species, (8) improve aesthetics, and (9) moderate environmental disturbance. I define restoration broadly, loosely, and inclusively. Restoration occurs when a single species is planted where it was previously extirpated and when changing habitat conditions favors natural revegetation. It includes restoring diversity to a monotypic, exotic-dominated plant community in some cases, and simply letting nature take its course in other cases. Seldom is an aquatic plant community completely restored or rehabilitated in the strictest sense, but thoughtful restoration promotes some recovery (Haslam 1996; Moss and others 1996; Munrow 1999). The most successful restorations alter habitat, making it more suitable to aquatic plants. Other successful strategies include stabilizing water levels, reducing or eliminating exotic species, making slow no-wake boating zones, increasing water clarity, consolidating or removing flocculent or toxic sediments, and building islands or break walls to reduce wind and wave action.

The Lake Wingra Story. Lake Wingra is a 137 ha, shallow urban lake in Madison. Surrounded by the University of Wisconsin Arboretum and city parkland, Wingra is unlike many urban lakes in that the shoreline is not heavily developed. In 1900, horsetails, wild rice, cattails, and bulrushes were common in the marshes surrounding the lake. Dense growths of stoneworts were interspersed between the emergents. Wild celery was particularly abundant. There were at least 34 species of aquatic plants in Lake Wingra, and the lake bottom was completely vegetated (Bauman et al. 1974). During the first half of the 20th century, dredging, filling, water-level fluctuation, and the introduction of carp decimated the aquatic vegetation. Macrophytes were sparse from the late 1920s through 1955 (Bauman et al. 1974). Eurasian water-milfoil invaded Lake Wingra in the early 1960s, and by 1966 it was the dominant species. In the early 1970s, EWM formed dense stands in shallow areas of the lake. Lake Wingra experienced an invasive meltdown.

For reasons still unexplained, the EWM population declined in 1977 (Carpenter 1980). Except for some minor plant harvesting around a public boat launch and a swimming beach, there was no lake management to speak of since the early 1950s, when carp were seined to low levels. Between 1969 and 1996 macrophyte species number increased slightly, the relative frequency of exotic species (EWM and curly-leaf pondweed) dropped from 70% to 35%, and the relative frequency of species sensitive to disturbance (Nichols et al. 2000) increased from near zero levels to 20%. Water quality improved, with the maximum depth of plant growth increased from 2.7 to 3.5 m. Wild celery and Illinois pondweed were observed for the first time since 1929. A recent carp exclosure (fig 29.5, p. 432) improved conditions even more dramatically.

The vegetation recovery in Lake Wingra was more dramatic than in the other Madison area lakes that had a similar history of EWM invasion (Nichols and Lathrop 1994). Historically, Lake Wingra had a rich aquatic flora. Even at the height of the EWM invasion, over 15 species of macrophytes inhabited the lake. Dane County also has many large lakes, so there is an abundant supply of aquatic plant propagules in the vicinity for recolonization. A seed bank also probably persisted in the Lake Wingra sediment. There has been no major disturbance of the plant beds in years, due to a slow no-wake boating ordinance on the lake. EWM declines occurred in other lakes, and once again native species are returning (Helsel et al. 1999; Nichols 1994; Smith and Barko 1992). The Lake Wingra experience is not unique.

Conclusion

Impacts to lake plant communities are probably less pronounced than impacts to many terrestrial or wetland areas. Few lakes are paved over for shopping malls. Invasive plants can become dominant in lakes, but they are still are relatively uncommon in Wisconsin's lake flora, and some exotics seem to have limited impacts on the native community. Human use represents a continuing threat. Until the value of macrophytes is realized, they will probably continue to be degraded by boat traffic, waves, eutrophication, turbidity, shoreline development, harvesting, and chemical control (chapter 13). Evidence from southern Wisconsin indicates that macrophytes do not occur at the depths they used to, and macrophyte communities produce less biomass then they did a century ago. Despite this decline, there are increasing complaints about the "aquatic weed problem." This view reflects changes in lake uses, population increases, and perceptions, not changes in the plant communities. Lakes are not manicured lawns—they are natural ecosystems that support diverse fish and wildlife communities. The perceived "aquatic weed problem" will disappear when invasive species decline and people learn to appreciate the beauty and importance of these fascinating plants.

References

Asplund, T., and C. E. Cook. 1997. Effects of motor boats on submerged aquatic macrophytes. Lake Reserv. Manage. 13:1–12.

———. 1999. Can no-wake zones effectively protect littoral zone habitat from boating disturbance? Lakeline 19(1):16.

Bauman, P. C., J. F. Kitchell, J. J. Magnuson, and T. B. Kayes. 1974. Lake Wingra, 1837–1973: A case history of human impact. Trans. Wis. Acad. Sci. Arts Lett. 62:57–94.

Beard, T. D. 1973. Overwinter drawdown: Impact on the aquatic vegetation of Murphy Flowage, Wisconsin. Wisconsin Department of Natural Resources, Technical Bulletin No. 61, Madison.

Buchan, L. A., and D. K. Padilla. 2000. Predicting the likelihood of Eurasian watermilfoil presence in lakes, a macrophyte monitoring tool. Ecol. Appl. 10:1442–1455.

Cahn, A. R. 1915. An ecological survey of the Wingra Springs region near Madison, Wisconsin. Bull. Wis. Nat. Hist. Soc. 13:123–175.

Carpenter, S. R. 1980. The decline of *Myriophyllum spicatum* in a eutrophic Wisconsin USA lake. Can. J. Bot. 58:527–535.

Cheney, L. S., and R. H. True. 1893. On the flora of Madison and vicinity, a preliminary paper. Trans. Wis. Acad. Sci. Arts Lett. 9:46–136.

Denniston, R. H. 1921. A survey of larger aquatic plants of Lake Mendota. Trans. Wis. Acad. Sci. Arts Lett. 20:495–500.

Engel, S. and S. A. Nichols. 1994. Restoring Rice Lake at Milltown, Wisconsin. Wisconsin Department of Natural Resources, Technical Bulletin No. 186, Madison.

Garrison, P., and R. Wakeman. 2000. Use of paleolimnology to document the effect of lake shoreland development on water quality. J. Paleolimnol. 24:369–393.

Garrison, P., and J. Winkelman, 1996. Paleoecological study of Little Bearskin Lake, Oneida County. Final report. Wisconsin Department of Natural Resources, Madison.

Haslam, S. R. 1996. Enhancing river vegetation: Conservation, development, or restoration. Hydrobiologia 340:345–348.

Helsel, D. R., S. A. Nichols, and R. W. Wakeman. 1999. Impacts of aquatic plant management methodologies on Eurasian water milfoil populations in Southeastern Wisconsin. Lake Reserv. Manage. 15:159–167.

Johnstone, I. M., B. T. Coffey, and C. Howard-Williams. 1985. The role of recreational boat traffic in the interlake dispersal of macrophytes: A New Zealand case study. Envir. Manage. 20:263–279.

Juday, C. 1914. The inland lakes of Wisconsin—The hydrography and morphometry of the lakes. Wisconsin Geological and Natural History Survey, Bulletin No. 26, Madison.

Kahl, R. 1993. Aquatic macrophyte ecology in the Upper Winnebago Pool Lakes. Wisconsin Department of Natural Resources, Technical Bulletin No. 182, Madison.

King, D. R., and G. S. Hunt. 1967. Effect of carp on vegetation in a Lake Erie marsh. J. Wildl. Manage. 31:181–188.

Lathrop, R. C., S. B. Nehls, C. L. Brynildson, and K. R. Plass. 1992. The fishery of the Yahara lakes. Wisconsin Department of Natural Resources, Technical Bulletin No. 181, Madison.

Les, D. H., and L. J. Mehrhoff. 1999. Introduction of nonindigenous aquatic vascular plants in southern New England: A historical perspective. Biol. Invas. 1:281–300.

Lillie, R. A., and D. L. Helsel. 1997. A native weevil attacks Eurasian watermilfoil. Wisconsin Department of Natural Resources, Findings No. 40, Madison.

Lillie, R. A., and J. W. Mason. 1983. Limnological characteristics of Wisconsin lakes. Wisconsin Department of Natural Resources, Technical Bulletin No. 138, Madison.

Madsen, J. D. 1998. Predicting invasion success of Eurasian watermilfoil. J. Aquat. Plant Manage. 36:28–32.

Mollenhoff, D. V. 1982. Madison, A History of the Formative Years. Dubuque, IA: Kendall/Hunt.

Moss, B., J. Madgwick, and G. L. Phillips. 1996. A Guide to the Restoration of Nutrient-Enriched Shallow Lakes. Norwich, UK: Broads Authority.

Munrow, J. 1999. Ecological restoration: Rebuilding nature. Vol. Monitor 11(1):1–6.

Nichols, S. A. 1975a. The impact of overwinter drawdown on the aquatic vegetation of the Chippewa Flowage, Wisconsin, Trans. Wis. Acad. Sci. Arts Lett. 63:116–128.

———. 1975b. The use of overwinter drawdown for aquatic vegetation management. Water Res. Bull. 11:1137–1149.

———. 1994. Evaluation of invasion and declines of submersed macrophytes for the Upper Great Lakes region. Lake Reserv. Manage. 10:29–33.

———. 1997. Seasonal and sampling variability in some Wisconsin lake plant communities. J. Freshwater Ecol. 12:173–182.

———. 1999a. Distribution and habitat descriptions of Wisconsin lake plants. Wisconsin Geological and Natural History Survey, Bulletin No. 96, Madison.

———. 1999b. Floristic quality assessment of Wisconsin lake plant communities with example applications. Lake Reser. Manage. 15:133–141.

———. 2001. Long-term change in Wisconsin lake plant communities. J. Freshwater Ecol. 16(1):1–13.

Nichols, S. A., and L. Buchan. 1997. Use of native macrophytes as indicators of suitable Eurasian watermilfoil habitat in Wisconsin lakes. J. Aquat. Plant Manage. 35:21–24.

Nichols, S. A., and R. C. Lathrop. 1994. Cultural impacts on macrophytes in the Yahara lakes since the late 1800s. Aquat. Bot. 47:225–247.

Nichols, S. A., and R. Martin, 1990. Wisconsin lake plant database. Wisconsin Geological and Natural History Survey, Information Circular No. 69, Madison.

Nichols, S. A., S. Weber, and B. H. Shaw. 2000. A proposed aquatic plant community biotic index for Wisconsin lakes. Envir. Manage. 26(5):491–502.

Nicholson, S. A. 1981. Changes in submersed macrophytes in Chautauqua Lake, 1937–1975. Freshwater Biol. 11:523–530.

Omernick, J. M., and A. L. Gallant. 1988. Ecoregions of the Upper Midwest States. U.S. Environmental Protection Agency, Report No. EPA/600/3–88/037, Corvallis, OR.

Phillips, G. L., D. Eminson, and B. Moss. 1978. A mechanism to account for macrophyte decline in progressively eutrophicated freshwaters. Aquat. Bot. 4:103–126.

Rickett, H. W. 1921. A quantitative study of the larger aquatic plants of Lake Mendota. Trans. Wis. Acad. Sci. Arts Lett. 20:501–527.

———. 1924. A quantitative study of the larger aquatic plants of Green Lake, Wisconsin. Trans. Wis. Acad. Sci. Arts Lett. 21:381–414.

Robel, R. J. 1961. The effects of carp populations on the production of waterfowl food plants on a western waterfowl marsh. Trans. N. Am. Wildl. Nat. Resourc. Conf. 26:147–159.

Roesler, C. P. 2000. The recovery of Rice Lake, a water quality success story. Wisconsin Department of Natural Resources, unpublished report, Spooner.

Ross, J. G., and B. M. Calhoun. 1951. Preliminary reports on the flora of Wisconsin, 33-Potamogetonaceae. Trans. Wis. Acad. Sci. Arts Lett. 40:93–110.

Sachse, N. D. 1965. A Thousand Ages. Madison: University of Wisconsin Regents.

Scheffer, M., S. H. Hosper, M.-L. Meijer, B. Moss, and E. Jeppesen. 1993. Alternative equilibria in shallow lakes. Trends Ecol. Evol. 8: 275–279.

Smith, C. S., and J. W. Barko. 1992. Submersed macrophyte invasions and declines. U.S. Army Engineers, Waterways Experiment Station, Aquatic Plant Control Research Program Report, Vol. A-92–1, Vicksburg, MS.

Swindale, D. N., and J. T. Curtis. 1957. Phytosociology of the larger submerged plants in Wisconsin lakes. *Ecology* 38:397–407.

Thwaites, R. G. 1902. Down Historic Waterways. Chicago: A. C. McClurg Co.

Wade, P. M. 1990. Physical control of aquatic weeds. Pp. 93–135 in A. Pieterse and K. Murphy, eds. Aquatic Weeds, the Ecology and Management of Nuisance Aquatic Vegetation. Oxford: Oxford University Press.

Wetter, M. A., T. S. Cochrane, M. R. Black, H. H. Iltis, and P. E. Berry. 2001. Checklist of the vascular plants of Wisconsin. Wisconsin Department of Natural Resources, Technical Bulletin No. 192, Madison.

17

Changes in the Wisconsin River and Its Floodplain

Monica G. Turner, Emily H. Stanley, Matthias Bürgi, and David J. Mladenoff

Traversing the state from north to south and transporting people and myriad goods to the mighty Mississippi, the Wisconsin River has long played a pivotal role in Wisconsin's history (Durbin 1997). From the fur trade, to the timber and paper industries, to manufacturing and power generation, the river has been essential to Wisconsin's commerce. The recreational opportunities provided by the river have assumed increasing prominence in recent years. However, few of the far-reaching changes in the structure and function of the river and its floodplain during the 20th century are visible in the contemporary landscape—the river still floods and returns to its banks each year, and the extensive forests of silver maple, river birch, American elm, and green ash look pristine to many. But the system has changed substantially. Uncovering and understanding the changes in this system and what these portend for the future requires a deeper look. Worldwide, river-floodplain ecosystems have been subjected to a wide array of anthropogenic changes, and the Wisconsin River is no exception. In this chapter, we focus on changes in the Wisconsin River—its landscape, its forests, and the flow of its water—primarily during the 20th century. We use historical sources and contemporary ecological studies to describe and interpret the changes in this dynamic system.

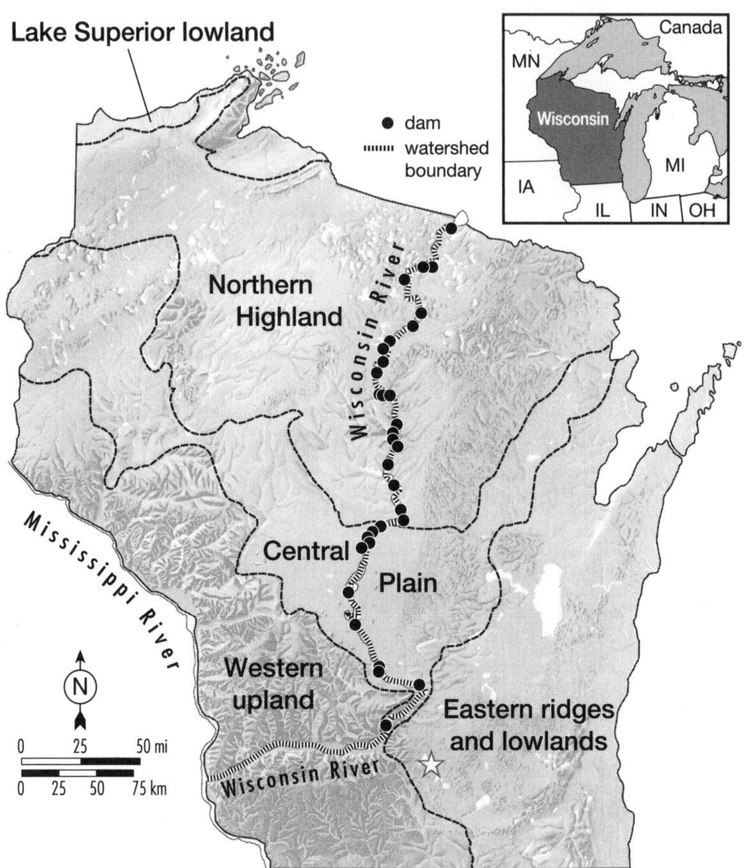

FIGURE 17.1 Wisconsin River and geographic provinces. The river traverses three provinces (Martin 1965), and the flow of the river has been modified by 26 main stem dams.

The Wisconsin River flows approximately 700 km from its source in northern Wisconsin to its confluence with the Mississippi River, draining an area of 31,440 km^2 (figure 17.1). The river traverses three geographic provinces: the Northern Highland, Central Plain, and Western Upland (Martin 1965; figure 17.1). Geologically, the Northern Highland province is characterized by multiple glacial moraines and glacial till soils. The Central Plain is composed of Cambrian sandstone lowlands and includes the sandy lakebed of Glacial Lake Wisconsin. The final 150 km to the Mississippi River are free of dams, include large amounts of protected lands, and traverse the unglaciated Western Upland province characterized by soft sandstones, limestone, and coarse-textured soils

(Durbin 1997). Today, the river-floodplain landscape is a mosaic of forest and wetlands, agriculture and urban development (Freeman et al. 2003). What was it like during earlier times? What might it be like in the future?

Changes in the Landscape

An enormous uncontrolled experiment in landscape alteration is underway in many of the world's river systems. Changes in land use and land cover have transformed the forests and wetlands surrounding rivers (Turner et al. 1998). For example, riparian forests once covered 30–40 million ha in the contiguous United States (Swift 1974). Much of this area has been converted to nonforest land uses with only 10–14 million ha remaining by the early 1970s. In many parts of the Midwest and in the lower Mississippi Valley, riparian forests were reduced by over 80% (Swift 1974). Today, floodplain forests are considered a threatened ecosystem (Yin et al. 1997; Knutson and Klaas 1998). Similarly, about 53% of the wetlands of the conterminous 48 states have been lost (Dahl 1990). Changes in the floodplain and surrounding landscape of the Wisconsin River since settlement provide us with a microcosm that illuminates the changes under way in similar systems. Such changes have strongly affected the connections among forests and wetlands. Habitat connectivity and its inverse, fragmentation, reflect the abundance and spatial arrangement of habitats as altered by land use.

Before European settlement, the Wisconsin River watershed was dominated by jack pine barrens, pine and deciduous forests at its northern reaches, and prairie, oak savanna, and oak woodland further south (Curtis 1959). Floodplain vegetation through much of the southern half of the river basin contained a mosaic of sedge meadow, marshes, prairie, oak savanna, and low and mixed floodplain forest (Ware 1955; Curtis 1959). Adjacent to the river, species-rich lowland forests were common and included river birch, honey locust, black willow, cottonwood, white oak, silver maple, and American elm.

European settlers moved into the region in the mid-19th century, advancing from southeast to northwest (Ostergren 1997). Population densities in the counties along the Wisconsin River rose during the 19th century, then remained fairly stable during the first decades of the 20th century. Active farmland increased in parallel fashion, leveling off early in the 20th century. After brief periods of lead mining and wheat production, southwestern Wisconsin land use became dominated by dairy farming (Conzen 1997). The proportion of land in farms has declined slightly but steadily since the 1940s, while population densities continue to increase.

These settlers profoundly changed the original land cover of forests, savanna, and prairie (Auclair 1976; Tans 1976; Lange 1990) in both the uplands and the floodplain forests through land use and fire suppression (see, e.g., Kline and Cottam 1979; Dorney 1981). Grazing and logging occurred in bottomland forests throughout the upper Midwest (see, e.g., Hosner and Minckler 1963; Nelson et al. 1994; Barnes 1997; Yin et al. 1997; Knutson and Klaas 1998), including along the Wisconsin River (Liegel 1988; Bürgi and Turner 2002). Fertile uplands were all under cultivation by1890 or so. Many farms were abandoned by the 1930s, although marsh hay mowing and cattle grazing continued in many wetlands and floodplain forests.

Land Use in the River Corridor in the 1930s and 1990s. Bürgi and Turner (2002) studied changes in land cover between 1938 and 1992 in a 20 km wide corridor along the lower 380 km of the Wisconsin River. This area encompassed 3,403 sections, each one square mile in size (Johnson 1976; chapter 2). Land-cover data for 1938 were obtained from the Wisconsin Land Economic Inventory, or Bordner Report (State of Wisconsin 1936). These 1938 data were compiled from unpublished tables (Archive of the State Historical Society of Wisconsin, Series 1956) summarizing the acreage of different land covers for all 3,403 sections. We compiled 1992 land-cover data from the Wisconsin Initiative for Statewide Cooperation on Landscape Analysis and Data database. Land cover in both maps was expressed as the proportion of each cover type by section using agricultural land, forests, and wetlands.

Our analysis showed that agricultural land has declined in the corridor surrounding the Wisconsin River, while forest cover has increased (figure 17.2). Agricultural lands declined from 54% in 1938 (44% cropland and 10% grassland) to 46% in 1992 (32% cropland and 14% grassland). Forest cover has increased from 32% in 1938 (27% deciduous and 5% coniferous) to 38% in 1992 (30% deciduous, 4% mixed, and 4% coniferous). Wetlands that occupied 10% of the landscape in 1938 as open (5%) and forested (4%) wetlands occupied 11% of the landscape in 1992.

There were also distinct regional patterns in land-cover change (Bürgi and Turner 2002). Agricultural cover declined and forest cover increased in 727 sections (21%), particularly in the mid- to lower sections of the river. Only 3% of the sections showed the opposite trend, and these occurred only in the Central Plain, probably reflecting cropping of pine

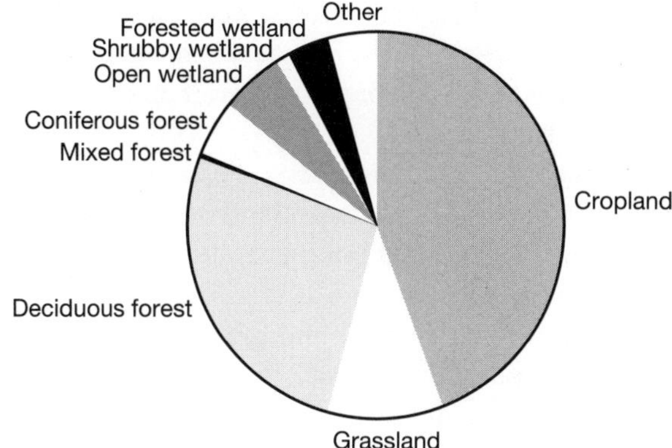

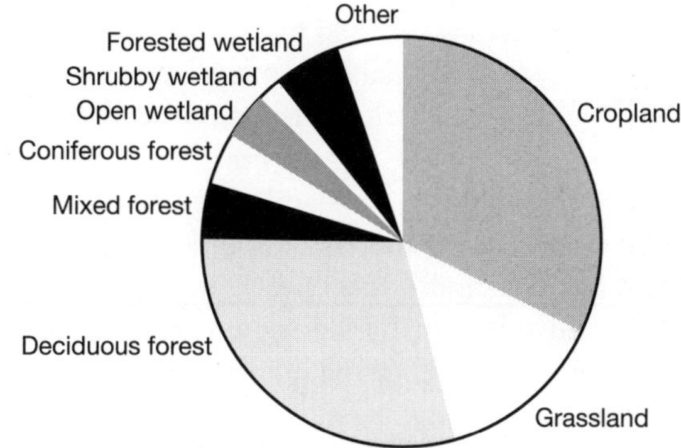

FIGURE 17.2 Dominant land covers in the corridor surrounding the Wisconsin River in 1938 and in 1992. Data are from Bürgi and Turner 2002.

plantations. Grasslands also often replaced croplands in 546 sections (16%), mostly in the mid- to upper part of the river. Only 91 sections (3%) near the confluence with the Mississippi River showed the opposite trend. Thus the abandonment of farms, declines in farming intensity, and locally intensified farming have all contributed to land-cover change. As expected, natural vegetation has increased the most in areas poorly suited for farming (Turner et al. 1996; Wear and Bolstad 1998).

Land Use in the Floodplain in the 1930s, 1960s, and 1990s. Freeman et al. (2003) used aerial photography to quantify changes in land use and land cover between 1930 and 1990 and to evaluate how forest connectivity changed during that period specifically within the 100-year floodplain of the Wisconsin River. They analyzed land cover at three time intervals in nine different reaches of the river between Stevens Point and Blue River. They analyzed over 200 historical aerial photographs, identifying a common set of land-cover classes.

During the 1930s, deciduous forests and agriculture dominated the Wisconsin River floodplain, with wetlands and grasslands occupying under 20% of the vegetation. As in the larger river corridor, land-cover change over the ensuing 60 years was characterized by increased forest extent and decreased agricultural and grassland areas. By the 1990s, deciduous forest covered the largest portion of the floodplain in every reach examined. Almost all the increase in forest cover reflects how forests have replaced crop and grasslands. There are fewer patches of forest in the 1990s than in the 1930s, and patches are now larger, indicating increases in forest connectivity. Open wetlands declined in the north but increased in the central region and more than doubled in extent in the southern region. Grasslands declined by two-thirds in all three regions between 1937 and 1990, more than any other land cover. These declines are paralleled by large reductions in the number, density, and size of grassland patches. Thus, unlike forests, grasslands are becoming more fragmented. Similar trends for grasslands are also occurring in upland areas where they often reflect succession following abandonment of agricultural lands and fire suppression (Leach and Givnish 1996). Finally, urban areas showed substantial relative increases in cover between the 1930s and 1990s, particularly in the north and central reaches, yet remained below 2% cover throughout.

Trends along the banks of the main channel differed from those for the floodplain as a whole. Forest cover was more prevalent along the river edge than across the entire floodplain; the length of channel bordered by deciduous forest has exceeded 74% for all three regions since 1937, increasing to 77%–89% for all regions in the 1990s. Agriculture bordering the river decreased through time.

Landscape Changes—Synthesis. The most striking change along the Wisconsin River in the 20th century has been increases in the amount of deciduous forest cover despite increases in human populations. Closed hardwood forests are more abundant and better connected, particularly in the floodplain. These increases in forest cover along the Wisconsin River contrast strongly with trends observed elsewhere in the state and in other large river floodplains (Décamps et al. 1988; Knutson and Klaas 1998). Across the state, total forestland cover has changed little in Wisconsin since the 1950s (Mauldin et al. 1999), yet forest patches tend to be smaller and more isolated, exposing them to increased edge effects (Sharpe et al. 1987). Increases in floodplain forest area and connectivity may reflect a growing awareness of the unsuitability of floodplains for residential land use and the environmental value of intact floodplain ecosystems as well as efforts to formally protect these lands by the WDNR.

Changes in River Flow and Water Quality

Like the surrounding landscape, water flow in the Wisconsin River has changed as the region was settled and populations grew (Durbin 1997). The Wisconsin River has been labeled the "hardest working river in the world," reflecting its 26 dams and 21 storage reservoirs strung along the northern and central sections (figure 17.1). The earliest dams appeared on the river in the mid-1800s to support the state's burgeoning timber industry (Durbin 1997). These early wood crib structures were often short lived, subject to washout by large spring floods. The oldest dam on the river today is the Rhinelander dam in Oneida County, constructed in 1905. Construction of new dams and conversion of old wooden structures continued until the 1950s with the completion of the Whiting-Plover dam and the upgrade of the Port Edwards dam. Today, most of these dams generate electricity and are owned by utility companies or paper producers. The levees and dikes (including the extensive Lewiston and Caledonia levees near the city of Portage) built to protect urban, residential, and agricultural areas also constrain the river's flow.

In contrast to its upper reaches, no dams exist along the lower 148 km of the Wisconsin River. This stretch gained legal protection as the 32,000 ha Lower Wisconsin State Riverway in 1988 following dramatic proposals to develop housing and recreation along the river. The Wisconsin Department of Natural Resources and a board of nine citizens manages the riverway under regulations intended to maintain its high quality natural and scenic areas, public hunting grounds, and recreational value (http://lwr.state.wi.us).

The extensive construction of levees and dams fundamentally altered both river flow and floodplain structure and function, encouraging human use of these landscapes. The dams considerably reduced annual flooding and overall variability in river flow (Krug and House 1980; Dixon 2001). These changes can be seen by comparing the average annual discharge of the river near Wisconsin Dells with a simulation where river flow is modeled in the absence of dams and levees (figure 17.3;

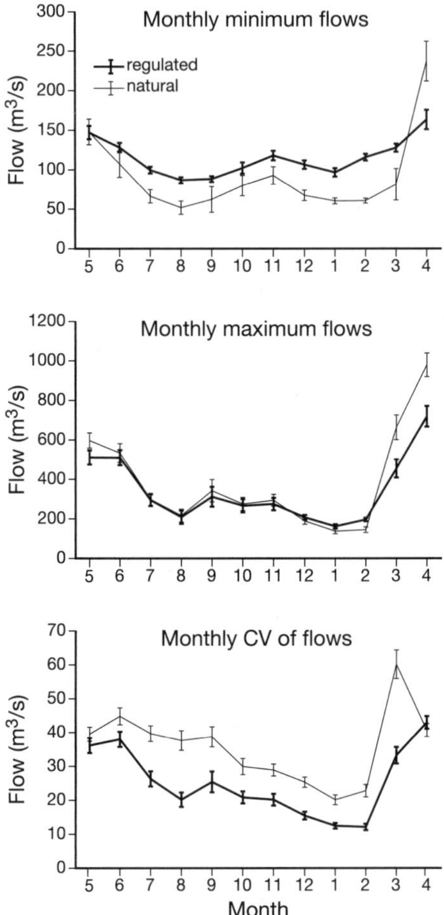

FIGURE 17.3 Effects of dams on river flow. Shown are the actual (regulated) and simulated (natural) annual hydrographs near Wisconsin Dells. The simulated hydrograph represents river flow in the absence of flow modifications such as dams, reservoirs, and levees. Data are from Dixon 2001. CV, coefficient of variation.

Dixon and Turner 2006). Note how dams have dampened the historical variability in the river's flow (particularly clipping peaks in March and April) while increasing flows through summer and fall.

Such major changes in the magnitude and timing of river flow have greatly affected the biota living in and along the river. Reduced flooding in spring and summer has probably favored seedling establishment in river birch, cottonwood, and willow (Dixon 2003) by reducing the chance that flood waters will dislodge newly established seedlings. Reductions in peak summer floods enhance seedling establishment, while diminished winter and spring floods probably favored overwinter survival (Dixon 2003). Reduced flooding may also favor upland species, shifting community composition. We observed such changes upland of the levees near Portage (Gergel et al. 2002).

Reduced flooding may also limit how much nitrogen is removed from the river by reducing the volume of water exposed to floodplain soils. Microbes in these soils can remove nitrate from overlying waters via denitrification (West 2001; Forshay and Stanley 2005). However, the amount of nitrogen removed depends on how large the flood is and how long it lasts. In fact, nitrate concentrations in the river have increased steadily since the 1970s (figure 17.4). This increase is usually assumed to reflect increases in nitrogen-laden runoff from the watershed. Although fertilizer use in the Wisconsin River watershed is considered moderate by midwestern standards (5,000–10,000 kg/km^2 annually; Goolsby and Battaglin 2001), nitrate and ammonium dissolve easily in water, allowing them to be quickly transported from lawns and fields into surface and groundwater. Thus, these elevated nitrate concentrations may reflect both increased inputs and declines in the nitrogen-removal capacity of the river's floodplains and wetlands associated with

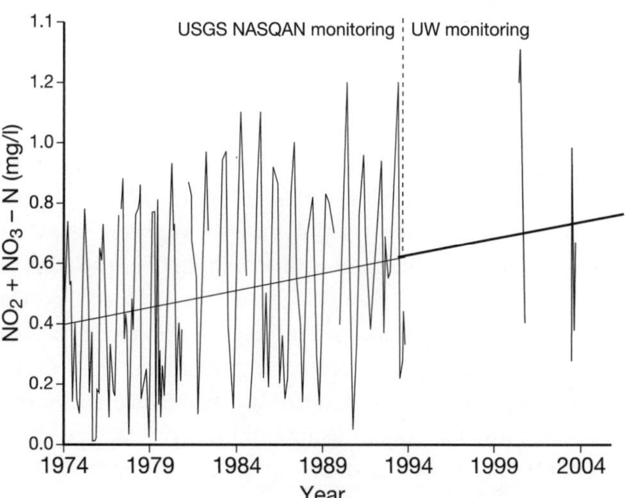

FIGURE 17.4 Nitrate concentrations in the Wisconsin River. Nitrate concentrations for the past 30 years have been increasing in association with the extensive agricultural and urban land uses in the watershed. USGS NASQAN, U.S. Geological Survey National Stream Quality Accounting Network; UW, University of Wisconsin.

land-use change and reduced flooding. Nitrogen loads in the Wisconsin River are of considerable importance as they travel down the Mississippi to the Gulf of Mexico, where they contribute directly to the hypoxic "Dead Zone" (Goolsby and Battaglin 2001).

Changes in the Floodplain Forest

The floodplain forests of the Wisconsin River are currently dominated by native, flood-tolerant species including green ash, silver maple, and American elm as we know from surveys by Turner and others (2004) of over 900 plots distributed over the same nine reaches studied by Freeman and others (2003). Green ash was most frequent (occurring in more than 60% of study plots), but silver maple and American elm each occurred in about half the plots. Which tree species occurred where and their abundance in the floodplain correspond reasonably well to differences in the geographic province and flooding regime (e.g., the relative elevation and distance from the main channel). Most tree species are most abundant in the less regulated Lower Wisconsin State Riverway. Land-cover history also helps to explain where late-successional species like basswood and bitternut hickory occur. However, understanding how the floodplain forest communities have changed in recent decades is challenging as baseline data are scarce. We draw on two analyses to compare contemporary with historical floodplain forests, then discuss the influence of the century-old levees near Portage on floodplain vegetation.

Floodplain Forests Then and Now. John Curtis (1959) and his students surveyed several floodplain forests as part of their broader surveys of Wisconsin's vegetation in the 1940s and 1950s. In 2000, Esther Alsum (2003) resampled five of these sites in the Lower Wisconsin Riverway, 6–45 km below the Prairie du Sac dam. Her analyses reveal increases in bitternut hickory, hackberry, and silver maple over the past 50 years. In contrast, American elm, swamp white oak, river birch, cottonwood, and black willow all decreased. Several trees dominant in the 1950s (silver maple, ash, and elm) had fewer saplings in 2000, apparently reflecting invasions of European buckthorn, an aggressive nonnative shrub (Alsum 2003). Elms have also declined along the Wisconsin River in response to Dutch elm disease since this deadly disease was introduced to America in the mid-1950s (Grittinger 1978; Dunn 1986). Hackberry and bitternut hickory often fill the canopy gaps left by dead elms (Larson and Barnes 1982), perhaps contributing to the increase in these species observed by Alsum in the resampled plots.

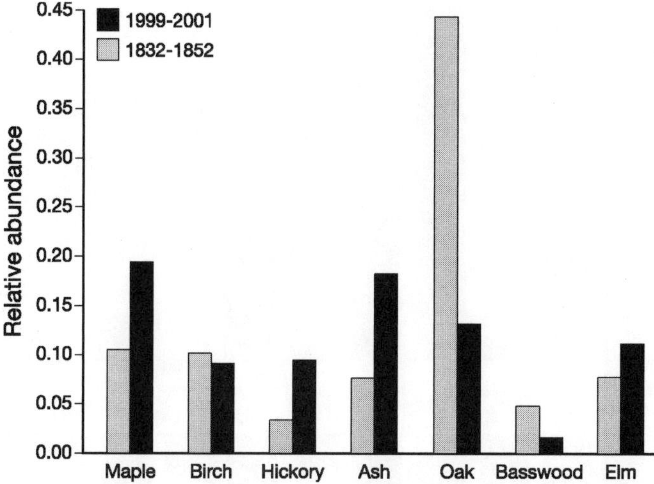

FIGURE 17.5 The relative abundance of tree genera in presettlement and contemporary floodplain forests of the Wisconsin River. Presettlement data were obtained from the General Land Office Surveys, and contemporary forest data are from Turner and others (2004) and M. G. Turner and others (unpublished data).

Another source of early data about Midwest forests comes from the General Land Office (GLO) Survey (Johnson 1976; chapter 2). These records provide a wealth of information about the landscape from an early phase of European settlement (see, e.g., Whitney 1994). By comparing forest composition from these GLO data with data from modern forests, we can infer significant changes across much of the Midwest (see, e.g., Curtis 1959; Mladenoff and Howell 1980; Liegel 1982; Radeloff et al. 1999). These data have also been used to study shifts in vegetation along the Platte River (Johnson 1994), the Upper Mississippi River (Yin et al. 1997; Knutson and Klass 1998), the Chippewa River (Barnes 1997), and the confluence of the Illinois and Mississippi rivers (Nelson et al. 1994).

We compared measures of current forest composition with pre–European settlement vegetation extracted from surveyors' notebooks as part of the original U.S. Public Land Survey. We tallied the identity of 1,146 trees recorded between 1832 and 1851 in each of nine study reaches by genus (as the original surveyors did not consistently identify species). Turner and others resurveyed these stretches between 1999 and 2001, identifying and measuring 4,689 trees. Because of the different sampling schemes, we compare only the proportion of sampled trees for the eight most common genera for each reach of the river between the two time periods. Since the mid-1800s, we observe several changes in relative abundance (figure 17.5). Maple, hickory, ash, and elm all

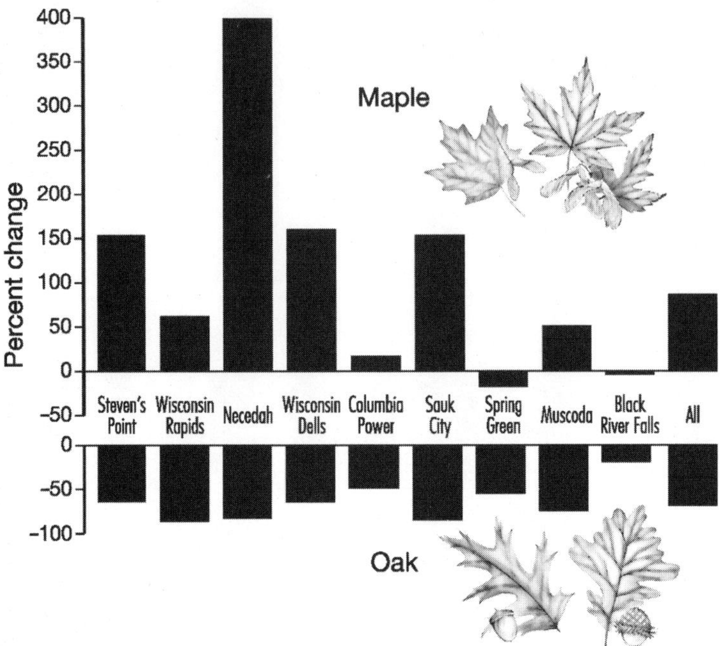

FIGURE 17.6 Change in the relative proportions of (*a*) maple and (*b*) oak in floodplain forests of nine study reaches along the Wisconsin River at presettlement and in contemporary forests. Presettlement data were obtained from the General Land Office Surveys, and contemporary forest data are from Turner and others (2004) and M. G. Turner and others (unpublished data).

increased in relative abundance during this interval with maple (primarily silver maple) increasing from 11% to 18% and ash from 8% to 17% (figure 17.6*a*). In contrast, oaks declined dramatically in relative abundance from 45% of trees seen by surveyors to 12% today (figure 17.6*b*). Birch, pine, and basswood also declined in relative abundance (from 10% to 8%, 3% to 0.2%, and 5% to 1.5%., respectively).

Thus, although floodplain forests of the Wisconsin River are still dominated by flood-tolerant species and contain a good mix of species, today's forests have shifted considerably since European settlement. Because we only compared the proportions of trees (rather than actual abundances), declines in the relative abundance of oak could reflect either of two processes. First, oaks could actually have declined numerically, consistent with the exclusion of fire that accompanied settlement, creating conditions less conducive to new oak establishment. Second, other tree species could have increased enough in abundance over the past 150 years to reduce the proportional abundance of oaks even as they persisted at a similar numerical abundance. Both of these have probably contributed to the declines in oak relative abundance that we observed (see chapter 7 for further discussion of oak decline).

The green ash, silver maple, and American elm that we observed frequently also dominate other floodplain forests in the region. Their abundance appears to reflect broad-scale changes in floodplain forest composition throughout the Midwest. On the lower Chippewa River in Wisconsin, the location and extent of floodplain forests have changed little since European settlement, but stand structure and composition have changed (Schulte and Barnes 1996). Trees in the contemporary floodplain forests are larger than at the time of settlement (ca. 1850), and tree species diversity has declined (Barnes 1997). In particular, silver maple is now three times more abundant than it was before settlement, replacing cottonwood and black willow as the major colonizing species (Barnes 1997). Fulton (1987) found that silver maple dominated the vegetation of islands formed between 1955 and 1962 in the lower Wisconsin River. Liegel (1982, 1988) noted similar vegetation changes in the Leopold Memorial Reserve near Wisconsin Dells. Silver maple has also increased in dominance relative to other species in unmodified forests along the Upper Mississippi in southwestern Illinois (Yin et al. 1997) and at the confluence of the Illinois and Mississippi rivers (Nelson et al. 1994).

Why has silver maple increased? This may reflect its fast growth, its intermediate shade tolerance, and/or its ability to exploit new site conditions (Nelson et al. 1994). Silver maple's ability to tolerate shade and establish on substrates rich in organic matter (Burns and Honkala 1990) may allow it to invade a wider set of sites than willow and cottonwood, which depend on open sediment bars for recruitment. Silver maple also tolerates saturated soils well, perhaps even growing faster when flooded (Hosner and Boyce 1962). Shifts in the timing of floods toward earlier in spring in the Upper Mississippi River Basin (Knox 2001) may also favor silver maple, which disperses its seeds before many other pioneer species (Dixon 2001). Despite these advantages and previous success, silver maple appears not to be recruiting well into the understory now, making its future position in floodplain forests uncertain.

A number of additional factors influence floodplain forests. Herbivory on tree seedlings, especially by deer, continues to influence forest development with particular impacts over the past few decades. Deer populations remain high throughout the study area, and intensive browsing depresses regeneration of preferred species (e.g., Rooney 2001; Rooney et al. 2002; chapter 19). Fire frequency has also declined in the region through the 20th century, likely affecting stand structure and composition (Curtis 1959). The effect of dams on the forests likely varies geographically; river regulation may decrease (Rood and Mahoney 1990) or increase (Johnson 1994) riparian tree recruitment depending on channel morphology, the type of regulation, and the species pool (Williams and Wolman 1984; Friedman et al. 1998; Johnson 1998; Jansson et al. 2000; Dixon 2001).

Is the composition of the current floodplain forest likely to change in the future? Tree saplings were counted by species between 1999 and 2001 in the same nine reaches in which landscape changes and tree community composition was studied. Green ash saplings are the most abundant and widespread, occurring in over one-third of the sample plots. In contrast, silver maple saplings are nearly absent despite being a current overstory dominant (S. E. Gergel et al., unpublished data). The future composition of the floodplain forests is thus likely to differ from what it is today and what it was historically. However, predicting future forests remains difficult. Although the sapling data suggest that we will see increases in green ash, the spread of the emerald ash borer (already in Indiana and Michigan) could dramatically reduce ash abundance (see chapter 30). Projected changes in climate could also alter the competitive balance among species (Kling et al. 2003; chapter 31). Such changes in species composition produce cascading effects on ecosystem processes because leaf characteristics vary among species, affecting rates of decomposition and nutrient release (Kang and Stanley 2004). These, in turn, affect the outcome of competition among seedlings of these species. Thus, shifts in the relative abundance of basswood, silver maple, and American elm will likely cause subtle long-term changes in ecosystem processes.

Effects of Levees on Floodplain Vegetation. Levees limit the lateral flow of sediment, nutrients, and organisms between rivers and their floodplains (Sparks 1995; Johnston et al. 2001). Not surprisingly, levees influence both the composition and productivity of floodplain forests. Along the Upper Mississippi, flood-intolerant oaks increased in abundance behind levees, while American elm, hackberry, and hickory declined (Yin et al. 1997).

The levees constructed upstream of Portage during the early 1900s offer a particular opportunity to explore how modifying rivers flows affects floodplains. Here, black oak and other flood-intolerant species again became more abundant upland of levees (Gergel et al. 2002).

Predick (2002) found that river birch, a highly flood-tolerant species, grew fastest between the river and the levee. Furthermore, relative growth rates of river birch inside the levee were positively related to maximum river flow—tree growth increased with increased flooding. Interestingly, between 1991 and 2000, the relative growth rates of green ash and two upland oaks (black oak and Hill's oak) were highest in 1993 when a large flood occurred. Active flooding thus appears to increase the growth rates of all four species. Riparian vegetation may be a sensitive indicator of environmental change in a river or its watershed. Tracking changes in these floodplain forests could therefore provide further insights into ecological change.

Bird Communities in the Floodplain Forest. Bird species may also be responding to changing habitat conditions in floodplain forests. Miller and others (2004) found a diverse assemblage of birds here (92 species) in 1999 and 2000 in the same reaches studied by Turner and others (2004). Ten forest generalist species were observed at over 90% of transects. Most such species reach their greatest abundance in edge habitats. Eight species that typically nest in forest interiors were also observed. Two species (Kentucky warbler and cerulean warbler) considered indicators of high quality floodplain forest were not observed during this study. This could reflect altered conditions associated with river regulation, but this requires further study. Local habitat characteristics explained most of the variation in the abundances of these forest birds as well as the number of species observed. Landscape composition and configuration mattered only for forest interior species. The fact that contemporary landscape pattern had little influence may reflect either the fact that the abundant habitat generalist birds are insensitive to these features or that these floodplain forests remain abundant and well connected. Interestingly, patterns of *former* land cover (Freeman et al. 2003), not usually included in avian studies, accounted for variation in the abundance of all the bird groups except edge species.

Summary

Although several stretches of the Wisconsin River appear pristine today, the river and its surrounding landscape have experienced dramatic changes over the past 150 years. Initial European settlement brought intensified agriculture and a loss of natural vegetation along the river. Since the 1930s, however, floodplain forests increased in extent and connectivity while agricultural lands and grasslands declined. Despite the recovery of forest cover, agricultural and urban land uses in the watershed have elevated fertilizer use and nonpoint sources of pollution, boosting nitrate concentrations in the river. Dams, reservoirs, and levees on the river have reduced its variability in flow, affecting, in turn, the composition of the floodplain forest and possibly impeding the ability of floodplain soils to denitrify nitrates in the water. The composition of floodplain forests continues to change as upland species invade areas where flooding is controlled. Although widespread flood-tolerant tree species still dominate floodplain forests along the Wisconsin, shifts in the understory suggest that changes in the overstory will continue through the 21st century.

Interactions between anthropogenic and ecological processes will continue to shape the Wisconsin River and its floodplains. Although natural vegetation has recovered along much of the river and its lower stretches are now legally protected from development, the river receives inputs from a predominantly developed watershed. Will nitrate loads continue to increase or decline? As in other ecosystems, we face challenges to manage the river and its lands wisely while preserving the beauty and services important to society now and in the future.

References

Alsum, E. M. 2003. Fifty years later: An assessment of the influence of common buckthorn (*Rhamnus cathartica L.*) and of change in overstory vegetation in several floodplain forests of the Lower Wisconsin State Riverway. MS thesis, Department of Botany, University of Wisconsin–Madison.

Auclair, A. N. 1976. Ecological factors in the development of intensive-management ecosystems in the midwestern United States. Ecology 57:431–444.

Barnes, W. J. 1997. Vegetation dynamics on the floodplain of the lower Chippewa River in Wisconsin. Journal of the Torrey Botanical Society 124:189–197.

Bürgi, M., and M. G. Turner. 2002. Factors and processes shaping land cover and land cover changes along the Wisconsin River, USA. Ecosystems 5:184–201.

Burns, R. M., and B. H. Honkala. 1990. Silvics of North America. Vol. 2, *Hardwoods*. U.S. Department of Agriculture (USDA) Forest Service, Agricultural Handbook 654. Washington, DC: USDA.

Conzen, M. P. 1997. The European settling and transformation of the Upper Mississippi Valley lead mining region. Pp. 163–196 in R. C. Ostergren and T. R. Vale, eds. Wisconsin Land and Life. Madison: University of Wisconsin Press.

Curtis, J. T. 1959. The Vegetation of Wisconsin. Madison: University of Wisconsin Press.

Dahl, T. E. 1990. Wetland Losses in the United States, 1780s to 1980s. Washington, DC: U.S. Fish and Wildlife Service, U.S. Department of the Interior.

Décamps, H., M. Fortune, F. Gazelle, and G. Patou. 1988. Historical influence of man on the riparian dynamics of a fluvial landscape. Landscape Ecology 1:163–173.

Dixon, M. D. 2001. Woody vegetation dynamics on Wisconsin River sandbars: Spatial and temporal controls on seedling recruitment. Ph.D. diss., University of Wisconsin–Madison.

———. 2003. Effects of flow pattern on riparian seedling recruitment on sandbars in the Wisconsin River, Wisconsin, USA. Wetlands 23: 125–139.

Dixon, M. D., and M. G. Turner. 2006. Simulated recruitment of riparian trees under natural and regulated flow regimes on the Wisconsin River, USA. River Research and Applications 22:1057–1083.

Dorney, J. R. 1981. The impact of Native Americans on presettlement vegetation in southeastern Wisconsin. Wisconsin Academy of Sciences, Arts and Letters 69:26–36.

Dunn, C. 1986. Shrub layer response to the death of *Ulmus americana* in southeastern Wisconsin lowland forests. Bulletin of the Torrey Botanical Club 113:142–148.

Durbin, R. D. 1997. The Wisconsin River: An Odyssey through Time and Space. Cross Plains, WI: Spring Freshet Press.

Forshay, K. J., and E. H. Stanley. 2005. Rapid nitrate loss and denitrification in a temperate river floodplain. Biogeochemistry 75:43–64.

Freeman, R. E., E. H. Stanley, and M. G. Turner. 2003. Analysis and conservation implications of landscape change in the Wisconsin River floodplain, USA. Ecological Applications 13:416–431.

Friedman, J. M., W. R. Osterkamp, M. L. Scott, and G. T. Auble. 1998. Downstream effects of dams on channel geometry and bottomland vegetation: Regional patterns in the Great Plains. Wetlands 18:619–633.

Fulton, M. R. 1987. The vegetation and development of young island surfaces in the lower Wisconsin River. M.S. thesis, University of Wisconsin–Madison.

Gergel, S. E., M. D. Dixon, and M. G. Turner. 2002. Consequences of human-altered floods: Levees, floods and floodplain forests along the Wisconsin River. Ecological Applications 12:1755–1770.

Goolsby, D. A., and W. A. Battaglin. 2001. Long-term changes in concentrations and flux of nitrogen in the Mississippi River Basin, USA. Hydrological Processes 15:1209–1226.

Grittinger, T. F. 1978. Loss of elm from some lowland forests in eastern Wisconsin. Transactions of the Wisconsin Academy of Sciences, Arts and Letters 66:195–205.

Hosner, J. F., and S. G. Boyce. 1962. Tolerance to water saturated soil of various bottomland hardwoods. Forest Science 8:180–186.

Hosner, J. F., and L. S. Minckler. 1963. Bottomland hardwood forests of southern Illinois—Regeneration and succession. Ecology 44:29–41.

Jansson, R., C. Nilsson, and B. Renofalt. 2000. Fragmentation of riparian floras in rivers with multiple dams. Ecology 81:899–903.

Johnson, H. B. 1976. Order upon the Land: The U.S. Rectangular Land Survey and the Upper Mississippi Country. New York: Oxford University Press.

Johnson, W. C. 1994. Woodland expansion in the Platte River Nebraska: Patterns and causes. Ecological Monographs 64:45–84.

———. 1998. Adjustment of riparian vegetation to river regulation in the Great Plains, USA. Wetlands 18:608–618.

Johnston, C. A., S. D. Bridgham, and J. P. Schubauer-Berigan. 2001. Nutrient dynamics in relation to geomorphology of riverine wetlands. Soil Science Society of America Journal 65:557–577.

Kang, H., and E. H. Stanley. 2004. Effects of levees on soil microbial activities in a large river floodplain. River Research and Management 20:1–7.

Kline, V. M, and G. Cottam. 1979. Vegetation response to climate and fire in the Driftless Area of Wisconsin. Ecology 60:861–868.

Kling, G. W., K. Hayhoe, L. B. Johnson, et al. 2003. Confronting Climate Change in the Great Lakes Region: Impacts on Our Communities and Ecosystems. Cambridge, MA: Union of Concerned Scientists; Washington, DC: Ecological Society of America.

Knox, J. C. 2001. Agricultural influence on landscape sensitivity in the Upper Mississippi River Valley. Catena 42:193–224.

Knutson, M. G., and E. E. Klaas. 1998. Floodplain forest loss and changes in forest community composition and structure in the Upper Mississippi River: A wildlife habitat at risk. Natural Areas Journal 18: 138–150.

Krug, W. R., and L. B. House. 1980. Streamflow Model of Wisconsin River for Estimating Flow Frequency and Volume. U.S. Geological Survey (USGS) Water-Resources Investigations Open-File Report 80–1103, USGS, Madison, WI.

Lange, K. I. 1990. A postglacial vegetational history of Sauk County and Caledonia Township, Columbia County, South Central Wisconsin. Wisconsin Department of Natural Resources, Technical Bulletin 168, Madison.

Larson, J. L., and W. J. Barnes. 1982. Succession and elm replacement in the Dunnville Bottoms. Transactions of the Wisconsin Academy of Sciences, Arts and Letters 70:52–60.

Leach, M. K., and T. J. Givnish. 1996. Ecological determinants of species loss in remnant prairies. Science 273:1555–1558.

Liegel, K. 1982. The pre-European settlement vegetation of the Aldo Memorial Reserve. Transactions of the Wisconsin Academy of Sciences, Arts and Letters 70:13–26.

———. 1988. Land use and vegetational change on the Aldo Leopold Memorial Reserve. Transactions of the Wisconsin Academy of Sciences, Arts and Letters 76:47–68.

Martin, L. 1965. The Physical Geography of Wisconsin. 3rd ed. Madison: University of Wisconsin Press.

Mauldin, T. E., A. J. Plantinga, and R. J. Alig. 1999. Land Use in the Lake States Region: An Analysis of Past Trends and Projections of Future Changes. U.S. Department of Agriculture Forest Service Pacific Northwest Research Station, Research Paper 519, Portland, OR.

Miller, J. R., M. D. Dixon, and M. G. Turner. 2004. Response of avian communities in large-river floodplains to environmental variation at multiple scales. Ecological Applications 14:1394–1410.

Mladenoff, D. J., and E. A. Howell. 1980. Vegetation change on the Gegebic Iron Range (Iron County, Wisconsin) from the 1860s to the present. Transactions of the Wisconsin Academy of Sciences, Arts and Letters 68:74–89.

Nelson, J. C., A. Redmond, and R.E. Sparks. 1994. Impacts of settlement on floodplain vegetation at the confluence of the Illinois and Mississippi Rivers. Transactions of the Illinois State Academy of Science 87:117–133.

Ostergren, R. C. 1997. The Euro-American settlement of Wisconsin, 1830–1920. Pp. 147–162 in R. C. Ostergren and T. R. Vale, eds. Wisconsin Land and Life. Madison: University of Wisconsin Press.

Predick, K. I. 2002. The importance of flood regime for tree growth and shrub productivity on the Wisconsin River floodplain and uplands. MS thesis, University of Wisconsin–Madison.

Radeloff, V. C., D. J. Mladenoff, H. He, and M. S. Boyce. 1999. Forest landscape change in the northwestern Wisconsin Pine Barrens from pre-European settlement to the present. Canadian Journal of Forest Research 29:1649–1659.

Rood, S. B., and J. M. Mahoney. 1990. Collapse of riparian forests downstream from dams in western prairies: Probable causes and prospects for mitigation. Environmental Management 14:451–464.

Rooney, T. P. 2001. Deer impacts on forest ecosystems: A North American perspective. Forestry 74:201–208.

Rooney, T. P., S. L. Solheim, and D. M. Waller. 2002. Factors affecting the regeneration of northern white cedar in lowland forests of the Upper Great Lakes region, USA. Forest Ecology and Management 163:119–130.

Schulte, L., and W. J. Barnes. 1996. Presettlement vegetation of the lower Chippewa River Valley. Michigan Botanist 35:29–37.

Sharpe, D. M., G. R. Guntenspergen, C. P. Dunn, L. A. Leitner, and F. Stearns. 1987. Vegetation dynamics in a southern Wisconsin agricultural landscape. Pp. 137–155 in M. G. Turner, ed. Landscape Heterogeneity and Disturbance. New York: Springer-Verlag.

Sparks, R. E. 1995. Need for ecosystem management of large rivers and their floodplains. BioScience 45:168–182.

State of Wisconsin. 1936. Division of Land Economic Inventory, Executive Office, Bulletin 3, Madison.

Swift, B. L. 1974. Status of riparian ecosystems in the United States. Water Resource Bulletin 20:223–228.

Tans, W. 1976. The presettlement vegetation of Columbia County, Wisconsin in the 1830's. Wisconsin Department of Natural Resources, Technical Bulletin 90, Madison.

Turner, M. G., S. R. Carpenter, E. J. Gustafson, R. J. Naiman, and S. M. Pearson. 1998. Land use. Pp. 37–61 in M. J. Mac, P. A. Opler, P. Doran, and C. Haecker, eds. Status and Trends of Our Nation's Biological Resources. Vol. 1. Washington DC: National Biological Service.

Turner, M. G., S. E. Gergel, M. D. Dixon, and J. R. Miller. 2004. Distribution and abundance of trees in floodplain forests of the Wisconsin River: Environmental influences at different scales. Journal of Vegetation Science 15:729–738.

Turner, M. G., D. N. Wear, and R. O. Flamm. 1996. Land ownership and land-cover change in the Southern Appalachian Highlands and the Olympic Peninsula. Ecological Applications 6:1150–1172.

Ware, G. H. 1955. A phytosociological study of lowland hardwood forests in southern Wisconsin. Ph.D. thesis, University of Wisconsin–Madison.

Wear, D. N., and P. Bolstad. 1998. Land-use changes in southern Appalachian landscapes: Spatial analysis and forecast evaluation. Ecosystems 1:575–594.

West, J. 2001. Denitrification in soils of the Wisconsin River floodplain: Patterns and potential controls. MS thesis, University of Wisconsin–Madison.

Whitney, G. G. 1994. From Coastal Wilderness to Fruited Plain. Cambridge: Cambridge University Press.

Williams, G. P., and M. G. Wolman. 1984. Downstream Effects of Dams on Alluvial Rivers. U.S. Geological Survey, Professional Paper 1286. Washington, DC: U.S. Government Printing Office.

Yin, Y., J. C. Nelson, and K. S. Lubinski. 1997. Bottomland hardwood forest along the Upper Mississippi. Natural Areas Journal 17: 164–173.

Part Four: Changing Animal Communities

Almost a century ago, zoologist Joseph Grinnell made extensive collections of vertebrate animals throughout California for Berkeley's Museum of Comparative Zoology. While these collections filled the pressing need for research specimens, Grinnell believed that the collection would also serve new purposes decades later. As he witnessed the growth of California's population and the expansion of agriculture, he realized that he created a baseline of the California fauna that could be used to evaluate human impacts on the land. With his eye to the future, he took detailed field notes so that future researchers could replicate his work (Grinnell Resurvey Project 2007). Today, researchers are revisiting many of Grinnell's more than 700 collection sites, resurveying the animals present, and analyzing the changes in their distribution and abundance. The Grinnell Resurvey Project is exceptional because it is the only place in North America where there is sufficient baseline data to study regional, decades-long changes in complete assemblages of mammals, reptiles, and amphibians.

Scientists have fewer data for detecting and interpreting changes in Wisconsin's animal communities over the past century or two. We lack a single repository of data to draw upon. Despite this limitation, we asked zoologists to tap what data sources they had to provide us with at least pieces of the puzzle. In the next chapter, Wisconsin

Department of Natural Resources (WDNR) zoologists Adrian Wydeven and Chuck Pils examine historical changes in the state's carnivore populations. They scoured agency hunting and trapping records, old agency reports, and the academic literature to reveal how populations of predators have shifted. Two themes emerge. First, populations of carnivores have changed in terms of both their abundance and their distribution in the state. Some species have done well, while others have fared poorly. Second, these shifts often reflect policy decisions. State bounties for certain animals like wolves and bobcats greatly depleted their populations. Later, legal protection and active restoration efforts by the same state have served to increase the densities of carnivores like fisher and wolf. Changes in public attitudes toward carnivores made these policy reversals possible. Perhaps there is a lesson here that we could extend to less charismatic species.

Wildlife biologists Scott Craven and Tim Van Deelen inform us about Wisconsin's wildlife icon—the white-tailed deer. Long hunted by Native Americans, deer declined in numbers soon after European settlement in response to overhunting and habitat loss. By the early 1900s, deer were only found in the northern third of the state. State conservation programs brought this species back from extinction, making deer recovery a great conservation success. A half-century later, the pendulum has swung back. Now conservationists contend with the impacts of too many deer: vehicle collisions, crop damage, failed tree regeneration, and general declines in biodiversity. By emphasizing deer as both a cause and a reflection of environmental change, the authors reveal some key links in the web of life and our relation to these.

Like most conservationists, we are alarmed by the persistent reports of global amphibian declines and midwestern amphibian deformities. Global declines in reptile abundance parallel those of amphibians, reflecting habitat loss, vehicle mortality, and overcollecting (Gibbons et al. 2000). How are these trends playing out in Wisconsin? Gary Casper addresses this question, drawing on his field research experience from two very different places—the Apostle Islands and Milwaukee County. Because they depend on different types of habitat throughout their life cycle and have limited dispersal abilities, reptiles and amphibians are particularly sensitive to habitat loss and fragmentation. Wetland losses throughout the state are taking their toll on amphibians and reptiles, along with ongoing habitat alteration and fragmentation of critical habitats. Many species have already declined 10-fold or more. Without directed conservation efforts, a large fraction of reptile and amphibian populations will continue to dwindle.

A recent survey indicated that roughly 30% of all Americans engage in bird watching (National Survey on Recreation and the Environment 2000). Some occasionally watch birds visiting their backyard feeders. At the other extreme, hard-core "twitchers," travel the world in their quest to add more species to their life list. The rest of us fall in between. Given all this interest, it is hardly surprising that biologists have more and better records for birds in North America than any other group of species. The annual Christmas Bird Count that started with 27 participants in 1900 draws 50,000 today. DNR ornithologists Dave Sample and Mike Mossman tell us how Wisconsin's grassland birds have changed since the 1700s. Given that Wisconsin is "The Dairy State," it might seem logical to conclude that agricultural fields benefit these birds. The reality, however, is that grassland birds are declining faster than any other group. The relationship between grassland birds and agriculture turns out to be complicated, tying the fate of these birds to socioeconomic forces, agricultural technology, and the conservation ethic of our society at large.

University of Wisconsin wildlife biologists Stan Temple and John Cary next lend us their considerable expertise on the distributions of Wisconsin's birds. They approach bird communities using some of the same approaches that plant ecologists use to explore changes in their composition across 10 distinct habitats over the past 55 years. They also interpret those changes in light of what they know about the birds themselves and their environment. Although species richness in most of those communities has increased over the past several decades, changes in individual species varied a lot, with some showing long-term declines and others increases. Bird communities will continue to change into the future, driven by shifts in climate, land use, and changing landscape patterns.

Insects are the most diverse and abundant class of animals. They also play critical and irreplaceable roles in most ecosystem processes. Although researchers know something of long-term changes in a handful of pest species, we know little about the distribution and abundance of most of our insect species and less about how these have changed over time. In fact, we have yet to even compile a full inventory of which insect species occur in Wisconsin (resembling the situation we have with lichens). Nevertheless, we do know a little about a few charismatic groups of insects. Entomologist Les Ferge introduces us to one such group: our butterflies, moths, and skippers. Even though this is the best-known group of insects in the state, we face many gaps in even our basic knowledge about these insects. These gaps are so great that we can only make informed conjectures about the general kinds of changes that are likely taking place. We know that butterflies, moths, and skippers are sensitive to extreme weather, climate change, invasive species, and pesticide use. All these factors loom large among the ecological changes we expect in our state over the next century. In the case of insects, we discover that what we don't know about our state's biota far exceeds what we know. Our lack of any statewide inventory and knowledge about how individual species will respond to coming challenges translates into a corresponding lack of any statewide conservation strategy for this important group.

References

Gibbons, J. W., D. E. Scott, T. J. Ryan, K. A. Buhlmann, T. D. Tuberville, B. S. Metts, J. L. Greene, T. Mills, Y. Leiden, S. Poppy, and C. T. Winne. 2000. The global decline of reptiles, deja vu amphibians. BioScience 50:653–666.

Grinnell Resurvey Project. 2007. Available at http://mvz.berkeley.edu/Grinnell/index.html. Accessed 26 February 2007.

National Survey on Recreation and the Environment. 2000. Available at http://www.srs.fs.usda.gov/trends/Nsre/Round1t4rptuw.pdf. Accessed 26 February 2007.

18 Changes in Mammalian Carnivore Populations

Adrian P. Wydeven and Charles M. Pils

Carnivores capture the imagination, arousing both fear and respect. Most people would quickly trade a backcountry experience with a wood turtle for the same experience with a wolf, or swap a sighting of a swamp metalmark for a marten. Carnivores also play critical functional roles in ecosystems, making their conservation a high priority. People have had a long and complex relationship with carnivores. Humans competed with carnivores for prey, trappers relied on carnivores for their livelihood, and governments sponsored both eradication and conservation programs, with the relative importance of these changing through time. The abundances of carnivores in Wisconsin today differ substantially from what they were 100 or 200 years ago and will continue to change in the future. Here, we explore these changes.

Postglacial, Presettlement Carnivore Communities

When glaciers retreated from Wisconsin, great herds of mammoths, mastodons, bison, musk ox, woodland musk ox, shrub ox, caribou, and stag-moose moved into the tundra steppe and boreal forest that covered the land (Kurten and Anderson 1980). Sabertooth cats, dire wolves, gray wolves, grizzly bears, short-faced bears, wolverines, and Paleo-Indians would have followed these migratory grazers. Within a few thousand years, mammoths, mastodons, woodland musk ox, and stag-moose disappeared. Large carnivores such as dire wolf, sabertooth cat, and short-faced bear became extinct as their major prey species disappeared. Musk ox, bison, and grizzly bears moved north and west as tundra and barrens contracted. The disappearance of the megacarnivores and change in ungulate communities allowed gray wolves and cougars to become the major large predators on ungulates in the region (Culver et al. 2000; Nowak 2003).

Between the glacial retreat and the arrival of Europeans, Wisconsin's flora and fauna changed drastically. The northern portions of the region were dominated by mixed deciduous/conifer forest with some boreal elements and supported white-tailed deer, moose, a few caribou, gray wolf, and black bear. The deciduous forest, oak savannas, and prairies to the south supported elk, white-tailed deer, bison, gray wolf, black bear, and cougar.

Native Americans influenced carnivore communities through controlled burning, creation of villages and croplands, and hunting. Prior to European invasion, Native American numbers were fairly high in the interior of North American, having major impacts on the landscape in some regions (Diamond 1997; chapter 2). By the time these Europeans began to explore the interior, their diseases preceded them, drastically reducing populations of Native Americans. Widespread pestilence may have allowed bison to reestablish east of the Mississippi into Wisconsin and eastward to the Atlantic coast (Martin and Szuter 2002) and might have increased the prey base for other predators. Alternatively, as Native Americans acquired European goods and began hunting with guns and horses, hunting efficiency improved. These hunters probably impacted elk and other ungulates by the time that Euro-American settlers arrived in the early 1800s and in turn would have indirectly impacted the large carnivores that hunted these ungulates.

The early fur trade emphasized beaver but also included some of the various carnivores used by Native Americans (McGee 1987). Changes in beaver populations probably had some indirect impacts on beaver predators such as wolf and bear. Changes in wetland habitat following beaver removal and perhaps incidental captures had substantial impacts on minks, river otters, and possibly raccoons.

The mammalian carnivore communities encountered by the first European settlers were not at equilibrium. The direct and indirect effects of climate, other predator and prey populations, and habitat alteration continuously influenced carnivore population numbers differently. Their stories follow.

The Gray Wolf: A Top Carnivore

Gray wolves apparently occurred throughout the state in 1800. Jackson (1961) speculated that as many as 20,000–25,000 may have existed in Wisconsin in 1835, but this would be much higher than typical densities of wolves found in recent research (Fuller et al. 2003). Wydeven and others (1995) provide a revised estimate of 3,000–5,000 wolves. As major predators on deer, elk, and moose, wolves probably affected distribution, behavior, and physical condition of these ungulates.

Wolves declined as Europeans settled Wisconsin. The territory of Wisconsin established a bounty on wolves in 1839, and state bounties were paid most years from 1865 to 1957 (Thiel 1993). At the same time, disappearing ungulates also impacted wolves. Elk were extirpated by about 1875 (Jackson 1961), and deer disappeared from much of southern Wisconsin by the late 1800s (Schorger 1953). These reductions, along with near extirpation of beaver (Schorger 1965), caused major reductions in food resources for wolves. Livestock and domestic animals became an important food source, increasing conflicts between people and wolves and reinforcing support for continued bounty payments. Wolves were eliminated from southern Wisconsin by 1900 and were extirpated from the state by 1960 (Thiel 1993).

Elimination of wolves might have eliminated trophic cascades, or progressive indirect effects of predators across successively lower trophic levels (Estes et al. 2001). Wolves and other top carnivores often play a key functional role in ecosystems by generating trophic cascades. Studies elsewhere show wolves can affect the growth of balsam fir (McLaren and Peterson 1994), aspen regeneration in Yellowstone (Ripple et al. 2001), and diversity and abundance of forbs in Michigan and Wisconsin (D. P. Anderson et al., unpublished data) through their impact on ungulates. The loss of top carnivores often magnifies the effects of herbivores on vegetation.

The elimination of wolves over a large area probably resulted in mesopredator release (Crooks and Soulé 1999) or increases in generalist, medium-sized predators, like coyotes, raccoons, and skunks. In response, these carnivores now prey more intensively on smaller animals like nesting songbirds, decreasing their abundance.

In 1957, wolves received formal protection (Thiel 1993). Gray wolves were absent from the state between 1960 and the mid-1970s (Wydeven et al. 1995). Michigan and Minnesota eliminated bounties on wolves in the 1960s, and the Endangered Species Act of 1973 extended protection to wolves. Wolves recolonized Wisconsin from a large source population in Minnesota (Wydeven et al. 1995). About 25 wolves occurred in the state in 1980, and this grew to nearly 500 in 2006 (Wydeven and Wiedenhoeft 2006a). Wolves mainly occupy heavily forested areas of northern and central Wisconsin (Mladenoff et al. 1995). Researchers are also beginning to detect trophic cascades in that wolves appear to increase forb diversity at least in cedar swamps by affecting local deer impacts (D. P. Anderson et al., unpublished data). This gives us hope that wolves are reestablishing some of their former functional ecological roles.

Other Canids: Coyote and Foxes

Red foxes were most abundant in the northern forests, where they preyed regularly on small mammals and ground-nesting birds and on fruits during summer. Gray foxes were more abundant in the deciduous forests of southern Wisconsin where they preyed upon small mammals. Gray and red fox ranges probably did not overlap. Coyotes lived mainly in prairies and savannas of southern Wisconsin. Some authors have questioned whether coyotes occurred east of the Mississippi River prior to European settlement, but older skeletal remains have been found in southern Wisconsin (Theler 2000). Coyotes would have been a major scavenger and predator on small- or medium-sized mammals, including ungulate fawns (Niebauer and Rongstad 1977). Wolves may have restricted coyote distributions in places lacking open habitats with low prey abundance.

By the early 1900s, coyotes were abundant in the cutover northern forest, where they were known as "brush wolves." These cutover areas attract deer, snowshoe hare, and smaller animals preyed upon by coyotes (Niebauer and Rongstad 1977). By the middle of the 1900s, wolf had been reduced to low numbers, and coyotes had become the dominant wild canid in northern Wisconsin. By the late 1990s, surveys of rural areas showed a major increase in reports of coyote observations across most of the state except in northern Wisconsin (Kitchell 2004). The coyote increase in southern Wisconsin also corresponded to major increases in the deer population (chapter 19). Coyote density is probably lowest where wolves range but remains high elsewhere.

European red foxes were introduced into the eastern United States by the British from 1650 to 1750 because of their love of fox hunting (Gilmore 1946). They soon hybridized to an unknown extent with native red foxes (Kamler and Ballard 2002). Red foxes are well adapted to highly modified landscapes. They also benefited from the reduced competition and predation by declining populations of cougars and wolves.

However, bounties were placed on foxes (Richards and Hine 1953; Pils 1977). Irregular bounties and varying fur prices probably drove fluctuations in fox abundance (Richards and Hine 1953). Interestingly, the Wisconsin Conservation Department bred and stocked foxes to provide hunting opportunities at the same time bounties were in place.

Foxes occupied much of the state by the mid-1900s. The two species probably competed more directly than they had in the past. Gray foxes were more abundant in 1930s, and red foxes more abundant in 1940s (Richards and Hine 1953). Gray foxes occurred over half the state in the 1940s and 1950s, extending to Lake Superior in extreme northwest Wisconsin (Petersen et al. 1977b). Gray fox declined to low levels by 1970s and were reduced to the southern third of the state by 1975 (Petersen et al. 1977b). Red foxes extended their range south and became established throughout southern Wisconsin. These animals most likely represent the European red fox or hybrids.

Wisconsin Cats

Bobcats apparently occurred throughout Wisconsin in the early 1800s, although they perhaps were less abundant in areas receiving heavy snowfall. Canada lynxes were probably not common at the time of European settlement (Jackson 1961). Both bobcat and lynx feed extensively on snowshoe hare and red squirrel, but bobcats are broader in their diet. During the cyclic decline of hare populations in the boreal forests of Canada, lynx dispersed into Wisconsin and other more southern locations (Thiel 1987). During these times, small breeding populations may have established in northern Wisconsin (Thiel 1987). Since bobcats have a competitive advantage over lynxes in areas with less snow cover, the two species might have shifted back and forth as climatic conditions fluctuated and during cooler periods. We can estimate total bobcat numbers from their average density (0.06 bobcats per km^2; Anderson and Lovallo 2003) and the fact that they occurred in all terrestrial habitats except boreal forest and sedge meadow. This leads to an estimate of over 8,000 bobcats in the state in 1800. Jackson (1961) considered that there may be some areas of the north that had more lynx, but bobcat pelts were 40–50 times more common in the furs shipped out of Green Bay.

Bobcats were bounty hunted until 1963, with annual harvests ranging from 180 to 1,048 throughout the 1940s (Creed and Ashbrenner 1976). More recently, the bobcat harvest ranged from 71 in 1991 to 497 in 2005 (Dhuey and Olson 2006a). In northern Wisconsin the population increased from about 1,500 in the early 1980s to about 3,000 in the early 2000s (Rolley and Woodford 2006b). Once largely confined to northern forests of Wisconsin, bobcats are spreading into southern portions of the state. In contrast, lynxes continue to be rare and sporadic, with the last dead lynx found in 1992; although a male lynx-bobcat hybrid was found in Polk County in 2005 (Wydeven and Wiedenhoeft 2006b).

Cougars probably were most abundant in southern Wisconsin where deer and elk densities were highest. As with wolves, cougars are adapted for preying on ungulates. They also kill smaller mammals, including porcupines (Pierce and Bleich 2003). Cougars were reported most often from river valleys and the Driftless Area of southwestern Wisconsin (Jackson 1961), where the topography would have aided their stealth strategy of hunting (Kunkel et al. 1999). At a typical density of 0.04 cougars per km^2 (Pierce and Bleich 2003), the population in southern Wisconsin may have been 2,500. Fewer cougars would probably have existed in northern Wisconsin, reflecting lower deer numbers and the less rugged topography. The cougar lasted until about 1909 in Wisconsin (Schorger 1942). Although up to 76 reports of cougar are received per year, it remains unclear whether any represent true wild cougars (Wydeven and Wiedenhoeft 2006b). However, the presence of individual cougars has been confirmed in Illinois, Iowa, Minnesota, and western Ontario, to the west and south of Wisconsin (Cougar Network 2007). The nearest known breeding population of cougars is located in the Black Hills of South Dakota, 800 km west of Wisconsin. Cougars from this population have traveled as far as 1,067 km (Thompson and Jenks 2005). Efforts to definitively test for cougar presence relying on hair snares at sites with special lures to attract cougars are currently being attempted by Eric Anderson and students of University of Wisconsin–Stevens Point.

Fisher and American Marten: A Tale of Two Furbearers

Fishers and American martens were once broadly distributed in northern and central Wisconsin (Scott 1939; Schorger 1942; Jackson 1961). Both species occur mainly in extensive tracts of intact forest, with martens more adapted to conifer and old growth stands (Powell et al. 2003). In the 1800s, martens were more abundant than fishers (Schorger 1942; Jackson 1961). This could be due to the cyclic nature of marten abundance, effects of climatic conditions, or impacts of large carnivores on fisher abundance. American martens feed extensively on voles and red squirrels. Fishers feed on a variety of small- and medium-sized birds and mammals, including porcupines. Martens may have occurred at densities of 1 marten per km^2

(Powell et al. 2003), and perhaps as many as 50,000 occurred in the state in 1800. Fishers may have occurred at densities of 0.1 fishers per km^2 (Powell et al. 2003) across the northern forest, or a population of 7,000.

Although mesopredator release has apparently allowed some medium-sized carnivores to increase, arboreal habitat specialists like fishers and martens usually do not respond to declines of large predators. Moreover, fishers and martens are relatively easy to trap because of their curious nature, making them susceptible to overharvest. Adapted to large blocks of midsuccessional, mature, and old-growth forests, these carnivores lost most of their habitat in the late 1800s and early 1900s. The last marten was taken in 1925, and the last fisher was found in 1932 (Scott 1939).

In the 1950s efforts began to return martens and fishers to the state, in part to replace valuable furbearers to Wisconsin and in part to reduce numbers of overly abundant porcupines. Sixty fishers were reintroduced into the Nicolet National Forest of northeast Wisconsin between 1957 and 1963, and another 60 fishers were released into the Chequamegon National Forest near Clam Lake between 1966 and 1967 (Petersen et al. 1977a). To facilitate the reestablishment of the fisher, the Wisconsin Conservation Department and U.S. Forest Service established special management areas where trapping of terrestrial furbearers was prohibited.

Fisher populations initially grew slowly, and by 1975 were broadly distributed across northern Wisconsin, numbering 1,200–2,500 animals (Petersen et al. 1977a). Public trapping of fishers resumed in 1983, as the population reached 4,000 (Kohn et al. 1993). The fisher population continued growing, topping 12,900 in 2004 (Rolley et al. 2004). Recent annual harvest have averaged about 1,500 fishers. The fisher reintroduction is a partial success; they are controlling porcupine populations (Powell 1980). Unfortunately, fishers are now important mortality agents for woodland raptors (Erdman et al. 1998). The negative impact on raptors and high population densities achieved by fishers may reflect mesopredator release, because wolves and other larger carnivores were uncommon during much of the recovery period.

An unsuccessful attempt to restore American martens occurred in 1953, when five martens were released on 39 km^2 Stockton Island (Jordahl 1954). Later, 172 martens were released into the Nicolet National Forests between 1975 and 1983 (Davis 1983; Kohn and Eckstein 1987). Between 1987 and 1990, 139 additional martens were released into the Chequamegon National Forest (Wydeven et al. 2003). Increase and expansion of these marten populations has been slow, however. By the mid-1990s, the state population had grown to only about 500–1,000 marten

(Wydeven and Ashbrenner 1996). By the early 2000s, marten appear mostly restricted to their reintroduction sites (Wydeven et al. 2003).

Lack of growth to American marten populations may be partially due to intraguild predation—that is, predation by predators at similar trophic levels. Important predators of martens include fishers (Krohn et al. 1995) and red foxes (Lindström et al. 1995). In other regions, researchers have shown that intraguild predation affects martens, as in Scandinavia, where pine marten populations grew when fox populations crashed in response to sarcoptic mange (Lindström et al. 1995). The abundance of foxes and fishers may thus be suppressing the growth of marten populations in Wisconsin.

Other Mustelids: Badger, Weasels, Mink, Otter, Skunk, and Wolverine

The badger was mainly a species of open prairies and savannas of southern Wisconsin (Jackson 1961). A powerful digger, it was a major predator on ground squirrels, pocket gophers, burrowing mammals, and ground-nesting birds (Long and Killingley 1983). Badgers lived at densities of around 1 badger per km^2 (Lindzey 2003), or about 40,000 animals statewide prior to European settlement. Although badgers were almost eradicated by the late 1800s, the cutover region in northern Wisconsin provided new habitat that allowed this species to persist (Hoy 1882). Badger harvests ranged from 128 to 4,597 annually between 1927 and 1955, but fewer than 500 have been harvested annually since 1947 (Petersen et al. 1976). In 1955, the badger was listed as a protected species, the first carnivore to be legally protected in Wisconsin. This move was due less to concerns about population status than interest in protecting the state symbol. After 1955, badger populations grew to an estimated 8,000–10,000 by 1975 (Petersen et al. 1976). By the 1990s, badgers occurred in every Wisconsin county, with their highest numbers in northern counties with extensive barrens (Wydeven et al. 1999).

Three weasels existed in Wisconsin in 1800 including the long-tailed weasel in southern Wisconsin, the short-tailed weasel in northern Wisconsin, and the least weasel in pockets throughout the state (Jackson 1961). The short-tailed and least weasels are circumpolar in their distribution, but long-tailed weasels are restricted to North America. Weasels are voracious predators on rodents and occupy a broad variety of habitats, although the least has an affinity for wetlands. Their distributions were probably similar to current conditions, but least weasels may have been much more abundant. Weasel populations vary greatly from year to year; harvests were nearly 100,000 in the 1920s but dipped to as low as a few hundred in both the early 1970s and the 1980s (Cunningham 1993). Current annual harvest is about 4,000 (Dhuey and Olson 2006b). Harvest declines probably represent reduced interest in weasel fur but perhaps also reduction of weasel densities in response to more abundant medium-sized predators. Weasel populations also respond sensitively to cycles in the abundance of small mammals (Johnson et al. 2000).

Minks apparently occurred throughout the state, living in wetlands and streams (Jackson 1961). The mink is an important predator on muskrat, other small mammals, frogs, crayfish, and fish. Large wetland complexes and extensive streams and rivers could have supported a high mink density. Mink harvests vary from 20,000 to 40,000 annually and show few long-term changes (Cunningham 1993; Dhuey and Olson 2006b).

River otters were fairly common throughout the state in the early 1800s. Like mink, the much larger otter lived in most rivers, larger streams, and lakes, feeding on fish, crayfish, frogs, birds, and mammals (Knudson and Hale 1968). Otters were once abundant throughout the Great Lakes region but have since declined (Schorger 1970). Only a few hundred otters were harvested annually in the 1930s (Cunningham 1993). Recent preharvest populations have been 13,000–15,000 (Kohn et al. 2003).

The striped skunk was originally most abundant is southern Wisconsin and probably mainly occurred in prairie and savanna areas. At densities of 5 skunks per km^2 (Rosatte and Lariviere 2003) in prairie and savanna, there could have been 190,000 skunks in southern Wisconsin in 1800. Skunk harvest declined from 35,000–70,000 annually in 1930s, to 6,000–10,000 today (Cunningham 1993; Dhuey and Olson 2006b). The decline may represent market changes in skunk fur and perhaps some reduction in the population due to succession of northern forests and reestablishment of medium- and large-sized predators.

The wolverine is one of the rarest and least studied carnivores in North America. It was present in Wisconsin before European settlement, probably existing at low densities (Jackson 1961). Wolverine would have been a scavenger and predator on ungulates and other medium- or large-sized mammals. Wolverines were eradicated from most of the state by 1880 (Jackson 1961). Today, occasional sightings of this large mustelid occur, but we lack solid evidence of its presence (Wydeven and Wiedenhoeft 2006b).

Black Bear and Raccoon, the Omnivorous Carnivores

Black bears occurred throughout the state but were probably less frequent in large prairie and savanna areas in southwest Wisconsin (Schorger

1949). Bears are powerful omnivores and can be important predators on ungulate fawns (Kunkel and Mech 1994; Payne et al. 1998). Bears disperse the seeds of many fruiting trees and shrubs (Rogers and Applegate 1983). At densities of 0.5 bears per km^2 of forest (Pelton 2003), 44,000 animals may have once roamed the state in 1800. Bears harvested since 1956 are registered with the Wisconsin Conservation Department and Department of Natural Resources, allowing accurate harvest estimates (Kohn 1982). Bear harvests have increased 10-fold since the 1950s (Kohn 1982; Dhuey and Kohn 2004), and the recent statewide population consisted of 13,000 animals (Rolley and Woodford 2006a).

Raccoons were originally more restricted to southern forests and probably most abundant in bottomland hardwoods and riparian woodlots (Jackson 1961). Raccoons are omnivores, feeding on a broad variety of plants and animals, and at times are important predators on the eggs of ground-nesting birds. Landscaping changes, stocking, and reduction of large carnivores allowed raccoons to spread throughout the state. Recent annual harvest of raccoons are usually between 100,000 and 200,000 (Dhuey 2004; Dhuey and Olson 2006b), the highest harvest of any Wisconsin carnivores.

The Future of Wisconsin's Carnivores

Most of Wisconsin's native carnivores should persist. Gray wolf populations may continue to expand somewhat, but suitable habitat is limited (Mladenoff et al. 1995, 1997). If additional development adds roads and eliminates habitat, it may instead decline. Cougars might eventually return to the state as a breeding population, but competition with wolves (Kunkel et al. 1999) may limit the areas that cougar will be able to occupy. Intraguild predation by wolves and other large predators may eventually reduce abundance of fishers and allow for further recovery of the American marten population. Successional changes on public forestland may also improve habitat for marten, but additional roads and development may limit its ability to disperse across the landscape. The lynx and wolverine will probably not reestablish in the state. Badgers will persist as long as suitable savanna and grassland habitat are maintained and connected via adequate corridors for dispersal. Edge species such as raccoons, skunks, and foxes might decline in northern forest but will remain abundant in southern Wisconsin and among human developments. Coyotes will likely remain abundant throughout the state, but less so among densely forested areas occupied by wolves. Minks and otters will continue to remain abundant if adequate protection is afforded riparian, aquatic, and wetland habitats. Increased development along rivers and lakes and in wetlands will reduce suitable habitat for these aquatic predators.

New exotic carnivores may also invade Wisconsin and affect our ecosystems. European stone martens were released into southeast Wisconsin, establishing a small population in the area of the Kettle Moraines (Long 1995). Domestic cats that roam in the wild can have extensive impacts on wildlife (Coleman et al. 1997). Domestic dogs have been present since Native Americans settled Wisconsin. Since European settlement, however, they have occurred at much higher numbers, and many are trained for hunting wildlife.

Effective carnivore conservation requires managing wildlife (and people) with thought and care. Population modeling, harvest registration, and carefully assigned quotas are needed to avoid population declines. Protecting, preserving, and reestablishing habitat will be key for maintaining future carnivore populations, especially in light of expanding development and human population growth. Human-carnivore conflicts will continue and probably expand, including depredation on domestic animals. This leads to pressure to cull "problem" animals. Wolves and even American martens may eventually be subject to periodic harvest as their populations continue to recover. For all these reasons, it will be important to monitor carnivore populations and their impacts carefully. By tracking their fluctuations and range expansions and contractions we will be in a better position to judge recovery and anticipate conflicts. Further research will also enable us to better understand the role each carnivore plays in Wisconsin's dynamic ecosystems.

Acknowledgments

Bruce Kohn and Bill Berg reviewed and provided suggestions on earlier versions of this chapter.

References

Anderson, E. M., and M. J. Lovallo. 2003. Bobcat and lynx. Pp. 758–786 in G. A. Feldhamer, B. C. Thompson, and J. A. Chapman, eds. Wild Mammals of North America: Biology, Management, and Conservation. Baltimore: Johns Hopkins University Press.

Coleman, J. S., S. A. Temple, and S. R. Craven 1997. Cats and wildlife: A conservation dilemma. University of Wisconsin–Extension, Cooperative Extension, Madison.

Cougar Network. 2007. Cougar Network Web site. Available at http://www.easterncougarnet.org/uppermidwest.html. Accessed March 2007.

Creed, W. A., and J. E. Ashbrenner 1976. Status report of Wisconsin bobcat in 1975. Wisconsin Department of Natural Resources, Research Report No. 87, Madison.

Crooks, K. R., and M. E. Soulé. 1999. Mesopredator release and avifaunal extinction in a fragmented system. Nature 400:563–566.

Culver, M., W. E. Johnson, J. Pecon-Slattery, and S. J. O'Brien. 2000. Genomic ancestry of the American puma (*Puma concolor*). Journal of Heredity 91:186–197.

Cunningham, P., ed. 1993. Wisconsin wildlife harvest summary, 1930–1992. Wisconsin Department of Natural Resources, Madison.

Davis, M. H. 1983. Post-release movements of introduced marten. Journal of Wildlife Management. 47:59–66.

Dhuey, B. 2004. Small game harvest, 2003–04. Wisconsin Wildlife Surveys 14(5):2–5.

Dhuey, B., and B. Kohn. 2004. Wisconsin black bear harvest report, 2003. Pp. 68–77 in The 2003 big game hunting harvest summary. Vol. 14. Wisconsin Department of Natural Resources, PUB-WM-284, Monona.

Dhuey, B., and J. Olson. 2006a. Bobcat harvest 2005. Wisconsin Wildlife Surveys 16(5):82–85.

———. 2006b. Fur trapper survey 2005–2006. Wisconsin Wildlife Surveys 16(5):130–135.

Diamond, J. 1997. Guns, Germs, and Steel: The Fate of Human Societies. New York: Norton.

Erdman, T. C., D. F. Brinker, J. P. Jacobs, J. Wilde, and T. O. Meyer. 1998. Productivity, population trend, and status of northern goshawks, *Accipiter gentilis atricapillus,* in northeastern Wisconsin. Canadian Field Naturalist 112:17–27.

Estes, J. A., K. Crooks, and R. Holt. 2001. Predators, ecological role of. Pp. 857–878 in S. A. Levin and J. Lubchenco, eds. Encyclopedia of Biodiversity. Vol. 4. San Diego: Academic Press.

Fuller, T. K., L. D. Mech, and J. F. Cochrane. 2003. Wolf population dynamics. Pp. 161–191 in L. D. Mech and L. Boitani, eds. Wolves: Behavior, Ecology and Conservation. Chicago: University of Chicago Press. Gilmore, R. M. 1946. Mammals in archaeological collections from southwestern Pennsylvania. Journal of Mammalogy 27:227–235.

Hoy, P. R. 1882. The larger wild animals that have become extinct in Wisconsin. Transactions of the Wisconsin Academy of Science, Arts and Letters 5:65–67.

Jackson, H. H. T. 1961. The Mammals of Wisconsin. Madison: University of Wisconsin Press.

Johnson, D. R., B. J. Swanson, and J. L. Edger. 2000. Cyclic dynamics of eastern dynamics of eastern Canadian ermine populations. Canadian Journal of Zoology 78:835–839.

Jordahl, H. C. 1954. Marten are back! Wisconsin Conservation Bulletin 19(2):26–28.

Kitchell, J. 2004. Summer wildlife inquiry. Wisconsin Wildlife Surveys 14(2):5–12.

Kohn, B. E. 1982. Status and management of black bear in Wisconsin. Wisconsin Department of Natural Resources, Technical Bulletin No. 129, Madison.

Kohn, B. E., and R. G. Eckstein, 1987. Status of marten in Wisconsin, 1985. Wisconsin Department of Natural Resources, Research Report No. 143, Madison.

Kohn, B. E., N. F. Payne, J. E. Ashbrennner, and W. A. Creed. 1993. The fisher in Wisconsin. Wisconsin Department of Natural Resources, Technical Bulletin No. 183, Madison.

Kohn, B. E., R. E. Rolley, and A. M. Roth. 2003. Otter population analysis, 2003. Wisconsin Wildlife Surveys 13(5):120- 127.

Knudsen, G. J., and J. B. Hale. 1968. Food habits of otter in the Great Lakes region. Journal of Wildlife Management 32:89–93.

Krohn, W. B., K. D. Elowe, and R. B. Boone. 1995. Relations among fisher, snow, and martens: Development and evaluation of two hypotheses. Forestry Chronicle 71:97–105.

Kunkel, K. E., and L. D. Mech. 1994. Wolf and bear predation on white-tailed deer fawns in northwestern Minnesota. Canadian Journal of Zoology 72:1557–1565.

Kunkel, K. E., T. K. Ruth, D. H. Pletscher, and M. G. Hornocker. 1999. Winter prey selection by wolves and cougars in and near Glacier National Park, Montana. Journal of Wildlife Management 63:901–910.

Kurten, B., and E. Anderson. 1980. Pleistocene mammals of North America. New York: Columbia University Press.

Lindström, E. R., S. M. Brainerd, J. O. Helldin, and K. Overskaug. 1995. Pine marten–red fox interactions: A case of intraguild predation. Annales Zoologica Fennici 32:123–130.

Lindzey, F. G. 2003. Badger. Pp. 683–691 in G. A. Feldhamer, B. C. Thompson, and Joseph A. Chapman, eds. Wild Mammals of North America: Biology, Management, and Conservation. Baltimore: Johns Hopkins University Press.

Long, C. A. 1995. Stone marten (*Martes foina)* in southeastern Wisconsin, U.S.A. Small Carnivore Conservation, No. 13, International Union for the Conservation of Nature, Gland, Switzerland.

Long, C. A., and C. A. Killingley. 1983. The Badgers of the World. Springfield, IL: Charles C. Thomas.

Martin, P. S., and C. R. Szuter. 2002. Game parks before and after Lewis and Clark: Reply to Lyman and Wolverton. Conservation Biology 16:244–247.

McGee, H. F., Jr. 1987. The use of furbearers by Native North Americans after 1500. Pp. 13–20 in M. Novak, J. A. Baker, M. E. Obbard, and B. Malloch, eds. Wild Furbearer Management and Conservation in North America. Toronto: Ontario Ministry of Natural Resources.

McLaren, B. E., and R. O. Peterson. 1994. Wolves, moose, and tree rings on Isle Royale. Science 266:1555–1558.

Mladenoff, D. J., R. G. Haight, T. A. Sickley, and A. P. Wydeven. 1997. Causes and implications of species restoration in altered ecosystems: A spatial landscape projection of wolf population recovery. BioScience 47:21–31

Mladenoff, D. J., T. A. Sickley, R. G. Haight, and A. P. Wydeven. 1995. A regional landscape analysis and prediction of favorable gray wolf habitat in the Northern Great Lakes region. Conservation Biology 9:279–294.

Niebauer, T. J., and O. J. Rongstad. 1977. Coyote food habits in northwestern Wisconsin. Pp. 237–251 in R. L. Phillips and C. Jonkel, eds. Proceedings of the 1975 Predator Symposium, University of Montana, Missoula.

Nowak, R. M. 2003. Wolf evolution and taxonomy. Pp. 239–258 in L. D. Mech and L. Boitani. Wolves: Behavior, Ecology, and Conservation. Chicago: University of Chicago Press.

Payne, N. F., B. E. Kohn, N. C. Norton, and G. G. Bertagnoli. 1998. Black bear food items in northern Wisconsin. Transactions of the Wisconsin Academy of Science, Arts and Letters 88:263- 280.

Pelton, M. R. 2003. Black bear. Pp. 547–555 in G. A. Feldhamer, B. C. Thompson, and Joseph A. Chapman, eds. Wild Mammals of North America: Biology, Management, and Conservation. Baltimore: Johns Hopkins University Press.

Petersen, L. R., M. A. Martin, and C. M. Pils. 1976. Status of badgers in Wisconsin, 1975. Wisconsin Department of Natural Resources, Research Report No. 90, Madison.

———. 1977a. Status of fisher in Wisconsin, 1975. Wisconsin Department of Natural Resources, Research Report No. 92, Madison.

———. 1977b. Status of gray foxes in Wisconsin, 1975. Wisconsin Department of Natural Resources, Research Report No. 94, Madison.

Pierce, B. M., and V. C. Bleich. 2003. Mountain lion. Pp. 744–757 in G. A. Feldhamer, B. C. Thompson, and J. A. Chapman, eds. Wild Mammals of North America: Biology, Management, and Conservation. Baltimore: Johns Hopkins University Press.

Pils, C. M. 1977. A case against red fox reduction in Wisconsin. Pp. 87–91 in R. L. Phillips and C. Jonkel, eds. Proceedings of the 1975 Predator Symposium, University of Montana, Missoula.

Powell, R. A. 1980. Stability in a one-predator–three-prey community. American Naturalist 115:567–578.

Powell, R. A., S. W. Buskirk, and W. J. Zielinski. 2003. Fisher and marten. Pp. 635–649 in G. A. Feldhamer, B. C. Thompson, and Joseph A. Chapman, eds. Wild Mammals of North America: Biology, Management, and Conservation. Baltimore: Johns Hopkins University Press.

Richards, S. H., and R. L. Hine. 1953. Wisconsin fox populations. Wisconsin Conservation Department, Technical Wildlife Bulletin No. 6, Madison.

Ripple, W.J., E. J. Larsen, R. A. Renkin, and D. W. Smith. 2001. Trophic cascades among wolves, elk and aspen on Yellowstone National Park's northern range. Biological Conservation 102:227–234.

Rogers, L. L., and R. D. Applegate. 1983. Dispersal of fruit seeds by black bears. Journal of Mammalogy 64:310–311.

Rolley, R. E., B. E. Kohn, and A. M. Roth. 2004. Fisher population analysis, 2004. Wisconsin Wildlife Surveys 14(5):87–90.

Rolley, R. E., and M. P. Woodford. 2006a Black bear population analyses, 2006. Wisconsin Wildlife Surveys 16(5):26–31.

———. 2006b. Bobcat population analyses, 2006. Wisconsin Wildlife Surveys 16(5):97–99.

Rosatte, R., and S. Lariviere. 2003. Skunks. Pp. 692–707 in G. A. Feldhamer, B. C. Thompson, and Joseph A. Chapman, eds. Wild Mammals of North America: Biology, Management, and Conservation. Baltimore: Johns Hopkins University Press.

Schorger, A. W. 1942. Extinct and endangered mammals and birds of the upper Great Lakes region. Transactions of the Wisconsin Academy of Science, Arts and Letters 34:23–44.

———. 1949. The black bear in early Wisconsin. Transactions of the Wisconsin Academy of Science, Arts and Letters 39:151–194.

———. 1953. The white-tailed deer in early Wisconsin. Transactions of the Wisconsin Academy of Science, Arts and Letters 42:197–247.

———. 1965. The beaver in early Wisconsin. Transactions of the Wisconsin Academy of Science, Arts and Letters 54:149–179.

———. 1970. The otter in early Wisconsin. Transactions of the Wisconsin Academy of Science, Arts and Letters 58:147–164.

Scott, W. E. 1939. Rare and extinct mammals of Wisconsin. Wisconsin Conservation Bulletin. 4(10):21–28.

Theler, J. L. 2000. Animal remains from Native American archaeological sites in western Wisconsin. Transactions of the Wisconsin Academy of Science, Arts and Letters 88:121–142.

Thiel, R. P. 1987. The status of Canada lynx in Wisconsin. Transactions of the Wisconsin Academy of Science, Arts and Letters 75:90–96.

———. 1993. The Timber Wolf in Wisconsin: The Death and Life of a Magnificent Predator. Madison: University of Wisconsin Press.

Thompson, D. J., and J. A. Jenks. 2005. Long-distance dispersal by a subadult male cougar from the Black Hills, South Dakota. Journal of Wildlife Management 69:818–820.

Wydeven, A. P., and J. E. Ashbrenner. 1996. Status if the American marten, 1995–1996. Wisconsin Department of Natural Resources, Wisconsin Endangered Resources Report No. 114, Madison.

Wydeven, A. P., R. N. Schultz, and R. P Thiel. 1995. Monitoring of a recovering gray wolf population in Wisconsin 1979–1991. Pp. 147–156 in L. N. Carbyn, S. H. Fritts, and D. R. Seip, eds. Ecology and Conservation of Wolves in a Changing World. Canadian Circumpolar Institute, Occasional Publication No. 35, Edmonton.

Wydeven, A. P., and J. E. Wiedenhoeft. 2006a. Gray wolf population, 2005–2006. Wisconsin Wildlife Surveys 16(5):140–155.

———. 2006b. Rare mammal observations, 2005. Wisconsin Wildlife Surveys 16(2):66–76.

Wydeven, A. P., J. E. Wiedenhoeft, and J. E. Ashbrenner. 2003. American marten surveys in northern Wisconsin, 2003. Wisconsin Wildlife Surveys 13(5):195–201.

Wydeven, A. P., J. E. Wiedenhoeft, and B. Dhuey. 1999. Status of badgers in Wisconsin, 1987–1998. Wisconsin Wildlife Surveys 9(2):59–62.

19

Deer as Both a Cause and Reflection of Ecological Change

Scott Craven and Timothy Van Deelen

A mangled deer lying on the roadside; the spread of chronic wasting disease; headlines touting hundreds of thousands of deer killed during a nine-day deer hunt—these images and thoughts capture public attention when it comes to white-tailed deer in Wisconsin. However, a large and growing body of research reveals a less visible and compelling relationship between an abundant deer herd and the ecological communities that support it. This might be the most important issue facing deer managers, landowners, and conservationists today. As a keystone herbivore (Waller and Alverson 1997), deer can reshape entire plant communities (plate 10). Changes in plant community composition and structure have a rippling effect, affecting many other animals, the plant community, and the deer themselves. Deer are not only an important agent of ecological change in Wisconsin. Their abundance and distribution also reflect the ecological changes brought about by human land use, deer hunting, weather, succession, and other forces.

White-tailed deer are not the only large herbivores with a past, present, or future in Wisconsin. Unlike other species, they are the only large herbivore that has a detectable impact over extensive areas. Bison must have been an important herbivore on Wisconsin prairies and savannas until the 1830s, but today they are relegated to game farms throughout the state. Woodland caribou once occupied a limited range in the extreme northern tier of Wisconsin counties near Lake Superior. This relict population typical of boreal forests and tundra to the north disappeared by 1910. Moose occupied the northern half of Wisconsin but were less numerous than deer and disappeared around 1900. Recently, moose have begun to move into northeastern Wisconsin from Michigan's upper peninsula. There may be a dozen or more present today, and in 2002 the first moose calf in a century was born in Wisconsin. Their return is of great public interest but still minor ecological significance.

Historical accounts confirm that elk occurred throughout Wisconsin but were most abundant southeast of a line extending from Green Bay to La Crosse. Despite their abundance, elk were extirpated by 1875. Attempts to restore elk were unsuccessful until 1995 when the Wisconsin Department of Natural Resources (DNR) established an experimental herd of 25 animals near Clam Lake in northwestern Wisconsin. That herd thrives but will likely remain a source of local interest. A similar reintroduction in central Wisconsin is being considered.

Small populations of moose and elk will likely persist, but bison and caribou are gone as wild species in Wisconsin. Other mammals also consume plants, modulate the rate and course of ecological succession through seed consumption or dispersal, or directly modify habitats. However, their impacts pale compared with those attributable to deer.

The White-Tailed Deer in Wisconsin

The white-tailed deer emerged in North America some 3 million years ago during the late Pliocene and survived the megafaunal extinctions of the late Pleistocene. Keys to their long-term persistence include their high reproductive rate, early maturation, effective long-distance dispersal, hardiness to temperature extremes, generalist food habits, and highly developed ability to avoid predators (Geist 1998). Deer were among the earliest postglacial colonizers of Wisconsin.

We will never know for sure what deer densities in Wisconsin were prior to quantitative monitoring efforts. Before European settlement, changes in white-tailed deer populations were driven by weather, habitat dynamics, and interactions with predators (particularly people and wolves) and competition (with moose and elk). The impact from cultural use and subsistence hunting by Native Americans is often underappreciated. Near villages and other centers of human activity, deer were hunted heavily (Schorger 1953). Our understanding of early deer densities is based on inferences drawn from the journal entries of early explorers and settlers and from estimates of how well the presettlement vegetation served as deer habitat (see, e.g., Swift 1946; Schorger 1953; Dahlberg and Guettinger 1956). In 1662, Radisson (a traveler with Joliet) described "small stags" (white-tailed deer) and "large stags" (elk) near Green Bay. During this period (the late 1600s) explorers noted that deer were scarce along Lake Superior's southern shore and plentiful as far north as Green Bay (Schorger 1953).

Dahlberg and Guettinger (1956) estimated that deer densities averaged 10–15 deer/sq mi in the northern forests and 20–50 deer/sq mi in the southern prairies and savannas. McCabe and McCabe (1997) studied early sources on deer numbers and found little support for the oft-repeated claim that North America's current deer population equals or exceeds that before European settlement. What about Wisconsin's deer population? We know deer show remarkable variation in density both temporally and spatially. It is quite likely that some areas (e.g., the Lake Superior region) today have much higher deer densities, while others (like Green Bay, Madison, and Milwaukee) have lower densities.

The fur trade quickly followed early exploration. The lucrative European market for North American furs led to massive increases in the hunting of deer and other species. McCabe and McCabe (1997) reported that continental deer populations were reduced by 30%–50%. By 1815, American fur trading companies were established in Wisconsin.

The flood of immigrant settlers after 1830 harvested timber and established farms. This conversion of the presettlement landscape both improved and degraded deer habitat. Initial logging of mature and old-growth forests benefited deer in the north. The flush of abundant early successional food plants enabled deer populations to rebound modestly from the earlier pressures of the fur trade (Swift 1946). At the same time, conversion to agriculture and intense subsistence hunting by settlers further reduced deer populations in the south. This brief growth in northern deer populations peaked sometime between 1850 and 1900 before it was overcome by further landscape change (Dahlberg and Guettinger 1956).

As the fur trade declined, logging and settlement accelerated. High quality oaks in southern Wisconsin were logged first, like the white pines in the north. With the logging infrastructure in place, subsequent waves of logging removed the less valuable remaining timber (other hardwoods, eastern hemlock, and lowland conifers). Exploitation of deer increased in tandem with exploitation of the forest. Professional hunters were hired to provide venison for lumber camps, and the new railroad systems provided access to a lucrative market for venison and other wild meat in the growing cities of Milwaukee and Chicago. By 1939, the presettlement forest was completely cut, with cutover areas being marketed as "cleared farmland" (Dahlberg and Guettinger 1956). At the same time, agricultural fields replaced the oak forests, oak savannas, and prairies of the south (chapters 8 and 21).

Extensive logging over a relatively short time left vast areas of logging slash to dry in the sun. The years between 1871 (when the tragic Peshtigo Fire occurred) and 1936 were marked by frequent and catastrophic wildfires (Swift 1946). These fires killed some deer directly but also altered deer habitat in ways that enhanced habitat quality in some areas while degrading it in others, depending on soil chemistry and fire intensity. The convergence of logging, fires, market hunting, and settlement led to the demise of many large mammals. Deer populations declined statewide after 1900, ebbing around 1910.

Deer Numbers in the 20th Century

Deer were extirpated from the southern two-thirds of Wisconsin by the early 1900s. Deer persisted at low densities in the north. In the "Northwoods," camps and roads built during the logging era began to be used by tourists. Hunting for sport grew steadily. While locally obtained venison was a menu staple for early resorts, it quickly became clear that tourists and sport hunters also placed a high value on seeing live deer. As tourism grew in northern Wisconsin, residents developed a protective attitude toward deer. Legislation reflected these attitudes. In 1900, the Lacey Act prohibited the interstate shipment of game birds and animals—effectively ending market hunting. In 1915 Wisconsin adopted a "one buck" law that restricted hunter harvest to a single male deer—the first in a series of dramatic restrictions on hunting.

The cutover forest began to recover, and forest conservation measures quickly followed (e.g., the 1927 Forest Crop Law, the establishment of the national forests, the county forest initiatives, and fire suppression). The 1920s and 1930s saw steady conversion of the northern forest from charred, burnt stumps, failed agricultural fields, and fireweed to brush and trees (Dahlberg and Guettinger 1956). By 1931 deer spread to the central forest (a discrete region of unglaciated forest) and the Wisconsin River areas of southwestern Wisconsin (Leopold 1931).

Northern forest recovery and hunting restrictions combined with wolf reduction, game refuge establishment, and a statewide game warden program set the stage for a rapid deer population recovery in the north. By the mid-1930s, the combination of too many deer with too little food led to the starvation of thousands of overwintering deer. Deer damage to agricultural crops prompted legislative action to pay for damages and construct deer-proof fences. Avid conservationists (including such luminaries as Aldo Leopold) advocated increasing the harvest of antlerless deer to reduce the northern deer population, thereby relieving the browsing impact on critical wintering areas. Calls to increase the antlerless kill were met with derision in the north, and the ensuing persistent controversy over doe killing during the 1930s and 1940s became known as the "deer wars." From 1934 to 1954, Wisconsin had a massive statewide supplemental feeding program intended to offset winter starvation (Creed et al. 1984). Regrettably, this did not appreciably diminish winter starvation, but it did unexpectedly help bolster the case to increase antlerless harvests to control deer populations (WDNR 2001).

Aldo Leopold (1931) was among the first to call for scientific research into the issues underlying and driving the deer wars. With the exception of deer drives conducted by the CCC, or Civilian Conservation Corps (Swift 1946), there was no scientific information available to inform debates over deer numbers and their impacts on deer range. CCC workers estimated 34–45 deer/sq mi on the Chequamegon National Forest from 1935 to 1941. With the 1937 passage of the Federal Aid in Wildlife Restoration Act, there was a reliable funding source for wildlife research. In 1940 a federal project began in Wisconsin to study winter range conditions, population dynamics, and hunting pressure. The results highlighted winter starvation and declining winter forage conditions in many northern Wisconsin forests—a conclusion also reached by a "Citizen's Deer Committee" chaired by Leopold in 1942 (Leopold 1943).

At about the same time, deer recolonized the farmland areas of southern Wisconsin. By 1947, deer were seen along the Illinois-Wisconsin border for the first time since the late 1890s (Swift 1946). There were now two deer problems: one in the south where local overabundance damaged farm crops, and one in the north where local overabundance was impacting forests (Swift 1946).

During the 1950s, sporadic antlerless harvests continued to generate controversy, as there were public fears that the deer herd was being depleted. Mandatory registration of hunter-harvested deer began in 1953. By 1959, deer had to be registered in one of the newly designated deer-management units. Data gathered on the sex and age composition of harvested deer produced the first quantitative estimates of deer density over large areas of the state. Similar registration data are still used to reconstruct the deer population through a mathematical technique known as the sex-age-kill model (because the model depends on the age and sex composition of the registered kill; WDNR 2001). Development of a quantitative estimate of deer numbers and use of ecologically meaningful deer-management units marked the beginning of "variable quota" management in Wisconsin. Since 1963, populations in each deer-management unit are evaluated relative to estimated carrying capacity with harvest levels set using variable quotas for antlerless deer (WDNR 2001).

Over the past two centuries, deer numbers have waxed and waned in response to a complex interaction of natural and anthropomorphic factors. Since about 1960, management strategies, hunter and landowner behavior, favorable winter weather, and superb habitat conditions have enabled continued deer population growth. More deer and more intensive human land use have exacerbated the problems of agricultural damage, deer-vehicle collisions, and ecological impacts. With 1.5–2 million Wisconsin deer, consuming 6–8 pounds of vegetation per day, impacts are inevitable and potentially dramatic.

Recognizing Deer Impacts

Attention to the impacts of deer herbivory is not new. Agricultural damage was a problem as early as the 1930s. Touring German forests in 1935, Aldo Leopold noted in his essay "Wilderness": "This effect of too many deer on the ground flora of the forest deserves special mention because it is an elusive burglary of esthetic wealth, the more dangerous because unintentional and unseen" (quoted in Jones et al. 1993). Leopold and others (1947) discussed overpopulated deer ranges in Wisconsin, and Webb and others (1956) discussed deer effects on hardwood forests. Swift (1946) developed a synthetic view of impacts, incorporating agricultural damage in southern Wisconsin and forest impacts in the north.

David Marquis and his colleagues (Marquis 1974, 1981) in the Allegheny hardwoods of northwestern Pennsylvania in the 1970s conducted research that stands out as some of the most useful early quantitative work on the relationship between deer densities and changes in forest composition. Since 1980, a host of researchers built on this body of knowledge. For an excellent review of that literature, see Waller and Alverson (1997). Also, a very detailed environmental assessment of deer impacts was completed by the WDNR in 1995 (Vander Zouwen and Warnke 1995). Finally, a key paper by Jones and others (1993) borrowed a subtitle—"Is Bambi Hogging the Forest?"—from a *Washington Post* article. These reviews and popular accounts brought the issue to the public; it was now clear that ecological impacts extended beyond trees and shrubs to include songbirds, small mammals, and other flora and fauna. The problem of deer impacts was now firmly established in the minds of most wildlife and conservation biologists and foresters.

Unfortunately, private landowners and other members of the public exhibit little awareness and concern. There are several explanations. Ecological change is often invisible (chapter 3), and its detection requires strong natural history skills. A survey of landowners in southern Wisconsin (Christoffel 1998) found that very few felt knowledgeable about native wildflowers and shrubs on their land; 44% indicated they could identify either no or only a few species. Landowners knew trees better; over a quarter thought they could identify all the species on their land, perhaps because of their commercial value and/or size. About 60% of landowners noted deer impacts, including both plant consumption and conspicuous sign, like buck rubs. When asked to evaluate changes in plant diversity and abundance, about half reported no changes during their tenure as owners, while fewer than 10% noted a decline in a specific plant group. Even when detected, deer damage was not always a concern: almost 60% of landowners agreed with the statement "I enjoy having deer on my property and I do not worry about the impacts they may have on plants." Only a third cited enjoyment of deer but expressed some concern over herbivory.

The Broad Scope of Ecological Impacts

In the second edition of "Wisconsin's Deer Management Program," the WDNR summarized the ecological effects of deer and deer herbivory as follows (McGown and Wallenfang 1998, 26):

- Herbaceous plants decline in abundance and diversity as deer numbers rise above 12–15 per square mile. A common example is the large white-flowered trillium. Examples of vulnerable rare species include the Indian cucumber, showy lady's-slipper, and white-fringed orchid.
- Tree and shrub species composition can change with reduced regeneration as deer numbers rise above 20–25 per square mile. Pines, white cedar, hemlock, oaks, and Canada yew are examples of vulnerable trees and shrubs.
- Large numbers of deer may affect rare insects that are dependent on one or a few plant species that are also preferred for food by deer. The federally endangered Karner Blue Butterfly is a good example; it depends on wild lupine for its larval stage.

- Small mammals dependent on forest floor vegetation may be reduced as deer numbers exceed 25 per square mile. A potentially affected small mammal is the red-backed vole.
- The number and diversity of the bird population may be reduced as deer populations rise from 15 to over 35 per square mile due to impacts on ground level vegetation, the shrub layer, and tree species composition. One vulnerable bird is the shrub-nesting hooded warbler.
- Moose may not be able to inhabit otherwise suitable habitat if deer numbers exceed 12–15 per square mile. A parasitic brainworm is carried and tolerated by deer, but it is often fatal to moose.
- The number of wolves that can be supported in an area generally increases with the size of the deer population, a primary prey species.

Scientists continue to quantify this list of general impacts (Vander Zouwen and Warnke 1995; Waller and Alverson 1997; Côté et al. 2004). These impacts of deer can be profound. As noted in chapter 6, forests in northern Wisconsin are changing in composition and declining in understory plant diversity. The fact that these shifts are most pronounced where deer are not hunted (like state parks) and least evident in areas with lower deer densities (like Indian reservations and some islands) clearly indicate that deer are a significant driver of ecological change.

Deer research by U.S. Department of Agriculture Forest Service scientists in northwestern Pennsylvania dates back to the 1940s. Using long-term monitoring and pen studies, they documented dramatic changes in the hardwood forests of the Allegheny Plateau. Over large areas, wildflowers, mid-level shrubs such as viburnums, and tree seedlings of sugar maple, white ash, and pin cherry have been replaced by dense stands of hay-scented and New York fern with black cherry as the dominant tree species. Horsley and others (2003) used fenced 160 acre plots, stocked with known densities of deer (10, 20, 38, and 64/sq mi) to test the effects of different deer densities on vegetation. They found that deer altered the abundance and density of wildflowers, shrubs, and birds. Collaborator Susan Stout, stated, "We think we know our forest. But in Pennsylvania and many other parts of the Northeast, deer overabundance has changed our forests so much and for so long that we don't know how our forests would look without too many deer" (Horsley and Stout 2004, 1).

Deer impacts are best assessed by repeatedly sampling plant communities as reported in Wisconsin and Pennsylvania. However, exclosures have long been used as a very visual means of demonstrating the effects of deer herbivory. Exclosures range in size from a small cage over specific or individual plants to fenced areas of hundreds of square meters. The intent is always the same—to prevent deer access to a patch of habitat. The famous Foulds Creek exclosure in Price County was built by the WDNR in 1945. The striking differences between the inside and outside of the Foulds Creek exclosure have been interpreted in various ways by different researchers, in part because snowshoe hare exclusion confounds matters. However, the inescapable conclusion from this (or any exclosure) is clear: herbivory dramatically alters forest regeneration and growth.

Exclosures provide a useful tool for any land steward (plate 10). They are easily constructed from light weight, inexpensive plastic mesh (or wire) and metal or wood posts. Within a single growing season, differences can become apparent between the protected space and the surroundings. While visually informative, it is important to remember that an exclosure represents an extreme and artificial "no-deer" scenario. Deer are a part of the ecosystem and native plant communities and deer have evolved together. Some degree of browsing occurs in every landscape, and usually without deleterious effects—provided that deer densities are not out of balance with available habitat.

Impacts of Deer Management

Beyond the immediate effect on deer numbers, some interactions between deer and people contribute to the ecological problems posed by the animals themselves. Deer feeding is both popular and economically significant, especially in northern Wisconsin. Deer feeding is ill advised as it can increase disease transmission. However, its popularity has thwarted every WDNR attempt to limit the practice. A ban currently exists in the southern part of the state only in the immediate vicinity of cases of chronic wasting disease (CWD). Feeding affects deer by altering their movement patterns. Animals become more concentrated near available food, putting increased pressure on vegetation in the immediate area. Feeding can thus greatly elevate deer numbers in some places, severely damaging vegetation near the feeding sites.

Some hunting and conservation groups advocate the creation of food plots, seeded trails, timber harvest, or other practices to improve deer habitat. This habitat management often impacts native vegetation and other animal species through its influence on deer populations. From about 1970 until the mid-1980s, the WDNR managed relict forest openings and created new openings in northern forests to improve deer habitat. Initial guidelines sought to manage 3%–4% of a forest in 5 acre (2 ha) openings, but this was later reduced to about 1%. Critics argued that these openings were misguided management that benefited already overabundant species. According to Wisconsin's iconoclastic retired deer biologist Keith McCaffery, the cost, concern over forest fragmentation, and dubious benefits have relegated the program to a small number of openings on public lands. Nevertheless, timber harvests, private food plots, abundant edge habitat, and trail development still serve to maintain elevated deer populations.

Deer-Management Dilemmas

Once we accept that deer impacts are a problem that requires us to adjust population levels, we are faced with the obvious question of how far to reduce deer populations to limit their intolerable impacts. A "one size fits all" benchmark for deer density ignores too many factors of deer biology, plant ecology, site characteristics, and human behavior. Drawing on several Wisconsin studies, Waller and Alverson (1997, 221) concluded that densities of less than 4.5 deer/km^2 (about 12/sq mi) "were most compatible with retaining a full complement of herbaceous species." This figure was derived for northern forests and would certainly be higher in the south, where deer carrying capacity is higher. Pennsylvania studies suggest that densities exceeding 20 deer/sq mi are problematic (Jones et al. 1993). Even here, there is substantial variation among sites. In Wisconsin, current WDNR overwinter population goals for over 130 deer-management units range from 10 to 35 deer/sq mi.

It is important to consider two factors that confound the relationship between deer densities and impact studies. First, deer population goals are expressed for overwinter populations when the deer population is at an annual *low.* Second, deer densities in Wisconsin are expressed as deer per square mile of "deer range," not total area. Thus, areas like backyards, greenways, and parks are not factored into the calculations even though deer use these areas.

Use of the term "overabundant" in deer impact discussions is also problematic. In Wisconsin, most people accept the idea that the deer herd is too large in a general sense. But because deer are not evenly distributed on the landscape, disagreement arises over where specifically they are overabundant. A few areas are even below WDNR management objectives, while others greatly exceed it. A landowner's back 40 may have high deer numbers and little deer damage but may also have mitigating factors such as the presence of alfalfa to buffer the impact of herbivory on native plants during the spring and summer (Augustine 1997). Further, there are some landowners who reject the idea that deer can have major ecological impacts (or they do not care) and instead welcome high deer numbers.

It is frustrating to us to hear people place responsibility for deer populations solely in the lap of the WDNR's deer managers. Agency managers can set regulations designed to change deer numbers, but the execution of those regulations is in the hands of the deer hunters willing to shoot does and the landowners who control access to a large proportion of deer habitat. As we have seen with CWD management in Wisconsin, management goals will not be attained if the public rejects the rationale for regulations.

The preservation of deer on some sites presents additional management difficulties with ecological implications. Without hunting pressure, deer herds can increase quickly, greatly exceeding the threshold for ecological impacts. These impacts are often seen on private lands where the landowners oppose hunting and in parks where public safety precludes hunting. In these places, deer populations often build up to the point where they seriously damage both that site and adjacent lands.

Finally, managers in Wisconsin have CWD to contend with. In early 2001, the WDNR learned that CWD had been discovered west of Madison. This poorly understood neurological disease is incurable, transmissible, and fatal. Wisconsin's outbreak marked the first time that CWD had been discovered east of Nebraska. Observations that the disease persisted in low-density populations and epidemiological models indicated that continued spread and higher prevalence were likely in Wisconsin's high-density deer herd. The WDNR responded by embarking on an intensive management program that included aggressive hunting in targeted areas and restrictions on baiting and feeding of deer. Despite support from animal health experts and professional wildlife managers, CWD management proved to be controversial among hunters and landowners. It is too early to predict whether management actions will eradicate the disease or what impacts CWD and its management will have on the deer herd. We are confident that the discovery of CWD will be remembered as a turning point in the history of Wisconsin's deer herd and the social milieu surrounding deer management. It may also pose a special opportunity to study how vegetation recovers from intense herbivory if CWD management succeeds in greatly reducing deer densities in this zone.

Conclusion

The white-tailed deer is arguably the most important wild animal in Wisconsin. Despite crop damage, vehicle collisions, and their important ecological role as keystone herbivores, deer generate enormous positive recreational and economic impacts. The deer hunting season adds over half a billion dollars to Wisconsin's economy. Despite concerns over disease transmission and already excessive deer densities, deer feeding also represents a multimillion dollar industry in the state. The experience of seeing a huge buck on opening day or a newborn fawn in spring cannot be quantified any more than the opportunity to see an explosion of wildflowers in the forest floor.

Deer are here to stay. Although most people do not recognize deer management as a long-term proposition with high stakes, it is exactly that. Deer numbers must be maintained at levels dictated by competing interests. Hunters, deer feeders, farmers, landowners, drivers, and wildlife managers need to understand deer impacts, support management efforts, and work together to improve how deer-management plans are developed and executed. Stakeholders must also realize that weather, disease, and other factors can confound the outcome of the best deer-management plan (Vander Zouwen and Warnke 1995). Deer management is an inexact science and an adaptive process.

Deer profoundly affect plant communities and wildlife habitat. These impacts should be considered when deer managers set population goals and regulations. These impacts of herbivory should also be communicated clearly to the landowners who control hunter access to deer habitats. We agree with Waller and Alverson (1997): Leopold's "Land Ethic" should be extended to concern for wildflowers. Deer impacts should be a central consideration when landowners make land stewardship decisions.

Deer managers are ecologists who understand the topics considered here, but they receive pressure from many different interest groups. Moreover, resource-management decisions are increasingly usurped and made within the political arena where the science may not always be the deciding factor. To date, there are more vocal supporters of deer than of trillium. Until the advocates of trillium begin hunting deer or providing hunters access to their land, it will remain so. Deer will continue to be an agent of ecological change and a reflection of it, and deer management will continue to present challenges, even for the most capable biologists.

References

Augustine, D. J. 1997. Grazing patterns and impacts of white-tailed deer in a fragmented forest ecosystem. M.S. thesis, University of Minnesota.

Christoffel, R. A. 1998. Ecological and sociological aspects of white-tailed deer herbivory in south-central Wisconsin. M.S. thesis, University of Wisconsin–Madison.

Côté, S. D., T. P. Rooney, J. P. Tremblay, C. Dussault, and D. M. Waller. 2004. Ecological impacts of deer overabundance. Annual Review of Ecology, Evolution, and Systematics 35:113–147.

Creed, W. A., F. Haberland, B. E. Kohn, and K. R. McCaffery. 1984. Harvest management: The Wisconsin experience. Pp. 243–260 in L. K. Hal, ed. White-tailed Deer: Ecology and Management. Harrisburg, PA: Stackpole Books.

Dahlberg, B. L., and R. C. Guettinger. 1956. The white-tailed deer in Wisconsin. Game Division, Wisconsin Conservation Department, Madison.

Geist, V. 1998. Deer of the World: Their Evolution, Behavior, and Ecology. Mechanicsburg, PA: Stackpole Books.

Horsley, S. B., and S. L. Stout. 2004. The forest nobody knows. Forest Science Review 1:1–7.

Horsley, S. B., S. L. Stout, and D. S. deCalesta. 2003. White-tailed deer impact on the vegetation dynamics of a northern hardwood forest. Ecological Applications 13(1):98–118.

Jackson, H. H. T. 1959. The Mammals of Wisconsin. Madison: University of Wisconsin Press.

Jones, S. B., D. deCalesta and S. E. Chunko. 1993. White-tails are changing our forests. American Forests 99(11/12):21–25, 53–54.

Leopold, A. 1931. Report on a Game Survey of the North Central States Made by Aldo Leopold for the Sporting Arms and Ammunition Manufacturer's Institute under Direction of Its Committee on Restoration and Protection of Game. Madison: Democratic Printing Company.

———. 1943. Deer irruptions. Wisconsin Conservation Bulletin 8(8): 3–11.

Leopold, A., L. K. Sowls, and D. L. Spencer. 1947. A survey of over-populated deer ranges in the U.S. Journal of Wildlife Management 11:162–177.

Marquis, D. A. 1974. The impact of deer browsing on Allegheny hardwood regeneration. U.S. Department of Agriculture Forest Service, Research Report No. NE-57.

———. 1981. Effect of deer browsing on timber in Allegheny hardwood forests of northwestern Pennsylvania. U.S. Department of Agriculture Forest Service, Research Report No. NE-47.

McCabe, T. R., and R. E. McCabe. 1997. Recounting whitetails past. Pp. 11–26 in W. J. McShea, H. B. Underwood, and J. H. Rappole, eds. The Science of Overabundance: Deer Ecology and Population Management. Washington, DC: Smithsonian Institution Press.

McGown, W., and K. Wallenfang, eds. 1998. Wisconsin's deer management program: The issues involved in decision-making. 2nd ed. Wisconsin Department of Natural Resources, Madison.

Shorger, A. W. 1953. The white-tailed deer in early Wisconsin. Transactions of the Wisconsin Academy of Sciences, Arts and Letters 42: 197–247.

Swift, E. 1946. A history of Wisconsin deer. Game Division, Wisconsin Conservation Department, Madison.

Vander Zouwen, W., and K. Warnke, eds. 1995. Wisconsin deer population's goals and harvest management environmental assessment. Wisconsin Department of Natural Resources, Madison.

Waller, D. M., and W. S. Alverson. 1997. The white-tailed deer: A keystone herbivore. Wildlife Society Bulletin 25(2):217–226.

Webb, W. L., R. T. King, and E. F. Patric. 1956. Effect of white-tailed deer on a mature northern hardwood forest. Journal of Forestry 54:391–398.

Wisconsin Department of Natural Resources (WDNR). 2001. Management workbook for white-tailed deer. 2nd ed. Bureaus of Integrated Science Services and Wildlife Management, WDNR, Madison.

20 Changes in Amphibian and Reptile Communities

Gary S. Casper

Amphibians and reptiles are an ancient group of vertebrates that has existed since long before the dinosaurs came and went. As a lineage, they survived the tremendous environmental upheavals that caused three mass extinctions over the last 250 million years including the cataclysmic Cretaceous-Tertiary event that wiped out their dinosaur relatives (Flannery 2001). Since then, they also survived the dramatic environmental changes that came with a succession of ice ages over the past 1.8 million years. During this time, all of Wisconsin was covered with a thick sheet of glacial ice except for the Driftless Area in southwestern Wisconsin (plate 1). This area surely sustained habitats for many reptiles and amphibians even as they retreated elsewhere (Martin 1965). As the glaciers retreated, reptiles and amphibians quickly recolonized the expanding wetlands, prairies, forests, and savannas left in their wake (Curtis 1959). Thus, the reptile and amphibian communities that survived, giving rise to those we see today in intact habitats, are substantially similar to those that have persisted for eons (Vogt 1981; Holman 1995; Casper 1996).

Losses of forest, savanna, prairie, and wetlands since Euro-American settlement have presented reptiles and amphibians with environmental changes on the scale of the ice ages. The loss of over half the state's wetlands and more than 99% of its prairies and oak savannas (described in detail in other chapters) have radically altered conditions for reptiles and amphibians, greatly shrinking the ranges of several now endangered species including Blanchard's cricket frog, queen snake, and eastern massasauga. These losses have been greatest and most permanent in southern Wisconsin as huge expanses of grassland and savanna were converted to agriculture and urban development. Changes in northern Wisconsin have generally been less severe, with rapid reforestation moderating the initial impacts of massive logging, wildfires, and failed agriculture in most areas (plate 4). More recently, reptiles and amphibians have confronted impacts from urban sprawl, shoreline development, persistent pollution problems (like mercury and polychlorinated biphenyls), invasive species, and global warming. We have yet to assess the cumulative impacts of habitat destruction and these more recent stresses on reptiles and amphibians, but the simple comparison presented below makes clear their severity.

Certain traits of reptiles and amphibians suggest how they will likely respond to shifts in habitat conditions and particular environmental stresses. For example, most reptiles and amphibians require several different types of habitats throughout their life cycle. The winter habitats required for denning, nesting, or larval development are often quite different from the habitats used for mating and feeding in spring and summer. Because many reptile and amphibian species need multiple habitats but have limited dispersal ability, their populations are highly susceptible to the fragmentation of natural areas resulting from paved highways, suburban developments, and agricultural fields (Driscoll 2004; Shine et al. 2004). Land use changes progressively subdivide and reduce the amount and quality of habitat available for reptiles and amphibians, isolating the smaller remaining populations into smaller patches of habitat. Even where habitat persists, invasive species, pollution, and siltation degrade habitat quality. Because they are sensitive to changes in the quality and quantity of habitat, reptile and amphibian communities often reflect patterns of human settlement and land use.

Amphibians play important roles in many ecosystems, sparking widespread interest in global amphibian declines (Blaustein and Wake 1995). Amphibians often represent a large proportion of the vertebrate biomass in the systems they inhabit (Petranka 1998). They also play important roles in nutrient cycling (Semlitsch 2003). Finally, they are good bioindicators of environmental stress owing to their complex life cycles, broad diets, permeable skin, and sensitivity to environmental contaminants in the egg and larval stages (Semlitsch 2003).

To understand how the state's reptile and amphibian fauna are responding to habitat conditions, let us examine two extremes along a continuum of anthropogenic disturbance. At one end of the continuum, we have the Apostle Islands. Although this is not the most pristine part of the state, many of the islands remain fairly wild. At the opposite extreme lies the heavily urbanized landscape of Milwaukee County (see chapter 25).

The Apostle Islands

The Apostle Islands are an archipelago of 22 islands in western Lake Superior. They are mostly forested, ranging in size from 3 to 10,000 acres (Judziewicz and Koch 1993). Land bridges probably connected these islands to each other and the mainland about 5,000 years ago. At this time, all the islands probably supported the same reptile and amphibian species as were present on the mainland. Rising water levels in Lake Superior then isolated the islands (Farrand 1969). This reduced the diversity of reptiles and amphibians on each island reflecting the well-known "species-area" relationship (the fact that larger areas support more species; Hecnar et al. 2002). Most species now absent from particular islands thus disappeared as a consequence of rising water levels and the growing isolation this produced. These declines in diversity probably took several generations, reflecting what ecologists term the "extinction debt." All but Madeline Island are now federally protected as national lakeshore managed by the National Park Service.

The species present today in the Apostle Islands are probably the same as those present over the last millennia. Although we have no data over this time, reptile and amphibian abundances surely fluctuated in response to shifting climate and rainfall patterns as they do elsewhere. When most of the islands were logged 50–100 years ago, conditions drastically changed, shifting the abundance of most animals. In particular, as microhabitats became warmer and drier after logging, they would have favored reptiles over amphibians. As canopies closed, conditions reverted to become cooler and wetter again.

Collectively, the islands support most of the species present on the adjacent mainland with any given island supporting 0%–88% of amphibians present on the mainland and 0%–71% of reptiles present on the mainland (Casper 2001a, 2001b; tables 20.1 and 20.2). Long Island often retains a connection to the mainland (subject to shifting sands) allowing it to maintain disproportionately more species of reptiles and amphibians than other islands relative to its area.

Table 20.1 Apostle Islands National Lakeshore amphibian species matrix

Island	Area, ha	BS	SS	CN	FS	RS	CM	AT	SP	CF	CT	GT	AB	GF	LF	MF	WF	Mainland, %
Basswood	779	X	X		X	X		X	X								X	44
Bear	741	X				X		X							X		X	31
Cat	550	X	X		X			X									X	31
Devils	130	X	X						?					?	?		X	38
Hermit	302	X	X		X	?		X	?					X			X	50
Ironwood	268																	0
Long	203	X			X		?	X	X			X		?	X	X	?	63
Manitou	554		X		X	?		X									X	31
Michigan	641	X	X	X	X			X	X					X		X	X	56
N. Twin	71																	0
Oak	2,064					X		X	X					X			X	31
Otter	542					X												6
Outer	3,252	X	X	X	X			X	X	X		X		X			X	63
Raspberry	120		X		X	X		X	X								X	44
Rocky	447	X	X		X			X	X			X					X	44
Sand	1,199	X	?		X			X	X	X	?	X		X			X	63
S. Twin	146	X	X		X			X	X								X	38
Stockton	4,087	X	X	X	X	X		X	X	X		X	?	X	X	X	X	88
York	130	X	X		X			X	X						X		X	44
Mainland	NA	X	X	X	X	X	X	X	X	X	X	X	X	X	X	X	X	100

Note: X, present; ?, questionable presence; BS, blue-spotted salamander; SS, spotted salamander; CN, central newt; FS, four-toed salamander; RS, eastern red-backed salamander; CM, common mudpuppy; AT, eastern American toad; CF, boreal chorus frog; SP, north spring peeper; GT, gray treefrog; CT, Cope's gray treefrog; AB, American bullfrog; GF, northern green frog; LF, northern leopard frog; MF, mink frog; WF, wood frog.

Table 20.2 Apostle Islands National Lakeshore reptile species matrix

Island	Area, ha	PT	ST	WT	GS	RS	RIS	SG	Mainland, %
Basswood	779	X			X	?			44
Bear	741				X				31
Cat	550				X				31
Devils	130				?				38
Hermit	302				X	?			50
Ironwood	268								0
Long	203	X	X		X	X		X	63
Manitou	554				X				31
Michigan	641	X			X	X			56
N. Twin	71								0
Oak	2,064	?			X	X	?		31
Otter	542				?				6
Outer	3,252	X			X	X			63
Raspberry	120	?			X				44
Rocky	447				X	X			44
Sand	1,199				X	?			63
S. Twin	146	?			X	?			38
Stockton	4,087	X	X		X	X	X		88
York	130				X	X			44
Mainland	NA	X	X	X	X	X	X	X	100

Note: X, present; ?, questionable presence; PT, painted turtle; ST, eastern snapping turtle; WT, wood turtle; GS, common gartersnake; RS, northern red-bellied snake; RIS, northern ring-necked snake; HS, eastern hog-nosed snake; SG, smooth greensnake.

Milwaukee County before European Settlement

Milwaukee County was an early industrial center in Wisconsin and is now the most heavily urbanized county in the state (see chapter 25). We can reconstruct which species of reptile and amphibians once existed here from historical records and biological inference. Historical records include museum specimens and early herpetological works (Pope and Dickenson 1928; Vogt 1981; Casper 1996). By knowing how species are distributed today, their habitat preferences, and which habitats were available before settlement, we can also infer a likely species list. These lines of evidence suggest that seven salamanders, eleven frogs and toads, five turtles, and twelve snakes originally occurred in Milwaukee County.

How sure are we of these numbers? Let's begin with the salamanders. These species are secretive, largely nocturnal, and thus often overlooked. Many can only be found during brief periods each year as they spend most of their adult life underground. These species also require both aquatic and terrestrial habitats (except for the terrestrial eastern red-backed salamander and the aquatic common mudpuppy). Of the seven salamanders that we think once inhabited Milwaukee County, three are not firmly established. The easily overlooked spotted, four-toed, and eastern red-backed salamanders all prefer mesic hardwood and mixed forests. These habitats were certainly present historically in northern Milwaukee County, and all three species were well documented from just north and south of Milwaukee County (Casper 1996; Phillips et al. 1999). Thus, I count these species as present.

Of the 11 species of frogs and toads present historically, three deserve special mention. Cope's gray treefrog is widespread and prefers savannas and mixed grassland/forest landscapes. These habitats occurred commonly before European settlement in Milwaukee County. However, because this species was not recognized as distinct from the gray treefrog until the early 1970s (Ralin 1968), presettlement records do not exist. Oddly, American bullfrogs were not reported from the county until 1987, despite much older records from surrounding cities. It is possible they recently expanded their range into Milwaukee, where they often colonize urban ponds. However, it seems more likely that they were present all along and remains a common frog. Pickerel frogs are found in clean streams, usually associated with spring seeps. These species are hard to detect as they look similar to the common northern leopard frog. They likely occurred historically in streams like Lincoln Creek and the Menomonee River but were never reported.

Turning to reptiles, five species of turtles originally occurred across a range of aquatic habitats in Milwaukee County. Stinkpots are secretive and nocturnal. While we know they occurred in surrounding counties, they were only confirmed in Milwaukee County recently. Blanding's turtles are also rare and were not recorded from the county until 1981. This species occurs statewide in marsh, pond, and wet meadow habitats like those that used to occur commonly in southern Milwaukee County.

We have but a single record for the common five-lined skink in the county, and this one record is problematic. Although one specimen creates a record, the location (New Coeln) was historically upland mesic forest, not the pine barrens and oak savannas this species inhabits (Vogt 1981). With no other records available, I do not count this lizard as originally occurring here.

Twelve species of snakes occurred historically in the county. Northern ring-necked snakes prefer mesic forests along with their salamander prey and are quite secretive. The single record is supported by appropriate available historical habitat. Likewise, the single record for the stream-dwelling queen snake was probably from the Kinnickinnic River. They also occupied the Milwaukee River, as we know from a 1928 record from Cedarburg, north of Milwaukee County. The marsh-dwelling eastern massasauga was reported to be common in 1883 when large areas of suitable habitat remained in the Menomonee Valley (chapter 25). Northern ribbonsnakes are known from two museum specimens collected in 1940 and 1951 when they were probably already rare and declining in wetland remnants. Both suitable habitat and historical records support the presence of the other eight species.

Present Day Conditions in Milwaukee County

Since European settlement, conditions for most amphibians and reptiles in Milwaukee County have declined greatly. To gauge which species have persisted, I first sought records since 1975. For species without such records, I considered habitat availability and how hard it is to detect a given species. I considered species lacking post-1975 records extirpated unless suitable habitat remains and the species is easily overlooked. Recent records for two species (Blanding's turtle and northern watersnake) likely refer to released animals as no breeding populations can be found. Thus, I count these species extirpated.

Only two of the original seven salamander species still persist: blue-spotted and eastern tiger salamanders. Eastern red-backed, spotted, and four-toed salamanders probably did not survive the initial deforestation.

The hardwood forests and most of the small ephemeral wetlands the latter two species require were effectively eliminated by about 1930. Central newts have not been seen for over 90 years but persist in adjacent Waukesha County. Their distribution tends to be spotty as they require intact landscapes including both aquatic and terrestrial habitats. Such landscapes are largely eliminated from the county. Mudpuppies still occur in Lake Michigan near Chicago and in inland lakes in Waukesha County but have not been reported from Milwaukee County since the 1930s.

Frogs and toads have fared better. Only three of the original 11 species have disappeared: Blanchard's cricket frog, pickerel frog, and wood frog. Blanchard's cricket frogs (a state endangered species) were common in southern Wisconsin through the 1950s. They have since experienced a significant range retraction and are now found only in southwestern Wisconsin (Lannoo 1998). They disappeared from Milwaukee County by the 1950s. The pickerel frog no longer finds its specialized habitats in the county. The wood frog suffered the same fate as the spotted salamander, losing the ephemeral ponds embedded within large forest tracts that it requires.

Turtles are one of the oldest and most resilient vertebrate groups alive today. Their body armor, generalist diets, and use of relatively stable aquatic environments have no doubt contributed to their persistence. Only one of five original species of turtles appears to have been lost: Blanding's turtle. Individuals of this state threatened species are, however, sometimes captured outside the county, held as pets, and then released in parks. Most contemporary records come from the Schlitz Audubon Center and Greenfield Park, but there is no evidence of breeding populations. We are also down to a single population of eastern spiny softshells with one turtle nest in Mallard Lake reported at the Wehr Nature Center in 1986. The only other modern records come from the Milwaukee River, where habitat is poor and turtles were probably released.

Seven of 12 snake species have been lost from the county: northern ring-necked snake, smooth greensnake, western foxsnake, northern ribbonsnake, queen snake, northern watersnake, and eastern massasauga. Northern ring-necked snakes, smooth greensnakes, queen snakes, and eastern massasaugas have not been reported since before 1911. They were probably victims of deforestation (northern ring-necked snake), the conversion of prairies and grasslands to agriculture (smooth greensnakes), stream siltation and channelization (queen snakes), and wetland filling (northern ribbonsnakes and eastern massasaugas). Western foxsnakes appear to have disappeared within the last 35 years. Northern water-

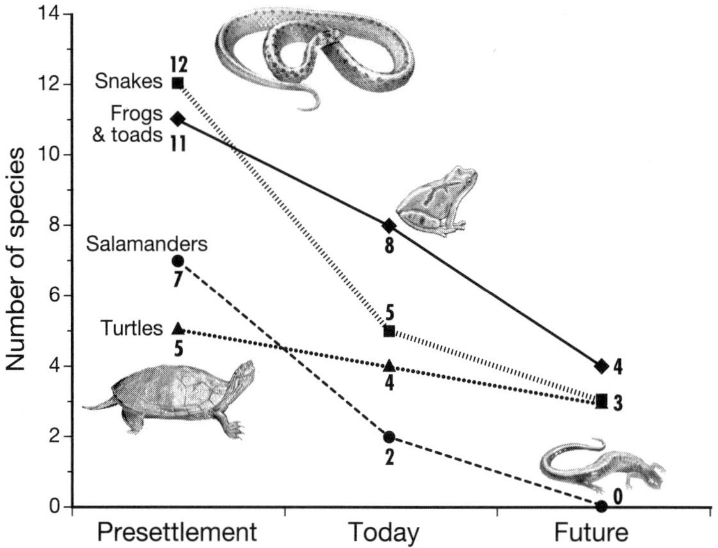

FIGURE 20.1 Historical and projected losses in amphibian and reptile species in Milwaukee County.

snakes are victims of shoreline development, with only one recent record (1986 from Scout Lake Park) probably reflecting a released individual.

Thus, Milwaukee County has lost many of it original amphibians and reptiles. Salamanders have experienced the greatest species losses (71%), followed by snakes (42%), frogs and toads (27%), and turtles (20%; figure 20.1). This sharply contrasts with the Apostle Islands, where present day conditions are similar to presettlement conditions (chapter 9) and no significant changes to the reptile and amphibian faunas have been documented. Reptile and amphibian faunas in the rest of the state are somewhere between these two extremes, with fewer species persisting in urbanized areas and more species found in wilder places (plates 8 and 11).

Shifts in the Distribution and Abundance of Reptiles and Amphibians

In addition to losing species, we see profound changes in the abundance and distribution of reptiles and amphibians. Terrestrial salamanders were probably at least 10 times more abundant before European settlement than they are today. Pond-breeding species, such as blue-spotted, eastern tiger, spotted, and four-toed salamanders and central newts, reach their highest abundance around fish-free ponds with at least 1,000 feet of undisturbed natural habitat surrounding (Semlitsch 1997; Petranka 1998). Such conditions were once common but are now rare in the county. While habitat loss clearly contributes the most to reducing salamander numbers, the common practice of stocking fish in ponds has also led to widespread declines in salamander populations. Salamanders cannot compete with fish during their aquatic larval stage.

Frogs and toads face similar problems. While naturalists can still find most species of frogs and toads in Milwaukee County, their numbers have declined greatly. Because routine surveys for frogs and toads are not conducted in Milwaukee County, we cannot be sure of recent trends. I estimate that the abundances of the semiterrestrial northern leopard frog and the remaining terrestrial frogs (northern spring peepers, western chorus frogs, eastern American toads, gray treefrogs, and Cope's gray treefrogs) have decreased by at least 90%. Like salamanders, these species require 300–1,000 feet of quality upland habitat around their breeding wetlands, and most are sensitive to introduced fish. Shoreline-restricted aquatic species such as American bullfrogs and northern green frogs are less vulnerable to fish stocking, and both of these species have fared better. American bullfrogs may, in fact, be more abundant now than historically. They respond well to simplified environments such as golf course ponds, where they outcompete other frog species.

Turtles depend on wetlands, lakes, and ponds with abundant aquatic vegetation and natural shorelines. Turtle population numbers have undoubtedly mirrored the general decline in these habitats, probably accelerated by shoreline development. Shallow weedy areas that comprise the best turtle habitat are often dredged or repeatedly damaged by motorized boats (chapter 16). The increased abundance of nest mesopredators (raccoons, skunks, cats, dogs, opossums, etc.) has further reduced reproductive success. At the same time, increases in traffic and road construction are killing more females on roads. Despite these threats, only one turtle species has been lost from the county.

Populations of many snake species are declining. The abundance of species like the eastern milksnake and common gartersnake hinges on how much good-quality habitat exists. As habitat extent and quality decline, so do population sizes. In contrast, Butler's gartersnakes, midland brownsnakes, and northern red-bellied snakes maintain high abundance within most occupied habitats, apparently because they are limited primarily by food (earthworms, slugs, and snails). For these species, we should worry more about declines in the number of colonies remaining than declines in the number of individuals within colonies.

Aside from contrasting the Apostle Islands with Milwaukee County, we should also be concerned about how the ranges of several species are contracting. Eastern massasauga rattlesnakes were once found throughout most of southern Wisconsin, wherever marsh, floodplain forest, and wet meadow habitats were available (Schorger 1967–68; Vogt 1981). Surveys over the past decade report this species from only a few locations (Bob Hay, personal communication). Populations are hunted illegally, while wetland loss, fire suppression, and hydrological manipulations eliminate habitats. Additionally, water drawdowns during the winter from river systems are thought to cause mass mortality in hibernating snakes.

Blanchard's cricket frogs were also once widespread throughout southern Wisconsin but declined rapidly beginning in the 1950s (Vogt 1981; Lannoo 1998). Bob Hay reports that recent surveys now find this Wisconsin endangered species in only a few southwestern counties (personal communication). Two ecological factors (landscape fragmentation and climate) and two life history factors (short life span and limited dispersal ability) probably contributed to declines. These frogs typically live less than 2 years, and their poor dispersal ability makes them especially prone to fragmentation arising from road building and agriculture. When populations disappear during extended droughts, habitats lacking connections are not recolonized when the rains return. Blanchard's cricket frogs face additional stress from being at the edge of their environmental tolerance for cold winters in Wisconsin.

Queen snakes have also disappeared from most of their southeastern Wisconsin range. The exact causes of this decline are mysterious, but we do know that the streams this aquatic snake once occupied have changed considerably as they become more loaded with sediment from agricultural and urban runoff. A suite of prairie reptiles is also declining statewide, including the ornate box turtle, prairie racerunner, western slender glass lizard, eastern racer, and bullsnake. These declines and range contractions appear to reflect the delayed effects of converting prairies into farm fields.

Trends Evident from the Frog and Toad Survey

The best source of trend data available for amphibians in the state is the Wisconsin Frog and Toad Survey (WFTS), administered by the Department of Natural Resources. These data comprise an over 20 year data set, dating back to 1981. Mossman and others (1998) analyzed the 1984–94 WFTS data and noted declines in northern spring peepers and possibly northern leopard frogs, pickerel frogs, and Cope's gray treefrogs. Gray treefrogs and eastern American toads appeared to be stable or increasing. Regionally, western chorus frogs declined in the eastern forest region, northern spring peepers declined in the central sands and southeast regions, northern leopard frogs declined in the north-central forest region, and eastern American toads increased in the Driftless Area.

While this analysis over a 10-year period suggests several trends, we need longer-term analyses to better understand how landscape conditions, precipitation patterns, and so on, are affecting variation in these populations. Herpetologists expect to see fewer breeding frogs following drought years. Consistent regional declines may reflect changes in the landscape such as obstacles that block needed linkages between terrestrial and aquatic habitats. If this is the case, I predict that amphibians will decline faster in those parts of the state undergoing rapid urbanization and similar changes in land use (plates 8 and 11).

The Future of Amphibians and Reptiles

The future for reptiles and amphibians in the Apostle Islands appears fairly secure because this national lakeshore is protected from the direct impacts of development. This security could prove illusory, however, if global warming causes a long-term drying and warming of this region. Such a climatic shift would generally favor reptiles while disfavoring amphibians. Lower water levels in Lake Superior could also result in expanded lagoons and warm water shoreline areas that favor many reptiles and amphibians. However, warmer and drier inland forests, soils, streams, and wetlands seem likely to foster amphibian declines.

In contrast, the future for most reptile and amphibian species in Milwaukee County appears bleak, barring major improvements in land use planning, land management, and conservation. We have already lost an estimated 16 of 35 amphibian and reptile species (48%). This represents about one species every 10 years over the last 150 years. These declines began with deforestation, agriculture, and wetland filling but continue with the intensification of agriculture and accelerating urban and suburban development. Unfortunately, more of Wisconsin is coming to resemble Milwaukee rather than the Apostle Islands.

Habitat losses combined with limited dispersal ability spell trouble for many reptiles and amphibians. These species generally cannot disperse as well as birds and most mammals—they must hop, walk, or crawl to a new destination instead of simply flying or running. As hostile terrain proliferates in the form of roads, parking lots, agriculture, lawns, golf courses, and gravel lots, these animals are increasingly exposed to hot, dry conditions, predators, and chemical contaminants. Once extirpated, habitat fragmentation also restricts opportunities for these species to recolonize suitable habitats. While biologists can sometimes assist, connections to other habitats are necessary if these populations are to persist and prosper. The limited dispersal ability of most reptiles and amphibians may also increase the risk of inbreeding and thus inbreeding depression. Butler's gartersnakes in Milwaukee County appear to have already suffered genetic bottlenecks in the past, resulting in low genetic diversity and perhaps limiting their ability to adapt to environmental changes, parasites, and disease (Burghardt et al. 2006).

If current trends continue, more species will likely be lost from Milwaukee County. If the remaining species at greatest risk are lost, we can expect to lose 25 of the original 35 species, or 71%. These include the blue-spotted salamander, eastern tiger salamander, northern spring peeper, gray treefrog, Cope's gray treefrog, northern leopard frog, eastern spiny softshell, eastern milksnake, and common gartersnake. All of these species have relatively large or complex habitat requirements. Should they be lost, total species losses will rise to 100% for salamanders, 64% for frogs and toads, 40% for turtles, and 75% for snakes (figure 20.1).

Several other factors also challenge our ability to preserve and manage habitats suitable to sustain amphibians and reptiles. We will, for example, need to control invasive species like reed canary grass and giant reed grass that degrade wetland quality. We may also need to limit the impacts of mesopredators like raccoons, skunks, feral cats, and opossums that have become increasingly abundant in our fragmented, human-dominated landscapes. Stream siltation, pollution, and disease add further stresses that compound when pollutants depress immune systems. Over the longer term, we should also be concerned about how global warming will affect amphibian and reptile populations.

As populations are lost one by one, remaining populations grow smaller and increasingly isolated. Similar scenarios are now playing out in other urbanizing regions like the counties around Milwaukee and areas around Green Bay and Madison. As these areas suffer parallel declines in habitat quality, quantity, and connectivity, local populations of amphibians and reptiles will decline across the region. Collectively, these local population extirpations also tend to accumulate to the point that they could eventually cause additional statewide extinctions.

To halt or reverse these losses will require us to preserve connected networks of habitat. We will also need to improve how we manage these habitats. This might be accomplished by pursuing cooperative land use planning efforts that take the needs of wildlife including reptiles and amphibians into account. Preserving, restoring, and better managing the habitat preserves that remain in urban areas could secure many populations of amphibians and reptiles. Doing so successfully, however, will require us to maintain the right kinds of habitat in the right configuration. Because reptiles and amphibians require different habitats for foraging, breeding and nesting, and overwintering, species often cannot persist when any habitat component is missing or inaccessible due to fragmentation. Such habitat recovery efforts would benefit many other species as well, including our own.

References

Blaustein, A. R., and D. B. Wake. 1995. The puzzle of declining amphibian populations. Scientific American 272:52–57.

Burghardt, G. M., J. S. Placyk, Jr., G. S. Casper, R. L. Small, and K. Taylor. 2006. Genetic structure of Great Lakes region *Thamnophis butteri* and *Thamnophis radix* based on mtDNA sequence data: Conservation implications for Wisconsin Butler's gartnersnake. Technical report to Wisconsin Department of Natural Resources, Bureau of Endangered Resources, Madison.

Casper, G. S. 1996. Geographic Distributions of the Amphibians and Reptiles of Wisconsin. Milwaukee: Milwaukee Public Museum.

———. 2001a. Amphibian Inventory of the Apostle Islands National Lakeshore, with an Evaluation of Malformity Rates, Monitoring Recommendations, and Notes on Reptiles. Bayfield, WI: National Park Service, Apostle Islands National Lakeshore.

———. 2001b. Reptile Surveys of Long, Michigan, and Stockton Islands, and Little Sand Bay, in the Apostle Islands National Lakeshore, with Notes on Amphibians. Bayfield, WI: National Park Service, Apostle Islands National Lakeshore.

Curtis, J. T. 1959. The Vegetation of Wisconsin. Madison: University of Wisconsin Press.

Driscoll, D. A. 2004. Extinction and outbreaks accompany fragmentation of a reptile community. Ecological Applications 14(1):220–240.

Farrand, W. R. 1969. The quaternary history of Lake Superior. Proceedings of the International Association for Great Lakes Research 1969:181–197.

Flannery, T. 2001. The Eternal Frontier: An Ecological History of North America and Its Peoples. New York: Atlantic Monthly Press.

Hecnar, S. J., G. S. Casper, R. W. Russell, D. R. Hecnar, and J. N. Robinson. 2002. Nested species assemblages of amphibians and reptiles on islands in the Laurentian Great Lakes. Journal of Biogeography 29:475–489.

Holman, J. A. 1995. Pleistocene Amphibians and Reptiles in North America. New York: Oxford University Press.

Judziewicz, E. J., and R. G. Koch. 1993. Flora of the Apostle Islands. Michigan Botanist 32(2):1–189.

Lannoo, M. J., ed. 1998. Status and Conservation of Midwestern Amphibians. Iowa City: University of Iowa Press.

Martin, L. 1965. The Physical Geography of Wisconsin. Madison: University of Wisconsin Press.

Mossman, M. J., L. M. Hartman, R. Hay, J. R. Sauer, and B. J. Dhuey. 1998. Monitoring long-term trends in Wisconsin frog and toad populations. In M. J. Lannoo, ed. Status and Conservation of Midwestern Amphibians. Iowa City: University of Iowa Press.

Petranka, J. W. 1998. Salamanders of the United States and Canada. Washington, DC: Smithsonian Institution Press.

Phillips, C. A., R. A. Brandon, and E. O. Moll. 1999. Field Guide to Amphibians and Reptiles of Illinois. Illinois Natural History Survey, Manual 8. Champaign: Illinois Natural History Survey.

Pope, T. E. B., and W. E. Dickinson. 1928. The amphibians and reptiles of Wisconsin. Bulletin of the Milwaukee Public Museum 8(1):1–138.

Ralin, D. B. 1968. Ecological and reproductive differentiation in the cryptic species of the *Hyla versicolor* complex (Hylidae). Southwestern Naturalist 13(3):283–300.

Schorger, A. W. 1967–68. Rattlesnakes in early Wisconsin. Transactions of the Wisconsin Academy of Sciences, Arts and Letters 56:29–48.

Semlitsch, R. D. 1997. Biological delineation of terrestrial buffer zones for pond-breeding salamanders. Conservation Biology 12(5):1113–1119.

———, ed. 2003. Amphibian Conservation. Washington, DC: Smithsonian Institution Press.

Shine, R., M. Lemaster, M. Wall, T. Langkilde, and R. Mason. 2004. Why did the snake cross the road? Effects of roads on movement and location of mates by garter snakes (*Thamnophis sirtalis parietalis*). Ecology and Society 9(1):9. Available at http://www.ecologyand society/vol9/iss1/art9.

Vogt, R. C. 1981. Natural History of Amphibians and Reptiles of Wisconsin. Milwaukee: Milwaukee Public Museum.

21

Two Centuries of Changes in Grassland Bird Populations and Their Habitats in Wisconsin

David W. Sample and Michael J. Mossman

The immense weed, grass, and fern grown marsh or low-land prairie, which has been the breeding grounds for Henslow's sparrows and short-billed marsh wrens since long, long before my time, is being slowly reclaimed. The cornfields and pastures are eating into it on all sides, and will, before many years, meet in its very center. . . . What will become of . . . [these birds], as well as the hordes of bobolinks, the marsh hawks, the prairie hens, and other characteristic nesting birds, when the last acre of virgin sod is ploughed for corn? **Hollister 1919**

: : :

Our grasslands have undergone profound changes since explorers found landscapes of "wide prairie, decked with flowers of the gayest hue; its long and undulating waves stretching away till sky and meadow mingle in the distant horizon" (Owen 1848, 25). These changes—from the near loss of the native prairies to shifts in agricultural practices and conversion of the farmlands that replaced them—have had huge impacts on grassland bird populations. No other group of birds in Wisconsin has declined more in recent decades (Sauer et al. 2005). As the original native grassland habitats were altered or destroyed, bird species adapted, exploited newly created agricultural habitats, shifted to other available habitats, or disappeared. This process continues, and the fate of grassland bird populations remains closely tied to socioeconomic forces, to agricultural technology, and to society's values. Here, we attempt to tell this story of change and adaptation, of loss and gain, and see what it forecasts for us and the grassland birds that resided here long before we did but now depend on the decisions we make.

We tell this story in four parts. The first regards the "recent presettlement" era of about 1700–1850, prior to the major changes wrought by Euro-Americans. Information on birds from this time is sketchy, derived mainly from the accounts of early explorers, ornithologists, or from early settlers who noted changes in birdlife. Most accounts come from Wisconsin, but others come from similar landscapes nearby. Though fascinating and evocative, most of this information is qualitative. Our assessment of bird populations for those early years involves some inference and prudent speculation based both on the historical accounts and on what we know about the habitat distribution of birds today. Our information on land cover comes from explorer accounts and the records of the General Land Office (GLO) Public Lands Survey (chapter 2).

The second period is the first century after settlement, 1850–1950. For this we rely partly on qualitative accounts of ornithologists and settlers, unpublished personal journals, and popular accounts of birdlife from reliable sources. The first scientific studies of birds in the state appeared during this period: the useful ones are quantitative or qualitative but thorough and well documented. Data on land use are mainly from the U.S. Census of Agriculture (U.S. Department of Agriculture 2002) but also from the GLO survey, especially in northern Wisconsin.

The third period spans 1950 to the present. We rely mostly on three major types of monitoring. The first is the North American Breeding Bird Survey (BBS), which started in 1966 and entails annual counts on 70 (1966–97) to 92 (1998–present) permanent 25-mile-long roadside routes (Robbins et al. 1996; Sauer et al. 2005). We also use Wisconsin Department of Natural Resources (WDNR) surveys like the annual greater prairie-chicken booming ground survey, which began in 1950 and continues to the present (Keir 2005). For some species we use the Wisconsin Society for Ornithology's Checklist Project, which, beginning in 1982, monitors the frequency at which individual bird species in each county are reported by bird-watchers (Temple et al. 1997). We also looked at several case studies that compare current bird populations with historical ones. Land use information is from the Census of Agriculture and the Wisconsin Initiative for Statewide Cooperation on Landscape Analysis and Data (Wisconsin State Cartographer's Office 2005). Finally, we look to the future of grasslands and grassland birds

Table 21.1 Breeding-season abundance of selected grassland birds in Wisconsin, from presettlement to present

Species	Pre–1850	1900	1950	2004	Recent population trend[a] (%)
Northern harrier	A	C	C	U	Stable
Greater prairie-chicken	A	C	U-L	R-L	Stable
Sharp-tailed grouse	A	C	C	R-L	Decline
Upland sandpiper	A	U	C	U	Decline (−3.5)
Long-billed curlew	C	X	X	X	—
Short-eared owl	C	C	FC	R	Stable
Horned lark	C	C	C	C	Stable
Sedge wren	A	C	C	FC	Stable
Dickcissel	C	C	FC	U	Decline (−10.2)
Vesper sparrow	A	A	A	C	Decline (−4.5)
Lark sparrow	C	FC-L	U-L	U-L	Stable
Savannah sparrow	A	A	A	C	Decline (−2.2)
Grasshopper sparrow	A	C	C	U	Decline (−8.9)
Henslow's sparrow	C	FC	U	U	Decline (−11.2)
Bobolink	A	A	A	C	Decline (−1.8)
Red-winged blackbird	U	U	A	A	Decline (−0.8)
Eastern meadowlark	A	A	A	FC	Decline (−2.8)
Western meadowlark	R?	R	A	U	Decline (−9.5)

Note: A, abundant; C, common; FC, fairly common; U, uncommon; R, rare; L, local; X, extirpated.

[a]Recent population trend is the mean annual percentage change ($p < 0.01$) during 1966–2004, based on the North American Breeding Bird Survey (Sauer et al. 2005). For species inadequately sampled by that survey, we base the trend on the Wisconsin Checklist Project (1983–2004; Rolley 2005) (short-eared owl and lark sparrow); the Wisconsin Department of Natural Resources prairie-chicken census (1950–2005; Keir 2005); and the Wisconsin sharp-tailed grouse census (1991–2006; Mezera 2006).

in Wisconsin, noting conservation needs based on projected trends and lessons from the past.

To keep the story concise, we focus on 18 bird species. These include 14 of our 17 obligate grassland birds—species that require relatively treeless grassland habitat for most or all of their breeding and foraging activities (Sample and Mossman 1997). We also include four other species for which the historical record is particularly instructive: long-billed curlew (extirpated in the state), sharp-tailed grouse (a bird of open barrens and shrub-grasslands), lark sparrow (a species intolerant of cultivation of the prairie), and red-winged blackbird (a habitat generalist that is now the most abundant bird in Wisconsin grasslands) (table 21.1).

Presettlement (circa 1830)

> The surface of the country . . . may be compared to the heavy and lazy-rolling waves of the sea after a tempest. These wave-like plains are often destitute of trees, except a few scattering ones, but present to the eye an almost boundless field of native herbage. Groves of oak sometimes diversify those native mead-

ows, or cover the ridges which bound them. . . . Numerous brooks of limpid water traverse the plains, and . . . the traveller is very often startled by flocks of the prairie-hen rising up in his path. **Schoolcraft 1834**

Habitat. This 1831 account, like those in chapter 8, typifies the awe of travelers from the eastern states and Europe, upon witnessing the wild grasslands that covered over a third of what today is the state of Wisconsin. Of the more than 5 million ha of grasslands encountered by the GLO surveyors, about 75% was savanna or barrens—characterized by scattered oaks or pines. The remaining 25% (1.3 million ha) was open prairie and sedge meadow, sometimes occurring in large blocks of over 55,000 ha (Curtis 1959; figure 21.1). Some extensive open barrens, large sedge meadows, and a few bracken-grasslands occurred in northern Wisconsin, but most grassland occurred in the southern and western portions of the state (plate 4). This area, within the midwestern ecotone between the

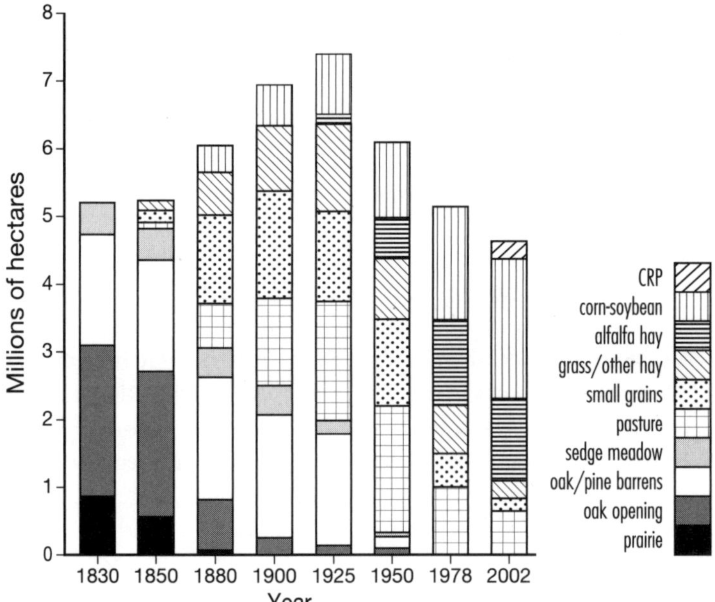

FIGURE 21.1 Changes in grassland and crop coverage in Wisconsin, 1830–2002. Data are from Curtis (1959), the U.S. Department of Commerce Census of Agriculture, the Wisconsin Crop and Livestock Reporting Service, and the Wisconsin Department of Natural Resources Natural Heritage Inventory Program. Numbers of hectares for native habitats from 1850 to 1978 are estimates inferred from the literature and expert opinion. Estimates for the amount of pasture from 1850 through 1900 are based on the ratio of the number of cattle: hectares of pasture from 1925 through 1978. CRP, Conservation Reserve Program.

continent's western prairies and eastern forests, was a dynamic mosaic of prairie, savanna, barrens, shrub, woodland and forest communities, sedge meadows, and—especially in glaciated areas—marshes and lakes. It was a landscape responding to the interplay of site conditions, topography, climate, fire, grazing, and succession (chapters 5, 7, and 8). Fires were often set by Native Americans. By the time of the GLO surveys (1832–66), this landscape had probably already become less open than in previous centuries as Indian populations declined due to translocations and disease (Curtis 1959).

Bird Populations. The power of flight allowed bird populations to respond readily to spatial and temporal variation in landscape pattern, as long as suitable habitat existed somewhere on the landscape. We can never have a complete picture of the presettlement avifauna in the state; but, for most grassland bird species, the historical record suggests that individuals and breeding pairs selected habitats with habitat structures roughly similar to those in which we find them today in Wisconsin or in other regions where they still occur. Moist sites with moderate to tall herbaceous vegetation supported species such as eastern meadowlark, dickcissel, savannah sparrow, and bobolink. When conditions had spared such sites from fire for one or more years, allowing for buildup of litter, species such as sedge wren and Henslow's sparrow probably occurred as well. In dry, sandy, or gravelly sites with sparse grass and forb cover, grasshopper, vesper, and lark sparrows plus horned larks probably nested. Some species with large territories or colonial breeding systems required large, open expanses of grassland but tolerated a range of habitats. Many of these species were widespread, including greater prairie-chicken (in open prairie), sharp-tailed grouse (in brushier areas), northern harrier, short-eared owl, upland sandpiper, and long-billed curlew.

Other grassland species were also common, but we do not examine them in detail. In grasslands near ponds nested a variety of "prairie" ducks such as blue-winged teal, gadwall, and northern pintail. In patches of shrubby growth created by oak sprouts or hazel, most open grassland birds tended to be replaced by other species like field and clay-colored sparrow, Bell's vireo, loggerhead shrike, and chestnut-sided warbler. Scattered live or dead trees also favored species that fed in open country but built their nests among tree limbs (e.g., swallow-tailed kite, red-tailed hawk, and eastern kingbird) or in cavities (e.g., American kestrel, red-headed woodpecker, northern flicker, and eastern bluebird).

An observant modern transported back to the prairie in 1830 would, we surmise, be amazed with the widespread abundance (table 21.1) and variety of these birds, many of which today are gone altogether or limited to a few plots and forgotten corners of the rural and suburban landscape. There would be other surprises as well. Western meadowlarks occurred rarely if at all, and red-winged blackbirds were restricted to wetlands. That great, seamless mosaic of natural communities contrasts strongly with today's world and suggests possibilities we might ponder for future landscapes. For the reader interested in such time travel, we suggest the firsthand accounts of explorers such as Carver (1781), Schoolcraft (1821, 1834), Smith (1838), Featherstonaugh (1847), Owen (1848), and Kinzie (1856); some of the early midwestern ornithologies (e.g., Allen 1868, 1871; Hoy 1853, 1885; Kennicott 1855; Baird et al. 1874; Kumlien and Hollister 1903); and modern reviews of historical records (e.g., Schorger 1943, Curtis 1959, 262–64, 295–305; Mossman 1988, 1994; Herkert 1991; Sample and Mossman 1994).

Postsettlement (1850–1950)

> There he sits; his whole being says it's your move to absent yourself from his domain. The county records may allege that you own this pasture, but the plover airily rules out such trivial legalities. He has just flown 4000 miles to reassert the title he got from the Indians, and until the young plovers are a-wing, this pasture is his, and none may trespass without his protest. . . . The upland plover [upland sandpiper] fits easily into the agricultural countryside. He follows the black-and-white buffalo, which now pasture his prairies, and finds them an acceptable substitute for brown ones. He nests in hayfields as well as pastures. . . . In farm country, the plover has only two enemies: the gully and the drainage ditch. Perhaps we will one day find that these are our enemies, too.
>
> **Leopold 1949**

Habitat. Euro-American settlement wrought massive changes in the composition, extent, and geographic distribution of Wisconsin's grassland bird habitats. South of the Tension Zone, native prairie, oak savanna, and some woodlands were swiftly replaced by pasture and cropland (Henderson and Sample 1995). In the absence of fire, most uncultivated, ungrazed, and some lightly grazed prairie and savanna succeeded rapidly into shrubs and eventually young woods (chapter 8). The open prairies disappeared by 1880, and 90% of the savannas were gone by 1900 (Curtis 1959; figure 21.1). Oak and pine barrens and sedge meadows were probably the only native grasslands to maintain significant acreage well after settlement. These, too, however, declined greatly as agricultural drainage accelerated in the early decades of the 1900s (WDNR 1976) and fire control became effective in the 1930s (WDNR 1970).

Farming was established in southeast Wisconsin by 1850 and quickly spread west and north. The crop fields of pioneers were small, weedy, and interspersed with pastures and areas that were too wet, dry, thin soiled, wooded, or inconvenient to cultivate. An era of intensive wheat farming quickly followed. Wheat could be planted even among the stumps of trees in former savanna and harvested by hand with a cradle (Hawkins 1940). Wheat peaked in 1878 at 809,717 ha, close to the original prairie acreage in the state (Wisconsin Crop and Livestock Reporting Service 1948; figure 21.1). Secondary crops in 1880 included grass and clover hay, pasture, other small grains, and corn.

Wheat farming depleted soils. As transportation infrastructure improved, Wisconsin agriculture shifted to livestock farming, and, with the critical aid of the silo for year-round storage, to dairy farming (Wisconsin Statistical Reporting Service 1967). Wheat was replaced by grass and clover hay, pasture, and oats—crops better suited to Wisconsin's geography and climate (Graber 1953; Wisconsin Crop and Livestock Reporting Service 1954). By 1900, the combined acreage of pasture, hay, and small grains (predominantly oats) equaled that of the original prairie, savanna, and sedge meadow (U.S. Department of Commerce 1952). Corn, grown mostly to feed livestock, remained a minor crop (figure 21.1).

As these changes were occurring in the prairie-savanna landscape of southern and western Wisconsin in the late 19th century, northern Wisconsin was being extensively logged. This left millions of hectares of open "stump prairies," many of which were converted to agriculture. Much of this cultivation was short lived, but farmland remains today in some areas, especially in north central and eastern Wisconsin. Wildfires often kept uncultivated areas open until fire suppression prevailed. The extent of these stump prairies was not well documented, so figure 21.1 includes only the area actually cropped or pastured. The decades around 1900 saw far fewer trees in Wisconsin than there are today.

As the human population increased through 1950, so did the number of cattle and the acreages of pasture and forage crops (Wisconsin Crop and Livestock Reporting Service 1948). Oats continued to increase through 1950, when it made up over 88% of small grains acreage. Grass hay acreage steadily increased until 1925, when it was the dominant crop in Wisconsin. It remained the predominant hay type through 1950, although alfalfa was becoming widely grown because of its superior drought resistance and nutrient value (Graber 1953). In 1950, corn was still subordinate to pasture and small grains.

This 100-year period saw the replacement of virtually all native grassland habitats with agricultural grasslands, or "surrogate prairie grasslands" (habitats dominated by European grasses and weeds, including pasture, grass and grass-legume hay, and small grains), row crops, native wooded habitats, and urban and farmstead development. Extensive tracts of northern and eastern forest were also converted to agricultural grasslands. The end of this period saw the peak development of relatively low-intensity, grass-based dairy agriculture in Wisconsin. Importantly, the structure of the agricultural landscape also changed, from a continuously varying mosaic to a more permanently fragmented, geometric pattern of fields, woodlots, hedgerows, and farmsteads (chapter 2).

Bird Populations. Although the wholesale loss of native grasslands during this era had drastic impacts on birds, many species adapted to this loss and the shifting mosaic of agricultural habitats. This reflects both their mobility and their dependence on vegetation structure more than on particular plant species (Sample and Mossman 1997). New landscapes with substantial grass, some weedy forbs, and scattered shrubs and trees were often suitable for many prairie and savanna breeding–bird species, most of which remained common through 1950 (table 21.1). The exceptions were generally species that require large, treeless expanses for nesting and foraging (e.g., northern harrier and short-eared owl), some of which were also hunted (e.g., greater prairie-chicken and sharp-tailed grouse). Fragmentation of the former prairie landscape into small farm fields meant that these species no longer had the room they require.

The long-billed curlew and lark sparrow also fared poorly, in part because they require unbroken prairie or prairie-like sod. The curlew remained common in southern Wisconsin through the 1850s (Hoy 1853). Skavlem (1912, 58) gathered its eggs after burning a southern Wisconsin prairie prior to breaking sod in the early 1850s; he reported that curlews were so numerous there that "a bird student might have been misled to the conclusion that they were nesting in colonies." This species was also hunted. The "sickle bill" was probably extirpated by 1900 (Kumlien and Hollister 1903). The decline was less rapid and complete for the lark sparrow, which survived in a few forgotten corners of the landscape (Schorger 1931; Buss and Mattison 1955).

The greater prairie-chicken, abundant in prairie and open savanna prior to 1850 (Schorger 1943; Anderson and Toepfer 1994), may have increased initially with the addition of cereal crops to the native landscape (Muir

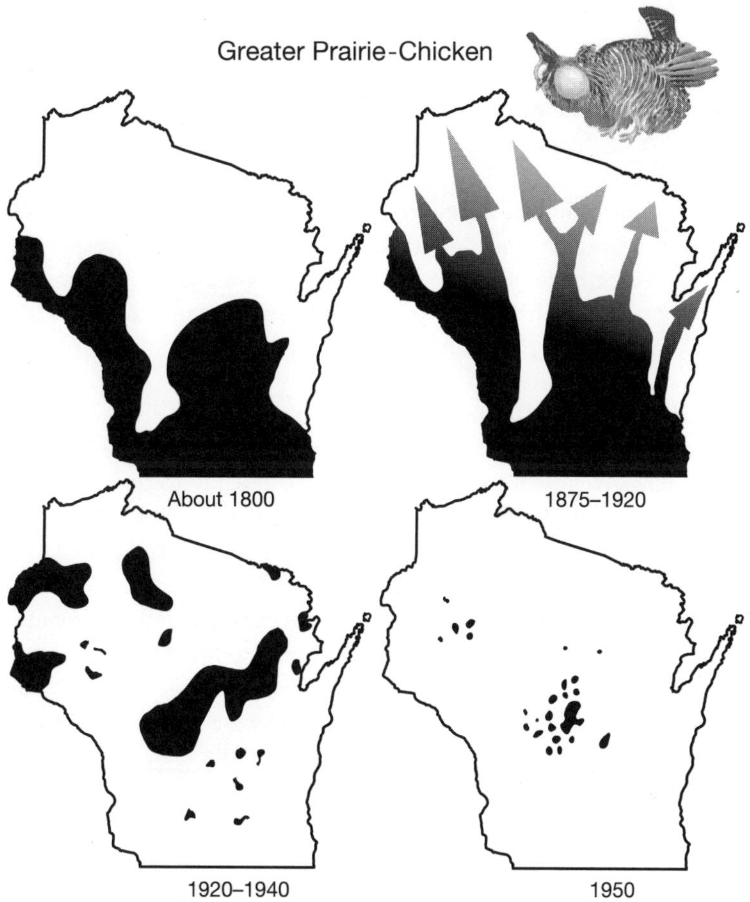

FIGURE 21.2 Greater prairie-chicken range expansion and contraction in Wisconsin, 1800–1950. Data are from Hamerstrom et al. (1957).

1965). It also expanded its range northward into newly cleared and fire-swept stump prairies in the late 1800s and early 1900s until it was present in almost every county (Schorger 1943; Hamerstrom et al. 1957; figure 21.2). This increase in range did not last long. They were heavily hunted, with 25,000 shipped to markets from Spooner in 1896 alone (Leopold 1949). The stump prairies soon grew back to brush and timber or were cultivated, rendering the habitat unsuitable (Hamerstrom et al. 1957; Bent 1932). By 1950, prairie-chickens were primarily limited to expansive grasslands in the drained marshes, bogs, and former forests of central Wisconsin.

The sharp-tailed grouse was common at settlement in brushy grasslands and oak openings south of the Tension Zone and northward in open bogs and barrens (Hoy 1853; Gregg 1987). It lost its southern range in the state even before the prairie-chicken and for the same reasons (Schorger 1943; Buss and Mattison 1955). It, too, quickly occupied the northern stump prairies. But as forests regenerated, it retreated. However, its preference for brushy habitat meant it persisted longer than the prairie-chicken. By 1950 it was found only in the northern half of the state (Gregg 1987).

Other grassland birds similarly expanded into the northern cutovers from southern or barrens habitats, especially species like vesper sparrow that tolerates some shrubs or trees (Jackson 1943). However, records for nongame birds are scant for this region until around 1920 by which time many of the stump prairies had already converted to crops, shrubs, or second-growth forest.

Extensive wheat farming probably contributed to declines in some grassland bird populations between 1850 and 1900. Horned lark and vesper sparrow, however, probably adapted quickly to the new monoculture as they did in Illinois (Graber and Graber 1963; Herkert 1991). Bobolink, eastern meadowlark, and savannah sparrow likely used wheat fields to a more limited extent.

The subsequent rise of dairy farming spread surrogate prairie grasslands across much of the state. This allowed population increases in some grassland species in Wisconsin as occurred in Ohio (Mayfield 1988a, 1988b). Bobolink; horned lark; dickcissel; Henslow's, vesper, grasshopper, and lark sparrows; eastern meadowlark; and upland sandpiper may all have increased in response to the low-intensity agriculture of this period. Buss and Hawkins (1939) stated that the early nesting of upland sandpipers and the late harvesting of hay rescued these birds from significant losses due to mowing. Between 1900 and 1950, when western meadowlarks invaded Wisconsin and red-winged blackbirds expanded from wetlands into uplands, both species benefited from this new landscape.

Direct human persecution caused some declines during this period, particularly the market hunting of greater prairie-chicken, sharp-tailed grouse, upland sandpiper, long-billed curlew, and even eastern meadowlark (King 1883; Bent 1929, 1958). Raptors like northern harrier and species known or suspected of destroying crops (e.g., bobolinks and red-winged blackbirds) were also shot (Hollister 1919; Bent 1958). Eventually, state game laws and the federal Migratory Bird Treaty Act of 1918 curtailed hunting pressure, allowing many species to recover temporarily. However, most species (except for the ever-increasing red-winged blackbird) failed to do so over the long term signaling the importance of other factors like land-use change. (See sidebar.)

Faville Grove: A Case History of Abundance, Loss, and Recovery

In the 1930s, Aldo Leopold, some graduate students, and farmers embarked on an experiment in land management. Their 2,400-acre Faville Grove Wildlife Experimental Area comprised 10 properties on part of the former Crawfish Prairie in Jefferson County—a landscape of low cultivated fields, pasture, tamarack swamps, woodlots, and "one of the best virgin prairie relics in the state." Leopold considered it "an excellent place to make a really serious test of the idea of reconnecting people with land," where the new science of wildlife management could be nurtured and demonstrated, students could be trained, and farmers would be assisted in providing for wildlife and native plant communities as well as crops and livestock (McCabe 1978, 26).

Among its outcomes was the state's first publicly protected prairie remnant, the 60-acre Stoughton Faville Prairie Preserve, named in honor of the local farmer-naturalist who ensured the project's success. Another was a study of the area's wildlife history (Buss and Hawkins 1939; Hawkins 1940), which entailed fieldwork and interviews with residents. It traced the conversion of the land to agriculture; the uses of native species and arrival of exotics; changes in farming practices and hunting pressures; and the fluctuations, eventual declines, and occasional increases of wildlife species. Of special interest was the upland sandpiper, or "prairie pigeon," whose populations here followed statewide trends: great abundance at settlement and into the late 1800s, followed by declines due to hunting and habitat conversion, then a gradual increase after protection was afforded by the 1918 Migratory Bird Act. It was common in the late 1930s, nesting in low pastures, hay meadows, and prairie, with northern harrier, sometimes short-eared owls, and the area's last remaining greater prairie-chickens. Faville's granddaughter recalled, "late in the afternoon we'd watch the Short-eared Owls from a haystack. We used to squeak them in and they'd make pass after pass, turning their anxious faces back and forth. . . . It was fun to watch their wing-clapping in the spring" (McCabe 1978, 43). Although the researchers reported little on passerine populations, these must have been abundant and diverse, based on the habitats present.

In search of areas with native grassland, and curious about how Faville Grove had changed since the 1930s, we censused birds in native and agricultural habitats there in the mid-1980s. Like much else, the management experiment had ceased during the War years, and it had not revived, except for the addition of a 32-acre abandoned field to the preserve. Conversion and succession had changed the landscape to one of woodlots, hedgerows, row crops, alfalfa, oats, some shrubby old fields, and the original, 60-acre prairie remnant—now isolated and filling with shrubs. Grassland birds had declined substantially from the 1930s, for where Buss and Hawkins estimated 3–10 upland sandpiper pairs per square mile, we found none, nor were there harriers or short-eared owls. Prairie chickens were last seen in 1940. Presumably because of these wholesale changes in the landscape, grassland songbirds were few even in the prairie remnant—primarily red-winged blackbird, bobolink, savannah sparrow, and common edge-loving species. However, in the uncropped grasslands of the protected Waterloo Wildlife Area 3 km away, the passerine community was more diverse and included sedge wrens, some Henslow's sparrows, and a single upland sandpiper sighting.

It was apparent that without a renewed effort to bring grassland back onto the Faville Grove landscape, even the remaining prairie—though rich floristically—was doomed ecologically. During the ensuing decades, Madison Audubon Society, Wisconsin Department of Natural Resources, and the University of Wisconsin rose to the challenge. By 2004 there were 600 acres in nine tracts under conservation ownership, easement, or management agreement to restore prairie and savanna and to connect the remaining remnants in the region with native and surrogate prairie grassland. Perhaps some day "plovers" will once again follow the black and white buffalo here as they had in Leopold's day.

The ditching and draining of wetlands across the state, like the Buena Vista Marsh of central Wisconsin, may have benefited certain grassland birds when these marshes or bogs were converted to low-intensity cropland. However, the primary effect was usually to replace sedge meadows, low prairies, and fens with agricultural habitats that were less productive or useless for grassland birds. Species that lost habitat due to drainage include the sedge wren, Henslow's sparrow (Temple and Temple 1976), bobolink, short-eared owl, and northern harrier.

Thus, most grassland bird species that occurred south of the Tension Zone became less common and widespread by 1950 relative to a century before (table 21.1). The advent of agriculture in the previously forested north undoubtedly allowed an increase in populations in that region. Statewide, most species probably declined, although a few that were "preadapted" (Beecher 1942) to agriculture thrived. These species (horned lark, savannah sparrow, vesper sparrow, eastern meadowlark, and bobolink) probably sustained population levels similar to, or even exceeding, 1850. A few birds (western meadowlark and red-winged blackbird) thrived for reasons that are not well understood.

Recent (1950–2004)

> Farmers are now told to cut alfalfa before it blooms. We always saw Dickcissels in alfalfa-clover fields in full bloom, and now we never see them anymore. I also wonder if other field birds such as Western Meadowlark, Bobolink and Upland Sandpiper can get their young off that quickly. **North American BBS cooperator Carol Rudy in 1980 (as reported by Robbins 1982)**

Habitat. This was a period of agricultural intensification characterized by shifts in cropping patterns and farming practices. The number of Wisconsin farms decreased from 168,561 in 1950 to 77,131 in 2002, while average farm size increased from 55.9 ha (138 acres) to 82.6 ha (204 acres) (U.S. Department of Commerce 1956, 2004). As farm machines grew bigger, field sizes grew to accommodate them. "Clean" cultivation resulted in fewer weeds, fewer uncultivated areas, and less grain waste. This transformation was aided by increasing dependence on chemical pesticides beginning by the late 1940s (Youngberg et al. 1984; Soil Conservation Society of America 1987). The classic dairy farm rotation of hay-oats-corn was replaced on many farms by the continuous cropping of corn or soybeans, abetted by heavy applications of fertilizer. Technological advances in draining, dredging, and irrigation, along with government incentives, encouraged farmers to convert wetlands and sand soil areas from prairie, pasture, and low-intensity farming to row crops (WDNR 1976).

The acreage of row crops (corn and beans) increased between 1950 and 2002 (figure 21.1), doubling from 22% to 44% of all cropland (U.S. Department of Commerce 1984, 2004). Alfalfa acreage increased from 39% of all hay in 1950 to 84% by 2002, while grass-dominated hay decreased substantially (figure 21.1). Alfalfa acreage became second only to corn, reflecting the development of improved varieties that matured earlier, recovered faster after early cutting, and were more winter hardy, nutrient rich, high yielding, and disease resistant than older varieties of alfalfa and grass hay (Smith and Rowheder 1977). The development of chopping equipment and large silos allowed a crop of alfalfa to be cut for haylage or green chop early in the spring, when the conditions were often too damp for baling. Because the new alfalfa varieties substantially improved milk production, many farmers switched to these more productive varieties (Hodgson 1983).

While these improvements benefited the farmer, they spelled trouble for grassland birds. Whereas grass hay and alfalfa were traditionally harvested once in late June or early July and a second time in late August, new alfalfa varieties could be cut three or four times per year (Smith and Rowheder 1977). Most southern Wisconsin farmers now harvest the first crop in mid- to late May. Statewide, the mean date by which 50% of the first crop of hay has been harvested advanced from June 29 in the latter half of the 1950s to June 10 from 1997 to 2006; for the years 2006 and 2007, the dates were June 5 and 8, respectively. Increases in row crops and alfalfa also came at the expense of small grains, pasture, and grass hay (figure 21.1). Small grains declined from 30% of the total cropland in 1950 to 5% in 2002. From 1954 to 2002, pasture acreage declined precipitously by over a half. Its percentage of total cropland declined from 43% in 1950 to 15% in 2002 (figure 21.1). Increasingly, cattle were confined to feedlots or small pastures near barns, where feed of consistently high quality could be brought to them year-round.

The loss of thousands of hectares of once suitable agricultural habitats affected many grassland birds during this period. Urban and exurban development also took its toll, spurred by rising property values, an increasing population, and cheap gasoline (chapter 26). Croplands ill suited to large equipment and new crop varieties gave way to forest. Statewide, forests matured but cover remained relatively constant (Vissage et al. 2005). The net result was a loss in agricultural land (figure 21.1) and rural landscapes that were either more open (where large fields were practical) or more fragmented by woody vegetation, homes, and roads than in the previous period. On the positive side, significant areas of grassland habitat were developed or maintained in federal- and state-owned wildlife areas. Two agricultural programs that have worked to maintain habitat for grassland birds on private lands are the U.S. Department of Agriculture Soil Bank of 1956–72 and the Conservation Reserve Program (CRP; 1986–present) (Berner 1988; Best et al. 1997). CRP enrollment in Wisconsin totaled 251,217 ha in 2004 (figure 21.1).

Bird Populations. The quote from Hollister that opened our chapter lamented the loss of native grassland bird communities. The quote from Rudy that opened this section laments the loss of the surrogate prairie bird communities that replaced them. In terms of grassland bird populations, the latter perhaps was more critical. Furthermore, these trends are not local. The precipitous declines in Wisconsin breeding-bird populations generally reflect broad trends across eastern North America (Peterjohn and Sauer 1999).

Of the 17 species considered here (table 21.1), 13 were sampled between 1966 and 2004 by roadside monitoring routes across the state as part of the BBS (Sauer et al. 2005). Of these, 10 (77%) declined significantly from 1966 to 2004, while three (23%) were stable. None increased. Grassland species declined more than birds in any other habitat group (Robbins et al. 1996). Declines were highest for Henslow's sparrow, dickcissel, western meadowlark, vesper sparrow, and grasshopper sparrow (figures 21.3 and 21.4). Western meadowlark dropped from being one of the 10 most common breeding birds during 1966–70 to 43rd in 1986–91 (Robbins et al. 1996). For the rare species sampled inadequately by BBS, other monitoring programs have shown that short-eared owl populations were stable and lark sparrow populations fluctuated (Rolley 2005); sharp-tailed grouse numbers were variable but appear to have declined slightly (Mezera 2006); and greater prairie-chicken populations were stable in the center of the range but declined on the edges (Keir 2005).

Declines for many of these species coincided with the loss of surrogate prairie grasslands in Wisconsin (Sample and Mossman 1997) and across the Midwest (Herkert et al. 1996). Only two grassland bird species, horned lark and vesper sparrow, regularly use the row crops that replaced these grasslands. Even these species generally occur in lower numbers here than in other suitable habitats and probably suffer high losses from farming operations in these fields (Rodenhouse and Best 1983; Dinsmore et al. 1984).

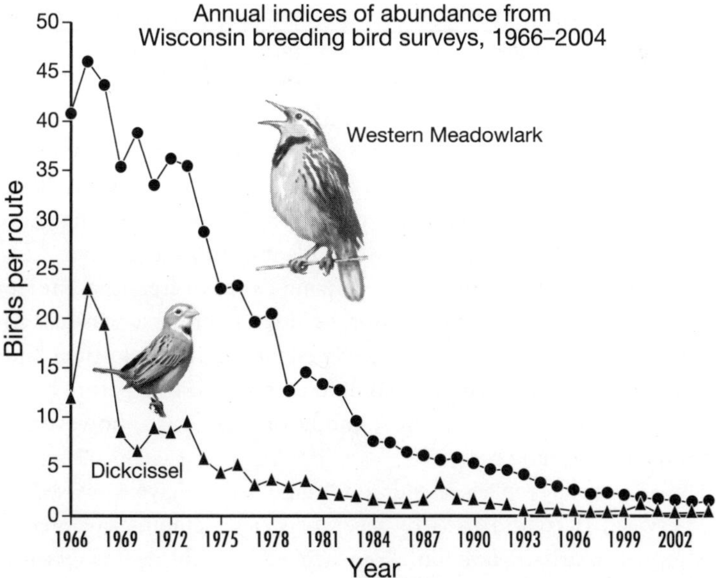

FIGURE 21.3 Population trend for western meadowlark and dickcissel in Wisconsin, 1996–2004. Data are from the North American Breeding Bird Survey (Sauer et al. 2005).

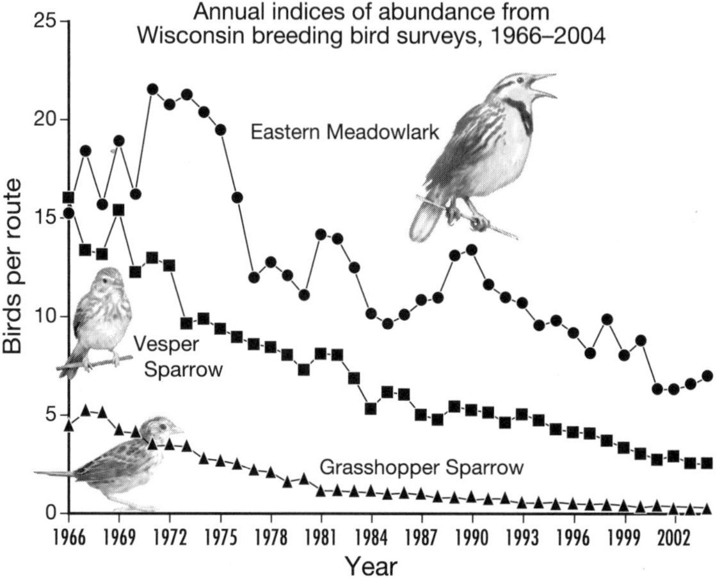

FIGURE 21.4 Population trend for eastern meadowlark, vesper sparrow, and grasshopper sparrow in Wisconsin, 1996–2004. Data are from the North American Breeding Bird Survey (Sauer et al. 2005).

Changes in haying practices also hurt grassland birds. In the early days of Wisconsin's history the cutting of hay, grass, or sedges typically occurred in mid- to late summer, mostly from low prairies and sedge meadows. Hoy (1885, 6) noted that sedge wrens, which had been abundant in the sedge meadows of southeastern Wisconsin in the 1840s, had scarcely been seen since the 1860s. Their song was "silenced by the click of the mower. The hay harvest comes before the young are fledged; hence the mower is fatal to this wren's best interests. They have gone, I hope, somewhere where *Carex* abounds and mowers do not." Sedge wrens are particularly sensitive to mowing as they often nest late in the season and require an accumulation of litter from past seasons. Most other grassland species continued to breed well in these old-time "mowing meadows" as they generally completed their nesting before hay cutting and benefited from the open conditions. By 1950, however, such places were becoming rare.

The alfalfa that replaced wild and "tame" grass hays was used regularly between 1950 and 2004 by several species including savannah and grasshopper sparrow, bobolink, red-winged blackbird, dickcissel, and both meadowlark species. As cuttings became more frequent, however, these habitats became ecological traps. Birds attracted to settle and nest in these open fields have their nesting cut short by the early harvest. In hayfields, harvest has been found to destroy 36% of all bird nests (including half of all dickcissel nests) in Iowa (Frawley 1989), 63% of meadowlark nests in Illinois (Roseberry and Klimstra 1970), and 94% of bobolink nests in New York (Bollinger et al. 1990).

Most hay-field species begin nesting too late to avoid alfalfa harvest (Buss and Hawkins 1939; Martin 1967; Basili 1997; Sample and Mossman 1997; Cutright et al. 2006). Red-winged blackbirds commonly, and eastern meadowlarks occasionally, nest early enough to fledge young in fields harvested after about June 1 (Sample 1989; Cutright et al. 2006). After hay mowing, the bobolink, red-winged blackbird, sedge wren, dickcissel, and Henslow's sparrow typically abandon their breeding territories or decline significantly in numbers (Sample 1989). Species typical of short, sparse vegetation (horned lark, upland sandpipers, and grasshopper, savannah, and vesper sparrows) may remain or move in. For grassland bird species, however, successful renesting takes at least 28 days *after* vegetation has regrown enough to support or conceal nests (George 1952; Bent 1958, 1968; Smith 1963; Harrison 1975). Such successful renesting is unlikely now as mowing occurs at monthly intervals.

Since the late 1900s, most grassland birds have occupied relatively rare or declining habitats, including pastures, late-cut grass hay, small remnant prairies, barrens, and idle grasslands such as CRP fields, old fields, fallow fields, sedge meadows, and public grasslands (Sample 1989; Sample and Mossman 1997). Small grains receive moderate use from some species, especially in landscapes that include other grassland (White 1983; Ribic and Sample 2001). Grassland birds also concentrate in formerly forested landscapes such as those in central and eastern Wisconsin (e.g., Marathon and Kewaunee counties), too far north to accommodate corn but good for grass.

Additional factors associated with the intensification and modernization of agriculture have affected grassland birds during this period. Increases in pesticide use prior to and early in this period contributed declines in at least one grassland species, northern harrier. Harrier populations began to recover following the ban of the organochloride DDT in 1972 (MacWhirter and Bildstein 1996).

Changes in landscape structure including exurban development and fragmentation of grassland by wooded fencerows continue to impact grassland birds as well, sometimes indirectly. Fragmentation of grassland habitat patches negatively impacts birds by excluding species that require large areas for nesting and foraging (Herkert 1994) and by lowering both nest density (Renfrew et al. 2005) and nest survival (Johnson and Temple 1990) near wooded edges. Populations of common nest predators, including raccoon, have benefited from these same changes in landscape structure (as well as from reduced persecution of varmints and low pelt prices) during this period (Petersen et al. 1988). Some predators use wooded fencerows as travel corridors and from them gain increased access to bird nests in the interior of small grassland patches (Bergin et al. 1997). Today, landscapes that are best suited for grassland birds are those that still retain significant amounts of grassland and limited low woody cover in the habitat matrix. In such landscapes the negative impacts of the small size of individual fields are lessened by the overall amount of open grass cover (Sample et al. 2003; Horn and Koford 2006).

Because most grassland birds in Wisconsin are migratory, additional perils faced in winter or during migration could compound their population declines. For example, dickcissels, which winter in large colonial groups in Venezuela, suffer from deliberate pesticide applications there (Basili and Temple 1995).

Several studies document changes in grassland bird populations and land use over the past 50 years. A transect across southern Wisconsin was surveyed for breeding meadowlarks in 1952–53 (Lanyon 1955) and again in 2003 (D. W. Sample and C. A. Ribic, unpublished data). Between these surveys, numbers of eastern and western meadowlarks declined by 55% and 98%, respectively. These declines parallel the loss of pasture land that was widespread during 1952–53 but remained common only in the western portion of the transect, where meadowlarks retained their highest numbers.

Another case study comes from two farms south of Madison. Here, Wiens (1969) studied grassland birds on a 32 ha pasture from 1964 to 1966. The diverse community was dominated by 26–37 savannah sparrows, 17–30 grasshopper sparrows, and 8–12 eastern meadowlarks, with a few vesper and Henslow's sparrows, western meadowlarks, bobolinks, and upland sandpipers. In 1986 we again surveyed bird populations here (Sample 1989). The entire pasture had been plowed and planted to corn and alfalfa with some hedgerows and upland brush present as well. Only five of the original eight common species were present, all at lower numbers. Savannah sparrow and bobolink were most common, a few individuals of eastern meadowlark, western meadowlark, and vesper sparrow remained, but both meadowlark species disappeared once hay was cut in early June.

Grassland birds persist in some places. The 11 ha hay meadow studied by Martin (1967) remained virtually unchanged between his 1966 study of bobolinks and our surveys on the same site in 1986–87 (Sample

1989). The vegetation was similar in both periods, and the bird community remained largely unchanged. Martin found six grassland bird species (the most common were bobolink, savannah sparrow, red-winged blackbird, and eastern meadowlark), while our surveys revealed five of these (Henslow's sparrow was missing). Of the common species, only savannah sparrow had dropped in abundance.

Conclusions

> Most of the interest in prairie restoration has been purely botanical; hence, most areas of attempted restoration are too small to harbor viable breeding populations of prairie birds. But an exciting possibility would be to upgrade a few prairie preserves to make them as large and complete as possible, favoring birds ranging from Bobolinks and Northern Harriers to Sedge Wrens and Greater Prairie-Chickens, and other animals ranging from lizards, snakes, and pocket gophers to badgers and bison. . . . It is not too soon to explore such possibilities, for agricultural practices could suddenly intensify further, while all open space continues to shrink under mounting pressures of human population.
>
> **Zimmerman 1991**

Euro-American pioneers and their successors transformed nearly all of Wisconsin's original prairies, meadows, barrens, and savannas within a few decades, yet the succeeding era of low-intensity, grass-based farming inadvertently sustained nearly all of the bird species native to the presettlement grasslands. Changes in farming since World War II, however, radically altered land use again. As farming became more efficient and dependent on artificial fertilizer and pesticides, farmlands came to be increasingly dominated by austere monocultures of corn, soybeans, and alfalfa. Consequently, most grassland-dependent birds declined. Yet none has been extirpated since the long-billed curlew disappeared with the last expanses of prairie sod a century ago. Most hang on where soils, climate, or a farmer's proclivity are not conducive to the new order and where preserves, or temporarily idle tracts, maintain suitable habitat in open landscapes.

Some lessons should be clear. Lesson 1: all but the most generalized or common grassland birds will continue to decline, and some will disappear from Wisconsin, without our intervention. For example, with expected climatic warming and advances in crop genetics, the grass-dominated farmscapes across central and eastern Wisconsin are likely to support more row crops in the future. Pressures to intensify agriculture and to develop land for urban expansion and exurban development continue to grow. Further, the rapidly expanding ethanol industry may mean extensive replacement of current grassland acreage in southern Wisconsin with corn grown as a biofuel crop. Lesson 2: suitable grassland bird habitat cannot simply be "set aside." Grasslands require active management to suppress succession to shrubs, trees, and invasive plants. Lesson 3: we cannot expect to preserve and manage public land enough to maintain healthy grassland bird populations, without also having substantial amounts of grass across the rural landscape on privately owned and managed properties.

The loss of grassland birds reflects larger problems with agricultural economies, land use, and dependence on petrochemical fuels, pesticides, and fertilizers. Although these issues are enormous, we also have opportunities and allies. To retain and restore grasslands, we need broad-based partnerships that include conservation groups, government agencies at various levels, farmers, other private landowners, educators, and policy makers. Civic and historic groups can also play a role. Several such grassland restoration partnerships have been created in recent years; some examples follow. The Military Ridge Prairie Heritage Area in southwestern Wisconsin comprises over 20,000 ha of mostly private land with many small but significant prairie remnants, many nonnative grasslands, and a vast, relatively treeless landscape with good populations of many critical grassland birds. The Nature Conservancy, WDNR, U.S. Fish and Wildlife Service, local conservation groups, and others work together with private landowners to attain conservation easements and acquire state and federal funds to help landowners manage their grasslands. They also work with local governments to manage residential development and prevent loss of agricultural land (Sample et al. 2003). A key part of the project is the creation of three core grassland areas, each with 600–1,000 ha of contiguous grassland habitat for area-sensitive bird species.

The planned closure of the 3,000 ha Badger Army Ammunition Plant in Sauk County brought together government agencies, the Ho-Chunk Nation, conservationists, historians, local civic leaders, chambers of commerce, farmers, and others to plan a future for the plant that incorporated conservation of the plant's rich grassland bird community, along with recreation, economic development, historic preservation, and agricultural research (Badger Reuse Committee 2001).

WDNR and private conservation organizations partnered for decades to save the state's largest remaining population of greater prairie-chicken in central Wisconsin, primarily in the 19,000 ha Buena Vista Grasslands. Recognition that this major property was insufficient to maintain a viable breeding population led to the creation of the 100 km^2 (39-township) Central Wisconsin Grassland Conservation Area. Here, a partnership works creatively with aquisitions, easements, leases, and federal cost-sharing programs to increase the amount of permanent grassland on the landscape and, in so doing, to reconnect isolated subpopulations of prairie-chickens that are now mainly restricted to several managed properties, including Buena Vista. In this manner, they strive to help farmers intersperse grassland among other crops and public preserves for chickens and other grassland birds, while maintaining a strong farm economy. As in many grassland conservation projects, substantial funding comes from hunters through license fees and voluntary contributions (WDNR 2004).

These practical, local projects follow the tradition of Leopold, the Hamerstroms, Jim Zimmerman, and other farsighted conservationists of the last century. If conducted at a large enough landscape scale, such projects will help sustain grassland bird populations plus other grassland fauna and flora as well. They serve as models for the projects we need and cultivate a committed, educated base of volunteers, landowners, and visitors who, in turn, can influence and inspire others. The success of these projects, however, will depend on having enlightened public policies at levels ranging from local land-use plans to federal farm and energy bills. Creative solutions could be pursued at both state and federal levels fashioned after existing, forest- and wetland-based tax incentives and cost-sharing programs. Because most grassland birds migrate, we should also expand partnerships among states and with Canada and Latin American countries.

Although grassland birds are in serious decline, we still have the opportunity to appreciate, rescue, and restore the populations that persist in Wisconsin. They deserve this attention and respect. We benefit them, ourselves, and our landscapes if we can succeed in protecting the habitats they need to survive.

References

Allen, J. A. 1868. Notes on birds observed in western Iowa, in the months of July, August and September; also on birds observed in northern Illinois, in May and June, and at Richmond, Wayne Co., Indiana, between June third and tenth. Memoirs Boston Society of Natural History 1:488–526.

———. 1871. The fauna of the prairies. American Naturalist 5:4–9.

Anderson, R. K., and J. E. Toepfer. 1994. Greater prairie chicken in Wisconsin. Pp. 49–73 in Wisconsin Grouse Symposium Proceedings.

Madison: Ruffed Grouse Society, Society of Tympanuchus Cupido, and Wisconsin Sharp-Tailed Grouse Society.

Badger Reuse Committee. 2001. Badger Army Ammunition Plant reuse plan. Sauk County Department of Planning and Zoning, final report, Baraboo, WI.

Baird, S. F., T. M. Brewer, and R. Ridgway. 1874. History of North American Birds: Land Birds. 3 vols. Boston: Little, Brown and Co.

Basili, G. D. 1997. Continental-scale ecology and conservation of dickcissels. Ph.D. thesis, University of Wisconsin–Madison.

Basili, G. D., and S. A. Temple. 1995. A perilous migration. *Natural History* 104:40–46.

Beecher, W. J. 1942. Nesting Birds and the Vegetative Substrate. Chicago: Chicago Ornithological Society.

Bent, A. C. 1929. Life histories of North American shorebirds, part 2. U.S. National Museum, Bulletin 146, Washington, DC.

———. 1932. Life histories of North American gallinaceous birds. U.S. National Museum, Bulletin 162, Washington, DC.

———. 1958. Life histories of North American blackbirds, orioles, tanagers, and allies. U.S. National Museum, Bulletin 211, Washington, DC.

———. 1968. Life histories of North American cardinals, grosbeaks, buntings, towhees, finches, sparrows, and allies, parts 1–3. U.S. National Museum, Bulletin 237, Washington, DC.

Bergin, T. M., L. B. Best, and K. E. Freemark. 1997. An experimental study of predation on artificial nests in roadsides adjacent to agricultural habitats in Iowa. Wilson Bulletin 109:437–448.

Berner, A. H. 1988. Federal pheasants—Impact of federal agricultural programs on pheasant habitat, 1934–1985. Pp. 45–95 in D. L. Hallett, W. R. Edwards, and G. V. Burger eds. Pheasants: Symptoms of Wildlife Problems on Agricultural Lands. Bloomington, IN: North Central Section of the Wildlife Society.

Best, L. B., H. Campa III, K. E. Kemp, R. J. Robel, M. A. Ryan, J. A. Savidge, H. P. Weeks, Jr., and S. R. Winterstein. 1997. Bird abundance and nesting in CRP fields and cropland in the Midwest: A regional approach. Wildlife Society Bulletin 25:864–877.

Bollinger, E. K., P. B. Bollinger, and T. A. Gavin. 1990. Effects of haycropping on eastern populations of the Bobolink. Wildlife Society Bulletin 18:142–150.

Buss, I. O., and A. S. Hawkins. 1939. The upland plover at Faville Grove, Wisconsin. Wilson Bulletin 51:202–220.

Buss, I. O., and H. M. Mattison. 1955. A half century of change in bird populations of the lower Chippewa River, Wisconsin. Milwaukee Public Museum, Publications in Ornithology No. 1, Milwaukee.

Carver, J. 1781. Travels through the Interior Parts of North America. London. Reprinted 1956 by Ross and Haines, Minneapolis.

Curtis, J. T. 1959. The Vegetation of Wisconsin. Madison: University of Wisconsin Press.

Cutright, N. J., B. R. Harriman, and R. W. Howe. 2006. Atlas of the Breeding Birds of Wisconsin. Waukesha: Wisconsin Society for Ornithology.

Dinsmore, J. J., T. H. Kent, D. Koenig, P. C. Petersen, and D. M. Roosa. 1984. *Iowa Birds*. Ames: Iowa State University Press.

Featherstonaugh, G. W. 1847. A Canoe Voyage Up the Minnay Sotor. 2 vols. London: R. Bentley.

Frawley, B. J. 1989. The dynamics of nongame bird breeding ecology in Iowa hayfields. M.S. thesis, Iowa State University.

George, J. L. 1952. The birds on a southern Michigan farm. Ph.D. thesis, University of Michigan.

Graber, L. F. 1953. A half century of alfalfa in Wisconsin. University of Wisconsin Extension Service, Bulletin 502, Madison.

Graber, R. R., and J. W. Graber. 1963. A comparative study of bird populations in Illinois, 1906–1909 and 1956–1958. Illinois Natural History Survey Bulletin 28:378–528.

Gregg, L. 1987. Recommendations for a program of sharptail habitat preservation in Wisconsin. Wisconsin Department of Natural Resources, Research Report 141, Madison.

Hamerstrom, F. N., Jr., O. E. Mattson, and F. Hamerstrom. 1957. A guide to prairie chicken management. Wisconsin Conservation Department, Technical Wildlife Bulletin 15, Madison.

Harrison, H. H. 1975. A Field Guide to Birds' Nests. Boston: Houghton Mifflin.

Hawkins, A. S. 1940. A wildlife history of Faville Grove, Wisconsin. Transactions of the Wisconsin Academy of Sciences, Arts and Letters 32:29–65.

Henderson, R. A., and D. W. Sample. 1995. Grassland communities. Pp. 116–129 in J. Addis, R. Eckstein, A. Forbes, D. Gebken, R. Henderson, J. Kotar, B. Les, P. Matthiae, W. McCown, S. Miller, B. Moss, D. Sample, M. Staggs, and K. Visser. Wisconsin's biodiversity as a management issue: A report to Department of Natural Resources managers. Wisconsin Department of Natural Resources, Madison.

Herkert, J. 1991. Prairie birds of Illinois: Population responses to two centuries of habitat change. Illinois Natural History Survey Bulletin 34:393–399.

———. 1994. The effects of habitat fragmentation on midwestern grassland bird communities. Ecological Applications 4:461–471.

Herkert, J. R., D. W. Sample, and R. E. Warner. 1996. Management of midwestern grassland landscapes for the conservation of migratory birds. Pp. 89–116 in F. R. Thompson, ed. Management of midwestern landscapes for the conservation of neotropical migratory birds. U.S. Department of Agriculture Forest Service North Central Experiment Station, General Technical Report NC-187, St. Paul, MN.

Hodgson, H. J. 1983. Wisconsin's alfalfa story. University of Wisconsin–Madison Cooperative Extension Program, College of Agricultural and Life Sciences, Research Publication R3192, vol. 1, no. 1, Madison.

Hollister, N. 1919. Some changes in the summer bird life at Delavan, Wisconsin. Wilson Bulletin 31:103–108.

Horn, D. J., and R. R. Koford. 2006. Could the area-sensitivity of some grassland birds be affected by landscape composition? Pp. 109–116 in D. Egan and J. A. Harrington, eds. Proceedings of the 19th North American Prairie Conference. Madison: University of Wisconsin.

Hoy, P. R. 1853. Notes on the ornithology of Wisconsin. Transactions of the Wisconsin Agricultural Society 2:341–364.

———. 1885. Man's influence on the avifauna of southeastern Wisconsin. Proceedings of the Natural History Society of Wisconsin (March):4–9.

Jackson, H. H. T. 1943. Summer birds of northwestern Wisconsin, part 7. Passenger Pigeon 5:24–35.

Johnson, R. G., and S. A. Temple. 1990. Nest predation and brood parasitism of tallgrass prairie birds. Journal of Wildlife Management 54:106–111.

Keir, J. 2005. Central Wisconsin prairie chicken census. Wisconsin Department of Natural Resources Web site. Available at http://dnr.wi.gov/org/land/wildlife/harvest/reports/prchickcensus05.pdf.

Kennicott, R. 1855. Catalogue of animals observed in Cook County, Illinois. Transactions of the Illinois State Agricultural Society 1:577–595.

King, F. H. 1883. Economic relations of Wisconsin birds. Pp. 441–610 in T. C. Chamberlin, ed. Geology of Wisconsin, Vol. 1. Madison, WI: Commission of Public Printing.

Kinzie, J. M. 1856. Wau-Bun, the "Early Day" in the North-west. New York: Derby and Jackson.

Kumlien, A. L., and N. Hollister. 1903. The Birds of Wisconsin. Madison: Wisconsin Society for Ornithology. Reprinted 1953 with revisions by A. W. Schorger.

Lanyon, W. E. 1955. The comparative ethology and ecology of sympatric meadowlarks in Wisconsin and other north-central states. Ph.D. thesis, University of Wisconsin–Madison.

Leopold, A. 1949. A Sand County Almanac. New York: Oxford University Press.

MacWhirter, R. B., and K. L. Bildstein. 1996. Northern harrier (*Circus cyaneus*). In A. Poole and F. Gill eds. The Birds of North America, No. 210. Philadelphia: Academy of Natural Sciences.

Martin, S. G. 1967. Breeding biology of the bobolink. M.S. thesis, University of Wisconsin–Madison.

Mayfield, H. F. 1988a. Changes in the bird life at the western end of Lake Erie. Part 1. American Birds 42:393–399.

———. 1988b. Changes in the bird life at the western end of Lake Erie. Part 2. American Birds 42:1259–1264.

McCabe, R. A. 1978. The Stoughton Faville Prairie Preserve: Some historical aspects. Transactions of the Wisconsin Academy of Sciences, Arts and Letters 66:25–49.

Mezera, A. 2006. Wisconsin sharptail grouse status. Wisconsin Department of Natural Resources Web site. Available at http://dnr.wi.gov/org/land/wildlife/harvest/reports/06stgstatus.pdf.

Mossman, M. J. 1988. A tory in the Wisconsin wilderness. Passenger Pigeon 50:314–320.

———. 1994. H. R. Schoolcraft and natural history on the western frontier, part 5: The 1831 expedition. Passenger Pigeon 56:39–72.

Muir, J. 1965. The Story of My Boyhood and Youth. Madison: University of Wisconsin Press.

Owen, D. D. 1848. Report of a geological reconnoissance [*sic*] of the Chippewa land district of Wisconsin, and, incidentally, of a portion of the Kickapoo country, and of a part of Iowa and of the Minnesota Territory, made under instructions from the United States Treasury Department. U.S. 30th Congress, 1st session, Sen. Ex. Doc. 7 (57), Serial 509, Washington, DC.

Peterjohn, B. G., and J. R. Sauer. 1999. Population status of North American grassland birds from the North American Breeding Bird Survey, 1966–1996. Pp. 27–44 in P. D. Vickery and J. R. Herkert, eds. Ecology and conservation of grassland birds of the Western Hemisphere. Studies in Avian Biology 19.

Petersen, L. R., R. T. Dumke, and J. M. Gates. 1988. Pheasant survival and the role of predation. Pp. 165–196 in D. L. Hallett, W. R. Edwards, and G. V. Burger, eds. Pheasants: Symptoms of Wildlife Problems on Agricultural Lands. Bloomington, IN: North Central Section of the Wildlife Society.

Renfrew, R. B., C. A. Ribic, and J. L. Nack. 2005. Edge avoidance by nesting grassland birds: A futile strategy in a fragmented landscape. Auk 122:618–636.

Ribic, C. A., and D. W. Sample. 2001. Associations of grassland birds with landscape factors in southern Wisconsin. American Midland Naturalist 146:105–121.

Robbins, S. 1982. Wisconsin's breeding bird survey results: 1966–1980. Passenger Pigeon 44:97–121.

Robbins, S. D., D. W. Sample, P. W. Rasmussen, and M. J. Mossman. 1996. The Breeding Bird Survey in Wisconsin: 1966–1991. Passenger Pigeon 58:81–179.

Rodenhouse, N. L., and L. B. Best. 1983. Breeding ecology of vesper sparrows in corn and soybean fields. American Midland Naturalist 110:265–275.

Rolley, R. E. 2005. Wisconsin checklist project. Wisconsin Department of Natural Resources Web site. Available at http://dnr.wi.gov/org/land/wildlife/harvest/reports/05checklist.pdf.

Roseberry, J. L., and W. D. Klimstra. 1970. The nesting ecology and reproductive performance of the eastern meadowlark. Wilson Bulletin 82:243–267.

Sample, D. W. 1989. Grassland birds in southern Wisconsin: Habitat preference, population trends, and response to land use changes. M.S. thesis, University of Wisconsin–Madison.

Sample, D. W., and M. J. Mossman. 1994. Birds of Wisconsin oak savannas: Past, present, and future. Pp. 155–159 in J. S. Fralish et al. eds. Proceedings of the North American Conference on Barrens and Savannas. Normal: Illinois State University.

———. 1997. Managing habitat for grassland birds: A guide for Wisconsin. Wisconsin Department of Natural Resources, Publication SS-925–97, Madison.

Sample, D. W., C. A. Ribic, and R. B. Renfrew. 2003. Linking landscape management with the conservation of grassland birds in Wisconsin. Pp. 359–385 in J. A Bissonette and I. Storch, eds. Landscape Ecology and Resource Management: Linking Theory with Practice. Washington, DC.: Island Press.

Sauer, J. R., J. E. Hines, and J. Fallon. 2005. The North American Breeding Bird Survey, Results and Analysis 1966–2004. Version 2005.2. Laurel, MD: U.S. Geological Survey Patuxent Wildlife Research Center.

Schoolcraft, H. R. 1821. Narrative Journal of Travels through the Northwestern Regions of the United States; Extending from Detroit through the Great Chain of American Lakes, to the Sources of the Mississippi River. Albany, NY: E. & E. Hosford. Reprinted by Arno Press.

———. 1834. Narrative of an Expedition through the Upper Mississippi to Itasca Lake, the Actual Source of this River; Embracing an Exploratory Trip through the St. Croix and Burntwood (or Broule) Rivers; in 1832. New York: Harper & Bros.

Schorger, A. W. 1931. The birds of Dane County, Wisconsin. Transactions of the Wisconsin Academy of Sciences, Arts and Letters 26:1–60.

———. 1943. The prairie chicken and sharp-tailed grouse in early Wisconsin. Transactions of the Wisconsin Academy of Sciences, Arts and Letters 35:1–59.

Skavlem, H. 1912. Recollections of bird-life in pioneer days. By the Wayside 13:57–59.

Smith, D., and D. A. Rohweder. 1977. Establishing and managing alfalfa. University of Wisconsin College of Agriculture and Life Sciences, Research Report R1741, Madison.

Smith, R. L. 1963. Some ecological notes on the grasshopper sparrow. Wilson Bulletin 75:159–165.

Smith, W. R. 1838. Observations on the Wisconsin Territory; Chiefly on That Part Called the "Wisconsin Land District." Philadelphia: E. L. Carey & A. Hart. Reprinted 1975 by Arno Press.

Soil Conservation Society of America, Wisconsin Chapter. 1987. Impacts of land-use changes: Agronomic/soils/wildlife relationships in southeastern Wisconsin 1900–1995. Soil Conservation Society of America, Wisconsin Chapter, Madison.

Temple, S. A., J. R. Cary, and R. E. Rolley. 1997. Wisconsin Birds: A Seasonal and Geographical Guide. Madison: University of Wisconsin Press.

Temple, S. A., and B. Temple. 1976. Avian population trends in central New York state, 1935–72. Bird-Banding 47:238–257.

U.S. Department of Agriculture. 2002. *2002* Census of Agriculture—Volume 1 Geographic Area Series. Washington, DC: National Agricultural Statistics Service. Available at http://www.nass.usda.gov/census/.

U.S. Department of Commerce. 1952. U.S. Census of Agriculture: 1950. Vol. 1. Counties and State Economic Areas. Part 7. Wisconsin. Washington, DC: U.S. Government Printing Office.

———. 1956. U.S. Census of Agriculture: 1950. Vol. 1. Counties and State Economic Areas. Part 7. Wisconsin. Washington, DC: U.S. Government Printing Office.

———. 1984. 1982 Census of Agriculture. Vol. 1. Geographic Area Series. Part 49. Wisconsin State and County Data. Washington, DC: U.S. Government Printing Office.

———. 2004. 2002 Census of Agriculture. Vol. 1. Geographic Area Series. Part 49. Wisconsin State and County Data. Washington, DC: U.S. Government Printing Office.

Vissage, J. S., G. J. Brand, and J. E. Cummings-Carlson. 2005. Wisconsin's forest resources in 2003. U.S. Department of Agriculture, Forest Service, North Central Research Station, Resource Bulletin NC-249, St. Paul, MN.

White, R. P. 1983. Distribution and habitat preference of the Upland Sandpiper (*Bartramia longicauda*) in Wisconsin. American Birds 37:16–22.

Wiens, J. A. 1969. An Approach to the Study of Ecological Relationships among Grassland Birds. Ornithological Monographs No. 8. Lawrence, KS: Allen Press.

Wisconsin Crop and Livestock Reporting Service. 1948. A century of Wisconsin agriculture, 1848–1948. Wisconsin State Department of Agriculture, Bulletin 280, Madison.

———. 1954. Wisconsin dairying in mid-century. Wisconsin State Department of Agriculture, Bulletin 331, Madison.

Wisconsin Department of Natural Resources (WDNR). 1970. Fire! Fire control and prevention in Wisconsin. WDNR, Publication 532–70, Madison.

———. 1976. Wetlands in Wisconsin: Historical perspective and present picture. WDNR, Madison.

———. 2004. Feasibility study and environmental analysis for the Central Wisconsin Grassland Conservation Area. Report on file at the WDNR, Madison.

Wisconsin State Cartographer's Office. 2005. Wisconsin Initiative for Statewide Cooperation on Landscape Analysis and Data home page. University of Wisconsin–Madison. Available at http://sco.wisc.edu/wiscland/index.php.

Wisconsin Statistical Reporting Service. 1967. Wisconsin Agricultural Statistics, 1967. Madison: Wisconsin Department of Agriculture.

Youngberg, I. G., J. F. Parr, and R. I. Papendick. 1984. Potential benefits of organic farming practices for wildlife and natural resources. Transactions of the North American Wildlife and Natural Resources Conference 49:141–153

Zimmerman, J. H. 1991. The landscape and the birds. Pp. 35–90 in S. D. Robbins, Jr. Wisconsin Birdlife. Madison: University of Wisconsin Press.

22

Wisconsin's Changing Bird Communities

Stanley A. Temple and John R. Cary

In the summer of 2003, one of us (Temple) revisited some of the same southern Wisconsin forests where Ambuel and Temple (1982, 1983) censused birds 25 years earlier and where Richard Bond (1957) censused birds 50 years ago. Walking through one of the woods on a late spring day listening to the chorus of territorial songs, it seemed that the bird community just didn't sound the same as it had 25 years earlier. There seemed to be fewer songs of the veery, yellow-billed cuckoo, and Baltimore oriole, and more of the blue-gray gnatcatcher, pileated woodpecker, and red-eyed vireo. Knowing that memories can be deceiving (chapter 3), a check of the census results confirmed impressions from the field. The bird community, the assemblage of species that are typically found together in a particular type of environment, had changed a lot between the visits in 1954, 1979, and 2003.

These three surveys at roughly 25-year intervals revealed that the bird community in southern Wisconsin forests differed every time ornithologists conducted a thorough census. Some newcomers joined the community. The tufted titmouse appeared sometime between 1954 and 1979, while wild turkey and house finch joined between 1979 and 2004. In contrast, some species had dropped out of the community. Between 1954 and 1979, Cooper's hawk had disappeared, while the red-headed woodpecker had almost disappeared. By 2004, however, Cooper's hawk returned. The abundance of many species changed dramatically. Populations of the cerulean warbler, American redstart, and several other migratory songbirds declined steadily over the past 50 years, whereas some permanent residents like red-bellied woodpecker and northern cardinal increased steadily. These southern Wisconsin forests are not unique—the composition of bird communities throughout Wisconsin is changing. Here, we take advantage of current and historic data to explore changes in the composition of 10 Wisconsin bird communities over the past 55 years (1950–2004) and interpret those changes in light of what we know about the birds themselves and their environment.

Bird Communities of Wisconsin

Bird communities are recurring assemblages of bird species distinguishable from one another and internally similar in terms of the identity, number, and relative abundance of their constituent species. For convenience ecologists often classify communities into somewhat discrete units. Whereas John Curtis's (1959) classification of Wisconsin's plant communities was based on detailed descriptions of the plant species composition in various environments, no similar, broadly accepted community classification exists for birds. While it might seem logical to examine bird communities in each different kind of plant community, not all plant community types have distinctive bird communities. For example, differences between the bird assemblages associated with Curtis's southern dry, dry-mesic, mesic, and wet-mesic forests are quite minor, even though plant differences are pronounced. As a result, ornithologists devised many ad hoc classification schemes to better describe how bird communities are organized (Zimmerman 1991; Temple et al. 2003). These schemes represent each ornithologist's expert opinion, not a rigorous, quantitative analysis of the actual compositions of the bird communities.

To classify the breeding bird communities of Wisconsin in a more systematic way, Temple and Cary (2007) examined recent (1976–2004) bird count data collected by experienced ornithologists in 18 of Curtis's native plant community types. They analyzed these data using cluster analysis, which compares characteristics of different groups and calculates their distinctiveness. Temple and Cary identified 10 bird assemblages distinct enough to be considered separate bird communities (and named them following Curtis's nomenclature): (1) southern dry, dry-mesic, mesic, and wet-mesic forests; (2) southern wet forest; (3) northern dry-mesic, mesic, and wet-mesic forests; (4) northern dry forest; (5) northern wet forest; (6) boreal forest; (7) dry, dry-mesic, and mesic prairies; (8) oak opening; (9) southern shrub-carr; and (10) emergent aquatic.

How Have Bird Communities Changed?

Our central challenge was to determine if and how these 10 recognizable bird communities changed over time. Temple and Cary (2007) analyzed how the characteristics of the recent (1976–2004) bird communities differed from those in the past (1950–75). To make the past counts comparable to recent counts, they used only bird counts made by highly skilled ornithologists within each of the 10 bird community types during the breeding season (May 15–August 1). They imposed no restrictions on the time each observer spent counting birds at a location (which varied from minutes to hours) or the way birds were counted (e.g., from fixed points or along transects). They summed all of the counts to produce a cumulative list of all the species detected in each plant community type and cumulative tallies of all individuals of each species. They considered a community list to be adequate to compare among periods if it included results from at least 10 counts. Each of these lists represents results from at least six hours of observing birds in a native plant community. Over the 55 years represented by these samples (1950–2004), 205 of the state's 226 breeding bird species were detected among the 10 communities (Temple and Cary 2007).

Species richness within most communities tended to increase slightly over the past 55 years (Temple and Cary 2007). Some new species were added to communities via range and habitat expansions. These species include the Carolina wren, tufted titmouse, and house finch. Other species were reintroduced, including wild turkey and trumpeter swan. Still others have recovered from formerly low abundance including the double-crested cormorant, sandhill crane, and Cooper's hawk. While rare species essentially disappeared from several communities, there were no statewide species extinctions over the past 50 years. The prairie bird community suffered the greatest decline in richness (a 17% loss of species). The oak opening community experienced the greatest gain (a 13% increase in species).

Why Have Bird Communities Changed?

The composition of a bird community shifts because of changes in the presence and abundance of constituent species. Most naturalists and

Table 22.1 Contrasting scenarios of population and habitat trends in three bird species, showing how these species are responding differently to shifts in habitat availability

	Scenario 1 (e.g., red-tailed hawk)	Scenario 2 (e.g., sandhill crane)	Scenario 3 (e.g., bobolink)
Breeding Bird Survey population trend (1966–2004)	2.4% per year increase	8.3% per year increase	1.9% per year decline
Primary habitat	Combination of woods and grasslands	Wetlands	Grasslands
Habitat availability	Increase—expanding into more developed landscapes, especially urban and suburban areas	Slight decrease	Steady and progressive decrease
Within-habitat population trend (1950–75 vs. 1976–2004)	Unchanged	Sharp increase (still recovering)	Steady decline

Note: See the text for an explanation of the scenarios.

conservationists in Wisconsin are well aware of the recent changes in certain bird species. Red-headed woodpeckers, western meadowlarks, and grasshopper sparrows, for example, have declined steeply in Wisconsin (chapter 21). In contrast, Canada geese, sandhill cranes, and house finches have all increased. Since 1966 when the North American Breeding Bird Survey established a standard methodology to track bird populations, 25% of the species monitored in Wisconsin declined in abundance, 35% increased, and the remaining 40% were relatively stable (Sauer et al. 2004).

Changes in Wisconsin's bird communities reflect complex changes in the relative and absolute abundances of species within and among communities. Temple and Cary (2007) distinguish three scenarios that could account for a statewide changes in the abundance of a species (table 22.1). (1) There has been either an expansion or reduction in the total area of the habitat that supports the given species, but within suitable habitat, the species remains as abundant as in the past. (2) The habitat that supports a species has not changed in area, but within that habitat, the species has become either more or less abundant. (3) Both the availability of suitable habitat and local abundance within the habitat have changed. Scenario 1 does not produce a change in bird community composition. Scenarios 2 and 3, in contrast, result in internal changes in community composition.

The red-tailed hawk reflects scenario 1 as it increased in abundance regionally by expanding into heavily developed landscapes while maintaining its relative abundance within its natural habitat (Stout and Temple 2004; table 22.1). Changes associated with scenario 2 can be related to environmental changes within habitat, rather than quantitative changes in availability of habitat. Habitat fragmentation, for example, has reduced the average patch size for many habitats, influencing bird communities in predictable ways (Ambuel and Temple 1983). Species showing regional declines are often affected by habitat fragmentation, especially many forest-dwelling, long-distance migrants. In contrast, northern harrier, bald eagle, osprey, Cooper's hawk, and other raptors have recovered much of their former abundance within their respective habitats since DDT has been banned. Changes in food availability within a habitat can also influence relative abundance. Turkey vultures, for example, may have increased across Wisconsin and within bird communities because white-tailed deer carcasses have become more abundant as their populations expanded.

In scenario 3, changes in abundance result from both habitat loss and reductions in quality of remaining habitat. Such a pattern appears to reflect what is happening with many grassland bird populations. Their regional declines are associated with losses of grassland habitat, but many of these birds have also experienced reductions in relative abundance within remaining patches of suitable prairie habitat (chapter 21). Regional changes in some migratory species have been paralleled by changes in relative abundance within their communities. Such patterns are evident in declines in loggerhead shrikes, purple martins, and dickcissels and increases in brown-headed cowbirds. These changes do not appear to be closely associated with changes in the availability or quality of breeding habitat in Wisconsin, instead they may reflect changes in availability of wintering habitat or other events during the nonbreeding season (Brittingham and Temple 1982; Basili and Temple 1995; Temple 1995).

Conclusions and Predictions

Several broad patterns will likely continue to affect bird communities (Temple and Cary 2007). Here, we summarize some of those changes. Over the past 55 years, shifts in overall species richness have been small compared with the shifts in relative abundances of species within communities. This trend seems likely to persist. We predict with moderate confidence that relatively few new native species will be added to Wisconsin's breeding bird communities in the next few decades, and few seem likely to succumb to local or regional extinctions. For example, the mid-20th century wave of northward range expansions into Wisconsin of birds with southern affinities (e.g., Carolina wren, tufted titmouse, and red-bellied woodpecker) appears to have run its course, even as the climate continues to become warmer. Most of the likely colonists may have already arrived. Since the 1970s, mandated recovery programs for threatened species are slowing the frequent global and local extinctions that characterized the early 20th century. Nonetheless, we are confident that complex shifts in patterns of relative abundance within communities will continue, as species populations experience changes in their dynamics, driven largely but not entirely by human-caused changes in the environment.

Those seeking to track changes in the composition of bird communities over time should ideally repeat their surveys at similar dates and the exact sites where previous surveys were conducted. Replicating survey work exactly, however, requires that we know the locations and methods of prior surveys, something that Temple and Cary (2007) found challenging to uncover in many historical records. Even so, the habitats may not persist at some sites or may change at others. Although this ideal approach is rarely feasible for most bird communities in Wisconsin, it is possible in a few cases. Ambuel and Temple (1982) documented 25 years of change in the bird communities of southern Wisconsin forests previously surveyed by Bond (1957), and a recensus of sites is now under way. Weise and others (2004) similarly resurveyed birds on a state natural area they had censused 30 years previously. Such ideal resurveys occur most commonly when sites are part of systematic monitoring programs like the ones that exist for many of the state's protected natural areas. Regular monitoring programs are also becoming an important part of evaluating management impacts on public lands like the Chequamegon-Nicolet National Forest (e.g., Howe et al. 1994). It should be possible to extend such systematic monitoring to encompass all regions and habitats of the state, especially if we enlist the state's many highly skilled amateur ornithologists. These efforts could eventually yield insights comparable to those based on resurveys of John Curtis's vegetation plots (see chapters 6 and 7).

Bird communities will certainly continue to change. Given the strong and increasing public interest in birds, ornithologists should be in a good position to continue detecting and interpreting those changes. Addressing their causes will be harder.

References

Ambuel, B., and S. Temple. 1982. Songbird populations in southern Wisconsin: 1954 and 1979. Journal of Field Ornithology 53:149–158.

———. 1983. Area-dependant changes in the bird communities and vegetation of southern Wisconsin forests. Ecology 65:1057–1068.

Basili, G., and S. Temple. 1995. A perilous migration. Natural History 104:40–48.

Bond, R. 1957. Ecological distribution of breeding birds in upland forests of southern Wisconsin. Ecological Monographs 27:325–349.

Brittingham, M., and S. Temple. 1983. Have cowbirds caused forest songbirds to decline? Bioscience 33:31–35.

Curtis, J. 1959. The Vegetation of Wisconsin. Madison: University of Wisconsin Press.

Howe, R. W., A. T. Wolf, and T. Rinaldi. 1994. Monitoring birds in a regional landscape: Lessons from the Nicolet National Forest Bird Survey. Pp. 83–92 in C. J. Ralph, J. Sauer, and S. Droege, eds. Monitoring Bird Populations by Point Counts. Generak Technical Report PSW-GTR-149. Albany, CA: Pacific Southwest Research Station, Forest Service, U.S. Department of Agriculture.

Sauer, J. R., J. E. Hines, and J. Fallon. 2004. The North American Breeding Bird Survey, Results and Analysis 1966–2003. Version 2004.1. Laurel, MD: U.S. Geological Survey Patuxent Wildlife Research Center.

Stout, W., and S. Temple. 2007. Growth, range expansion and density dependence of an urban red-tailed hawk population. Journal of Wildlife Management (in press).

Temple, S. 1995. When and where are shrike populations limited? Proceedings of the Western Foundation for Vertebrate Zoology 6:5–11.

Temple, S., and J. Cary. 2007. Wisconsin's bird communities: Their composition and dynamics. Passenger Pigeon 69:133–158.

Temple, S., J. Cary, and R. Rolley. 2003. Wisconsin Birds: A Seasonal and Geographical Guide. 2nd ed. Madison: University of Wisconsin Press.

Weise, C., G. Meyer, and H. O'Brian. 2004. A long-term survey of breeding birds of the Cedarburg Bog and Cedarburg Beech Woods State natural Areas. Passenger Pigeon 66:101–112.

Zimmerman, J. 1991. The landscape of birds. Pp. 53–69 in S. D. Robbins, ed. Wisconsin birdlife: Population and distribution, past and present. Madison: University of Wisconsin Press.

23 Changes in the Butterfly and Moth Fauna

Les Ferge

"Why are there so few butterflies this year?" This question weighed on the minds of many naturalists during the summer of 2004 when numbers of most butterfly species appeared alarmingly lower than usual. It was even worse than a similar decline seen in 2002, since more species seemed affected. Is it habitat loss? Pesticide impacts? Adverse weather conditions? Will butterfly populations recover as they have from past declines, or are we seeing a major shift in our natural heritage? As with most invertebrates, we lack the data necessary to even begin addressing these questions.

Butterflies (including skippers), moths, and other insects make up the majority of all animal species. According to the University of Wisconsin–Green Bay's Cofrin Center for Biodiversity, there are four times as many species of butterflies and moths in the United States and Canada as there are fish, amphibians, reptiles, birds, and mammals combined. While we have a fairly complete list of all 693 native vertebrate animal species in Wisconsin, we have nothing close to a complete inventory of insects for the state. There are certainly thousands of Lepidoptera native to Wisconsin. However, butterflies, moths, and other invertebrates receive little attention from taxonomists and conservation professionals. Invertebrates make up less than 30% of the state-listed endangered and threatened animals. This low percentage does not reflect the conservation security of invertebrates so much as our state of ignorance. The actual fraction of biologically threatened animals that are invertebrates is probably much higher.

Given these gaps in our knowledge, any analysis of changes in Wisconsin's Lepidoptera fauna will be incomplete. This chapter explores what is known and what is likely happening to Wisconsin's moths and butterflies. Many species of Lepidoptera can serve as extraordinarily sensitive indicators of environmental change, given the dependence of many species on a single host plant and habitat type. Many of these plants and habitats are threatened, reduced to small isolated populations and remnants. While the vast majority of Lepidoptera species now present were probably here a century or more ago, we must rely on educated guesswork to reconstruct their historic distributions. Without complete baseline and contemporary data, we do not know for sure what species may have disappeared from the state over the past 150 years. Invasive, nonnative plants now occupy large areas of native habitat and threaten areas rich in butterflies and moths. Outbreaks of, and our efforts to suppress, pest insects, both native and introduced, could affect many native species. Extreme weather conditions also take their toll. Excessive rainfall promotes the spread of fungal, bacterial, and viral diseases, while drought can reduce larval host plants or the density of nectar flowers. Large-scale climatic changes associated with global warming could have both positive and negative effects on native Lepidoptera populations.

Limited Baseline Historic Data Restricts Our Ability to Document Change

Lepidoptera have highly specialized ecological requirements. Most species clearly prefer a specific habitat type. Some depend on a single species host plant during their larval stages. Yet we still don't sufficiently know the life cycle and associated habitat and resource requirements for most species. Some published host plant data for moths are suspect because they are based on plants offered to larvae in laboratory experiments. Feeding choices in the laboratory do not always reflect preferences in the field, and laboratory experiments cannot always capture true field preferences of adult moths for egg-laying sites. Natural host plant data for most Lepidoptera remain incomplete. Even when we have such data, they often only apply in a portion of a species' geographic range.

Most of Wisconsin's moth and butterfly species breed once per year. Adults of many species are highly seasonal and are only present 2–3 weeks of the year. While the occurrence of individual butterfly species is fairly well known, the status, distribution, and habitat affinities of many moth species is poorly documented. Many species appear rare, but they may not be. Rarity is often an artifact reflecting insufficient searching, lack of knowledge of habitat, seasonal occurrence, or a species that is missed using customary collecting methods. Many seemingly rare species may turn out to be common or even abundant if sampling used different methods, happened more frequently, or occurred at a different time of year. Other rare species may be transients from other regions, far from their normal habitat. Reliably tracking changes in abundance in creatures that are so seasonally limited and strongly affected by daily weather conditions is difficult.

Identifying long-term changes in Wisconsin moth and butterfly populations is also hampered because we have so little historic data. Museum collections, the most reliable and useful source of information, contain few Wisconsin specimens collected before 1945. Label data accompanying these older specimens are often vague or incomplete, giving little or no information regarding the specific locality, habitat, or abundance. The late 1960s marked the beginning of a growth in avocational Lepidoptera collecting throughout the state, resulting in the accumulation of a large amount of reliable data useful as a baseline.

Historic data on the moths (which make up about 93% of Lepidoptera) are particularly scant. Activities of the pioneering collectors were usually limited to a few accessible or convenient localities and focused on the most conspicuous, easily identified moths. Only in recent years has our knowledge of Wisconsin moths approached that of the butterflies. Much of this occurred over the last few decades when about a half-dozen dedicated amateur moth collectors documented a large number of moths not previously known in Wisconsin. These discoveries reflect collectors systematically investigating specialized habitats along with technological advances in batteries and electronics used to operate portable, moth-attracting ultraviolet light rigs. Published information specifically covering significant portions of Wisconsin's Lepidoptera appeared relatively recently (Ebner 1970; Ferge and Balogh 2000; Ferge 2002). Despite this progress, the most challenging work remains—namely, inventorying the poorly known, difficult to study, small-bodied species making up the microlepidoptera.

Factors Affecting Lepidoptera Populations

Habitat loss has been, and continues to be, the most obvious and significant threat to many species of Lepidoptera. Many species are inherently uncommon, due to their host plant specificity. Large areas of native habitat are necessary to support populations of uncommon plants large enough to support these less common Lepidoptera and other insects associated with them. Bogs, sedge meadows, prairies, savanna, and barrens have distinct lepidopteran faunas. Prairie-, savanna-, and barrens-associated Lepidoptera are particularly at risk due to the small, fragmented, and isolated nature of their habitats. Other detrimental factors are also at work, particularly invasive alien plant species and the loss of host plant diversity from overabundant white-tailed deer.

The proliferation of invasive, nonnative plant species in native plant communities reduces the diversity of native Lepidoptera. Sedge meadows, for example, once supported a distinctive butterfly fauna, including the mulberry wing, broad-winged, dion, black dash and two-spotted skippers, Acadian hairstreak, Baltimore, and eyed brown. Extensive tracts of sedge meadow are now covered by reed canary grass and purple loosestrife. These aggressive invaders outcompete and displace the native host plants these butterflies depend on. As a consequence, these once widespread butterflies are becoming restricted to the remaining uninvaded sedge meadows.

Aside from displacing their host plants, invasive plants can affect moths and butterflies in other ways. Garlic mustard presents a double threat to the mustard white and West Virginia white butterflies, which historically relied on toothwort, rock cress, and watercress as host plants in rich deciduous forests. Garlic mustard outcompetes the native host plants for these species and then attracts both butterfly species to lay eggs on it instead. Although the eggs hatch and the larvae begin feeding, they abruptly cease feeding and ultimately die of starvation (Bowden 1971). The West Virginia white is particularly affected by increasing garlic mustard because adults preferentially lay eggs on this plant (Bowden 1971). These plants create a population sink for both species, since larvae from eggs laid on garlic mustard fail to complete their development. Where these plant species have proliferated, both butterfly species have been locally extirpated (Chew 1995). There may be some hope in that some mustard white populations appear to be slowly adapting to garlic mustard in Massachusetts (Courant et al. 1994).

The introduction of certain invasive plants has not been entirely detrimental to moths and butterflies. Some species, such as orange and yellow hawkweed, provide nectar sources frequently used by a variety of butterflies. Such weedy plants sometimes provide their only reliable nectar source. Another invasive, bouncing bet, is a highly attractive nectar source for sphingid moths. The wild indigo duskywing has been reported to switch larval host plants from wild indigo to the invasive crown vetch (Opler and Malikul 1992). Although this species was previously constrained by having few host plants in Wisconsin, it is increasingly observed in association with crown vetch.

Increases in Wisconsin's white-tailed deer population have been linked to dramatic losses of plant diversity (chapter 6). Two parks that banned deer hunting lost more than half their plant species (Rooney and Waller 2003; Rooney et al. 2004). We do not yet have evidence that links such plant declines to declines in lepidopteran populations. This may reflect the lack of historic data on Lepidoptera presence and abundance and incomplete knowledge of host plants rather than a true lack of effect. Losses of this magnitude are likely affecting many Lepidoptera given their diverse array of host plants and nectar sources.

The spread of the gypsy moth and other invasive insects into Wisconsin affects several native species. Although these invaders may compete for larval food resources, they pose a greater threat by provoking the widespread use of Bt (*Bacillus thuringiensis*) insecticide. Although touted as an environmentally safe product, these bacteria can infect and kill most lepidopteran species. Treatments of Bt are applied in the spring, when a large fraction of Lepidoptera species are in their larval stage and thus susceptible. Applications of Bt are associated with high larval mortality in many Lepidoptera species (Miller 1990, 1992; Wagner et al. 1996; Peacock at al. 1998; Severns 2002). Reductions and local extinctions of adult butterfly populations were observed in one Bt-treated park, for example (Severns 2002).

Introduced parasites and predators pose yet another threat to native Lepidoptera. A tachinid fly species, the so-called friendly fly, is particularly successful in controlling forest tent caterpillar outbreaks in Wisconsin. It was introduced from Europe in an effort to control the gypsy moth but is known to attack a wide variety of other Lepidoptera. For example, it is associated with declines in giant silkworm moths in the Northeast (Berenbaum 2004). The German yellowjacket, a voracious predator of caterpillars, invaded Wisconsin in the 1970s. Likewise, the multicolored Asian lady beetle, which was introduced to control aphids, appears to consume any slow-moving soft-bodied insect, including lepidopteran caterpillars (Berenbaum 2004).

Some native species also influence the abundance of Lepidoptera. The widespread and severe outbreak of the native forest tent caterpillar that occurred in northern Wisconsin in 2001 may have depressed numbers of Lepidoptera in subsequent years. The forest tent caterpillar is a native insect characterized by cyclical outbreaks, eventually brought under control by natural enemies such as parasites, predators, and viral, fungal, protozoan, or bacterial diseases. Forest tent caterpillars have many natural insect enemies, including 14 species of Hymenoptera egg parasites, 52 Diptera and 61 Hymenoptera species parasitic on larval and pupal stages, and 18 Hemiptera, 9 Coleoptera, and 1 Dermaptera that prey on various life stages (Witter and Kuhlman 1972). It is likely that some generalized diseases, predators, and parasitoids persist at higher than normal levels after forest tent caterpillar outbreaks, posing a risk to other species of caterpillar.

Effects of Weather and Climate Change

Extreme weather conditions can also have significant effects on insect populations. Both excessive rainfall and high humidity facilitate the spread of fungal, bacterial, and viral diseases of insects. Conversely, extreme drought can reduce the availability of larval host plants and adult nectar flowers, possibly extirpating local populations. Karner blue butterflies and other savanna Lepidoptera are vulnerable to drought, particularly where large numbers of trees are removed in the course of restoration. In drought years, lupine host plants wither and senesce early where they receive full sun before the second Karner blue brood larvae has time to mature. Lupine plants along the edges of openings shaded by trees part of the day remain in better condition. Wetland Lepidoptera are also impacted by drought. The demise of the swamp metalmark in several southeastern Wisconsin localities is likely a consequence of its habitat becoming excessively dry during the drought of 1977. Searches for the butterfly in 1980 at known sites were unsuccessful, and swamp thistle, its host plant, was far less abundant.

Early peaks in temperature can also wreak havoc with insect populations by causing them to emerge prematurely. This would not be a problem if mild conditions persisted, but once insect dormancy is broken and development resumes, they lose the ability to tolerate freezing. The unusually mild February and March of 2001 and 2002 probably broke dormancy in many lepidopteran species that subsequently fared poorly during the freezes of April and May. These observations indicate that a warming climate may spell trouble for some of Wisconsin's moth and butterflies but could favor other species. For example, there have been significant influxes or migrations of nonresident migratory lepidopteran species into Wisconsin in association with unusually early and warm seasons. Among the butterflies, the monarch and 14 other species have been recorded periodically in Wisconsin. A number of moth species in eastern

North America migrate northward every season, some with such regularity they are often considered resident (Ferguson et al. 1991). Many of the migrants recorded in Wisconsin originate from breeding ranges in the southern states, while others are from the west. A few, including the monarch butterfly, are of tropical or subtropical origin. Some species have been able to locate suitable larval host plants and establish temporary breeding populations but are unable to survive Wisconsin winters. Unlike the monarch, however, these other species are not known to undergo late-season reverse migrations out of Wisconsin leaving their fate uncertain. Many likely die here, as species seen just days before the first freeze would not have enough time to escape southward.

Large influxes of migratory and stray butterfly species were observed in Wisconsin each season from 1998 through 2001, including unprecedented numbers during the 2001 season. This remarkable phenomenon was also documented during 1977 and 1987, but four such years in a row is unprecedented. Weather conditions were similar in all of these years: a mild winter followed by an early, mild spring and average yearly temperatures near or exceeding record highs. Thus, some butterflies' ability to disperse may allow them to respond opportunistically to climate change.

The most notable visitor was the cloudless sulfur, a striking, large, yellow subtropical butterfly considered to be a rare late-season stray in Wisconsin before 1987. In late June of that year, numerous individuals were seen flying northward near the Mississippi River in Grant and Crawford counties. This was regarded as an once-in-a-lifetime experience by many lepidopterists. However, similar flights occurred again in 1991 and 1999. Even more amazing was the discovery that a population had successfully bred here on partridge pea in 1999.

In addition to the periodically migrating species, 21 butterfly species recorded from Wisconsin are regarded as accidental strays, meaning there have been less than four historic records. Strong winds and storm fronts carry many of these species out of their normal breeding range. If the climate continues to warm, a number of these species may be able to expand their range northward and appear in Wisconsin on a more regular basis.

Changes in Wisconsin's Lepidoptera Fauna

Several species of European Lepidoptera have been introduced into North America and have become established in Wisconsin. The earliest known arrival was the cabbage butterfly. This species was introduced into Quebec, Canada, about 1860 and spread quickly through eastern North America (Scudder 1887). It was first reported from Wisconsin in

1879 (Hoy 1883). It would take about 80 years for the next exotic butterfly species to arrive in Wisconsin. The European skipper moved into Wisconsin from both the north and south around Lake Michigan. This species was discovered near Milwaukee in 1960 and in Vilas County in 1981 and had spread statewide by the late 1980s. Its biology greatly favored its spread. It feeds on grasses and eggs overwinter on grass leaf sheaths and seed heads of timothy. First found in North America in Ontario in 1910, its eggs arrived in imported timothy seed and possibly hay (Layberry et al. 1998).

The rate of new introductions has risen sharply in last few years, and the speed at which some have spread across the state is remarkable. The large yellow underwing feeds on grasses and a wide variety of weedy and cultivated herbaceous plants (Passoa and Hollingsworth 1996). First recorded in North America in Nova Scotia in 1979 (Neil 1981), it appeared in Wisconsin in Appleton and Ashland in 1995. It quickly spread across the state, reaching Grant County by 1998. The double-lobed was found in two northeastern Wisconsin sites in 1999 and the rest of the state by 2002. The small-clouded brindle was found in Oneida and Shawano counties in 2004, and it, too, may be found statewide in a few years. Both the double-lobed and the small-clouded brindle are riparian moths, feeding on common reed grass, reed canary grass, and manna grass. They were both first detected in northeastern North America in 1991 (Mikkola and Lafontaine 1994). The toadflax brocade, first recorded in Door County in 2002, was intentionally introduced into Canada in 1965 and elsewhere in the United States in 1968 as a biological control agent of yellow toadflax, an invasive plant found in several western states.

Although historic data are often meager, significant changes in range have been documented for a few native butterflies. The causes are not known and are the subject of much speculation. Consider the case of the greenish blue butterfly, a northern species widespread in Canada. Museum collections contain a surprising number of older Wisconsin specimens. Most were collected from Door to Sawyer counties and northward from 1921 to about 1940, with large numbers found in some localities. Since then, its range has contracted to Forest and Bayfield counties where it is quite local and found in very small numbers. Its larval host plant is reported to be species of clover. A warming climate may be a contributing to this range contraction, but the extensive, post-logging reforestation may also have diminished the open habitats this species requires. Selective browsing by deer may have eliminated an unknown preferred host plant. On the other hand, the range of the common ringlet has expanded considerably eastward and southward in Wisconsin during the last 30 years. Historically reported only in Burnett and Douglas counties in the 1960s, it reached Oconto County by 1990, Marathon County in 2004, and LaCrosse County in 2007. The common ringlet is a butterfly of open habitats, most often found in somewhat damp areas along roads and highways where the various grasses making up its larval host plants abound. Open roadside corridors likely facilitated the movement of the common ringlet through densely forested areas otherwise unsuitable as habitat.

What does the future hold for Wisconsin's moths and butterflies? Will they recover from the 2004 decline? Continued losses of native habitat will continue to affect our Lepidoptera, particularly in heavily populated southern and eastern Wisconsin. Except for scattered fragments of native habitat, this developed and agricultural landscape already largely lacks suitable habitat for anything other than generalized, "weedy," or pest species of Lepidoptera. It is ironic that forested areas of central and northern Wisconsin, once regarded as ecologically devastated by logging, now support the most diverse Lepidoptera fauna in the state. These areas offer the best opportunity to maintain Lepidoptera diversity into the future. Even in the northern forests, Lepidoptera face challenges from large deer populations, invasive plants, introduced predators and parasites, and extreme weather flucuations. Because even the most common species of Lepidoptera are sensitive to these threats, the northern fauna is not immune to dramatic change.

Given the lack of any comprehensive statewide survey, gaps in our knowledge about species-specific host plant requirements, the absence of basic research into the importance of natural enemies in driving population dynamics, and the lack of conservation strategies for most of our native moths and butterflies, we cannot say what the future holds. We would first need to understand the present and the forces that brought us here. With butterflies, moths, and other understudied groups (including all invertebrates), the gaps in our basic knowledge are too great to make anything beyond broad, general predictions. We should therefore strive to increase our stock of observations and analyze data from more species before generalizing from the changes we see so far.

References

Berenbaum, M. R. 2004. Friendly fire. Wings 27(1):8–12.

Bowden, S. R. 1971. American white butterflies (Pieridae) and English food-plants. J. Lepid. Soc. 25:6–12.

Chew, F. S. 1995. From weeds to crops: Changing habitats of Pierid butterflies (Lepidoptera: Pieridae). J. Lepid. Soc. 49:285–303.

Courant, A. V., A. E. Holbrook, E. D. Van Der Reijden, and F. S. Chew. 1994. Native Pierine butterfly adapting to naturalized crucifer? J. Lepid. Soc. 48:168–170.

Ebner, J. A. 1970. Butterflies of Wisconsin. Milwaukee Public Museum, Popular Science Handbook No. 12, Milwaukee.

Ferge, L. A. 2002. Checklist of Wisconsin butterflies. Wisconsin Entomological Society, Miscellaneous Publication No. 2, Madison.

Ferge, L. A., and G. J. Balogh. 2000. Checklist of Wisconsin moths (superfamilies Drepanoidea, Geometroidea, Mimallonoidea, Bombycoidea, Sphingoidea and Noctuoidea). Milwaukee Public Museum, Contributions in Biology and Geology No. 93, Milwaukee.

Ferguson, D. C., D. J. Hilburn, and B. Wright. 1991. The Lepidoptera of Bermuda: Their foodplants, biogeography and means of dispersal. Memoirs of the Entomological Society of Canada, Monograph No. 158, Ottawa.

Hoy, P. R. 1883. A catalog of Wisconsin lepidoptera. Pp. 406–421 in vol. 1 of Geology of Wisconsin—Survey of 1873–1879. Madison: Commissioners of Public Printing.

Layberry, R. A., P. W. Hall, and J. D. Lafontaine. 1998. The butterflies of Canada. Toronto: University of Toronto Press.

Mikkola, K., and J. D. Lafontaine. 1994. Recent introductions of riparian Noctuid moths from the palaearctic region to North America, with the first report of *Apamea unanimis* (Hübner) (Noctuidae: Amphipyrinae) J. Lepid. Soc. 48:121–127.

Miller, J. C. 1990. Field assessment of the effects of a microbial pest control agent on non-target Lepidoptera. Am. Entomol. 36:135–139.

———. 1992. Effects of a microbial insecticide, *Bacillus thuringiensis kurstaki,* on non-target Lepidoptera in a spruce budworm-infested forest. J. Res. Lepid. 29:267–276.

Neil, K. 1981. The occurrence of *Noctua pronuba* (L.) (Noctuidae) in Nova Scotia: A new North American record. J. Lepid. Soc. 35:248.

Opler, P. A., and V. Malikul. 1992. A field guide to eastern butterflies. Boston: Houghton Mifflin.

Passoa, S., and C. S. Hollingsworth. 1996. Distribution, identification and rate of spread of *Noctua pronuba* (Lepidoptera: Noctuidae) in the northeastern United States. Ent. News 107:151–160.

Peacock, J. W., D. F. Schweitzer, J. L. Carter, and N. R. Dubois. 1998. Laboratory assessment of the effects of *Bacillus thuringiensis* on native Lepidoptera. Environ. Entomol. 27:450–457.

Rooney, T. P., and D. M. Waller. 2003. Direct and indirect effects of deer in forest ecosystems. For. Ecol. Manage. 181:165–76.

Rooney, T. P., S. M. Wiegmann, D. A. Rogers, and D. M. Waller. 2004. Biotic impoverishment and homogenization in unfragmented forest understory communities. Conserv. Biol. 18:787–798.

Scudder, S. H. 1887. The introduction and spread of *Pieris rapae* in North America, 1860–1885. Mem. Boston Soc. Nat. Hist. 4:53–69.

Severns, P. 2002. Evidence for the negative effects of BT (*Bacillus thuringiensis* var. *kurstaki*) on a non-target butterfly community in western Oregon, USA J. Lepid. Soc. 56:166–170.

Wagner, D. L, J. W. Peacock, J. L. Carter, and S. E. Talley. 1996. Field assessment of *Bacillus thuringiensis* on non-target Lepidoptera. Environ. Entomol. 24:1444–1454.

Witter, J. A., and H. M. Kuhlman. 1972. A review of the parasites and predators of tent caterpillars (*Malacosoma* spp.) in North America. Minnesota Agricultural Experiment Station, Technical Bulletin 289, St. Paul, MN.

Part Five: Nature Meets Us

The Social and Political Context

Wisconsin's ecosystems are undergoing profound changes, many of which result from human activities. Relationships between social and ecological systems, though, are not simple. As ecosystems change, the people living in those ecosystems innovate to respond to those changes. Cultural changes and adaptations drive further changes in ecosystems. These complex interactions between ecological and social systems represent a form of cultural coevolution. An essential feature of this coevolution, however, is that most species and ecosystems lack the ability to adapt quickly to rapid cultural change. The lesson here is that we should be careful to limit and adapt our culture to restrict its impacts on the biotic systems that surround and sustain us.

In the next chapter, former U.S. Forest Service chief and Wisconsin native Mike Dombeck examines biocultural landscapes through the dual lenses of biology and policy. He observes that great advances in conservation were always preceded by changes in public attitudes. Today, few believe that we have a moral duty to squander our natural resources, yet the opposite was true 150 years ago when clearing the forests for timber and agriculture was deemed a moral imperative. The great conservation movement of the early 20th century shifted the dominant paradigm, making it possible to set aside public lands, protect threatened birds and mammals, and assign the Civilian Conservation

Corps the job of restoring habitats. Paradigms shifted again during the 1960s and 1970s as we began to protect air and water quality in earnest and extended protection to a wide set of endangered species. Dombeck concludes that future generations will only have the opportunity to experience and enjoy the forests, waters, and wildlife we have today if we collectively embrace the notion that these are communities "to which we belong."

The human population is undergoing a period of unprecedented growth. Every year, 38,000 people are added to Wisconsin's population, and 2.1 million to the population of the United States. Worldwide, we add another 77 million people. These people demand land on which to live and work, plus ample surface and groundwater for drinking, agriculture, and industry. Just 200 years ago, few people lived in modern-day Milwaukee. The rapid growth of our largest city provides a very concrete example of how population growth typically brings declines in habitats and biodiversity. Biologists Larry Leitner, John Idzikowski, and Gary Casper describe what was once there, what persists today, and what may remain in the future in Milwaukee County. Although much has already been lost, biologists also recognize that further losses will continue as the "extinction debt" is paid. When habitats are reduced in size, they inevitably support fewer species. There is often a time lag, however (sometimes decades long), between when habitats shrink and when these local extinctions occur. Targeted conservation and restoration efforts can sometimes offset this extinction debt. We should therefore be alert to these opportunities even in heavily urbanized areas and support the organizations that promote and pursue them.

After reading a chapter about biodiversity loss in Milwaukee, you may be surprised to hear Madison mayor Dave Ciezlewicz's counterintuitive argument that cities are good for the environment. He observes that far more land is being developed in Midwest than would be predicted based on our population growth. This reflects sprawl and our continuing hunger to live on the edge of cities (often in ever larger houses). How we live on the land matters. People living in high-density urban areas typically produce far fewer air pollutants, greenhouse gases, and nonpoint water pollution than suburban and rural residents. Ironically, people who move to rural areas and the suburban fringes professing to love nature create the very sprawl they disdain. Mayor Dave concludes that we should extend Aldo Leopold's land ethic to incorporate a city ethic that embraces livable urban landscapes as an effective way to protect and heal the land.

Why do so many streams lack buffer zones? If researchers know that streams without protective riparian areas support fewer invertebrates and fish, why isn't this knowledge translated into effective action? Scientists deeply knowledgeable about environmental impacts are often befuddled about why their knowledge is not applied in terms of policy. Professor of urban and regional planning and former Department of Natural Resources board chair Steve Born brings the biology in this book down to earth with a chapter focused on how policy decisions are actually made in our state. Policy decisions often have broad impacts, shaping a multitude of individual decisions throughout the state. He displays and explains some of the tools that agencies and politicians use to guide policy, carefully noting the differences between successful and unsuccessful approaches to policy.

24

Public Lands and Waters and Changes in Conservation

Mike Dombeck

Over the past five decades, I have driven from central Wisconsin to the northwestern part of the state hundreds of times. I made the trip first as a small boy when my family relocated from rural Marathon County to Moose Lake in Sawyer County. and later, as a college student, I made the trek from my family's home to University of Wisconsin–Stevens Point. Today, I continue to drive the route from my house on the sloughs of the Wisconsin River near Stevens Point to hunt and fish and visit with old friends and family. My course crosses the Wisconsin River four times and the Flambeau and Chippewa rivers twice. Looking through the eyes of a biologist and a conservationist, now old enough to have an appreciation of history, what I see is not just a landmass—a 56,000 square mile place on a map—but also our heritage and, in certain respects, our future.

Along the route, I drive through second- and third-growth mixed hardwood forests of primarily aspen where the ancient white and red pine forests once stood. I look out upon the Wisconsin River, which has ebbed and flowed with man's every step forward and back—a river that at one time had a dam every seven miles from Plover upriver to Vilas County and was once so polluted with industrial and municipal waste that the fish were totally inedible below Rhinelander. As I travel down a four-lane interstate that, in my youth, was two lanes of blacktop, I see a love of the outdoors in the canoes, mountain bikes, snowmobiles, boats, jet skies, and four-wheelers strapped to cars and trailers. The imprint of man—both the good and the bad—is ubiquitous.

Prior to the advent of European settlement, the slow-moving rivers produced an abundance of wild rice, known to the Ojibwa as manoomin or "delicacy from the Great Spirit." People often burned the oak savannas to promote berries and fresh grass. The rivers and lakes they lived by were clean enough to drink out of. With the advancing populations of European explorers, traders, and new settlers, man's imprint on Wisconsin's landscape quickly changed. The fur trade—the system of commerce that attracted early French explorers and traders like Jean Nicolet to the region—overharvested the beaver. On the heels of the declining fur trade—due both to a lack of beaver pelts and changing fashion styles—the westward expansion of the United States began to move into Wisconsin in earnest as waves of settlers came to mine and farm what would soon become the 30th state admitted into the Union.

During the initial period of European settlement, the immense forests of the Great Lakes region were seen as little more than obstacles. Trees stood in the way of a plow's straight furrows and thus of America's expanding agrarian backbone. Trees slowed down the progress of roads and railroads. Forests contained wild animals that threatened families—they were wild places, out of step with how the young nation viewed itself. Because they were so abundant, wetlands were viewed as wasted space. Later, technology made it possible to drain these lands for crop production. The new settlers set about to tame the untamed.

By the end of the great cutover (chapters 5 and 6) slash gave rise to tremendous forest fires. The great Peshtigo Fire of 1871 burned 1.28 million acres, killing an estimated 1,500 people. While it remains the most disastrous forest fire ever in U.S. history, it was not the only devastating fire to visit Wisconsin. Forest fires became commonplace, and catastrophic blazes scorched the landscape from the 1860s to the 1930s. Whether intentionally or unintentionally set, the fires exposed fragile soils to the eroding effects of rain and snow. The burned off areas were aggressively farmed—often with mixed results due to the lack of nutrients in the soil and the seemingly endless fields of stumps—causing further erosion. Soils were swept into Wisconsin's rivers, lakes, and wetlands.

As Wisconsin's lands were changing by the day, the landscape of public policy as it pertained to trees and water was changing as well, although much more slowly. Beginning in the second half of the 19th century, the attitude toward trees and water—especially those on public lands—began to shift and once again was mirrored in the state's landscape. This new attitude had its roots in the eastern United States with people that recognized the value of forests beyond commerce.

In his writings of 1864, Henry David Thoreau had called for the creation of national forest preserves, "not for idle sport or food, but for inspiration and our own true recreation." That same year, President Abraham Lincoln signed legislation granting that Yosemite Valley and the Mariposa Big Tree Grove to California be held forever "for public use, resort, and recreation." A decade later, Congress established Yellowstone National Park. States began to join the movement, with New York establishing the Adirondack Forest Preserve in 1885 so that the preserve "shall be kept forever as wild forest lands" (Williams et al. 2003, 18–19).

Not surprisingly, this early effort aimed at preserving the nation's forests and waters experienced halts and delays and was surrounded by controversy. The same year that the Adirondack Forest Preserve was created, Congress voted down a half dozen bills to create public forest reserves. When in 1891, legislation was finally passed giving the president authority to create forest reserves by withdrawing forestlands from the public domain, western states balked and tried to abolish the law. These were, after all, radical notions for the period and not in line with the tame and conquer mind-set that until recently been the norm.

In Wisconsin, trepidation over the state's changing landscape and the desire to better manage public lands for the future had its beginnings around the same period as Thoreau's writings. In 1867, the Wisconsin legislature authorized the Forestry Commission to study forest destruction in the state. Twelve years later, 50,000 acres of state park lands had been established in Vilas and Iron counties. The concern was not necessarily for aesthetics and public enjoyment, as Thoreau and other naturalists had called for, but for utilitarian needs. Wisconsin's future, at that time, was economically linked to the forests. While there were other industries in the state—like agriculture—the timber industry dominated the economy.

What at one time had seemed like an inexhaustible and boundless landscape—what one Wisconsin member of Congress had described in 1852 as having enough trees to supply American wants forever—was exhausted—both literally and figuratively. The state's waters were terribly polluted, having served as a receptacle for waste from the milling industry and as a sewage discharge system for cities.

But by the turn of the century, as logging on public lands was reaching its fevered pitch in Wisconsin, the growing conservation ethic became ingrained throughout the United States. In 1891, the ethic helped to spawn congressional passage of the Forest Reserve Act, which authorized the president to set aside forest reserves from the public domain. A few years later, in 1897, the Forest Management Act was approved. The act specified that forest reserves were to "improve and protect the forest, or for the purpose of securing favorable conditions of water flows, and to furnish a continuous supply of timber for the use and necessities of citizens of the United States" (Williams et al. 2003, 20).

Although the Reserve and Management acts establishing the forest reserves were designed to preserve, maintain, and manage the great tracts of forests in the West, they also had a marked effect on public opinion east of the Mississippi River. This resulted in the passage of the Weeks Act of 1911, which gave the federal government the authority to purchase burned-over woodlands and cutover stump lands to conserve and protect the nation's water supply. Unlike the Forest Reserve and Forest Management acts, the Weeks Act was designed to target eastern lands near navigable waters. An amendment to the law, approved in 1924, allowed the government to purchase of lands for timber production. The eventual creation of Wisconsin's Chequamegon and Nicolet National Forests were the direct result of these laws.

The most remarkable change to Wisconsin's public lands after the turn of the century came, not through efforts to preserve, but through the work to restore and heal. In 1933, the Depression-era Civilian Conservation Corps (CCC) was created by the Roosevelt administration to put unemployed young men to work across the United States. The jobs program became a metaphor for the expression "to give is to receive." At its onset, there were 47 CCC camps scattered across Wisconsin. In exchange for $30 per month, young men were employed to fight soil erosion and to restore Wisconsin's public forests. By the end of 1942, the CCC had assigned nearly 165,000 men to 128 camps throughout Wisconsin, planting an estimated 265 million trees in the state to repair watersheds.

The legacy of the CCC can be seen not only in the forests of the Chequamegon and in the preservation of the ancient Driftless Area but in signs marking the location of their camps and in plaques memorializing their work. The labor of the CCC employees and the efforts of the early conservation movement are also reflected in the present-day attitudes of Wisconsinites toward the state's public lands and waters. A recent survey found that a full 89% believe conservation is important to future generations.

Today, there are more acres of forest in Wisconsin than when the first inventory was taken in 1936. The number of acres of forested land in the state has actually increased by 1.2 million acres since 1980, now reaching nearly 50%. There are nine state forests encompassing over a half million acres and 1.5 million acres of national forest land. While many states have experienced a decline in timber harvests—especially in the West—Wisconsin's timber industry has actually seen an increase in harvest levels since 1990.

Since the dawn of the conservation movement in Wisconsin, we see great improvements in the abundance of clean, clear water flowing off our forests. Fish and wildlife now thrive in our rivers, lakes, and forests, contributing to a sporting industry that generates $8 billion a year. Wisconsin ranks second only to Florida in the number of fishing licenses sold each year (though Florida's population is three times greater than Wisconsin's).

Although Wisconsin's landscape and our public lands and waters appear to be doing well, certainly in contrast to the turn of the 20th century, our state is at a crossroads. We see progress in many areas, but challenges to our forests and waters continue to mount because of the ever-growing imprint of mankind. For example, half the wetlands here at statehood are now gone, having been drained for farming and developments (chapter 15). The others continue to face a multitude of threats including urban sprawl. Expanding shoreline recreational development throughout the state directly and indirectly threatens the aquatic health of many of our rivers and lakes (chapters 13 and 16).

In spite of an increase of wooded acres and cleaner water than existed at the turn of the 20th century, many species throughout the state are in decline or threatened with wholesale extinction. There are currently 73 endangered, 65 threatened, and 185 special concern species, including such magnificent forest dwellers as snow trillium, northern gooseberry, ram's-head lady's slipper, and blue ash. The understory plant diversity of our forests is far lower than it should be partly due to over browsing by deer (chapter 6).

Erosion is also a growing problem on our public lands. Increasingly, this reflects impacts from recreational visitors taking enjoyment from the land more than impacts from those harvesting trees from the forests. Off-road vehicles and four-wheel drive trails cause serious damage to our forests—the source of our cleanest water. In addition, their use is rapidly expanding with a 36% increase in all-terrain vehicle registrations in the state from 2000 to 2005. Not only do these vehicles cause irreparable harm to the soil and contribute to erosion, their tires also help spread exotic (nonnative) plant species in our public forests.

Buckthorn, zebra mussels, Eurasian water-milfoil plants, and a host of other alien invaders are quickly spreading throughout our public and private lands and waters. Free of the natural predators that checked their growth in their countries of origin, these species threaten our forests, waters, plants, and animals. With more people moving into the forest and planting exotic landscape plants, the threat will only increase if steps aren't taken to halt their spread.

It's been said that the only constant is change. One hundred years from now, as my descendants drive along the back roads of Wisconsin, the landscape they will see will be far different than what exists today. The question will be whether or not the public forests and waters they look out upon will be healthier than they are today—whether those ecosystems positively or negatively reflect what we do today to preserve and nurture them.

If Wisconsin is to assure that future generations have the opportunity to access natural forests, clean water and an abundant and diverse population of fish and wildlife we must recognize today, as Aldo Leopold did more than 50 years ago, that the our lands and waters are communities, "to which we belong." Like all species, mankind's future is tied to the earth. When we preserve the lands—especially those lands held in the public realm—and the species they support, we preserve opportunities for future generations to not only experience true wild places but to live in a healthy, balanced world. When we heal the land and waters, we heal ourselves.

We can never go back in time. Our descendants will never experience the sights and surroundings that the early explorers witnessed in their journeys through the region. But we can move forward with an understanding of the importance of healthy public forests and waters to not only our heritage but also our collective well-being.

Reference

Williams, J. E., M. P. Dombeck, and C. A. Wood. 2003. From conquest to conservation: Our public lands legacy. Washington, DC: Island Press.

25

Urbanization and Ecological Change in Milwaukee County

Lawrence A. Leitner, John H. Idzikowski, and Gary S. Casper

At 600,000 people, Milwaukee is Wisconsin's largest city. It lies within the state's third smallest, but densest, county along the western shore of Lake Michigan. As urban and suburban areas like this expand, ecological change follows. Most conspicuously, as housing, roads, and other developments spread over the landscape, natural habitats shrink and become more isolated (plate 4). Simple ecological theory predicts that smaller and more isolated habitats will retain fewer species, but how quickly is this "extinction debt" paid? Without adequate records and monitoring, we can neither document the species that have disappeared nor those that remain. However, the baseline that we have for Milwaukee exposes these losses, making the biotic costs of urban development all too clear.

In this chapter, we ask, how has Milwaukee County changed? This area is typical of metropolitan areas elsewhere, where centuries of dense human settlement have eroded natural habitats and the species they supported. We focus on three major groups: vascular plants, birds, and reptiles and amphibians to consider species losses, current species composition, and future trends. These well-studied groups give us a picture of the dramatic ecological changes that have occurred since European settlement and so serve to reflect how metropolitan areas are changing around the world. For more details on how reptile and amphibian populations have changed, see chapter 20.

Early Conditions—Flora and Fauna

Conspicuous differences in climate and vegetation separate northeastern Wisconsin from its southwestern regions. The same Tension Zone (Curtis 1959) bisects Milwaukee County. The original surveyors' records of 1836 (SEWRPC 1997a) reveal that dry-mesic oak forests, oak savannas, and small, localized prairies dominated southwestern Milwaukee County. Mesic forests of beech, sugar maple, and basswood occurred to the northeast and south along the Lake Michigan shore. Lowland hardwood swamps were scattered through the county, with bogs and tamarack swamps dispersed from the northern part of the county all the way downtown. There, the Menomonee River estuary supported a large complex of open wetlands dominated by grasses, sedges, and forbs (figure 25.1) with fen species occurring on seeps on the clay banks bordering Lake Michigan.

Changes in the natural vegetation of Milwaukee County since settlement have been profound (table 25.1). In 1836, upland woods (oaks, sugar maple, beech, basswood, hickories, etc.) covered 84% of the land. By 2000, only 3% of these forests remained (although they remain the most widespread type of natural vegetation). Other vegetation types fared even worse. Settlement obliterated all the oak savannas that once existed as well as over 99% of the prairie. The thousands of acres of conifer (tamarack) swamp noted in 1836 are now represented by a handful of tamaracks in a few degraded swamps. The impressive Menomonee River wetlands have morphed into an "industrial valley." Remaining patches of native vegetation are further degraded by the successive waves of invasive exotic species that sweep the county, outcompeting and displacing native plants. Overall, nearly 94% of native plant habitats have been destroyed.

How Has the Flora Changed?

Excellent botanical records provide a clear picture of the original flora of Milwaukee County. We compiled a list of some 944 vascular plant species by examining plant specimens deposited in the state's herbaria, species lists of local botanists, Wisconsin Department of Natural Resources (WDNR) records, and plant surveys conducted by Southeastern Wisconsin Regional Planning Commission (SEWRPC) botanists. This

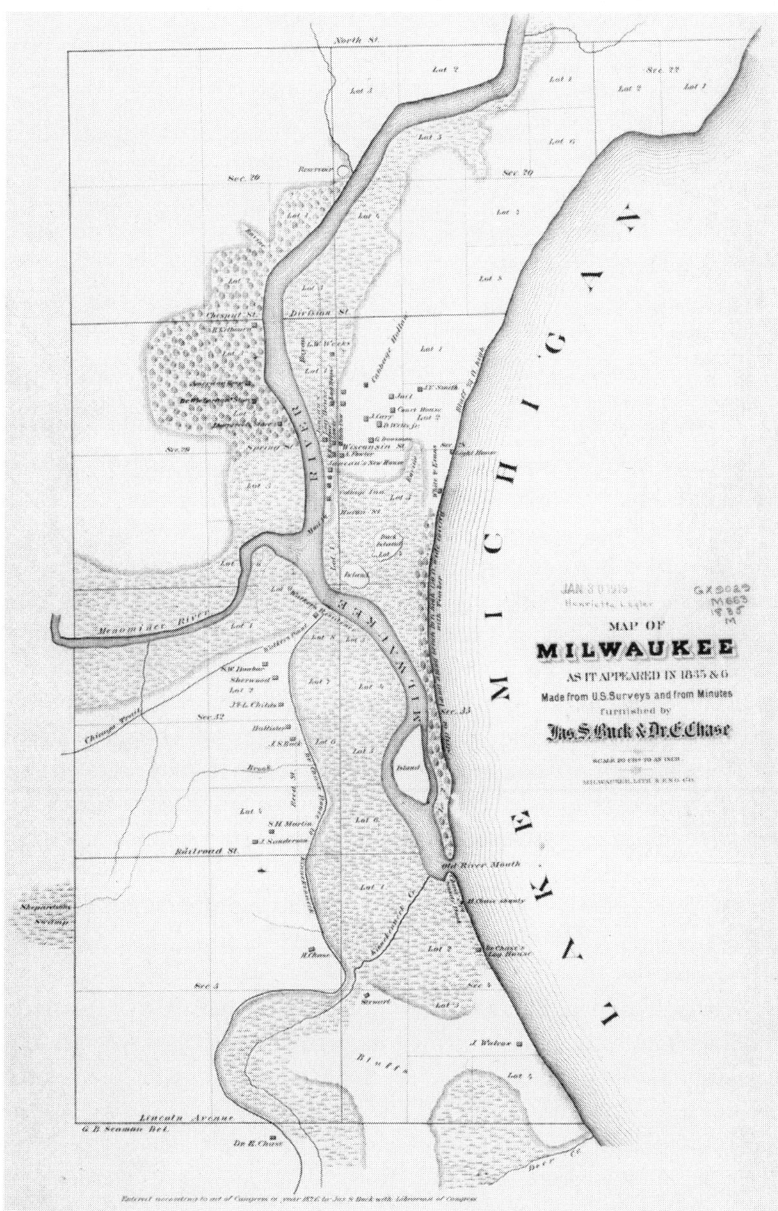

FIGURE 25.1 The Menomonee River estuary. (Reproduced by permission of the Wisconsin Historical Society, image no. WHi-40965.)

Table 25.1 Natural vegetation of Milwaukee County, 1836 and 2000

Vegetation type	Areal extent of vegetation (hectares)		% of county land area		% of county natural vegetation	Net loss	
	1836	2000	1836	2000	2000	Hectares	%
Prairie	572	3	0.9	<0.1	0.1	569	99.6
Oak savanna	2,822	0	4.5	0.0	0.0	2,822	100.0
Upland woods	52,877	1,933	84.4	3.1	50.3	50,944	96.3
Wetlands	6,392	1,904	10.2	3.0	49.6	4,488	70.2
Total	62,664	3,840	100.0	6.1	100.0	58,824	93.9

total reflects its diversity of plant communities and compares favorably with nearby Ozaukee (791), Racine (948), Washington (736), and Waukesha (965) counties.

Surprisingly, it is more difficult to determine just how many plant species remain in Milwaukee County. Nevertheless, we have substantial knowledge of today's flora from many reliable sources, providing an excellent opportunity to catalog just what has been lost and gained. This knowledge reflects what we know about the fate of habitats as well as detailed inventories. We consider a species extirpated if it lacks any reliable reports over the past 25 years. This approach is reasonable, as local botanists continually survey remaining habitats and eagerly share reports of new or unusual species. In particular, SEWRPC (1997a) routinely conducts extensive field surveys to delineate wetlands and environmental corridors. They also began in 1991 to protect natural areas across seven counties via intensive floristic surveys of remaining natural areas and habitats. Together, these efforts give us an accurate picture of the present-day flora.

As noted above, many habitats were obliterated or so extensively modified that little remains of their original flora. In cases where a species historically occupied only a handful of sites, all of which have been destroyed, and when searches of these areas fail to detect the species, we can be confident the species is extirpated. This is particularly true when these are showy species, like the snow trillium, or species restricted to unique habitats. The only remaining stand of tamaracks in the county is so extensively degraded that heath and orchid species that once grew here are gone. One of the state's rarest and most beautiful wildflowers, the ram's-head lady's-slipper orchid, was collected here in 1890. Its herbarium label now reads like a naturalist's fantasy: "Center of tamarack swamp, with [*Cypripedium*] *acaule* [i.e., moccasin flower orchid] . . .

growing in abundance everywhere." No trace remains of this large tamarack swamp located in western Milwaukee County.

These surveys reveal that 598 native vascular plant species still occur in Milwaukee County. This implies that we have lost some 346 species or 37% of the original flora. Species differ, of course, in their vulnerability. Particularly at risk are species at the limits of their range, those restricted to certain habitats, and those sensitive to human-caused disturbance. Certain plant families have experienced particularly acute losses. The entire heath family (with 10 species) is now extirpated from the county. The greatest losses among those families that persist are 46% of the sedges (49 species), 64% of the legumes (16 species), and 84% of the orchids (27 species).

Which species have lost out? Not surprisingly, rare species and those restricted to lost habitats have vanished most often. Of the 29 vascular plant species native to the county listed by the WDNR as endangered or threatened, 72% (21) can no longer be located. These included some of our prettiest and most distinctive species, including kittentails, harbinger-of-spring, ram's-head lady's-slipper, small white lady's-slipper, dwarf lake iris, prairie white-fringed orchid, and snow trillium. Two species restricted to shaded rock outcrops—cliff brake and walking fern—have vanished. Along with the tamarack swamps and bogs went many associated species including winterberry, mountain holly, twinflower, roundleaf sundew, bog buckbean, bluebead-lily, several species of lady's-slipper orchids, goldthread, chokeberry, and pitcher plant. Along with the prairies or savannas went their corresponding species including butterflyweed, Indian-plantain, rough blazing-star, wild quinine, white wild indigo, cream wild indigo, lupine, and Indian paintbrush. Interestingly, several northerly species at the southern limits of their range have also disappeared including mountain maple, rosy twisted stalk, showy orchis, Canada yew, and Canadian white violet. Could this be related to climatic warming?

Thus, the county has seen particular declines in pretty and rare wildflower species of high conservation value (see sidebar on p. 368). As common natives and invasive exotic species have replaced rarer, more habitat-specific species, we see corresponding declines in average conservation (C) values from 5.6 in 1850 to 5.0 in 2003. Correspondingly, the mean C-value of the species lost was a high 6.7 (figure 25.2). Not only are there fewer species today than in 1850, but those that remain are more "weedy" generalists, tolerant of degraded conditions, with less fidelity to remnant natural communities. Of the 62,307 ha (about 240 sq mi) in the county, about 89.6% is classified as residential, commercial,

Measuring Floristic Quality

Lawrence A. Leitner

From a conservation perspective, all species are not equivalent. Some species are common and widespread, requiring no conservation measures. Other species are rare and depend on having specialized habitats and/or disturbance regimes. Botanists rate plants according to their rarity and fidelity to particular habitats by assigning them a "coefficient of conservatism" (or C-value; Swink and Wilhelm 1994; Oldham et al. 1995; Lopez and Fennessey 2002; Bernthal 2003). These species-specific C-values range from 0 (indicating a weedy species that shows no fidelity to any particular plant community) to 10 (a highly specialized species intolerant of anthropogenic disturbance and restricted to a nondegraded natural community). Botanists can then evaluate the overall floristic quality of a site by computing an average C-value for all species at that site. These differences in mean C-values among sites provide a basis for comparing floristic quality. Sites with mean C-values above 4.5 have potential as significant natural areas while those above 3.5 are still considered to be of at least marginal natural area quality (Swink and Wilhelm 1994).

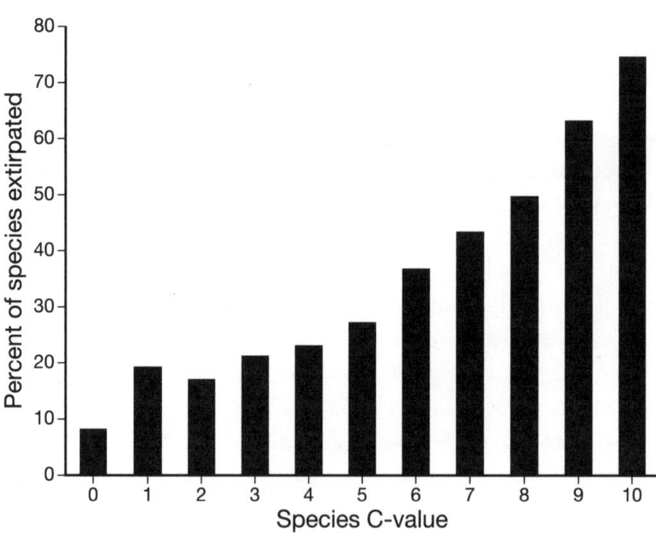

FIGURE 25.2 Percent of plant species lost from Milwaukee County by conservation (C) value.

industrial, or institutional (SEWRPC 1997b). These areas support only native species that are common, widespread, and weedy, with C-values between 0 and 2. On the remaining 10.4% of the land, less than 2% (1,177 ha) has even modest natural area quality (with a mean C-value of 3.5 or greater). Thus, nonnative plants and common native species dominate 98% of Milwaukee County.

How Have Bird Populations Changed since Settlement?

Although inventories for most animal groups are less extensive than those for plants, we can also estimate the original diversity of birds, mammals, and other vertebrates. What is harder to visualize is their staggering numbers. Anecdotal accounts of birds in Milwaukee prior to settlement far exceed what any modern birder would expect. Native Americans knew the confluence of the Milwaukee, Kinnickinnic, and Menomonee rivers for the abundance of wildlife in the marshes and natural embayment that became the Milwaukee Harbor. William Donahoe provided an early account of the marshes surrounding Deer Creek in present-day Bay View, noting the plentiful "ducks, geese, [passenger] pigeons, squirrels, rabbits, mink, muskrats and deer." At least 16 species of waterfowl nested in these marshes and those extending through the Menomonee Valley. Its abundant wild rice attracted thousands of migrating waterfowl every spring and fall. Thousands of ducks including greater scaup and common goldeneye, wintered there. Herring and ring-billed gulls also used these wetlands and the lakeshore. Visitors in coaches and trains in the mid-1800s noted large flocks of "Prairie Hen" (greater prairie-chicken and sharp-tailed grouse).

Because there was no systematic effort to document birds in Milwaukee County in the 19th century, we rely instead on Kumlien and Hollister's *Birds of Wisconsin* (1903), which compiled reports of many collectors and ornithologists. A modern species list appears in Mueller and Idzikowski (2004) based on extensive birding throughout the county over the past 30 years and on records published in Robbins (1991) and the *Passenger Pigeon.*

These records suggest that there were 166 bird species present before European settlement. Most of these species occurred in forests (37%), wetlands (31%), and grassland and prairie/oak savanna (23%). More "northern" species like Canada and black-throated green warblers occupied deep mesic forests, cool lakeside ravines, and the relict bogs and tamarack swamps typical of northern Wisconsin (Idzikowski 1982). The local and scattered distributions of these habitats made these species

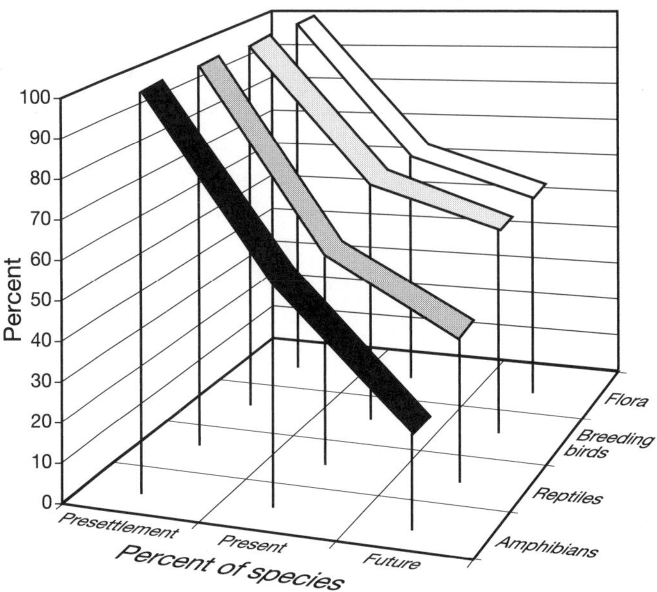

FIGURE 25.3 Relative losses in plant, bird, reptile, and amphibian species since European settlement and expected future extirpations.

sensitive to habitat loss. The Carolina paroquet was probably an occasional wanderer in late summer to southeast Wisconsin, while the passenger pigeon had a major migration corridor along the western shore of Lake Michigan. Both these species were driven extinct by 1918.

Today, only 102 bird species breed in Milwaukee County, representing at least a 39% loss. This is surprisingly close to the magnitude of plant species losses (figure 25.3). As with plants, these birds tend to be more common and less specific to particular habitats. Their numbers have also declined greatly. Many forest and wetland species remain in small numbers within their remnant, fragmented habitats. Other species, including several from savannas and prairies and a few from wetlands (such as red-winged blackbirds), adapted to fallow fields and second-growth forest of varying ages. Remaining forest tracts vary in quality for forest birds. As these habitat patches continue to shrink, migrant birds become increasingly susceptible to nest predation by crows, raccoons, and blue jays as well as brood parasitism by brown-headed cowbirds. Larger cavity-nesting species such as hairy woodpecker can be displaced by starlings.

Birds that are rare in the Midwest are now particularly scarce in Milwaukee County. Only two threatened species still occur in the county—the Henslow's sparrow and the yellow-crowned night heron (both uncommon and local). Milwaukee's few sizable remaining wetlands only support breeding populations of certain species in some years, including yellow-headed blackbirds, yellow-crowned night herons, moorhens, and least bitterns. In the past 30 years, Forster's tern, a Wisconsin endangered species, has attempted to nest in the far southwestern corner of the county but is not yet a regular breeder. Two other listed species, red crossbills and pine siskins, occasionally invade in winter but rarely breed.

In contrast to these declines, other species have reinvaded or are now increasing. The wild turkey, extirpated from the county by the mid-1800s, is again breeding here, spreading in from an introduced flock in the northern Kettle Moraine State Forest. Several southern species such as the Carolina wren and northern mockingbird are also increasing in apparent response to recent mild winters. Mockingbirds are now seen regularly and are likely nesting. Carolina wrens, however, remain at low numbers, and nesting pairs are rare. A one-half mile section of high, eroded bluff overlooking Lake Michigan hosts one of the largest colonies of bank swallows in southeastern Wisconsin. This spot also provides one of the few nesting spots suitable for belted kingfishers.

We also observe recent increases in several adaptable cosmopolitan and nuisance birds. Since the 1970s, urban (giant) Canada geese have proliferated in Milwaukee County to over 5,000 birds. The lakeshore and Menomonee River embayment still host thousands of nonbreeding, subadult gulls that use the breakwater and beaches. A summer population of 10,000 birds is typical, and, during migration, we see over 50,000 gulls. The Milwaukee Harbor remains a wintering haven for greater scaup and small numbers of lesser scaup, both supported by the recent proliferation of invasive zebra mussels. By early January up to 20,000 birds are seen near mussel beds at South Shore and North Point. By the early 1970s, siltation from the Milwaukee River required the U.S. Army Corp of Engineers to dredge the harbor. They constructed a large disposal facility at South Shore where fill has been deposited for 33 years. As the fill dries, early successional vegetation colonizes producing stands of grasses and emergent vegetation including cattails. This has given the site a marshlike character, attracting several nesting species. It also provides shelter and food for migrant shorebirds and waterfowl. Notable breeders include spotted sandpiper, sora and Virginia rails, song and swamp sparrows, and, recently, moorhen. This site demonstrates how even a small restoration effort (unplanned in this case) can attract desirable species in an urban environment.

Changes in the Avifauna

Experienced observers are noting declines in many species, including during peak May migration. Of 160 presettlement breeding species, 58 (36%) are now extirpated from the county (see sidebar on p. 373). Losses of exploited game species to settlers was obvious by the mid-1800s when wild turkey, northern bobwhite, greater prairie chicken, and sharp-tailed and ruffed grouse all disappeared. Not surprisingly, all 10 bird species that bred in tamarack bogs disappeared along with that habitat. We see the greatest declines in wetland species, where 23 species (45%) have disappeared as breeders (including 10 waterfowl species). These losses likely reflect both unregulated hunting and the draining and filling of wetlands. The black rail, the most secretive of all North American birds, may have nested in Menomonee marshes, but it has disappeared as well (although ornithologists recently noted two migrating birds near the South Shore Coast Guard Station). The nesting status and distribution of this species through much of its range is unknown.

The red-headed woodpecker, a conspicuous bird that prefers forest edge and oak savanna, has declined markedly in recent years, probably reflecting a loss of dead wood. As farming intensified, hedgerows disappeared. In addition, the number of snags today has declined relative to 30–40 years ago when many elms died from Dutch elm disease. Competition with starlings for nesting holes may also be a factor (although, ironically, starling numbers appear to have declined as well; Mueller 2002).

The golden-winged warbler, a species of forest edges and early second-growth woodland, has been displaced by the more southern blue-winged warbler with which it hybridizes. Golden-wings now occur only in the northern portions of its range, and its genetic extinction may be near. The habitat for both species is common in Milwaukee County, but only the blue-winged and some hybrids remain. Three other neotropical migrant woodland birds—Canada, hooded, and cerulean warblers—have essentially disappeared as well. A few lingering singing birds attempt to nest, but usually disappear by June 15.

In contrast to these declines of most native birds, some introduced birds have enjoyed remarkable success in their new land. Of six introduced breeding birds, only the rock pigeon appeared alongside early European settlements. House sparrows were then introduced in 1875. By 1900, Kumlien and Hollister (1903) noted that these sparrows oc-

Extinct, Extirpated, and Introduced Breeding Bird Species in Milwaukee County

EXTINCT SPECIES

Passenger pigeon
Carolina paroquet

EXTIRPATED FOREST SPECIES

Sharp-shinned hawk
Red-shouldered hawk
Broad-winged hawk
Ruffed grouse
Solitary sandpiper
Barn owl
Barred owl
Long-eared owl
Whip-poor-will
Pileated woodpecker
Acadian flycatcher
Least flycatcher
Cerulean warbler
Hooded warbler
Canada warbler

EXTIRPATED WETLAND SPECIES

Trumpeter swan
Gadwall
American wigeon
Northern pintail
Green-winged teal
Canvasback
Redhead
Ring-necked duck
Hooded merganser
Black-crowned night heron
Ruddy duck
Osprey
Northern harrier
Black rail
King rail
Common moorhen
Sandhill crane
Piping plover
Wilson's phalarope
Forster's tern
Black tern
Yellow-headed blackbird
Brewer's blackbird

EXTIRPATED GRASSLAND–OAK SAVANNA SPECIES

Sharp-tailed grouse
Greater prairie-chicken
Northern bobwhite
Upland sandpiper
Short-eared owl
Loggerhead shrike
Golden-winged warbler
Grasshopper sparrow
Henslow's sparrow
Western meadowlark

EXTIRPATED RELICT BOG–TAMARACK SWAMP SPECIES

Northern saw-whet owl
Alder flycatcher
Brown creeper
Winter wren

Nashville warbler	Northern waterthrush
Blackburnian warbler	Black-and-white warbler
White-throated sparrow	Black-throated green warbler

INTRODUCED SPECIES (*NONBREEDING)

Gray partridge*	Ringed-necked pheasant
Rock pigeon	Monk parakeet*
European starling	Great tit
Eurasian collared dove*	House finch
House sparrow	

curred throughout the state (though since the 1950s, they have decreased in apparent response to the scarcity of horses, as they fed on seeds in horse dung). The ring-necked pheasant was intentionally introduced into southeastern Wisconsin in 1916, and gray partridge became established in the region by 1920. This species may occur in the Little Menomonee River Parkway in the northwestern corner of the county. On February 17, 1923, Herbert Stoddard of the Milwaukee Public Museum found Wisconsin's first European starling, emaciated and unable to adapt to a severe winter. Stoddard prophetically reported "there will be more."

Bird invasions continue in Wisconsin. Although native to western North America, the house finch spread to the Midwest from the East where they were illegally sold as cage birds. The first documented breeders settled in Wisconsin in 1986. Similarly, the Eurasian collared dove spread to the upper Midwest from birds introduced in the Southeast. Nesting birds now occur in Wisconsin and probably in Milwaukee. This bird also hybridizes with mourning doves, representing a potential genetic threat to this native bird. Warmer winters and extensive bird feeding in winter have attracted at least six more exotic European species in the last few years. The source of these birds is unclear but may include escapes from the pet trade and ships in the Great Lakes. In 2004, great tits successfully nested in Milwaukee. We can thus expect other new exotics to arrive in coming years, particularly as winters become milder.

Change in Reptiles and Amphibians

The changes described above in plant communities and habitats also spelled trouble for amphibian and reptile populations in Milwaukee

County (chapter 20). Unlike birds, these "herptiles" have limited powers of dispersal. Thus, present-day communities largely reflect collections of species that have managed to survive the isolation and habitat changes over the past century. Estimated species losses in these groups range from 20% for turtles and 27% for frogs and toads to 42%–45% for snakes and 71% for salamanders. Population losses are surely much greater. The abundance of terrestrial frogs, toads, and salamanders is likely now a tenth or less of what it was, reflecting the loss of suitable habitats and the introduction of predatory fish. Declines in the extent and quality of snake habitats have brought similar declines in remaining snake populations. Despite the massive losses and degradation of wetland habitats and large declines in abundance, only one turtle species has been lost. Two aquatic frogs restricted to shoreline habitats (American bullfrog and northern green frog) remain secure, reflecting their tolerance to introduced fish and habitat degradation. American bullfrogs may even be more abundant than they were in presettlement times. In sum, herptile biodiversity and particularly abundance have declined greatly over the past 150 years.

What Will the Future Hold?

It is difficult to predict what Milwaukee County's future plant communities will be. Our two data sets from circa 1850 and 2003 represent just two points in time. Without data from intervening years, we cannot yet judge whether rates of species loss are declining or accelerating. Did most of these losses occur in the early years of European settlement as large expanses of land were cleared or later with urban spread and industrial expansion? Did the losses occur early in direct response to landscape change or progressively over time as the "extinction debt" incurred by these changes was paid? We may now be past the first "bottleneck" when sensitive habitat specialists were extirpated. We generally expect that those plants that have persisted are resilient and may find stable refuges in our remaining parks and preserves. Some "extirpated" species might even reinvade or be discovered. We recently added three orchid species to the county flora: purple twayblade and late coralroot appear new to the county, while large yellow lady-slipper was rediscovered.

This hope, however, may be misguided. Some species are so rare that their survival is in doubt. Heartleaf plantain, for example, is a state endangered species only found today in two relict populations in the state, one of which is in Milwaukee County. Another endangered species, blue-stem goldenrod, remains abundant in only a few woodlots in southern Milwaukee County. Continuing urbanization, high deer populations, and human use all place heavy stresses on our remaining natural areas. If this is the case, we expect that biodiversity will continue to decline (figure 25.3). The small remnant populations that remain of many rare habitat specialists would then represent not survivors, but rather the "living dead," ultimately destined for oblivion in their isolated habitats. Species present at just a few locations, like the orchids noted above, are particularly at risk. Loss of a single woodlot or wetland would mean the extirpation of that species from the county. As random events gradually eliminate small and increasingly isolated populations, the chances of these species reestablishing themselves elsewhere are dim given how far seeds must now travel to reach suitable habitat. Local extirpations increasingly signal countywide extinctions. Of the 598 native plant species still present, 92 (15.4%) are known from a single site. Not surprisingly, almost half these species are highly conservative (C = 7–10). If we lose them, the county's floristic quality will decline further.

The drastic declines we see in floristic quality for Milwaukee County represent an extreme for Wisconsin. Nevertheless, we should pay close attention to what they foretell for the rest of the state and nation. As cities and their suburbs spread, more and more counties across the country are coming to resemble Milwaukee County. The changes we document here predict the changes we should expect in these other rapidly urbanizing areas. These include the replacement of habitat specialists by the same impoverished set of cosmopolitan and increasingly weedy species. As natural areas dwindle in size and number and grow increasingly isolated, we will also learn more about the ability of native species to persist in our increasingly fragmented landscapes. Will 2% of an urban area be enough to sustain a reasonable complement of native species? The experiments have begun, complete with replicates.

Bird Futures

Continuing urban sprawl seems likely to claim the remaining old fields and farms of Milwaukee County. These losses and continuing fragmentation of habitat will, in turn, lead to further declines in bird abundance and diversity. Declines in habitat cover and quality in tropical wintering habitats are likely to further depress populations of migratory birds (a majority of our species). How great will these losses be? We predict the loss of up to seven forest, six wetland, and four grassland species within the next 20 years (figure 25.3). Most recently, the grasshopper sparrow has ceased to breed here. Forest fragmentation and associated cowbird parasitism limit the nesting success of species like the red-eyed vireo despite yearly attempts. Can we extrapolate from past trends? Over the last 150 years, we have lost 36% of our breeding species, suggesting a loss of four birds per decade. More than half those bird species nested in bogs, swamps, and marshes. Future losses could accelerate to five to eight bird species per decade over the next 20–40 years. This would doom 20% of our currently breeding species (figure 25.3). Populations of the remaining species seem likely to continue to decline as they become more fragmented, local, and unpredictable.

What can we do about these declines? To sustain bird populations into the future, we must provide them with the habitats they need to successfully nest. This, in turn, requires that we protect lands to provide both a diversity of habitats and adequately sized habitats. These efforts should be based on systematic surveys of breeding birds, particularly on public lands (e.g., the floodplains held by the county) and tracts being considered for acquisition by various agencies. The Milwaukee Metropolitan Sewerage District is presently setting priorities to acquire selected tracts. Surveys of breeding birds would efficiently indicate how suitable these areas are for particular species. However, it is often difficult to detect species present in only small numbers. With infrequent surveys, new species spreading northward and remnant species are sometimes missed. We should also survey remaining forested tracts on both public and private land for species like the wood thrush, which is declining across the region. How many remaining woodlots are large enough to support nesting pairs of this species? Only repeated annual surveys of good quality wetlands can reveal the presence of secretive species like the least and American bitterns and rails. Further losses of these wetlands or a decline in their size or buffer areas could eliminate these species from the county. Forster's tern could perhaps be attracted to suitable sites with nesting platforms. The ravines along the lakeshore often have a cooler microclimate and should be routinely surveyed for northern species occurring on the margins of their range. State conservation agencies will soon use radar units to estimate how many birds migrate in and out of selected habitats, one element of habitat quality. The National Oceanic and Atmospheric Administration's four Wisconsin weather radar stations have already provided valuable data on how spring and fall migration occurs along the western shore of Lake Michigan.

In addition to conserving inland habitats for breeding birds, we must also provide quality habitat areas for migrant birds to rest and feed. Nearly 200 species of migrant birds stop here, and all need quality habitat.

Such cover within urban spaces would also reduce proximity to windows where reflections of trees can prove deadly. Domestic cats and an increasing feral cat population pose an additional hazard that is compounded when cover is scarce. Cats and collisions with buildings and tall antennae account for high rates of mortality during migration. Migrant birds over Lake Michigan at dawn often struggle against headwinds to make it to shore. Such birds require some cover along the lakeshore, even if it is not quality habitat. These migrants flock to even poor cover along the shore, including small plantings of shrubs on parking lot islands. We should arrange landscape plantings to provide as continuous a strip of lakeshore cover as possible for these migrants. Fallow fields on undeveloped parkland should also be carefully managed to benefit particular bird species. Controlled burning and habitat restoration would benefit many grassland birds including meadowlarks and bobolinks. As the Dredge Confinement Facility at South Shore is filled and as soil contamination is reduced, plans to use the fill site should include habitat management for both nesting and migrant birds. The success of this site serves as an example for other, small-scale wetland restoration projects.

As climatic warming extends their ranges north, several southern species can be expected to increase as breeders, including white-eyed and bell's vireos, blue grosbeak, orchard oriole, prairie warbler, yellow-breasted chat, summer tanager, Carolina wren, and northern mockingbird. There are also reports of hooded mergansers nesting in southeastern Wisconsin near small ponds and drainage ditches. While there is a small summer population of yearling birds in the county, nesting has not yet been documented.

The Future of Amphibian and Reptile Populations

Amphibians and reptiles in Milwaukee County face a particularly difficult combination of habitat loss and poor dispersal ability. Recolonization of restored habitats is not likely without assisted translocations. Declines and species losses are therefore likely to continue. Estimated future species loss rates could rise to 100% for salamanders, 64% for frogs and toads, 40% for turtles, and 73%–75% for snakes (figures 25.3 and 20.1). One trend evident in amphibians and reptiles is an ongoing loss of biodiversity and consequent simplification of ecological communities. For example, many of the remaining wetlands in the county now support only two snake species, one preying on earthworms (Butler's gartersnake), and the other upon slugs and snails (northern red-bellied snake).

Where frogs remain abundant, the common gartersnake will also occur, illustrating the ecological linkages between predator and prey. The overall species loss rate to date is estimated at 15 of 34 species (44%), or one species lost every 10 years over the last 150 years. Losses may increase to 24 of 34 species (71%), in the near future. If this rate of loss extends to other regions with a similar pace of development, we will see more local extirpations and eventually the extinction of endemic species. Stemming, or reversing, the biodiversity losses illustrated here will require us to preserve, connect, and manage all remaining extensive habitat areas.

Conclusions

Despite substantial losses, we retain significant native species and natural communities in Milwaukee County. Residents must now choose whether to sustain and restore these communities or allow them to degrade. The nature that was once abundant in our backyards is fading, forcing future residents to travel tens to hundreds of miles to view anything similar. We have documented 150 years of profound changes in this county's plant, bird, amphibian, and reptile communities. These changes continue. The losses of biodiversity we described here parallel those found in other studies of urbanization, including the disappearance of half the lichens from Madison (chapter 11). We suspect that urbanization is driving similar changes in insects, fishes, crustaceans, and other less well-studied groups.

Continuing ecological change may be inevitable given continued invasion by exotic species, further air and water pollution, emerging diseases, global climate change, and the predictable collapse of small, isolated populations. Nevertheless, certain proactive measures would do much to sustain and enhance the region's native flora and fauna. Foremost among these is the need to expand and connect natural habitats across landscapes. Milwaukee needs a holistic, ecosystem approach to conserving natural areas with an emphasis on protecting and restoring whole communities and their associated ecological services. The Chicago Wilderness Network just to the south provides a positive example. This network is bringing citizens and organizations together to protect and restore a remarkable set of remnant natural areas in and around Chicago. Their lessons could benefit us. This work is not easy and the challenges are daunting. Nevertheless, we owe it to those who will look back in 150 years to ask, what did this generation do to protect nature and stem the tide of species losses?

References

Bernthal, T. W. 2003. Development of a floristic quality assessment methodology for Wisconsin. Final Report to U.S. Environmental Protection Agency—Region V. Wisconsin Department of Natural Resources, Bureau of Fisheries Management and Habitat Protection, Madison.

Curtis, J. T. 1959. The Vegetation of Wisconsin. Madison: University of Wisconsin Press.

Idzikowski, J. H. 1982. Summer birds reaching the margins of their range at the Cedarburg Bog and the UWM Field Station. Field Station Bulletin 15(1):1–15.

Kumlien, L., and N. Hollister. 1903. The birds of Wisconsin. Bulletin of the Wisconsin Natural History Society 3(1–3):1–143.

Lopez, R. D., and M. S. Fennessey. 2002. Testing the floristic quality assessment index as an indicator of wetland condition. Ecological Applications 12(2):360–369.

Mueller, W. P. 2002. The biogeography and recent decline of the red-headed woodpecker in Wisconsin. Master's thesis, University of Wisconsin–Milwaukee.

Oldham, M. J., W. D. Bakowski, and D. L. Sutherland. 1995. Floristic quality assessment system for southern Ontario. Natural Heritage Information Centre, Ontario Ministry of Natural Resources, Peterborough.

Robbins, S. D., Jr. 1991. Wisconsin Birdlife: Population and Distribution, Past and Present. Madison: University of Wisconsin Press.

SEWRPC (Southeastern Wisconsin Regional Planning Commission). 1997a. A natural areas and critical species habitat protection and management plan for southeastern Wisconsin. SEWRPC, Planning Report No. 42, Waukesha.

———. 1997b. A regional land use plan for southeastern Wisconsin. SEWRPC, Planning Report No. 45, Waukesha.

Swink, F., and G. Wilhelm. 1994. Plants of the Chicago Region. 4th ed. Indianapolis: Indiana Academy of Science.

26 Ecological Footprints of Urbanization and Sprawl: Toward a City Ethic

Dave Cieslewicz

The United States produces about a third of all the greenhouse gasses emitted worldwide. When someone hears about greenhouse gasses, thoughts inevitably proceed to the effects—climate change. We could just as easily turn our attention to causes. A third of those emissions come from the transportation sector. I have concluded that Americans drive more than any other nation because our land use patterns demand it. I also view land use as a key driver of many water and air quality issues we face. While point sources of pollution have been dramatically reduced, nonpoint sources of air pollution grow. Millions of tailpipes emit tons of greenhouse gasses and other air pollutants daily. Land use also influences water quality, as runoff from construction site erosion, overfertilized suburban lawns and oily parking lots and roads contribute extensively to water pollution. Current levels of air and water pollution are not inevitable consequences of a growing population with growing affluence. Instead, air and water pollution levels reflect the way we develop land, where we develop land, and ultimately, where we choose to live on the land.

Land: Consumption beyond the Need

A growing population will consume some land for development, and this will greatly influence biodiversity (chapter 25). Yet we are consuming far more land than simple population growth would predict. Between 1982 and 1997, the population of the United States grew by 17%, and the amount of urbanized land increased by 47% (Fulton 1997). That pattern is repeated in every major metropolitan area in America—whether they are growing rapidly or shrinking. In Los Angeles, between 1970 and 1990 the population expanded 45% and land area grew 300%. Cleveland lost 11% of its population during those same decades but consumed an additional 33% for development (Benfield et al. 1999). Between 1990 and 2000, an area twice the size of New Jersey has crossed over from rural to suburban or urban use in the United States.

Once, people argued that land consumption was not a problem, because there was so much of it in the United States. Frank Lloyd Wright made this argument, noting that there were 57 acres for every person in America. That was 1932 when there were 130 million Americans. By 2008, there were 24 acres for every one of the 305 million people in the continental United States. That included every acre of prime farmland, deserts, and mountains and every acre of protected park, habitat area, and green space in the nation. The view that the American landscape is so vast that it does not demand any constraint on development is flawed; it neglects the need for agricultural and recreational land, functional ecosystems, biological diversity, and even the American myth of "wilderness." Ironically, one of the key tenets of American folklore—the room to roam and to be independent—is being obliterated by that same desire to live apart. As more of us move out into the "wide open spaces," they become less wide open.

In addition to the amount and the manner in which land is developed in America, another important factor is where development is taking place. There is an unfortunate association between sprawling suburban areas and some of our best farmland. Many cities grew precisely because of their proximity to good farmland, providing the interface between farmers and their markets. Unfortunately, the deep, well-drained soils that were attractive for farming are also attractive for development (Buttel 1994). According to the American Farmland Trust, counties with an abundance of both prime farmland and development pressure account for 79% of our nation's fruit, 69% of our vegetables, 52% of our dairy products, and over one-fourth of our meats and grains. The trust calculates that we are losing prime farmland at the rate of 46 acres *per hour* (Benfield et al. 1999). As farms are relocated from these more productive regions to less suitable land, increased chemical inputs are needed to provide similar yields.

Climate: Driving Up the Temperature

Disproportionate land consumption is not the only issue. The way in which land is developed matters. Nearly every new development since World War II has been designed for auto travel. By strictly separating uses into vast large-lot single-family house subdivisions connected to large shopping malls and business "parks" by wide highways and streets, we have made driving mandatory in virtually every new development built in America in the last 50 years. In fact, due to this development pattern even short trips demand auto travel. One in four automobile trips is less than one mile in length (Benfield et al. 1999). In both in the United States and Europe, about 90% of all trips are less than 10 miles. Yet Americans drive much more than Europeans, because the U.S. pattern of development leads to more driving for even short distances. The key difference is not so much that Americans have farther to go, but that they drive more frequently while Europeans tend to substitute walking, biking, or mass transit for these short trips (Nivola 1999). Compact European development patterns make this possible.

Transportation accounts for a third of all the greenhouse gases produced in the United States, and the contribution from the transportation sector is growing faster than the others. The average car burns 550 gallons of gasoline per year, producing four metric tons of carbon dioxide. Sport utility vehicles and minivans burn about twice as much gas, releasing twice as much carbon dioxide. Furthermore, sales of these light truck now account for about half of all vehicle sales. Vehicular greenhouse gas emissions produced are projected to leap 55% over the next 10 years if current trends in increased travel and vehicle preference continue (Benfield et al. 1999). So, the connection between how we live and our climate is very real. Sprawling land use patterns in the United States require more driving, which leads to the production of more greenhouse gases that fuel global warming, leading to changes in the landscape and the culture that is shaped by it.

Air: Squandering the Gains

Air quality in the United States has improved in the last three decades, but this improvement has been in spite of, not because of, our land use patterns. The gains have been impressive. Airborne lead declined 97% since 1977, carbon monoxide is down 61%, and smog has been cut by 30%. Today's cars are 70% cleaner than 1960s models for nitrogen oxides and 80%–90% cleaner for hydrocarbons. These gains are largely due to government-mandated improvements in vehicle emissions and from improvements in point sources such as utilities and industry (Benfield et al. 1999). But these improvements would have been even greater if increases in vehicle miles traveled merely reflected increase in the driving population.

While each car was becoming cleaner, the number of cars and the number of vehicle miles driven was skyrocketing. Between 1969 and 1990, the number of miles driven per capita rose over three times faster than the U.S. population (Benfield et al. 1999). The U.S. Department of Energy now predicts that U.S. carbon emissions will grow at an average rate of 1% per year, with transportation sources contributing disproportionately. The U.S. Environmental Protection Agency (EPA) has found that total hydrocarbon emissions could start to edge up again in the next several years because of increased driving. Total nitrogen oxide emissions from vehicles are already at higher levels then they were 20 years ago, even with the much cleaner burning engines in each vehicle. Ozone and particulate pollution are also both increasing (Benfield et al. 1999).

We are giving back air quality gains because sprawling development patterns demand more driving. Figure 26.1 compares the land and air impacts of development at densities of one lot per five acres (a typical rural subdivision in Wisconsin), one lot per one acre (Frank Lloyd Wright's idea of utopia, "broadacre city"), eight lots per acre (a typical "suburban" neighborhood built in the early part of the 20th century), and 50 units per acre (a dense urban development by midwestern standards, but trivial compared with New York City). It demonstrates that development at the density of even the relatively leafy "suburban" neighborhoods of 80–100 years ago would have half the air quality impact and only 2.5% of the land consumption of the five-acre lot scenario.

Some hope that new technological advances will make up for the dramatic increases in vehicle miles driven. For example, in 1999 Honda introduced the Insight, a hybrid vehicle that featured an electric motor combined with a three-cylinder gasoline engine. The gas engine can be smaller and lighter because the electric motor supplies additional power when needed. Meanwhile, the electric batteries never need recharging because the motor acts as a generator when the car is decelerating. Honda combined this technology with the latest in lightweight construction to achieve EPA mileage ratings of 61 miles per gallon in the city and 70 miles per gallon on the highway. The Insight meets California's ultralow vehicle emission standard, which is driving the industry toward greater fuel efficiency. Still, even Honda

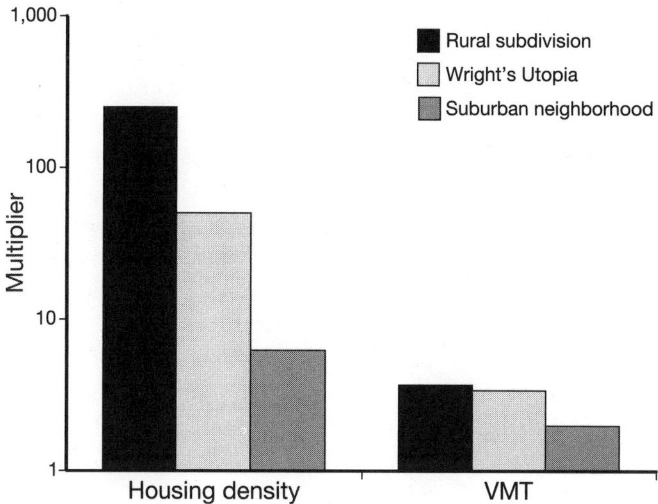

FIGURE 26.1 How development patterns influence housing densities and vehicle miles traveled (VMT). VMT is a surrogate for carbon monoxide and dioxide, nitrous oxide, and volatile organic compound emissions. All values are relative to an urban density of 50 units/acre.

claims improvements only for emissions that cause smog, not for greenhouse gases.

Water: Missing the Point

As with air pollution, we have made great progress in the United States over the last three decades in cleaning up point sources of water pollution, like municipal sewage treatment plants and paper mills. The remaining water quality problems we face largely originate from nonpoint sources—places like farm fields, lawns, roads, parking lots, and construction sites. Nonpoint pollution is now the leading cause of water pollution in America, impacting 40% of the nation's surveyed waterways (Benfield et al. 1999).

Water pollution becomes apparent when impervious surfaces, like roads, parking lots, and rooftops, exceed 10% of the area inside a watershed. The problem grows when the makeup of the impervious surface is transportation related. Parking lots, roads, and driveways are usually interconnected, and they hold oil, grit, and road salt. When it rains, larger quantities of water move at faster speeds carrying more pollutants. The attempt to solve the problem by increasing lot sizes only worsens the problem. Because large-lot developments require more driving per unit of housing, they require longer driveways, wider roads, and more parking lots. Large lot developments are thought to contribute up to three times more sediment than traditional, dense urban developments (Benfield et al. 1999)

There might be at least one positive water quantity impact of sprawl. In some large municipal water systems, water is drawn from high capacity wells, used, and sent to municipal sewerage treatment plants where it is treated and discharged. As a result, groundwater is drawn down, reducing springs, stream flows, and surface water levels. This harms species fish and other aquatic life dependent on cool, rapidly moving streams. Sprawling rural developments on private septic systems return the effluent to the same groundwater table and watershed. As a result, there is no net loss of groundwater and related surface water flow rates and levels (Hall 1998).

The Environmentally Good City

Cities provide antidote to the problems of sprawl. Their benefits are described in Milwaukee mayor John Norquist's book *The Wealth of Cities.* He writes:

> Cities are, on balance, good for the environment. New Yorkers pollute far less, on average, than their suburban neighbors. More gasoline is needed to support the auto-dependent lifestyle; more electricity must be generated to heat and cool the large, standalone homes; more resources must be used to provide roads, pipes, and utility lines to the scattered sites; more energy must be consumed to supply water and return sewage from homes farther and farther away from municipal plants; more trucks must use more gas to move products farther and farther; more chemicals are applied to control the weeds on larger and larger lawns and more water is needed to keep those lawns green; and, most important, more land must be cleared and leveled to accommodate the same amount of living. (Norquist 1998, 139–40)

The policy answers to sprawl are numerous and complex, but few of them are possible in a practical political sense until we resolve the confusion that clouds popular discussion—and even discussion among sophisticated environmental activists—about sprawl, cities, and the environment. Polls show that American attitudes are somewhat schizophrenic, as they oppose both sprawl and high density housing. A recent survey by the Pew Center for Civic Journalism (2000) found that sprawl came out at the top of an open-ended question about the most important issues facing Americans in their own communities. A survey of Wisconsin residents found that 34% believed that most development should take place in Wisconsin's largest cities, but only 6% would live there themselves. A national survey found that 77% of Americans oppose building even single family homes at higher densities in their own neighborhoods (Gould 2000). They recognize the problem of sprawl but oppose the solution. We will not solve the problems of sprawl until we resolve this contradiction and learn to embrace city life—with its advantages as well as disadvantages—as the most positive environmental choice an individual can make.

A City Ethic

Over half a century ago, Aldo Leopold recognized that one of the greatest threats to the natural environment was society's very fascination with—and attraction to—that environment.

"Man always kills the thing he loves, and so we the pioneers have killed our wilderness," he writes in his essay "The Green Lagoons" (Leopold 1966, 157). But while Leopold's concerns in the 1940s focused on the hunters, bird-watchers, and other enthusiasts that America's fledgling car culture allowed to visit the countryside frequently, today our natural resources face the greatest threat not from those who visit the rural landscape, but from those who increasingly choose to inhabit it. I suspect sprawl is the primary remaining environmental problem in America—underlying most of the others—and that we will not solve it until we convince people that city life is the best way to live as plain members and citizens of a biotic community (Leopold 1966). To me, this "city ethic" is a natural extension of Leopold's work.

Cities are good for the environment. Each city resident uses less land then his suburban brethren. The city resident contributes less to water pollution through runoff from lawns and from concrete simply because there is less lawn and less impervious surface per person in the city. The city resident drives less, making a smaller contribution to air pollution and to global warming, sending fewer pipelines into the wilderness, and fewer oil tankers into the water.

Despite the advantages of city living for the environment, many of us feel that country—or at least large-lot suburban—life is best for our personal environment. Polls show that we see sprawl as a problem, but we are reluctant to accept its cure in choosing city life for ourselves. The irony is that so many people move to the country because they profess a love for nature. The ethic we need to develop is just the opposite: if you love nature, make your home in the city. It's just this simple: sprawl is a problem because too many people want to live in the country. If fewer people wanted to live in the country, sprawl would cease to be a problem. If we do not like sprawl, we should not live sprawl.

How would a city ethic change our views of what it means to live as citizens of a biotic community? We might begin to take as much care with cities as we do with nature. We would take a greater interest in the magnificent subtleties of urban design that spell the difference between a place that works and a place that does not. We would begin to understand that it is as important to be a good urbanist as it is to be a good naturalist. Too often, when environmentalists think about cities at all, we think about think about importing nature back into them. Urban parks are certainly wonderful, but in Wisconsin—as in most places in America—the problem is not that we do not have enough urban open space. The problem is that we do not have enough urban. A good, dense urban neighborhood with sidewalks, porches, corner stores, good schools, and strong neighborhood associations is not only a good place to live, it makes fewer demands per unit of housing on land, air, and water than sprawling but more grassy and superficially green large-lot subdivisions or country estates. The city ethic is not easy. We cannot pass the blame to developers or the government. Everyone shares responsibility. We cannot tell others to live in greater density. Rather, the picture this book paints makes clear our need to construct cites in a manner that will preserve and enhance our quality of life while protecting the ecosystems we love and depend on.

References

Benfield, F. K, M. D. Raimi, and D. D. T. Chen. 1999. Once There Were Greenfields. New York: Natural Resources Defense Council.

Buttel, F. 1994. Agricultural Change, Rural Society and the State in the Late Twentieth Century. Pp. 41–65 in D. Symes and J. J. Anton, eds. Agricultural Restructuring and Rural Change in Europe. Wageningen, the Netherlands: Agricultural University.

Fulton, W. 1997. The Reluctant Metropolis: The Politics of Urban Growth in Los Angeles. Point Arena, CA: Solano Press Books.

Gould, W. 2000. Growing Smarter: The Struggle with Sprawl. Milwaukee Journal Sentinel, January 30.

Hall, M. W. 1998. Extending the Resources: Integrating Water Quality Considerations into Water Resources Management. Water Resources

Update, No. 111, Universities Council on Water Resources, Carbondale, IL.
Leopold, A. 1966. A Sand County Almanac. New York: Oxford University Press.
Nivola, P. S. 1999. Laws of the Landscape: How Policies Shape Cities in Europe and America. Washington, DC: Brookings Institution Press.
Norquist, J. O. 1998. The Wealth of Cities: Revitalizing the Centers of American Life. Cambridge, MA: Perseus Books Group.
Pew Center for Civic Journalism. 2000. Research Straight Talk from Americans. Available at www.pewcenter.org/doingcj/research/r_ST2000.shtml.

27 Influences of Policy, Planning, and Management on Ecological Change

Stephen M. Born

Wisconsin has a long and illustrious history in the field of conservation (Scott 1967), populated by such giants in the field as Increase Lapham, John Muir, Charles Van Hise, Aldo Leopold, Sigurd Olson, Gaylord Nelson, and many others. Since the great cutover of the northern forests, chronicled in Lapham's Forestry Commission "Report on the Disastrous Effects of the Destruction of Forest Trees Now Going on So Rapidly in the State of Wisconsin" published in 1867 (Scott 1967), conservation and management of the state's natural resources have been ongoing and remain highly controversial issues. Special recognition must be accorded to Robert M. LaFollette and his Progressive politics; in the first quarter of the 20th century, he placed an indelible imprint on Wisconsin conservation by creating a strong role for government and establishing conservation as a deeply ingrained political movement (Huffman 1989). Given the character of Wisconsinites, the quality of the state's resources and environment, a University committed to applying its intellectual resources to public policy issues (Haveman and Shroder 1989; Corry and Gooch 1992; Cronon 1994), and the state's progressive political traditions, it is not surprising that Wisconsin has been a national leader in natural resources policy and planning—indeed a national laboratory for innovation and diffusion of ideas (Huffman 1989). As noted by

Jacobs, Jordahl, and Roberts (1990), Wisconsin has been the incubator of many "firsts" in natural resources policy and management. These include the application of the urban concept of zoning to rural land use problems; the first national watershed-based soil conservation project in southwestern Wisconsin's Coon Valley; the first shore land–floodplain management program in the nation—the basis of the national flood management and coastal management programs; and precedent-setting legal decisions including the first state to ban DDT and the 1972 *Just v. Marinette County* Supreme Court decision that improved wetland protection.

As documented throughout this book, Wisconsin's lands, waters, and wildlife have been changing in response to changing land use and development pressures. These changes are partly due to public policy and program decisions but also reflect the effects of the aggregation of myriad unplanned private and individual actions. My focus is the important influence of public policy, planning, and management interventions have on ecological systems. While science can create an informative knowledge base that helps shape the public and political opinions that lead to policy and management actions, it is the cumulative impacts of public (and private) policy and management interventions themselves that bring about change. The principal drivers of change include population growth, development levels and distribution, land use, agriculture and industrial production, energy development, and transportation and infrastructure choices.

Public policy and management decisions involve choosing among options that ultimately shape the interaction of society and the environment. These decisions have intended and unintended effects on ecosystems. Consider actions taken early in state history to foster economic growth through water development (the 1840 Milldam Act; Kanneberg 1946). Or consider efforts to increase agricultural acreage by encouraging wetland drainage (private drainage and drainage district laws; Kent 1994; URPL/IES 2002). What would have happened if Wisconsin never created a system of county forests following the cutover era and consequent economic crisis (Jordahl 1984; Harkin 1987)? These and myriad others have had profound effects on ecological conditions. More recent activities—developing our state highway system, stocking Pacific salmon in the Great Lakes (chapter 12), removing dams to restore rivers like the Baraboo, and establishing floodplain and shore land regulations along our waterways—have had equally significant consequences. Land acquisition initiatives over past decades have protected rare and threatened resources, biodiversity, and critical fish and wildlife habitat.

Policy decisions to preserve land helped Wisconsin protect some of its ecological heritage—in state parks and forests, scientific and natural areas, wild and scenic rivers, trail systems, and environmental corridors—while often providing natural resource-based outdoor recreation to citizens. In short, public policies and actions have played a major role in shaping today's Wisconsin landscape and ecological communities.

A Context for Planning and Management

Although many policy choices and management decisions affect short- and longer-term ecological conditions, ecological consequences are seldom considered in decision making. Many major policies and programs emerge from political processes that may be strategic and carefully thought out but are unrelated to any systematic planning. The planning process helps identify appropriate future actions by "applying knowledge to action" (Friedman 1987). Planning is designed to clarify policy approaches and alternatives so decision makers can make informed judgments (Randolph 2004). In contemporary practice, it is also an open and inclusive process that fosters civic engagement and identifies conflicts among competing interests (Forester 1999). When effective, planning prepares us to manage change, and thus it has the potential to strongly influence future ecological conditions.

In this chapter, I emphasize public sector planning. Much of governmental planning that influences ecological conditions involves planning for valued environmental resources, like air, water, fish, and wildlife. The resultant plans can be quite broad in scope or quite narrow and specific. For example, a policy-level plan for future transportation infrastructure may be general and easily adapted, while a plan for a new state park is necessarily specific with respect to the design and location of roads, campgrounds, parking lots, and foot trails. Both types of plans can have short- and long-term ramifications for ecological conditions.

The "Toolkit" for Management

Planning is a cyclic process. It involves evaluating the results of past intervention efforts while identifying new problems or opportunities and setting new goals, much like adaptive environmental management (Holling 1978). The management strategies presented here represent the "toolkit" for implementing plans and programs to achieve goals and objectives. These tools are deployed singularly or in combination.

Regulation, the "police power" of the state, is the pillar of point source pollution abatement programs to improve water and air quality. Regulation through land use controls is central to efforts to protect shore lands, floodplains, and wetlands and also plays a key role in shaping the physical form of the communities in which we live. Regulation also has been a primary tool in fish and game management.

Education is embedded in most environmental management programs. It often goes beyond informing citizens and affected interests about programs; it offers new knowledge and ultimately attempts to change attitudes and social behaviors. Education is a key strategy, for example, in voluntary programs to address habitat and ecological resource protection on private lands, in efforts to prevent the spread of invasive species (chapter 30), in programs to encourage recycling of residuals, and in working with landowners to address polluted runoff issues confronting waterways.

Economic incentives and disincentives are also key components of the "toolkit." Tax credits for preserving farmland and upgrading pollution abatement equipment are good examples of using market-based tools. Financial penalties for violating environmental laws are a form of economic disincentives.

New *technology* can have varied long-term environmental consequences. In 2000, new domestic waste disposal systems opened up great expanses of land in Wisconsin to development, lands previously unsuitable because of natural site limitations. Such technological choices have major potential ecological implications for water resources, habitat fragmentation, and biodiversity (LaGro 1998). Adoption of solar and wind power generation technologies can have profound effects on ecological systems, altering the scale and location of energy-generating and transmission facilities while creating new land use patterns. Geographic information systems software is used by governments and the citizenry to make better-informed land use and environmental decisions.

The "power of the public purse"—that is, *spending and land acquisition* programs—is a fundamental management tool. Expenditures for purchasing lands for public parks, natural areas, and open spaces from the state's stewardship fund are intended to benefit ecological communities and systems while providing major recreational benefits for humans. Federal spending that provides payments to farmers who improve the environment through conservation programs like the Conservation Reserve, Wetlands Reserve, Environmental Quality Improvement, Wildlife Habitat Improvement, and Conservation Reserve Enhancement programs dramatically alter ecological conditions, at least as long as these programs continue. Transportation system expenditures lead to major landscape modifications. And spending to support citizens groups concerned about their natural resources—for example, via river protection grants to conservation organizations—can have significant long-term ecological consequences by increasing local resource stewardship and capacity. Collectively, the deployment of this assemblage of management tools directly influences the health of ecological systems.

Temporal and Spatial Concerns in Policy and Planning

Good planning is by definition future oriented, and good plans frame the likely future consequences of alternative management options. Consider the years of planning, analysis, and citizen participation that went into the establishment of the Lower Wisconsin State Riverway. The land use and scenic protection standards developed in the planning process will indelibly influence the landscape far into the future (chapter 17). Similarly, plans for acquisition, protection, and management of important wetland and estuary complexes along Wisconsin's Great Lakes shorelines—like the Mink River estuary and the Kakagon and Bad River sloughs—help assure the long-term health of these systems (chapter 14). Plans made for dam removal, environmental effects mitigation, and river environment restoration along rivers like the Baraboo and the Prairie in north-central Wisconsin also have huge long-term consequences for affected aquatic and riparian ecological communities. The Wisconsin Land Legacy initiative was started by the Wisconsin Department of Natural Resources (WDNR) and aimed at identifying special land and water resources in the state that warrant protection or acquisition over the next 50 years represents the leading edge of planning for long-range outcomes and a sustainable environment. This process identifies special land and water resources in the state that should be protected over the next half century.

Enacted in 1971, the Wisconsin Environmental Policy Act (WEPA) was intended to assure that long-term environmental impacts are considered in all too often short-term–oriented state government policy making. WEPA established a state policy that will "encourage productive and enjoyable harmony between man and his environment; promote efforts which will prevent or eliminate damage to the environment and biosphere and stimulate the health and welfare of man, and enrich the understanding of the important ecological systems and natural resources (Wisconsin Statutes Section 1.11). While ideally such considerations would be part of a proactive government planning process, WEPA is applied post facto, requiring all state agencies to prepare environmental impact statements for legislation and other management functions and regulatory activities that have the potential to significantly affect the environment. Agencies are required to develop and evaluate alternatives to proposed actions, while providing opportunities for public involvement in governmental decision making. While it is not "planning" in the strict sense and is sometimes difficult and controversial in it implementation, WEPA is designed to influence decisions affecting the environment, having an overall positive effect.

Nevertheless, major legislative enactments—intended to resolve current problems not directly related to environmental policy—can have enormous future influences on ecosystems. Policy decisions involving tax laws provide a good illustration. Responding to the belief that increasing property taxes threatened Wisconsin farms and farmers, the state constitution's tax uniformity clause was changed in 1974 to allow for preferential assessment of agricultural and conservation land for property tax purposes. While over the succeeding years, farmers received reduced tax payments by enrolling in the state Farmland Preservation Program, legislators felt this tax credit program was insufficient. The 1995 Budget Act changed the state law again, establishing "use value" assessment provisions for agricultural land allowing reduced taxes on lands classified as agricultural. The legislature did not consider how this might affect farms serving conservation purposes, like maintaining riparian buffers along streams or eliminating grazing on erosion-prone wooded hillsides. Under the new law, these lands were not defined as agricultural (based on estimated value for growing crops), and therefore shared in bearing the tax shift, which in many cases was substantial. Landowners had fewer choices: resume grazing, plant crops, or incur large property tax increases. Thus embedded in the use-value legislation were conservation disincentives with the potential for widespread ecological degradation. Other tax policy decisions—from gasoline taxes to home ownership tax deductions—are rarely considered in ecological terms even though they can have large unintended or unanticipated effects.

Ecological systems do not follow political boundaries. Unfortunately, environmental plans and policies are executed by units of government whose jurisdiction does not match up with the relevant ecological region, or "problemshed." While the necessary levels of intergovernmental and regional cooperation can be difficult to achieve (Knight and Landres 1998), it can be done. For example, the WDNR is restructuring along geographic management units (roughly corresponding to river basin boundaries). Likewise there is collaboration between agencies and nongovernmental organizations to protect the Baraboo Hills region (http://dnr.wi.gov/org/caer/cfa/LR/stewardship/baraboo.html).

When regional planning and policy initiatives rely on affected local governments and other stakeholders for implementation, there seldom are the lines of authority needed to facilitate participation. Fragmented and uncoordinated decisions and actions are commonplace. For example, consider the "Regional Natural Areas and Critical Species Habitat Protection and Management Plan" prepared for the southeastern region of the state by the Southeastern Wisconsin Regional Planning Commission (1997). It provides a solid framework for land conservation and acquisition programs and guidance to prioritize public funding opportunities. However, achievement of the plan's goals requires the concerted voluntary actions of a large array of governmental units, land conservancies, and individual property owners. Current efforts at "smart growth"/ comprehensive land use planning by local governments face this same challenge. There are opportunities for protection and/or restoration of ecosystems, but they require a high level of sustained, intergovernmental cooperation. This mismatch—absent mandates or incentives for working together—has proved problematic.

The challenges of scale and intergovernmental cooperation only become more vexing at larger multistate and international levels. Comprehensively protecting and managing vast ecological landscapes like the Mississippi River basin or the Great Lakes region are illustrative of the complexity and difficulty. Addressing water quality, levels, and flows in these institutional settings typically involves protracted negotiations and compromises among the parties at interest. These large ecoregions/ landscapes are shaped by many "masters," with the ensuing changes to ecological systems being a result of decisions by literally thousands of actors acting largely independently.

New Directions in Planning and Management and Implications for Ecological Change

Since the 1972 United Nations Conference on the Human Environment and the publication of the report of the Brundtland Commission (Brundtland 1987), there has been increasing attention to issues of *sustainability*. Ultimately, societal values and attitudes will determine if sustainability forms the basis for planning and policy efforts. Fortunately, some new approaches hold promise. The old incremental approaches—one problem, one solution at a time—are giving way to more *integrative* approaches to environmental management that consider the interrelationships among ecosystem elements and human demands on systems (Born and Sonzogni 1995; Margerum and Born 1995). Embedded in integrated approaches is the notion of *adaptive management,* which acknowledges the uncertainties associated with management options and treats each planning or policy intervention as experimental, subject to careful monitoring, evaluation and learning, and subsequent modification (Holling 1978; Lee 1993). Adaptive planning and management follows a "learn by doing" model.

Another dimension of the changing environmental planning and management paradigm involves a new focus on more *decentralized, collaborative, community-based approaches* (Selin and Chavez 1995; Duane 1997; Agrawal and Gibson 1999; Wondolleck and Yaffee 2000). These approaches are commonly characterized as "grassroots" or partnership initiatives (Born and Genskow 2000; Weber 2000). They are more inclusive, less "top-down," and bring a wider and more diverse array of interests into more participatory approaches to environmental decision making. The associated planning and decision-making processes aim to preemptively resolve disputes and reach more consensual decisions. In regions with a mixture of public and private lands, there is growing recognition that *private lands stewardship*—facilitated by governmental programs—play a critical role in achieving environmental management goals (Freyfogle 2003).

There is substantial experimentation going on with these innovations. The WDNR has assumed leadership for applying these new approaches in their geographic management units, identifying integrated ecosystem management projects in each unit (WDNR 1997). The various river basin partnerships, facilitated by University of Wisconsin–Extension and supported by WDNR, represent major efforts at collaborative decision making (http://dnr.wi.gov/org/gmu/). Across the state there is a burgeoning movement of watershed associations, lake associations, land conservancies, conservation groups, land use planning alliances, and others breaking new ground in applying these new approaches. While it is premature to claim success, these efforts have great potential to produce and implement plans and policies that are sensitive to the long-term protection and functioning of ecological systems and communities.

In a world of competing values and interests, scientific uncertainty, political vacillation, economic and budgetary stress, and widespread global inequity and unrest, I cannot forecast with any degree of assurance that future policies and plans will be adequately responsive to secure the long-term health of ecological communities and systems. While our rich environmental policy heritage and traditions offer some basis for optimism, the forces of population growth, development, and urbanization are daunting. Further, it has been politically difficult to establish effective institutions at supra-local levels with the geographic reach and requisite powers to assure that growth and development go forward in environmentally sustainable ways. Proactive and progressive leadership across the Wisconsin political landscape—public leadership that works to avert rather than respond to environmental crises—has too often been absent. While civil society has made many important contributions, it should be a complement to rather than a substitute for government action to protect and restore Wisconsin's ecological systems. Whatever public policies, plans, and management actions are adopted (or not adopted) in the Badger State, they will have enormous long-term consequences for the state's ecosystems.

References

Agrawal, A., and C. C. Gibson. 1999. Enchantment and disenchantment: The role of community in natural resource conservation. World Development 27(4):629–649.

Born, S., and K. D. Genskow. 2000. Toward Understanding New Watershed Initiatives. University of Wisconsin–Madison Workshop, Madison.

Born, S., and W. Sonzogni. 1995. Towards integrated environmental management: Strengthening the conceptualization. Environmental Management 19:167–183.

Brundtland, H. 1987. Our Common Future. Oxford: Oxford University Press (for the World Commission on Environment and Development).

Corry, J., and J. Gooch. 1992. The Wisconsin idea: Extending the boundaries of a university. Higher Education Quarterly 46:305–320.

Cronon, W. 1994. Planning another century of good government: The Wisconsin idea in the twenty-first century. Remarks before the Wisconsin Commission for the Study of Administrative Value and Efficiency, January 7.

Duane, T. P. 1997. Community participation in ecosystem management. Ecology Law Quarterly 24:771–797.

Forester, J. 1999. The Deliberative Practitioner: Encouraging Public Participatory Planning Processes. Cambridge, MA: MIT Press.

Freyfogle, E. 2003. The Land We Share—Private Property and the Common Good. Washington, DC: Island Press.

Friedman, J. 1987. Planning in the Public Domain: From Knowledge to Action. Princeton, NJ: Princeton University Press.

Harkin, D. A. 1987. Land Use Decisions: Issues in the Evolution of Wisconsin's County Forest Program 1963–1985. University of Wisconsin–Extension, Publication No. G3475, Madison.

Haveman, R., and M. Shroder. 1989. Roots of the Wisconsin idea—The university and public policy since the Progressive Era. L & S Magazine 6(1):35 (University of Wisconsin–Madison).

Holling, C. S. 1978. Adaptive Environmental Assessment and Management. New York: John Wiley.

Huffman, T. R. 1989. Protectors of the land and water: The political culture of conservation and the rise of environmentalism in Wisconsin, 1958–1970. Ph. D. thesis, University of Wisconsin–Madison.

Jacobs, H. M., H. C. Jordahl, Jr., and J. C. Roberts. 1990. Land resource policy and planning in Wisconsin: An interpretive history. Pp. 9–25 in S. M. Born, D. A. Harkin, H. M. Jacobs, and J. C. Roberts, eds. Future Issues Facing Wisconsin's Land Resources. University of Wisconsin–Madison, Institute for Environmental Studies, Report 138, Madison.

Jordahl, H. C., Jr. 1984. County Forests in Transition—An Account of the Wisconsin County Forest Crop Revolt, 1960–63. University of Wisconsin–Extension, Publication No. G3262, Madison.

Kanneberg, A. 1946. Wisconsin law of waters. Wisconsin Law Review 345–385.

Kent, P. 1994. Wisconsin Water Law—A Guide to Water Rights and Regulations. University of Wisconsin–Extension, Publication No. G3622, Madison.

Knight, R. L., and P. B. Landres, eds. 1998. Stewardship across Boundaries. Washington, DC: Island Press.

LaGro, J. 1998. Landscape context of rural residential development in southeaster Wisconsin (USA). Landscape Ecology 13:65–77.

Lee, K. 1993. Compass and Gyroscope—Integrating Science and Politics for the Environment. Washington, DC: Island Press.

Margerum, R., and S. Born. 1995. Integrated environmental management: moving from theory to practice. Journal of Environmental Planning and Management 38(3):371–391.

Randolph, J. 2004. Environmental Land Use Planning and Management. Washington, DC: Island Press.

Scott, W. S. 1967. Conservation's first century in Wisconsin: Landmark dates and people. Pp. 14–42 in N. Cournow-Camp, ed. Conservation

Centennial Symposium: The Quest for Quality in Wisconsin. University of Wisconsin, Madison.
Selin, S., and D. Chavez. 1995. Developing a collaborative model for environmental planning and management. Environmental Management 19:189–195.
Southeastern Wisconsin Regional Planning Commission (SEWRPC). 1997. A Regional Natural Areas and Critical Species Habitat Protection and Management Plan. SEWRPC, Planning Report 42, Waukesha.
Urban and Regional Planning/Institute for Environmental Studies. 2002. The Tumultuous World of Drainage Districts: An Analysis of Existing Management Arrangements, with Recommendations. University of Wisconsin–Madison, Department of Urban and Regional Planning, Working Paper Series 2002–1, Madison.
Weber, E. P. 2000. A new vanguard for the environment: Grass-roots ecosystem management as a new environmental movement. Society and Natural Resources 13:237–259.
Wisconsin Department of Natural Resources (WDNR). 1997. Integrated Ecosystem Management (IEM) Project Summaries 1997–98. Water and Land Divisions, WDNR, Madison.
Wondolleck, J. M., and S. L. Yaffee. 2000. Making Collaboration Work: Lessons from Innovation in Natural Resource Management. Washington, DC: Island Press.

Part Six: Trajectories

We should all be concerned about the future because we will have to live the rest of our lives there. **Charles Kettering (1949)**

: : :

Anyone who has read this far has concerns about how wildlife and habitat conditions are faring. You may also wonder what these trends portend for the future of Wisconsin's waters, landscapes, and wildlife. What future can we expect for Wisconsin's ecosystems? While it is tempting to simply take recent trends and extrapolate them, such predictions inevitably fail sooner or later. Because ecological systems often display rapid, delayed, or nonlinear responses, simple predictions usually fail sooner. Coupled human-ecological systems are even less predictable. But the most relevant question here is, Can we direct ecological change toward desired outcomes?

Ecologist Steve Carpenter asks these questions and helps us to think about the challenges we face in seeking answers. He explains why ecologists face difficulties in making predictions. The more detailed our prediction becomes, the more likely it is to fail. Ecosystems are not deterministic systems in that chance factors play an important role in their dynamics. This is further complicated by volition—many of the decisions people make that will ultimately affect ecosystems have not happened yet. He argues that scenario planning—the development of structured narratives about possible futures—is therefore well suited for understanding changes in complex systems. By accepting the unpredictability and lack of control in complex systems, it may paradoxically become easier to identify drivers of change, major uncertainties, options for action, and plausible outcomes. He explains how this works using an exercise he helped conduct in Wisconsin's Northern Highlands Lake District.

International travel, trade, and commerce have transformed our world economically, culturally, and biologically. The oceans that once acted as barriers to separate far-flung floras and faunas no longer do this. New exotic plants and animals from faraway places continue to establish themselves in North America, often displacing native species. Their remarkable success may reflect their ability to leave coevolved predators, parasites, and competitors behind; their ability to deploy novel weapons; and/or their ability to reallocate resources into efficient early reproduction. Chapters 29 and 30 contemplate these invasions of nonnative species and how they may shape our biota in the future. Aquatic ecologists Jake Vander Zanden and Jeff Maxted note a shift away from describing the impacts of individual invasive species towards forecasting future invasions and their likely impacts. Focusing on five invasive species of Wisconsin's inland waters, they project impacts and predict which lakes will ultimately be invaded based on their water chemistry. Department of Natural Resources ecologist Kelly Kearns then shares her concerns about the species invading terrestrial habitats: where they came from, what factors contribute to their success, their current and projected impacts, and, most importantly, how individuals, governments, and private organizations are beginning to respond to these threats. We also learn about what both individuals and organizations can do to stop the spread of invasive species, including explicit suggestions for action.

Wisconsin's forests will also continue to change, but not necessarily in the way they have in the past. Exurban sprawl, rapid climate change, and invasive species seem likely to interact, altering forests in novel ways. Echoing Steve Carpenter, ecologists Rob Sheller and David Mlandenoff note that our biggest obstacle in understanding how global change will play out in Wisconsin's forests is knowing how people will use or alter forests in the future. They provide a general scenario to predict how different tree species will respond to climatic warming. However, because trees grow slowly while weather changes from year to year (even with steady warming), systematic shifts in forest conditions may be subtle and slow to emerge.

28 Seeking Adaptive Change in Wisconsin's Ecosystems

Stephen R. Carpenter

Ecosystems have always changed, and, as far as we know, they always will. New species colonize communities and resident species sometimes disappear. The ecosystems of today are novel outcomes of the long series of past changes. Wisconsin's ecosystems we see today are vanishing; they are in transition, becoming something different.

If change is so pervasive, one might ask, why are scientists alarmed by it? At present, ecological change is unusual in both its magnitude and speed. Humanity is driving extraordinary changes in climate, geology, and biology of the entire planet (Steffen et al. 2004). Entire habitats, species, and genomes are disappearing. These are the elements from which the constituents of new ecosystems emerge. In other words, ecosystems are losing their capacity for renewal. This is why scientists are worried. It is precisely at times of great change that capacity for renewal is most needed.

The issues are not just academic. Throughout history, people have depended on ecosystems for fundamental support of their livelihoods. Ecosystem goods like food, fiber, and timber are essential commodities, and ecosystems services like flood abatement and crop pollination underscore human well-being. Both goods and services are in critically short supply in many regions of the world and are growing more scarce (Millennium Ecosystem Assessment 2005a). Declining ecosystem services, combined with deteriorating ecosystems, are causing serious damage to human well-being. To understand and address the problem, we cannot think of social systems and ecological systems as separate entities. Rather, they both form part of a larger, social-ecological system.

The consequences of human-driven change in Wisconsin's ecosystems are highlighted throughout other chapters. What future can we expect for Wisconsin's ecosystems? To what extent can we direct ecological change toward desired outcomes? This chapter will sketch some approaches to these questions. The chapter begins with the limits to ecological prediction and our limited capacity to control change in ecological systems. Existing mechanisms for governance of social-ecological systems are not well suited for circumstances of high uncertainty and limited control (Dietz et al. 2003). These challenges will be framed in terms of ecosystem regime shifts, using concepts of boundaries, resilience, and adaptive change—concepts that will become clearer later in the chapter. Scenario development is a tool to help us understand the high uncertainty and limited control found in social-ecological systems. I present a set of social-ecological scenarios developed for the Northern Highland Lake District (NHLD). The chapter concludes with some speculations about prospects for Wisconsin's ecosystems in the turbulent decades to come.

Four Limits to Ecological Prediction

Complexity limits our ability to predict social-ecological change. While ecologists have made reliable predictions in a few particular, narrowly prescribed circumstances, in general we cannot predict important changes in social-ecological systems. Some of the barriers to successful prediction for regional social-ecological change are as follows.

The "long now": In ecology, "now" is not an instant but a long period of time. The present condition of ecosystems reflects events that occurred last year, last decade, and even last century. This gives rise to an important corollary: actions taken now can have consequences that extend far into the future (Carpenter 2002; chapter 31). For example, the algae blooms of southern Wisconsin's lakes reflect the legacy of decades of overfertilization and erosion in farmlands, and it could take a century or more to restore water quality by decreasing the mass of phosphorus in the uplands (Bennett et al. 1999). Long time horizons make prediction difficult. This is a common theme in this book. Ecological changes in Milwaukee County (chapter 25), along the Wisconsin River (chapter 17), and in Lake Michigan (chapter 12) provide a few of the many examples of ecology's long now.

Scientific uncertainty: Our scientific knowledge of the conditions and trends of whole ecosystems is limited, in part because ecosystem change is strongly influenced by random processes. At best, ecological predictions can be represented as probabilities of possible future conditions. Even the science of estimating such probabilities is in its infancy (Carpenter 2002). For social-ecological systems, the science has scarcely been imagined. Because many current changes in ecosystems have no historical analog (Steffen et al. 2004), past changes are at best an unreliable guide to the future.

Surprise: Complex systems are subject to rapid change, and social-ecological systems are no exception (Carpenter 2003; Folke et al. 2005; Scheffer et al. 2001). The 20th century brought many important ecological surprises, such as the biomagnification of toxins in food chains, rapid evolution of resistance of pests to biocides, and the contribution of land-use change to diverse syndromes including desertification, eutrophication, and disease emergence (Bennett et al. 2003). Important, unexpected changes in social-ecological systems seem to be increasing in frequency (Steffen et al. 2004). In fact, novel changes may be emerging faster than we can devise solutions (Homer-Dixon 2000).

Volition: Even if ecology had great predictive capacity, social-ecological systems would exhibit great uncertainty because people are embedded in the systems (Millennium Ecosystem Assessment 2005b). The future is subject to human choices that have not yet been made, and the very process of thinking about the future can affect these choices. While volition diminishes the predictability of social-ecological systems, it evokes the possibility of changing the future through the use of scenario planning and related tools for looking forward. Scenarios can help envision the new worlds that might be created by transcending present boundaries.

Regimes and Boundaries

A regime shift is a change in the nature and strength of feedbacks that affect an ecosystem. Lake eutrophication is one such regime shift that will be elaborated on shortly. A regime shift can bring change in ecosystem organization, trends, and variability (Scheffer et al. 2001; Carpenter 2003; Folke et al. 2005). Sometimes the different regimes of an ecosystem have important consequences for ecosystem services and human well-being (Millennium Ecosystem Assessment 2005b). Although the most spectacular examples of ecological regime shifts are fairly rapid (Scheffer et al. 2001), they are not always fast. While the boundary between regimes may be crossed in an instant, the impacts of the regime shift may be gradual.

Organizational changes set in motion by crossing a boundary may not be evident until long after the boundary was crossed (Carpenter 2003).

Lake eutrophication, in which lakes undergo a regime shift from low to high productivity, is among the best-understood ecological regime shifts (Carpenter 2003). During eutrophication, excessive enrichment with phosphorus (P) pushes the ecosystem across a boundary and creates an organizational change—a persistent condition of turbid water. The turbidity is due to high concentrations in the water of P-limited microscopic plants, often toxic blue-green algae. Even if P load (annual input) is decreased, the turbid state may persist due to recycling of P that has built up in the sediments. Many Wisconsin lakes are now eutrophic. Prior to the advent of European agriculture in Wisconsin, most of Wisconsin's lakes had low P loads, low P recycling, and clear water. Currently, most of the excess P enrichment in Wisconsin comes from agricultural fertilizers.

The concept of multiple regimes separated by slowly changing boundaries also operates in social-ecological systems (Gunderson and Holling 2002). Social-ecological examples tend to be more complex than the lake regimes, although the basic ideas of regimes and boundaries are the same. For example, models with regimes and boundaries have been used to explore social traps, such as the persistence of harmful ecosystem management practices (Scheffer et al. 2003).

Figure 28.1 illustrates an abstract case of multiple regimes of a social-ecological system. The topography represents the full range of possible social-ecological systems, with social systems along one dimension and ecological systems along the other. Two points close together in graph space represent similar social-ecological systems, while two points far apart represent less similar systems. Valleys represent a stable, attainable social-ecological system, or regime. Peaks represent highly unstable combinations of social-ecological systems. Ridges between valleys reflect boundaries. To make matters more complex, the topography changes slowly. The ball moves freely across the surface, and its location reflects the current state of the social-ecological system. The ball stops moving when it rolls into a valley—the system becomes stable. It can move rapidly if there is a perturbation from outside the system, or if people drive it from one regime to another (figure 28.1*A*). More fundamental changes, like climate change, alter the topography (figure 28.1*B*), representing changes in the boundaries and possible regimes of the social-ecological system. Changes in the topography of possible regimes can be driven by ecological or social factors or by perturbations from outside the system. In complex systems, the topography is constantly changing and the ball is often in motion.

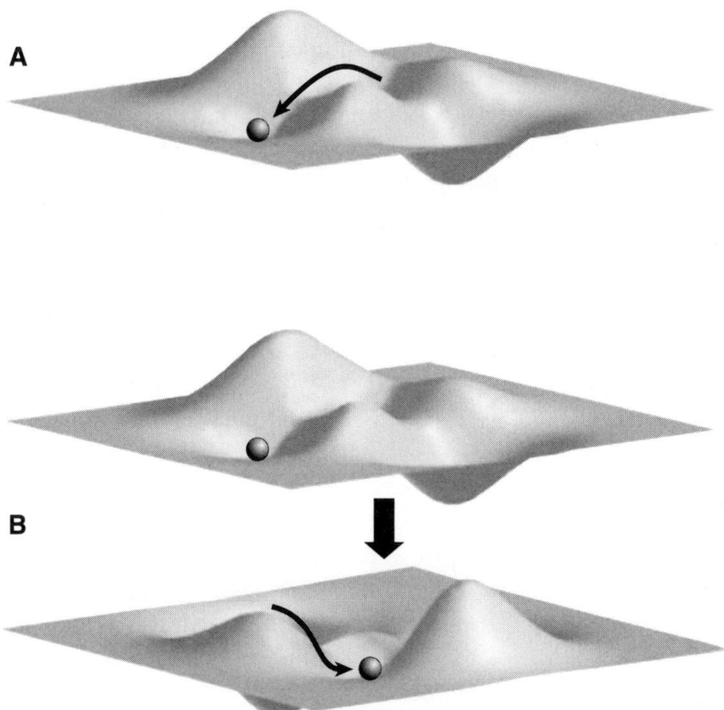

FIGURE 28.1 Potential surfaces illustrating attainable regimes (valleys) of a social-ecological system. Changes in the surface are relatively slow. The ball represents the current state of the system, which may change rapidly. *A,* The arrow represents a shift from one regime to another as a result of a rapid change in an external driver or a brief perturbation. *B,* The potential surface is altered by gradual changes in underlying variables that control the types of regimes that can exist. Changes of this type may be more long lasting than those that result from instantaneous perturbations.

People often think that the sustainability of social-ecological systems is captured by a single regime, the combination of a socially and ecologically sustainable state. In fact, sustainability can be defined in terms of multiple regimes and their boundaries (Walker et al. 2004). In view of the constant change of ecosystems and societies, it makes no sense to think in terms of single, stable states. There are several conditions that can give rise to sustainability, but some paths to those conditions are more sustainable than others.

Scenarios: A Tool for Envisioning Change

Anyone who attempts to understand or manipulate change in a social-ecological system must confront enormous complexity. How is the system organized? What is changing, how is it changing, and why? What are the regimes and boundaries? What makes particular regimes vulnerable or resilient? What features are desirable, and what kind of system do we want? What features are attainable, and what kinds of system can we get? The vast complexity of these questions makes it hard to think about the future in a coherent way.

Scenario planning developed as a process for addressing change in systems that are not predictable and not controllable. Social-ecological systems fit this profile: change cannot be predicted accurately, and the people making decisions have only limited and narrow capabilities to control change in social-ecological systems. Additional history of scenario planning in relation to ecosystem change appears in Bennett and others (2003), Peterson and others (2003b), and the Millennium Ecosystem Assessment (2005b).

Here, a scenario is a structured narrative about a possible future path of a social-ecological system. A scenario is not a forecast; instead scenarios stress the unpredictable and the uncontrollable in order to capture key uncertainties about the future of the social-ecological system. In a typical project, three to five scenarios are developed. If more scenarios were used, it would be impossible for people to grasp the implications. The small number of scenarios forces us to prioritize the most critical variables. Comparison of a few scenarios reveals drivers of change, major uncertainties, options for action, and plausible outcomes.

Scenarios for the NHLD

The NHLD is a social-ecological system centered on Vilas County, Wisconsin (figure 28.2). The NHLD contains a mix of public, private, and tribal lands, and it is changing rapidly (Peterson et al. 2003a). Visitors to the region in 2004 see a very different place than they would have seen 30 years ago. Both resident and visitor populations have grown substantially. Highways from big cities have expanded, bringing more traffic. The NHLD's urban centers are larger and still growing. International or national chains are more prominent in the business community. Almost all the lakeshore that can be developed has been developed. Redevelopment (replacement of old, smaller cottages with new, large houses) is under way. There is frequent conflict about regulations for development, such as setbacks designed to protect lakeshore habitat. The Lac du Flambeau tribe is growing economically and bringing youth to the region as more tribal members with young families return to the reservation. In contrast, the age distribution of people off-reservation is older and gray-

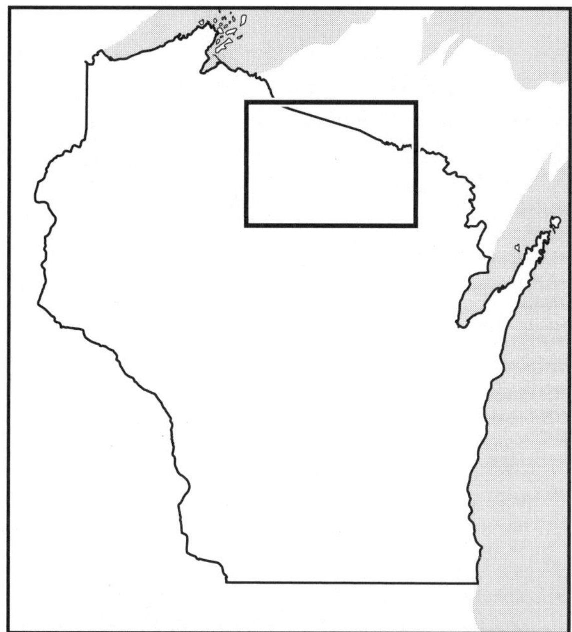

FIGURE 28.2 Outline map of Wisconsin and the Upper Peninsula of Michigan, showing the location of the Northern Highland Lake District.

ing, as the young adults move elsewhere and more retirees move in. A comanagement system for the walleye fishery sometimes creates conflict but also has increased the quality of fishing on some lakes. Angling has thinned the larger size classes of fish populations on most public access lakes. Deer populations have expanded. Heavy browsing by deer, combined with losses of older forest stands, is a threat to some plant species and the animals that depend on them. Invasive species are a growing problem for both terrestrial and aquatic ecosystems. Invasions are associated with increases in visitors, traffic, boats, all-terrain vehicles, and snowmobiles. Overall the NHLD seems more crowded—there are growing numbers of people using the same, finite area of land and lakes. Conflict over use, such as the tension between motorized recreation and the silent sports, is intensifying.

The Resilience Alliance (www.resalliance.org) selected the NHLD as one of several "regions in transition" for an international comparative study of regional resilience in 2000 (Walker et al. 2002). Later, the NHLD was accepted as an Associated Sub-Global Assessment of the Millennium Ecosystem Assessment (www.maweb.org). We initiated an assessment process that included the development of scenarios (Peterson et al.

2003a). A "Workshop on Theories of Adaptive Change" was held for residents (managers, businesspeople, conservationists, local politicians, and the media) at Minocqua, Wisconsin, in March 2002. A Scenarios Workshop with scientists and residents was held at Kemp Station, Wisconsin, in September 2002. At the scenarios workshop, we reviewed scientific information about change in the NHLD and heard accounts of change from residents with long experience in the region. After an introduction to scenarios and presentation of examples from other regions, the group developed 18 different scenarios for the next 25 years in the NHLD. During subsequent discussions, it became clear that these scenarios contained many similarities and parallel events. Therefore, we condensed the 18 original scenarios to four scenarios that captured the main issues. After the workshop, a writing team quickly developed drafts of the scenarios, which were distributed to the workshop attendees for review. After revision to incorporate these review comments, we visited leaders of the Lac du Flambeau tribe, the Vilas County Board of Supervisors, and the Vilas County Lake Association to tell the stories and listen to comments and criticisms. Following these visits, the scenarios were revised again. In May 2003, the scenarios were placed on a Web site (http://lakefutures.wisc.edu) in several formats. We also printed and distributed hard copies of the scenarios. The scenarios were publicized widely to people of the region through advertising and media coverage. We initiated a survey to assess responses to the scenarios. This assessment process continued through summer 2004. A long sampling period was necessary to include a full range of seasonal visitors in the responses. At the time of writing, a full analysis of the survey results is not yet available.

The NHLD scenarios can be seen online (http://lakefutures.wisc.edu) and in a booklet available in the library of the University of Wisconsin Center for Limnology (Carpenter et al. 2002). Brief summaries of the four stories follow.

Anaheim North: Development accelerates, centering around theme parks (figure 28.3*B*). Population and commercial activity increase, but many of the jobs in the NHLD are low-paying ones and much of the profit of the theme parks does not stay in the NHLD. Locally owned businesses become less common. Problems with urban sprawl and pollution intensify. Motorized recreation replaces muscle-powered recreation, except in the most remote areas and on private tracts of land. Public hunting and fishing lands are heavily harvested, and quality hunting and fishing experiences are found only in a few remote sites and on large private landholdings.

Walleye Commons: The visitor population declines as a result of intensifying conflicts over resource use, environmental deterioration, and

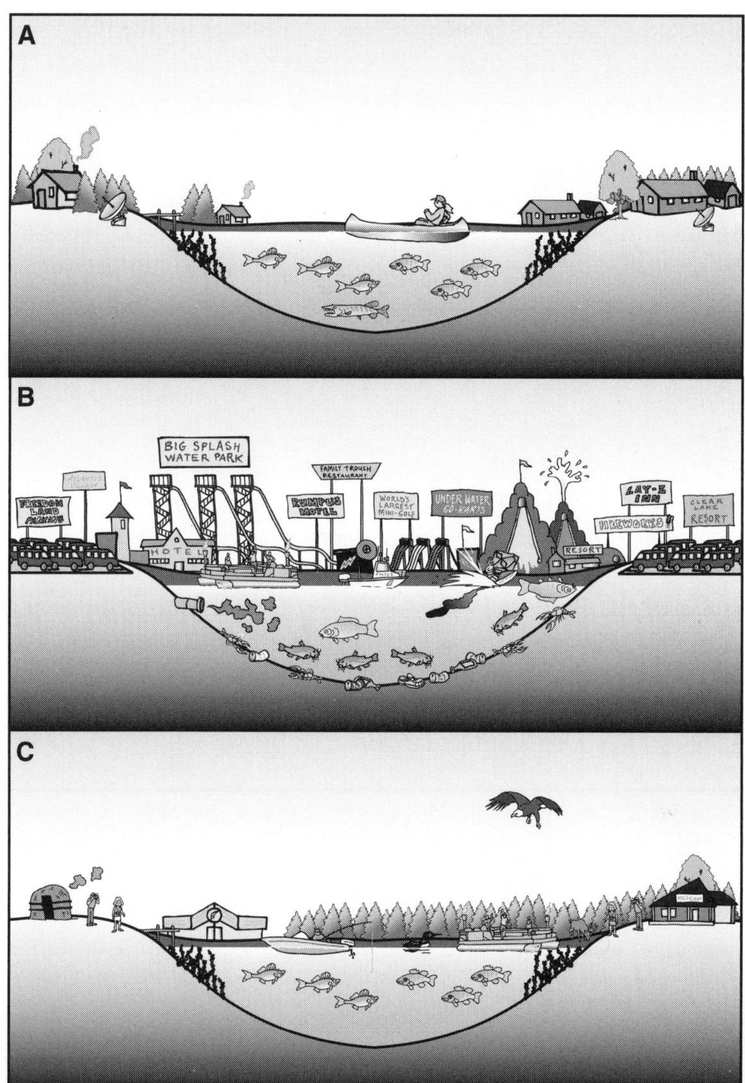

FIGURE 28.3 Selected examples from the illustrations created for the Northern Highland Lake District development scenarios. *A,* Strong lake associations support silent sports around some lakes (as shown in the illustration) and motorized recreation on other lakes (not shown) in Northwoods Quilt. *B,* Theme parks become common, especially around the larger lakes near population centers, in Anaheim North. *C,* Tribal innovations diversify the tourist economy in Walleye Commons. (Illustrations by Bill Feeny, from Carpenter et al. 2002. Reprinted by permission.)

collapse of a real-estate bubble. Despite economic hardship, the Lac du Flambeau tribe persists (figure 28.3*C*). Ecosystems recover slowly. The economy is smaller in 2027 than in 2002 but more diverse with contributions from ethnotourism and slow recovery of recreational opportunities on feral ecosystems.

Northwoods Quilt: The retiree population expands and becomes more influential in the politics and economics of the NHLD. The economy diversifies because some retired professionals work part-time via travel or telecommuting. Resource conflict resolves in a multitiered system of regulations and incentives that allocates considerable power to lake associations. By 2027 the NHLD is a mosaic of diverse ecosystem uses (figure 28.3*A*).

Refugee Revolution: Terrorism makes urban life chaotic and dangerous. Many people abandon cities for rural areas. Owners of recreational properties in the NHLD move there to stay. Initially the infrastructure is severely stressed, but strong interventions by state and federal governments eventually create a viable economic base for a much more populated NHLD. By 2027, working ecosystems producing water, cranberries, fish and game for market, and forest products dominate the NHLD landscape.

Collectively, the scenarios explore aspects of vulnerability, resilience, and innovation in the NHLD (table 28.1).

- The region is vulnerable because of the low diversity of economic opportunity and its susceptibility to economic and political forces from outside the NHLD. Ironically, the self-reliance that is valued by many residents may perpetuate this vulnerability by undermining the networking and collaboration efforts.
- Resilience is conferred by several features of the NHLD. One source is the tribes, who intend to stay in the region. The capacity for renewal of the ecosystems of the NHLD is a source of regional resilience as well as the foundation of the ecosystem services on which the society is built. Ecological breakdowns can occur due to poor stewardship of shoreline habitats, biotic invasions, overharvesting, and so forth. Boundaries of ecological resilience are a source of tension in the scenarios.
- Key sources of innovation in the scenarios are the tribes and the newly retired or semiretired professionals who migrate to the region. The tribes are an important source of young people who want to stay in the region. In addition, they diversify the perspectives on resource management and the kinds of tourism opportunities in the re-

Table 28.1 Comparison of the scenarios for the Northern Highland Lake District

	Scenario			
Characteristic	Anaheim North	Walleye Commons	Northwoods Quilt	Refugee Revolution
Theme	Expansion of tourist industry, loss of local control, ecosystem decline	Economic and ecological breakdown, population decline, tribal persistence, ecological recovery	Diversification of economy, expansion of lake associations, diverse management goals, heterogeneous landscape	Urban refugees drive economic and ecological transformation; intensive use of ecosystems for services
Triggers of change	Development of megaresorts, theme parks	Resource conflict, ecological breakdown, environmental health risks	Resource conflict	Terrorism in urban centers
Drivers of innovation	Transnational tourism corporations	Native Americans	Active semiretirees, lake associations	State and federal agencies and the refugees
Economics in 2027 (vs. 2002)	Much larger economy, more dependent on tourism, more variable over time, higher proportion of low-wage jobs	Smaller economy but more diversification of tourism and resource management jobs	Larger and more diverse economy; more telecommuting, consulting, service, resource management jobs	Much larger and more diverse economy; more resource-extraction and service jobs
Environment in 2027 (vs. 2002)	Degraded water quality, fisheries, forests, and wildlife, except in a few remote or privately held pockets	Feral ecosystems; recovering and diversifying landscape	Heterogeneous landscape, diverse recreational opportunity	Working landscape-water supply, forest products, game farms, aquaculture

gion. Incoming older residents bring different viewpoints on resource management, different economic activities, and new problem-solving skills to the region.

The alternative futures depicted in the scenarios derive from different mixtures of these three key elements: vulnerability, resilience, and innovation.

Can Scenarios Change the Future?

We do not know if the scenarios project will change the future. In one sense, we can never know, because there is only one NHLD and the scenarios are now in play, with no control or reference system to help us interpret the outcome.

The scenarios have stimulated debate and new thinking. In our surveys, most respondents hope that the future brings something like

Northwoods Quilt or Walleye Commons. However, they believe that the future is most likely to resemble Anaheim North. About 70% of respondents say they would become involved in a group working for desirable change in the NHLD. Although they are willing to act, most respondents believe that they have little influence on the future of the NHLD. A quarter of respondents say they will move away if the NHLD begins to change in undesirable ways. One correspondent stated that the most important goal for the NHLD is "making people aware that they have options, that there is still time to affect the future." Other correspondents have sent descriptions of proposed new institutions for planning sustainable growth for the NHLD. These are positive, creative ideas that demonstrate the adaptability of the NHLD. Clearly there are people in the region who are ready to act in forward-looking ways.

Better networking is a key to building the adaptive capacity of the NHLD. The workshops that led to the scenarios have already formed new networks of contacts in the NHLD. More connections among key people and groups are necessary for adaptive change in the region. Substantial benefits could emerge from more frequent exchange of ideas among the innovative institutions in the region, such as the tribes, lake associations, and research organizations. A few interesting experiments in governance, collaboration, and ecosystem management are already under way in the NHLD. More experiments will be needed as the residents of the NHLD invent new ways to live in the future.

The NHLD is changing into a different region from what it was just a generation ago. It is not clear, however, what the NHLD is becoming. The present already contains elements of all four scenarios, and the same is likely to be true of the future. Also, the future will contain many surprises that are not in the scenarios. Which scenario elements and what unforeseeable surprises will dominate the future? What parts of the past will people choose to carry in the future, and what parts of the past will be abandoned? What boundaries will be accepted by the people of the NHLD? What boundaries will people revolt against and overcome? As the NHLD reorganizes, what new boundaries will be created? These questions will be answered over time, as the people of the NHLD act on the expectations and visions for the future.

Conclusions

Adaptability and transformability depend on the capacity of people to change the social-ecological system in which they live (Walker et al.

2004). In the NHLD, as in other social-ecological systems, adaptability depends on ecosystem resilience and human innovation. Ecosystem resilience is substantial but finite and threatened by forces external to the NHLD (e.g., climate change and species invasion) and practices within (e.g., poor stewardship of shorelines, deer overpopulation, and overharvest of some living resources). Sources of human innovation include the tribes, lake associations, research groups, and many other organizations. Adaptability is limited by several features of the NHLD, including the tradition of rugged individualism, limited capacity of networks that span across the entire region, and the narrow economic base. These constraints on adaptability underlie the NHLD's vulnerability to exogenous physical, biotic, and social forces.

The NHLD is at a crossroads, each leading to different futures. Leadership from within the community will have a powerful effect on the next directions of the NHLD. It is clear that emergence of key stewards has been critical in the conservation of other regions around the world (Olsson et al. 2004). However, the emergence of leadership is impossible to predict.

Throughout the world, social-ecological systems are changing rapidly. It is not clear which elements of the present will continue into the future. We are headed for a world of degraded ecosystems, feral ecosystems, working ecosystems, richly diverse ecosystems, a heterogeneous patchwork, or something we have not yet imagined. While the outcome is unknown, it is certain that the ecosystems of the future will affect the lives and livelihoods of people. Adaptability to upcoming challenges depends on human choices being made now. Better choices are likely if evolving changes are faced clearly and collaboratively, with our minds open to the surprises to come.

References

Bennett, E. M., S. R. Carpenter, G. D. Peterson, G. S. Cumming, M. Zurek, and P. Pingali. 2003. Why global scenarios need ecology. Frontiers in Ecology and the Environment 1:322–329.

Bennett, E. M., T. Reed-Andersen, J. N. Houser, J. R. Gabriel, and S. R. Carpenter. 1999. A phosphorus budget for the Lake Mendota watershed. Ecosystems 2:69–75.

Carpenter, S. R. 2002. Ecological futures: Building an ecology of the long now. *Ecology* 83:2069–2083.

———. 2003. Regime Shifts in Lake Ecosystems. Oldendorf/Luhe, Germany: Ecology Institute.

Carpenter, S. R., E. A. Levitt, G. D. Peterson, E. M. Bennett, T. D. Beard, J. A. Cardille, and G. S. Cumming, with illustrations by B. Feeny. 2002. Future of the Lakes. Center for Limnology, University of Wisconsin, Madison. Available at http://lakefutures.wisc.edu.

Dietz, T., E. Ostrom, and P. C. Stern. 2003. The struggle to govern the commons. Science 302:1907–1912.

Folke, C., S. R. Carpenter, T. Elmqvist, L. Gunderson, C. S. Holling, M. Scheffer, and B. Walker. 2005. Regime shifts, resilience and biodiversity in ecosystem management. Annual Review of Ecology Evolution and Systematics 35:557–581.

Gunderson, L. H., and C. S. Holling, eds. 2002. Panarchy: Understanding Transformation in Human and Natural Systems. Washington, DC: Island Press.

Homer-Dixon, T. 2000. The Ingenuity Gap. New York: Random House.

Kinzig, A., and D. Starrett. 2003. Coping with uncertainty: A call for a new policy forum. Ambio 32:330–335.

Millennium Ecosystem Assessment. 2005a. Conditions and Trends. Washington, DC: Island Press.

———. 2005b. Scenarios. Washington, DC: Island Press.

Olsson, P., C. Folke, and F. Berkes. 2004. Adaptive co-management for building resilience in social-ecological systems. Environmental Management 34:75–90.

Peterson, G. D., T. D. Beard, Jr., B. E. Beisner, E. M. Bennett, S. R. Carpenter, G. S. Cumming, C. L. Dent, and T. D. Havlicek. 2003a. Assessing future ecosystem services: A case study of the Northern Highlands Lake District, Wisconsin. Conservation Ecology 7(3):1. Available at http://www.consecol.org/vol7/iss3/art1.

Peterson, G. D., G. S. Cumming, and S. R. Carpenter. 2003b. Scenario planning: A tool for conservation in an uncertain world. Conservation Biology 17:358–366.

Scheffer, M., S. Carpenter, J. Foley, C. Folke, and B. Walker. 2001. Catastrophic shifts in ecosystems. Nature 413:591–596.

Scheffer, M., F. Westley, and W. Brock. 2003. Slow response of societies to new problems: Causes and costs. Ecosystems 6:493–502.

Steffen, W., A. Sanderson, J. Jäger, P. D. Tyson, B. Moore, III, P. A. Matson, K. Richardson, F. Oldfield, H.-J. Schellnhuber, B. L. Turner II, and R. J. Wasson. 2004. Global Change and the Earth System: A Planet under Pressure. New York: Springer-Verlag.

Walker, B., S. Carpenter, J. Anderies, N. Abel, G. Cumming, M. Janssen, L. Lebel, J. Norberg, G. D. Peterson, and R. Pritchard. 2002. Resilience management in social-ecological systems: A working hypothesis for a participatory approach. Conservation Ecology 6(1):14. Available at http://www.consecol.org/vol6/iss1/art14.

Walker, B., C. S. Holling, S. R. Carpenter, and A. Kinzig. 2004. Resilience, adaptability and transformability in socialecological systems. Ecology and Society 9(2):5. Available at http://www.ecologyandsociety.org/vol9/iss2/art5.

29 Forecasting Species Invasions in Wisconsin Lakes and Streams

M. Jake Vander Zanden and Jeff T. Maxted

We now live in the age of globalization, one consequence of which has been an explosion in international travel, trade, and commerce. The result is that the world has become smaller and more connected, contributing to a trend of cultural homogenization (Olden et al. 2005). For example, prior to World War II, regional isolation in the United States allowed the development of distinct regional cultures. With the rise of postwar mass culture, these differences have largely been lost. Today's strip malls, restaurants, and hotels are mostly the same everywhere in the United States. A similar trend is seen at the global level, where thousands of local languages and indigenous cultures are on the verge of extinction.

Similarly, every part of the world was historically inhabited by a unique and locally adapted flora and fauna. With globalization, human activities are dissolving the barriers that have separated animal and plant populations for the history of life on Earth, enabling some species to establish in new places and new habitats. Biotic composition is becoming increasingly similar across the globe, and we are entering a new period in the history of life characterized by a thorough mixing of the global biota—recently referred to as the "Homogecene" by Rosenzweig (2003). An unintended consequence of this mixing is that the imperilment of freshwater fauna in North America now rivals that of tropical rainforests (Ricciardi and Rasmussen 1999), with invasive species ranking as a leading threat to aquatic biodiversity (Richter et al. 1997; Wilcove et al. 1998; Sala et al. 2000). Annual economic losses resulting from invasive species in the United States alone were recently estimated at $137 billion (Pimentel et al. 2000).

What does this change mean for lakes and streams in Wisconsin? The state's 15,000 lakes and 45,000 miles of streams are among our most valuable natural resources. The abundance, diversity, and quality of Wisconsin's aquatic resources provide the cornerstone of the state's $12 billion annual travel and tourism industry, in addition to a wide range of ecosystem services, recreational opportunities, and aesthetic benefits. Here, we highlight the ecological change caused by the invasion of Wisconsin's aquatic ecosystems by a series of "emerging" exotic species.

Invasion Biology and Management

Introduction of nonnative species may be either intentional or accidental. The common carp, brown trout, and rainbow trout were all intentional introductions (Becker 1983). Because the economic and ecological costs of nonnative species continue to grow, natural resource agencies are moving away from the policy of stocking or introducing nonnatives. However the accidental introduction of exotic species is on the rise. More than 160 exotics have established in the Great Lakes, many during recent decades through the release of ballast water of transoceanic ships (Ricciardi and MacIsaac 2000). Exotic species now dominate the food webs of the Great Lakes resulting in profound ecological and economic impacts (Mills et al. 1994; chapter 12). Some of these exotics are now spreading to inland lakes and streams through interconnected waterways and canals and by hitchhiking on recreational watercraft. Following Lodge (1993), "colonists" are individuals of a species introduced into an ecosystem beyond their native range. If a population establishes, spreads, and becomes a nuisance, it is considered "invasive." Species native to other continents are "exotic," while "nonnative" refers simply to species occurrences beyond their native range.

Interestingly, most colonists do not successfully establish, and most established populations do not become invasive (Williamson 1996). Two critical challenges facing researchers are predicting which systems will be invaded and which systems will be adversely impacted. To address such questions for the lakes and streams of Wisconsin, we need to consider the invasion process as comprised of three sequential steps or "filters" (figure 29.1). The first filter determines whether colonists can reach an

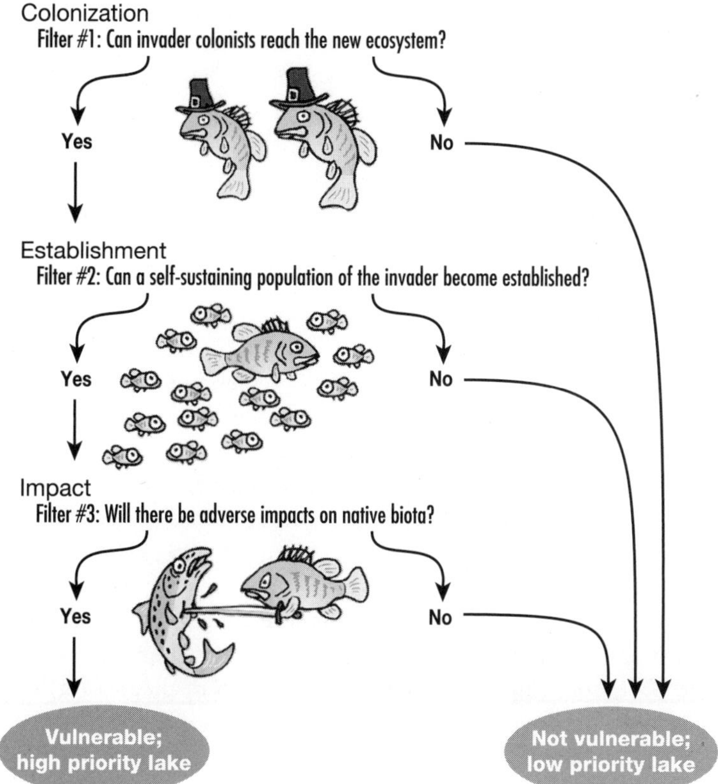

FIGURE 29.1 Sequential "filters" in the species invasion process.

uninvaded ecosystem. This depends on the dispersal mode of the invader, the frequency of human visitation, and the potential for dispersal through stream networks. The second filter determines whether the invader is capable of surviving, reproducing, and establishing a self-sustaining population in the new ecosystem. In cases where colonists reach an ecosystem, they often fail to establish a population. This may be due to inappropriate environmental or biotic conditions, or the suite of problems encountered by populations at low numbers (Pimm 1991). The third filter determines whether an established invader adversely impacts the native ecosystems or biota. In some systems, invaders have little or no impact. In others, invaders wreak ecological and economic havoc.

The science of invasion biology is moving away from simple descriptions of impacts toward forecasting invasions and their impacts (Kolar and Lodge 2001, 2002; Vander Zanden, Olden, et al. 2004; Vander Zanden, Wilson, et al. 2004). Such forecasts allow us to target our efforts to control invaders to particular lakes most likely to benefit. For example, which lakes in Wisconsin are likely to receive colonists of an invader such as the zebra mussel? Of these lakes, which is likely to support a self-sustaining population? And of these lakes, which will be ecologically disrupted? This type of ecological forecasting can play an important role in invasive species management. By identifying vulnerable ecosystems, invasion prevention efforts can be targeted to sites where they will achieve the greatest benefit.

Species Accounts

We highlight five notorious species we see as emerging invaders of inland waters in Wisconsin: rusty crayfish, zebra mussels, spiny water flea, rainbow smelt, and common carp (see the distributions of three of these species in Wisconsin in figure 29.2). With the exception of common carp, species were chosen based on the following criteria: (1) their invasion poses a potential risk to aquatic ecosystems of the state, (2) they are early in the invasion process and have not yet realized their potential distribution, and (3) humans are responsible for spreading the species, implying that their spread can be slowed or halted through changes in human behavior. (Additional aquatic invaders are discussed in chapter 16.) Focusing on these emerging invaders provides the best opportunity to prevent future impacts. Fortunately, the number of invasive species impacting inland waters of Wisconsin is still relatively low, though the Great Lakes will undoubtedly remain an important source of new invaders to inland systems (chapter 12).

Rusty crayfish: This crayfish species is native to streams of the Ohio River basin (Ohio, Kentucky, Indiana, and Tennessee) and since the 1960s has spread across large parts of North America. In Wisconsin, they occupy a broad range of lakes and streams and have had pronounced impacts upon northern lakes (Wilson et al. 2004). Prior to being banned in 1983, rusty crayfish were widely used as live bait, making bait bucket release a major vector of introductions. Capelli and Magnuson (1983) found that rusty crayfish in Wisconsin's northern highlands lake district colonized areas close to major roads and highly developed lakeshores, indicating the importance of humans in its transport. Once in a watershed, rusty crayfish spread through interconnected waterways, though dispersal is slow relative to many other invaders. Nevertheless, comparison of survey data through time indicates rapid

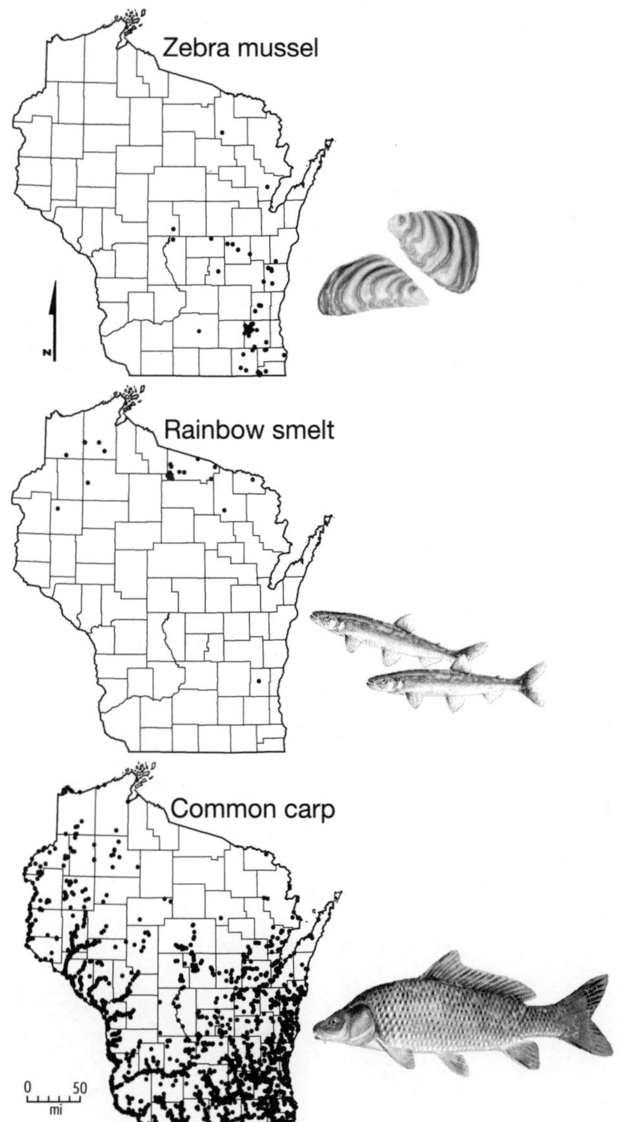

FIGURE 29.2 Maps showing the known distributions of three aquatic invasive species in Wisconsin.

expansion across the state. Comparison of pre-1980 and 2004–6 survey data reveals expansion from 3% to over 50% of sites sampled (figure 29.3).

What factors might limit the future distribution of rusty crayfish in Wisconsin? Rusty crayfish do not survive in waters with dissolved calcium

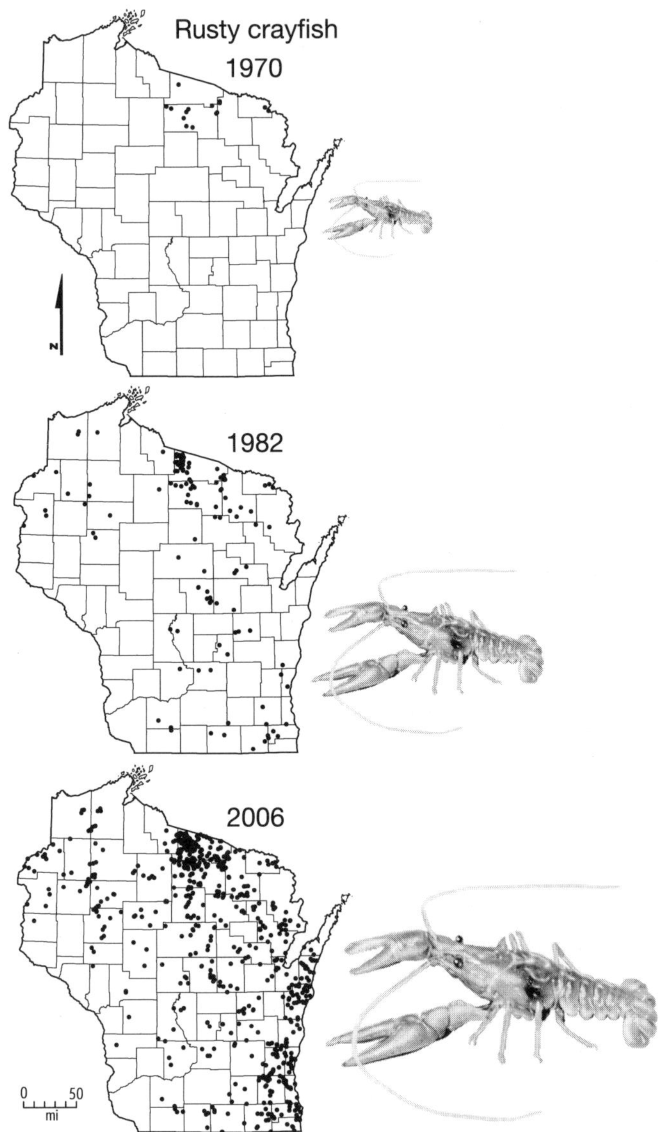

FIGURE 29.3 Progressive expansions in the range of rusty crayfish in Wisconsin.

(Ca^{2+}) concentrations under 2–3 mg/L (Capelli and Magnuson 1983). In Wisconsin, relatively few aquatic systems fall below this threshold level, indicating little potential to limit rusty crayfish distributions (figure 29.4). Rusty crayfish also have a strong preference for rocky substrate, which could influence their presence and abundance. When small, they are con-

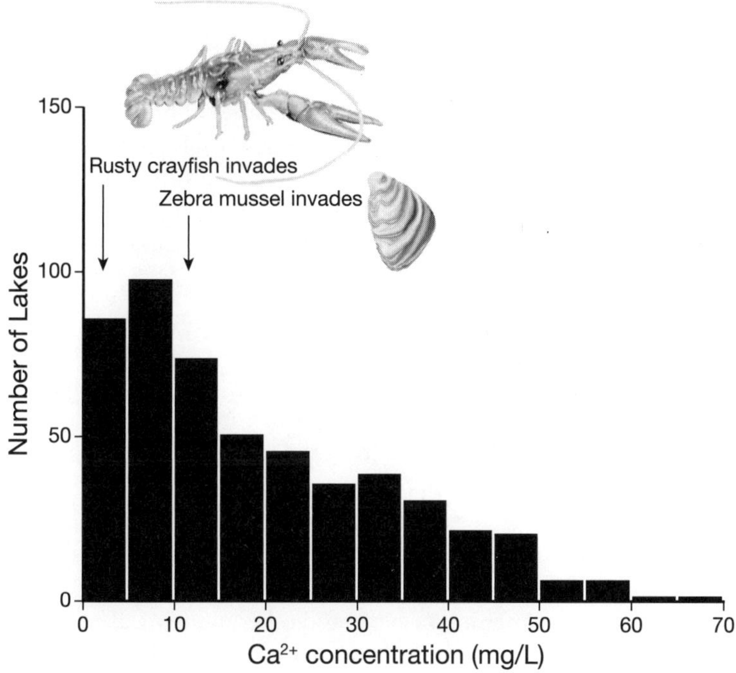

FIGURE 29.4 Calcium (Ca^{2+}) as a limiting factor for rusty crayfish and zebra mussels in Wisconsin.

sumed by fish like smallmouth bass, though they quickly become too large for predators.

Rusty crayfish displace native crayfishes (Capelli 1982) and often reach densities much higher than native crayfishes. Rusty crayfish are both voracious and omnivorous, foraging opportunistically on aquatic plants, detritus, invertebrates, and fish eggs (Lodge and Hill 1994). Invasion is associated with declines in snails, other invertebrates, and littoral fishes, likely through reductions in aquatic plants (Lodge and Hill 1994; Wilson et al. 2004; McCarthy et al. 2006; chapter 13). In short, this species has disrupted littoral zones and food chains and is of growing management concern. Concern is greatest in northern Wisconsin, but based on their rapid expansion during the past decades, this species could be a statewide threat. Perhaps the majority of aquatic ecosystems in Wisconsin are vulnerable to rusty crayfish, though the implications for most regions of the state remain unknown.

Zebra mussels: These mussels were a ballast water introduction from the Caspian Sea, first discovered in the Great Lakes in 1988. Zebra mussels quickly spread throughout the commercial shipping waterways of the Mississippi River and Great Lakes drainages. Colonization of inland waters has been slower although the invasion rate is now increasing. Recreational boaters and anglers are the major vector for dispersal (Johnson and Padilla 1996; Johnson et al. 2001), and studies of boaters have been used to identify lakes likely to receive zebra mussel colonists (Padilla et al. 1996). Zebra mussels have spread to a number of lakes in Wisconsin, although not all lakes are capable of supporting zebra mussels; many Wisconsin lakes lack the low dissolved calcium concentrations required to support a zebra mussel population (figure 29.4).

Zebra mussels are successful because they fill an empty niche in North American ecological communities. They physically modify the aquatic environment and habitats, earning them the label "ecosystem engineers" (Karatayev et al. 2002). They accomplish this by efficiently removing phytoplankton and other particles from the water column. Zebra mussels not only clear the water but also excrete large amounts of organic material. This organic material accumulates on the lake bottom, enriching bottom algae growth. Economically, they are also among the most notorious biofouling organisms in the world (Ludyanskiy et al. 1993), readily attaching to water intake pipes and other mechanical equipment, thereby damaging infrastructure. In addition, they adhere to (and kill) native mussels, accelerating the decline of our already imperiled freshwater mussel fauna (Ricciardi et al. 1998).

Spiny water flea: The spiny water flea (SWF) is a free-swimming predatory crustacean native to lakes of northern Europe and Asia. This species arrived in North America in ship ballast water and was first discovered in Lake Huron in 1984. It quickly spread to the other Great Lakes and has since spread to over 50 inland lakes in Ontario and numerous lakes in Michigan, Minnesota, New York, Wisconsin, and Ohio by hitchhiking on recreational watercraft (Yan et al. 1992; MacIsaac et al. 2004). SWF is relatively ineffective at moving from lake to lake by hitchhiking on recreational watercraft. Thus, only lakes near the Great Lakes (or other invaded lakes) are considered most vulnerable. Studies from North America and Europe indicate that SWF tend to inhabit large, deep, clear lakes (MacIsaac et al. 2000). Based on this, a large number of lakes in Wisconsin are capable of supporting this species.

The first SWF population in Wisconsin was discovered in 2003 in the Gile Flowage in Iron County. This impoundment was not considered a likely candidate for SWF invasion based on its poor water clarity. On the other hand, this impoundment lies in close proximity to Lake Superior. The location of the Gile Flowage allows it to serve as a stepping stone for SWF to colonize the hundreds of potentially vulnerable lakes of the

Northern Highlands Lake District that offer suitable habitat for the SWF (Havel et al. 2005).

SWF can become abundant in lakes and are a voracious predator upon native zooplankton. Their introduction in North American lakes has resulted in dramatic declines in the native zooplankton community (Yan et al. 2002). SWF are a preferred prey of large-sized zooplantivorous fishes (Coulas et al. 1998), but their long spine inhibits consumption by smaller fishes including juvenile game fish. The replacement of edible zooplankton species with largely inedible SWF could have negative impacts on small fishes, though these food web interactions are poorly understood at present.

Rainbow smelt: This anadromous species is native to northern coastal regions of North America. Rainbow smelt were successfully introduced into Crystal Lake in Michigan almost a century ago and spread through the upper Great Lakes during the 1920s and 1930s. From there, they effectively dispersed through inland lakes and rivers and now occupy portions of Mississippi and Hudson Bay drainages (Franzin et al. 1994). Smelt continue to colonize isolated inland lakes and now occupy at least 24 inland Wisconsin lakes (figure 29.2; Becker 1983; Lyons et al. 2000). While smelt can disperse through rivers, smelt introductions in Wisconsin are closely associated with lakeshore development, indicating an important role for human introductions (Hrabik and Magnuson 1999). There is anecdotal evidence indicating some anglers have intentionally introduced rainbow smelt into northern Wisconsin lakes. Another likely vector is the unintentional introduction of fertilized eggs into lakes while cleaning and processing smelt collected from other lakes.

While rainbow smelt prefer deep, oligogrophic lakes, they can inhabit lakes spanning a wide range of conditions (Evans and Loftus 1987). Mercado-Silva et al. (2006) estimated that more than 500 lakes in Wisconsin are candidates for smelt invasion, indicating that there remains great potential for further spread of this species. Rainbow smelt have had dramatic negative impacts on important native fish species such as lake whitefish, lake herring, yellow perch, and walleye in Wisconsin and elsewhere (Evans and Loftus 1987; Hrabik et al. 1998). Rainbow smelt predation was responsible for the decline of cisco in Sparkling Lake, while competition with smelt caused the extirpation of yellow perch in Crystal Lake (Hrabik et al. 1998). In addition, numerous lakes in Vilas County have lost reproducing walleye populations following smelt infestation. Smelt introductions also correspond with increased levels of pollutants such as mercury and PCBs in game fish (Vander Zanden and Rasmussen 1996). Though smelt are a small-sized forage fish, they commonly feed on other fishes, thereby adding an additional link to the food chain and generating greater pollutant biomagnification.

Common carp: First shipped to Wisconsin in 1880, carp were immediately propagated in hatcheries and intentionally introduced widely throughout the state (Becker 1983). Today, carp are scarce in the colder, cleaner lakes and rivers of northern Wisconsin but remain widespread and abundant in the shallow, warm lakes and rivers of southern Wisconsin (figure 29.2; Becker 1983). Carp occupy habitats that are often highly degraded, with high water temperatures, high sediment and nutrient loading, and low oxygen.

Not only do carp inhabit degraded waters, but the presence of carp further degrades aquatic ecosystems and worsens water quality problems (Cahn 1929; Becker 1983; Parkos et al. 2003). Carp directly consume and uproot aquatic plants . They actively resuspend bottom sediments, thereby increasing turbidity and reducing light levels and macrophyte growth (figure 29.5). In turn, the loss of macrophytes allows for further increases in turbidity due to wind-induced sediment resuspension (Scheffer et al. 1993). Carp are now widely recognized as a nuisance species with large impacts on aquatic habitats and water quality.

FIGURE 29.5 The effects of common carp on water quality and clarity. The effects are directly evident in this aerial photo of a carp exclosure in Lake Wingra near Edgewood College, Madison. Carp cause turbidity by consuming and uprooting aquatic plants via feeding and nesting, resuspending sediments, and reducing light levels and macrophyte growth.

Carp removal efforts, such as those undertaken at Horicon Marsh, have not proven to be particularly efficient or effective. However, dam removal and other habitat improvements hold tremendous promise. The more than 4,000 man-made impoundments dotting Wisconsin's landscape typically provide ideal habitat for carp—shallow, weedy, warm water. Removal of the Milwaukee River's Woolen Mills Dam resulted in a 80% decline in carp and a corresponding 10-fold increase in smallmouth bass (Kanehl et al. 1997). Similar declines in carp and recovery of game fish are occurring in response to the recent dam removals on the Baraboo River in Wisconsin.

Invasive species of the future: Though we have focused on a handful of emerging aquatic invaders in Wisconsin, there are many other exotic species that pose a potential threat to the aquatic ecosystems of Wisconsin. A giant snakehead was captured in the Rock River (September 2003), and a closely related species, the northern snakehead, was captured in Lake Michigan near Chicago (October 2004). Fortunately, there is no evidence that these species have established self-sustaining populations. Asian carp species are moving northward through the Mississippi River system and are poised to enter Lake Michigan. Other exotics such as the round goby, tubenose goby, rudd, Eurasian ruffe, threespine stickleback, and white perch currently inhabit coastal Great Lakes habitats (Lyons et al. 2000) and populations could spread to inland waters.

Summary

Invasive species are a key driver of ecological change and contribute to biotic homogenization and the loss of ecosystem services (Lodge 1993). Some of these changes are apparent, while others, particularly those involving interactions among invaders, are difficult to predict. For example, there is concern that the current suite of invaders may actually create conditions favorable for future invasions, a process known as "invasional meltdown." When it comes to the invaders, the future will undoubtedly hold many more surprises.

Fortunately, much can be done to minimize the spread and impacts of aquatic invaders, and the targeted prevention of future invasions should be a central pillar of management efforts (Kolar and Lodge 2002; Vander Zanden, Olden, et al. 2004; Vander Zanden, Wilson, et al. 2004). As is the case with human health, an ounce of prevention is worth a pound of cure (Leung et al. 2002). An effective management strategy will involve a mix of preventing the further spread of invasives while simultaneously adapting to the presence of exotics in many of our lakes and streams.

Finding ways of sustaining native species in the face of this onslaught of invaders poses a unique management challenge. It will require the commitment of diverse stakeholders—lake associations, local and tribal governments, resource agencies, researchers, nonprofit groups, anglers, educators, and the general public. Legislative efforts should ensure that aquaculture, aquarium trade, biological supply and live bait trade—all potential vectors of aquatic invasive species—do not further contribute to the problem. In cases where invaders are already established, there is a need for thoughtful and effective control and eradication efforts.

One common feature of these aquatic invaders is the role of human activities in aiding their spread. Thus, the future state of aquatic ecosystems in Wisconsin undoubtedly depends upon whether the present generation is willing to take the necessary steps to halt the further spread of invasives. Simple behavior changes among citizens can make a tremendous difference in the future spread of aquatic invasives: (1) clean plants, mud, and any other aquatic materials from boats, trailers, and equipment before leaving boat landings; (2) drain bilge, live-well, bait-well, and motor water before leaving boat landings; (3) thoroughly wash and dry anything in contact with the water (boats, trailers, and equipment) before launching a boat on another lake; and (4) never release plants or animals into a body of water unless they originate from that body of water, and dispose of unused live bait (including earthworms) in the trash. Perhaps more than any other form of ecological change examined in this book, collective acts of personal responsibility could make a tremendous difference.

Acknowledgments

Financial support was provided by the Wisconsin Department of Natural Resources, the Wisconsin Coastal Management Program, the University of Wisconsin Sea Grant Program, and the North-Temperate Lakes Long Term Ecological Research Program. Lucas Joppa, Pieter Johnson, Julian Olden, and Norman Mercado-Silva contributed in various ways to the work presented here.

References

Becker, G. C. 1983. Fishes of Wisconsin. Madison: University of Wisconsin Press.

Berrill, M., L. Hollett, A. Margosian, and J. Hudson. 1985. Variation in tolerance to low environmental pH by the crayfish *Orconectes rus-*

ticus, *O. propinquus*, and *Cambarus robustus*. Canadian Journal of Zoology 63:2586–2589.

Cahn, A. R. 1929. The effect of carp on a small lake: The carp as a dominant. Ecology 10:271–275.

Capelli, G. M. 1982. Displacement of northern Wisconsin crayfish by *Orconectes rusticus* (Girard). Limnology and Oceanography 27:741–745.

Capelli, G. M., and J. J. Magnuson. 1983. Morphoedaphic and biogeographical analysis of crayfish distribution in northern Wisconsin. Journal of Crustacean Biology 3:548–564.

Coulas, R. A., H. J. MacIsaac, and W. Dunlop. 1998. Selective predation on an introduced zooplankter (*Bythotrephes cederstroemi*) by lake herring (*Coregonus artedii*) in Harp Lake, Ontario. Freshwater Biology 40:343–355.

Evans, D. O., and D. H. Loftus. 1987. Colonization of inland lakes in the Great Lakes region by rainbow smelt, *Osmerus mordax:* Their freshwater niche and effects on indigenous fishes. Canadian Journal of Fisheries and Aquatic Sciences 44(Suppl. 2):249–266.

Franzin, W. G., B. A. Barton, R. A. Remnant, D. B. Wain, and S. J. Pagel. 1994. Range extension, present and potential distribution, and possible effect of rainbow smelt on Hudson Bay drainage waters of Northwestern Ontario, Manitoba, and Minnesota. North American Journal of Fish Management 14:65–76.

Havel, J. E., C. E. Lee, and M. J. Vander Zanden. 2005. Do reservoirs facilitate invasions into landscapes? BioScience 55:518–525.

Hrabik, T. R., and J. J. Magnuson. 1999. Simulated dispersal of exotic rainbow smelt (*Osmerus mordax*) in a northern Wisconsin lake district and implications for management. Canadian Journal of Fisheries and Aquatic Sciences 56:35–42.

Hrabik, T. R., J. J. Magnuson, and A. S. McLain. 1998. Predicting the effects of rainbow smelt on native fishes in small lakes: Evidence from long-term research on two lakes. Canadian Journal of Fisheries and Aquatic Sciences 55:1364–1371.

Johnson, L. E., and D. K. Padilla. 1996. Geographic spread of exotic species: Ecological lessons and opportunities from the invasion of the zebra mussel *Dreissena polymorpha*. Biological Conservation 78:23–33.

Johnson, L. E., Ricciardi, A., and Carlton, J. T. 2001. Overland dispersal of aquatic invasive species: A risk assessment of transient recreational boating. Ecological Applications 11:1789–1799.

Kanehl, P. D., J. Lyons, and J. E. Nelson. 1997. Changes in the habitat and fish community of the Milwaukee River, Wisconsin, following removal of the Woolen Mills dam. North American Journal of Fish Management 17:387–400.

Karatayev, A. Y., L. E. Burlakova, and D. K. Padilla. 2002. Impacts of zebra mussels on aquatic communities and their role as ecosystem engineers. Pp. 433–446 in E. Leppakoski, S. Gollasch, and S. Olenin, eds. Invasive aquatic species of Europe—Distribution, impacts, and management. Dordrecht: Kluwer Academic Publishers.

Kolar, C. S., and D. M. Lodge. 2001. Progress in invasion biology: Predicting invaders. Trends in Ecology and Evolution 16:199–204.

———. 2002. Ecological predictions and risk assessment for alien fishes in North America. Science 298:1233–1236.

Leung, B., D. M. Lodge, D. Finnoff, J. F. Shogren, M. A. Lewis, and G. Lamberti. 2002. An ounce of prevention or a pound of cure: Bioeconomic risk analysis of invasive species. Proceedings of the Royal Society of London Series B–Biological Sciences 269:2407–2413.

Lodge, D. M. 1993. Biological invasions: Lessons for ecology. Trends in Ecology and Evolution 8:133–137.

Lodge, D. M., and A. M. Hill. 1994. Factors governing species composition, population size, and productivity of cool-water crayfishes. Nordic Journal of Freshwater Research 69:111–136.

Ludyanskiy, M. L., D. McDonald, and D. MacNeill. 1993. Impact of the zebra mussel, a bivalve invader. BioScience 43:533–544.

Lyons, J., P. A. Cochran, and D. Fago. 2000. Wisconsin fishes 2000: Status and distribution. Madison: University of Wisconsin Sea Grant Institute.

MacIsaac, H. J., J. V. M. Borbely, J. R. Muirhead, and P. A. Graniero. 2004. Backcasting and forecasting biological invasions of inland lakes. Ecological Applications 14:773–783.

MacIsaac, H. J., H. A. M. Ketelaars, I. A. Grigorovich, C. W. Ramcharan, and N. D. Yan. 2000. Modeling *Bythotrephes longimanus* invasion in the Great Lakes basin based on its European distribution. Archiv für Hydrobiologie 149:1–21.

McCarthy, J. M., C. L. Hein, J. D. Olden, and M. J. Vander Zanden. 2006. Coupling long-term studies with meta-analysis to investigate impacts of invasive crayfish on zoobenthic communities. Freshwater Biology 51:224–235.

Mercado-Silva, N., J. D. Olsen, J. T. Maxted, T. R. Hrabik, and M. J. Vander Zanden. 2006. Forecasting the spread of invasive rainbow smelt (*Osmerus mordax*) in the Laurentian Great Lakes region of North America. Conservation Biology 20:1740–1749.

Mills, E. L., J. H. Leach, J. T. Carlton, and C. L. Secor. 1994. Exotic species and the integrity of the Great Lakes. BioScience 44:666–676.

Olden, J. D., M. E. Douglas, and M. R. Douglas. 2005. The human dimension of biotic homogenization. Conservation Biology 19:2036–2038.

Olsen, T. M., D. M. Lodge, G. M. Capelli, and R. J. Houlihan. 1991. Mechanisms of impact of an introduced crayfish (*Orconectes rusticus*) on littoral congeners, snails, and macrophytes. Canadian Journal of Fisheries and Aquatic Sciences 48:1853–1861.

Padilla, D. K., M. A. Chotkowski, and L. A. J. Buchan. 1996. Predicting the spread of zebra mussels (*Dreissena polymorpha*) to inland waters using boater movement patterns. Global Ecology and Biogeography Letters 5:353–359.

Parkos, J. J., V. J. Santucci, and D. H. Wahl. 2003. Effects of adult common carp (*Cyprinus carpio*) on multiple trophic levels in shallow mesocosms. Canadian Journal of Fisheries and Aquatic Sciences 60:182–192.

Pimentel, D., L. Lach, R. Zuniga, and D. Morrison. 2000. Environmental and economic costs associated with nonindigenous species in the United States. BioScience 50:53–64.

Pimm, S. L. 1991. The balance of nature? Chicago: University of Chicago Press.

Ricciardi, A., and H. J. Maclsaac. 2000. Recent mass invasion of the North American Great Lakes by Ponto-Caspian species. Trends in Ecology and Evolution 15:62–65.

Ricciardi, A., R. J. Neves, and J. B. Rasmussen. 1998. Impending extinctions of North American freshwater mussels following the zebra mussel (*Dressena polymorpha*) invasion. Journal of Animal Ecology 67:613–619.

Ricciardi, A., and J. B. Rasmussen. 1999. Extinction rates of North American freshwater fauna. Conservation Biology 13:1220–1222.

Richter, B. D., D. P. Braun, M. A. Mendelson, and L. L. Master. 1997. Threats to imperiled freshwater fauna. Conservation Biology 11:1081–1093.

Rosenzweig, M. L. 2003. Win-win ecology. Oxford: Oxford University Press.

Sala, O. E., F. S. Chapin, J. J. Armesto, E. Berlow, J. Bloomfield, R. Dirzo, E. Huber-Sanwald, L. F. Huenneke, R. B. Jackson, A. Kinzig, R. Leemans, D. M. Lodge, H. A. Mooney, M. Oesterheld, N. L. Poff, M. T. Sykes, B. H. Walker, M. Walker, and D. H. Wall. 2000. Biodiversity:

Global biodiversity scenarios for the year 2100. Science 287:1770–1774.

Scheffer, M., S. H. Hosper, M. L. Meijer, and B. Moss. 1993. Alternative equilibria in shallow lakes. Trends in Ecology and Evolution 8:275–279.

Vander Zanden, M. J., J. D. Olden, J. H. Thorne, and N. E. Mandrak. 2004. Predicting occurrences and impacts of bass introductions in north temperate lakes. Ecological Applications 14:132–148.

Vander Zanden, M. J., and J. B. Rasmussen. 1996. A trophic position model of pelagic food webs: Impact on contaminant bioaccumulation in lake trout. Ecological Monographs 66:451–477.

Vander Zanden, M. J., K. A. Wilson, J. M. Casselman, and N. D. Yan. 2004. Species introductions and their impacts in North American Shield lakes. Pp. 239–263 in J. Gunn, R. A. Ryder, and R. Steedman, eds. Boreal shield watersheds: Lake trout ecosystems in a changing environment. Boca Raton: CRC Press.

Wilcove, D. S., D. Rothstein, J. Dubow, A. Phillips, and E. Losos. 1998. Quantifying threats to imperiled species in the United States. Bioscience 48:607–615.

Williamson, M. 1996. Biological invasions. New York: Chapman and Hall.

Wilson, E. O. 1994. The diversity of life. London: Penguin.

Wilson, K. A., J. J. Magnuson, D. M. Lodge, A. M. Hill, T. K. Kratz, W. L. Perry, and T. V. Willis. 2004. A long-term rusty crayfish (*Orconectes rusticus*) invasion: Disperal patterns and community change in a north temperate lake. Canadian Journal of Fisheries and Aquatic Sciences 61:2255–2266.

Yan, N. D., W. I. Dunlop, T. W. Pawson, and L. E. MacKay. 1992. *Bythotrephes cederstroemi* (Schoedler) in Muskoka lakes: First records of the European invader in inland lakes in Canada. Canadian Journal of Fisheries and Aquatic Sciences 49:422–426.

Yan, N. D., R. Girard, and S. Bourdreau. 2002. An introduced invertebrate predator (*Bythotrephes*) reduces zooplankton species richness. Ecology Letters 5:481–485.

30 Nonnative Terrestrial Species Invasions

S. Kelly Kearns

A great change has taken place on our landscape in the last 50 years. In the 1930s, farmers were encouraged to plant reed canary grass for forage and Eurasian shrubs for wildlife habitat. In just a few decades, these and other introduced species have exploded. Invasive nonnative species are rapidly inundating our native landscape, resulting in one of our most serious environmental issues. These species can eliminate wildlife habitat, displace native plants, drastically diminish farm incomes, and interfere with forest regeneration. For example, the emerald ash borer—accidentally introduced from Asia into the Midwest—was first detected in 2002 in Detroit, Michigan, and Windsor, Ontario. Within two years, the introduction spread to become an infestation, damaging and killing over 6 million ash trees in southern Michigan and Ontario. Despite strenuous efforts to prevent its spread to Upper Michigan, egg-infested firewood made it to a campground there in the summer of 2005, risking its spread to Wisconsin's 727 million ash trees. Even if this northern infestation is contained, Wisconsin's trees remain at risk from the south because an established infestation was discovered near Indianapolis in late 2005 and several more in northern Illinois in 2006. Some of these infestations appear to date to 1998, suggesting that current efforts to contain the emerald ash borer in the Midwest may be too little and too late (Cumming-Carlson and Walker 2004; see dnr.wi.gov/forestry/fh/ash).

Unfortunately, we do not face just one or a few invaders but an increasing swarm of invasive species whose impacts cascade through many of Wisconsin's ecosystems. Eurasian shrub honeysuckles and buckthorns now form dense stands under forest canopies, often shading out tree seedlings struggling to survive. With few native trees to replace them, many of our forests are slowly becoming Eurasian shrub thickets.

Earthworms, which many presume to be good for soil health, are actually not native to glaciated regions of North America. Most earthworm species in Wisconsin were introduced from Europe, traveling with potted plants in soil. Research in Minnesota reveals that these worms are eliminating the leaf litter layer in forests, which limits the establishment of many native forest plants, including sugar maple (Hale 2003). These worm invasions may initiate irreversible changes that threaten the ecological health of our deciduous forests (Bohlen et al. 2004).

Invasive plants, animals, and disease organisms strongly affect both our biological resources and economy. Some scientists believe that invasions are inevitable and feel that it is futile to attempt to stop them. However, most who work with invasives feel strongly that much can and should be done to protect natural areas from the impacts of invasive species. A broader awareness of which species are of concern and the problems they cause is key to containing the current infestations and preventing the import of new harmful species. This chapter examines the status of invasive terrestrial species in Wisconsin: the history of their introduction and spread, their impacts, projections for future change, a summary of what is currently being done at different levels, and recommendations for further actions. Effects of invasive aquatic species are discussed in chapters 12, 16, and 29.

This chapter focuses on exotic plants as well as plant pests and associated invasive animals. While researchers know a great deal about the insects and pathogens that impact forest trees and agricultural crops, little is known about the pests that impact native plants that are not harvested commercially. Except for feral cats and hogs, mute swans, pigeons, and a few other birds and mammals, we have few troublesome nonnative terrestrial vertebrates in Wisconsin.

A History of Invasive Nonnative Species

Ecologically, the flora of Wisconsin is young (chapter 5). As the glaciers receded, plants migrated into the land that is now Wisconsin. They came by wind and water and on the hooves, hair, and feathers of wild animals. As each new species arrived, it found a niche and became established, or it failed to adapt and disappeared. The ecological communities that developed were driven by these patterns of species immigration and extinction. Native people accelerated the movement of plants and animals across the continent, largely through trade. Europeans greatly accelerated the process. They arrived in North America with European plants, livestock, soil, invertebrates, and disease organisms. Invasive European diseases ravaged Native American populations. Early settlers to the Midwest brought domestic livestock and European plants for food and medicines and to remind them of their homeland. Both the intentional crops and the incidental weeds and pests took hold as the prairie sod was tilled and the forests were felled. Plants were imported, bred, and distributed for livestock forage, food, and erosion control. The nursery trade developed, and plants were often selected for their hardiness and ability to withstand northern climates and pest damage. With economic globalization, invasions have accelerated. Species from anywhere in the world can now enter Wisconsin via many pathways, including vehicles (mowers, all-terrain vehicles, logging trucks, tractor trailers, campers, boats, etc.); hay, feed, and seed; gravel, soil, and mulch; firewood, lumber, packing crates, and live plants; livestock, horses, pets, and humans; and wildlife, water, and wind.

Perhaps because Wisconsin is located in the center of the continent, it has suffered fewer invasions by Eurasian species than have the coastal states. Many of the plants and pests that could become troublesome in Wisconsin are not yet successfully established. Cold winters have excluded many warmer climate species. However, growth in commerce and the warmer and shorter winters recorded in recent years (chapter 3) improve chances of success even for less hardy species. Throughout North America there are dozens of invasive plants in environments similar to Wisconsin that have not yet been introduced to the state. These would probably establish rapidly if they were not quickly detected and contained.

Characteristics of Invasive Plants

There are thousands of nonnative species established in Wisconsin including over 800 plants. Most of these are established as small populations and of little ecological concern. Other nonnative plants are widespread throughout much of the state. A subset of these naturalized plants, in turn, are invasive (see sidebar on p. 442). With increased movement of

Plants in Wisconsin's Flora

Data are from Wetter et al. (2001) and Reinartz (2003).

- Total taxa = 3,243
- Native taxa = 2,366
- Introduced taxa = 877 (27% of the flora)
- Serious current invasives in natural areas ≈ 35
- Less dominant, locally invasive, or disturbance related ≈ 148
- Potential for becoming serious ≈ 40 (approximately 17 of these are not yet found in the state)

plant material, rates of disturbance, and climate change, we can expect this list to grow in coming years.

Several factors affect whether a species will adapt to and thrive in a new environment, and most invasive plants display some combination of weedy characteristics (see sidebar below). Many invasive plants produce large numbers of seeds and spread by root suckers, rhizomes, or other vegetative means. In their native environments, these species were kept in check by locally coevolved predators, diseases, and parasites. When brought to a new environment, however, such species are often freed of such constraints, allowing them to spread rapidly. Without natural enemies, natural selection can favor the reallocation of resources away from defense into growth and reproduction. In fact, some of these plants were intentionally selected for traits that rendered them aggressive (e.g., reed canary grass, crown vetch, and kudzu). Some of these plants

Characteristics Found in Many Weedy Invasive Plant Species

- Large numbers of seeds
- Vegetative reproduction
- The ability to resprout from roots
- The ability to quickly colonize disturbed sites
- The ability to form symbioses with nitrogen-fixing bacteria in the soil
- Chemical defenses to herbivory
- Few if any predators, parasites, and diseases
- Allelopathy (toxic chemicals that affect nearby plants)
- Growth early and/or late in the season
- The ability to adapt to new environments and disturbance
- Rapid growth rates, especially in the presence of increased nutrients

have beneficial uses in agriculture, erosion control, and land reclamation but are invasive when they spread to nearby natural areas.

Characteristics of Invaded Sites

Invasive species are not randomly distributed, because certain sites are more vulnerable to invasion. These sites include fragmented (and roaded) landscapes, those that are actively grazed and browsed, and sites where fires are suppressed. Soil disturbances include the draining and filling of wetlands, residential and commercial development, and certain animal-caused disturbances (e.g., by exotic earthworms and feral hogs). These are often accompanied by inputs of nutrients like nitrogen and shifts in climate. All of these factors can interact to favor invasions of species like reed canary grass, which greatly outcompete native species (Kercher et al. 2004; chapter 15).

Certain disturbances promote invasion and establishment, while other invasive species thrive under a lack of appropriate disturbance, such as fire. It is therefore difficult to generalize about how disturbance will affect patterns of invasion. Some argue that areas not heavily disturbed by humans or natural events like flooding will resist invasions. There are some data to support this. However, even relatively undisturbed systems like natural areas are increasingly being invaded as surrounding landscapes become more fragmented and human dominated. Species such as garlic mustard and purple loosestrife, for example, readily invade if seeds or other propagules are introduced into appropriate habitats from nearby roads, trails, or invaded habitats. Among natural communities, some are more vulnerable than others. Cliffs, dunes, and bogs contain relatively few invasive plants. Most lands, however, are vulnerable to bird-dispersed plants, including buckthorns and honeysuckles. Riparian zones and wetlands are being invaded by water-dispersed plants, like Eurasian water milfoil and purple loosestrife. Even closed-canopy forestlands are being invaded by garlic mustard, and high quality remnant prairies now often contain invasive plants, like yellow sweet-clover and multiflora rose.

Impacts of Invasives

How do invasive plants restructure native communities? Some alter soil chemistry and/or microbial communities. Others like spotted knapweed are allelopathic, exuding chemicals that interfere with the growth of neighboring plants (Callaway and Aschehoug 2000). Still others like buckthorn shade out the ground flora, slowing the accumulation of litter and discouraging fires in communities such as savannas that depend on fires. Invasive plants also affect native animals in unexpected ways. At Chicago's Morton Arboretum, certain native birds selected nest sites in the early leafing buckthorn and honeysuckle that were lower to the ground and were therefore more likely to be attacked by predators (Schmidt and Whelan 1999).

Forest diseases and insect pests provide further insights into the changes wrought by invasive species. Chestnut blight killed every American chestnut tree in the eastern United States, and Dutch elm disease had similar effects on the American elm. Major insects and diseases looming on the horizon threaten most hemlock, spruce, oak, maple, and ash. Impacts of invasive plants on forests are complex, subtle, and less studied. Eurasian shrubs and vines can limit tree regeneration, outcompete seedlings and saplings, and even damage and slow the growth of mature trees (Frappier et al. 2003; Hartman 2005). These impacts are so apparent that few scientists study or quantify them.

The economic costs of controlling invasive shrubs are better quantified. In the course of timber production and land management, invasive shrub removal and restoration of native species costs upward of $5,000/acre. Economic costs of other invasive plants are also striking, amounting to more than $15 billion for weed control and crop loss in 1994. Efforts to control weedy plants along roadsides and in forestry and aquatic systems totaled at least an additional $5 billion in 1994 (Westbrooks 1998).

The impacts of invasive plants on rare species are largely unknown. Rare species often have specific habitat needs and could be the first to disappear with invasion. Some rare species are directly affected; the invasive spotted knapweed outcompetes the federally threatened dune thistle and eliminates lupine habitat critical for federally endangered Karner blue butterflies (U.S. Fish and Wildlife Service 2003).

Projected Changes

How will factors including climate change (chapter 31), increased nutrient inputs, increased global trade, hybridization, and genetic modifications to existing organisms affect rates of invasion? More species will likely become significant problems, and infestations will likely worsen in response to these changes. The Internet makes it easy to purchase plants and animals from all parts of the country and around the world; most orders enter the United States without being inspected. We can expect problems with some of these species, not to mention the organisms that hitchhike along.

Why hasn't the importation of invasive species been made illegal? At the federal level, the Noxious Weed Law is restricted to those species proven to cause extensive harm but not yet widespread. Even if such legislation were passed and was strictly enforced, it would not stop invasions by extant introduced species that are still expanding their geographical range like Kudzu, Japanese stilt grass, and hemlock wooly adelgid. These species are not yet in Wisconsin but appear likely to invade.

Of the many invasive plants already here, how many have already reached their maximum range and abundance, and how many will continue to spread? Unfortunately, probably only reed canary grass has already filled much of its potential range in the state. Most other plants are still spreading. Some, such as garlic mustard, are doing so at a rapid rate. Furthermore, we do not always know which naturalized plants already present will become invasive later. Education plays a key role in giving a concerned public a sense of responsible stewardship and concern for uninvaded natural areas. These areas can be kept relatively protected, but only if we make concerted efforts to monitor them carefully each year and report and remove invaders as soon as they arrive. Already widespread invasive plants are too abundant to eradicate. We can, however, keep uninfested areas weed free, especially in priority natural areas. We outline how citizens can participate in these important efforts below.

A concerted effort to stall the march of invasive species will require action at all levels of government. Funding is needed for education, research, prevention, and containment efforts. Public awareness of biological pollution should become as widespread as it was for air and water pollution in the 1970s.

Taking Action against Invasives

The National Response. Because invasive species do not stop at state lines, regulations and coordination are needed at the federal level. The recent accidental introduction of sudden oak death (SOD) reflects the importance of a federal response. SOD affects dozens of species of native and ornamental plants. Because it is particularly damaging to oaks, SOD has the potential to significantly alter oak forests throughout North America. This pathogen entered the United States on infested nursery stock. It was rapidly detected and partially contained through a well-organized and well-funded federal program that monitors for plant diseases and regulates the movement of nursery stock. In Wisconsin, all nurseries that received stock from infested nurseries were carefully inspected for the disease. There is no analogous program for invasive plants, although one is sorely needed.

In recent years federal agencies have been more responsive to problems posed by invasive species. The National Invasive Species Council (NISC; see www.invasivespecies.gov) was established through an executive order issued by President Clinton. This body provides some coordination at the federal level. A more action-oriented group of staff from key federal agencies formed the Federal Interagency Committee on the Management of Noxious and Exotic Weeds. This group works with NISC and the Invasive Species Advisory Committee to propose policies and programs. As a result, most federal resource management agencies now have invasive species teams, some staff and funding, and at least drafts of invasive species management plans. Despite these efforts, there has been little change in federal funding or policies. Free trade agreements and e-commerce are increasing importation, escalating the risk of new invasive species establishing. The transfer of many port customs duties to the Office of Homeland Security has resulted in decreased inspection for pests and other organisms (despite the clear and present danger they present to our national economic and ecological security). Unless the federal government increases restrictions on nonnative species imports while increasing inspections, prevention strategies, and funding, even the best state efforts to combat invasive species will be impaired. At a regional level, the Midwest Natural Resources Group has formed. Consisting of all of the regional supervisors of federal agencies, they have appointed a staff-level group working across agencies to implement actions aimed at combating invasive species in the Great Lakes region.

Wisconsin State Responses. The Department of Natural Resources (DNR) and Department of Agriculture, Trade, and Consumer Protection (DATCP) share authority and responsibilities for some invasive species in Wisconsin. However, these agencies lack adequate authority, coordination, staff, and funding to fully address invasive species issues. Coordinating education, research, inventory, prevention, and control efforts and the policies to oversee these requires staff and funding. Efforts by private landowners, municipalities, counties, and other state agencies partially fill these gaps, but more statewide (and nationwide) leadership is needed. One clear priority would be to establish a rapid response program capable of tracking, containing, and eradicating newly invading species.

DATCP has broad authority over all plant pests and has the authority to establish quarantines and to mandate the destruction of infested host plants. The DNR has an effective and well staffed Forest Health Program that combats harmful forest insects and diseases, sharing responsibilities with the DATCP for pests such as gypsy moth and emerald ash borer. In recent years gypsy moth containment has received a large amount of federal and state funding. Additionally, the DNR has an Invasive Species Team that coordinates agency efforts on invasive species issues. Current funding and staffing levels to address invasive plants are surprisingly small. The DNR's small Endangered Resources Program has provided most of the coordination to date, with funding coming from voluntary donations in the form of endangered resource license plate fees, income tax refund donations, and grants. The DNR's Forestry Division has recently reallocated funds within their program, placing additional emphasis on plants that might compromise forest health. They have hired an invasive plant coordinator, surveyed state forests for invasive plants, and initiated the development of Best Management Practices to minimize the spread of invasives.

Invasive plants are treated far differently than forest pests. Unlike most states, Wisconsin has no single agency with broad authority over weeds. The limited and largely ineffective noxious weed law only authorizes municipalities and counties to conduct enforcement and containment. The nuisance weed law limits the sale of only purple loosestrife and multiflora rose. DATCP does inspect nurseries and limits sales of these species.

Attempts have been made to develop a comprehensive state weed law, including a six-year effort by a diverse group of stakeholders. Because the proposed plan would require financial resources and agency staff from DATCP, DNR, and the University of Wisconsin–Extension to implement the program, it has not advanced. With severe state budget and staff cuts, these agencies lack the staff and the capacity to move forward with the plan.

The 2001 state budget established the Wisconsin Council on Invasive Species (WCIS; see www.invasivespecies.wi.gov) to prevent and reduce the harmful impacts of invasive species. It also authorized the DNR to classify invasive species. This work is largely accomplished through committees and agency staff. In 2004, WCIS, DNR, and DATCP began work on an invasive species classification system including legal restrictions and allowable activities for all categories of invasives. This system is being developed as a DNR administrative rule. In addition, revisions of some laws will be needed to fill in gaps in authority and enforcement. The Wisconsin Council on Forestry is also concerned about the impacts of invasive species on forest health. They created an Invasives Task Group, which in turn provided recommendations to the council.

These governor-level councils have some political clout, leading many to hope that the legislature and governor's office may respond with substantial legislation, administrative rules, and funding to implement these recommendations.

Inventory and monitoring. To effectively limit the spread of invasive species, we need an early response network that would detect new potentially invasive species as soon as they arrive and move quickly to contain new infestations before they spread. Within Wisconsin, several dozen projects gather, record, and map invasive plant occurrences. We are developing a centralized system where data can be entered from many sources and shared widely. The University of Wisconsin–Madison (www.botany.wisc.edu/wisflora) and University of Wisconsin–Stevens Point herbaria provide range maps for all vascular plants in the state, including nonnatives. However, these maps only include records from collected specimens, and invasive species are often underrepresented in herbarium collections. To address this issue, these herbarium maps are being expanded to include all reports of invasive plants. The DNR and the University of Wisconsin–Madison Herbarium also initiated an early detection effort in 2004. This project aims to identify potentially invasive plants when they are still localized or before they have spread to Wisconsin. Trained volunteers identify, report, collect, and map target species where they occur. With immediate follow-up, such populations can often be eradicated or contained. Control efforts are under way on dozens of infestations of new invaders, including black swallow-wort, Japanese hops, and Japanese hedge parsley.

Research. Research on invasive species biology and control has accelerated in recent years, but information gaps remain. Many scientists are now investigating why invasive species are so successful, whether invasions can be predicted, and how invasions displace native species and alter invaded environments. However, we still know little about the ecological and economic impacts that most invasive species cause. Much of our information comes from qualitative observations or anecdotal reports. We also need to learn more about how invasive species respond to particular biotic and abiotic factors and how they interact with other stresses to influence ecosystems. Information is lacking on how to effectively control some invasive species. Biological control (using natural enemies) can be inexpensive and surprisingly effective but requires careful testing in advance to ensure that native species will not suffer "collateral damage." Mechanical and chemical control are generally more expensive and labor intensive. Land managers often know a single method that is at least partially effective but may not know the most efficient methods, timing, tools, herbicides, and adjuvants to use to control each invasive species. Finally, we need research that explores how to restore ecosystems following invasive species control or removal.

Nongovernmental Organizations and Outreach. Many private organizations in the region confront invasive species. The Invasive Plants Association of Wisconsin (IPAW) formed in 2001. This nonprofit organization seeks to increase awareness of and take action against invasive plants. Measurable progress has been made in recent years. Today, most citizens recognize the problem of invasive species, and more landowners are becoming aware of the invasive species present on their property. Organizations including the University of Wisconsin–Extension have developed brochures, species identification cards, Web sites, displays, and slide shows. IPAW offers a speakers' bureau and electronic presentations (see www.ipaw.org). The University of Wisconsin Press recently published the first invasive plant manual for the Midwest, with hundreds of color photos and control recommendations (Czarapata 2005). WCIS, IPAW, DNR, and others sponsor Invasive Species Awareness Month each June. Field trips, volunteer workdays, and talks around the state help bring this important issue to a wide audience. At the regional level, the Midwestern Invasive Plant Network (www.MIPN.org) acts as a clearinghouse for outreach materials and research studies.

There is also a need to reach specific audiences. Roadside maintenance crews need to learn how to identify and time their mowing to control roadside weeds. Arborists need to know the symptoms of attacks by emerald ash borer, Asian long-horned beetle, and sudden oak death, as well as how to properly dispose of infested material and how to report infestations. Landowners and volunteers need information about effective weed control strategies and tactics. The opportunities for outreach are endless.

Individual and Local Actions. Individuals can do much to combat invasive species. One generally starts by learning more about the invasive species found in a region. The Web sites and books mentioned above are logical places to start learning species identification, impacts, and control methods. People who like to learn by doing can participate in volunteer work parties in local parks and natural areas to remove invasive species. Likewise, landowners can stop new infestations before they become uncontrollable. Because groups working together often accomplish much more than individuals working alone, many communities organize groups to cooperate on habitat restoration and removal of invasive species.

Individuals can locate and join an existing group or start their own group to monitor local natural areas, organize invasive species work parties, and share information. MPN has trained hundreds of people throughout the eastern states to develop Cooperative Weed Management Areas. These are local coalitions that work together to address local weed management challenges.

Legislators, county board members, and other decision makers need to hear from citizens as to the problems caused by invasives. Most municipalities are unaware of the threats posed by invasive species, and some local ordinances actually encourage their spread. Citizens can meet and share information with their local lawmakers, highway and parks maintenance staff. They can also take the initiative to revise local weed ordinances. Model ordinances already exist, and several communities around Milwaukee have passed strong revised weed laws.

Conclusion

The current spread of invasive species and our limited countermeasures to contain and eradicate these species offer little basis for optimism. New species continue to arrive, attracting only limited attention from the public. As additional species expand their ranges into new communities and new invaders arrive each year, the limited resources we have to combat them are spread ever more thinly. There are, however, many reasons to be optimistic. A growing segment of the public is aware of the problems posed by invasive plants, and many are active in controlling their spread. Government agencies and politicians are slowly awakening to the need to craft more effective policies and allocate more resources to this problem. Nonprofit organizations, municipalities, and even neighborhood organizations are mobilizing to eradicate invasive species from parks and preserves. Land management agencies now share their expertise and tools to help landowners control invasive species on their properties. New tools and approaches continue to emerge. Biological control agents show particular promise against certain invaders. Increased communication and research allows us to better predict species likely to invade. With more partner organizations and volunteers trained, we should be able to detect and contain new invasions more rapidly. If we had known 50 years ago only a fraction of what we now know of invasive ecology, we might have been able to prevent many of these invasions. However, looking ahead to the next 50 years, we have every reason to expect more invasions, but now we will be better prepared to contain them, ensuring that the efforts we make now will benefit our future ecosystems.

References

Bohlen, J. J., S. Scheu, C. M. Hale, M. A. McLeaen, S. Migge, P. M. Groffman, and D. Parkinson. 2004. Non-native invasive earthworms as agents of change in northern temperate forests. Frontiers in Ecology and the Environment 2:427–435.

Callaway, R. M., and E. T. Aschehoug. 2000. Invasive plants versus their new and old neighbors: A mechanism for exotic invasion. Science 290:521–523.

Cummings-Carlson, J., and M. Walker, eds. 2004. State Action Plan for Emerald Ash Borer. Madison: Wisconsin Department of Natural Resources, Wisconsin Department of Agriculture, Trade, and Consumer Protection, University of Wisconsin, U.S. Department of Agriculture (USDA) Forest Service, and USDA Animal and Plant Health Inspection Service.

Czarapata, E. 2005. Invasive Plants of the Upper Midwest: An Illustrated Guide to Identification and Control. Madison: University of Wisconsin Press.

Frappier, B., R. T. Eckert, and T. D. Lee. 2003. Potential impacts of the invasive exotic shrub *Rhamnus frangula* L. (glossy buckthorn) on the forests of southern New Hampshire. Northeastern Naturalist 10:277–296.

Hale, C. 2003. Ecological consequences of exotic invaders: interactions involving European earthworms and native plant communities in hardwood forests. Ph.D. diss., University of Minnesota, Duluth.

Hartman, K. 2005. The impacts, invasibility, and restoration ecology of an invasive shrub, Amur honeysuckle (*Lonicer maackii*). Ph.D. thesis, Ohio University, Athens.

Kercher, S. M., Q. J. Carpenter, and J. B. Zedler. 2004. Interrelationships of hydrologic disturbances, reed canary grass (*Phalaris arundinacea* L.), and native plants in Wisconsin wet meadows. Natural Areas Journal 24:316–325.

Reinartz, J. 2003. Invasive Plants Association of Wisconsin (IPAW) working list of the invasive plants of Wisconsin. IPAW newsletter, no. 4 (March). Available at http://www.ipaw.org/list/columns.htm.

Schmidt, K. A., and C. J. Whelan. 1999. Effects of exotic *Lonicera* and *Rhamnus* on songbird nest predation. Conservation Biology 13:1502–1506.

U.S. Fish and Wildlife Service. 2003. Final recovery plan for the Karner blue butterfly *(Lycaeides melissa samuelis)*. U.S. Fish and Wildlife Service, Fort Snelling, MN.

Westbrooks, R. 1998. Invasive Plants, Changing the Landscape of America: Fact Book. Washington, DC: Federal Interagency Committee for the Management of Noxious and Exotic Weeds.

Wetter, M. A., T. S. Cochrane, M. R. Black, H. H. Iltis, and P. E. Berry. 2001. Checklist of the Vascular Plants of Wisconsin. Madison: University of Wisconsin Press.

31 The Potential Futures of Wisconsin's Forested Landscapes

Robert M. Scheller and David J. Mladenoff

As you learned in chapters 5–7, Wisconsin's forests have changed in many different ways, reflecting shifts in climate, variable soils, the migration of species following glaciation, natural disturbances, past and current logging, fragmentation from roads, and continuing shifts in human land use. Forest ecologists, historians, and sociologists use data from many sources to infer how Great Lakes states forests have changed and how these changes reflect broader geographic and historical contexts. In this era of global environmental change, can we use the past to anticipate and understand the future? Or will future changes be unique and unpredictable? We grapple with these questions as we try to imagine Wisconsin's forests 100 years from now, exploring the consequences of factors like population growth and climate change.

People Intentionally Change the Forest

A significant obstacle to understanding the future of Wisconsin's forests—and, by extension, its rivers, lakes, and wetlands—lies in understanding how humans will use, reduce, or even expand forests in the future. In the past, patterns of human settlement and resource use shaped the forests (chapter 5). In northern Wisconsin, most lands deforested during the great cutover were slowly replaced by second-growth forest; others became homes or farms. After World War II, new groups began joined the resident farmers, loggers, and miners. These new arrivals often came for recreation rather than employment in extractive industries (Radeloff et al. 2001). In southern Wisconsin, settlement and land use changed drastically with the farms that arrived prior to the 20th century (chapters 2 and 8). Since then, change slowed, and then land use patterns changed direction as rapidly expanding cities and suburbs began to consume more land. Most farmland remained in crop or pasture (often intensified; chapter 21), but some of the most marginal, erosion-prone fields have been reforested (Heasley and Guries 1998).

The forests and lakes continue to draw more people into northern Wisconsin. Many of these new residents are seasonal, maintaining a cabin or vacation home (Clendenning et al. 2005). This population shift is directly affecting Wisconsin's forests and is indirectly changing the sociological and political context in which these forests exist. Seasonal residents from nearby urban centers, for example, often have very different values and attitudes toward forest management than permanent residents. The new urbanites often oppose intensive extraction, while favoring larger preserved areas and greater government regulation of land use (Clendenning et al. 2005).

Can we predict where and how future development will occur? Research shows clear links among housing density, land cover, and property ownership (Radeloff et al. 2000, 2001). As one might expect, housing density is increasing fastest near bodies of water but is limited by large tracts of publicly owned land. How housing density has developed over the last 60 years has also been used to project likely changes in housing density over the next 20 years (Radeloff et al. 2001). Inferring how this future housing development will affect forests is more difficult. Clearly the type and magnitude of disturbances have changed greatly since European settlement (chapter 5). Increasing numbers of seasonal and permanent residents in northern Wisconsin will further shift disturbance regimes as they impose their own values and cultural perspectives on this landscapes. Higher housing density will likely limit the amount of intensive timber management (Ward et al. 2005). We therefore expect areas with higher housing density to experience declines in the dominance of early successional aspen and birch and a shift toward older, more shade-tolerant trees. This, in turn, could increase rates of tree mortality in populated areas, biasing perceptions of forest health.

People Unintentionally Change the Forest

While alterations of the land such as farms, residential tracts, and timber harvests are local and obvious, people also generate more subtle, unintentional changes at much larger scales. Shifts in atmospheric composition and climatic change, for example, are difficult to see when viewing particular forest stands over periods of a decade or two but become clear when we expand our frame of reference (chapters 3 and 4). Wisconsin's forests will surely change in response to shifts in climate and carbon dioxide levels, and these changes may be enormous. We know that fossil fuel combustion is driving up the concentration of carbon dioxide and other heat-trapping gases in the atmosphere dramatically. Computer models ("global circulation models") predict how these increases in greenhouse gases will alter global climate in coming years (Intergovernmental Panel on Climate Change 2001). We know that climate change is already under way (Magnuson et al. 2000). Annual average temperatures have already increased by 1°C–2°C (2°F–4°F) in Wisconsin, compared with the 30-year (1961–90) average, and are expected to increase another 1°C–4°C (2°F–7°F) in the winter and 3°C–11°C (5°F–20°F) in the summer (Wuebbles and Hayhoe 2004). These numbers are alarming. They also indicate that what we once imagined to be a distant problem confronts us now and in the immediate future (chapters 3 and 4).

Climate and soils form the template upon which all plants depend. If the temperature warms, some tree species will thrive, growing faster and increasing their reproductive output. Other species adapted to a cooler climate will suffer. Here, history can be a valuable guide for understanding forest change. During past climate changes, all temperate tree species have undergone dramatic and often unique shifts in their geographic range (Delcourt and Delcourt 1988). Many populations went extinct in portions of their range, contracting their range, while others thrived, extending their range. Soils and climate patterns modulate these shifts. The hemlocks persist in small refuges in the Baraboo Hills where steep north-facing cliffs create cool, moist microclimates that resemble sites hundreds of kilometers north.

Do not expect our existing forests to die suddenly. Some species may die out quickly, but this will probably reflect invading diseases (chapter 30). Other changes will be more subtle. Some tree species are likely to benefit from climate change, including aspen and sugar maple. Beech may continue its postglacial expansion westward. However, other important species will likely lose their ability to reproduce and compete (Scheller and

Mladenoff 2005). Even during a warming period, climates still vary from year to year. A species that cannot reproduce due to high temperatures for a decade may reproduce well during a cool year. In addition, not all age groups are equally vulnerable to climate-related mortality. Conditions severe enough to kill seedlings and saplings may not affect older trees. Thus, there will be considerable inertia to overstory composition. The ability of each species to adapt to changing climates also depends on human influences, including logging and fragmentation (Scheller and Mladenoff 2005).

With climate change, we use the past as a guide to what the future may hold. For other kinds of change, we often lack any clear analogy to the past. For example, the chemical makeup of the atmosphere is changing rapidly. Air pollutants such as nitrogen oxides and ozone are increasing (Vitousek et al. 1997). There are now more deer in northern Wisconsin than ever. Hungry deer are eliminating the ability of many trees, shrubs, and wildflowers to persist and reproduce (chapters 6 and 19). We also see increasing numbers of nonnative, invasive plants, pathogens, and insects (chapter 30) including gypsy moths, which are currently spreading across Wisconsin causing extensive defoliation and mortality (Sharov et al. 2002). European buckthorn and garlic mustard outcompete native wildflowers. European earthworms are changing forest floor conditions by eliminating much of the forest floor litter critical for the germination of many native herbs (Bohlen et al. 2004). As nonnative species continue to proliferate, we can expect more new species to appear in coming decades (Mills et al. 1994).

All of these changes will interact with each other and with human dimensions of landscape change. Currently, we have almost no information on how and how strongly these various factors will interact. As scientists seek to study these various agents of change and their interactions, both scenarios and experiments should prove useful (chapter 28).

Projecting Wisconsin's Future Forests

To project long-term forest change in response to climate change, land use change, and other expected ecological drivers, forest ecologists often use computer models. They typically begin by first attempting to represent the current-day landscape, including soil types, species locations, dominant forest cover, and climate. These models seek to represent a very complex system often via a large set of interrelated processes including photosynthesis, tree growth, leaf fall, plant reproduction, fire occurrence, and windstorm damage. Each process is represented by mathematical formulas. After determining what they hypothesize to be the right set of processes for a given question, ecologists test the resulting model on whether it produces reasonable results. Ecologists then use such models to study research questions like how natural, intentional, and unintentional future changes will affect forests. These models simulate the changes forests are likely to experience in response to changing climate, human development, and invasions by exotic species and pests. Models invariably include at least one (but never all) of the various drivers of forest change (Scheller and Mladenoff 2007).

Our computer models suggest that Wisconsin's forests will face disturbing trends as they respond to climate warming. One model predicts that many species now commonly found in northern Wisconsin (including red pine, jack pine, paper birch, white spruce, and balsam fir) will cease to reproduce and eventually disappear from the state (Scheller and Mladenoff 2005). Where loamy and silty soils soils hold enough water, species like sugar maple, red maple, and white pine are likely to grow faster and to larger sizes. Other species like aspen may not respond at all. We often lack enough information to predict how species will respond (as with tamarack). Climates are now changing faster than tree species can adapt and evolve. Forests show a lot of inertia, reflecting how long most tree species live. This inertia, plus limited dispersal, may limit how quickly many tree species can shift their ranges, particularly for the southern oaks and hickories whose climate is predicted to change quickly (plate 16). Shifts in climate may therefore reduce tree diversity and forest growth for decades to centuries. Logging and natural disturbances will also interact with these changes and the climate/soil/disturbance template to influence what can grow where across our landscapes.

Although history and models can inform our expectations of forest change, there are still many unknowns (Stainforth et al. 2005). Of the dozens of available climate models, some predict an increase in precipitation in Wisconsin, others a decrease. Changes in precipitation will greatly affect how our forests change and where. Even if we could predict precipitation patterns, we would still face uncertainty regarding our models and their ability to make accurate predictions. Despite these uncertainties, models still help us anticipate forest change. We can test how different processes are likely to interact under various circumstances, simulating controlled experiments. These projections help us to identify areas of uncertainty and which assumptions matter the most in projecting how forest change depends on climate change. Thus, both models and the scenarios that Carpenter describes (chapter 28) provide tools to help us anticipate, and prepare for, the future.

Summary

We live in an age of great change, and our landscapes reflect these changes. We cannot know precisely how land use, climate, pollution, and invasive species will change in the future, nor do we fully understand how forests will respond to every potential cause or combination of change (see sidebar). Our greatest limitation lies in not knowing how people will continue to use and change the landscape. For example, if climate changes, will people move? Will they harvest more trees or less? How will further dispersed development enhance invasions of new exotic species? These and similar questions will continue to challenge both scientists and society as we enter an era of unprecedented change. Our ability to anticipate the risks and challenges ahead will require that we understand past changes, that we research how forests respond to change, and that we use every tool available to understand how the future may unfold.

The Future of Forest Conservation

Thomas P. Rooney and David J. Mladenoff

Traditionally, foresters managed forests for specific end points. By identifying a desired future condition of tree species and ages for a stand, they could select the most appropriate management tools to bring about that condition and move the stand in that direction. For example, a forester can designate the desired future condition of a 70-year-old, 40-acre red pine plantation as a stand that continuously produces high-quality sawtimber (logs of 12 inch diameter or greater) over the next 50 years. To move the stand in that direction, a fraction of the smaller trees might be removed at 10–15-year intervals using a management tool called "thinning," improving the growth of the remaining trees.

But, the world is changing. Efforts to manage forests in the next century are likely to be thwarted by climate change, habitat fragmentation, new diseases, and insect pests (chapter 30), as well as interactions among these factors. Returning to our red pine example, suppose that a new strain of a fungal canker disease of Scots pine began infecting red pines and, within 5 years, most red pine stands Wisconsin are dead. The desired future condition becomes impossible to attain, so the stand is salvage logged, removing all trees. In another 10 years, new pathogens rapidly eliminate red oak, sugar maple, and white ash. While salvage logging can recover some quality timber, it will fail to satisfy the demands of the growing population and economy for forest products. The idea that we can reliably manage for specified end points during an era of rapid environmental change is unrealistic.

How should we manage our forests, given likely increases in both environmental uncertainty and demand for wood and fiber? Any viable strategy should rest on diversity and flexibility. Landowners and managers would be wise to maintain a diversity of species and management approaches. Single-species plantations may be appropriate where we have a narrow focus on timber production, but relying on one species (like red pine) or genotype (like a new hybrid poplar) poses clear risks. Emerging diseases could wipe out both in the next 50 years. Instead, it would be wiser to establish more mixed species stands and experimental plantations of other species, including ash, oak, walnut, and valuable softwoods like white pine.

Where production is not the primary goal, maintaining diverse, mixed stands will likely meet more objectives, particularly in light of shifts in climate and threats from new pests. We now face the real possibility that many of the tree species that have thrived for millennia in northern Wisconsin may lose their ability to persist here in the next 200 years! This is less than the normal life span of many trees. Combining a diversity of silvicultural treatments and rotation ages with a diversity of species provides the safest way to manage forests with so much uncertainty. Additionally, management plans need to be flexible, perhaps with built-in contingencies for improbable (but inevitable) events.

If conditions become warmer and drier, it makes sense to establish stands with more southern species. However, it may also be risky to assume that southern species will thrive in a warming climate or further north. Pathogens or interactions with other species may limit their success. It would also be a mistake to ignore ecologically important northern species like hemlock and white cedar. We do not know what the future holds for these species—they may adapt to and thrive in new conditions. We are frequently surprised by the actual behavior of tree species in nature. We often see species growing in locations we assumed were unsuitable or where we believed they could not persist. If we assume that hemlock and white cedar will not persist in a warmer drier Wisconsin, we may take actions that make this a self-fulfilling prophecy.

The past and present are at best imperfect guides to the future. Given the complexity of forest ecosystems, we would be wise to prepare for multiple futures instead of trying to manage for specific outcomes.

References

Bohlen, P. J., P. M. Groffman, T. J. Fahey, M. C. Fisk, E. Suarez, D. M. Pelletier, and R. T. Fahey. 2004. Ecosystem consequences of exotic earthworm invasion of north temperate forests. Ecosystems 7:1–12.

Clendenning, G., D. R. Field, and K. J. Kapp. 2005. A comparison of seasonal homeowners and permanent residents on their attitudes toward wildlife management on public lands. Human Dimensions of Wildlife 10:3–17.

Delcourt, H. R., and P. A. Delcourt. 1988. Quaternary landscape ecology: Relevant scales in space and time. Landscape Ecology 2:23–44.

Heasley, L., and R. P. Guries. 1998. Forest tenure and cultural landscapes: Environmental histories in the Kickapoo Valley. pp. 182–207 in H. M. Jacobs, ed. Who Owns America? Social Conflict over Property Rights. Madison: University of Wisconsin Press.

Intergovernmental Panel on Climate Change. 2001. Climate Change 2001: The Scientific Basis, edited by J. T. Houghton, D. Yihui, D. J. Griggs, M. Noguer, P. J. van der Linden, X. Dai, K. Maskell, and C. A. Johnson. Cambridge: Cambridge University Press.

Magnuson, J. J., D. M. Robertson, B. J. Benson, R. H. Wynne, D. M. Livingstone, T. Arai, R. A. Assel, R. G. Barry, V. Card, E. Kuusisto, N. G. Granin, T. D. Prowse, K. M. Stewart, and V. S. Vuglinski. 2000. Historical trends in lake and river ice cover in the northern hemisphere. Science 289:1743–1746.

Mills, E. L., J. H. Leach, J. T. Carlton, and C. L. Secor. 1994. Exotic species and the integrity of the Great Lakes: Lessons from the past. BioScience 44:666–677.

Radeloff, V. C., A. E. Hagen, P. R. Voss, D. R. Field, and D. J. Mladenoff. 2000. Exploring the spatial relationship between census and land-cover data. Society and Natural Resources 13:599–609.

Radeloff, V. C., R. B. Hammer, P. R. Voss, A. E. Hagen, D. R. Field, and D. J. Mladenoff. 2001. Human demographic trends and landscape level forest management in the northwest Wisconsin pine barrens. Forest Science 47:229–241.

Scheller, R. M., and D. J. Mladenoff. 2005. A spatially interactive simulation of climate change, harvesting, wind, and tree species migration and projected changes to forest composition and biomass in northern Wisconsin, USA. Global Change Biology 11:307–321.

———. 2007. Forest landscape simulation models: Tools and strategies for projecting and understanding spatially extensive forest ecosystems. Landscape Ecology 22:491–505.

Sharov, A. A., D. Leonard, A. M. Liebhold, E. A. Roberts, and W. Dickerson. 2002. "Slow the Spread": A national program to contain the gypsy moth. Journal of Forestry 100:30–35.

Stainforth, D. A., T. Aina, C. Christensen, M. Collins, N. Faull, D. J. Frame, J. A. Kettleborough, S. Knight, A. Martin, J. M. Murphy, C. Piani, D. Sexton, L. A. Smith, R. A. Spicer, A. J. Thorpe, and M. R. Allen. 2005. Uncertainty in predictions of the climate response to rising levels of greenhouse gases. Nature 433:403–406.

Vitousek, P. M., H. A. Mooney, J. Lubchenco, and J. M. Melillo. 1997. Human domination of Earth's ecosystems. Science 277:494–499.

Ward, B. C., D. J. Mladenoff, and R. M. Scheller. 2005. Landscape-level effects of the interaction between residential development and public forest management in northern Wisconsin, USA. Forest Science 51:616–632.

Wuebbles, D. J., and K. Hayhoe. 2004. Climate change projections for the United States midwest. Mitigation and Adaptation Strategies for Global Change 9:335–363.

Conclusion

32 The Big Picture

Donald M. Waller

Thank you, reader. Arriving here suggests that you have a serious interest in Wisconsin's lands, waters, and wildlife. I might also guess that you enjoy spending time outside; know something about birds, trout, or ferns; and care about how nature is faring in the 21st century. I hope you enjoyed learning more about the familiar and obscure corners of the state and its biota. You may have taken particular delight in learning something new about a species that lives here, its interactions with other species and its environment, or the more or less natural areas it calls home. If you are now more aware of and interested in Wisconsin species and habitats and how they have changed, this book has been a success.

Science, like other fields, rewards specialization. The individual chapters of this book reflect that specialization as scientists share with you their insights from years of field work and data analysis. Although we scientists and passionate amateurs know a great deal about our own favorite system or group of organisms, we don't always take the opportunity to learn about parallel changes in other systems. We may also hesitate to ponder what these changes might collectively imply about the nature and extent of regional ecological change or how to apply this knowledge to better protect nature.

The authors of the science chapters share their fascination with natural history and ecological history by exploring what we know about a group of species or habitats. A few historians and policy experts add their insights to complete these stories and explore their social context. These stories are rich, interesting, and important, and perhaps these individual stories justify this book. However, the real value of the book you hold lies in the more complete picture of ecological change that emerges collectively from our individual accounts. Understanding that each of us held individual "pieces of the puzzle," we sought to assemble our fragmentary stories into a broader narrative so that readers could understand their cumulative significance. As noted in chapter 1, our knowledge will always be incomplete, as many pieces of the puzzle are missing or disconnected from the rest. Nevertheless, we have enough information to see the big picture and its implications. Public discussions and decision making, however, often fail to recognize these overall patterns of ecological change and their long-term implications. We therefore sought to share our results broadly by writing not only for other scientists but also for teachers, students, policy makers, natural resource professionals, and interested citizens. This book represents the first time so many specialists have shared their collective knowledge about the causes and implications of ecological change for one region. It is unlikely to be the last.

This book focuses on assessing and interpreting the past century and a half of ecological change in the specific context of one state—Wisconsin. Ecological history tends to be particular to its geographic context. If we had written a book about the Great Plains or intermountain West, for example, you would find far more about the role of fire. The book benefits, however, from the landscape approach many chapters take to ecology as well as our regional strength in ecological history. We particularly benefit by inheriting such exceptional baseline information, allowing us to infer particular kinds of ecological change with precision. These rich historical data sets help us lift the veils on Magnuson's (1990) "invisible present" in a way that is difficult or impossible elsewhere.

Bringing knowledge on these regional patterns of ecological change to light addresses several goals. Increasing the reader's wonder and appreciation for species, natural systems, and the many ecological services they provide is always worthwhile. Wonder and appreciation, in turn, can inspire understanding and concern. Readers of this book are alert to the several factors that individually and collectively threaten the persistence of native species and the habitats they depend on. Such knowledge is critical for translating our concern for species and ecosystems into actions that can serve to sustain the beauty, diversity, and ecological integrity of our lands, waters, and wildlife into future centuries. The most significant problem facing modern humans, as Aldo Leopold (1966) noted, is how to live upon the land without destroying its capability to sustain life.

What Makes Wisconsin Unique?

Wisconsin is not home to dense, tropical forests, coral reefs, or alpine meadows. We have few endemic species and few threatened or endangered species. Nevertheless, Wisconsinites take justifiable pride in their state's unique history, qualities, natural beauty, and wild areas and use these to promote tourism.

What gives Wisconsin its particular ecological context and history? Those who live and work in Wisconsin sense its unique qualities. Wisconsin lies in the northern heart of North America where once the great western prairies merged into the savannas, forests, and wetland habitats of the eastern United States. Its residents know both the subzero blasts of arctic air in the winter and the rapidly advancing squall lines that spawn summer thunderstorms and tornadoes.

Our state lies between the Mississippi River and the Great Lakes, taking its name from the great river that bisects its length. "Wisconsin" derives from the French word "Ouisconsin," translated perhaps from an Ojibwa word referring to a "red-stone place" along the river or a general gathering of the waters, used first to refer to the river and later to the territory around it. Water defines the state in more ways than its boundaries. We have such abundant surface and groundwater that then governor L. S. Dreyfus once seriously proposed that Wisconsin should build a pipeline to the arid Southwest and become the OPEC for water.

The Indian tribes that migrated into Wisconsin over the centuries before and after European settlement were attracted by the food, fiber, and shelter they found in its forests, grasslands, and wetlands. They fished for sturgeon, walleye, trout, bass, and whitefish. They hunted elk and bison in the prairies and savannas, white-tailed deer in the forests, and moose and caribou in the north. The Ojibwa were particularly drawn to "manomin," the wild rice beds lining sloughs and clear lakes throughout Wisconsin. Wetlands also gave the Indians tubers from arrowhead and cattails and great flocks of geese and ducks to hunt. They felled large paper birches and stripped their bark to build light and maneuverable canoes. The mound-building Indian culture that thrived along the Mississippi and Wisconsin rivers cultivated fields of squash, beans, and maize.

Wisconsin also gave sustenance, fiber, and shelter to the early European settlers drawn to the region, though these took radically different forms. French voyageurs spread out over the region to trap fur-bearing animals and trade with the Indians for pelts. Paul Bunyan era loggers came for logs from the giant white and red pines to float down the rivers to sawmills with spring floods. The loggers' cooks clearly relished the nearby abundance of game. Demand for hemlock bark to tan hides and timber to build barns, houses, and the growing city of Chicago and a proliferating railroad network soon leveled old-growth forests, leaving burning slash and expanses of open land soon colonized by young aspen and birch. Aspen remains the primary source of pulp for the paper from mills on the Wisconsin and Fox rivers. Open lands and John Deere's steel plow brought successive waves of farmers, whose efforts transformed the state's prairies and savannas into the rural agricultural landscapes we see today. Many cows now graze the rich pastures of the dairy state where bison and elk once roamed. The rich soil built up by centuries of prairie plants now support large fields of genetically improved soybeans and corn with yields far higher than any Indian or early settler could have imagined.

The rapid transformation of Wisconsin's landscapes in the late 19th and early 20th century left few huge pines and only scraps of native prairie or old-growth forest. The elk and herds of bison are gone as are the wolverines and cougars that used to hunt here. These species survive elsewhere and might one day return. Passenger pigeons, however, never will again darken our skies for hours or days at a time. Extinction is forever. Witnessing such rapid ecological devastation may have spawned the conservation ethic that took root in Wisconsin. John Muir's boyhood in Portage, college experiences in Madison, forest work in Ontario, and industrial work in Indianapolis spurred a lifetime of exploration, scientific essays on glacial geomorphology, and an inspiring commitment to protect wild spaces in nature. We now associate his name with redwood groves in California, the movement to establish national parks, and the Sierra Club.

Half a century later, Aldo Leopold traced a curiously antisymmetric route that began in Dubuque, moved east, and then west before settling in Wisconsin. We remember Leopold, like Muir, for his lyrical writing, contributions to science, and fierce dedication to conserving land and wildlife. He virtually founded the field of professional game (later wildlife) management, urged strict protection for threatened species, and worked to establish the nation's first wilderness area. He was also a keen observer whose views grew with his experience. The man who had once eagerly joined in killing wild wolves to protect "game" later warned us about the dangers of overabundant deer and the need to protect predators. Sales of

A Sand County Almanac continue to climb 60 years after it was written, helping to support a family foundation dedicated to carrying on work in restoration ecology. The Wilderness Society he cofounded still fights to broaden protection for the wildlands he so loved and understood.

Wisconsin thus claims a proud tradition in conservation. This tradition extends beyond Muir and Leopold to the mid-20th century when John Curtis helped convince the state to establish the first state natural areas program in 1951. The man from Clear Lake, Gaylord Nelson, made path-breaking efforts to protect land and waters as governor, senator, and chair and counsel to the Wilderness Society. He played key roles in passing the 1964 Wilderness Act and the Scenic and Wild Rivers Act, in controlling phosphates and pesticides, and in establishing Earth Day in 1970. We honor his legacy via the Knowles-Nelson Stewardship Fund dedicated to acquiring and protecting public land. The state has also become a hotbed for conservation land trust activity.

What Makes Wisconsin Typical?

If Wisconsin is so special, you may be wondering, are all the results we report here just local and specific to Wisconsin? Sadly, Wisconsin is not unusual or exceptional in terms of the trends documented in this book. Despite the fact that all the places and examples in this book are local to one midwestern state, the patterns, trends, and threats that emerge are numbingly familiar. Problems here are problems everywhere. This was, in fact, a premise for this book. The ecological change we observe in Wisconsin serves as a synecdoche for ecological changes around the world.

Wetlands continue to be filled in for agriculture or development or are polluted by runoff here and around the world (Crumpacker et al. 1988). The declines in many native grassland and forest songbirds that we describe extend at least across temperate North America (Terborgh 1989). States across the continent are grappling with overabundant deer, as are parts of Europe and New Zealand (Côté et al. 2004). The diversity of wildflowers appears to be declining in most forests where anyone has monitored closely (Waller and Rooney 2004). Many state foresters cringe in fear at what gypsy moths, Asian long-horned beetles, emerald ash borers, and unknown future pest arthropods are doing and will do to their forests. State and regional networks have sprung up to track and fight a succession of weedy plant invasions. International commerce, roads, and vehicles accelerate these trends. Birds now die from West Nile virus halfway around the world from its source. A 2007 headline—"Deadly fish disease circulating through the Great Lakes"—announces the arrival of viral hemorrhagic septicemia to Wisconsin. Expect more. As travel and commerce shrink our world, roads and suburbs proliferate, and agriculture intensifies, global invaders find easier paths and more suitable hosts and habitats. These, along with other abundant weedy species, continue to displace species with more specialized, particular, and local requirements. The result? Wisconsin, like the world, grows ever simpler and more homogenous. What we can perhaps say about Wisconsin is that we know more—and should therefore know better.

The Nature of Cumulative Effects

Many of the changes described in this book may seem minor, or local, perhaps reflecting temporary shifts in habitat conditions (like succession). Any change in one species or one location can hardly be deemed a trend. But as we assemble data from many species and many locations and return to resurvey these years later, a sharper, broader picture emerges. While our image remains fragmented, both encouraging and disturbing trends are evident. There is no doubt that sandhill crane populations are recovering steadily across much of the state. Wolf numbers continue to climb, particularly in northeastern Wisconsin, and surpassed 500 in 2007. Many forests in northern Wisconsin continue to mature, reestablishing forest communities that could eventually come to resemble those that cloaked these lands 200 years ago. Steady efforts have increased the amount of public land, the number of designated natural areas, and the acres dedicated to conserving natural values under private efforts. We are also gaining scientific expertise and public enthusiasm for restoring prairies, wetlands, and forests. Some also look forward to chaining these habitats together into larger, more biologically functional networks capable of supporting ungulates beyond deer and carnivores beyond raccoons.

Although these trends are encouraging, it is difficult to be optimistic about other parts of the big picture. Grassland birds and many forest interior songbirds continue to decline in abundance, as do butterfly, moth, and amphibian populations in many parts of the state. Deer continue to decimate wildflower populations as well as seedling populations of oak, pine, cedar, yellow birch, and hemlock. Even if the deer dilemma is addressed more effectively, reestablishing healthy populations of these species may take decades to centuries. Levels of atrazine in our wells and PCBs and mercury in our fish and wildlife are declining only slowly. Groundwater depletion, nutrient runoff, and road salt threaten too many streams and wetlands. Land use changes across the state reveal steady declines in natural habitats and a steady climb in roads, towns, and cities.

Like many biotic declines, the population and economic growth that drive landscape changes usually creep along at a steady rate in a manner that attracts little notice. Each incremental change seems minor, and we are all now used to these changes. Indeed, politicians and chambers of commerce urge us to pursue and celebrate this growth, boasting about the benefits it will bring. Those concerned about too much growth or growth in the wrong places are accused of being elitist, myopic, or antiprogress. Local skirmishes increasingly erupt, but city and rural zoning codes still view natural habitats as undeveloped real estate more often than valuable assets deserving protection. This will continue to be the case until we recognize the threats posed by cumulative environmental effects. Although ecology teaches limits to growth, many pursue a different gospel.

A theme in this book has been the creeping, cumulative nature of ecological change. Because most habitat and species losses occur slowly, most of us remain unaware of them. Those who are attuned tend to notice fewer flowers or birds in a favorite patch of woods, cloudier lakes, or the advancing fronts of invasive species. However, these changes often remain invisible to an increasingly plugged-in and urban population. More media attention is lavished on celebrity gossip than on bird and butterfly population trends. More and more of what we know about nature comes secondhand, from books, papers, and TV, rather than from what we experience directly. Natural habitats are becoming more distant and foreign to us. In his perceptive book, Richard Louv (2006) notes that on average, between 1970 and 1990, the area around the home where children can roam on their own shrunk to one-ninth of what it had been. As urban populations spend less time outside observing wild plants and animals directly, the danger grows that they will feel less connected and care less about wild places. Worse, the outdoors looms increasingly as a menace, harboring disease-carrying ticks, mosquitoes that might transmit West Nile virus, or dangerous people engaged in illicit activity. As children lose their connections to nature, they may also be losing creativity and forms of social interaction while increasing their risks of obesity and attention-deficit hyperactivity disorder. How many teenagers today would accept Aldo Leopold's assertion that being able to watch a woodcock's "sky-dance" is more important than being able to watch TV?

The Growing Importance of Ecological Monitoring

Ecologists from a variety of subdisciplines, using a variety of approaches, are focusing increased attention on general themes of ecological change (Vitousek et al. 1997). Although the public now pays considerable attention to global climate change, ecological change represents a much broader class of events. These extend from local changes in physiological function and species composition to shifts in habitat structure and community composition to regional shifts in species ranges to widespread habitat destruction and shifting landscape dynamics. In addition, these ecological changes interact with increasing atmospheric concentrations of carbon dioxide and climate changes in known and unknown ways. Given the increasing number of these impacts, the prevalence of nonlinear effects in ecology, and the complexity of their interactions, we may soon face a mounting and confusing profusion of impacts including several of unanticipated size and direction.

Understanding these complex patterns of ecological change and accurately forecasting their effects on ecosystems will doubtless increase the significance of ecological monitoring in the future. In the near term, it seems assured that natural ecosystems will continue to suffer the effects of habitat fragmentation, invasive species, altered disturbance regimes, disrupted trophic dynamics, and climate change. As these stresses accumulate, losses of populations, species, and ecological functions will accelerate and interact. As natural systems grow more scarce, they will also grow more valuable, though tracking their direct and indirect economic value will remain challenging. At the same time, other resources will also be growing scarcer and costlier, maintaining or increasing pressure on natural areas. As accounting for and tracking the values of natural systems becomes increasingly important, we can expect to see the emergence of a new field we might call ecological accounting. Ecological accountants will purse ever more accurate and inclusive methods to track the ecological benefits and costs of various actions.

The importance of ecological monitoring and accounting is already evident in the rapid increase in economic trading of greenhouse gas emissions and carbon credits. Here, the goals are to cut greenhouse gas emissions (often relatively easy to estimate) and increase the amount of carbon being sequestered either by ecosystems or via industrial processes. Carbon accounting is fast emerging as a vital subfield demanding both economic and ecological expertise. A key aspect of this accounting consists of understanding how different kinds of ecosystem (agricultural fields, grasslands, wetlands, and various kinds of forest) function to absorb or release greenhouse gases, both in the short term and over longer cycles of disturbance (and ultimately in response to ongoing climate change). Fire frequencies, the fate of coarse woody debris, belowground carbon dynamics, and microbial processes in soil and animal guts all assume much greater significance in this context, demanding corresponding increases in research and monitoring activity. At the same time, the few existing baselines and monitoring programs will grow in value. The current dearth of reliable baseline data and active monitoring programs, however, will slow progress and reduce our certainty about carbon sources and sinks. Slowly, policy makers will come to appreciate the complexity of ecosystems and the need to include short- and long-term dynamics into their calculations as well as our uncertainty about these.

Increasing Visibility

Although we see frequent headlines now about global warming, habitat destruction, new emerging diseases, and invasive weeds, these stories usually emerge piecemeal, one at a time, disconnected from their broader ecological context. Sound bites rob these stories of their historical and landscape context. Such snippets reflect both the narrow, specialized way we conduct our research and the way important scientific advances are usually simplified by reporters to make their stories more "newsworthy." It may also reflect the reticence of scientists who usually prefer doing research to speaking publicly on controversial issues.

Consider the lesson offered by the unfolding global warming story. Although concerns about greenhouse gases and global climate effects have existed for decades, it took a string of dramatic disasters and personal interest stories to really mobilize public interest and concern. The heat wave and drought across the United States in 1988, the Mississippi River floods (and outbreaks of enteric disease) of 1993, the lethal 2003 heat wave in Europe that felled thousands, and the devastating effects of Hurricane Katrina in 2005 all primed audiences for Al Gore's 2006 book and movie, *An Inconvenient Truth*. Suddenly, stories about polar bears and polar ice cap melting were front and center, displacing stories on biodiversity and tropical deforestation. As in that case, initial predictions from scientists were dismissed as speculative, premature, fraught with error, or unrelated to human activities. As empirical evidence on shifts in climate started to build up, some argued that these were anecdotal, local, or temporary. These arguments routinely came from lobbyists for various industries or their hired experts who took advantage of the "invisible present." Once the data became overwhelming, tactics switched, with the same voices arguing that changes should be slow and deliberate to allow time for more research and analysis lest the economic costs of our reforms be too high. In the 1990s, an interesting scientific structure emerged in the form of the Intergovernmental Panel on Climate Change. This group of some 1,500 experts on climate change and its causes and effects was assembled to provide consensus statements to governments on the scope and severity of the problem. Its most recent report and the United Kingdom's Stern Report also discuss the economic costs and potential benefits of various actions. We have here both a concrete example of how useful it can be to link scientific expertise to pressing environmental issues and how slow this process can be when the public is confused by a fog of conflicting statements.

As we become more aware of pervasive ecological changes, ecologists have also become more aware of the need to share their research results with the broader public and decision makers. This is what motivated this book and directed its format. These concerns are also spurring sweeping assessments of ecological conditions across the country and around the world, including the Millennium Ecosystem Assessment program and major reports from the Pew and Heinz foundations. They have also spurred the Ecological Society of America's "Sustainable Biosphere Initiative and Ecological Visions Committee and Report" (Palmer et al. 2004). This report notes that ecologists will have to forge partnerships at scales and in forms they have not traditionally used and strongly advocates public information campaigns to raise awareness of ecological sustainability.

Focusing on the Right Issues

Global warming presents us with a double-edged sword. It is, on the one hand, an exceptional opportunity to alert a broad cross-section of society (and the politicians who follow) to the alarming plight of our planet and the necessity of taking strong action. The Big Message here is that humans have become a global force—a clear symptom that human growth has outstripped the capacity of Earth to sustain our species (certainly in the style we are accustomed to). Climate change thus presents a "bridge" issue to connect the public with to the broader set of ecological issues we confront. We have a golden opportunity to educate people about the large and complex web of environmental and ecological crises in which we are enmeshed and how these might be managed in an integrated and strategic manner. Most obviously, going "green" to reduce our greenhouse gas emissions could also reduce our collective ecological footprint in many other ways (e.g., by favoring cleaner, denser, and more livable cities; see chapter 26).

We also, however, face dangers if we focus attention only on climate change. While global warming clearly poses an immediate and dramatic threat to human well-being, it represents at least as large a threat to other species living in increasingly isolated fragments of habitat. Just as we were once admonished to buy a hat and sunglasses to respond to ultraviolet exposure from ozone thinning, we should be leery of proposed "solutions" to global warming that focus only on saving humans. Environmentalism of the kind that focuses on threats to human comfort, well-being, and commerce ignores the cataclysmic threat that climate change and other human impacts pose to the biosphere. Buying more air conditioners, rerouting rivers, and shifting agricultural regions treats symptoms rather than causes. Thus we face the risk that proximal concerns about how global warming threatens humans will eclipse appropriate concerns for protecting habitats and other species. Our current crises demand deeper, more ecological, and more integrated approaches that focus on the core issues of human population growth and social and geographic patterns of overconsumption.

Human wants and needs show no signs of abating. We are not peculiar in this trait. No species in the history of life on Earth has ever evolved traits to limit its own acquisition of resources or reproductive output. On the contrary, natural selection favors individuals that acquire as many resources as possible and efficiently convert these into new progeny. Yet selection that makes sense on the individual level can be malignant at a higher level. Morality may have evolved to limit and guide human behavior so as to promote actions tied to collective success and limit behaviors harmful to our communities. As we gain a better view of how destructive our cumulative actions can be across landscapes and over time, can we also accept Leopold's suggestion to extend our ethics to encompass the wider biotic systems that sustain us?

References

Côté, S. D., T. P. Rooney, J.-P. Tremblay, C. Dussault, and D. M. Waller. 2004. Ecological impacts of deer overabundance. Ann. Rev. Ecol. Evol. System. 35:113–147.

Crumpacker, D. W., S. W. Hodge, D. Friedley, and W. P. Gregg. 1988. A preliminary assessment of the status of major terrestrial and wetland ecosystems on federal and Indian lands in the U.S. Conserv. Biol. 2:103–115.

Leopold, A. 1966. The land ethic. Pp. 237–264 n A Sand County Almanac with Essays on Conservation from Round River. New York: Ballantine Books.

Louv, R. 2006. Last Child in the Woods: Saving Our Children from Nature-Deficit Disorder. Chapel Hill, NC: Algonquin Books.

Magnuson, J. 1990. Long term research and the invisible present. BioScience 40:495–501.

Palmer, M., E. Bernhardt, E. Chornesky, et al. 2004. Ecology for a crowded planet. Science 304:1251–1252.

Terborgh, J. 1989. Where Have All the Birds Gone? Princeton, NJ: Princeton University Press.

Vitousek, P. M., H. A. Mooney, J. Lubchenco, and J. M. Melillo. 1997. Human domination of Earth's ecosystems. Science 277:494–499.

Waller, D. M., and T. P. Rooney. 2004. Nature is changing in more ways than one. Trends Ecol. Evol. 19:6–7.

Glossary

biomass. The total mass of living organisms in a given area or volume of habitat.
biotic homogenization. The loss of taxonomic distinctness among ecological communities through time.
bottomland forests. Forested areas that occupy floodplains of rivers and large streams. During the growing season, these forests can flood for days or weeks.
conductivity. A measure of the ability to conduct electricity. The conductivity of water and soils is influenced by the concentration of the ionic forms of nutrients like calcium, potassium, bicarbonate, and chloride.
cover type. A descriptive classification of the land cover or land use of an area
detritus. Nonliving, partially decomposed organic material.
drainage lake. Lakes that have surface water inflows and outflows.
drawdown. A reduction of water in a lake or river.
eutrophic. Often referring to lakes, an ecosystem that is characterized by high nutrient concentrations, murky water, high productivity, and low quantities of dissolved oxygen.
extirpation. The local extinction of a species.
exurban sprawl. Sprawl in rural areas, typically with two or more acres consumed for each housing unit.
floodplain. Low-lying areas adjacent to streams and rivers that are periodically covered by water during peak flows.
fragmentation. The subdivision of one continuous habitat into two or more smaller isolated habitats.
hydrograph. A graphical representation of water flow of a river or stream through time.

hydroperiod. Cyclical changes in the amount of water present in a wetland.
intraguild predation. the killing and eating of other predators that compete for the same prey.
land bridge. A connection between two land masses that once existed but has since been covered by a lake, ocean, or other large body of water.
land cover. A description of the vegetation of an area of land, such as forest, grassland, or marsh.
land use. A description of how an area of land is used, such as urban, cropland, or pasture.
loam. A fertile type of soil with nearly equal parts of sand, clay, and silt.
mesic. An environment with a moderate amount of moisture.
mesopredator. A midlevel predator in a food chain or web that serves as prey for larger predators.
oligotrophic. A lake ecosystem that is characterized by low nutrient concentrations, clear water, low productivity, and large quantities of dissolved oxygen.
oxidation. A chemical reaction that involves the loss of electrons from an element or compound
physiography. Related to natural geographic features and processes.
phytoplankton. Vascular plants, algae, and photosynthetic protists usually smaller than one centimeter that drift with water currents. Examples include diatoms and blue-green algae.
Pleistocene. Sometimes (imprecisely) called "the ice age," the epoch that started 1.8 million years ago and ended 11,500 years ago. The epoch was marked by four major glacial events.
productivity. The rate of new biomass production in an ecosystem. It indicates how much energy is captured by and therefore available in an ecosystem.
seepage lake. Lakes lacking surface inflows or outflows; most water in the lake originates groundwater flow.
shrub carr. A type of wetland habitat occupied by tall shrubs, frequently red osier dogwood and willows.
sprawl. The growth in developed land at a rate higher than population growth, resulting in dispersed, low-density development.
succession. The change in species composition through time at a particular site.
surficial geology. The branch of geology related to surface features, such as soil, exposed bedrock, and glacial features.
synecdoche. a figure of speech in which part of something is used to refer to the whole thing or when a specific thing is used in place of a more general thing.
upland. Areas of high ground, not subject to flooding.
xeric. An environment with little moisture.
zooplankton. Animals usually smaller than one centimeter that drift with water currents. Examples include rotifers, protists, water fleas, and copepods.

Scientific Names

Common Name	Latin Binomial
Acadian flycatcher	*Empidonax virescens*
Acadian hairstreak	*Satyrium acadium*
Acutetip cup lichen	*Cladonia acuminata*
Alder flycatcher	*Empidonax alnorum*
Alewife	*Alosa pseudoharengus*
American bittern	*Botaurus lentiginosus*
American black duck	*Anas rubripes*
American brook lamprey	*Lampetra appendix*
American bullfrog	*Rana catesbeiana*
American coot	*Fulica americana*
American crow	*Corvus brachyrhynchos*
American elm	*Ulmus americana*
American goldfinch	*Carduelis tristis*
American kestrel	*Falco sparvarius*
American redstart	*Setophaga ruticilla*
American robin	*Turdus migratorius*
American wigeon	*Anas americana*
American woodcock	*Scolopax minor*
Asian lady beetle	*Harmonia axyridis*
Badger	*Taxidea taxus*
Balsam fir	*Abies balsamea*
Baltimore	*Euphydryas phaeto*
Baltimore oriole	*Icterus galbura*
Banded darter	*Etheostoma zonale*
Banded killifish	*Fundulus diaphanus*

Bank swallow	*Riparia riparia*
Barn owl	*Tyto alba*
Barn swallow	*Hirundo rustica*
Barred owl	*Strix varia*
Bass	*Micropterus* spp.
Basswood	*Tilia americana*
Beard lichens	*Usnea* spp.
Beaver	*Castor canadensis*
Bedstraw	*Galium* spp.
Beech	*Fagus grandifolia*
Bell's vireo	*Vireo bellii*
Belted kingfisher	*Ceryle alcyon*
Big bluestem	*Andropogon gerardii*
Bison	*Bos bison*
Bitternut hickory	*Carya cordiformis*
Black and white crust fungus	*Cystostereum murraii*
Black and white warbler	*Mniotilta varia*
Black ash	*Fraxinus nigra*
Black bear	*Ursus americana*
Black cherry	*Prunus serotina*
Black chokeberry	*Aronia melanocarpa*
Black dash skipper	*Euphyes conspicua*
Black rail	*Laterallus jamaicensis*
Black snakeroot	*Sanicula gregaria*
Black spruce	*Picea mariana*
Black swallow-wort	*Vincetoxicum nigrum*
Black tern	*Chlidonias niger*
Black willow	*Salix nigra*
Black-billed cuckoo	*Coccyzus erythropthalmus*
Blackburnian warbler	*Dendroica fusca*
Black-capped chickadee	*Poecile atricapilla*
Blackchin shiner	*Notropis heterodon*
Black-crowned night heron	*Nycticorax nycticorax*
Black-eyed Susan	*Rudbeckia hirta*
Blacknose shiner	*Notropis heterolepis*
Black-throated green warbler	*Dendroica virens*
Blanchard's cricket frog	*Acris crepitans blanchardi*
Blanding's turtle	*Emydoidea blandingii*
Blue grosbeak	*Cyanocomposa parellina*
Blue jay	*Cyanocitta cristata*
Blue sucker	*Cycleptus elongatus*
Bluebead lily	*Clintonia borealis*
Blueberry	*Vaccinium angustifolium*
Blue-gray gnatcatcher	*Polioptila caerulea*
Blue-joint grass	*Calamagrostis canadensis*
Blue-spotted salamander	*Ambystoma laterale*

Bluestem goldenrod	*Solidago caesia*
Blue-winged teal	*Anas discors*
Blue-winged warbler	*Vermivora pinus*
Bobolink	*Dolichonyx aryzivorus*
Bog buckbean	*Menyanthes trifoliata*
Boreal chorus frog	*Pseudacris maculata*
Boreal oakmoss lichen	*Evernia mesomorpha*
Boulder lichens	*Porpidia* spp.
Bouncing bet	*Saponaria officinalis*
Box elder	*Acer negundo*
Brewer's blackbird	*Euphagus cyanocephalus*
Brittle naiad	*Najas minor*
Broad-winged hawk	*Buteo platypterus*
Broad-winged skipper	*Poanes viator*
Brook trout	*Salvelinus fontinalis*
Brown creeper	*Certhia americana*
Brown thrasher	*Toxostoma rufum*
Brown-headed cowbird	*Molothrus ater*
Bullsnake	*Pituophis catenifer sayi*
Bulrush	*Scirpus* spp.
Burbot	*Lota lota*
Burreed	*Sparganium* spp.
Bushy beard lichen	*Usnea strigosa*
Butler's gartersnake	*Thamnophis butleri*
Butterflyweed	*Asclepias tuberosa*
Butternut	*Juglans cinerea*
Butterwort	*Pinguicula vulgaris*
Cabbage butterfly	*Pieris rapae*
Calypso orchid	*Calypso bulbosa*
Canada bluegrass	*Poa compressa*
Canada goldenrod	*Solidago canadensis*
Canada goose	*Branta canadensis*
Canada warbler	*Wilsonia canadensis*
Canada yew	*Taxus canadensis*
Canadian white violet	*Viola canadensis*
Canvasback	*Aythya valisineria*
Carmine shiner	*Notropis percobromis*
Carolina paroquet	*Conuropsis monachus*
Carolina wren	*Thryothorus ludovicianus*
Catnip	*Nepeta cataria*
Cedar waxwing	*Bombycilla cedrorum*
Central newt	*Notophthalmus viridescens louisianensis*
Cerulean warbler	*Dendroica cerulea*
Chestnut-sided warbler	*Dendroica pensylvanica*
Chimney swift	*Chaetura pelagica*

Chipping sparrow	*Spizella passerna*
Cisco	*Coregonus artedi*
Clasping-leaf pondweed	*Potamogeton richardsonii*
Clay-colored sparrow	*Spizella pallida*
Cliff swallow	*Petrochelidon pyrrhonota*
Cloudless sulfur	*Phoebis sennae eubule*
Common arrowhead	*Sagittaria latifolia*
Common bur-reed	*Sparganium eurycarpum*
Common carp	*Cyprinus carpio*
Common five-lined skink	*Eumeces fasciatus*
Common gartersnake	*Thamnophis sirtalis*
Common goldeneye	*Bucephala clangula*
Common grackle	*Quiscalus quiscula*
Common hound's-tongue	*Cynoglossum officinale*
Common moorhen	*Gallinula chloropus*
Common mudpuppy	*Necturus maculosus maculosus*
Common nighthawk	*Chordeiles minor*
Common ringlet	*Coenonympha tullia inornata*
Common script lichen	*Graphis scripta*
Common yellowthroat	*Geothlypis trichas*
Compass plant	*Silphium laciniatum* var. *laciniatum*
Coontail	*Ceratophyllum demersum*
Cooper's hawk	*Accipiter cooperi*
Cope's gray treefrog	*Hyla chrysoscelis*
Cottonwood	*Populus deltoides*
Cougar	*Puma concolor*
Coyote	*Canis latrans*
Crack willow	*Salix fragilis*
Cream gentian	*Gentiana alba*
Cream wild indigo	*Baptisia bracteata*
Crown vetch	*Coronilla varia*
Curly-leaf pondweed	*Potamogeton crispus*
Dandelion	*Taraxacum officinale*
Deer tick	*Ixodes scapularis*
Dickcissel	*Spiza americana*
Dion skipper	*Euphyes dion*
Double-crested cormorant	*Phalacrocorax auritus*
Double-lobed	*Apamea ophiogramma*
Downy woodpecker	*Picoides pubescens*
Draba	*Draba reptans*
Duckweeds	*Lemna* spp.; *Wolffia* spp.; *Spirodela polyrhiza*
Dune goldenrod	*Solidago simples* subsp. *randii* var. *gillmanii*
Dune thistle	*Cirsium pitcheri*
Dutchman's breeches	*Dicentra cucullaria*
Dwarf lake iris	*Iris lacustris*
Dyers' weed	*Solidago nemoralis*

Earthscale lichen	*Placidium squamulosm*
Eastern American toad	*Bufo americanus americanus*
Eastern bluebird	*Sialia sialis*
Eastern hemlock	*Tsuga canadensis*
Eastern hog-nosed snake	*Heterodon platirhinos*
Eastern kingbird	*Tyrannus tyrannus*
Eastern massasauga	*Sistrurus catenatus catenatus*
Eastern meadowlark	*Sturnella magna*
Eastern milksnake	*Lampropeltis triangulum triangulum*
Eastern phoebe	*Sayornis phoebe*
Eastern racer	*Coluber constrictor*
Eastern red-backed salamander	*Plethodon cinereus*
Eastern screech-owl	*Otus asio*
Eastern snapping turtle	*Chelydra serpentina serpentina*
Eastern spiny softshell	*Apalone spinifera spinifera*
Eastern tiger salamander	*Ambystoma tigrinum tigrinum*
Eastern towhee	*Pipilo erythrophthalmus*
Eastern wood-peewee	*Contopus virens*
Elk	*Cervus elaphus*
Emerald ash borer	*Agrilus planipennis*
Eurasian (water) milfoil	*Myriophyllum spicatum*
Eurasian collard dove	*Streptopelia decaocto*
Eurasian ruffe	*Gymnocephalus cernuus*
European buckthorn	*Rhamnus cathartica*
European earthworm	*Lumbriscus* spp.
European frogbit	*Hydrocharis morsus-ranae*
European skipper	*Thymelicus lineola*
European starling	*Sturnus vulgaris*
European water fern	*Marsilea quadrifolia*
Evening primrose	*Oenothera biennis*
Eyed brown	*Satyrodes eurydice*
False-pimpernel	*Lindernia dubia*
Fan lichen	*Peltigera venosa*
Fanwort	*Cabomba caroliniana*
Fern pondweed	*Potamogeton robbinsii*
Field sparrow	*Spizella pusilla*
Flat-stem pondweed	*Potamogeton zosteriformis*
Fleabane	*Erigeron* spp.
Floating-leaf pondweed	*Potamogeton natans*
Flowering rush	*Butomus umbellatus*
Forest tent caterpillar	*Malacosoma disstria*
Forster's tern	*Sterna forsteri*
Four-toed salamander	*Hemidactylium scutatum*
Fox sparrow	*Passerella iliaca*

Gadwall	*Anas strepera*
Garlic mustard	*Alliaria petiolata*
German yellowjacket	*Paravespula germanica*
Giant goldenrod	*Solidago gigantea*
Giant ragweed	*Ambrosia trifida* var. *trifida*
Giant silkworm moths	family Saturniidae
Giant snakehead	*Channa micropeltes*
Glossy buckthorn	*Rhamnus frangula*
Golden-winged warbler	*Vermivora chrysoptera*
Goldspeck lichens	*Candelariella* spp.
Goldthread	*Coptis trifolia*
Grass carp	*Ctenpharyngodon idella*
Grasshopper sparrow	*Ammodramus savannarum*
Gray catbird	*Dumetella carolinensis*
Gray dogwood	*Cornus racemosa*
Gray fox	*Urocyon cinereoargenteus*
Gray partridge	*Perdix perdix*
Gray treefrog	*Hyla versicolor*
Gray wolf	*Canis lupus*
Great blue heron	*Ardea herodius*
Great crested flycatcher	*Myiarchus crintus*
Great horned owl	*Bubo virginianus*
Great tit	*Parus major*
Greater prairie chicken	*Tympanuchus cupido*
Greater redhorse	*Moxostoma valenciennesi*
Greater scaup	*Aythya marila*
Green ash	*Fraxinus pennsylvanica*
Green heron	*Butorides virescens*
Greenish blue butterfly	*Plebejus saepiolus*
Green-winged teal	*Anas crecca*
Ground dove	*Columbina passerina*
Ground squirrel	*Spermophilus* spp.
Gypsy moth	*Lymantria dispar*
Hackberry	*Celtis occidentalis*
Hairy woodpecker	*Picoides villosus*
Harbinger-of-spring	*Erigenia bulbosa*
Hawthorn	*Crataegus* spp.
Hay-scented fern	*Dennstaedtia punctilobula*
Heartleaf plantain	*Plantago cordata*
Hemlock	*Tsuga canadensis*
Hemlock wooly adelgid	*Adelges tsugae*
Henslow's sparrow	*Ammodramus henslowii*
Herring gull	*Larus argentatus*
Hickory trees	*Carya* spp.
Hill's oak	*Quercus ellipsoidalis*
Honewort	*Cryptotaenia canadensis*

Honey locust	*Gleditisia triacanthos*
Hooded merganser	*Lophodytes cucullatus*
Hooded warbler	*Wilsonia citrina*
Horned lark	*Eremophilia alpestris*
Horsetails	*Equisetum* spp.
House finch	*Carpodacus mexicanus*
House sparrow	*Passer domesticus*
House wren	*Troglodytes aedon*
Huron sulphur shelf	*Laetiporus huroniensis*
Hydrilla	*Hydrilla verticillata*
Illinois pondweed	*Potamogeton illinoensis*
Indian cucumber root	*Medeola virginica*
Indian grass	*Sorghastrum nutans*
Indian paintbrush	*Castilleja coccinea*
Indian plantain	*Arnoglossum plantagineum*
Indigo bunting	*Passerrina cyanea*
Iowa darter	*Etheostoma exile*
Jack pine	*Pinus banksiana*
Jack-in-the-pulpit	*Arisaema triphyllum*
Japanese hedge parsley	*Torlis japonica*
Japanese hops	*Humuls japonicus*
Japanese stilt grass	*Microstegium vimineum*
Joe-pye weed, Joe pye-weed	*Eupatorium perfoliatum*
Karner blue butterfly	*Lycaeides melissa samuelis*
Kentucky bluegrass	*Poa pratensis*
Kentucky warbler	*Oporornis formosus*
Killdeer	*Charadrius vociferous*
King rail	*Rallus elegans*
Kittentails	*Besseya bullii*
Kudzu	*Pueraria montana*
Labrador tea	*Ledum groenlandicum*
Lake chubsucker	*Erimyzon sucetta*
Lake herring	*Coregonus artedi*
Lake Huron tansy	*Tanacetum huronense*
Lake sedge	*Carex lacustris*
Lake sturgeon	*Acipenser fulvescens*
Lake trout	*Salvelinus namaycush*
Lake whitefish	*Coregonus clupeaformis*
Larch	*Larix laricina*
Large yellow lady's slipper	*Cypripedium parviflorum* var. *pubescens*
Large-flowered trillium	*Trillium grandiflorum*
Large-leaf pondweed	*Potamogeton amplifolius*
Lark sparrow	*Chondestes grammacus*

Late coralroot	*Corallorhiza odontorhiza*
Leafy pondweed	*Potamogeton foliosus*
Least bittern	*Ixobrychus exilis*
Least darter	*Etheostoma microperca*
Least flycatcher	*Empidonax minimus*
Least weasel	*Mustela nivalis*
Leatherleaf	*Chamaedaphne calyculata*
Lesser scaup	*Aythya affinis*
Liverwort	*Riccia fluitans*
Loggerhead shrike	*Lanius ludovicianus*
Long-billed curlew	*Numenius americanus*
Longear sunfish	*Lepomis megalotis*
Long-eared owl	*Asio otus*
Long-leaf pondweed	*Potamogeton nodosus*
Long-tailed weasel	*Mustela frenata*
Loosestrife beetles	*Galerucella* spp.
Lousewort	*Pedicularis* spp.
Lung lichen	*Lobaria pulmonaria*
Lupine	*Lupinus perennis*
Mallard	*Anas platyrhynchos*
Maple	*Acer* spp.
Marsh marigold	*Caltha palustris*
Marsh milkweed	*Asclepias incarnata*
Marsh wren	*Cistothorus palustris*
Marten	*Martes martes*
Mead's milkweed	*Asclepias meadii*
Mealy pixie-cup lichen	*Cladonia chlorophaea*
Mealy rosette lichen	*Physcia millegrana*
Methuselah's beard lichen	*Usnea longissima*
Midland brownsnake	*Storeria dekayi wrightorum*
Milfoil beetle	*Euhrychiopsis lecontei*
Mink	*Mustela vision*
Mink frog	*Rana septentrionalis*
Monarch	*Danaus plexippus*
Monk parakeet	*Myiopsitta monachus*
Mooneye	*Hiodon tergisus*
Mossy maple polypore	*Oxyporus populinus*
Motherwort	*Leonurus cardiaca*
Mottled sculpin	*Cottus bairdii*
Mountain holly	*Ilex mucronatus*
Mountain maple	*Acer spicatum*
Mourning dove	*Zenaida macroura*
Mourning warbler	*Oporornsis philadelphia*
Mud darter	*Etheostoma asprigene*
Mulberry wing	*Poanes massasoit*

Multiflora rose	*Rosa multiflora*
Muskellunge	*Esox masquinongy*
Muskrat	*Ondatra zibethicus*
Mustard white	*Pieris oleracea*
Naiads	*Najas* spp.
Narrow-leaved cattail	*Typha angustifolia*
Nashville warbler	*Vermovora ruficapilla*
Nettle	*Urtica dioica* subsp. *gracilis*
New York fern	*Thelypteris noveboracensis*
Northern bobwhite	*Colinus virginianus*
Northern cardinal	*Cardinalis cardinalis*
Northern flicker	*Colaptes auratus*
Northern gooseberry	*Ribes hirtellum*
Northern green frog	*Rana clamitans melanota*
Northern harrier	*Circus cyaneus*
Northern hog sucker	*Hypentelium nigricans*
Northern leopard frog	*Rana pipiens*
Northern mockingbird	*Mimus polyglottos*
Northern pike	*Esox lucius*
Northern pintail	*Anas acuta*
Northern red-bellied snake	*Storeria occipitomaculata occipitomaculata*
Northern ribbonsnake	*Thamnophis sauritus septentrionalis*
Northern ring-necked snake	*Diadophis punctatus edwardsii*
Northern rough-winged swallow	*Stelgidopteryx serripennis*
Northern saw-whet owl	*Aegolius funereus*
Northern shoveler	*Anas clypeata*
Northern snakehead	*Channa argus*
Northern spring peeper	*Pseudacris crucifer crucifer*
Northern watersnake	*Nerodia sipedon sipedon*
Northern waterthrush	*Seiurus noveboracensis*
Oaks	*Quercus* spp.
Orange bush lichen	*Teloschistes* spp.
Orange hawkweed	*Hieracium aurantiacum*
Orchard oriole	*Icterus spurius*
Orchids	family Orchidaceae
Ornate box turtle	*Terrapene ornata ornata*
Osprey	*Pandion haliaetus*
Ovenbird	*Seiurus aurocapillus*
Ozark minnow	*Notropis nubilus*
Pacific salmon	*Oncorhyncus* spp.
Paddlefish	*Polydon spathula*
Painted turtle	*Chrysemys picta*

Paper birch	*Betula papyrifera*
Passenger pigeon	*Ectopistes migratorius*
Perforated ruffle lichen	*Parmotrema perforatum*
Pickerel frog	*Rana palustris*
Pickerelweed	*Pontederia cordata*
Pie-billed grebe	*Podilymbus podiceps*
Pileated woodpecker	*Dryocopus pileatus*
Pin cherry	*Prunus pensylvanica*
Pin lichens	morphological group of microstalked species (<1 mm); in families Caliciaceae, Coniocybaceae, Mycocaliciaceae, etc.
Pine	*Pinus* spp.
Pine siskin	*Carduelis pinus*
Piping plover	*Charadrius melodus*
Pirate perch	*Aphrododerus sayanus*
Pitcher plant	*Sarracenia purpurea*
Plains gartersnake	*Thamnophis radix*
Pocket gopher	*Geomys* spp.
Pondweeds	*Potamogeton* spp.
Porcupine	*Erethizon dorsatum*
Powder-headed tube lichen	*Hypogymnia tubulosa*
Prairie cinquefoil	*Potentilla arguta*
Prairie panic grass	*Panicum leibergii*
Prairie parsley	*Polytaenia nuttallii*
Prairie racerunner	*Cnemidophorus sexlineatus viridis*
Prairie sunflower	*Helianthus pauciflorus*
Prairie thistle	*Cirsium discolor*
Prairie warbler	*Dendroica discolor*
Prairie white-fringed orchid	*Platanthera leucophaea*
Pugnose minnow	*Opsopoeodus emiliae*
Pugnose shiner	*Notropis anogenus*
Purple loosestrife	*Lythrum salicaria*
Purple martin	*Progne subis*
Purple prairie clover	*Dalea purpurea*
Purple twayblade	*Liparis lilifolia*
Pussy-toes	*Antennaria* spp.
Quackgrass	*Elytrigia repens*
Quagga mussel	*Dreissna bugensis*
Quaking aspen	*Populus tremuloides*
Queen Anne's lace	*Daucus corata*
Queen snake	*Regina septemvittata*
Quillworts	*Isoetes* spp.
Quinine fungus	*Fomitopsis officinalis*
Rainbow smelt	*Osmerus mordax*
Ram's-head lady's slipper	*Cypripedium arietinum*

Rattlesnake master	*Eryngium yuccifolium*
Rayless ragwort	*Packera (Senecio) indecora*
Red beard lichen	*Usnea rubicunda*
Red crossbill	*Loxia curvirostra*
Red fox	*Vulpes vulpes*
Red maple	*Acer rubrum*
Red pine	*Pinus resinosa*
Red raspberry	*Rubus idaeus* subsp. *strigosus*
Red squirrel	*Tamiasciurus hudsonicus*
Red-backed vole	*Clethrionomys gapperi*
Red-bellied woodpecker	*Melanerpes carolinus*
Red-berried elder	*Sambucus racemosa* subsp. *pubens*
Red-breasted nuthatch	*Sitta canadensis*
Red-eyed vireo	*Vireo olivaceus*
Redfin shiner	*Lythrurus umbratilis*
Redhead	*Aythya americana*
Red-headed woodpecker	*Melanerpes euthrocephalus*
Red-osier dogwood	*Cornus stolonifera*
Red-shouldered hawk	*Buteo lineatus*
Redside dace	*Clinostomus elongatus*
Red-tailed hawk	*Buteo jamaicensis*
Red-winged blackbird	*Agelaius phoeniceus*
Reeds	*Phragmites* spp.
Reed canary grass	*Phalaris arundinacea*
Rim-lichen	*Lecanora* spp.
Ring-billed gull	*Larus delawarensis*
Ringed-necked pheasant	*Phasianus colchicus*
Ring-necked duck	*Aythya collaris*
River birch	*Betula nigra*
River grape	*Vitis riparia*
River otter	*Lontra canadensis*
River rush	*Bolboschoenus fluviatilis*
Rock bass	*Ambloplites rupestris*
Rock cress	*Arabis lyrata*
Rock pigeon	*Columba livia*
Rockshag lichen	*Ephebe lanata*
Rose-breasted grosbeak	*Pheucticus ludovicianus*
Rosy-twisted stalk	*Streptopus roseus*
Rough blazing star	*Liatris aspera*
Round goby	*Neogobius melanostomus*
Roundleaf sundew	*Drosera rotundifolia*
Ruby-throated hummingbird	*Archilochus colubris*
Rudd	*Scardinius erythropthalmus*
Ruddy duck	*Oxyura jamaicensis*
Ruffed grouse	*Bonasa umbellus*
Rusty crayfish	*Orconectes rusticus*

Saffron-colored polypore	*Rigidoporus crocatus,*
Sagebrush	*Artemisia tridentata*
Sago pondweed	*Stuckenia pectinata*
Sandhill crane	*Grus canadensis*
Savannah sparrow	*Passerculus sandwichensis*
Scarlet tanager	*Piranga olivacea*
Sea lamprey	*Petromyzon marinus*
Seaside spurge	*Chamaescyce polygnifolia*
Sedge wren	*Cictothorus platensis*
Shagbark hickory	*Carya ovata*
Sharp-shinned hawk	*Accipiter striatus*
Sharp-tailed grouse	*Tympanuchus phasianellus*
Shooting star	*Dodecatheon meadii*
Short-eared owl	*Asio flammeus*
Short-tailed weasel	*Mustela erminea*
Shovelnose sturgeon	*Scaphirhynchus platorynchus*
Showy lady's-slipper	*Cypripedium reginae*
Showy orchis	*Galearis spectabilis*
Showy tick-trefoil	*Desmodium canadense*
Shrub honeysuckles	*Lonicera morrowii, tatatrica,* and x *bella*
Side-oats grama grass	*Bouteloua curtipendula*
Silver lamprey	*Ichthyomyzon unicuspis*
Silver maple	*Acer saccharinum*
Skunk cabbage	*Symplocarpus foetidus*
Sky-blue aster	*Aster oolentangiensis*
Slender madtom	*Noturus exilis*
Slender naiad	*Najas flexilis*
Small pondweed	*Potamogeton pusillus*
Small white lady's-slipper	*Cypripedium candidum*
Small-clouded brindle	*Apamea unanimis*
Smallmouth bass	*Micropterus dolomieu*
Smooth brome grass	*Bromus inermis*
Smooth cliff brake	*Pellaea glabella*
Smooth greensnake	*Opheodrys vernalis*
Sneezeweed	*Helenium autumnale*
Snow trillium	*Trillium nivale*
Snowshoe hare	*Lepus americanus*
Solitary sandpiper	*Tringa solitaria*
Song sparrow	*Melospiza melodia*
Sora	*Porzana carolina*
Spatterdock	*Nuphar* spp.
Speckled alder	*Alnus rugosa*
Spiked water-milfoil	*Myriophyllum sibiricum*
Spikerushes	*Eleocharis* spp.
Spiny naiad	*Najas marina*
Spiny water flea	*Bythotrephes longimanus*
Spotted knapweed	*Centaurea biebersteinii*

Spotted salamander	*Ambystoma maculatum*
Spotted sandpiper	*Actitis macularia*
Starhead topminnow	*Fundulus notti*
Stinkpot	*Sternotherus odoratus*
Stoneworts	*Chara* spp., *Nitella* spp.
Striped skunk	*Memphitis memphitis*
Sugar maple	*Acer saccharum*
Summer tanager	*Piranga rubra*
Swallow-tailed kite	*Elanoides forficatus*
Swamp aster	*Aster puniceus*
Swamp metalmark	*Calephelis muticum*
Swamp milkweed	*Asclepias incarnata*
Swamp sparrow	*Melospiza georgiana*
Sweet cicely	*Osmorhiza claytonii*
Sweetflag	*Acorus calamus*
Tamarack	*Larix laricina*
Threespine stickleback	*Gasterosteus aculeatus*
Toadflax brocade	*Calophasia lunula*
Toothwort	*Dentaria* spp.
Tree swallow	*Tachycineta bicolor*
Treeflute	*Menegazzia terebrata*
Trillium	*Trillium* spp.
Trumpeter swan	*Cygnus buccinator*
Tubenose goby	*Proterorhinus marmoratus*
Tufted titmouse	*Baeolophus bicolor*
Tussock sedge	*Carex stricta*
Twinflower	*Linnea borealis*
Two-spotted skippers	*Euphyes bimacula*
Upland sandpiper	*Bartramia longicauda*
Various-leaved water-milfoil	*Myriophyllum heterophyllum*
Veery	*Catharus fuscescens*
Vernal sweet grass	*Hierochloe hirta* subsp. *arctica*
Vesper sparrow	*Pooecetes gramineus*
Viburnum	*Viburnum* spp.
Virginia creeper	*Parthenocissus quinquefolia*
Virginia rail	*Rallus limicola*
Walking fern	*Asplenium rhizophyllum*
Walleye	*Sander vitreus*
Warbling vireo	*Vireo gilvus*
Water hyacinth	*Eichornia crassipes*
Water lilies	*Nymphaea* spp.
Water marigold	*Bidens beckii*
Water sedge	*Carex aquatilis*

Water smartweed	*Polygonum amphibium*
Water star-grass	*Zosterella dubia*
Watercress	*Nasturium officinale*
Water-lettuce	*Pistia stratiotes*
Water-milfoils	*Myriophyllum* spp.
Water-shield	*Brasenia* sp.
Waterweed	*Elodea canadensis*
West Virginia white	*Pieris virginiensis*
Western chorus frog	*Pseudacris triseriata*
Western foxsnake	*Elaphe vulpina*
Western meadowlark	*Sturnella neglecta*
Western sand darter	*Ammocryta clara*
Western slender glass lizard	*Ophisaurus attenuatus attenuatus*
Whip-poor-will	*Caprimulgus vociferus*
White ash	*Fraxinus americana*
White avens	*Geum canadense*
White birch	*Betula papyrifera*
White cedar	*Thuja occidentalis*
White mandarin	*Streptopus amplexifolius*
White oak	*Quercus alba*
White perch	*Morone americana*
White pine	*Pinus strobus*
White prairie fringed orchid	*Platanthera leucophaea*
White snakeroot	*Eupatorium rugosum*
White spruce	*Picea glauca*
White water crowfoot	*Ranunculus longirostris*
White water lily	*Nymphaea odorata*
White wild indigo	*Baptisia alba*
White-breasted nuthatch	*Sitta carolinensis*
White-eyed vireo	*Vireo griseus*
White-tailed deer	*Odocoileus virginianus*
White-throated sparrow	*Zonotrichia albicollis*
White-winged dove	*Zenaida asiatica*
Wide-leaf cattail	*Typha latifolia*
Wild celery	*Vallisneria americana*
Wild geranium	*Geranium maculatum*
Wild indigo duskywing	*Erynnis baptisia*
Wild lily of the valley	*Maianthemum canadense*
Wild quinine	*Parthenium integrifolium*
Wild rice	*Zizania aquatica* and *Z. palustris*
Wild turkey	*Meleagris gallopavo*
Willow flycatcher	*Empidonax traillii*
Wilson's phalarope	*Phalaropus tricolor*
Winter wren	*Troglodytes troglodytes*
Winterberry	*Ilex verticillata*
Wolf	*Canis lupus*
Wolverine	*Gulo gulo*

Wood duck	*Aix sponsa*
Wood frog	*Rana sylvatica*
Wood thrush	*Hylochchla mustelina*
Wood turtle	*Glyptemys* (*Clemmys*) *insculpta*
Woodcock	*Scolopax minor*
Woodland caribou	*Rangifer tarandus-caribou*
Woolly fruit sedge	*Carex lasiocarpa*
Yellow birch	*Betula alleghaniensis*
Yellow floating-heart	*Nymphoides peltata*
Yellow hawkweed	*Hieracium canadense*
Yellow perch	*Perca flavescens*
Yellow sweet-clover	*Melilotus officinalis*
Yellow underwing	*Noctua pronuba*
Yellow warbler	*Dendroica petechia*
Yellow-billed cuckoo	*Coccyzus americanus*
Yellow-breasted chat	*Icteria virens*
Yellow-bud hickory	*Carya cordiformis*
Yellow-crowned night heron	*Nyctanassa violacea*
Yellow-headed blackbird	*Xanthocephalus xanthocephalus*
Yellow-throated vireo	*Vireo flavifrons*
Zebra mussel	*Dreissena polymorpha*

Index